SOCIAL RIGHTS IN EUROPE

Social Rights in Europe

Edited by
GRÁINNE DE BÚRCA
Professor of European Law, European University Institute, Florence

and

BRUNO DE WITTE
Professor of European Law, European University Institute

With the assistance of
Larissa Ogertschnig
Researcher, European University Institute

OXFORD
UNIVERSITY PRESS

OXFORD
UNIVERSITY PRESS

Great Clarendon Street, Oxford OX2 6DP

Oxford University Press is a department of the University of Oxford.
It furthers the University's objective of excellence in research, scholarship,
and education by publishing worldwide in

Oxford New York

Auckland Cape Town Dar es Salaam Hong Kong Karachi
Kuala Lumpur Madrid Melbourne Mexico City Nairobi
New Delhi Shanghai Taipei Toronto

With offices in

Argentina Austria Brazil Chile Czech Republic France Greece
Guatemala Hungary Italy Japan Poland Portugal Singapore
South Korea Switzerland Thailand Turkey Ukraine Vietnam

Oxford is a registered trade mark of Oxford University Press
in the UK and in certain other countries

Published in the United States
by Oxford University Press Inc., New York

British Library Cataloguing in Publication Data

Data available

Library of Congress Cataloging in Publication Data

Social rights in Europe / edited by Gráinne de Búrca and Bruno de Witte with
the assistance of Larissa Ogertschnig.
   p. cm.
  Includes bibliographical references and index.
  "This volume of essays originates in a conference organized by the Academy
of European Law at the European University Institute in Florence"—Preface.
  ISBN 0–19–928617–5 (hardback: alk. paper)—ISBN 0–19–928799–6
(pbk.: alk. paper) 1. Social legislation—Europe. 2. Social rights—Europe.
3. Social legislation—European Union countries. 4. Social rights—European
Union countries I. De Búrca, G. (Gráinne) II. Witte, Bruno de.
III. Ogertschnig, Larissa
  KJC2838.S66 2005
  344.24—dc22   2005018241

Typeset by Newgen Imaging Systems (P) Ltd., Chennai, India
Printed in Great Britain
on acid-free paper by
Biddles Ltd., King's Lynn
ISBN 978–0–19–928799–4

Preface

This volume of essays originates in a conference organized by the Academy of European Law at the European University Institute in Florence. There the participants examined the evolution of the protection of fundamental social rights in Europe in the light of recent developments in the constitutional law of the European Union and in the monitoring system of the Council of Europe's Social Charter. The idea for the conference originally came from Régis Brillat and Gisella Gori, of the European Social Charter's Secretariat in Strasbourg, who wondered aloud why so many academics and politicians spoke and wrote about the European Union's Charter of Fundamental Rights, and the social rights contained therein, and why so few seemed to be aware of the recent developments concerning the Council of Europe's Social Charter mechanism. Together with Olivier De Schutter, who was involved in this project from the start, we decided to take up this question as a project of the Academy of European Law. We saw it as a more focused if less ambitious follow-up to the volume which the Academy of European Law had, under the direction of Philip Alston, devoted to the *EU and Human Rights* in 1999. In the spirit of that earlier project, we invited the contributors to this volume to reflect on social rights protection in Europe in a comprehensive way, looking at the role of both the European Union and the Council of Europe, and from a policy-oriented perspective.

Even though the likely failure of the Treaty establishing a Constitution for Europe has placed a shadow over the EU's Charter of Fundamental Rights enshrined therein, it seems likely that the Charter will survive in some form, given that it was separately drafted, politically approved, and proclaimed by the EU institutions several years before the Convention on the future of Europe even began to draft a constitutional treaty.

Both during the preparation of the conference and in the process of editing this volume, the role of Larissa Ogertschnig was essential. Without her untiring and efficient coordinating efforts, this volume would not have appeared. She is also responsible for directing us to the work of Savina Tarsitano, whose artistic image appears on the cover of the book. Thanks also to Evangelia Psychogiopoulou for careful copyediting work, and to Euan Macdonald and Kate Elliot for their translation and language revision. Finally, warm thanks are once again due to John Louth, Gwen Booth and their collaborators at Oxford University Press for their friendly and professional publishing skills.

Gráinne de Búrca and
Bruno de Witte

Florence/New York
March 2005

Table of Contents

List of Abbreviations

CESCR	United Nations Committee on Economic, Social, and Cultural Rights
CETS	Council of Europe Treaty Series
CFI	European Court of First Instance
CLP	*Current Legal Problems*
CMLRev.	*Common Market Law Review*
CRI	Commission against Racism and Intolerance
EAPN	European Anti-poverty Network
ECHR	European Convention on Human Rights
ECJ	European Court of Justice
ECtHR	European Court of Human Rights
ECOSOC	UN Economic and Social Council
ECR	European Court Reports
ECRI	European Commission against Racism and Intolerance
ECSR	European Committee of Social Rights
ECTUC	European Confederation of Trade Unions Confederations
EEC	European Economic Community
EES	European Employment Strategy
EHRLR	*European Human Rights Law Review*
EJIL	*European Journal of International Law*
ELJ	*European Law Journal*
ELRev.	*European Law Review*
EPL	*European Public Law*
ESC	European Social Charter
ETS	European Treaty Series
ETUC	European Trade Union Confederation
EU	European Union
EUCFR	Charter of Fundamental Rights of the European Union
HRC	UN Human Rights Committee
ICCPR	International Convention on Civil and Political Rights
ICESCR	International Covenant an Economic, Social and Cultural Rights
ICFTU	International Confederation of Free Trade Unions
IGC	Intergovernmental Conference
IJCLLIR	*International Journal of Comparative Labour Law and Industrial Relations*
ILJ	*Industrial Law Journal*
ILO	International Labour Organization
Int'l Com J Review	*International Commission of Jurists Review*

JCMS	*Journal of Common Market Studies*
JDI	*Journal du droit international*
JEPP	*Journal of European Public Policy*
JIA	*Journal of International Affairs*
JTDE	*Journal des tribunaux—droit européen*
LIEI	*Legal Issues of European Integration*
MJ	*Maastricht Journal of European and Comparative Law*
MLR	*Modern Law Review*
NAFTA	North American Free Trade Agreement
NGO	Non-governmental Organization
OECD	Organization for Economic Cooperation and Development
OJLS	*Oxford Journal of Legal Studies*
OMC	Open Method of Coordination
OMCT	World Organization Against Torture
(Rev)ESC	Revised European Social Charter
RGDIP	*Revue générale de droit international public*
RIDE	*Revue internationale de droit économique*
RTDH	*Revue trimestrielle de droit européenne*
RUDH	*Revue universelle des droits de l'homme*
TEC	Treaty on the European Community
TEU	Treaty on European Union
TUAC	Treaty Union Advisory Commitee
UDHR	Universal Declaration of Human Rights

Notes on the Contributors

Jean-François Akandji-Kombé is Professor of European and Human Rights Law at the Université de Caen Basse Normandie.

Philip Alston is Professor of Law and Director of the Center for Human Rights and Global Justice at New York University.

Diamond Ashiagbor is Lecturer in the Faculty of Laws at University College London.

Mark Bell is Senior Lecturer at the Centre for European Law and Integration, University of Leicester.

Brian Bercusson is Professor of European Social and Labour Law at King's College, University of London.

Régis Brillat is Executive Secretary of the European Social Charter, Directorate General of Human Rights—DG II, Council of Europe.

Gráinne de Búrca is Professor of European Law at the European University Institute.

Olivier De Schutter is Professor at the University of Louvain.

Bruno de Witte is Professor of European Law at the European University Institute.

Cécile Fabre is Lecturer in Political Theory at the London School of Economics.

Alexandra Gatto is Researcher at the European University Institute.

Gisella Gori is Administrator in the Secretariat of the European Social Charter, Directorate General of Human Rights—DG II, Council of Europe.

Tamara K. Hervey is Professor of Law at the University of Nottingham.

Marie-Ange Moreau is Professor of Labour and Social Law at the European University Institute.

Larissa Ogertschnig is Researcher at the European University Institute.

Gerard Quinn is Professor of Law at the National University of Ireland, Galway.

Silvana Sciarra is Professor of Law in the Department of Private and Procedural Law, University of Florence.

Stijn Smismans is Post-doctoral Researcher at the Faculty of Sociology of the University of Trento.

PART I

INTRODUCTION

1

The Future of Social Rights Protection in Europe

GRÁINNE DE BÚRCA

This volume sets about appraising the current legal position of social rights in Europe, looking in particular at the two regional regimes of rights protection, that of the Council of Europe's European Social Charter (ESC) on the one hand, and that of the European Union (EU) on the other, in the light of recent developments and changes within the two systems.

Rights are both a way of thinking about the priorities of human existence, as well as a legal way of categorizing recognition of and access to such priorities. And despite the discourse of indivisibility which has characterized the international human rights movement over the past half century or more, those values which are more readily categorized as 'civil and political rights' are legally and politically privileged over those normally categorized as 'economic and social rights'. The fact that the categories themselves are contested and ambiguous—for example that freedom from forced labour, although categorized as one of the core social rights, can also be understood as a negative personal liberty, and the right not to be discriminated against can as readily be described as a civil right as it can a social or economic right[1]—or indeed that they 'dynamically intersect',[2] does not undermine the thrust of this point. Civil and political rights, traditionally understood as negative freedom from governmental intervention, are more often accorded national constitutional status, and are usually enforceable by sharper and more direct legal and judicial means. Social and economic rights, the so-called second generation rights, are often perceived as aspirational or programmatic rather than concretely defined entitlements, and as collectively rather than individually enjoyed. They are generally believed to necessitate more extensive and immediate expenditure and intervention than traditional civil and political liberties, and they normally enjoy weaker legal enforcement.[3] While it is undoubtedly the case that

---

[1] See the discussion by G. Quinn, Chapter 14 of this volume, on the different 'social rights' and 'civil rights' conceptions of disability discrimination emerging from the ESC and the EU respectively.

[2] See J.- F. Akandji-Kombé, Chapter 6.

[3] For discussion of programmatic versus justiciable social rights, see B. Bercusson, Chapter 9.

certain civil or political rights—the right to life, to privacy or to bodily integrity in the context of abortion, or freedom of expression in the context of racial hatred, for example—can be highly contentious in legal and political terms, it seems that the very *idea* of social and economic rights raises deeply redistributive questions in such a direct and immediate way that it gives rise to sharper political and ideological opposition. Given the focus of social rights on economic justice rather than on personal liberty, these rights are particularly challenging in political, ideological, and economic terms for governments in the developed world. Liberal capitalism, many argue—pointing *inter alia* to the refusal of the United States to ratify the United Nations Covenant on Economic and Social Rights—is more readily compatible with a traditional conception of civil and political rights rather than with clear legal recognition for social and economic rights.[4]

The focus of this book is on the protection of social rights in Europe—'social rights' being used broadly to refer to the category of rights which concern economic and social well-being, and 'Europe' referring primarily to the overlapping systems of the European Union and the Council of Europe. The profile of social rights has been raised in recent years by the debates during the drafting of the EU's Charter of Fundamental Rights and during the Convention leading to the drafting of an EU Constitution about the status of social rights within the European economic and social model. It has also been raised—to a lesser extent, despite the more impressive substantive content and focus of its provisions—by the revision of the European Social Charter which came into force in 1999. While the term 'social rights' is used in different ways within different academic and policy literatures,[5] sometimes in order to place particular emphasis on the subcategory of labour rights (including the rights to associate and organize, to strike, to earn a living, fair working conditions, etc.) or on 'fundamental' social rights, it is used in this volume in a broad sense to include many kinds of economic and social rights, and the choice of case studies—while necessarily selective and inevitably vulnerable to the criticism of under-inclusiveness or specific emphasis—has deliberately been made with this broader category in mind.

All of the authors who have contributed to this volume share an interest in the idea of social rights as a possible means to promote a greater degree of social justice, as well as an interest in the operation of the European regional mechanisms of social rights protection. Several of the chapters dealing with the ESC are written by authors who are working within or alongside the relevant Council of Europe organs—either as members of the ESC secretariat (Régis Brillat and

---

[4] See for a contrary argument, C. Sunstein, *Why does the American Constitution Lack Social and Economic Guarantees?*, University of Chicago Public Law and Legal Theory Working Paper No. 36 (2003).

[5] The difficulties of definition and classification became evident in the preparation of the bibliography for this volume by Larissa Ogertschnig, during which questions about the appropriate classification of particular literature regularly arose. See also the opening comments by Brian Bercusson in his chapter in this volume.

Gisella Gori) or as members of the European Committee of Social Rights (ECSR) of the ESC (Gerard Quinn). These chapters contain both practical insights about the workings of the systems, as well as a measure of scholarly reflection on their strengths and—to a lesser extent—their limitations. And several of the chapters dealing partly with the EU are written by authors who have been members of EU-appointed human rights networks (Olivier De Schutter, of the network of experts on fundamental rights, and Mark Bell, of the network of experts on anti-discrimination law). All of the contributions, however, whether written from a primarily academic perspective or from a more internal or policy-oriented perspective, seek to engage both reflectively and in a practically relevant way on the subject. While individual chapters obviously differ significantly in their orientation and emphasis, the collection as a whole aims both to inform as well as to offer a critical appraisal of the two systems of social rights protection in Europe and their interaction: on the one hand, of the muscular European Union with its considerable economic and political resources but its belated and contingent interest in human rights, and on the other hand the 'twilight existence' of the European Social Charter[6] with its thoughtful and extensive jurisprudence on social rights but its minimal resources, low visibility, and uncertain impact.

The book begins with a philosophical reflection by Cécile Fabre on the place of social rights within national constitutions in Europe, in which she argues that—despite the impossibility of proving the premise of human equality on which the commitment to protect social rights rests—a common 'European culture of social justice' can be perceived through a study of these differing constitutional provisions. The book closes with a section containing two chapters by Alexandra Gatto and Marie-Ange Moreau respectively, which consider the impact and relevance of European social rights protection beyond Europe's borders. Alexandra Gatto asks whether the EU in its externally oriented policies seeks to promote social rights, and gives at best a mixed response, arguing that human rights clauses are not necessarily a useful instrument for promoting them, but also that the language of 'rights' is avoided in dealing with subjects such as food, health and education, and is used mainly with reference to civil and political rights. While the EU does address certain social concerns in its external policies, it appears more ready to embrace a wider array of social rights *qua* rights in its internally oriented policies. Marie-Ange Moreau's chapter then considers a rather different aspect of the question whether Europe's protection for social rights is inappropriately territorially limited, arguing that the European legal regimes for social rights protection do not adequately address the reality of economic globalization and the contribution by multinational corporations and other private actors to the spread of social injustice. Indeed, a third and even more fundamental weakness of the limited 'European' focus of the two systems of social rights protection emerges

---

[6] See M. Bell, Chapter 13, n. 7, referring to the phrase of D. Harris and J. Darcy, *The European Social Charter* (2001), at 12.

from other contributions in the book, that is that both the EU and the ESC are at best ambivalent and at worst clearly exclusionary in relation to the protection of non-nationals. Social rights, given the redistributive fears they raise, are considerably less 'universal' than other human rights claim to be, and any extension from favoured Member State nationals to non-nationals tends to be marginal or slight.[7]

In between the first and final sections, there are three main parts to the book. Part II focuses on the mechanisms and functioning of the revised European Social Charter, with particular emphasis on its monitoring mechanism and on the domestic implementation of ESC jurisprudence. Régis Brillat asserts the increasingly judicial nature of the European Committee of Social Rights, the increasingly authoritative character of its decisions and the dynamic character of its interpretation, and argues that its relationship vis-à-vis the Committee of Ministers has been strengthened following the revision of the ESC in 1996. Both he and Gisella Gori emphasize the significance of the new collective complaints mechanism in sharpening the interpretative and enforcement instruments of the ESC. Philip Alston responds with a more critical appraisal of the functioning of the monitoring mechanism and the role of the European Committee of Social Rights, and makes a number of suggestions for strengthening it, including by focusing and targeting its scrutiny more effectively. Gisella Gori examines the different ways in which the ESC has been implemented or enforced by legislation in the various member states of the Council of Europe, given that its provisions are not in themselves directly applicable. Whereas Cécile Fabre's chapter looks briefly at the extent to which various national constitutions in Europe provide for the justiciability of social rights, Gisella Gori's builds on this in considering the justiciability at national level of provisions of the ESC, despite the 'classical arguments' for their non-enforceability. While noting that legislative enforcement of the Charter has been considerably more effective and positive than judicial enforcement, she argues for a more nuanced ('normative') idea of justiciability which could also have a 'standstill' effect, as well as an evolving idea of justiciability through the progressive clarification of particular provisions and the increasing practice of national courts adjudicating on social rights and interpreting national laws and practices in their light. Jean-François Akandji-Kombé complements the analysis of Brillat and Gori by providing an assessment of the methods of the European Committee of Social Rights, and emphasizing its juridical nature especially but not only in relation to the collective complaints mechanism. He points to the efforts of the Committee to strengthen the acceptance of social rights as human rights, in part by pointing to the dynamic process of *rapprochement* of the respective regimes for the protection of social rights and civil rights, as well as to the fact that the ESC mechanism does not operate in isolation (sometimes indeed involving

---

[7] See in particular J.- F. Akandji-Kombé, Chapter 6 and M. Bell, Chapter 13.

'bitter exchanges between the ECSR and the ECtHR', as on the right of association), but rather as one element of the Council of Europe system, and within the broader international human rights system.

The next part of the book (Part III) looks at the EU's contribution to the protection of social rights, focusing not only on the past EU *acquis* in this field, but also on the EU Charter of Rights, the Constitution, and the newer trends in EU social and employment policy, including the use of soft law and the 'Open Method of Coordination' in particular. The first chapter in this part, by Olivier De Schutter, links with the preceding part on the ESC by looking directly at the relationship between the EU and the ESC. He argues that the EU, in building and enhancing its own system of protection for social rights, should not sideline or seek to replace the ESC, but rather should both benefit from and strengthen it by accession. He claims that accession of the EU to the revised ESC would be entirely compatible with the EU's constitutional law and with its limited competence, and he sets forth a range of arguments in favour of accession: first, to prevent those states with the fewest and weakest commitments under the ESC from under-cutting other states and taking advantage of variable levels of protection for social rights in EU measures, secondly because of the improved and strengthened nature of the revised ESC, thirdly to avoid possible conflicts between ESC and EU inter-pretations of the same issues, fourthly because the EU now explicitly recognizes social rights within the Charter of Fundamental Rights, fifthly because of the complementarity of the ESC and the ECHR, and in view of the EU's decision to accede to the ECHR; and finally because of the desirability of coordinating the actions of the states and of the EU in areas of shared external competence which touch on social rights covered by the ESC. Bruno de Witte follows this chapter by tracing the evolution of social rights in the *acquis* of the EU, both through the ECJ's case law and through the various legal instruments and social policies adopted over the years. Echoing conclusions reached in other chapters, including Tamara Hervey's and Alexandra Gatto's on the absence (until recently, at least in the context of the Charter of Rights) of the language of rights within the EU's social policies, he argues nonetheless that social rights, even if not in traditionally justiciable form, may now be coming to the forefront of a new EU policy-oriented human rights agenda.

Three essays on social and labour rights in the current EU context then follow within this Part. Brian Bercusson addresses the recurrent question of justiciability, and, relatedly, indivisibility, tackling the question of social rights under the new, although now ill-fated EU Constitution, and in the Charter of Fundamental Rights. He provides a critical account of the debates which led to the provision of the Charter distinguishing between 'principles' and other rights, and moves on to consider sev-eral different ways in which the various social rights contained in the Charter may come to be given domestic effect, whether through indirect interpretative methods, or non-judicial methods including administrative and industrial relations mech-anisms, or, more likely, through varying 'equilibria' of these mechanisms. He rejects a simple justiciability/non-justiciability dichotomy in the social rights field, and identifies at least three groups of social rights: those that are clearly justiciable and simply need effective implementation, those that are moving towards greater justiciability as positive enforceable rights, and finally those that are programmatic in nature and that require greater ongoing monitoring of governmental policy together with a form of 'consistency' review (similar to Gori's category of 'normative justiciability'). Silvana Sciarra and Stijn Smismans then in different ways consider the interaction of the idea of social rights with the EU's Lisbon Agenda, and the operation of the Open Method of Coordination (OMC) in the context of the European employment strategy in particular. Stijn Smismans, highlighting the ambiguity of the notions of hard and soft law when contrasting rights and the OMC, adopts a more pessimistic view than Bercusson of the likely justiciability of social rights under the EU Charter. He concludes that social rights are very unlikely to be justiciable in the context of the operation of the OMC, other than in interpreting relevant national or EU legislation, or in influencing the cognitive framework set by the OMC itself, and he discusses the possibility of a genuinely participative OMC on fundamental rights policy (including social rights) which could be integrated into other policy fields. Silvana Sciarra also looks to see how the discourse and commitments of social rights might be harnessed to the Open Method of Coordination, or, in her own words, how to establish a language of rights in EU labour law reforms. She considers how the absence of traditional legal sanctions within the OMC has been countered by an increase in monitoring mechanisms, and looks at a number of examples where soft law structures interact with more familiar enforcement of rights. Proposing a further and different classification within the category of social rights, she argues that certain fundamental 'procedural' social rights such as the right to training, to employment services, or to the freedom to reconcile work and family life, could be detached from the contract of employment and could be attached to 'flexible' working paths as preconditional rights, following the individual rather than the employment relationship. Finally, in common with Marie-Ange Moreau, she argues for a raising of the profile of human rights, and for the creation of a human rights culture through greater publicity and attention to social rights, whether by means of monitoring, collective complaints systems or otherwise, if more creative mechanisms for responding to violations are to be found.

The fourth Part of the book contains four case studies, which examine specific social rights and the way in which they have been interpreted and developed in the EU and the ESC contexts respectively. In each case, the authors set out to inquire whether a common substantive core of legal protection for the right can be detected, and what the added value of each of the two systems is, assuming that it is not simply replicating or duplicating the other's work. In none of the four cases does the author conclude that there is no added value, but perhaps the more difficult question is whether there is any 'common core' to the conception of each of the social rights within the two systems. Tamara Hervey's chapter identifies the strongest disjuncture, arguing—as we have seen, in common with other chapters in the book—that although the EU in many ways is involved in exercising health policy powers, it does not acknowledge or address a 'right to health' in this context, even though the European Committee of Social Rights has begun to shape such a right under Article 11 of the revised Charter. She suggests that the absence of a language of rights in the EU context is explicable in part by reference to the assumption that the 'right to health' is protected at national level and secondly by reference to competence concerns: that it is neither the EU's role nor within its power to promote or to require states to promote the right to health. Diamond Ashiagbor examines the 'right to work' within the two systems respectively, and finds the concept itself a multifaceted and definitionally complex one, lacking a readily identifiable core. While the EU emphasizes individual economic freedom to choose employment, the ESC and its Committee focus more on the program-matic obligations of the state in relation to labour market policies. As in Tamara Hervey's analysis, the limited competence of the EU in this field provides part of the explanation for the difference in emphasis as between the EU and the ESC in relation to the right to work, even though the explanatory memorandum to the EU Charter consciously links the right to work with the right contained in the ESC. However, in the case of the 'right to work', unlike the right to health, Ashiagbor points out that explicit differences in emphasis and tensions between the ESC and the EU conceptions are apparent: for example, in relation to the approach to 'full employment', in the respective approaches to the provision of paid employment services, and in relation to the linking of entitlement to social security benefits and availability for work. The chapters by Mark Bell and Gerard Quinn then examine the area of anti-discrimination, Mark Bell looking at the general principle and Gerard Quinn considering the specific area of disability, in which the underpinning of equality was made explicit in the ESC only after the 1996 revision of the Charter. Mark Bell examines the respective approaches of the two systems in their concepts of equality and in tackling diversity, as well as their mechanisms for enforcement: looking at individual and collective enforcement as well as monitoring. He finds that while the EU has evolved towards greater preci-sion in definition, it has also spelt out the limits to positive action in a way that the ESC with its evolving approach has not (yet) done, but that the EU in the areas of gender equality and race equality has perhaps given a lead to the ESC, and certainly—at least in so far as gender equality is concerned—influenced the draft-ing of the ESC's 1988 Additional Protocol. As far as individual enforcement is concerned, the EU has the edge over the ESC where directly effective provisions of law are concerned, whereas the EU—despite the provisions of the recent anti-discrimination directives on the role of equality bodies—lacks the ESC's collective enforcement mechanism. Ultimately, he argues that there is room for comple-mentarity and mutual reinforcement of the two systems of anti-discrimination, given some of their respective strengths and weaknesses. Gerard Quinn analyses the developing contribution of the ESC on the question of disability discrimination, in particular following the significant decision in a collective complaint brought by a European autism group against France. He argues that the EU, now that it has introduced legislation dealing with disability discrimination in employment, could learn from the ESC's human rights approach to defining disability and from its understanding of the notion of 'reasonable accommodation' as simply an adjustment of the non-discrimination norm to meet the circumstances of persons with disabilities.

Is the conclusion to be drawn from these accounts that—apart from the specific area of anti-discrimination law and gender equality in particular—it is essentially the ESC that adds value, as far as social rights are concerned, while the EU lags behind in definitional sophistication, in the degree of its commitment to social justice, and even in its initial willingness to adopt a 'rights' approach within its spheres of social policy? The answer is perhaps not so simple. While clearly the ESC has been formulating a reasonably sophisticated jurisprudence of social rights, unmatched by the EU, the EU has nonetheless made some substantive progress through its policies and laws in a number of these fields, without necessarily having used the language of rights. Looking ahead, however, the question for the future is whether, given that the EU Charter of Rights does give explicit recognition to social rights such as the right to health care, as fundamental rights, the stronger legal and policy instruments of the EU and the far greater resources at its disposal are likely to lead gradually to the marginalization and even to the eventual redundancy of the ESC.

The respective roles of the two European systems in the promotion and protection of social rights, and the relationship between them, forms the central theme of this book. The Council of Europe has clearly suffered something of a crisis of identity and function with the expansion of both membership and scope of the European Union, and perhaps in particular as a result of the recent 'turn to rights' in the EU. Given that the most significant and distinctive feature of the Council of Europe's contributions has been in the area of human rights, in the operation of the European Convention on Human Rights (ECHR) on the one hand, and to a lesser extent in the functioning of the European Social Charter, the drafting and proclamation of the Charter of Fundamental Rights has raised renewed questions about the relationship between the two systems. Given that the EU Charter not only integrates both civil and political as well as economic and social rights, but also incorporates many provisions which are based directly on provisions of the ECHR and to a lesser extent of the ESC, the continuing significance of these Council of Europe instruments at least for the twenty-five Member States of the European Union might seem to be called into question. As far as the ECHR is concerned its ongoing relevance seemed to have been settled at least in a formal sense by the political and legal decision, encapsulated in Article I-9 of the EU constitutional text, to mandate accession by the EU to the ECHR, thus subordinating the former regime to the latter in significant respects. Even though the constitutional treaty may fall, the political commitment to accede to the ECHR seems clear. No such decision has been made, on the other hand, in the case of the revised ESC.

More specifically, apart from the fact that no formal relationship between the EU and the ESC has been envisaged, the ESC has always had a considerably lower profile than the ECHR in terms of knowledge of its substantive content and of its domestic enforcement. Reflecting the typical asymmetry between legal regimes for the protection of civil and political rights and those for the protection of social and economic rights, the ESC unlike the ECHR has been enforced by a reporting and monitoring mechanism without an individual right of complaint, and its 'jurisprudence' has been developed by a committee of experts (even after the changes to the committee's functioning introduced by the revision of the ESC) rather than a court. The EU itself—including both the political institutions and the Court—has paid relatively little attention to the ESC, and in 1989 adopted its own Community Charter on the Fundamental Social Rights of Workers, rather than incorporating the ESC into EU law. Both the ESC and the 1989 Charter are now referred to, in similar vein, in Article 136 of the EC Treaty on social policy, but the possible impact of the substantive content of the ESC and of the jurisprudence of its committee is difficult to discern. Indeed, as indicated in the contribution to this volume by Bruno de Witte, the influence of the EC's own 1989 Charter on the social policy programme and legislation pursued by the EU has equally always been difficult to ascertain, and it remains to be seen whether the new Charter of Fundamental Rights, which contains quite a number of social rights, however weakly phrased and uncertain in their justiciability, will have greater impact on the development of EU social policy, whether as a 'platform',[8] through alternative mechanisms of enforcement,[9] or otherwise.

Apart from the specific question of the impact of the ESC on the EU and its policies, however, the respective positions of the ESC and the EU as two very different regional systems engaged in different ways in the protection and promotion of social rights is a subject worth revisiting, particularly in the light of the adoption of the Charter of Fundamental Rights. To what extent do the two organizations complement each other, by focusing on different issues, using different instruments, availing of different incentives to induce compliance with social standards, and to what extent do they overlap, duplicate, or even perhaps disrupt one another's functioning? Does the extension of the scope and range of activities of the EU in the field of social policy and social rights necessarily point in the direction of the further marginalization of the ESC, or does it, on the contrary, underscore the continued importance of an organization which—unlike the EU—is not focused on the promotion of economic growth, but which has as its mandate the protection of social rights as human rights even in the face of serious economic challenges?

The debate on the existence of overlapping European human rights regimes has more often taken place in relation to the respective roles of the EU and the

---

[8] T. Hervey and B. de Witte, Chapters 15 and 8 in this volume.
[9] See B. Bercusson, Chapter 9 in this volume.

ECHR, with commentators asking whether the role of the European Court of Human Rights is likely to be taken over by the European Court of Justice (at least as far as the EU Member States are concerned) as its jurisdiction to deal with human rights questions gradually expands. One of the answers given to this question has been that the EU is not a 'human rights organization', but an emergent constitutional polity focused mainly on economic integration and growth; and that the European Court of Justice is not purely a human rights court, but a court charged primarily with overseeing the enforcement of the EU treaties and with EU laws and policies, and whose teleological approach has always been informed by the priorities and goals embodied in those treaties. The ECJ's approach to human rights protection, it has been argued, is likely to continue to be influenced by this teleology, meaning that the Court of Human Rights will continue to have an important role—perhaps an increasingly important one, as the EU grows in power and scope—in focusing exclusively on human rights, maintaining a high benchmark for their protection and promotion, and guarding against any normative dilution. The force of this argument can perhaps be seen even more clearly when applied to the relationship between the EU and the ESC, rather than the ECHR. The relative weakness of the European social model, when confronted by the legal and political commitments to economic liberalization at EU level, has been the cause for much debate and contestation, not least during the 2005 referenda on the EU Constitution. New strategies, such as the so-called Lisbon Agenda, which claim to integrate the economic, social (and environmental) dimensions in equal measure, have not reassured those who fear the further marginalization of social concerns and the prioritization of economic growth and monetary stability rather than social well-being within these macro-processes. This suspicion gains some support from Diamond Ashiagbor's analysis of the 'right to work' and the idea of full employment under the ESC and in the context of the EU's Lisbon Agenda.[10] The chapters by Silvana Sciarra and Stijn Smismans also reflect similar concerns, and they consider ways in which the language of rights could be introduced into the Lisbon strategy and into its main policy instrument, the Open Method of Coordination, although they do so with varying degrees of conviction about the likely results.

The problem for the European Social Charter, on the analysis set out above, is not that the EU is taking over its norms and functions and rendering it redundant, but rather that the ESC could be all the more important as a mechanism for maintaining a strong commitment to social and economic justice, even though its profile remains low and its impact weak. If the ESC is to play a role in shaping a stronger European social model, as Gerard Quinn in his chapter suggests it might,[11] serious thought therefore needs to be given to the ways in which its profile and its relationship with the more powerful entity, the EU, might be

[10] Chapter 12 of this volume.
[11] G. Quinn, Chapter 14, argues that the value of the ESC 'resides in how effectively it can become an expositor of social values—values that supposedly lie at the heart of social Europe'.

strengthened. Some suggestions to this effect are made in various chapters of the book which address the relationship between the two systems. To give some examples: Philip Alston argues for the importance of the committee producing better targeted reports which focus greater attention on particular violations, and for strategies to mobilize civil society—the real engine and energy of the human rights movement—around the ESC in the context of its supervision and monitoring mechanism. Olivier De Schutter sets out the arguments for accession by the EU to the revised ESC, so as to anchor itself to the standards being set by the latter. Mark Bell suggests that the two systems can learn from one another in a complementary way at least in the field of anti-discrimination law and policy, and his suggestion that the reporting system of the ESC would be taken much more seriously if the conclusions of the European Committee of Social Rights were to be given some impact within the EU legal framework has obvious relevance for the whole range of social rights and policy.

The attempt in this book to generate some constructive proposals for a revitalized and complementary relationship between the EU and the ESC as far as social rights are concerned does not, however, mean that the complexity inherent in the notion of social rights, or the tensions not only between the two European systems but also in the range of views about how economic and social justice might be pursued through social rights, can be ignored. On the one hand, we can see that certain policy goals of the EU—the idea of activation of social benefits in the context of employment policy, for example—may be in tension with values articulated by the organs of the ESC, for example on the importance of freedom to choose a suitable employment.[12] On the other hand, the tensions which emerge in such conflicts may also be reflected in other contexts, and may point to different conceptions of the specific role which social rights should play in the pursuit of greater social and economic justice. Thus, while a policy of quasi-punitive conditionality based 'activation' is objectionable from the perspective of freedom to choose employment (linking social security to an obligation to work), a policy of passive 'maintenance' rather than active and supportive integration of marginalized persons such as disabled people, into society (delinking social welfare from positive measures of integration) may also be objectionable from the point of view of social citizenship and belonging.[13] The relationship between welfare and freedom is undeniable, but complex, and while the notion of social rights provides a normative structure for addressing the complexities of that relationship, amongst other things, it certainly does not resolve them.

More generally, however, the reluctance of the EU to use the language of social rights in the context of many of its policy fields—in external cooperation and development policy,[14] for example, or in the area of health policy[15]—reflects precisely a fear of giving strong legal recognition and priority to particular social

---

[12] O. De Schutter, Chapter 7, at pp. 124–25 and D. Ashiagbor, Chapter 12 at pp. 250–51.
[13] G. Quinn, Chapter 14.   [14] A. Gatto, Chapter 16.   [15] T. Hervey, Chapter 15.

values in the face of competing economic interests. And it may be this paradoxical fact that in the end best explains why the existence of these two separate organizations for the protection of social rights in Europe—provided that they interact more intensively and constructively in the future—could be a valuable asset rather than wasteful institutional duplication. It is because the organization which is legally, institutionally, and economically weaker (the ESC within the Council of Europe) may in the end be more likely than the organization which has greater legal, institutional, and economic power (the EU) to maintain a strong and ongoing normative commitment to high standards of social justice in the face of changing economic circumstances.

2

Social Rights in European Constitutions

CÉCILE FABRE*

I. INTRODUCTION

Individuals, it is commonly argued within and without academic circles, have civil and political rights such as the rights not to be tortured, not to be detained and not to be tried without due process, as well as rights to freedom of speech, freedom of association, voting, and running for office. Those rights have defined democratic and liberal regimes for over two centuries, and are set out, sometimes in great detail, in many a constitution. By contrast, as is often noted, social rights, which historically became part of liberal-democratic discourse at a later stage, are more controversial.[1] Some philosophers and policy-makers deny that the state should get into the business of re-distribution; others maintain that the language of rights is not appropriate in that context. More numerous still are those who claim that, although individuals do have social rights, those rights should not be entrenched in the constitution of a democratic state. And yet, most democratic constitutions do have them. In fact, twenty-five out of the twenty-nine constitutions of the countries which now form the EU (or aspire to become members) have social rights: constitutional practice belies philosophical, juridical, indeed political discourse.[2]

My aim in this chapter is to explore how European constitutions deal with social rights—by which I mean rights to adequate income, education, housing, and health care, as well as rights in the workplace. It is a particularly urgent task in the

* For their incisive comments on this chapter, I am grateful to participants at the European University Institute conference on Social Rights in Europe—where it was first presented—as well as to an anonymous referee for Oxford University Press.

[1] For a classical exposition of the history of rights, see Marshall, 'Citizenship and Social Class', in T. H. Marshall, *Sociology at the Crossroads* (1963).

[2] Sources for constitutional texts: http://www.ecln.net/elements/euro_constitutions.html, and http://www.oefre.unibe.ch/law/icl/index.html. I do not restrict my account to the constitutions of the Member States; I also consider Bulgaria, Croatia, Romania, and Turkey, all four of which are candidates for accession.

present political and economic context. Whilst welfare states are a central plank of the European liberal and democratic model, they are currently under threat from the combined pressures of, amongst others, globalization, an ageing population, and (relatedly) ever expanding medical needs. Examining constitutional social rights in Europe will enable us to see whether there are discrepancies between legal texts and local practices, and whether it is possible to challenge the latter in the light of the former. It will also enable us to contest the view that civil and political rights have primacy over social rights: as we shall see, not all European constitutions rank social rights below their historical predecessors. More broadly, the study of constitutional social rights in Europe is a lens through which we can perceive that there is a European culture of social justice—with some variations between countries of course, but a common culture nonetheless. In a nutshell, most European constitutions, in their spirit if not always in their letter, claim that human beings have dignity, are equal to one another, and should all be treated accordingly—that is, should receive material help in the form of social assistance.

In unearthing social rights in all twenty-nine European constitutions, we shall walk down the following road. We shall begin by examining, in Section II, which constitutions enshrine social rights, and how specific those constitutions are. We shall then look in Section III at the difficult issue of justiciability, and assess how, if at all, European courts can deal with constitutional social rights. Finally, we shall explore the two foundational ideas of fundamental equality and human dignity. In particular, we shall see that the principle of fundamental equality to which they give rise, namely the principle whereby individuals should treat one another with equal concern and respect, simply cannot be proven. And that is a rather worrying thought: for if one cannot prove that principle, then the entire edifice of Western moral and political philosophy, from the 17th century onwards, and more specifically the European constitutional order which it underpins, rests on extremely shaky philosophical foundations. The question, which I shall address at the close of Section IV, is the extent to which that really matters.

Two caveats, before I begin. First, in order to get to grips with what I have called the European constitutional culture of social justice, one would also have to examine the role played by the European Social Charter in each of the countries which has adopted it. I shall not do so here: many of the contributions to this volume do precisely that. Rather, I shall restrict myself to the letter and spirit of the constitutions of the twenty-nine countries which are members of the EU or are aspiring to become so. To be sure—and this is my second caveat—the political and social context within which a country drafts and adopts a constitution matters a great deal to getting a full understanding of its constitutional fabric. A full comparative study of the European constitutions would require careful scrutiny of such context, of the debates—parliamentary and otherwise—leading up to the adoption of the constitution and of its amendments, and so on. To do so is beyond the scope of this chapter. Accordingly, I do not claim to engage in sophisticated comparative constitutional law. My aim, rather, is to offer a broad and comprehensive overview of what those constitutions say. In so doing, I am merely scratching the surface of Europe's constitutional culture of social justice. Scratching the surface, however, can give us enough of an appetite for discovering what lies underneath it—a task I leave to those better qualified than I am.

II. WHICH SOCIAL RIGHTS IN WHICH CONSTITUTIONS?

Reviewing each European constitution one by one would be both cumbersome and not particularly interesting. Instead, let me make six general observations. For a start, although social rights are rights which individuals have against those who are in a position to help them, generally welfare assistance is financed from tax proceeds and provided by the state. In so far as bills of rights are thought to enshrine the rights of individuals and citizens against the state, as opposed to against one another, it is not surprising that the constitutions of European countries should adopt a very state-centrist, and national, language when delineating social rights. To many, this is a dated view of conceiving of social rights, since the latter are more often than not respected, or rather violated, by private actors such as firms and corporations, and by foreign actors such as foreign states and international institutions. There is a sense, then, in which European constitutions have failed to take on-board some of the most important causes of deprivation.

Secondly, many European constitutions specify that such rights should be respected to an adequate standard. But what does constitute an adequate standard of provision? Consider, for example, the right to a minimum income. Whatever income we get helps meet subsistence needs, such as food, water, clothing, as well as socially determined needs—that is, needs which we have by virtue of living in a particular society, such as, in Europe, the cost of using public transport, a television, and so on. If those latter needs are not met, we lack well-being, and are not in a position to frame, revise, and pursue our conception of the good life—we are not, in short, autonomous, and therefore do not lead a minimally decent life. An *adequate* income must thus be calculated by taking into account both kinds of needs, and to that extent will vary from country to country and, within a country, over time.[3] Accordingly, when entrenching social rights, constitution-makers must be careful not to be too specific, since levels of provision may have to vary depending on the country's level of economic and social development. However, they must also be careful not to be too vague, so as to give courts a sense of how best to respect the constitution when adjudicating those rights.[4]

---

[3] For an extended argument to that effect, see C. Fabre, *Social Rights under the Constitution: Government and the Decent Life* (2000), Ch 1.   [4] Ibid., at 154ff.

When assessing how European constitutions deal with social rights, and in particular which rights they enshrine and in which terms, we shall need to bear those considerations in mind. However, there is no need to do so as far as Austria, Germany, and the United Kingdom are concerned, since they (alone out of twenty-nine constitutions) do not enshrine social rights as such. I say 'as such' because both the German and the British constitutions (such as the latter is) mention the right to education; they do not, however, enshrine it as a *social right*—that is, as a right the fulfilment of which is grounded in the importance of ensuring that a basic need is met. Rather, the German Basic Law of 1949 stipulates a right to set up private schools, and is rather detailed on the role of religion in education. It thus sees the right to education as part of the broader civil right to religious freedom. As to the British Human Rights Act of 1998, which incorporates some provisions of the European Charter on Human Rights in British law, it explicitly grants individuals a right to education, but as part of what is necessary for the effective exercise of (political) citizenship. On those views, then, education is not to be valued for its contribution to individual welfare alongside minimum income, housing, and health care; rather, it is to be valued for its connections to those long-standing elements of bills of rights, to wit, civil and political rights.

Whereas the aforementioned three countries are silent on social rights, at the other end of the scale, the Portuguese Constitution is very detailed, without falling into the trap of being too specific. It lists all social rights under study, distinguishes between various categories of people who might need, and deserve, material assistance: the young, the elderly, the disabled, workers, the unemployed. In that it is not alone, as we shall see. But it is unusual in that it suggests a number of ways in which the state can meet its obligations to the needy. For example, Article 64 states that all individuals have a right to health care, and goes on to specify that such a right can be respected through preventive, curative, and rehabilitative care, and that the state ought to supervise private medicine. Article 60, which deals with consumers' rights, notes that consumers' health must be protected through ensuring the quality of goods of consumption. When dealing with the right to housing, at Article 65, again this Constitution lists various measures which the state can take: setting a housing policy based on urban planning sensitive to the importance of transport networks; promoting housing cooperatives as well as individual buildings; introducing a system of rent 'compatible with family income and individual ownership of dwelling', and so on.

All other twenty-five countries fall somewhere in between: some enshrine all social rights, others focus on one or two. Some use rather terse language; others take greater care to elucidate the content of those rights. For example, the Constitution of Cyprus merely stipulates at Article 9 that individuals have a right to 'decent existence and social security', without specifying further what that could mean. Nor does it mention housing or health care. Sweden's Instrument of Government also rather succinctly states, at Article 2 of Chapter One, 'that it shall be incumbent upon the public administration to secure the right to work, housing and education, and to promote social care and social security': no mention of the right to health care, one may note. By contrast, to name a few, Italy, the Netherlands, France, Spain, and Malta are fairly expansive on the rights to be secured, the categories of people to whom they are granted, and the levels at which they are granted. On the latter point, the Italian Constitution at Article 34 and the Constitution of Malta at Articles 10–11 specify that education shall be free at primary level and that deserving pupils at subsequent levels should get financial assistance. The Dutch Constitution states at Article 22 that individuals should have 'sufficient living accommodation'. In a similar vein, Article 47 of the Spanish Constitution provides for the right to 'decent and adequate housing', and Article 41 asks for 'adequate social assistance'.

So far, I have mentioned only those social rights the promotion of which is incumbent on governments. It is worth noting, though, and thirdly, that many European constitutions enshrine a number of rights in the workplace—in other words, rights which ought to be protected by law, but which it is incumbent upon employers to respect. Thus, Articles 22 and 37 of the Greek and Spanish Constitutions respectively make it very clear that working conditions and labour conflicts should be solved through collective bargaining; Article 56 of the Croatian Constitution stipulates not only that workers should be granted weekly rest and paid holidays, but also that they should be given rights to take part in firms' decision-making procedures. The point is worth noting precisely because constitutions are thought, generally, to regulate the relationship between citizens and their governments, not to set the rules of citizens' interaction *qua* employees and employers. European constitutions thus display awareness that individuals' fates depend, not merely on governmental decisions, but also on their employers'. To put the point differently, the European culture of social justice is, as it were, 'complete', delineating as it does principles for individuals' status as citizens and workers.

As we have seen, European constitutions vary considerably in their degree of precision, the kind of social provision they mention, and the categories of individuals they cater for. But—and this is my fourth general observation—they also vary in the ways in which they conceive of social provision. The majority clearly state that they are a matter of rights; others do not use rights discourse, in keeping with the view, often held in the past but not so prevalent nowadays, that the only rights are those which only impose on others, including the state, a duty of non-interference, not those which impose on them a positive duty to act. One may think that whether or not the language of rights is used is irrelevant, that what matters is that the constitution guarantees that individuals' needs will be met. And yet, it does matter (as indeed other contributions in this volume note). For to say that someone, P, has a right to something, A, is not merely to say that it would be good or desirable for P to get A. It amounts to the much stronger claim that P *must* get A, and that third parties, upon whom it is incumbent to respect the right, do not have a choice in the matter (unless P releases them from their obligation). More deeply, it makes it clear that whatever obligation the right imposes is owed *to P*, and is grounded in P's interests, and not in some other value. Rights discourse, in short, rests on the view—rooted in Judæo-Christian thought—that the individual matters, that his or her interests are the primary focus of our concern. Accordingly, those constitutions which unambiguously assign social rights to individuals are more faithful, or so it seems, to the moral and political traditions of our continent than those which do not.

A fifth interesting point about social rights in European constitutions is their importance relative to civil and political rights. In the Anglo-American tradition, bills of rights are bills of civil and political rights. Indeed it is no coincidence that the British Human Rights Act of 1998 should be one of three constitutional texts, in Europe, which do not mention social rights. By contrast, as should be clear by now, European constitutions easily incorporate social rights. But some of them nevertheless do subscribe to the widely held view that those rights are subordinate to civil and political rights—that the right not to be killed, for example, is more important, more central, than the right not to be left to die of hunger. Thus, most of them list civil and political rights first, social rights last (in fact, not a single one of them begins with social rights). But some of them, interestingly, begin with a few civil rights (such as the right not to be killed or tortured), carry on with social rights, and end with other civil rights which are thus, implicitly, considered as less important.

Finally, many European constitutions (for example, the Danish and Finnish Constitutions) tend to rely, sometimes explicitly, sometimes implicitly, on the distinction between those who are needy through no fault of their own, and those who are responsible for their predicament. The phrases 'those who cannot work', or 'those who cannot secure the means for their own subsistence' are often used in connection with the right to a minimum income. In so doing, European constitutions strongly distinguish between the deserving and the undeserving poor. That they should do so is worth noting. For in drawing that distinction, they are not in keeping with a still marginal, but growing number of European philosophers and policy-makers who, instead of according individual responsibility the place it currently has in contemporary welfare states, advocate that *all* individuals, whether they want to work or not and regardless of the reasons why they do not work, be given an *unconditional* basic income.[5] In fact, European constitutions are firmly anchored in the Christian ethical norms of individual responsibility and work ethics.

Moreover, the distinction between the deserving and the undeserving poor is a cornerstone of 'right-wing' thinking on welfare policies (alongside the view that the state should intervene as little as possible in the economic and social life of the nation). By contrast, left-wing parties and movements have been charged for being too lenient with the undeserving poor. However, the fact that those parties, when

---

[5] The best defence of an unconditional basic income is P. Van Parijs' brilliant book *Real Freedom for All: What, if Anything, Can Justify Capitalism?* (1995).

in power, have endorsed the view that, at constitutional level, some poor individuals deserve to be helped, whilst others do not, suggests that the European left has more common ground with its foes than is usually acknowledged. Not that this should be surprising: the view that individuals are able to make the decisions that affect them most and should be left free to do so is central to liberalism—Europe's dominant ideology, whether left or right. In so far as its correlate is, precisely, that individuals should be held responsible for such decisions, not only is it politically expedient for the left to restrict constitutional social rights to those who are not responsible for their predicament, it is also in keeping with some of its core values.

Having said that, it pays to note that in Europe at least, constitutional discourse and actual practices somewhat diverge. No welfare policy can hope exactly to implement the distinction between the deserving and undeserving poor in all the areas in which it applies. For we simply cannot gather enough information about individuals' precise circumstances, which include not merely their current situation, such as unemployment, and its direct causes, such as poor interpersonal skills, but also what in their education, background, etc., contributed to it. We cannot, in short, know precisely the extent to which someone is responsible for being poor. However, we can, up to a point, at least in some cases, know whether someone is responsible for requiring medical treatment: someone who can, but does not, get vaccinated against serious diseases; a driver who has a car accident while driving under the influence of alcohol or using the phone, and so on. If European practices were in line with the spirit of their constitutions, such individuals should not be given medical treatment for free. And yet, they are: notwithstanding their (at times) stern constitutional languages, European societies simply cannot accept the idea that someone who is responsible for his predicament, but does not have the wherewithal to pay for medical treatment, should be left to die. One cannot help thinking that this is as it should be—that in the area of social rights, one should not stick to the letter of the constitutional law, but rather to its spirit—that no matter what they do, individuals are entitled to be treated in ways which are compatible with the idea of human dignity. More precisely, they are entitled to social rights to minimum income, education, housing, and health care.

III. JUSTICIABILITY

I shall come back to human dignity in section 4. For now, I want to focus on the second feature of constitutional entrenchment, namely justiciability. For it is one thing for a constitution to say, for example, that all individuals have a right to a decent income; it is quite another to allow the courts to ensure that public authorities, most notably the legislative power, actually respect that right. The issue of justiciability raises three questions: (1) Are constitutional social rights within the remit of the courts?; (2) How can the courts intervene so as to protect those rights from legislative and executive attempts to undermine them?; (3) How difficult is it for the legislative power to override courts' decisions?

Not all European constitutions allow the courts to adjudicate conflicts between public authorities and individuals regarding constitutional social rights. The Constitution of Denmark is entirely silent on the issue. Others, such as the Dutch Constitution, explicitly disallow judicial interference with legislative action; still others explicitly disallow judicial interference with social policy specifically. Thus, the Constitution of Ireland enshrines the right to free and adequate education for all children, but 'relegates' other social rights to a section called 'Directive Principles of Social Policy'—principles which, under Article 45, do not fall within the remit of the courts. Similarly, the Constitution of Malta, which as we saw does enshrine rights to education and to social assistance for the needy, explicitly rules out at Article 21 the possibility of allowing the courts to intervene in those areas. As to the Spanish Constitution, it allows for judicial review of constitutional rights by the Constitutional Court as well as lower courts, but only for breaches of the right to equal treatment before the law, civil and political rights, as well as the right to education (Articles 53, 161). Under Article 53(2), it does not allow for judicial review of other constitutional social provisions such as adequate social assistance and the rights to health protection and adequate housing.

However, the majority of countries provide for justiciability, although in one case, that of Romania, the legislative power can override courts' decisions without having to amend the constitution. In and of itself, this does not mean that individuals have extensive recourse, at the bar of the constitution, against their governments, indeed against their elected representatives. For whilst some constitutions allow any court to make a judgment of unconstitutionality (such as Cyprus and Estonia), many others do not, and restrict this possibility to a Constitutional Court (for example Bulgaria, Belgium, and Greece). Some constitutions (such as the Estonian Constitution) allow individuals to petition the constitutional courts, whereas others only allow them to raise the question of the constitutionality of a law or decision in the course of any judicial proceedings (as is the case in Cyprus); still others, such as the French Constitution, simply rule out individual petition altogether. Finally, some countries allow not merely for judicial review, whereby the constitutionality of a law is assessed after the law is passed or upon a complaint from a party in judicial proceedings, but also for judicial preview, whereby the constitutionality of the law is assessed before the law is passed. Such is the case with Romania and Bulgaria. And whereas some constitutions explicitly rule out judicial preview (see Article 128 of the Slovakian Constitution as well as Articles 156 and 160 of the Slovenian Constitution), France, by contrast, is the only country which makes constitutional social rights justiciable *and* rules out judicial review: neither the Council, nor the Council of State, which is the highest court to adjudicate conflicts between the state and individuals residing in France, can invoke the constitution once a law is passed to annul the latter.

What is the significance of all this? The easier a constitution makes it for an individual to petition a court on the grounds that his constitutional rights have been violated, the greater the strength of entrenchment. Judicial review is crucial in that respect, since it works on the assumption that a law may well appear to be congruent with the constitution as it is passed, but turn out not to be once it is applied to individual cases. This is not to say that judicial preview is unnecessary: one can imagine situations where a law clearly violates the constitution, or is phrased in such a way that it can obviously be applied in violation of it, in which case it is better to strike it down before it is promulgated—in other words, before it can do any damage. European constitutions which allow for one, and not for the other, of those modes of adjudication, fail to protect individuals' constitutional rights, and thereby their constitutional *social* rights, to the full extent of their power. Needless to say, those which rule out constitutional social rights from the remit of the courts fail on that count to an even greater degree.

In so doing, however, they thereby accord greater importance to democratic decision-making than those constitutions which provide for judicial review, judicial preview, and individual petition. For the greater the strength of constitutional entrenchment, the more restricted the scope for legislative and executive decision-making. Justiciability, or the lack of it, is crucial, then, in particular when constitutional social rights are concerned, in so far as it gives us an indication of a given country's understanding of the relative importance of social justice and democracy.

I am presupposing here that social rights matter in and of themselves, that they are not instrumental to democracy. This is a controversial view, particularly in academic circles, where it is widely held that one cannot be an effective citizen if one does not know where one's next meal is coming from. I have rebutted that argument at length elsewhere, and I shall not repeat myself here.[6] Suffice it to say that European constitutions do not ground social rights on the claim that they are part and parcel of political citizenship. In fact, some of them say very little on the fundamental values to which social rights give expression. But quite a few invoke the importance of two ideals, of human dignity and fundamental equality. To examining those two ideals, which in those constitutions at least are the explicit basis for constitutional social rights, I now turn.

IV. FUNDAMENTAL PRINCIPLES: DIGNITY AND EQUALITY

Some European constitutions (such as, for example, the Czech, Finnish, Italian, and Portuguese Constitutions) clearly state that human beings have dignity and should be treated as such; more specifically, that they should be treated as having *equal* moral worth. Unsurprisingly, those constitutions do not in any way

---

[6] See Fabre, *supra* n. 3, Ch 4.

elucidate what they mean by 'human dignity' or 'equal moral worth'. But in so far as they avail themselves of a vocabulary to be found in the philosophical, religious, and political discourses which constitute the foundation of European public culture, one can easily and plausibly understand them to mean the following: human beings have a special moral status, in that they have attributes such as the capacity for moral and rational agency which no other being has. Moreover, they have that capacity to the same degree. Accordingly, in so far as they have equal moral worth, they should be treated with equal concern and respect.[7]

My aim in this section is first to explore the view I have just sketched out, and which for convenience's sake I shall dub the *principle of fundamental equality*, in relation to European constitutions' treatment of social rights. It is then to assess whether the principle can be proven.

Notice, first, that 'treating with concern' and 'treating with respect' are two different ways of treating someone, although the words 'concern' and 'respect' are often lumped together. To treat them with concern is to have solicitous regard for their interests; it is to recognize that their interests are important in and of themselves, irrespective of whatever importance they might have to us; it is, accordingly, to refrain from harming those interests as well as to help promote them, on those very grounds. Thus, to treat someone with concern is to attach importance to their interest in continuing to live a minimally decent life, which in turn means not killing them *and* helping them to get the resources which they need in order to live such a life. Hence the attention paid, in most European constitutions, to such necessities as minimum income and housing.

By contrast, to treat someone with respect is to recognize that they are capable of acting rationally and morally so as to promote their interests. Thus, although I treat my cat with concern (I feed him not because it is in my interest that he remain alive, but because it is in *his* interest to do so, and because he depends on me), I do not respect him. I do not mean that I *dis*respect him: I mean that he is not the kind of creature which warrants respectful or, indeed, disrespectful, treatment. Some of the social rights enshrined in European constitutions are founded on the importance of respectful treatment. To insist that individuals should receive an adequate income, either from the state directly, or at work thanks to the protection afforded by minimum wage legislation[8] is not merely to have concern for them: it is to pay respect to them, by recognizing that they are able, through work, to raise the resources they need; and if not in work, that they need an all-purpose resource such as money in order to further their own interests, even if they end up squandering such resources. European constitutions would have been far less respectful of the needy if they had provided, instead, for help in kind rather than in cash, by way of food and clothing vouchers.

---

[7] The best contemporary philosophical accounts of the view sketched here are J. Rawls, *A Theory of Justice* (1999, 2nd edn.); R. Dworkin, *Sovereign Virtue* (2000).

[8] As stipulated by, e.g., Article 59 of the Portuguese Constitution and, in France, Article 28 of the Preamble of Constitution of the Fourth Republic—which is part of the current Constitution.

Although the principle of fundamental equality dictates that we treat one another with equal concern and respect, the two requirements may conflict with each other: I may be led, out of concern for someone, to act so as to promote his interests in what I think is the best way, thereby failing to recognize that he has a say over how his interests should be promoted, and thereby failing to show him respect. Conversely, I might, out of respect for him, decide not to take any step to help him promote his interests, thereby contributing to his downfall. European constitutions emphasize the importance of respecting, by contrast with showing concern for, individuals, in two ways. First, as we saw in Section II above, they guarantee material help to those who are not causally responsible for their predicament and not to those who are. In so doing, they imply that we should respect individuals for their ability to take charge of their lives, the correlative of which is that those individuals are held morally responsible for their predicament. Secondly, unlike instruments such as the International Declaration of Human Rights, they do not characterize individual rights in general and social rights in particular as inalienable. If an individual decides *not* to avail herself of the material provision to which she has a constitutional right, then so be it: it is her choice, which has to be respected.

The fact that concern and respect denote different dispositions towards others does bear on the requirement that we treat them with *equal* concern and respect. For it may be that, in some cases, the interests of some individuals outweigh those of other individuals. For example, although we ought to show concern for individuals by helping them get the material resources they need, we ought not to bring about full equality of resources through extensive distributive policies. For if we were to do so, we would jeopardize the interests of those in a position to help, by asking them to give far more of their own resources than is reasonable to expect. There is, in other words, a limit to our obligation to help others. European constitutions are, by and large, sensitive to this, since they understand social rights as ensuring that individuals have enough resources to meet their needs, not that everyone has as much as others. I say 'by and large', for the Italian and the Portuguese Constitutions (Articles 3 and 9 respectively) provide for more extensive, more egalitarian measures.

So far, so good. But to elucidate the relationship between having equal moral worth and being under a duty to treat one another with equal concern and respect, and in turn to define with greater precision than is (perhaps) usually done what those terms mean, does in no way show *why* we should, indeed, believe that human beings have equal moral worth, and why we should treat them accordingly. Unsurprisingly, European constitutions do not do this: for that is not their role. However, it pays to assess whether it is possible to show the truth of that belief. For if it turns out that the principle of fundamental equality is not justifiable, then we may well have cause to worry that the European constitutional culture of justice rests on shaky foundations.

Remember the basis upon which the principle of fundamental equality is asserted. Human beings, it is said, have a special moral status, in that they have attributes such as the capacity for moral and rational agency which no other being has. This in turn suggests that they should be treated with concern and respect. Moreover, they have that capacity to the same degree. Accordingly, in so far as they have equal moral worth, they should be treated with equal concern and respect.

There are various familiar problems with that argument. First, human beings who share that capacity, actual or potential, do not have it to the same degree. Egalitarians readily acknowledge that some people are better able than others at furthering their own interests and at understanding what is morally right and wrong. Yet, they claim that, notwithstanding those variations, human beings must be treated with *equal* concern and respect. However, if it is true that the capacity for moral and rational agency is what warrants treating one another with concern and respect, why not say that we should treat one another with concern and respect to the degree to which we have that capacity?

Some philosophers, many of them Kantians, and certainly Kant himself, have argued that the capacity for agency is independent of the mental and psychological capacities we are empirically found to have, and is therefore not vulnerable to the challenge posited at the end of the last paragraph. But their response to that challenge is clearly false. For it makes sense to state that human beings have, and trees lack, the capacity for agency, only in virtue of the fact that human beings have capacities that trees do not. In order to distinguish between human beings and trees in respect of their moral status, one cannot but appeal to that fact. The problem, of course, is that this argument for the principle of equal concern and respect under study rests on a naturalistic fallacy. It seeks to derive a moral requirement from a set of facts, whereas no such derivation is possible: to acknowledge that human beings are capable of acting rationally and morally does not in any way commit us to agreeing that we should treat them with equal concern and respect.

Now, there are other justifications for the principle of fundamental equality than the one mentioned so far, most notably the Golden Rule. On that view, if, as a human being, you wish to be treated with concern and respect by others, you should treat them in exactly the same way. However, I do not believe that the Golden Rule is in the spirit of most European constitutions. For those constitutions deem that human beings are inherently worthwhile, and equally so, and it is *that* which grounds our obligations to others, rather than our (legitimate) desire to be so treated by them. In any event, even if the Golden Rule is a tenet of European constitutional orders, it does not provide a more successful defence of fundamental equality than the aforementioned alternative. For it will not work against someone who does not already believe in fundamental equality. Imagine a white supremacist, who systematically discriminates against, or abuses, members of other races. Were you to point out to him that he should treat them with the same degree of concern and respect he demands of them, he could, in reply to your criticism, point out that the reason why he asks them to show to him concern and respect is precisely because he belongs to the superior race. The Golden Rule, he could go on to say, only dictates that he show to fellow white supremacists the kind of concern and respect he demands of them; it does not dictate that he so behave towards other races.

However repugnant the supremacist's reasoning may sound, I do not think it can be countered in a non-question-begging way. To counterclaim to him, for example, that he should not believe in the superiority of the white race in the first instance, begs the question, since this is precisely what is at issue. The Golden Rule, then, is powerless to defend fundamental equality, when fundamental equality applies to all human beings who share moral and rational agency, irrespective of race, gender, sexual orientation, etc.

Thus, neither of the justifications for fundamental equality which I have examined works. It could be, of course, that some other justification could work. Somehow, though, I doubt it. For it is unclear to me that any such justification can avoid the charge of question-beggingness, or avoid relying on the naturalistic fallacy. If so, what then? As I pointed out in Section I, if one cannot prove the truth of the principle of fundamental equality, European constitutions rest on extremely shaky philosophical foundations. For, to the extent that the principle of fundamental equality dictates that we respect others, it thereby requires that we be able to give those who disagree with us reasons for subjecting them to the power of the law. Of relevance here, it requires that we be able to give them a reason as to why they ought to contribute part of their income to help the needy. If we cannot give them such a reason—if we cannot justify subjecting them to taxation by appealing to equality—then are we not, in fact, violating the very principle which we aim to respect?

I submit that we are not guilty of such violation. For the main reason why we may think that we have cause to worry, if the principle cannot be proved, is that opponents of the principle may use its improvability as evidence that the principle of fundamental *in*equality is true. However, the fact that the principle cannot be proved need not worry us too much, because its opponents are vulnerable to some of the objections which they deploy against it. For consider: some of them might indeed adduce the claim that, as egalitarians themselves must acknowledge, human beings are not equal in strength, intelligence, capacity for rational thoughts, and that they should therefore be treated with concern and respect to the degree to which they possess those qualities. Others might adduce the claim that only members of a particular race or gender should be so treated. In the field of social rights, then, they might claim that only White children should get the benefit of state education as Black children are by nature not as intelligent, that only men should enjoy full protection in the workplace since women's place is, by nature, at home, that the mentally and physically disabled should not get health care treatment since they are a drain on the nation's resources, and so on. However, in so arguing, anti-egalitarians *themselves* are guilty of the naturalistic fallacy, since they assume that the possession, or lack thereof, of certain features by some human beings justifies unequal treatment. But that *does* amount to deriving values from facts.

If I am correct, the fight between egalitarians and anti-egalitarians is a fight between people who can never hope to convince one another of the truth of the fundamental principles on which their theories respectively rest. All egalitarians can hope to do, *vis-à-vis* anti-egalitarians, is to show them that the facts which they use to justify their policies are false, and that some of the policies they advocate cannot be justified by the principle of fundamental *in*equality. For example, they can point out that women have skills and talents above and beyond the care and nurturing of children, and that men are capable of being good carers; that many Blacks are intelligent whilst many White children lag behind at schools, and that such differences as exist between minorities with respect to educational achievement can be traced not to natural differences, but to social and economic conditions. And so on.

Egalitarians, then, are not powerless when faced by anti-egalitarians. And even if they were, that still would not mean that they should give up on constructing normative arguments which appeal to the principle of fundamental equality; more concretely, it does not mean that they should tear apart those constitutions which rest on it. True, the principle has not been proven yet; and true, one may never be able to prove it. In so far as most people hold it to be true, and in so far as most philosophical and political fights occur between them, the whole enterprise of working out the implications of fundamental equality (Should we help those in need by way of coercive taxation? How much if at all should we distribute?) remains worthwhile. So does the business of forcing transient democratic majorities, by way of constitutional entrenchment, to respect the norms of fundamental equality.

V. CONCLUSION

In conclusion, we have seen that although European constitutions differ on the kinds of social provision they protect, as well as on the level of such provision they guarantee and the ways in which they do so, they (with the exception of the Austrian, British, and German Constitutions) converge to enough of a degree that it is appropriate to speak of a European constitutional order with respect to social justice. And although the ideal which underpins such order, fundamental equality, is philosophically shaky in the face of inegalitarian challenges, it is not so shaky as to warrant abandonment.

PART II

THE EUROPEAN SOCIAL CHARTER

3

The Supervisory Machinery of the European Social Charter: Recent Developments and their Impact

RÉGIS BRILLAT*

I. INTRODUCTION

Over the last ten years, the European Social Charter (hereinafter the 'Charter') has ceased to be the minor or unknown document that it was in the first decades of its existence. It has become one of the Council of Europe's major treaties, alongside the European Convention on Human Rights, which served as its model and continues to do so. The indivisibility and interdependence of human rights are now—at least in official declarations—generally accepted. At the same time, the unprecedented geographical extension of the countries bound by the Charter gives it an indisputable pan-European dimension. As of October 2004:

- Forty-five of the forty-six member states had signed either the Charter or the Revised Charter or both (ten the Charter and thirty-five the Revised Charter).[1] The only country not to have done so is Serbia and Montenegro, which only recently joined the organization.

- Thirty-six had ratified the 1961 Charter, the Revised Charter or both (seventeen the Charter, nineteen the Revised Charter).[2]

- Thirteen member states had accepted the collective complaints procedure.

Other ratifications expected in the coming months include Georgia, 'The former Yugoslav Republic of Macedonia' and the Ukraine. The ratification procedure is also under way in Russia and Bosnia-Hercegovina.

---

* The views expressed in this chapter are purely those of the author and do not represent the views of the Council of Europe.

[1] Monaco acceded to the Council of Europe on 5 October 2004 and signed the Revised Social Charter on the same day. The Parliamentary Assembly asked Monaco to ratify it within two years.

[2] Azerbaijan and Andorra are the states that most recently ratified the Revised Charter. Azerbaijan deposited its instrument of ratification on 2 September 2004.

So far twenty-eight collective complaints have been registered, the number increasing significantly over the last year.[3] The reforms of the 1990s had a major impact on the rights embodied in the Charter and on the way the implementation by ratifying states is monitored. It forms part of the curriculum of numerous European universities and is increasingly frequently referred to in legal publications, not to mention works entirely devoted to the Charter.

So what can we now add? That the reform continues to bear fruit and that the quasi-judicial nature of the procedure is becoming more and more evident, thus reinforcing the dynamic interpretation of the rights.

II. THE QUASI-JUDICIAL NATURE OF THE PROCEDURE

A. *A Judicial Procedure*

This has been a central aspect of the reform.[4] According to Rule 2 of the March 2004 Rules of the European Committee of Social Rights:

1. The Committee makes a legal assessment of the conformity of national situations with the European Social Charter, the 1988 Additional Protocol and the Revised European Social Charter.

2. It adopts conclusions in the framework of the reporting procedure and decisions under the collective complaints procedure.

This removes the ambiguity overshadowing the Charter's first thirty years. There is no longer any doubt about the role of the different committees active in the supervision process.

The European Committee of Social Rights makes the legal rulings, and its findings of Charter violations cannot be challenged. In the great majority of cases, governments accept these findings and make the necessary changes to secure compliance. Admittedly, it is sometimes a long process, but this is hardly surprising given the complexity of the reforms and the number of actors—government and legislature, regional authorities, social partners, and so on—involved. The list of changes, in law and practice, arising from the Committee's conclusions is becoming longer each year and of ever-growing significance.[5]

Naturally, there are cases where states have failed—or have so far failed—to make the necessary changes. One of the main challenges facing the supervisory procedure is how to resolve these situations and persuade the countries concerned to take

---

[3] The number of collective complaints registered has been 1 in 1998, 5 in 1999, 4 in 2000, 1 in 2001, 2 in 2002, 10 in 2003, and 5 in 2004.

[4] See, in particular, R. Brillat, 'Le système de contrôle de la Charte sociale européenne', in J.-F. Akandji-Kombé and S. Leclerc (eds), *La Charte sociale européenne* (2000).

[5] See, for example, Council of Europe, *Implementation of the European Social Charter—Survey by Country* (2001 and 2002). See also the country situations on www.coe.int (Human Rights/European Social Charter/Reporting Procedure/Survey by Country).

action. However, it is reassuring to note that in the great majority of cases such disagreements occur in countries that ratified the Charter prior to the 1991 Turin Protocol amending the Charter. States that ratified it more recently, in contrast, have abided by the new supervisory rules with a lot more conviction. In this respect, the Governmental Committee reports to the Committee of Ministers speak volumes.[6]

The Governmental Committee's role is to ensure that states do follow up the conclusions. If this does not happen after a certain period, the Governmental Committee can request the Committee of Ministers to issue a recommendation to the member state concerned, calling on it to bring the situation into conformity.

Certain commentators[7] have tried to measure the Charter's effectiveness in terms of the number of Committee of Ministers recommendations adopted. This seems to imply that recommendations are the only way of securing compliance. They then generally add that such recommendations have little binding force. Such an approach no longer corresponds to reality, if it ever did.

Recommendations are political documents and are not intended to be findings of violations, which are solely the competence of the European Committee of Social Rights. The aim of such recommendations is to remind states of their obligations to comply with a treaty they have ratified and take account of the conclusions of the body responsible for ruling on violations, which is the treaty's judicial organ.

Admittedly, there have been stand-offs of the sort referred to where the Governmental Committee has not played a very active role. Violations that have been pinpointed for years, if not decades, and where it seems that the government has refused to take the necessary action, would certainly have justified a Committee of Ministers recommendation. Such cases are fairly rare however and the practice according to which states comply with the Committee's conclusions and decisions is becoming established practice, even though such an obligation is not explicitly written in the Treaty.

In a few years it will be possible to tell whether all findings of violations are followed by the necessary measures to bring the situation into compliance, as is the case with the European Convention on Human Rights, where all the Court's judgments are implemented by the countries concerned.[8]

---

[6] The reports are available on www.coe.int (Human Rights/European Social Charter/Reporting Procedure/Follow up to the Conclusions: Governmental Committee).

[7] See, *inter alia*, R. Churchill and U. Khaliq, 'The Collective Complaints System of the European Social Charter: An Effective Mechanism for Ensuring Compliance with Economic and Social Rights?', 15 *EJIL* (2004) 417.

[8] Sometimes, after a certain time has elapsed. In addition to the formal obligation enshrined in Article 46 of the ECHR, the Committee of Ministers' role in the execution of Court judgments and the key contribution of the Directorate General of Human Rights should not be underestimated.
Article 46 reads as follows :

'Article 46—Binding force and execution of judgments

1 The High Contracting Parties undertake to abide by the final judgment of the Court in any case to which they are parties.
2 The final judgment of the Court shall be transmitted to the Committee of Ministers, which shall supervise its execution.

Turning to collective complaints, recent years have further demonstrated the binding nature of the European Committee of Social Rights' decisions. The Committee adopts a 'decision' on the merits of each complaint that it has declared admissible. It sends it to the parties to the complaint, and to the Committee of Ministers in a report. This decision may not be published until four months have elapsed. The—regrettable—lack of transparency at this critical stage of the proceedings has led to fears that the Committee of Ministers might question the Committee's decisions. Experience shows that this is not usually the case. In fact, there has only been one case where the Committee of Ministers has adopted a resolution effectively challenging the Committee's decision.[9] In every other case,[10] the Committee of Ministers has noted the decision and either urged the defendant state to bring the situation into conformity if it did not show immediate signs of doing so[11] or taken note of the government's undertaking to bring the situation into conformity and of any measures already taken to achieve this.[12] It is also significant that in both content and style, Committee of Ministers resolutions have become increasingly explicit when describing the legal situation and the steps defendant states are expected to take.[13]

These changes all show how far the Committee has evolved towards a more judicial role, since it interprets the law and states are bound by that law, whether laid down in the conclusions of the reporting procedure or decisions in response to collective complaints. To a certain extent, in exercising this responsibility the Committee has the status of and acts as a judicial body.

B. A Quasi-judicial Body

1. The Collective Complaints Procedure   The collective complaints procedure has been the most obvious focus of the Committee's increasingly judicial method of proceeding. Its very first rules of procedure[14] showed that it wished to give a

---

[9] *CFE-CGC v. France*, Decision on the merits of 1 November 2001, Complaint No. 9/2000: Res ChS(2002) 4 of 26 March 2002. The CFE-CGC has since submitted a further complaint based on similar grounds: *CFE-CGC v. France*, Complaint No. 16/2003, which was declared admissible on 16 June 2003 and is currently being considered on the merits.

[10] Seven so far, since of the 13 complaints for which the Committee has completed its examination, one was declared inadmissible and four others led to a non-violation finding.

[11] *Syndicat des professionnels du tourisme v. France*, Complaint No. 6/1999, Resolution Res ChS(2001) 1 of 31 January 2001.

[12] In 6 other cases: *International Commission of Jurists v. Portugal*, Complaint No. 1/1998: Resolution Res ChS(99) 4 of 15 December 1999; *FIDH v. Greece*, Complaint No. 7/2000: Resolution Res ChS(2001) 6 of 5 April 2001; *Quaker Council for European Affairs (QCEA) v. Greece*, Complaint No. 8/2000: Resolution Res ChS(2002) 3 of 6 March 2002; *STTK ry and TEHY ry v. Finland*, Complaint No. 10/2000: Resolution Res ChS(2002) 2 of 21 February 2002; *Confederation of Swedish Enterprises v. Sweden*, Complaint No. 12/2002: Resolution Res ChS(2003) 1 of 26 September 2003; *Autism-Europe v. France*, Complaint No. 13/2002: Resolution Res ChS(2004) 1 of 10 March 2004.   [13] As *supra* nn. 11 and 12.

[14] Adopted in 1998 and published in *Conclusions XIV-1*, at 29–31.

judicial orientation to implementing the Protocol. The adoption of new rules on 9 September 1999 represented further progress in this direction and this was taken still further with the rules of 29 March 2004.15

Several aspects of the procedure offer a clear indication of the Committee's orientation.

(a) The Committee Adopts Decisions

The report that the Committee submits to the Committee of Ministers, after it has been seen by the parties to the proceedings, contains a brief introduction followed by the decisions on the merits and on admissibility.

Decisions are reasoned and detailed, and in several respects draw inspiration from the format of judgments of the European Court of Human Rights: description of the situation in law and practice in the defendant state, the arguments of the parties to the proceedings and the Committee's conclusion, with the reasoning and the majority by which the decision was reached.

(b) Both Parties Participate in the Proceedings

In accordance with the adversarial principle, any document supplied to the Committee by one of the parties is communicated to the other, which then has the opportunity to respond. At the hearing the parties present either the complaint or the government's response and then reply to questions from Committee members. Hearings[16] have been held in one of the European Court's hearing rooms, which strengthens the impression of a judicial procedure.

(c) Reinforcing the Public Nature of the Procedure

Under the new rules, all case documents, submitted by the parties to the complaint, are to be made public on registration with the secretariat, unless the President of the Committee decides otherwise.

(d) Moving Away from the Tripartite Model

Under the new rules, European organizations of employers and European trade unions authorized to take part in the procedure may participate in hearings only if they have presented written observations on the case in question and have indicated that they wish to intervene in support of the complaint or for its rejection. The role of the European social partners, who in any case have always had the

---

[15] Available on www.coe.int (Human Rights/European Social Charter/European Committee of Social Rights); the new rules have applied since their adoption, other than in the case of collective complaints already underway, which are still covered by the 1999 rules. In practice, they have applied as of *Syndicat des Agrégés de l'Enseignement Supérieur (SAGES) v. France*, Complaint No. 26/2004.

[16] There have been 5 hearings concerning 8 of the 13 complaints whose proceedings have been completed: 1 in the 3 EUROFEDOP cases declared admissible, 9 October 2000; 1 in *CFE-CGC v. France*, Complaint No. 9/2000, 11 June 2001; 1 in *Confederation of Swedish Enterprise v. Sweden*, Complaint No. 12/2002, 31 March 2003; 1 in *Autism-Europe v. France*, Complaint No. 13/2002, 29 September 2003; and 1 in *ERRC v. Greece*, Complaint No. 15/2003, 11 October 2004.

right to submit complaints, even if they have not so far done so, is therefore to present arguments for or against complaints, in other words support or oppose the complainant organization. They are not involved in the decision-making process. The European Committee of Social Rights is not a tripartite body.

2. Impact on the Examination of Reports Procedure The quasi-judicial dimension now extends to the examination of national reports, as the following examples show.

(a) The Reasons Behind the Conclusions
Consideration of recent conclusions adopted under the reporting procedure shows that the Committee has made a real effort to explain its reasoning. This development can be illustrated with reference to Article 31 of the 1961 Charter and Article G of the Revised Charter. These two provisions correspond to paragraph 2 of Articles 8 to 11 of the European Convention on Human Rights. They set out the conditions under which rights embodied in the Charter may be restricted. For many years, the Committee has assessed whether the conditions were fulfilled when one of the rights concerned was subject to restriction. However, over the last few supervision cycles, the Committee has set out its reasoning in detail, examining the following three issues:[17]

- Is the restriction prescribed by law?
- Is it necessary in a democratic society for one of the purposes specified in Articles 31 or G?
- Is it proportionate to the objective pursued?

(b) More Systematic Drafting and Presentation
The presentation of conclusions has become increasingly systematic and follows a specific pattern: description of the situation in law and practice in the country concerned (or more simply recent changes from the previously described situation), aspects considered by the Committee to raise problems of compliance with the Charter, and a detailed statement of the reasons of the finding of conformity or non-conformity. The conclusion ends with a short sentence stating whether or not the situation is in conformity and in the latter case a brief summary of the grounds of non-conformity.

(c) The Systematic Examination of Situations for all States (Interaction between Complaints and Reports)
Once it has reached a decision on a collective complaint, the Committee then systematically examines the issues raised by the complaint in all the parties to the

---

[17] See, e.g. *Conclusions XVII-1*, Vol.1, at 101–02.

Charter when it next considers the reports on the relevant provision. The most striking example concerns the length of alternative service for conscientious objectors. After deciding that the situation in Greece was contrary to Article 1(2) because the period of alternative service was disproportionate to that of military service,[18] the Committee raised the matter with every country and concluded that the situation was not in conformity in certain other states.[19]

The strengthening of the procedure has also led to the reinforcement of the dynamic interpretation of the rights.

III. DYNAMIC INTERPRETATION OF THE RIGHTS

The strengthened supervisory machinery has had an undoubted impact on the rights embodied in the Charter. Since 1969,[20] the Committee, through interpretation, has developed the rights embodied in the Charter. However, since its role in the procedure has been re-affirmed, the Committee has to exercise this function more rigorously: indeed the recognition of its position in the procedure increases its responsibility. The term 'case law', used somewhat inappropriately for many years,[21] has never been as fully justified as it is now, in terms not only of the Committee and the procedure but also of what has been achieved by a dynamic approach to interpreting the Charter.

The Charter now concerns new issues to add to its 'traditional' ones, but in addition all the rights are now tangible, rather than mere aspirations, the fate that some wished to reserve for these so-called economic and social human rights.

A. *Different Rights*

In recent years, the Committee's case law has expanded through its interpretation of the new provisions of the Revised Charter. However it has also extended its interpretation of the older provisions, which appear in both the 1966 and revised 1996 versions, to new areas that were not originally considered to come within the Charter's scope.[22]

---

[18] *Quaker Council for European Affairs v. Greece*, Complaint No. 8/2000, Decision on the merits, para. 25.

[19] See, *Conclusions 2004* (Cyprus), at 91–92, (Romania), at 450–51; *Conclusions XVII-1* (Finland), at 165–66.

[20] The Committee was established in 1967. It held its first session in December 1968 and published its first conclusions in 1969.

[21] See J.-F. Akandji-Kombé, 'L'application de la Charte sociale européenne: la mise en œuvre de la procédure de réclamations collectives', *Droit social* (2000) 888.

[22] Many observers and commentators view the Social Charter as a treaty concerning work and employment-related matters. This is particularly reflected in the long-standing but now revitalized debate on the so-called 'social Europe'. The adjective 'social' attached to the Charter must be understood in its wide sense, 'relating to society' rather than concerned only with employment-related issues.

1. Interpreting the New Articles of the Revised Social Charter   In the last few years, the Committee has considered the first reports on the application of the Revised Social Charter, thus enabling it to interpret the new articles.[23] Over the coming years its interpretations will be refined as a growing number of reports on the Revised Charter are presented for examination. For example, the Committee has interpreted Article 26 'Right to Dignity at Work'[24] to include, *inter alia*, somewhat of a shift in the burden of proof and the existence of effective legal remedies providing for reinstatement and appropriate compensation.

The Committee has interpreted Article 31 'Right to Housing'[25] as follows:

- states must establish procedures to limit the risk of evictions and ensure that when these do take place, they are carried out under conditions which respect the dignity of the persons concerned;

- legal protection for persons threatened by eviction must include, in particular, an obligation to consult with the affected parties in order to find alternative solutions to eviction and the obligation to fix a reasonable notice period before eviction. The law must also prohibit evictions from being carried out at night or during winter and provide legal remedies and offer legal aid to those who are in need to seek redress from the courts. Compensation for illegal evictions must also be provided. When an eviction is justified by the public interest, authorities must adopt measures to re-house or financially assist the persons concerned.

2. Extending the Interpretation of Older Articles   The Committee has for many years extended its interpretation of Charter provisions to include areas that fall outside the traditional sphere of economic and employment rights. Even before the European Court of Human Rights *Mazurek* judgment,[26] the Committee had concluded that the situation in France was contrary to Article 17 of the Charter because of differences in inheritance rights between children born out of wedlock and other children.[27]

Several recent examples show how the Committee uses all the Charter's potential to apply it to new areas.

---

[23] The Conclusions on the Revised Charter are classified by the year of their publication. Three sets of conclusions have been adopted and published so far: 2002 (hard-core provisions); 2003 (non-hard-core provisions); and 2004 (hard-core provisions).

[24] See, *inter alia*, *Conclusions 2003* (Bulgaria), at 85: '... from the procedural standpoint, effective protection of employees requires somewhat of a shift in the burden of proof, making it possible for a court to find in favour of the victim on the basis of sufficient prima facie evidence and the personal conviction of the judge or judges; The victims of sexual harassment should have effective legal remedies. In particular, these should provide for reinstatement—when a sexual harassment case has led to dismissal—and appropriate compensation that is sufficient to deter the employer and fully compensate the victim.'

[25] See, *inter alia*, *Conclusions 2003* (France), at 221–37.

[26] *Mazurek v. France*, Case No. 34406/97, judgment of 1 February 2000, ECHR 2000-II.

[27] *Conclusions XIII-2*, at 159 and *Conclusions XIII-4*, at 313; Recommendation No. R ChS (98) 1 of 4 February 1998.

(a) The Right to Environment
The Committee has interpreted Article 11(1) of the Charter—'remove as far as possible the causes of ill-health'—as implying that States Parties should ratify the Kyoto Protocol and take effective measures to secure its objectives.[28]

(b) The Length of Alternative Service for Conscientious Objectors[29]
The need for compulsory military service and its duration are matters for states to decide. However, the Committee has ruled that making alternative civilian service longer than compulsory military service raises problems of compliance with Article 1(2), since during this additional period those concerned are deprived of their right to earn a living in an occupation freely entered upon. For the situation to be in compliance with the Charter, therefore, this additional period must not be excessive. In accordance with its normal methods of interpretation, the Committee has not specified what additional period is acceptable but has highlighted situations that are manifestly contrary to the Charter, from which it can be deduced that in normal circumstances an additional period of more than half the length of normal military service is excessive.

(c) The Prohibition of all Forms of Corporal Punishment of Children
The Committee has ruled that Article 17 requires a legal ban on any form of corporal punishment of children in the home, at school, or in other institutions.[30] When this

---

[28] *Conclusions XV-1*, Article 11§1, for all states.

[29] *Quaker Council for European Affairs v. Greece*, Complaint No. 8/2000, Decision on the merits of 25 April 2001. However the Committee rejected the NGO's arguments concerning the organization of alternative service: working conditions, working hours, length (or absence) of holidays.

[30] It explained its reasoning in the General Introduction to *Conclusions XV-2*, at 28–29 as follows:

The Committee attaches great importance to the protection of children against any form of violence, ill-treatment or abuse, whether physical or mental. Like the European Court of Human Rights it emphasizes the fact that children are particularly vulnerable and considers that one of the main objectives of Article 17 is to provide adequate protection for children in this respect.

—The Committee observes that in the last decades corporal punishment of children has been explicitly prohibited by law in several Contracting Parties. It observes that Recommendation No. R (90) 2 on social measures concerning violence within the family adopted by the Committee of Ministers on 15 January 1990 in its Appendix, point 14 emphasizes the general condemnation of corporal punishment and other forms of degrading treatment as a means of education.

—The Committee does not find it acceptable that a society which prohibits any form of physical violence between adults would accept that adults subject children to physical violence. The Committee does not consider that there can be any educational value in corporal punishment of children that cannot be otherwise achieved.

—Moreover, in a field where the available statistics show a constant increase in the number of cases of ill-treatment of children reported to the police and prosecutors, it is evident that additional measures to come to terms with this problem are necessary. To prohibit any form of corporal punishment of children, is an important measure for the education of the population in this respect in that it gives a clear message about what society considers to be acceptable. It is a measure that avoids discussions and concerns as to where the borderline would be between what might be acceptable corporal punishment and what is not.

is not the case, it finds that the situation is not in conformity with the Charter, as in the case of France.[31] In this respect, the Committee's finding is the same as that of the United Nations Committee on the Convention on the Rights of the Child.[32]

It is interesting to note that in cases where the Committee has not adopted conclusions for certain states and has asked for more information before ruling on the situation, an NGO, the World Organization Against Torture (OMCT), has lodged collective complaints on the subject.[33] It argues that the situation in the countries concerned is not in conformity and invites the Committee to rule as such.

Nevertheless, this activist approach to interpretation must be matched by the prudence appropriate to a quasi-judicial body. There are probably other areas where the Charter could be applied in the coming years but its sometimes excessively restrictive wording would require additions or changes.[34]

B. *Tangible Rights*

1. *Implementation at National Level* If rights and machinery to monitor their application provided for by international treaties are to be really effective, states must also be required to incorporate those rights into domestic legislation.

> —For these reasons, the Committee considers that Article 17 requires a prohibition in legislation against any form of violence against children, whether at school, in other institutions, in their home or elsewhere. It furthermore considers that any other form of degrading punishment or treatment of children must be prohibited in legislation and combined with adequate sanctions in penal or civil law.

[31] *Conclusions 2003* (France), at 176, which reads as follows:

As regards corporal punishment of children, the Committee notes that according to the report corporal punishment of children is not explicitly prohibited in the home, in school or in other institutions. Although the Penal Code prohibits violence against the person and provides for increased penalties where the victim is under 15 years of age or where the perpetrator is related to the child or has authority over the child. The Committee notes that these provisions of the Penal Code do not necessarily cover all forms of corporal punishment and therefore finds that the situation is not in conformity with the Revised Charter.

[32] Though, it should be noted that the wording is very different as between the two committees:

The Committee welcomes the fact that the State party considers corporal punishment totally unacceptable and inadmissible, however it remains concerned that corporal punishment is not explicitly prohibited in the family, in schools, in institutions and in other childcare settings. The Committee encourages the State party to expressly prohibit corporal punishment by law in the family, in schools, in institutions and in other childcare settings. It further recommends awareness raising and promotion of positive, non-violent forms of discipline, especially in families, schools and care institutions in light of Article 28(2) of the Convention.

(4 June 2004, Unedited Version CRC/C/15/Add.240, paras. 38 and 39).

[33] *OMCT v. Greece*, 17/2003; *OMCT v. Ireland*, 18/2003; *OMCT v. Italy*, 19/2003; *OMCT v. Portugal*, 20/2003; *OMCT v. Belgium*, 21/2003. These complaints were declared admissible on 9 December 2003 and the Committee is now considering the merits.

[34] See various proposals in R. Brillat, 'L'activité pré-conventionnelle et para-conventionnelle du Conseil de l'Europe dans les droits sociaux', in J.-F. Flauss (ed), *Droits sociaux et droit européen: bilan et prospective de la protection normative* (2002).

For several years now, the Committee has used both the collective complaints and the reporting procedures to describe in detail how governments should apply the Charter in practice. Three related areas illustrate this point.

(a) Practical and Effective Rights

In the well-known wording of the European Court of Human Rights, the rights embodied in the Charter must be practical and effective rather than theoretical and illusory. The Committee emphasized this point in its first decision on the merits, in Complaint No. 1/1998, *International Commission of Jurists v. Portugal* (§32):

... the Committee recalls that the aim and purpose of the Charter, being a human rights protection instrument, is to protect rights not merely theoretically, but also in fact. In this regard, it considers that the satisfactory application of Article 7 cannot be ensured solely by the operation of legislation if this is not effectively applied and rigorously supervised (see for example Conclusions XIII-3, pp. 283 and 286).

(b) Collective Bargaining and Legislation

In Collective Complaint No. 12/2002, *Confederation of Swedish Enterprise v. Sweden*, the Committee described the relationship that should exist between collective bargaining and the law and states' resulting obligations in domestic law:

26. The Committee observes firstly that Article 5 must be interpreted in the light of Article I, which reads as follows:

'Without prejudice to the methods of implementation foreseen in these articles the relevant provisions of Articles 1 to 31 of Part II of this Charter shall be implemented by:
    a. laws or regulations;
    b. agreements between employers or employers' organisations and workers' organisations;
    c. a combination of those two methods;
    d. other appropriate means.'

27. It results from the combination of these provisions that when, in order to implement undertakings accepted under Article 5, use is made of agreements concluded between employers' organisations and workers' organisations, in accordance with Article I.b, States should ensure that these agreements do not run counter to obligations entered into, either through the rules that such agreements contain or through the procedures for their implementation.

28. The commitment made by the Parties, under which domestic legislation or other means of implementation under Article I, bearing in mind national traditions, shall not infringe on employers' and workers' freedom to establish organisations, implies that, in the event of contractual provisions likely to lead to such an outcome, and whatever the implementation procedures for these provisions, the relevant national authority, whether legislative, regulatory or judicial, is to intervene, either to bring about their repeal or to rule out their implementation.

(c) Financial Implications

In its decision on the merits of Complaint No. 13/2002, *Autism-Europe v. France* §53, the Committee clarified states' obligations when the implementation of Charter provisions has significant financial implications:

When the achievement of one of the rights in question is exceptionally complex and particularly expensive to resolve, a State Party must take measures that allows it to achieve the objectives of the Charter within a reasonable time, with measurable progress and to an extent consistent with the maximum use of available resources. States Parties must be particularly mindful of the impact that their choices will have for groups with heightened vulnerabilities as well as for other persons affected including, especially, their families on whom falls the heaviest burden in the event of institutional shortcomings.

2. Judicial Implementation   Domestic courts' application of the Charter is a development that is clearly to be encouraged. The Committee has considered its own role in relation to this. It has done so in both the collective complaints and examination of reports procedures. In the former case, Complaint No. 12/2002[35] offers an illustration:

The Committee considers therefore that it is for the national courts to decide the matter in the light of the principles the Committee has laid down on this subject or, as the case may be, for the legislator to enable the courts to draw the consequences as regards the conformity with the Charter and the legality of the provisions at issue.

In the context of its examination of national reports, the Committee has stated:[36]

In its previous conclusions (Addendum to Conclusions XV-1, at 27–30; Conclusions XVI-1, at 248–251), the Committee examined the principles of proportionality and fairness as they applied to strikes and their resulting obligations, in the light of the case-law of the Federal Labour Court. It asked for examples of decisions declaring strikes unlawful because of failure to respect the proportionality principle. The report makes a very brief reference to a decision dated April 2003 (outside the reference period). The Committee points out that it examines the decisions of domestic courts to determine whether these are consistent with the principles it has laid down (see, *mutatis mutandis*, Collective complaint No. 12/2002, *Confederation of Swedish Enterprises v. Sweden*, Decision on the merits, 15 May 2003, §43). The Committee has indeed a responsibility to ensure that domestic courts act reasonably and that in particular their interventions do not strike at the very substance of the right to strike, thus depriving it of its effectiveness. In the absence of any information to allow it to assess the situation in this case, the Committee asks for a detailed description in the next report and reserves its position on this point.

---

[35] *Confederation of Swedish Enterprise v. Sweden*, Complaint No. 12/2002, Decision on the merits of 15 May 2003, para. 42.   [36] *Conclusions XVII-1* (Germany) Art. 6(4), at 205.

IV. CONCLUSION

Now that the supervisory machinery has reached this stage of development, what are the next steps? What further challenges does the Social Charter face?

The main challenge is undoubtedly to publicize all these developments and disseminate information on the Charter to all the Council of Europe member states and beyond. The formidable efforts over the last twenty years to raise awareness of the European Convention on Human Rights provide an obvious model. The Charter will only achieve its full potential if individual citizens are willing to recognize and use it as a point of reference and invoke it in their domestic courts. In countries where the Charter is not part of domestic law its incorporation would encourage its development and more general application. Finally, the forthcoming 'Constitution' of the European Union, which will give binding force to the Charter of Fundamental Rights, has revitalized the debate on the Union's accession to the Social Charter and, more generally, the Charter's role in EU law, particularly in the context of the role of the European Court of Justice in Luxembourg.

4

Assessing the Strengths and Weaknesses of the European Social Charter's Supervisory System

PHILIP ALSTON*

I. INTRODUCTION

For almost half a century, the European Social Charter (ESC) has been the flagship of international instruments aiming to promote the integrated protection of a comprehensive range of social rights. While a large number of conventions and recommendations adopted by the International Labour Organization (ILO) blazed the social rights trail at the international level, these did not add up to a comprehensive social rights agenda. At the United Nations level, the International Covenant on Economic, Social and Cultural Rights (ICESCR)[1] did not enter into force until fifteen years after the adoption of the Social Charter. Similarly, the equivalent instrument within the Inter-American human rights system—the Protocol of San Salvador—entered into force only in 1999 (exactly eleven years after its adoption).[2]

The ESC is thus of major importance both in its own right and as a benchmark against which other international standards and supervisory arrangements in this field have come to be judged.[3] It has been said to provide 'the social and economic

* I am grateful to Alexandra Gatto for her assistance in gathering materials for use in the Italian case study contained in this chapter.

[1] Available at www.ohchr.org/english/law/cescr.htm.

[2] Additional Protocol to the American Convention on Human Rights in the Area of Economic, Social and Cultural Rights ('Protocol of San Salvador'). Available at www.cidh.oas. org/Basicos/basic6.htm.

[3] This is best exemplified by regular reference to the ESC system in the debates over the adoption of an optional complaints procedure under the ICESCR. Although that debate began in the early 1990s it has only recently engaged the systematic attention of governments and it will not be until 2006 at the earliest that a definite decision is taken on the question of whether to draft such a protocol and on the extent to which it should follow the characteristics reflected in the collective complaints procedure adopted under the ESC. See for example the advice offered to the Working Group of the UN Commission on Human Rights by Mr Kristensen, Deputy Executive Secretary of the Committee of Independent Experts established under the ESC. *Report of the Open-ended Working Group to Consider Options regarding the Elaboration of an Optional Protocol to the International Covenant on Economic, Social and Cultural Rights on its Second Session*, UN doc. E/CN.4/2005/52, paras 50–53.

foundations of human rights protection on the continent of Europe'.[4] But despite its undoubted achievements, which have been amply documented elsewhere in this volume and in other recent publications,[5] the ESC has not succeeded in having quite the impact for which its proponents would have wished. Moreover, its place in the overall scheme of European human rights mechanisms in the twenty-first century remains somewhat uncertain.

The principal objective of this chapter is to identify a range of initiatives that might be considered in order to make the Charter's supervisory arrangements more effective and more likely to be able to respond to the various challenges which it confronts, especially those arising out of the continuing expansion of the European Union, and the pressures to prioritize economic liberalization over social justice and cohesion. While much has been written on the European Social Charter in its various permutations, very few empirical studies have been undertaken in an effort to evaluate its impact or to assess the effectiveness of the procedures that have been devised over the years. While the present study cannot pretend to constitute a systematic or comprehensive case study, it is sufficiently grounded in the actual practice of the European Committee of Social Rights (ECSR) in relation to a representative case as to provide a basis for identifying possible reforms.

The chapter is divided into several parts. The first seeks to locate the ESC and its supervisory system within the overall European human rights regime. The second introduces an element of comparison with the ICESCR, on the assumption (which will come as a surprise at least to some European social rights proponents) that the latter might have some useful lessons for the Charter system. The third, and perhaps the most important part of the chapter, seeks to contextualize the ESC system by examining its strengths and weaknesses through the lens of a detailed case study of the Charter's operation in practice. The final parts of the chapter aim to conceptualize the role of the Committee and then to identify some of the means by which the supervisory system could be made more effective.

II. THE PLACE OF THE ESC WITHIN THE OVERALL EUROPEAN HUMAN RIGHTS REGIME

It is often said that the ESC is the 'counterpart' of the European Convention for the Protection of Human Rights and Fundamental Freedoms (the ECHR).[6] The Council of Europe's website refers to the former as the 'natural complement' to the

---

[4] S. Evju, 'The European Social Charter', in R. Blanpain (ed.), *The Council of Europe and the Social Challenges of the XXIst Century* (2001) 19.

[5] See R. Brillat, 'The Supervisory Machinery of the European Social Charter: Recent Developments and Their Impact', chapter 3 in this volume; and more generally D. Harris and J. Darcy, *The European Social Charter* (2nd edn, 2000).   [6] Ibid., inside front dust jacket.

latter.[7] Similarly, Brillat notes that the Charter 'has become one of the Council of Europe's major treaties, alongside the European Convention on Human Rights, which served as its model and continues to do so'.[8] These claims to some form of equivalence with, and complementarity to, the ECHR are generally also mediated through references to the principle of the indivisibility of the two sets of rights.

It needs to be acknowledged, however, that despite the desirability of a situation in which economic and social rights are accorded equal importance with civil and political rights, this is far from being the actual situation. While there are many reasons which can be offered for the discrepancies that exist in practice,[9] and not all of the differences in treatment are necessarily problematic, the bottom line is that social rights remain the poor step-sister of civil and political rights and this is every bit as true within the Council of Europe as elsewhere. The fact that membership of the Council requires ratification of the ECHR but not of the ESC, the discrepancies in staff and resources devoted to the respective supervisory systems, the unequal roles accorded to the different rights within the broad promotional activities of the Council, and a variety of other indicators all tell a story which helps to explain at least some of the challenges confronted by those who would wish to reform the ESC supervisory system.

III. INTRODUCING A COMPARATIVE DIMENSION: THE ICESCR

One of the aims of this chapter is to consider whether there are any lessons that might be learned in relation to the monitoring arrangements under the ESC from the experience of the comparable tasks undertaken within the United Nations framework in relation to the ICESCR. The Charter itself only predated the adoption of the Covenant by five years, but whereas the Charter set up a system of supervision which began functioning in the late 1960s, its UN counterpart was not established until 1987. Such comparisons are potentially useful insofar as the two monitoring bodies face many of the same challenges. They seek to evaluate compliance with comparable normative obligations, they face similar problems of mobilizing civil society and of obtaining alternative sources of information, and they are dealing with similar levels of scepticism in relation to the role of international supervisory organs in influencing domestic social policies.

By the same token, it needs to be recognized that while such comparisons can be instructive, they are also potentially fraught to the extent that techniques which work in one setting might be almost irrelevant in another, or might even be counter-productive. This follows from the fact that each of the two systems has its

---

[7] 'What is the European Social Charter?', available at www.coe.int/T/E/Human_Rights/Esc/1_ General_Presentation/default.asp#TopOfPage. [8] *Supra* n. 5, 1.

[9] See P. Alston, 'The Importance of the Inter-Play between Economic, Social and Cultural Rights and Civil and Political Rights', in *Human Rights at the Dawn of the 21st Century* (1993) 59.

own separate texts with very different drafting histories, a quite different set of assumptions motivating the original drafters, different governmental actors and traditions, and different inherent strengths and weaknesses which cannot necessarily be transplanted in any meaningful way. In addition to this general caveat there are two other factors which caution against taking the comparison in this case too far. The first is that the ESC mechanism is considerably more advanced and sophisticated, in some respects at least, than its UN counterpart.

The second is more complicated and goes to the ethos of legalism and the processes of change and reform in the two systems. While the ICESCR system has evolved very significantly in the space of only some fifteen years from the basis of a very vague and general resolution of the UN's Economic and Social Council (ECOSOC), the development of procedures within the ESC system has tended to be much more legalistic. Several factors account for these differences and they are of direct relevance to the focus of this chapter. One is the stronger role of the Council of Europe Secretariat than its United Nations counterpart in the Office of the High Commissioner for Human Rights. It serves to restrain the opportunities open to the Committee to innovate and to adopt flexible interpretations of its rules and procedures. Another is the greater feasibility of careful governmental scrutiny of all that is done under the ESC system, both through the active involvement of the Strasbourg permanent delegations and through the role accorded to the Governmental Committee and the Committee of Ministers. While the UN Commission on Human Rights and even the ECOSOC (the nominal parent body of the UN Committee on Economic, Social and Cultural Rights) might be supposed to play this role they have not in practice and the Committee tends, as a result, to have much more leeway in terms of systemic innovations.

The differences can be illustrated by the example of past reforms in the two systems. In the very early 1990s I was asked by the then Director of Human Rights at the Council of Europe to join a small expert group, the purpose of which was to explore the type of reforms that might be undertaken in order to make the European Social Charter system more effective. The group met in private and I doubt that its report was ever made public. It nevertheless began a process which was remarkably successful, one that led to the revision of the Social Charter, a major upgrading of its provisions, and the introduction of a collective complaints procedure. The lessons that I took from this experience with the ESC were that major and far-reaching reforms were feasible, personalities were important (Peter Leuprecht and a couple of key ambassadorial allies played a key role in the whole process), and that intergovernmental processes are the principal means of achieving progress.

In sharp contrast, the experience under the ICESCR points to the opposite conclusion in most respects. Big ideas are rarely appreciated within the UN system and are more likely than incremental strategies to attract strong opposition. They tend to frighten governments and to bring out all sorts of active and passive resistance strategies. The inability of governments within the UN Commission on Human Rights context to come to grips with the proposal put forward for a complaints system under the ICESCR is a good example. A draft Optional Protocol was proposed by the UN Committee in 1993. The same year the Vienna World Conference on Human Rights 'encouraged' the Commission, in cooperation with the Committee, to continue its examination of that proposal.[10] The Committee sent a completed draft to the Commission four years later. In 2004, after a whole series of procedural debates and the appointment of an independent expert whose reports seemed not to move the process forward significantly, the Commission decided to continue for another two years the work of an open-ended working group which first met in 2003 with a mandate of considering 'options regarding the elaboration of an optional protocol'.[11] As a result, it is unlikely that the Commission will have a complete draft of a possible protocol before it in less than fifteen years after the general idea was endorsed by the World Conference. And the adoption and entry into force of such an instrument would be likely to take an additional five years or so.

In contrast, however, to the snail's pace at which formal reform processes work within the UN context, the Committee on ECSR has introduced a large number of important procedural innovations without any express authorization by the Commission or by the Meeting of States Parties to the Covenant. These innovations have been acquiesced in by the governments concerned and the result has been to achieve a considerable transformation of the procedures applied and accepted by reporting governments.

The relevance of this reflection on comparative reform processes is to underscore the fact that the contexts in which reforms of the monitoring systems under the ESC and the ICESCR are implemented are very different. Nevertheless, it seems unlikely that the member states of the Council of Europe are likely to embark again in the near future on a revision of the ESC and that there are thus good reasons for the ECSR to reflect on ways in which it can develop its own procedures in order to respond to the particular challenges that are now confronting it. It is in that perspective that the experience of the UN Committee might have something to offer.

IV. EVALUATING THE STRENGTHS AND WEAKNESSES OF THE ESC REPORTING SYSTEM

There is no shortage of useful analyses documenting the work of the European Committee of Social Rights and its predecessors in monitoring social rights in Europe.[12] But almost all of these studies are relatively abstract or decontextualized

---

[10] UN doc. A/CONF.157/23 of 12 July 1993, Part II, para. 75.

[11] See generally the *Report of the Open-ended Working Group*, UN doc. E/CN.4/2005/52, *supra* n. 3.

[12] In addition to those cited *supra* nn. 4 and 5, see J.-F. Akandji-Kombé and S. Leclerc (eds), *La Charte sociale européenne* (2001); L. Wasecha, *Le Système de contrôle de l'application de la Charte sociale européenne* (1980); and A. Jaspers and L. Betten (eds), *25 Years: European Social Charter* (1988).

in the sense that they look at the system as a whole rather than at the ways in which it has functioned in response to a particular country situation. This orientation is not surprising. Much of the analysis has been undertaken by those with a stake of some sort or a role within the ESC system and anyone thus involved is more or less obliged to avoid country-specific analyses and instead to opt for a more detached focus on the overall system.

Thus, one way in the present context to add value to the existing literature is to undertake a case study of the Committee's approach to the situation in one particular country in order to get a sense of the practical strengths and weaknesses of the system. While the experience of none of the thirty-four reporting states is necessarily typical in any generalizable sense, there are good reasons to take a large country with considerable resources available to engage in the exercise, with extensive experience in reporting under the ESC and a wide range of other international procedures, and a vibrant civil society. Based on these criteria, Italy is an appropriate case study and there is no reason to believe that it is atypical as a case study or that it shows symptoms that are not widely present in relation to the experience of other countries.

A. *Timing and Role of the Different Committees*

The best way to get a sense of the timelines and chronology involved in reporting under the ESC is to look at the specifics of a given country's reporting obligations. For present purposes the focus is on Italy, which ratified the original European Social Charter in October 1965. It ratified the Revised Social Charter in July 1999, which rendered it liable to report on the two-year period from 1 January 1999 until 31 December 2000 by a deadline of 31 March 2002. While the report was late, it was impressively timely by the standards that operate within the United Nations where states' reports are usually a year or so late at best. Italy sent in its report on 7 July 2002. The report was considered by the Committee in the course of 2003 and its conclusions were adopted in June 2003,[13] some two and a half years after the legislative and policy developments which it describes, but only one year after the report was presented. The Committee's conclusions were then subjected to the next round of scrutiny by the Governmental Committee which published its full report for 2004 only in April 2005.[14] The latter report is then sent to the Committee of Ministers which will finalize the process by determining whether or not any further action is required.

The focus of the Italian report is on the 'non-hard core' provisions of the Charter,[15] and the Committee requests the government to submit its report on

[13] European Committee of Social Rights, *Conclusions 2003*, Vol. 1 (Bulgaria, France, Italy).
[14] Governmental Committee of the European Social Charter, *Report concerning Conclusions 2004*, Council of Europe doc. T-SG (2004) 26 of 8 April 2005, available at www.coe.int/T/E/Human_Rights/Esc/3_Reporting_procedure/3_Follow-up_to_the_Conclusions/ETSG2004_26_Det_Report_Conclusions_2004-1.pdf.
[15] This term refers to the following articles of the Revised ESC: Arts 1 para. 4, 2, 3, 4, 9, 10, 15, 21, 22, 24, 26, 28, and 29.

the 'hard core' provisions[16] by 31 March 2006. It also asks that the answers to the questions that it has signalled as having gone unanswered in this round should be provided by 31 March 2004, thus giving the government an additional two years in which to complete its report for the period ending December 2000.

Several conclusions emerge from this information. First, the proceedings are complex, and a non-specialist will have to make a significant effort to understand the distinction between the hard core and non-hard core provisions, as well as the precise roles being played by each of the levels of supervision. Secondly, the staggering of the overall exercise, both in terms of governmental reporting on different issues, and the timing of the contributions by each of the three committees (expert, governmental, and ministerial), means that there is no conclusive date until the last of the committees has finally pronounced itself, by which time the likelihood of attracting any significant public attention has long since passed. Thirdly, a single round can take close to a decade to complete by the time both cycles have been finished and each of the instances has had its say. These are hardly the hallmarks of a system designed to have a significant impact on public opinion or to ensure timely interventions in response to important concerns.

B. *The Governmental Report*

The Italian report was some 130 single-spaced pages in length and written in French.[17] It is not clear whether it was also available in Italian, but this seems unlikely and the present author was unable to track it down if it was. The report contains no general introduction and no information as to how it was compiled, no indication as to whether there was any consultation within the government at large or with civil society groups, and no details of whether, once completed, it had been disseminated within Italy by the government. It consists of a dry factual statement describing various legislative and administrative initiatives systematically and in detail. Those elements are supplemented with extensive statistics from official Italian and European sources. It does not seek to situate itself within the context of previous reports submitted by the government on the same issues, or of comments made in earlier rounds by the Committee. Nor does it flag major criticisms of government policies which might have been made by social policy groups or others. It is, in brief, a detailed technocratic accounting which will be inaccessible to the great majority of Italians, whether because they do not read French or because they do not have the necessary background to give meaning to an otherwise lifeless report.

---

[16] This term refers to the following Articles of the Revised ESC: Arts 1, 5, 6, 7, 12, 13, 16, 19 and 20 (except Art. 1 para. 4).

[17] Ministère du travail et des politiques sociales, Direction générale de la protection des conditions du travail, Division II—affaires internationales du travail, 1er rapport biennal du gouvernement italien sur l'état d'application de la Charte sociale européenne, révue, articles 1–5–6–7–12–13–16–19–20, période de référence : 1er janvier 1999–31 décembre 2000, at www.coe.int/T/E/Human%5FRights/Esc/4%5FReporting%5Fprocedure/1_State_Reports/Revised_Social_Charter/2002/Italy%201st%20report.pdf.

C. *The Report of the ECSR*

The Committee's analysis of the government report is detailed and not only addresses every single paragraph of each article of the Revised ESC, but also specifies the information it needs in order to assess conformity. Thus, for example, in relation to the right to adequate remuneration (Article 4(1)) it seeks information on 'the net value . . . of the average wage' after deductions, a comparison between wages under collective agreements and those outside them, and inflation-adjusted figures over time.[18] The conclusions reached by the Committee take up 110 single-spaced pages and arrive at a conclusion in respect of every paragraph of the relevant articles, a total of fifty-seven. In nine cases it found the situation to be in conformity. In another fifteen cases,[19] it decided that there was a discrepancy (i.e. non-conformity). But the most revealing outcome was the deferral of any conclusion in relation to thirty-three of the articles, or over 60 per cent of the issues under review. In those cases, the Committee concluded that it needed 'further information in order to assess the situation'.[20]

Even more surprising is that at least some of the findings of conformity are also based on a lack of relevant information, leading the Committee to conclude that '[s]ince there is no information in the report, the Committee considers that the situation, which was held to be in conformity with the Charter, has not changed'.[21] On its face, such a methodology is surprising. In order to be valid it would have to reflect a finding, based on independent research, that there is no reason to conclude that problems have arisen. But if that is the case it would seem appropriate to give some indication to that effect and to refer to the sources used.

But while a 60 per cent governmental non-response rate is very high, the problem is compounded by the fact that in many of those instances, the Committee had sought and failed to receive the same information in the context of its previous examination of the situation in Italy. Thus, for example, the whole procedure is paralysed in relation to Article 14, the right to benefit from social welfare services. In relation to each of the two paragraphs the Committee takes note of a very limited amount of information contained in the government's report, repeats in detail the information previously sought and not provided, and accordingly 'defers its conclusion' pending receipt of the information. No intimation is given that a negative conclusion would follow from the non-provision of information. As a result, the approach adopted effectively rewards the government and provides very little incentive for a detailed reckoning in the future.

The report does not suggest reasons for the very high rate of non-response, nor does it seek to draw attention to it in any concerted way. The reasons can thus only be surmised. The failure to penalize significantly non-reporting would seem to be

---

[18] Ibid., 257.

[19] Although there were two dissenting opinions, which related to Arts 4(5), 26(1) and 26(2). Ibid., 352–53.   [20] Ibid., 244.

[21] Ibid., 278, in relation to Art. 10(5)(c) on the provision of training during working hours.

one explanatory factor. The amount of detail sought by the Committee and its decision not to prioritize any particular issues over others might be another. The fact that this was one of the very first reports under the Revised Social Charter might explain some of the gaps in information, but that seems unlikely given that in many cases the same information was absent from the previous report.

Another aspect of the report which is especially revealing is the list of sources of information to which reference is made. The breadth of available sources and their reliability has long been a key indicator of the effectiveness of international monitoring and supervision of human rights obligations. For many years in the United Nations context, the assumption pushed by governments was that the only reliable information that could be invoked was that emanating from governmental or intergovernmental sources.[22] In fact, of course, the opposite was often true and the only way to measure the reliability of official information was to test it against other, usually non-official, information whether from the media or non-governmental organizations.

The ECSR report does not list in any one place the range of sources used, nor does it provide any explanation as to which sources were chosen and on the basis of what criteria. A careful reading of the report indicates that Internet-based sources have been consulted to a significant extent but that the Committee is rather loath to rely on information from non-governmental organizations (NGOs) or to contrast governmentally provided information with that from other sources. Thus the report is assiduous in making use of information from official Italian sources, including the websites of the Ministries for Education,[23] Labour and Welfare,[24] and for Universities.[25] In addition, reference is made to the report submitted by Italy under the United Nations Convention on the Rights of the Child,[26] and to the views of a government advisory body.[27] The major sources of information cited are other international organizations such as the ILO,[28] the European Union,[29] the Organization for Economic Co-operation and Development (OECD),[30] the World Health Organization,[31] the Council of Europe,[32] and statistical agencies such as the European Statistical Office,[33] and its Italian counterpart.[34]

Only two NGO sources are cited. One is the European Anti-Poverty Network (EAPN) and reference is made to its comments on the Italian Government's Action Plan on Social Inclusion.[35] This is information available on an EU website.[36] Another reference is to a report on housing prepared jointly by the main Italian trade union umbrella groupings.[37] Somewhat paradoxically, one of the Committee's observations in relation to the problem of sexual harassment at

---

[22] See Report of Independent Expert, UN doc. A/44/668 (1989), para. 119.
[23] Italian Report, *supra* n. 17, 263 and 276.   [24] Ibid., 264–65 and 345.
[25] Ibid., 269–70.   [26] Ibid., 302.
[27] Consiglio Nazionale Economia e Lavoro (CNEL), ibid., 343, 344, and 347.
[28] Ibid., 254.   [29] Ibid., 271, 273, 274, and 345.   [30] Ibid., 279–80.
[31] Ibid., 280–82 and 284.   [32] Ibid., 336.   [33] Ibid., 254, 273–74, and 345.
[34] Istituto Nazionale di Statistica, ibid., 283.   [35] Ibid., 338.   [36] Ibid., 343 n. 2.
[37] Ibid., 343 and 347.

work is to note that 'intensive information campaigns are carried out by a variety of actors (trade unions, law firms, NGOs, etc.) in particular via the Internet'. The Committee then asks the government what steps it has taken to 'make sure that [this information] reaches all corners of the Italian labour world'.[38] This is paradoxical in two respects. First, the Committee is acknowledging that it has searched the Internet in order to bolster its conclusions, and that it is prepared to take cognizance of civil society reporting, but in the entire report it makes only this single reference to the material thus available. Secondly, while drawing attention to the significance of this issue in practice, the Committee gives no details of the problem and does not draw attention to the incongruence of the empirical situation and the government's failure to address the issue in its report.

The apparent paucity of non-official sources has a variety of consequences for the nature of the reporting procedure and its potential effectiveness. First, it leaves the government report and related sources as the predominant basis of deliberation, and does not put the government under any particular pressure to establish either the veracity of its claims or to respond to concrete information which would show that while necessary legislation is in place, the practice on the ground is not in conformity with the Charter. Secondly, in the absence of any 'alternative' sources of information, the evaluation is a very tame affair and the overwhelming focus is on the legislative and formal administrative framework. Thirdly, there is no incentive for the civil society groups to engage. Their information is apparently not solicited, and is certainly not used.

This final point is borne out by a brief survey of the extent to which the European Social Charter is an element in the work of the main Italian NGOs active in the social field. While the survey that was undertaken was confined to Internet sources, there is no reason to think that a more broadly-based survey would have yielded different results. As far as trade union groups are concerned, there are three main Italian labour confederations and each of them has shown an active interest in Europe, which is hardly surprising given the extent to which national labour law in the EU countries is increasingly dependent upon the EU framework.

The Unione Italiana del Lavoro (UIL) is the most internationally focused of the groups. Its European Office closely monitors EU legislative and political initiatives, and its website carries news and documentation in relation to the social and labour rights-related activities of the ILO, the OECD, and the United Nations.[39] The Council of Europe, however, is absent except for a generic link to the website of the Parliamentary Assembly of the Council. There is no specific mention at all of the ESC.

The Confederazione Italiana Sindacati Lavoratori (CISL) is the second largest Italian labour group and participates actively in the Trade Union Advisory Group to the OECD (TUAC), the International Confederation of Free Trade Unions

---

[38] Ibid., 325.   [39] See www.uil.it.

(ICFTU), and the European Confederation of Trade Unions Confederations (ECTUC). Its website also carries documentation on the work of the other regional and international groupings but not on the Council of Europe or the ESC.[40] The same applies to the Confederazione Italiana del Lavoro (CGIL), which has a European Secretariat monitoring EU developments but gives no more than a general link to the Council of Europe website. It is also worth noting that the websites of all three groups carry many reports which would be of direct relevance to the monitoring of the situation in Italy in relation to the rights dealt with in the ESC, which makes the Committee's failure to draw on the relevant materials all the more surprising.

The ESC also seems to have had a limited impact on the work of other civil society groups concerned with social rights in Italy. It seems that such groups are not exactly plentiful,[41] in part because of a strong tradition of relying upon trade unions to pursue a wide range of social issues, extending well beyond traditional labour matters. Reliance upon the Catholic Church and the ubiquitous role it plays in society is another possible explanatory reason. Nevertheless, the absence of a powerful 'welfare lobby' of the type found in many other countries is all the more noteworthy given the very strong presence of civil society groups in the debates over development cooperation, immigration, and trade. But the bottom line remains the same. Whether we take account of the work of the three major civil society groups involved with social rights,[42] or of the groups participating in the European Social Forum in Florence in 2003,[43] the ESC remains entirely invisible.

Thus, despite a strong international orientation, it appears that neither the major trade union groupings nor the major civil society groups concerned with social rights more generally has a significant interest in the ESC or the work of the

---

[40] See www.cisl.it.

[41] The website of the Ministry of Labour and Social Affairs is required by the Legge 7 dicembre 2000, no. 383 to maintain a register of associations involved in social affairs (the Registro Nazionale delle Associazioni di Promozione Sociale) at www.welfare.gov.it/EaChannel/MenuIstituzionale/Sociale/associazionismo+sociale/documenti/elenco+associazioni+promozione+sociale.htm. Most of the groups listed pursue very specific aims and are active in the cultural, entertainment, or religious fields.

[42] Among those civil society groups that do have a significant focus on social rights, mention might be made of three in particular. The Associazioni Cristiane Lavoratori Italiani (ACLI), created in 1945, does provide on its website extensive references to a broad range of Italian and European social issues, including a reference to the EU Charter of Rights at Work. See www.acli.it. The Associazione Ricreativa Culturale Italiana (ARCI) is a left of centre group, created in 1994, which has a particularly strong focus on international social policy and broader issues such as the new European Constitution. See www.arci.it. Finally, the Associazione per la Tassazione delle Transazioni finanziarie e per l'Aiuto ai Cittadini (ATTAC), which defines itself as an 'international movement for democratic control of financial markets', was created in 1998 in Paris. The Italian section is particularly concerned with labour rights issues such as the reform of the Italian pension system and efforts to amend Art. 18 of Legge no. 300/70 (the so-called Statuto dei Lavoratori) regarding the right to reinstatement following unfair dismissal (Reintegrazione nel posto di lavoro). Its website carries significant information about the activities of the EU and the WTO. See www.attac.it. But none of these three organizations refers at all on its website to either the ESC or to the Council of Europe more generally.

[43] See www.firenzesocialforum.net.

ECSR. This brings us back to the findings of comparable research on the impact of the complaints process provided for under the North American Free Trade Agreement (NAFTA) to the effect that:

arrangements which are applied as though their essential purpose is to facilitate dialogue are highly unlikely to be very effective in the absence of a range of additional measures designed to ensure broad-based participation, and to make it worth the while for individuals and non-state actors to invest an effort in the process.[44]

The relevant groups perceive themselves as having no stake in either the input or the output side of the Strasbourg exercise, and so they behave accordingly. It would appear that they have concluded that it is either too difficult to make submissions to the Committee or that if made, those submissions would not be taken into account. The lack of a formal invitation to submit information or alternative reports, the inability to participate in any way in the relatively anonymous proceedings of the committee, and the sense that individual members are not worth lobbying in order to have a significant impact, all serve to reinforce that impression. Equally problematic, from the perspective of trade union groups and those dealing more broadly with social rights, is the fact that while the output (the report of the ECSR) is careful, professional, and legally sound, it is not seen to add enough value to the bargaining power of the relevant groups within the domestic political arena as to warrant a significant investment of time and resources.

Where, however, there are opportunities to make inputs and where the outputs have achieved sufficient public recognition as to make a difference, these groups do tend to be active. Thus the ILO and the OECD, esoteric bodies by general standards of public opinion, both offer significant participatory opportunities to the trade union groups and are able to attract some attention. Where the ILO has moved to introduce a procedure which is more clearly cosmetic, the level of interest on the part of the social partners is low. Where it continues to operate a system, like that overseen by its Committee on Freedom of Association, which is capable of having an impact, there is a continuing flow of inputs from trade union groups.[45]

This is not the sole explanation, however. There would also seem to be a failure on the part of the ESC and its supporters to publicize their conclusions adequately. This is apparent from the fact that although two of the issues highlighted by the ECSR have been extremely newsworthy in Italy, the Committee's adverse findings have failed to gain any significant publicity.[46] The first of the issues concerns the rights of Italy's three million persons with disabilities,[47] a subject to

---

[44] P. Alston, ' "Core Labour Standards" and the Transformation of the International Labour Rights Regime', 15 *EJIL* (2004) 457, at 503.   [45] Ibid., 513.

[46] Neither of the two principal associations devoted to the situation of persons with disabilities devoted any attention on their websites to the findings of the ECSR. See www.disabili.com and www.affarisocialihandicap.it/soggetti/r_associazioni.asp.

[47] Italian Report, *supra* n. 17, 292.

which the Committee devoted considerable attention and on which it concluded that Italy had failed to conform to the Charter in relation to each of the three paragraphs of Article 15.[48] It should be noted, however, that the Committee's conclusion in each case focused solely on the absence of appropriate anti-discrimination legislation rather than on a range of government policies which have been widely portrayed as discounting the difficulties faced by persons with disabilities.[49]

The second issue addressed by the Committee and which subsequently received major media attention concerns the right to reinstatement following a finding of unfair dismissal.[50] But the Committee's conclusion that Italian law excludes far more workers from protection in that regard than is permitted under the ESC[51] drew little, if any, attention from civil society or the media.

D. The Report of the Governmental Committee

It took almost two years for the Governmental Committee to evaluate the recommendations made by the Expert Committee on the Italian Report and the result was to diminish any pressure that might have been generated by the experts and, in effect, to defer to the positions once again urged by the Italian government. This can be illustrated by the response to the problems identified by the ECSR in relation to child labour.

The government argued that the situation in practice 'was not as serious as originally estimated to be or as serious as that in other Contracting Parties'. Nevertheless, it had undertaken 'a wide ranging series of measures to address the problems' such as the adoption of 'a Programme of Action, a special training programme for the Labour Inspectorate, and family support policies'.[52] In response to such reassurances the Governmental Committee welcomed the steps taken and 'expressed the hope that the de facto situation would soon be in conformity with the revised Charter'.[53]

In relation to allowances paid to apprentices, on which the ECSR had insisted on receiving specific figures which had again not been provided, the Italian delegate insisted that there was no problem and argued that there was no need for a warning. In response '[t]he Committee took note of the information provided by the Italian delegate; asked the Italian Government to provide detailed information in its next report; and considered that the warning previously addressed to Italy was still in force'.[54] That, in essence, was the outcome of the very lengthy process described above.

---

[48] Ibid., 292–99.

[49] Thus, e.g., funding for special teachers for students with disabilities in the schools has been withdrawn (see www.scuolaitalia.com/genitori/escuola/rubriche/) and the government has refused to provide special funding to facilitate employment opportunites for persons with disabilities (see www.vita.it/articolo/index.php3?NEWSID=44766).   [50] See *supra* n. 42.

[51] Italian Report, *supra* n. 17, 323.   [52] Governmental Committee, *supra* n. 14, para. 133.

[53] Ibid., para. 134.   [54] Ibid., paras 177–82.

V. CONCEPTUALIZING THE ROLE OF THE COMMITTEE

There are two essential elements required in order to be able to make suggestions as to the types of reforms that should be contemplated in order to make the ESC process more effective. The first is to obtain a clear sense of how it operates and of its principal strengths and weaknesses. This we have endeavoured to do on the basis of the foregoing case study of Italy and we will return shortly to the principal lessons that might be learned from that case.

The second is to have a reasonably clear idea of the roles played by the European Committee of Social Rights and of the expectations that key actors have for it. This is, however, not quite as straightforward as might have been assumed. The problem is well illustrated by the previous chapter in this volume in which Régis Brillat, the Executive Secretary of the European Social Charter, whose contribution to professionalizing the work of the Committee has been immense, suggests that the procedures of the Committee should be characterized as judicial or quasi-judicial.[55] While it would be difficult to contest the contention that the collective complaints procedure is a quasi-judicial one, it is more problematic to suggest that the procedure involving the supervision of states' reports amounts to 'a judicial procedure'. While the importance of such terminological questions can easily be overstated, they nonetheless serve to highlight an important question as to the aspirations of the system.

Some observers would challenge the very notion that a function performed by a body such as the Committee can be quasi-judicial, arguing that it either is judicial or it is not. But this is not the place to engage in such semantic (or alternatively foundational) questions. Suffice it to say that the term 'quasi-judicial' must mean that at least some of the essential elements of judicial decision-making are present.[56] In the case of the Committee, neither the assumptions which apply when electing the experts, nor the consequences that attach to a failure to abide by the Committee's conclusions, would seem to possess the hallmarks of a judicial process. Similarly, an analogy might be drawn in other respects to the role of the UN's Human Rights Committee (HRC) which examines reports submitted by states under the International Covenant on Civil and Political Rights (ICCPR). As McGoldrick concluded in that respect:

Having regard to the absence of any judicial determination, binding decisions or recommendations, and enforcement powers it is apparent that the key to the effectiveness

---

[55] Chapter 3 above, p. 32 ff.

[56] One definition of 'quasi-judicial' notes that: '[B]etween routine government policy decisions and the traditonal court forums lies a hybrid, sometimes called a "tribunal" or "administrative tribunal" and not necessarily presided by judges. These operate as a government policy-making body at times but also exercise a licensing certifying, approval or other adjudication authority which is "judicial" because it directly affects the legal rights of a person.' Duhaime's *Online Legal Dictionary*, available at www.duhaime.org/dictionary/dict-qr.aspx.

of the reporting procedure established by the ICCPR will be the HRC's powers to persuade.[57]

Similarly, a former President of the Committee has noted that '[t]he ECSR is not a judicial body, certainly not in the strict sense'. He added that this is precisely the reason why various proposals have been made to incorporate social rights into the European Convention on Human Rights and to establish a European Court of Social Rights.[58]

It must be conceded, however, that a plausible counter-argument could be mounted to the effect that the ECSR does behave judicially to the extent that it considers both sides of the question when examining compliance, confines itself to applying the applicable legal norms to the facts before it, and formulates its reasoned views in a judicious fashion. And, it might be added, at least some of those involved in the procedure aspire to make it increasingly more judicial in nature.

On balance, however, it is difficult to conclude that a body which operates as this one does, which relies heavily upon sets of draft conclusions prepared by a full-time staff rather than undertaking its own analyses from scratch,[59] and whose recommendations are subject to a form of review by the Committee of Ministers, is primarily a quasi-judicial one when performing its reporting function. More importantly, it can be argued that it is counter-productive to characterize it in this way since its methods of work and general approach are then less likely to be framed so as to take full advantage of those techniques and functions which might be appropriate to a monitoring body but not to one which aspires to be seen in judicial terms. The type of functions that might be performed by a monitoring body can be illustrated by reference to the list of seven objectives identified by the UN Committee on ESCR in relation to its reporting procedure. It suggested that the process should be designed: (i) to ensure that a comprehensive initial review is undertaken of national legislation, administrative rules and procedures, and practices; (ii) to ensure regular monitoring of the situation by the state party in relation to each of the rights; (iii) to encourage a process of 'principled policy-making' on the part of the government; (iv) to facilitate public scrutiny of relevant government policies; (v) to provide a basis on which both the government and the Committee can evaluate progress over time; (vi) to enable the government to acknowledge the problems it faces in meeting its obligations; and (vii) to enable the Committee to develop a better understanding of the common problems faced by states in relation to these rights.[60]

---

[57] D. McGoldrick, *The Human Rights Committee* (1994) at 55.

[58] Evju, *supra* n. 4, 22–23.

[59] It seems that the examination of state reports is undertaken primarily by the Secretariat and, while there is every opportunity for inputs by the expert members, the great majority of the findings are those first flagged by the Secretariat. In this respect the procedure is faithful to the ILO model, on which it was originally largely based.

[60] Committee on Economic, Social and Cultural Rights, General Comment No. 1 (1989): Reporting by States Parties, UN doc. HRI/GEN/1/Rev.7 (2004), at 9.

The proposals that follow in relation to enhancing the effectiveness of the ESC system draw upon the assumptions underpinning that model of the roles which should be played by a reporting procedure at the international level. The situation is, of course, different in relation to the collective complaints procedure, which is also briefly addressed below.

VI. ENHANCING THE EFFECTIVENESS OF THE ESC SYSTEM

Critiques of the shortcomings of the ESC's monitoring arrangements are hardly new. Five years ago Andrew Drzemczewski identified what he termed its 'four major weaknesses' in the following terms:

> its heavy and slow procedure, uncertainty as to the respective roles of the Committee of Independent Experts and of the Governmental Committee, the absence of actual participation of the social partners in the supervisory procedure, and the lack of any significant political sanction as the outcome of the procedure.[61]

The case study contained in the present chapter serves both to illustrate the ways in which these shortcomings affect the procedure and to demonstrate that most of the weaknesses endure. In this final section of the chapter an effort is made to suggest ways in which the system could be strengthened so as to mitigate the impact of the relevant structural defects and to take action in areas in which the Council of Europe or the ECSR retains a degree of initiative or discretion which could be used to strengthen the procedures.

A. Status of the Charter in National Law

The starting point for most international human rights monitoring mechanisms is the assumption that the principal level of engagement is at the national level and that the international level is no more than a complement or catalyst to national action. This serves to highlight the importance of ensuring that the ESC is given appropriate status within the domestic law of the states parties. Yet one of the conclusions that emerges from various of the chapters contained in the present volume[62] is that the present situation in this regard is far from optimal. One conclusion to be drawn from this observation is that the Committee itself might devote more attention and effort to encouraging governments to ensure that the Charter does have a meaningful role within the national legal system. This is an element to which the UN Committee on ESCR paid particular attention in one of its early General Comments.[63]

---

61 A. Drzemczewski, 'Fact-finding as Part of Effective Implementation: The Strasbourg Experience', in A. Bayefsky (ed.), *The U.N. Human Rights Treaty System in the 21st Century* (2000) 115, at 130.   62 See especially the chapters by C. Fabre, G. Gori and M. Bell.
63 General Comment No. 9 (1998): The Domestic Application of the Covenant, UN doc. HRI/GEN/1/Rev.7 (2004), at 55.

B. *Composition of the Committee*

One of the largely unspoken issues in relation to the ECSR relates to its composition. Although the Charter was originally cast in broad terms, it was designed on the basis of very significant inputs from the ILO, and in many respects followed a labour rights model. Indeed, an ILO representative was long accorded a uniquely important role in the work of the Committee's predecessor. Unsurprisingly, the majority of the experts who have served on the Committee have been labour law experts. The Charter's scope was significantly extended by the Additional Protocol of 1988 and in the revised (consolidated) Charter of 1996. As a result of these changes the narrowly defined labour rights component of the Charter was diluted and an expanded range of social rights matters, more broadly defined, brought within the remit of the Charter.[64] The predilection for labour lawyers continues to apply despite the expansion of the scope of the Charter and the fact that the regime now aspires to play a broad-ranging role in relation to social rights.

As the labour rights dimension becomes less important because of the strong influence of the European Union in that area, even on the standards followed by non-member states, the Committee will need to develop a broader base and draw upon professional constituencies reaching well beyond the labour law field. Labour unions should not necessarily be the principal interlocutors, labour law should not necessarily define the target groups, and labour lawyers should not dominate the jurisprudential debate over the interpretation of the Charter. While governments will need to respond by nominating a more diverse range of candidates for election to the Committee, the role of civil society is also of particular importance in ensuring that the nomination process at the national level yields qualified nominees reflecting diverse fields of expertise.

C. *Reaching Out to Civil Society*

In relation to social development policy in general it has been argued that:

A social rights perspective needs to continually move between micro-, meso- and macro-levels so that the links between issues of governance, provision, innovation, access and voice are continually addressed.

Perhaps above all, partnerships for social justice cannot be technical but, rather, must involve attention to power issues. In this way, allies can be found.[65]

---

[64] It should be noted here that there is a continuing terminological debate within Europe as to the proper scope to be accorded to labour rights and the extent to which that category can or should be interpreted broadly so as to encompass a range of social rights. See e.g. the comment that identifying the labour law aspects of the EU Charter of Fundamental Rights is 'not necessarily an easy task' since it might include 'only the rights dealing with employment relationships' or might extend to a much broader range of social rights. P. Lorber, 'Labour Law', in S. Peers and A. Ward (eds), *The EU Charter of Fundamental Rights: Politics, Law and Policy* (2004) 211.

[65] P. Stubbs, *International Non-State Actors and Social Development Policy*, Globalism and Social Policy Programme, Policy Brief No. 4 (2003), at 8.

Such an analysis is entirely consistent with the vision suggested above of the ECSR as playing the role of a catalyst, rather than that of a primary or principal actor. It follows that it is important for the Committee to reflect on its current or potential relationships with other actors and its ability to mobilize, inform, assist and work with them. In this respect, civil society has proven to be the key ally of most international human rights bodies, yet it has not featured prominently in any dimension of the work of the ECSR.

There are many options available to the Committee to correct this self-defeating approach. One is to suggest that national NGOs be given a stake in the process by either encouraging governments to give them a role in the preparation of the report (as some have advocated, but which I consider to be unrealistic in practice) or, more feasibly and more conceptually defensible, by alerting the key NGO groups at the national level to the fact that the report has been prepared and soliciting a separate and critical response to it (an 'alternative report' as they are sometimes called in the UN context). Under the ESC, governments are supposed to disseminate the reports and to consult, but it seems that such practices are not very common, at least in a meaningful sense. In the case of the Committee on the Rights of the Child, and to a lesser extent some of the other UN human rights treaty bodies, the dissemination of government reports and the preparation of alternative reports have facilitated a significant mobilization of civil society and ensured an important alternative input into the international supervisory process.

Another option is to give national NGOs some more direct role, either in relation to the actual examination of the report, or in following up on the recommendations that emerge from the process of examination. But the picture that emerges from the Italian case study is somewhat dispiriting in this respect. The views of the key domestic players were not solicited in a meaningful way,[66] the relevant information they generated was barely taken into account, and the issues of most concern to them were not necessarily even addressed by the Committee. There are many creative ways in which the Committee could expose itself to the sunlight of civil society if it so chose and such a move would have the potential to transform the minimalist and rather bureaucratic profile currently adopted in this respect into one which would demand and warrant the attention and energies of civil society.

D. Reaching Out to Other Key Institutional Actors

The future of the ESC is, to a significant extent, inextricably linked to the approach and the fortunes of two other organizations—the ILO and the EU—and it will need to re-evaluate and recalibrate its relationship with each in the years ahead.

---

[66] Some letters seeking further information were sent, but apparently rather few. The resulting impression seemed most unlikely to stimulate any particular sense that it is worthwhile to contribute to or to seek to participate in the process.

Its close relationship with the ILO stems, as noted above, from the largely ILO-derived nature of many of the Charter's standards. As Stein Evju, a former President of the European Committee of Social Rights, has noted, the 1961 Charter was 'inspired by and patterned on ILO conventions and recommendations in the field of social and economic rights'. In his view, even the new standards adopted in the 1990s 'are not novel inventions by the Council of Europe but draw, largely speaking, on corresponding, more recent ILO instruments and, in part, on EU directives'.[67] To the extent that the ESC provisions track the traditional approach of the ILO, the ECSR will need to take account of the fact that the ILO itself has, since 1998, opted to devote much of its effort to a very different approach which reflects flexible standards, a greatly diminished emphasis on centralized supervision, and considerably more deference to national preferences.[68] As this approach takes up more and more of the labour standards-related energies of the ILO, the ESC approach will risk becoming anachronistic and being painted as rigid and poorly adapted to the demands of a globalized economy, unless the ECSR explicitly addresses the resulting challenges.

In terms of the EU, there is little to indicate that the relationship between the impact of the EU Charter of Fundamental Rights on the ESC has been given the attention it would warrant within the Council of Europe.[69] While commentators have long urged that the EU should accede to the ESC,[70] there is little reason to think that the EU will proceed down that path given the contentious nature of economic and social rights in that context and the reluctance of EU governments and institutions to submit themselves to external scrutiny when alternatives can be devised which keep the decision-making within the family. If this (hopefully over-pessimistic) prediction is correct then it means that the ESC runs a strong risk of marginalization unless it is able, through force of reasoning and promotional initiatives, to compel the EU to pay attention to its jurisprudence and treat it as a relevant reference point for determinations relating to the EU Charter.[71] Indeed, it is significant that Evju observes in relation to the EU that 'where the two systems diverge, the [ESC] will clearly suffer'.[72]

---

[67] Evju, *supra* n. 4, 20.

[68] See P Alston, ' "Core Labour Standards" and the Transformation of the International Labour Rights Regime', 15 *EJIL* (2004) 457; and P. Alston and J. Heenan, 'Shrinking the International Labor Code: An Unintended Consequence of the 1998 ILO Declaration on Fundamental Principles and Rights at Work', 36 *New York University Journal of International Law and Politics* (2004) 221.

[69] See P. Alston, 'The Contribution of the EU's Fundamental Rights Agency to the Realisation of Economic and Socials Rights', in P. Alston and O. De Schutter (eds), *Monitoring Fundamental Rights in the EU: The Contribution of the Fundamental Rights Agency* (2005) 159.

[70] See P. Alston and J. H. H. Weiler, 'An "Ever Closer Union" in Need of a Human Rights Policy: The European Union and Human Rights', in P. Alston, with M. Bustelo and J. Heenan (eds), *The European Union and Human Rights* (1999) 32; and O. De Schutter, *L'adhésion de l'Union européenne à la Charte sociale européenne révisée*, European University Institute Working Paper LAW No. 2004/11.

[71] For a detailed analysis of this issue see J.-F. Akandji-Kombé, 'Charte sociale et droit communitaire', in J.-F. Akandji-Kombé and Stéphane Leclerc (eds), *La Charte sociale européenne* (2001) 149.

[72] Evju, *supra* n. 4, 32.

The same point has been made by Churchill and Khaliq in their analysis of the collective complaints procedure. They urge the ECSR to promote compatibility between the standards they define under the ESC and those reflected in the EU and elsewhere. In their view, such an approach 'is more likely to mean that [the Committee's] findings will not be ignored because similar breaches under other treaties are more likely to be enforceable, especially in the case of EU law'. They concede, however, that such an approach increases the 'risk that the ECSR may need to water down its approach to the obligations imposed by certain Charter provisions, thus to some extent defeating the object of the exercise'.[73]

The first step towards finding a solution lies in acknowledging the problem. The ECSR needs to recognize that in some areas it is operating under the shadow of the EU, that its best hope is to seek to collaborate and interact, and that this will involve a systematic effort to shape compatible jurisprudence and to develop presidential dialogue with the key institutions, including the Commission and the European Court of Justice.

E. *Making Inputs and Outputs Accessible*

The ESC is close to being a disaster area when seen from a public relations perspective. It must suffice for present purposes to note several dimensions of this problem. The first is obvious, but has no simple solution. It is that the complex system resulting from the combination of the *à la carte* range of rights to which states subscribe and the complex set of texts which result from the efforts to update and revise the Charter almost guarantee that only the most dedicated and skilled of observers will be able to navigate their way through the labyrinth that has been created. As a result, the Charter's potential to resonate easily with the broader public is close to zero. But instead of leading to resignation, this should lead to steps designed to make the process more accessible and comprehensible. In the first place, the format of the Committee's current reports is badly in need of improvement. The existing format is about as unappealing as it possibly could be and an effort should be made to make it more user friendly.

Secondly, the jurisprudential contributions developed by the Committee need to be made more obvious and accessible. At present they too often remain buried deep in verbiage. The formal output of the Committee's procedures provides useful grist for the academic mill but little material in a form likely to be picked up by civil society, national courts, or legislators. The point has been made in more gentle terms by Harris and Darcy who observe that 'the Committee has not articulated in general terms the principles that it applies; instead they are usually mostly to be inferred from its rulings on . . . particular situations'.[74] Thus, for

---

[73] R. R. Churchill and U. Khaliq, 'The Collective Complaints System of the European Social Charter: An Effective Mechanism for Ensuring Compliance with Economic and Social Rights?', 15 *EJIL* (2004) 417, at 456.   [74] Harris and Darcy, *supra* n. 5, 31.

example, the recent breakthroughs on the right to housing and the right to environment mentioned in the chapter in this volume by Brillat[75] are at best barely visible to most observers. While the UN human rights treaty bodies have made very effective use of the technique of adopting General Comments, the ECSR has failed to devise any equivalent means by which to distil and highlight the interpretations of specific rights which they have adopted. The introduction to the annual report would provide an appropriate opportunity for the Committee to highlight its contributions in this regard. This is a technique generally used by the ILO Committee of Experts and one which has been tried but not pursued by the ECSR. It should be revived and developed.

Thirdly, the Committee needs to pay more attention to the ways in which its conclusions are presented and disseminated. The response of the media, of specialist civil society groups, and of the general public which emerges from the Italian case study is not encouraging in this respect. The Committee's recommendations were not taken up with any notable enthusiasm by civil society even when they were critical of the government and were supportive of positions which civil society had been at pains to push at the national level. The Committee needs to be able to translate its conclusions from legalese into everyday discourse and to find ways to disseminate the conclusions which will reach (and more importantly, touch) the general public.

F. Holding Governments to Account

The number of unanswered issues, leading to a large proportion of matters deferred for consideration in the next report, is a sign that the process is not working optimally, especially in the days of Internet and video-link communication. To say that issues will, in effect, be deferred for five years is not a sign that opportunities provided by new technologies are being exploited. Nor is it likely to inspire civil society to engage actively when governmental failures to provide information are rewarded so handsomely.

The role still accorded to the Committee of Ministers in the overall ESC supervisory system is a strong reminder both of the fact that governments remain extremely sensitive in relation to social rights and that the autonomy accorded to the European Court of Human Rights under the Protocol 11 reforms is a far cry from the continuing second-guessing role retained by governments under the ESC system. Thus, for example, in relation to the complaints procedure, Churchill and Khaliq have observed of the Committee of Ministers that:

While it has generally acted speedily, its handling of those complaints where the ECSR has found non-compliance with the Charter by the defendant State has been quite unsatisfactory . . . If [the present trend] continues, it will serve only to discredit the system and

---

[75] Chapter 3 above.

discourage complaints because complainants will feel that there is little point in utilising the system if a finding of non-compliance by the ECSR will not be endorsed.[76]

G. *Importance of the Collective Complaints Procedure*

The most significant innovation in the ESC system in recent years was the adoption of the collective complaints procedure. In the seven years since the first complaint was lodged, the balance sheet offers a mixed picture. On the one hand, the fact that a complaints procedure has been introduced in relation to social rights constitutes a major breakthrough in terms of the general resistance of governments to submit such matters to international adjudication of any sort. The fact that twenty-five complaints have been registered between October 1998 and February 2005 is not insignificant given the stakes that are involved in some of the cases. And the preparedness of the ECSR to adopt far-reaching decisions in several cases augurs well for the contribution which the procedure might make in the future.

On the other side of the balance sheet, reference may be made to several less encouraging elements. First, neither national nor international NGOs have yet been sufficiently mobilized to push for acceptance of the complaints procedure by governments. The result is that only thirteen states, or less than one-third of the forty-four which have signed (thirty-four have ratified) either the Charter or the Revised Charter, have accepted it. Secondly, only one country, Finland, has agreed that complaints can be lodged by its national NGOs (the optional fourth category), rather than requiring the involvement of an international organization of employers or trade unions or a national group certified for this purpose. These restrictions help to maintain the labour law (or employment rights) orientation of the Charter and hence its limited relevance to many of the major social movements at the national level.

And thirdly, the relative paucity of complaints to date, twenty-nine as of May 2005, is surprising. It would seem to suggest that national social action groups are loath to confront their governments in an international forum, whether for fear of losing government sympathy or financial support or because national resolution of such issues is seen as the appropriate norm. While the labour movement has made reasonable use of the procedure, there is a clear need to encourage the involvement of a more traditional human rights constituency in bringing cases under the procedure.

The bottom line, however, is that the collective complaints system represents an important development in the procedure and one which has the potential to transform the effectiveness of the ESC system as a whole. Because the procedure also has the potential to convince governments that complaints systems in relation to these rights represent a step too far, it is important for the ECSR to tread carefully and to ensure that its case law is strongly reasoned and consistent.

[76] Churchill and Khaliq, *supra* n. 73, 455.

VII. CONCLUSION

The picture that emerges of the supervisory system under the ESC, as illustrated by the recent experience in relation to Italy, points to the need for significant reforms to be adopted. The thrust of the present analysis is that the great majority of these reforms are within the grasp of the existing institutions and that a concerted effort by the Council of Europe, and especially by the ECSR itself, could transform a relatively ineffectual system into one that could have a far greater impact.

5

Domestic Enforcement of the European Social Charter: The Way Forward

GISELLA GORI*

I. INTRODUCTION

Discussing the domestic enforcement of the European Social Charter (for the purpose of this chapter this term covers both the 1961 Charter and the 1996 Revised European Social Charter)[1] would appear to be a simple exercise: in reality it is rather the opposite. Domestic enforcement of the European Social Charter (also referred to as the ESC or Charter), that is its legislative and judicial implementation into national legal systems, has always been a difficult process, more often avoided than pursued. First, the implementation of this treaty into national legal orders has followed a variety of diverse patterns. Secondly, the direct impact of the Charter on national legislation is rather fragmented and circumscribed. Finally, the amount of national case law on the Charter is limited and, with few exceptions, fails to acknowledge any 'direct applicability' or 'justiciability' of the social rights contained in the instrument.

It is common to view an international treaty as relevant only if its main effect is to confer individual rights which can be asserted before national courts. But it should also be emphasized that, in international law, this attribute is the exception rather than the rule. In the European context, only two treaties, the Convention on Human Rights and Fundamental Freedoms and the European Union Treaty and their case law—and secondary law in the case of the EU legal order—are currently recognized as having direct effect in national legal orders. Their enforceability,

---

* The opinions expressed in this chapter are those of the author and do not necessarily reflect those of the Council of Europe.

[1] The situation at September 2004 was: 18 states had ratified the Revised European Social Charter (Albania, Armenia, Azerbaijan, Belgium, Bulgaria, Cyprus, Estonia, Finland, France, Ireland, Italy, Lithuania, Moldova, Norway, Portugal, Romania, Slovenia, and Sweden) and 17 the 1961 European Social Charter (Austria, Croatia, the Czech Republic, Denmark, Germany, Greece, Hungary, Iceland, Latvia, Luxembourg, Malta, the Netherlands, Poland, Slovakia, Spain, Turkey, and the United Kingdom).

however, differs to the extent that only the European Convention on Human Rights and Fundamental Freedoms provides for an individual right of appeal, while in the EU context individuals have seen their rights protected mainly through the mechanism of the preliminary ruling.

Generally speaking, traditional international treaties are not accorded direct applicability. Often their provisions are held not to be self-executing, which means that 'for them to produce effects domestically, the passing of implementing legislation proves necessary'.[2] But this does not diminish their relevance: these treaties remain binding instruments whose final goal is the effective protection of, for example, the fundamental social rights of individuals. In the social rights sphere, it is particularly true that the state remains the main actor, its intervention being necessary to ensure that this protection for individuals is in fact effectively enforced.

The state is relevant first in its role as legislator since, generally, it is through legislation that the benefits contemplated by the provisions of the treaty are guaranteed in the form of subjective rights. In other words, legislation operates to transform the principles into individual rights (*subjectivisation par la loi*). Alternatively, legislation will not itself carry out this transformation but will ordain how national authorities are to act to guarantee the benefits to individuals.

Secondly, the role of the state is relevant from the standpoint of judicial review of action taken by means of legislation. An application may be lodged before the ordinary courts against legislation considered not adequately to guarantee a fundamental social right. In such an application, both constitutional provisions and international treaty provisions may be relied upon in argument against the legislation. The state in fact may not have respected its international obligations when implementing a right. This is the so-called 'normative justiciability' of social rights.[3]

In this chapter I first review the domestic enforcement of the ESC that has been undertaken hitherto by way of both national legislation and case law. Secondly, I attempt to outline how this enforcement could be improved by way of the evolving interpretation of the Charter given by the European Committee of Social Rights and the development of the notion of justiciability. Taking into consideration the fact that international treaties are binding upon the states that ratify them and, thus, they have binding legal effects in national legal orders, the purpose of this chapter is to demonstrate that a broader notion of justiciability can lead to the strengthening of individual social rights deriving from the ESC.

II. DOMESTIC ENFORCEMENT: WHERE DO WE STAND?

As an international treaty guaranteeing fundamental social rights, the ESC has from its earliest days suffered from the presumption of non-justiciability[4] of social

---

[2] See A. Cassese, *International Law* (2001), at 173.

[3] G. Braibant, *La Charte des droits fondamentaux de l'Union européenne* (2001), at 46.

[4] See F. Sudre, 'Le protocole additionnel à la Charte social européenne prévoyant un système de réclamations collectives', 100 *RGDIP* (1996) 739.

rights. In the past it was usual to consider that social rights relied upon state intervention and, consequently, were principles of a programmatic nature rather than subjective rights. It follows from this that the provisions guaranteeing them, being constitutional or flowing from international treaties, could not be accorded direct applicability until the legislator intervened. Notwithstanding the efforts of some academics to move this view on[5] and the increasing individualization by national courts of social rights contained in constitutions or other national acts, this view still appears to hold fast.[6] Indeed, at least as regards international provisions guaranteeing social rights, the recognition by national courts of their direct applicability is still quite limited.

In particular, as far as the Charter is concerned, there was, and still appears to be, consensus in the literature[7] on the fact that the intention of its authors was set out with absolute clarity from the beginning, as demonstrated by certain clauses of the Treaty. Article I of Part V of the Charter and Part III of the Appendix to the Charter and Article 12 of the Protocol on Collective Complaints have been held to rule out any direct applicability of the Charter.[8] As a consequence, almost all Charter provisions have been considered to be programmatic provisions which need state intervention to put them into effect, in line with the long-standing theory about social rights as *droits des créance*.[9]

This presumption has influenced the way in which the ESC has—or has not yet—been implemented into national legal orders and its legislative and judicial enforcement.

A. *Implementation of the ESC into National Legal Orders*

Any international treaty must first be implemented into national law in order fully to acquire binding effect.[10] States are free to choose how to give effect to such

---

[5] See generally K. Drzewicki, C. Krause, and A. Rosas (eds), *Social Rights as Human Rights, a European Challenge* (1994); A. Eide, C. Krause, and A. Rosas (eds), *Economic, Social and Cultural Rights, a Textbook* (1995).

[6] For an overview of the legal protection of social rights in the EU Member States see J. Iliopoulos-Strangas (ed.), *La protection des droits sociaux fondamentaux dans les etats membres de l'Union européenne* (2000).

[7] See O. Khan-Freund, 'The European Social Charter', in F. G. Jacobs (ed.), *European Law and the Individual* (1976), at 193; more recently see O. De Schutter's contribution to this book.

[8] Art. I(1) reads: 'Without prejudice to the implementation foreseen in these articles the relevant provisions of Article 1 to 31 of Part II of this Charter shall be implemented by: a. laws or regulations; b. agreements between employers or employers' organizations and workers' organizations; c. a combination of those two methods; d. other appropriate means'; Part III of the Appendix reads: 'It is understood that the Charter contains legal obligations of an international character, the application of which is submitted solely to the supervision provided for in Part IV thereof'; Art. 12 of the Protocol providing for a system of Collective Complaint repeats Part III of the Appendix and completes it with 'and in the provisions of this Protocol' after 'thereof'.

[9] See C. Grewe and H. Ruiz Fabri, *Droits constitutionnels européens* (1995), at 168.

[10] On the implementation of the ESC see A. P. C. M. Jaspers and L. Betten (eds), *25 Years of the European Social Charter* (1988); more recently see J.-F. Akandji-Kombé, monograph under redaction on the European Social Charter, provisional Chapter 1 of Title II, and C. Sciotti, 'L'applicabilité de la

treaties and how nationally to fulfil their international obligations according to the characteristics of their legal orders.

Generally speaking,[11] there are two main implementation mechanisms. The first is automatic standing incorporation, which means that a national rule provides for the automatic incorporation of international treaty provisions without any need for the passing of *ad hoc* legislation. This approach is followed by the so-called monist states, which, as far as the Charter is concerned, number twenty-two: Albania, Armenia, Azerbaijan, Belgium, Bulgaria, Croatia, Cyprus, the Czech Republic, Estonia, France, Greece, Lithuania, Luxembourg, Moldova, the Netherlands, Poland, Portugal, Romania, Slovakia, Slovenia, Spain, and Turkey.[12] Latvia cannot be considered as falling into this category—nor the second one described below—because of the lack of a constitutional provision on human rights and the fact that its accession to human rights instruments is regulated by a declaration.[13] By way of a constitutional provision, a law (Latvia)[14] or the case law (Belgium),[15] these states, in principle, recognize the Charter as having immediate legal effects in the domestic legal order upon its ratification and publication.

The second mechanism consists of legislative *ad hoc* incorporation, by which international treaties become effective in the domestic legal order upon the passing of specific implementing legislation.[16] Such legislation is of one of two kinds: the first translates the international provisions into national ones that reproduce them in detail (statutory *ad hoc* incorporation). The second consists of the automatic *ad hoc* incorporation of international provisions, without any reformulation, through a specific act adopted for the purpose. As far as the Charter is concerned, the following dualist states have adopted legislative *ad hoc* incorporation: Austria, Denmark, Finland, Germany, Hungary, Iceland, Ireland, Italy, Malta, Norway, Sweden, and the United Kingdom. Of these, Finland, Germany, Hungary,[17] Italy,[18] and Sweden, have implemented the Charter by way of the automatic *ad hoc* incorporation mechanism, while the others have not yet implemented it.[19] In both automatic standing incorporation and legislative *ad hoc* incorporation, and according to national traditions, the Charter provisions may be recognized as ranking higher than normal law,[20] or at least as equivalent

---

Charte sociale européenne dans l'ordre juridique des etats contractants', in J.- F. Flauss (ed.), *Droits sociaux et droit européen, bilan et prospective de la protection normative* (2002), at 175.

11 Cassese, *supra* n. 2, at 168 ff.

12 For more details about national implementation see Sciotti, *supra* n. 10, at 179.

13 See Ziemele, 'Incorporation and Implementation of Human Rights in Latvia', in M. Scheinin, *International Human Rights Norms in the Nordic and Baltic Countries* (1996), at 73.

14 Act of 15 December 1992 on the judicial power in Latvia.

15 Belgian *Cour de Cassation*, 27 May 1971, *Le Ski* [1971] PB 887.

16 See Cassese, *supra* n. 2, at 169.   17 Act No. 32/1989, s. 1.

18 Act No. 30/1999, Legge recante ratifica ed esecuzione della Carta sociale europea riveduta con annesso fatta a Strasburgo il 3 Maggio 1996.

19 See Sciotti, *supra* n. 10, at 183 for more details.

20 Albania (Art. 122), Armenia (Art. 6), Azerbaijan (Art. 148(II)), Bulgaria (Art. 5(4)), Croatia (Art. 140), Cyprus (Art. 169(3)), Czech Republic (Art. 10), Estonia (Art. 123), France (Art. 55),

to it.[21] At one end of the spectrum are the Netherlands, where the Charter is in principle accorded a supra-constitutional value, and at the other end is Sweden, which implemented the Charter by means only of a regulation as a consequence of the non-enforceability of social rights.

From the above overview it appears that, with some exceptions, the Charter has been incorporated into domestic legal orders mainly through automatic standing incorporation for many countries and legislative *ad hoc* incorporation for a few others, and, as such, is ready for enforcement or direct applicability in those orders. But, as the next section will show, this has not really been the case so far. This can be explained by the type of the provisions guaranteeing social fundamental rights. Independently of the term used to define this type, that is self-executing[22] or directly applicable[23] provisions, the point is that the passing of national legislation is deemed necessary for them to have domestic effects. This seems to apply, at least at a first reading, to the Charter, whose provisions, like constitutional provisions guaranteeing social fundamental rights, require the legislative intervention of the state.

B. *The Legislative and the Judicial Enforcement of the ESC*

Domestic enforcement occurs through the adoption of legislation adapting national law to the requirements laid down in international provisions (see Subsection 1. below) or through the ability of social rights provisions contained in an international instrument to be invoked in domestic courts of law (see Subsection 2. below).

1. *The Legislative Enforcement of the ESC*   Article I of the Charter reads:

Without prejudice to the implementation foreseen in these articles the relevant provisions of Article 1 to 31 of Part II of this Charter shall be implemented by: a. laws or regulations; b. agreements between employers or employers' organizations and workers' organizations; c. a combination of those two methods; d. other appropriate means.

Greece (Art. 28(1)), Hungary (Art. 7), Moldova (Art. 4), the Netherlands (Art. 94), Poland (Art. 91(2)), Portugal (Art. 8), Romania (Art. 20), Slovakia (Art. 7(5)), Slovenia (Art. 153(2)), and Spain (Art. 96(1)). Belgium and Luxembourg recognized this rank through the case law. The situation of Latvia and Lithuania is unclear.

[21] Turkey (Art. 90(5)) and the countries that used legislative *ad hoc* incorporation (Finland, Germany, and Italy). Norway did not include the Charter in a recent Act incorporating various human rights instruments, which even included the UN Covenant on Economic, Social and Cultural Rights.

[22] For the current use of this terminology see Cassese, *supra* n. 2, at 173. Non-self-executing provisions are 'provisions that cannot be directly applied within the national legal system because they need to be supplemented by additional national legislation for them to be implemented'.

[23] See M. Scheinin, 'Direct Applicability of Economic, Social and Cultural Rights: A Critique of the Doctrine of Self-Executing Treaties', in Drzewicki, Krause, and Rosas (eds), *supra* n. 5, at 75.

This list indicates how the Charter shall be enforced. Certain provisions of the Charter or the Appendix further suggest which instrument is most appropriate for their enforcement, but in general the choice is left to states. According to the academic view the law must be used every time states are under an obligation to recognize a precise right, to define precise regulations or to prohibit certain types of behaviour.[24] It must however be taken into consideration that almost all national constitutions contain a catalogue of social and economic rights and that these provisions generally form the legal basis for the adoption of national legislation to make these rights operative in the domestic legal order. Therefore, the relevance of the Charter consists rather in reinforcing standards, also set by national constitutions, fostering equality of treatment for non-nationals, and requiring legal remedies to be provided.

The case law of the European Committee of Social Rights (hereinafter 'ECSR') contains several examples of states adopting measures in order to bring their situations into line with the Charter. The kinds of measures taken by states vary: the adoption of new legislation, amendments to existing legislation, judicial action, administrative measures, and collective agreements by social partners. States take measures often as a result of a finding of non-conformity by the ECSR, usually after the further intervention of the European Social Charter Governmental Committee (warnings) and the Council of Europe Committee of Ministers (recommendations), rather than as a spontaneous development. Nonetheless, this process is producing visible results.[25] From this perspective the collective complaints procedure is particularly apt to further the adaptation of legislation because it brings to light specific problems and failures of national rules guaranteeing one or the other social fundamental right. Moreover, it is worth noting that states are more and more keen, once again particularly in the collective complaints procedure, to try to bring their situations into conformity with the Charter even during the course of the proceedings by amending their existing legislation, as in Collective Complaint No. 11/2001, *European Council of Police Trade Unions v. Portugal*,[26] or adopting, or at least planning to adopt, new rules, as in Collective Complaint No. 13/2002, *Autism-Europe v. France*. As regards the latter, the French government undertook before the Council of Europe Committee of Ministers to implement a whole series of measures aimed at improving the right of access to education of autistic people, while a new Act on people with disabilities was introduced into the French Parliament.[27]

---

[24] Akandji-Kombé, *supra* n. 10.

[25] For an overview see Council of Europe, *Implementation of the European Social Charter, Survey by country* (2001 and 2002), as well as the fact-sheets in www.coe.int (Human Rights/European Social Charter/Reporting Procedure/Survey by country).

[26] The Portuguese Government adopted Act 14/2002 of 19 February 2002, which removed the basis of non-conformity with Arts. 5 and 6(2) of the ESC.

[27] See Appendix to Resolution ResChS (2004) 1 of the Committee of Ministers of the Council of Europe, adopted on 10 March 2004 (www.coe.int); Projét de loi pour l'égalité des droits et des chances, la participation et la citoyenneté des personnes handicapées, 28 January 2004, in www.handicap.gouv.fr/point_presse/doss_pr/loi_egalite/sommaire.htm.

From among the many available examples,[28] I will here highlight a few concerning the amending of legislation to bring national situations into line with the Charter in the field of family benefits, mainly from the perspective of equal treatment of non-nationals.

Belgium recently adopted amendments to the 1971 Act on Guaranteed Family Allowances to ensure equal treatment for nationals of Contracting Parties to the European Social Charter by removing the residence condition for family allowances under the non-contributory guaranteed family allowance scheme.[29] Malta extended the entitlement to family benefits to nationals of other Contracting Parties by means of the European Social Charter Order of 1999. Finally, Germany extended to Turkish nationals entitlement to the supplement to the child-rearing allowance provided by certain *Länder*. Generally speaking, as regards equal treatment of non-nationals, it is worth noting a new trend which is developing. Rather than taking *ad hoc* measures, as regards the personal scope of the legislation at issue for the purpose of equal treatment, Slovenia and the Netherlands opted for a general reference to any ratified international treaty, thereby including the ESC. This is welcome progress towards ensuring that equal treatment is comprehensively guaranteed to all nationals of the Parties to the Charter.

It is finally worth noting the interest in the European Social Charter recently shown by the United Kingdom Parliament, and in particular the House of Lords and the Joint Committee on Human Rights, in their debates. In the procedure for the adoption of the Children Act, the Charter was taken into consideration in the discussion of the reasonable chastisement clause. In both the House of Lords[30] and the Joint Committee on Human Rights, the case law of the ECSR was quoted in support of the view that the continuing availability of the defence of reasonable chastisement was incompatible with the United Kingdom's obligations under the European Social Charter.

2. The Case Law on the ESC Judicial domestic enforcement of social rights provisions means in its most developed form that these can be invoked in courts and be directly applicable in national legal orders. This means that these provisions have direct effect for individuals, giving them subjective rights, and eventually

---

[28] E.g., in Poland the right to reunion of migrant workers' family members was expressly guaranteed by an Act of 1 July 2001. In Malta, since 1996, part-time employees have benefited from maternity leave. In Turkey, a new Civil Code ensuring equality between spouses and parents was adopted in January 2002. In France, the Civil Code was revised in 2001 to eliminate any discrimination against children born out of wedlock with respect to heritage rules. In Portugal, the right to organize was in 1999 extended to all public employees, while children under the age of 16 are prohibited from working. In Italy, since 1999 there has been the prohibition on the employment of children under 15, etc.

[29] See Loi Progr., 24 December 2002 (I), Art. 106(1): 'la personne non visée au 1° qui est ressortissante d'un Etat qui a ratifié la Charte sociale européenne . . .'.

[30] House of Lords Hansard, 20 May 2004 (240520–07); House of Lords, House of Commons, Joint Committee on Human Rights, Children Bill, Nineteenth Report, Session 2003–04, at 45, available at www.publications.parliament.uk/pa/jt/jtrights.htm.

replacing incompatible national provisions. The case law on the Charter demonstrates that national courts have largely considered this text not to be directly applicable, with the exception of a few provisions which these same courts have held to be clear enough to provide an individual right that they could guarantee.[31] This 'state of the art' may appear disappointing, but the fact that some of the Charter provisions have been recognized as directly applicable demonstrates that, when this does not happen, the reasons are found in the classical arguments for the non-enforceability of the ESC provisions, such as the nature of these rights, the wording of the articles,[32] the clauses in Part III and in the Appendix, the non-jurisdictional nature of the supervisory mechanism, etc. These arguments lose much of their relevance when there are taken into account the increasing justiciability of social rights at national level; the content of the ESC rights themselves as developed by the case law; the way the Charter has been incorporated into national legal orders; and, finally, the evolution of the supervisory mechanism.

Indeed, the view that Part III of the Appendix, which reads: 'It is understood that the Charter contains legal obligations of an international character, the application of which is submitted solely to the supervision provided for in Part IV thereof', precludes any direct applicability of the Charter appears quite odd.[33] The plain interpretation of this provision appears to be that the Charter, at international level, is subject only to the control of its own supervisory mechanism(s). Such a drastic interpretation seems rather to be the inheritance of old conceptions of social rights widespread after the Second World War, where a mixture of feelings of devotion to civil and political rights and fear of social rights prevailed. But it is almost inconceivable in contemporary society, where social rights assume greater and greater relevance. As is demonstrated by academic writing,[34] this interpretation of Part III of the Appendix is not even fully supported by the *travaux préparatoires* to the Charter and, therefore, notwithstanding its use also in German case law, it cannot be upheld.[35] In any event the example of Finland—see below—demonstrates that treaty provisions may become 'self-executing—or directly applicable, even if this was against the actual intent of their framers'.[36]

---

[31] The example of the Netherlands is particularly enlightening on this approach: see Jaspers and Betten (eds), *supra* n. 10, at 134 ff.

[32] The articles that have been recognized as directly applicable use the formula 'the Parties recognize', while the others use 'the Parties undertake to . . .'. This same approach was used by the European Court of Human Rights in *Ireland v. United Kingdom*, ECHR (1978) Series A, No. 25, 90.

[33] See Wierbringhaus, 'Les effets de la Charte sociale européenne en droit interne', in F. Gamillscheg (ed.), *In Memoriam Sir Otto Kahn-Freund* (1980), at 756; W. Wengler, 'Reflexion sur l'application du droit international public par les tribunaux internes', *RGDIP* (1968) 935; D. Gomien, D. Harris, and L. Zwaak, *Convention européenne des droits de l'homme et Charte sociale européenne: droit et pratique* (1997), at 492.   [34] See Sciotti, *supra* n. 10, at 196.

[35] For a different opinion on the *travaux préparatoires* see also Akandji-Kombé, *supra* n. 10.

[36] Scheinin, in Eide, Krause, and Rosas (eds), *supra* n. 5, at 60. See also O. De Schutter, commentary on the *Henry* decision in O. De Schutter and S. Van Drooghenbroeck, *Droit international des droits de l'homme devant le juge national* (1999), at 397.

As regards the case law, Dutch courts, for example, have recognized Article 6(4) as directly applicable, as also have German and Belgian courts, and this irrespective of whether they finally found non-violation (Germany and the Belgian *Cour d'Arbitrage*). In 1986, the Dutch Supreme Court held Articles 6(4) and 31 (Article G of the Revised Charter) to be directly applicable in national law by virtue of both Article 93 of the Netherlands Constitution and the wording of these two provisions.[37] The Supreme Court considered that the action brought by railway workers in 1983 could be regarded as a means of defending their right to negotiate their working conditions. The action concerned a conflict of interests and, therefore, fell within Article 6(4). As a result of the Supreme Court decision, strikes, at least those involving private employees, have to be reviewed by Dutch national courts in the context of the Charter. This judgment was preceded by two other decisions taken in the context of the ratification process of the Charter and recognizing the right to strike, first, as regards private employees and, secondly, as regards public employees.[38]

The main reason Dutch courts acknowledged Article 6(4) to be directly applicable was the lack of a similar provision in national law. In the Netherlands, the issue of the right to strike had long been controversial, thereby preventing the ratification of the European Social Charter. However, it is interesting to note that the recognition of direct effect does not automatically imply that the country also complies with the ESC. The interpretation given by the Dutch courts of the right to strike does not accord with that in the ECSR case law, in so far as a Dutch court is accorded the jurisdiction to decide whether collective action is premature.[39] The ECSR considers this to impinge 'on the very substance of the right to strike as this allows the judge to exercise one of the trade unions' key prerogatives, that of deciding whether and when a strike is necessary'.[40]

In the *Henry* decision, the Belgian *Conseil d'Etat* based its legal reasoning on, among other international instruments, Article 6 of the ESC in order to conclude that an internal administrative act should be annulled, thereby recognizing it as a source of individual rights.[41] In particular, Article 6(4) was used to annul a disciplinary sanction against a worker on strike since this measure was considered excessively to restrict his right to strike. In this decision, the recognition of the direct applicability of the provision followed from the court's capacity to base its reasoning on the international provision without exceeding its own competence with regard to the division of powers at national level.[42] Neither the intentions of

---

[37] Supreme Court (*Hoge Raad*), 30 May 1986, NJ 1986/688; see also Jaspers and Betten (eds), *supra* n. 10, at 134.

[38] Arrondissementsrechtbank (District Court), Amsterdam, 13 April 1972, NJ 1972/192; President of the Arrondissementsrechtbank, Utrecht, 11 March 1982, NJ 1982/346; President of the Arrondissementsrechtbank, Arnhem, 12 March 1982, NJ 1982/347.

[39] *Hoge Raad*, 19 April 1991.　　　　[40] ECSR, *Conclusions XVII-1*, Vol. 2, at 319.

[41] *Conseil d'Etat* (VI ch.), 22 March 1995, *Henry*, No. 52424, A.P.T. (1995), at 228.

[42] See De Schutter and Van Drooghenbroeck, *supra* n. 36, at 397.

the Contracting Parties to the international instruments, nor the self-executing nature of the provision are taken into consideration. The Belgian *Cour d'Arbitrage* seems also, though implicitly, to recognize the direct applicability of certain ESC provisions. In a 1993 decision, it seemed to acknowledge the direct applicability of Articles 5 and 6 since it accepted all the grounds invoked by the complainants, including the Charter provisions.[43] Similarly, in a 1998 decision, it seemed to accept the direct effect of Article 13 by affirming that it could be invoked only by nationals of the States Parties to the Charter who were legally present in the territory in question.[44]

Finally, Finland has gone much further when ratifying the Charter, since the Finnish Parliament Social Affairs Committee expressly indicated that, as a consequence of its incorporation, the provisions of the ESC would become applicable in domestic courts and by administrative authorities.[45] So far case law on the Charter has mainly concerned Article 13.

It is true that these same courts have been broadly cautious in according direct applicability to the Charter provisions. In the Netherlands, they have denied any direct effect to other Charter provisions (Articles 1(2), 6(1) and (2), 12, 13(4), 18(1)–(3), 19(8)), often on the ground of their 'nature and contents'. It appears that there were often political reasons behind such decisions, as for example the wish not to challenge the official aliens policy. In Belgium, the need for national implementing measures of a substantial nature, which implied the exercise of a power of appreciation, was the ground for the denial by the *Conseil d'Etat* of the direct applicability of other ESC provisions. In the *Hoefkens* case, this court considered that the ESC provisions in issue, that is Articles 1, 2, 3, and 15, could be directly applicable only if they were clear and complete enough and needed no further implementing measure of a substantial nature.[46] The same occurred as regards Article 4(4).[47] In Germany, several judicial decisions, mainly relating to Articles 5 and 6(4), took the ESC into account, but refrained from taking a position on its direct applicability. They rather cited it as a mere parallel to or

---

[43] *Cour d'Arbitrage*, No. 62/93, 15 July 1993, *Syndicat progressiste pour le personnel de la gendarmerie*, M.B., 5/08/1993, in De Schutter and Van Drooghenbroeck, *supra* n. 36, at 517.

[44] *Cour d'Arbitrage*, 22 April 1998, *A.s.b.l. Mouvement contre le racisme, l'antisémitisme et la xénophobie et crts*, No. 43/98, M.B., 29 April 1998, in De Schutter and Van Drooghenbroeck, *supra* n. 36, at 624.   [45] Parliament of Finland, Social Affairs Committee, Opinion No. 14/1990.

[46] '*Considérant qu'une règle de droit international ou supranational a des effets directs lorsqu'elle peut être appliquée dans l'ordre juridique où elle est en vigueur sans aucune mesure interne d'exécution d'ordre substantiel; qu'en revanche n'a pas de tels effets la règle de droit international ou supranational qu'impose à l'Etat une obligation d'agir, ou de s'abstenir, conformément aux principes que la règle contient; que les dispositions d'un traité qui sont dépourvues d'effets directs ne produisant aucun effet normatif à l'égard des individus, elle ne peuvent investir les individus de droits subjectifs, leur seul effet étant d'imposer des obligations aux parties contractantes; . . . que les articles invoqués, 1, 2, 3, et 15 de la Charte sociale européenne n'ont pas d'effect direct dans l'ordre juridique belge; . . .': Conseil d'Etat* (X ch.), 10 December 1996, *Hoefkens v. Etat Belge*, No. 63473, T.B.P., at 580.

[47] *Conseil d'Etat*, 16 October 1997, *V.*, No. 68914, R.W., 1998–1999, at 331.

repetition of rights already guaranteed under national law, thereby being able to affirm that national law was compatible with the Charter.[48] In a particular case on strikes not called by a trade union, the Berlin Labour Court went so far as explicitly to deny the direct applicability of Article 6(4) ESC.[49] This meant interpreting the Charter provision in the light of domestic law and ignoring the case law to the contrary of the, at the time, Committee of Independent Experts (today the ECSR).

The French case is particularly interesting, as it shows agreement among courts to deny any direct effect to the Charter without providing much explanation.[50] In the *Valton and Crepeaux* case, as in many others,[51] the *Conseil d'Etat* confined itself to affirming that Article 4(4) of the ESC '*ne produit pas d'effet direct à l'égard des nationaux des états contractants*'.[52] One rather interesting and partly dissenting judgment was delivered by the Lyon Administrative Court, which denied direct effect to Article 19(6), while according it to the Appendix to the Charter relating to this same provision.[53] In many other cases, both the *Conseil d'Etat* and the *Cour de Cassation* considered the arguments based on the ESC insufficiently reasoned[54] or ill-founded.[55] In the light of the dubious *Glaziou* judgment, where it was unclear whether the *Cour de Cassation*, in contrast to its previous case law, acknowledges that the Charter has direct effect,[56] we shall wait for more case law in order to be able to draw a conclusion about the legal reasons for the French

[48] Federal Constitutional Court, Decision of 20 October 1981, in *Entscheidungen des Bundesverfassungsgerichts* (BVerfGE) 58, 233; Federal Labour Court, Decision of 12 March 1985 in *Entscheidungen des Bundesarbeitsgerichts* (BAGE) 48, 195.

[49] Arbeitsgericht Berlin, Decision of 10 October 1974 in AP No. 49 on Art. 9 Grundgesetz, Arbeitskampf; see also Bundesarbeitsgericht (Federal Labour Court), Decision of 21 April 1971, BAGE 23, 292.

[50] See Akandji-Kombé, *supra* n. 10, for a full description of this case law.

[51] Conseil d'Etat (hereinafter C.E.), 15 May 1995, *J.-P. Raut*, No. 152417, Recueil Lebon, as regards Arts. 11 and 12; C.E., 2 April 2004, *Christophe X*, No. 249482, Recueil Lebon, as regards Art. 1.

[52] C.E., 20 April 1984, *Ministre de l'économie et des Finances v. Valton et Crepeaux*, Recueil Lebon, at 148. See also the *Fédération des services CFDT* case, 28 January 1994, 4 *Revue de Jurisprudence sociale* (1994), at 480.

[53] Tribunal Administratif de Lyon, 28 May 1995, inédit au Recueil Lebon, which reads: '*si les stipulations du paragraphe 6 de l'article 19 . . . ne produisent aucun effet direct à l'égard des particuliers, les stipulations de l'annexe à l'article 19 (6) . . . sont directement exécutoires en droit interne*'.

[54] C.E., 5 May 2000, *Pinault*, No. 205043; 6 Nov. 2000, *GISTI*, No. 204784; 28 May 2004, *Catherine X*, No. 252159; 7 July 2004, *FNSA PTT*, No. 220697. *Cour administrative d'appel de Nancy*, 24 June 2002, No. 97NC00465.

[55] C.E., 28 January 1994, *CFDT*, No. 14111; 9 July 1997, *Chambre de Commerce et de d'Industrie de Dunderke*, No. 149306; 30 July 2003, *Bernard X*, No. 237720; 7 June 2004, *Jean-Pierre X*, No. 260631. See also *Cour de Cassation*, 13 November 2003, *M. and Mme X*; No. 01–15611; and *Cour administrative d'appel de Paris*, 9 March 2004, *Syndicat des agrégés de l'enseignement supérieur*, No. 03PA03412.

[56] *Cour de Cassation*, CH. Soc., 17 December 1996, pourvoi No. 92–44.203, where the Court affirms that '*la règle de compétence dont la Cour d'appel a fait application n'est pas contraire ni à l'article 4 de la Convention EDH, ni à aucune disposition de toute autre convention internationale signée par le gouvernement et ayant en France un effet direct*'. The ESC provisions at issue were Articles 1 to 5, 10, and 12.

jurisdictions' attitude. But it must also be borne in mind that the *Conseil d'Etat* has consistently demonstrated a conservative attitude towards international courts and monitoring bodies, one which for long was also applied to the European Court of Human Rights and the European Union Court of Justice. The treatment reserved for the European Social Charter, which may eventually improve, is nowadays shared by the United Nations Convention on the Rights of the Child.

Review of the case law on direct applicability of the Charter is indeed not very encouraging. The impact of the Charter on domestic legal orders has been far greater in the context of legislative enforcement. If there has been recognition, direct applicability has been limited to a few Charter provisions. If recognition has been denied, the case law is far from rehearsing in depth the reasons for the non-recognition of social rights as individual rights. The nature of social rights and the over-caution of national courts are indeed two of the reasons behind such an attitude. But, in the case of the Charter, this is also due to its weak recognition by States Parties over a long period. The political and normative process for relaunching the Charter, begun by the Council of Europe member states in the 1990s and culminating in the adoption of the Protocol providing for a system on Collective Complaints in 1995 and the Revised European Social Charter in 1996, will eventually improve the recognition of the Charter as the basic European instrument for the protection of social rights. The sharp increase in the number of States Parties, especially to the Revised Charter, in a short time-span witnesses its growing recognition as one of the fundamental treaties protecting human rights.

But beyond merely looking for progress on the direct applicability of the Charter, which is the perspective adopted by almost all national courts so far, it is now worth examining whether the notion of justiciability can also cover other, more fruitful, dimensions of the domestic enforceability of the Charter.

III. DOMESTIC ENFORCEMENT: THE WAY FORWARD

Beyond the pertinent ESC case law, the justiciability of social rights has already been proved in the context of the Convention for the Protection of Human Rights and Fundamental Freedoms. Many decisions of the European Court of Human Rights (hereinafter ECtHR) fleshed out the protection of individual fundamental social rights using certain Convention provisions, such as Articles 3, 8, and 14, to guarantee or at least to take into consideration the right to health (Article 11 ESC), the right to social security benefits (Articles 12 and 13 ESC), the right of people with disabilities to social integration (Article 15 ESC), and the right of children and young people to protection from negligence, violence, and exploitation (Article 17(1)(b) ESC).[57] This extension of the material scope of the Convention

---

[57] See, respectively, Application 44599/98; *Bensaid v. United Kingdom*, ECtHR, judgment of 6 February 2001; *Gaygusuz v. Austria*, ECtHR (1996) Reports 1996–IV; Application 56869/00;

has occurred as a result of the various techniques used by the Court, that is, autonomous notions, indirect protection, the theory of the inherent elements of the law, positive obligations, horizontal effect, and will be reinforced by the entry into force of Protocol No. 12 containing a non-discrimination clause.[58] How all these techniques can be most efficiently used for the further extension of the ECtHR jurisdiction on social rights on the basis of the current Convention for the Protection of Human Rights and Fundamental Freedoms[59] is demonstrated in masterly fashion by the literature.[60]

Moreover, on certain occasions the ECtHR has explicitly referred to the case law of the European Committee of Social Rights.[61] This happened first with regard to Articles 5 and 6 of the Charter. In *Sigurdur A. Sigurjónsson v. Iceland*,[62] in order to define the content of Article 11 of the Convention (the right to freedom of association), reference was made to the Committee of Independent Experts' (the former incarnation of the ECSR) case law, according to which the right to organize, covered by Article 5, also included the negative freedom not to join a professional organization. In the case law that followed,[63] the ECtHR developed the content of Article 11 on the basis also of the ECSR's case law, finally to interpret it explicitly in the light of the European Social Charter. This occurred in *Sanchez Navajas v. Spain* where the Court affirmed that: 'it may infer from Article 11 of the Convention, read in the light of Article 28 of the European Social Charter (Revised), that workers' representatives should as a rule, and within certain limits, enjoy appropriate facilities to enable them to perform their trade-union functions rapidly and effectively'.[64] More recently, in the *Koua Poirrez* judgment,[65] the ECtHR quoted the ECSR's conclusions to support its finding that the reciprocity clause awarding an allowance for disabled adults to non-nationals was in breach of Article 14 read together with Article 1 of Protocol No. 1 of the Convention. The same happened in

Larioshina v. Russia, ECtHR, judgment of 23 April 2002; *Botta v. Italy*, ECtHR (1998) Reports 1998–I; Application 29392/95, *Z and others v. United Kingdom*, ECtHR, judgment of 10 May 2001.

[58] For an overview of the existing case law see F. Tulkens, 'Les droits sociaux dans la jurisprudence de la nouvelle Cour européenne des droits de l'homme', in C. Grewe and F. Benoît-Rohmer (eds), *Les droits sociaux ou la démolition de quelque poncifs* (2003), at 117.

[59] A proposal is currently under scrutiny in the Council of Europe bodies to enlarge the scope of the Convention to include certain social rights.

[60] See F. Sudre, 'Exercice de "jurisprudence-fiction": la protection des droits sociaux par la Cour européenne des droits de l' homme', in Grewe and Benoît-Rohmer (eds), *supra* n. 58, at 145.

[61] For an overview, see J.-F. Flauss, 'Les interactions normatives entre les instruments européens relatifs à la protection des droits sociaux', in Flauss (ed), *supra* n. 10, at 89.

[62] *Sigurdur A. Sigurjónsson v. Iceland*, ECtHR (1993) Series A, No. 254, 35.

[63] See *Gustafsson v. Sweden*, ECtHR (1996) Reports 1996–II on collective bargaining (Art. 6 of the ESC); Applications 30668/96, 30671/96 and 30678/96, *Wilson & the National Union of Journalists, Palmer, Wyeth & the National Union of Rail, Maritime and Transport Workers, Doolan & others v. United Kingdom*, ECtHR, judgment of 2 October 2002, paras. 30–33 and 48 (Arts. 5 and 6 ESC).

[64] Application 57442/00, *Sanchez Navajas v. Spain*, ECtHR, decision on admissibility, para. 2.

[65] Application 40892/98, *Koua Poirrez v. France*, ECtHR, judgment of 30 September 2003, paras. 29 and 39.

Sidabras and Džiautas v. Lithuania,[66] where the Court 'attach[ed] particular weight...to the text of Article 1(2) of the European Social Charter and the interpretation given by the European Committee of Social Rights'. Legal authors also began to argue extensively in favour of the justiciability of social rights and provided arguments against the classical vision analysed in the previous section.[67] According to Olivier De Schutter, for example, the justiciability of social rights consists in '*la capacité pour le juge de prendre appui sur la stipulation de tel droits afin de motiver le dispositif de sa décision de justice*'. J.-F. Akandji-Kombé provides a threefold definition of justiciability. From the perspective of the judge, it means his capacity to ensure the effectiveness of a provision and the effective protection of individuals. From the perspective of the individual, it consists in his capacity effectively to invoke the provision as an argument before the Court. Finally, from the perspective of the norm, it is the ability of the provision to be applied in the course of judicial proceedings.

Bearing these definitions in mind, I will first examine how the evolution of the Charter provisions which, as interpreted by the ECSR, progressively asserted individual rights, can contribute to the justiciability of social rights (see Subsection A. below). Secondly, I will consider which options are left open for achieving the justiciability of social rights beyond the direct applicability of the Charter provisions in the domestic legal order (see Subsection B. below).

A. *The Individualization of Social Rights in the ECSR Case Law*

The presumed unenforceable nature of social rights can evolve both at domestic and international level. At international level, there are two elements which can further justiciability: evolution in the interpretation of the international provisions and the improvement of supervisory mechanism.

The development of the ECSR case law can help individual social rights to emerge from the restrictive wording of the Charter provisions and, thereby, to improve the use of the instrument in the national context. Indeed, the progressive clarification carried out by the ECSR of the scope of the obligations set out in the Charter permitted, and will continue to permit, individual rights to be extracted from the Charter provisions. For example, from the beginning of its operation, the ECSR interpreted at least certain provisions of the Charter, for instance Article 13, in terms of individual rights, and this notwithstanding their classical formulation.[68] This evolution, coupled with the fact that almost all States Parties

---

[66] Applications Nos. 55480/00 and 59330/00, ECtHR, judgment of 27 July 2004, paras. 31 and 47.

[67] See O. De Schutter, 'L'interdépendance des droits et l'interaction des systèmes de protection: les scénarios du système européen de protection des droits fondamentaux', in *Les mécanismes de contrôle de l'application de la Charte sociale européenne* (L'Europe des libertés, Special issue 2000), at 19. Most recently see Akandji-Kombé, *supra* n. 10.

[68] Art. 13, on the right to social and medical assistance, reads: 'With a view to ensuring the effective exercise of the right to social and medical assistance, the Parties undertake: 1. to ensure that

have implemented the Charter in their legal orders and some, like Finland, go so far as to award it direct applicability, should improve the use of the Charter provisions before national courts.[69]

There are many Charter provisions whose interpretation has resulted in the affirmation of subjective rights. Since supervisory cycle 1, the ECSR has affirmed that social and medical assistance, as provided by Article 13, shall be granted 'as of right'.[70] In the case law that followed, the ECSR affirmed that 'the right to social and medical assistance means that anyone who satisfies the conditions has an individual right to receive this assistance, the granting of which may not be left solely to the authorities' discretion. Furthermore, provision must be made for the right to appeal to an independent body.'[71] The following is a non-exhaustive list of provisions which, according to the ECSR interpretation, give rise to individual rights: Article 1(2) sets out the right not to be discriminated against or to be subjected to forced labour; Article 2 enshrines the right to just conditions of work; Article 4(2) to (5) provides for workers' rights to adequate and non-discriminatory remuneration and to reasonable notice of termination of employment; Articles 5, 6(3), and 6(4) provide for the individual right to join or not to join a trade union and the right to collective action; Article 7 gives certain rights to children and young people in relation to employment; Article 17 guarantees the right to free primary education; Article 19(6) and (8) provides for the right of migrant workers to family reunion and housing; Article 20 sets out the right to non-discrimination on the ground of sex as regards employment; Articles 24 and 25 concern the rights of workers to protection on termination of employment or the insolvency of the employer; Article 28 sets the right of workers' representatives to protection in the undertaking; Article 31(1) provides for the right to adequate housing. Finally, many of these rights are complemented by the right to non-discrimination for nationals of other parties to the Charter who are lawfully resident or regularly working on the territory of another party.

Moreover, while evolution at international level can indeed exert pressure for similar progress in the national field, the increasing justiciability of social rights at national level would easily allow for international norms to be invoked in the context of national judicial proceedings. Indeed, the time has come for an increase in the juridification of social rights.[72] In the Nordic countries, various benefits and services in the fields of social security, health, and education are secured as individual rights. In Finland, the right to municipal day-care for small children, the right to social assistance, and the right to housing have been recognized by

any person who is without adequate resources and who is unable to secure such resources either by his own efforts or from other sources, in particular by benefits under a social security scheme, be granted adequate assistance, and, in case of sickness, the care necessitated by his condition . . .'.

[69] See Scheinin, in Eide, Krause, and Rosas (eds), *supra* n. 5, at 61.
[70] *Conclusions I*, at 64.   [71] See *Conclusions XVI-1* and *XVII-1* on Art. 13.
[72] For an overview see Iliopoulos-Strangas, *supra* n. 6, at 801.

Acts of Parliament[73] as subjective rights. In Italy, the following social rights have been construed by the Constitutional Court as subjective rights: the right freely to enter employment and the right not to be arbitrarily dismissed, the right to leave, the right to adequate remuneration, the right to compulsory education,[74] the right to social assistance and social security, and the right to physical and mental health, and, more generally, the right to health.[75] Finally, many countries recognize as individual rights the so-called social liberties, that is, the rights to choose a profession, to organize, to collective action, etc. (Germany, Austria, Greece, Spain, Portugal), and the right to non-discrimination. The bulk of the case law of the ECSR can then be used as a sort of common standard against which to measure the scope of the right guaranteed at national level. Eventually, this can bring to an end the situation where the social right is not correctly guaranteed at national level and, therefore, reveal a violation of the obligations imposed by the Charter on the States Parties.

The increasing individualization of social rights in the interpretative work of the ECSR can be further legitimated by the corresponding improvement in the mechanism of control provided by the Charter, the 1995 Protocol providing for a system of Collective Complaints. Indeed, the collective complaints procedure may prove fundamental to this process, as it allows the ECSR to evolve a more precise and systematic case law starting from specific cases of violation of the social rights brought to its attention. Springing out of a quasi-judicial process, the decision of the ECSR can define in legal terms the meaning and scope of an individual social right protected by the Charter. This case law not only can be easily invoked before national courts, but it can also strengthen the notion of justiciability of social rights, demonstrating that international bodies can lay down common core definitions. Moreover, this role is even more justified by the fact that the collective complaint procedure is, today, the only existing European procedure allowing the collective interests of individuals to be represented, which is particularly relevant in the context of social rights.

B. *The Normative Justiciability of Social Rights*

Apart from the direct applicability of its provisions, there are two other mechanisms by which an international instrument such as the European Social Charter can be made relevant in the domestic legal order in order to protect the social rights of individuals: normative justiciability and the *téchnique de l'interprétation conforme*.

---

[73] The Norwegian Supreme Court (*Høyesterett*) in the *Fusa* case, 25 September 1990, recognized a legal right to social assistance for a person with a disability and deemed the court able to determine the content of the right in the case in point and to order the municipality to pay compensation for the services which had been refused; see Scheinin, in Eide, Krause and Rosas (eds), *supra* n. 5, at 61.

[74] Decision No. 7/1967 [1967], Giurisprudenza costituzionale 56.

[75] Decisions Nos. 559/1987, 455/1990, and 304/1994.

1. The Notion of Normative Justiciability and its Application The first mechanism is normative justiciability. This is defined as the mechanism which 'permet de défendre devant des instances constitutionnelles ou juridictionnelles l'existence de la mise en œuvre d'un droit'.[76] The purpose of normative justiciability is to ensure that Charter provisions setting objectives can also be invoked in the courts in order to assess whether national implementing measures (law, regulations, administrative measures implementing the legal sources, etc.) properly ensure the attainment of these objectives. States Parties to the Charter are obliged to respect the rights provided in it and to ensure their effectiveness by adopting measures to facilitate their exercise by individuals. Thus, normative justiciability means that the provisions of the Charter can be invoked before domestic courts for the purpose of giving them the task of ensuring that national implementation first has occurred and, secondly, has done so in a form which accords with the provisions of the treaty as interpreted by the ECSR, thereby realizing the objectives contained in them and not contravening them.

The first step takes place when the Charter is invoked before a national court because a state has failed to fulfil an obligation deriving from it, for instance to guarantee the right to social and medical assistance provided therein. It could be counter-argued that it is not the role of the judge to interfere with the procedure states consider appropriate for putting social rights into practice (timing and budgetary issues may be relevant in such a context). But the literature has argued in abundance that there is space for the court to ensure the effectiveness of the right without exceeding national competences.[77] However, as was rightly pointed out,[78] the weakness of this mechanism consists in the fact that, at national level, few legal systems permit the bringing of an action before the Constitutional Court in respect of the inaction (*carence*) of the state.[79]

The second step aims at assessing that the way in which the state implements the social right accords with the objectives set by a certain provision of the Charter as interpreted by the ECSR. The consequence of such review ought to be the annulment or amendment of the national enactment that does not accord with the Charter.[80] In this sense normative justiciability also plays the role of a standstill clause to the extent that it prevents national norms from reducing the protection already afforded through international instruments. Collective Complaint

---

[76] Braibant, *supra* n. 3, at 46.

[77] See De Schutter as regards the competence and the legitimacy of the court to play this role, *supra* n. 67, at 21. [78] See Akandji-Kombé, *supra* n. 10.

[79] See, e.g., the Portuguese Constitution (Art. 238), never used so far as the Charter was concerned, where two controls of constitutionality are provided: '*inconstitutionnalité par omission*' or '*par action*' according to whether the legislator had not acted at all or had not done enough to ensure the minimum level of realization of the right: see de Andrade, 'Portugal', in Iliopoulos-Strangas, *supra* n. 6, at 679.

[80] According to Braibant, '*les juges pourront écarter ou annuler des normes qui porteraient atteinte à leur mise en œuvre*', *supra* n. 3, at 46.

No. 13/2002, *Autism-Europe v. France*, illustrates how normative justiciability functions. In its decision, the ECSR provides an interpretation of Article 15, which in the main sets the objectives to be achieved as regards people with disabilities, clarifying that states are obliged to achieve these objectives and indicating the criteria by which to measure this achievement:

When the incorporation of one of the rights in question is exceptionally complex and particularly expensive to achieve, a state party must take measures that allow it to achieve the objectives of the Charter within a reasonable time, with measurable progress and to an extent consistent with the maximum use of available resources.[81]

This interpretation could easily be invoked before and used by a national court in order to achieve the normative justiciability of the objectives laid down in Article 15 ESC, that is the review of the national measures ensuring the application of Article 15 in the domestic legal order in order to assess the extent of the achievement of these objectives or whether these same measures conflict with the objectives.

2. The 'Technique de l'Interprétation Conforme' The second mechanism is the use of the Charter and its case law as a source of law when interpreting existing national law (*technique de l'interprétation conforme*). This technique does not raise particular problems since it is currently used within the national legal order with respect to constitutional norms. It is worth considering that a few national courts, such as those of Belgium, Sweden, Italy, and Germany, already use the Charter in this way.

Belgian courts construed their decisions interpreting the national law with reference to its conformity to the Charter, eventually annulling contrary national legislation.[82] As regards Article 13, even the Swedish Supreme Administrative Court, although the Charter is not accorded the status of law in that domestic legal system, referred to this instrument in order to reverse a lower court decision denying social assistance benefits to two asylum-seekers.[83] In its 2001 decision on the requirement to organize into a trade union (the closed shop clause) the Norwegian Supreme Court referred to Article 5 ESC, which has been interpreted by the ECSR as prohibiting closed shop clauses and including the negative right to organize, in order to find the clause of a collective agreement in question null and void because it breached national law as well as Article 5.[84]

The Italian Constitutional Court and regional courts often used the Charter provisions in interpreting national legislation. The Constitutional Court referred

---

[81] ECSR, *Autism-Europe v. France*, Collective Complaint No. 13/2002, para. 53, in www.coe.int/T/E/Human_Rights/Esc/.

[82] *Cour d'Arbitrage*, Decision of 15 May 1996 with respect to Art. 1.

[83] Case No. 4642/1989: 'It is to be added that Sweden has acceded to the European Social Charter according to which, i.e., a principle of equal treatment is valid in the field of social assistance.'

[84] *A. v. Norwegian People's Aid*, Supreme Court judgment of 9 November 2001; the national law at issue was s. 55A(1) and (3) of the 1977 Worker Protection and Working Environment Act.

to Article 8 of the Charter in order to review the constitutionality of Act No. 1204/1971, Article 1(3) of which denies maternity leave to domestic employees.[85] Likewise, it referred to Articles 15 and 24 to strengthen its interpretation of national legislation dealing with, respectively, a pension regime for people with disabilities[86] and dismissal.[87] Several Regional Administrative Courts referred to Articles 3, 4, 11, and 12 of the European Social Charter when interpreting Act No. 327/2000 and collective agreements as prohibiting derogations from the minimum salary.[88] Like the Italian Constitutional Court, the Romanian Constitutional Court, too, has often referred to the ESC (Articles 1, 21, 29, and E) when interpreting and reviewing the constitutionality of national legislation.[89]

The German Federal Labour Court in a 1984 decision affirmed that national courts were bound by the obligations set by the Charter whenever they had to fill in gaps in the law on industrial disputes.[90] Like the legislator, courts were deemed to respect Article 31 (G in the revised Charter) of the Charter when restricting the right to strike. The Charter therefore has become a guideline instrument whenever national legislation is lacking. Following this guideline, the Gelsenkirchen Labour Court[91] reaffirmed that the Charter, as an obligation of international law, must be taken into account when interpreting national rules. In that case, the question was whether the prohibition on calling a non-union strike accorded with the Charter. Finally, in this perspective, in 2002 the Federal Labour Court[92] indicated that a review of the principle that, in Germany, a strike is admissible only for the enforcement of the objectives covered by a collective agreement might take place. The Federal Administrative Court also indicated that, despite their international nature, the obligations established by the ESC have to be taken into account when discretionary administrative powers are exercised at internal level.[93]

IV. CONCLUSION

The purpose of this chapter has been to remove the preconceived idea that the European Social Charter is a soft instrument, lacking normative and judicial impact. This chapter has tried to show that it has had, and is having, an impact on the protection of fundamental rights at European level. Certainly, many national organs deputed to apply the Charter in the domestic legal order, like the House

---

[85] Judgment No. 86/1994, in www.cortecostituzionale.it.

[86] Judgment No. 163/1983, in www.cortecostituzionale.it.

[87] Judgment No. 46 of 3 February 2000, in www.cortecostituzionale.it.

[88] Regional Administrative Court (TAR) Emilia Romagna, judgment No. 272/2002, para. 3.2; TAR Sardinia, judgments Nos. 659 and 660/2003; TAR Sicily, judgment No. 79/2004, para. 5.3, in www.giustizia-amministrative.it.

[89] Decisions Nos. 24/2003, 25/2003, 108/2003, and 351/2003.

[90] BAGE 46, 350; see also Hohnerlein, 'Germany', in Jaspers and Betten (eds), *supra* n. 10, at 125.   [91] Judgment of 13 March 1998.

[92] Judgment of 10 December 2002, 1 AZR 96/02, para. 43.   [93] BWerfGE 66, 268.

of Lords[94] and others, have declined to do so even when the argument was raised before them. But others seized the opportunity. If indeed the impact of the Charter in the domestic legal order has, since the beginning of its existence, been weakened by many factors (the widespread doctrinal presumptions regarding the nature of social rights, the rather political nature of the original supervisory mechanism, etc.), it can safely be argued that many of these factors are no longer as relevant as they were in the past. This should allow the Charter to gain in authority at international and national level. What strikes one most is that, probably, much of the potential of the Charter has been lost by reason of its not being as well known in the domestic legal order as it might be. And this notwithstanding its long existence (fifty years!).

---

[94] House of Lords, judgment in the case *Associated Newspapers Ltd. v. Wilson*, and *Associated British Ports v. Palmers and others* [1995] 2 LR: App. cas. 454.

6

The Material Impact of the Jurisprudence of the European Committee of Social Rights

JEAN-FRANÇOIS AKANDJI-KOMBÉ

I. INTRODUCTION

The basic role of the European Committee of Social Rights (ECSR) is to assess the conformity of national legislation and practices with the requirements of the European Social Charter (ESC). This role, often referred to as 'jurisprudential', is, materially speaking, a means of supplying a legal interpretation of each of the clauses of the Charter; that is, of clarifying its content and its scope. From this, it follows that the impact of the Committee is essentially—but not exclusively—juridical in nature.

This impact can be assessed from different standpoints, the most obvious being that of the Social Charter system itself. This system has, in the course of the last decade, been profoundly revised with the aim of reinforcing the rights protected on one hand, and a control mechanism whose efficacy was, at best, doubtful, on the other. We could, therefore, legitimately content ourselves with an examination of the extent to which the activity of the ECSR contributes to the realization of these objectives.

However, interesting though such an approach may appear, it seems neither the most useful nor the most appropriate—if only because it neglects the external influence of the instruments that make up the Charter system. It is a fact that this is not a closed system, but one existing in interrelation with others; most notably with the European Convention on Human Rights (ECHR), an instrument to which the Charter is, in principle, the counterpart. Such a relation also exists, objectively at least, between the Charter and various other international conventions due to the fact that they protect, in part, the same rights. This material overlap confers on the interpretations of the Committee a scope that necessarily extends beyond the framework of a single Council of Europe instrument. The assessments of this body can be viewed as being of general interest within the field of social rights, and of human rights more broadly. It is at this level that the observations that follow are located.

One question, therefore, must be asked: is the impact of the ECSR, internally speaking, limited to one particular procedural framework? This is an important question within the charter system, given the differentiation in control procedures and, following from this, in the working methods of the Committee. The attention of the jurist risks being completely monopolized by what happens in terms of collective complaints, because here the juridical process is neater. Here we find disputes that are clearly defined and formulated in terms of law, exchanges of legal argumentation between the parties and, at the end, a decision that resolves the issues involved and articulates the law. Moreover, the Committee now habitually formulates its decisions with a rigour that we normally consider reserved to courts of law: they are, generally speaking, concise (more concise, in any event, than the 'conclusions' adopted in the context of reports), well structured, and solidly argued in law. There are thus many factors that could combine to create an *a priori* bias in favour of the complaints procedure. If we add to these the fact that certain decisions taken within this context have allowed the Committee to develop its jurisprudence, notably in terms of emphasizing what the protected rights require of states, there may be a strong temptation to limit the inquiry to that which is produced here. This, however, would be an error because, although they may lack the above attractions, the conclusions adopted in the context of the periodic supervision of reports also contain expositions of the law that are both interesting and important for the purposes of this chapter. Moreover, often the decisions rendered within the context of collective complaints are based upon the jurisprudence formed during the examination of national reports; indeed, the interpretative innovations so common to the decisions have their roots in the evaluations of the Committee in the latter context.

In light of the decisions of other treaty organs charged with the task of protecting human rights, and also of the intense doctrinal debate well known to this sphere, the jurisprudence of the ECSR—all of it—can be read as a plea in favour of the indivisibility of human rights; or, better than a plea, as an illustration of that indivisibility at work. An important part of this development has been the conception that has emerged from the work of the Committee of social rights in general: they are treated as fully-fledged human rights (see Section II. below). Another contributing factor is the fact that the Committee contributes, through its jurisprudence, to the enrichment of the content not only of those rights on the border between civil rights and social rights, but also of certain rights that belong without doubt to the first category.

II. 'SOCIAL RIGHTS EQUAL HUMAN RIGHTS': THE PROMOTION OF SOCIAL RIGHTS AS HUMAN RIGHTS

The indivisibility of human rights has become a *leitmotiv* of all discourse on the subject, political or doctrinal, at both the regional and the international levels.

The following example is commonplace: 'all human rights are universal, indivisible, interdependent and interrelated, be they civil, political, economic, social or cultural'.[1] At the same time, however, it is clear that this 'truth' is far from having been successfully translated into practice. It is thus not the least of the ECSR's merits that it has demonstrated, from the basis of the Social Charter, that all human rights require the same protection. And if it has not been possible to bring this demonstration to its conclusion, it is due to the fact that there are a number of obstacles within the Social Charter itself that are still, for the moment, proving difficult to overcome.

A. The Principle

It was in the context of two cases brought before it under the collective complaints procedure that the ECSR laid down the principle in the clearest manner. The first case—and this is doubtless no coincidence—was also the first ever to be brought before the Committee under this new procedure. The International Commission of Jurists alleged that Portugal, on the basis of the situation actually prevailing in that country, had violated Article 7(1) of the European Social Charter, which places strict limitations on the employment of children under fifteen years of age. In this case, the respondent state did not contest the fact that a significant proportion of children under fifteen were employed in businesses, particularly family businesses, but emphasized the fact that complementary legislative measures had been adopted with a view to reinforcing the ban on children working, as well as administrative measures to increase supervision by means of workplace inspections and action programmes. The defending state thus argued that the article in question imposed only a weak obligation that could be satisfied merely by the adoption of internal measures. The ECSR nevertheless concluded that there had been a violation of the Charter. What is most striking is the justification for the reasoning that led to this result. For the Committee, the Charter is 'a human rights protection instrument' whose 'aim and purpose... is to protect rights not merely theoretically, but also in fact'.[2] The same justification was used by the Committee in another case in which it was alleged that France was discriminating against freelance interpreter guides.[3] Regular followers of European case law would have recognized here the *obiter dictum* of the European Court of Human

---

[1] Declaration of 10 December 1998 adopted by the Committee of Ministers of the Council of Europe on the occasion of the 50th anniversary of the Universal Declaration of Human Rights.

[2] ECSR, *International Commission of Jurists v. Portugal*, Complaint No. 1/1998, 10 September 1999. For a commentary, see Akandji-Kombé, 'L'application de la Charte sociale européenne: la mise en œuvre de la procédure de réclamations collectives', *Droit social* (2000) 888.

[3] ECSR, *Syndicat national des professions du tourisme v. France*, Complaint No. 6/1999, 10 October 2000, para. 26. For a commentary on this decision, see Akandji-Kombé, 'La France face au Comité européen des droits sociaux', *Droit social* (2001) 977f. See also the author's chronicle, *RTDH* (2001) 1035f.

Rights (ECtHR) in the case *Airey v. Ireland*, in which the Court acknowledged clearly for the first time that there was no strict boundary between civil rights on the one hand and social rights on the other.

In the two cases, the principle laid down expresses the fundamental unity of all human rights. However—and this must be emphasized—it leads to different requirements depending on the instrument under consideration. In effect, while the position adopted by the Court tends to introduce the problem of social rights to the Convention system through the theory of positive obligations or the theory of 'inherence' (that certain social rights are inherent elements of civil and political rights), that of the Committee aims to apply to social rights a process that until then had seemed reserved to civil and political rights. In the context of the Social Charter, the affirmation of this principle led, first and foremost, to the introduction of a system of *concrete supervision* of the enjoyment of protected rights. The Committee emphasized very early on, in their conclusions adopted during the third cycle of supervision of national reports, that it was necessary to 'look for the reality behind the appearances', and in this sense, to ensure in particular that legislation that appears satisfactory on paper is applied effectively.[4] This position has remained constant. In the two cases cited above, the Committee again reaffirmed that conformity with a requirement of the Charter 'cannot be ensured solely by the operation of legislation if this is not effectively applied' in practice.[5]

Moreover, the requirement that the rights protected by the Charter must be effective in practice has led the Committee to read a role for judges into the clauses of that instrument that was not expressly included. This introduction of the judge to the national strategy for guaranteeing social rights has been confirmed in a striking manner in a number of cases,[6] in particular one recent one involving Sweden, concerning the freedom to organize.[7] The complainants, the Confederation of Swedish Enterprise, alleged that the situation in their country was not in conformity with Article 5 of the Charter, due, first, to the existence of closed shop clauses in a number of collective agreements, and, secondly, to the fact that all salaries of one section of the workforce were subject to deductions paid to a particular union as wage monitoring fees. In the first case, in which the violation of the Charter was not contested but in which the tradition of the autonomy of social partners prevented the Swedish government, or even the Parliament, from intervening, the Committee stressed that:

The commitment made by the Parties, under which domestic legislation or other means of implementation . . . shall not infringe on employers' and workers' freedom to establish

---

[4] *Conclusions III*, General introduction, at xiv et seq.

[5] ECSR, *International Commission of Jurists v. Portugal*, Complaint No. 1/1998, 10 September 1999, para. 32. In this regard, see also the decision of 10 October 2000, *supra* n. 3.

[6] See in particular the decision in *Syndicat national des professions du tourisme v. France*, *supra* n. 3, in which the Committee recalled that the requirement of effectiveness implied judicial intervention.

[7] ECSR, *Confederation of Swedish Enterprise v. Sweden*, Complaint No. 12/2002, 22 May 2003. See the author's observations in *RTDH* (2004) 225.

organisations, implies that, in the event of contractual provisions likely to lead to such an outcome, and whatever the implementation procedures for these provisions, the relevant national authority, whether legislative, regulatory or judicial, is to intervene, either to bring about their repeal or to rule out their implementation.[8]

The Committee went even further in pronouncing on the second claim. It considered that, after it had laid down the basic principles relevant to the matter in hand, 'it is for the national courts to decide' on the legality of the contested deductions in the light of these principles, 'or, as the case may be, for the legislator to enable the courts to draw the consequences as regards the conformity with the Charter and the legality of the provisions at issue'.[9]

There is nothing exceptional about the adoption of such positions within the Charter system. They are based upon well-established case law, drawing on Articles 6 and 13 of the ECHR, which oblige states to put in place effective and efficacious legal mechanisms for the protection of the rights set out in this instrument, and upon which the Committee has based its definition of the criteria for judging the effectiveness and efficacy of national remedies.[10] There is no space to go into this in detail here; it is enough to note that the role of judges in this regard has not stopped expanding. Limited at first to a few particular rights set out in certain clauses of the Turin [Social] Charter—Article 1(2) (the right to non-discrimination in employment-related matters); Article 4(3) (the right to equal pay for equal work); Article 13(1) (the right to social and medical assistance); and Article 19(8) (the right of foreigners against expulsion)—it is today almost certain that it applies to all substantial rights, notwithstanding the fact that only Article 24 of the Revised Social Charter (the right to protection in cases of termination of employment) makes explicit reference to it.[11] This follows from the recent finding of the ECSR that Article 1 of the additional protocol of 1988 (Article 20 of the revised Social Charter) necessarily implies the recognition of such a right,[12] and is confirmed by the form for submission of reports on the application of the revised Charter. Moreover, this form states clearly that this applies equally to the rights set out in Articles 21 to 31; in effect, states are being systematically invited to describe the remedies open to those who believe themselves to be victims of violations of these rights.

This evolution is remarkable if we take into account standard doctrinal conceptions of social rights. In fact, we have moved far from the image of these rights as mere legislative objectives set for states, or as simple petitions filled with political principles that do not imply any legal obligations upon states and are not susceptible to judicial protection. It remains true, however, that this dynamic

---

[8] Decision of 22 May 2003, *supra* n. 7, para. 28.   [9] Ibid., para. 42.

[10] On this point, we can refer the reader to the book the author is currently working on, on the European Social Charter.

[11] Also noteworthy in this regard is Art. 19(7), which sets down the principle of non-discrimination between national and migrant workers in matters relating to legal proceedings.

[12] See e.g. *Conclusions XIII-5*, at 27.

process of *rapprochement* between the legal regime of social rights and that of civil rights is still subject to certain important limits.

B. The Limits

The limits of the process that has just been described are imposed by different factors that are fundamentally linked to the Charter itself. First of all, of course, is the fact that the manner in which the clauses of this instrument are formulated makes it, on occasion, impossible to deduce any immediately applicable obligations.[13] Most importantly, however, the Charter contains a number of clauses that are particularly alien to the logic of human rights, a logic at once expressive of the individualization of protection (*each* person has the right to protection) and of the universality of the same (*all* people have the right to protection).

The first of such clauses that we encounter is that in Article 33 of the Turin Charter, taken up with only minor adjustments in Article I of the revised European Social Charter ((Rev)ESC). In the terms of the latter article, that has a broader scope than that of Article 33 of the ESC, 'Compliance with the undertakings deriving from the provisions of paragraphs 1, 2, 3, 4, 5 and 7 of Article 2, paragraphs 4, 6 and 7 of Article 7, paragraphs 1, 2, 3 and 5 of Article 10 and Articles 21 and 22 of Part II of this Charter shall be regarded as effective if the provisions are applied... to the *great majority of the workers concerned*.'[14] Traditionally, according to the jurisprudence of the Committee, this clause was called into play as soon as at least 80 per cent of workers could be considered as beneficiaries of the satisfactory application of one of the provisions cited in the article. Or, to put it another way, if it transpired that one of the provisions cited was not enjoyed by a group making up 5, 10, or even 20 per cent of workers, the Committee was obliged to find that the above clause has been satisfactorily applied. This rule was viewed as worrying even within the European Committee of Social Rights. Pierre Laroque, who was its first President, set out the position of this body in the following terms:

Il existe dans de nombreux Etats des groupes marginaux qui, à certains égards, ne sont protégés par aucune règle législative, conventionnelle ou autre. Le Comité... estime que, compte tenu de l'évolution des idées et des valeurs éthiques, il semble aujourd'hui injustifié

---

[13] This is the case, for example, in a number of provisions of the Charter commonly referred to as 'dynamic', in that they include a commitment on behalf of the Contracting Parties to make legislative progress and to improve the situation of their respective populations: for example, to achieve and maintain the highest and most stable level of employment possible, with a view to the attainment of full employment (Art. 1(1)); to progressively reduce the working week (Art. 2(1)); to raise progressively the system of social security to a higher level (Art. 12(3)); to liberalize regulations governing the employment of foreign workers (Art. 18(3)).

[14] Emphasis added. Compared with the old Art. 33 of the ESC, the effect of this new clause is extended to para. (7) of Art. 2, to para. (5) of Art. 10 and to Arts. 21 and 22 of Part II. Para. (4) of Art. 10 drops out of the list of provisions affected.

d'exclure d'une protection sociale normale certaines catégories de la population, si faibles soient-elles en nombre, et il exprime le regret que la Charte consacre ... la possibilité d'une telle exclusion.[15]

More than three decades later, the new President of this body would express the same criticisms.[16]

The second clause, which appears in the Appendix to the Charter and to the Revised Charter, defines the scope of these instruments in terms of the persons protected, from which it excludes foreigners. It states that the provisions of the text in question 'include foreigners only in so far as they are nationals of other Parties lawfully resident or working regularly within the territory of the Party concerned'.[17] The Charter is thus the only human rights instrument whose provisions are not applicable to all persons under the jurisdiction of a contracting state.

The ECSR has gone to considerable lengths in attempting to move beyond these limits, without, however, ever fully succeeding. The most remarkable developments in the case law without doubt have been in terms of the above-mentioned clause in Article I of the (Rev)ESC (Article 33 of the ESC), whose scope has been markedly restricted. The case that began these developments— known as the '35 hours' case—also arose within the context of the complaints procedure.[18] The claimant organization, the *Confédération française de l'encadrement* (CFE-CGC), alleged that the 'Aubry II' Act adopted by the French Parliament, on the reduction of working hours, ignored the right of managerial staff to benefit from a working time of reasonable length, in conformity with Article 2(1) of the (Rev)ESC. The French Government, however, without ever contesting these allegations, argued that, as managerial staff represented a proportion not exceeding 5 per cent of the total wage-earning population, there could not in any event be a violation of the provision in question. The Committee dismissed this argument, holding that 'in view of the reference made in its very wording to the workers concerned, the application of Article I of the revised Social Charter cannot give

---

[15] P. Laroque, 'La Charte sociale européenne', *Droit social* (1979) 107. ('In numerous states there exist marginalized groups who, in certain respects, are not protected by any law, treaty-based or otherwise. The Committee ... considers that, taking into account the evolution of ethical ideas and values, it seems unjustified today to exclude certain categories of the population from normal social protection, however small they may be in number; and it expresses regret that the Charter establishes ... the possibility of such an exclusion.')

[16] J.-M. Belorgey, 'De quelques problèmes liés à la prohibition et à l'élimination des discriminations, essai de clarification des concepts et eléments de droit comparé', *Droit social* (2002) 683, at 686. The author condemns the fact that 'an entire social category [can] be removed from the protection of the law for the sole reason that they are in a minority, trapped in a position more or less oppressed or servile'.

[17] See e.g. Appendix to the (Rev)ESC, para. 1. It is noteworthy that, by exception to this rule, refugees and stateless persons are eligible for protection in accordance with the Charter; see the same Appendix.

[18] ECSR, *Confédération Française de l'Encadrement-CGC v. France*, Complaint No. 9/2000, 11 December 2001.

rise to a situation in which a large number of persons forming a specific category are deliberately excluded from the scope of a legal provision'.[19] The exclusionary effect of the clause was thus limited in this manner: it becomes inapplicable if the purported victims of the alleged violation constitute a distinctive category, treated as such by the state authorities, whatever the number of affected persons might be. This being so, it must nonetheless be noted that the threat from Article I does not appear completely neutralized. At the most, the Committee has challenged the automatic application of a threshold rule, and set up the possibility of a genuine case-by-case evaluation. Despite this, however, there has undoubtedly been progress; considerable progress even, considering the prior state of the law.

Recently, the Committee has also decided to re-examine its interpretation of the Appendix that defines the 'scope of the Charter in terms of persons protected'. The purpose of this was to redefine the position of foreigners, taking into account all of the provisions of the Appendix, in particular the second sentence of its first paragraph, from the perspective of the universalization of protection. In order to understand this debate properly, it is helpful to recall the structure of the provisions in question. The first sentence of the paragraph cited above provides that 'the persons covered by Articles 1 to 17 and 20 to 31 include foreigners only in so far as they are nationals of other Parties . . .'. The second sentence, however, adds that 'This interpretation would not prejudice the extension of similar facilities to other persons by any of the Parties.' Certainly, this last sentence could constitute the basis for a general protection of foreigners under the Charter. The central idea is that each time a state extends one of the rights protected by the Charter to foreigners who are not nationals of a Contracting Party, either unilaterally through its domestic law, or in cooperation with other states through international commitments, it extends at the same time the sphere of protection of the Social Charter, and enlarges the domain under the control of the Charter organs. Put otherwise, the violation of a right accorded to foreigners under domestic law or stemming from an international treaty that implicates a right otherwise guaranteed to Contracting Party nationals by the Charter would constitute a violation of the Charter itself, and would in turn authorize the involvement of the ECSR either through the supervision of reports or the collective complaints procedure. When applied, for example, to the ECHR, this would mean that, to the extent that all States Parties to the Charter are also parties to this instrument, we should consider those rights protected by the Charter that are also recognized in the Convention as guaranteed *by the Charter* to all persons under the jurisdiction of the state in question. This would be the case in particular for the right not to be subject to forced labour (Article 1(2) ESC and (Rev)ESC and Article 4 ECHR) and the right to organize (Article 5 ESC and (Rev)ESC and Article 11 ECHR). The same reasoning could be applied to provisions of the Charter that protect, in one way or another, the right to family life (Articles 16, 17, and 19(6) ESC and

---

[19] Ibid., para. 40.

(Rev)ESC),[20] or that guarantee or imply the recognition of a right to appeal (which is the case for most of the provisions of the Charter),[21] or that set out a right to social security benefits (Articles 12 and 13 ESC and (Rev)ESC).[22] Admittedly, such an interpretation of the Charter would be revolutionary in terms of the effects that it could produce. Between national legislation and international treaties, the whole Charter would be of general scope in terms of its beneficiaries, although there would, nevertheless, be variations due to the web of other obligations linking each State Party.[23] It is, however, very far from certain that such a reading of the text of the Appendix would be acceptable in law. In any event, there are two major objections that may be raised against it.

First of all, there is nothing that allows us to maintain that the Appendix may constitute the basis for an expansion of the obligations between states, let alone that it attributes competence for the control of these new obligations to the ECSR. In effect, by providing that 'this interpretation would not prejudice the extension of similar facilities to other persons by any of the Parties', the Appendix is content to grant states the freedom to decide for themselves. It doesn't establish this freedom, it merely recognizes it. In effect, even in the absence of such a clause, there would be nothing to forbid states from extending the protection of the rights recognized by the Charter to foreigners. In doing so, they would certainly be bound in law, but not by the Charter itself. In this regard, there exists a certain analogy between this situation and that surrounding Article 32 of the Turin Charter (Article H (Rev)ESC). In providing that 'The provisions of this Charter shall not prejudice the provisions of domestic law or of any bilateral or multilateral treaties, conventions or agreements which are already in force, or may come into force, under which more favourable treatment would be accorded to the persons protected', this article also emphasizes, although this time in terms of rights and duties, that States Parties can go further and pass stricter legislation. Now, it is generally accepted that to do so in no way implies a reinforcement of the material requirements of the Charter. The point in such clauses, common in instruments of social protection or for the protection of social rights, is rather to insert a progressive principle into the relation between the different sources of social law and social rights, without, however, affecting the independent identity of each source or the distinction between them. It may be added that, given that the attachment of external obligations to the Charter in this manner is not conceivable, the ECSR would not claim a reinforced or extended competence from the mere fact that a State Party to the Charter had contracted other obligations of broader scope; as with all organs of this type, its competence is based exclusively on the instrument that established it, and consists solely in 'assess[ing] from a legal

---

[20] With reference to Art. 8 ECHR.   [21] With reference to Arts 6 and 13 ECHR.
[22] With reference to Art. 1 of Protocol 1 to the ECHR, combined with Art. 14 of the Convention.
[23] For a summary of this approach, see R. Brillat, 'La Charte sociale européenne', in C. Grewe and F. Benoît-Rohmer (eds), *Les droits sociaux ou la démolition de quelques poncifs* (2003) 93.

standpoint the compliance of national law and practice *with the obligations arising from the Charter* for the Contracting Parties concerned'.[24]

Another argument, which although purely formal is nonetheless powerful for that, also militates in favour of such a conclusion. It is that to support this 'universality by rebound' thesis in terms of the Charter amounts to claiming that the States Parties can bind themselves without going through the procedures explicitly provided for in the text of that instrument, which state that all modifications must be notified to the Secretary General of the Council of Europe; something that is scarcely conceivable. Neither the principle of the security of legal relations, nor the rule of international law according to which limitations on sovereignty cannot be presumed,[25] would allow any place for such a theory of implied obligation.

The ECSR was, it seems, sensitive to these objections, as is illustrated by the position that it finally adopted. It is true that, in its conclusions on the 17th supervision cycle of national reports,[26] it recalls 'that states Parties to the Charter can extend its scope beyond the minimum laid down in the Appendix' and notes

... that the Parties to the Charter (in its 1961 and revised 1996 versions) have guaranteed to foreigners not covered by the Charter rights identical to or inseparable from those of the Charter by ratifying human rights treaties—in particular the European Convention of Human Rights—or by adopting domestic rules whether constitutional, legislative or otherwise without distinguishing between persons referred to explicitly in the Appendix and other non-nationals. In so doing, the Parties have undertaken these obligations...

The Committee, however, goes on explicitly to recognize that 'these obligations do not in principle fall within the ambit of its supervisory functions'.

However, the Committee manifestly does not intend to deny totally its own competence in these matters as it 'does not exclude that the implementation of certain provisions of the Charter could in certain specific situations require complete equality of treatment between nationals and foreigners, whether or not they are nationals of member states, Party to the Charter'. It is, however, difficult to see how, given the current state of the law, they could provide this protection to nationals of non-Contracting Parties: either their situation is regulated by the same rules as nationals of Contracting Parties, and they are thus the *indirect and passive* beneficiaries of an application of the Charter to this latter category, necessitating a modification in domestic law; or their situation is regulated by specific national rules, in which case the Committee should, logically, consider itself incompetent to pass judgment on their compatibility with the Charter. The situation seems all the more at an impasse given that states have, during the recent revisions of the

---

[24] Article 24(2) of the European Social Charter, as amended by the 1991 Turin Protocol. (Emphasis added.)

[25] *Lac Lanoux* arbitration (*France v. Spain*), 16 November 1957, *RSA*, XII, 281.

[26] *Conclusions XVII-1*, at 8–9.

Charter, clearly confirmed their wish to exclude foreigners from the scope of that instrument.[27]

The realization of the prospect that the Charter system will evolve towards a genuine universality, fully inscribed within the problematic of fundamental human rights, thus depends more now on the will of states, by means of revision of the Charter according to the proper procedures, than it does on the interpretative dynamism of the ECSR. If there remains one area in which this dynamism can continue to express itself, then it is that of the development of substantial rights.

III. THE CONTRIBUTION TO THE DEVELOPMENT OF THE LEGAL REGIME OF RIGHTS

During almost three decades, the ECSR has carried out a considerable amount of work in terms of analysing the rights contained in the Charter, clarifying their content, and specifying, even enforcing, the obligations they give rise to.[28] In this regard, it has contributed to the whole area covered by the instrument it is charged with policing. In terms of the limited context of this chapter, it is not possible to give a detailed account of this; instead, the discussion will be limited to a number of particularly salient elements that are characteristic of the process employed by the Committee.

These elements are related to one of the fundamental characteristics of the international law of human rights: the material overlapping of systems of protection. This overlapping comes before all texts, a result of the same right being proclaimed by a number of instruments at the same time. In principle, to the extent that each of these texts is unique, legally distinct from the others, there could be as many competing definitions of the right in question as there are texts. We know, however, that the reality, driven in particular by claimants and supervisory bodies, is somewhat different. It is more often the case that the meaning of the norms under consideration is elaborated in a multi-authored and multifaceted process. It is in this sense that the idea of a 'contribution' best expresses the role played by any given authority in the process. However, the overlapping systems also result from the actions of supervisory and enforcement

---

[27] Contrary, however, to the wishes of the Parliamentary Assembly of the Council of Europe. On this point, see Opinion No. 185 (1995) on the draft revised European Social Charter, para. 5: 'As regards the scope of the revised Charter in terms of persons protected, the Assembly fully understands that it should be limited as far as foreigners are concerned to those lawfully residing or working regularly within the territory of the party concerned. However, it shares the view that the scope should not in addition be limited only to nationals of the Contracting Parties since the scope of the Charter should be as similar as possible to that of the European Convention on Human Rights. Therefore, the Assembly is in favour of deleting the text between brackets at the beginning of the appendix.'

[28] For an overview of the case law of the Committee, see L. Samuel, *Droits sociaux fondamentaux, jurisprudence de la Charte sociale européenne* (2002).

organs, and in particular from the tendency common to a number of them to interpret rights in a very broad manner, to discover in them new implications, and to establish new rights using the technique of 'protection by rebound'. On both of these grounds, it must be acknowledged that the impact of the ECSR has been far from negligible.

A. *The Impact of the ECSR on the Consolidation of Social Freedoms*

Among the most important of the rights protected at once by the Social Charter, by international instruments both for the protection of social rights *lato sensu* (the International Covenant on Economic, Social and Cultural Rights—ICESCR) and civil rights (the International Covenant on Civil and Political Rights—ICCPR, and the ECHR), are social freedoms such as the freedom to organize and the freedom to work. In this context, there can be no doubt that the approach of the ECSR, due to the particular problematic of the Charter, and taking into account the voluntaristic nature of this organ, has been and continues to be more audacious than that, for example, of the Human Rights Committee of the United Nations (HRC) or of the ECtHR. It is even possible to claim that, in some respects, the jurisprudence of the Committee of the Council of Europe has functioned as a stimulus for the consolidation of the status of these freedoms in the other two contexts.

1. The Freedom to Organize   The most obvious example is that of the freedom to organize, which has until now been at the centre of the conflictual, dynamic relationship between the ECtHR and the ECSR. It is useful at this point to recall that this particular freedom is itself explicitly guaranteed by Article 5 of the Charter,[29] whereas it is only *implied* in the freedom of association proclaimed in Article 11 of the Convention.[30] If both organs are in agreement in considering that the right to organize implies the right to form and join trade unions (a positive right to organize), their positions have contrasted since the beginning on the issue of whether this right could include other elements, such as the right not

[29] Article 5 reads: 'With a view to ensuring or promoting the freedom of workers and employers to form local, national or international organisations for the protection of their economic and social interests and to join those organisations, the Parties undertake that national law shall not be such as to impair, nor shall it be so applied as to impair, this freedom. The extent to which the guarantees provided for in this article shall apply to the police shall be determined by national laws or regulations. The principle governing the application to the members of the armed forces of these guarantees and the extent to which they shall apply to persons in this category shall equally be determined by national laws or regulations.'

[30] Article 11 reads: '1. Everyone has the right to freedom of peaceful assembly and to freedom of association with others, including the right to form and to join trade unions for the protection of his interests. 2. No restrictions shall be placed on the exercise of these rights other than such as are prescribed by law and are necessary in a democratic society in the interests of national security or public safety, for the prevention of disorder or crime, for the protection of health or morals or for the protection of the rights and freedoms of others. This article shall not prevent the imposition of lawful restrictions on the exercise of these rights by members of the armed forces, of the police or of the administration of the state.'

to join a trade union (a negative right to organize) and the right to collective bargaining.

In terms of the negative right to organize, the position affording the greatest degree of protection has without doubt been that of the ECSR, since the first cycle of supervision. According to this body, 'any form of obligatory unionism imposed by law must be considered incompatible with the obligation arising under this article of the Charter'.[31] This position has remained constant since. Moreover, it was confirmed recently, in the decision in *Confederation of Swedish Enterprise v. Sweden*, in more general terms, drawing on previous statements: '. . . the freedom guaranteed by Article 5 of the Charter implies that the exercise of a worker's right to join a trade union is the result of a choice and that, consequently, it is not to be decided by the worker under the influence of constraints that rule out the exercise of this freedom'.[32] This interpretation is above all remarkable because of its voluntaristic character. In fact, the freedom not to join a trade union is not explicitly countenanced by this article. What is more, the Appendix to Article 1(2) of the Charter (the right to earn a living in an occupation freely entered upon) provides that 'this provision shall not be interpreted as prohibiting or authorizing any union security clause or practice', which could be interpreted, as the Committee itself has admitted,[33] as an illustration of the intention of the drafters of the Charter to accord to States Parties, regarding this aspect of the right to organize, a wide margin of appreciation at the very least. It was only by basing its argument on the utility of the freedom under consideration that the Committee was able to decide in the manner that it did.[34] This interpretation is even more remarkable given the status that it confers on the negative freedom to organize: it is now the equal of the positive freedom to organize, endowed with the same value, and requiring a strict supervision of any interference with its exercise.

It took the ECtHR almost forty years and much procrastination in order to achieve the same result, illustrative, according to Judge Morenilla, 'of a certain reluctance to "open the door" to the negative freedom of association'.[35] As is well known,[36] the Court refused up until 1993 to acknowledge explicitly the negative freedom to organize as an element of the right of association, most notably in the cases *Young, James and Webster v. United Kingdom* (1981) and *Sibson v. United Kingdom* (1993).[37] This was changed in the cases of *Sigurdur A. Sigurjónsson v. Iceland* (1993) and

---

[31] *Conclusions I*, at 31. See also, Samuel, *supra* n. 28, at 118f.
[32] Decision of 22 May 2003, *supra* n. 7, at 29.   [33] *Conclusions I*, at 32.
[34] See in particular *Conclusions VIII*, at 77.
[35] Dissenting opinion of Judge Morenilla, in *Gustafsson v. Sweden*, No. 15573/89, ECHR (II-1996), para. 1.
[36] See in particular F. Sudre, *Droit européen des droits de l'homme* (2003), at 437f.; see also F. Sudre et al., *Les grands arrêts de la Cour européenne des droits de l'homme* (1999), at 480f.; J.-M. Larralde, 'Charte sociale et Convention européenne des droits de l'homme', in J.-F. Akandji-Kombé and S. Leclerc (eds), *La Charte sociale européenne* (2001).
[37] *Young, James and Webster v. United Kingdom*, No. 7601/76, ECHR (1981) Series A, No. 55; *Sibson v. United Kingdom*, No. 14327/88, ECHR (1993) Series A, No. 258-A. In these two cases the

Gustafsson v. Sweden (1996),[38] albeit in a cautious manner, as the Court was careful to allow states a wide margin of appreciation, weakening its own supervisory power and the value of the freedom that it finally recognized in the process. It was not until the case of *Chassagnou v. France* (1999) that the negative freedom to organize was raised to the same level as the positive right.[39]

What must be emphasized above all is that this evolution occurred in a dialectical manner, as a result of sometimes bitter exchanges between the ECSR and the ECtHR.[40] After the first two decisions of the Court, the Committee came under considerable pressure to modify its own case law. Nevertheless, it firmly held its ground; to the point at which it was systematically handing down negative conclusions to states, despite their contention that their national situation was in conformity with the requirements of the ECHR as they were interpreted in those early cases. Faced with the systematic resistance of certain states, in particular the United Kingdom and Denmark, and their insistence that the case law of the Committee must be brought into conformity with that of the Court, the former even thought it necessary to recall the fact that 'the European Convention on Human Rights and the Social Charter are two distinct instruments'.[41] This reminder is without doubt testament to the Committee's exasperation rather than its unwillingness to take the other major document of the Council of Europe into consideration. On the contrary, the conclusions adopted demonstrate a particularly attentive monitoring of the case law of other European jurisdictions (including the ECJ),[42] with the Committee noting with pleasure any progress made, in particular when the Court finally undertook to protect the negative right to organize.[43] It is a fact that the jurisprudential reversal occasioned by the *Sigurjónsson* case resulted from the Court taking into consideration the Committee's interpretation of Article 5

Court, performing some of the esoteric legal acrobatics that it sometimes indulges in, examined whether certain constraints imposed upon workers who were unwilling to affiliate themselves with a trade union posed a threat to the substance of the right of association, without, however, being prepared to pronounce on whether this right also gave rise to the freedom not to join a trade union.

[38] *Sigurdur A. Sigurjónsson v. Iceland*, No. 16130/90, ECHR (1993) Series A, No. 264; *Gustafsson v. Sweden*, *supra* n. 35.

[39] *Chassagnou v. France*, No. 25088/94, ECHR (1999). What this case explicitly lays down is the equal value of the negative and positive aspects of the right of association. It should be noted that, in the preceding cases specifically concerning the right to organize, the Court opted to '[leave] open whether the negative right is to be considered on an equal footing with the positive right'. *Gustafsson v. Sweden*, *supra* n. 35, para. 45. See also *Sibson v. United Kingdom*, *supra* n. 37.

[40] It is going a little too far to argue 'qu'à partir du moment où la Cour européenne est amenée à commenter la signification des dispositions de la Charte, il en résulte une érosion de l'autonomie du pouvoir d'appréciation du [CEDS]' ['that from the moment the European Court begins to comment upon the meaning of the provisions in the Charter, there results an erosion in the autonomy of the discretionary power of the Committee'] and that the ECHR would thus become an 'obligatory [point of] reference' for the former. J.-F. Flauss, 'Les interactions normatives entre les instruments européens relatifs à la protection des droits sociaux', in J.-F. Flauss (ed.), *Droits sociaux et droit européen, bilan et prospective de la protection normative* (2002), at 98.   [41] *Conclusions XIV-1*, at 186.

[42] Regarding the case law relevant to the negative right to organize, see e.g. *Conclusions X-1*, at 67–68, *XI-1*, at 83–84 and *XIV-1*, at 185–86.

[43] See in particular *Conclusions XIII-3* (1994), handed down after the *Sigurjónsson* case.

of the Charter.[44] The application—to be hoped for—of the *Chassagnou* case to the issue of trade unions, establishing the status of the negative right to organize relative to its positive counterpart, may well draw on the same source of inspiration.

The emergence of a right to collective bargaining and, to a lesser degree, of a right to strike as components of the right to organize guaranteed by Article 11 of the ECHR has come about, *grosso modo*, under the same conditions as that of the negative right to organize. In fact, if the Committee has constantly upheld the indissociability thesis with regard to these rights, the Court in the first instance refused to transpose this analysis into the framework of the Convention, holding instead that the right to collective bargaining and the right to strike were not 'indispensable to the exercise of the freedom to organize' and that they could thus not be considered as 'necessarily inherent elements' of the right guaranteed by Article 11.[45] This changed only belatedly, in the case of *Wilson and the National Union of Journalists and Others v. the United Kingdom*,[46] in which the Court once again relied upon the conclusions of the ECSR, and in particular on the fact that the particular practice in contention in the case had already been condemned by the latter.[47]

2. The Freedom to Work   On top of its contribution to widening the scope of the right to organize, including, indirectly, within the framework of the ECHR, the ECSR has also participated, through its jurisprudence, in widening the material scope of the freedom to work. However, in contrast with the contribution outlined above, this one is more limited in scope, and has not (yet) had any effect outwith the Charter system itself. Its significance lies for the moment solely in the fact that it

[44] In particular, the Court notes that 'Even in the absence of an express provision, the Committee of Independent Experts set up to supervise the implementation of the Charter considers that a negative right is covered by this instrument and it has in several instances disapproved of closed-shop practices found in certain States Parties, including Iceland. With regard to the latter, the committee took account of, inter alia, the facts of the present case (see *Conclusions XII-1* (1988–89), at 112–13, of the aforementioned committee). Following this, the Governmental Committee of the European Social Charter issued a warning to Iceland (by ten votes to four with two abstentions; see the Governmental Committee's 12th Report to the Committee of Ministers of 22 March 1993, at 113).' *Sigurdur A. Sigurjónsson v. Iceland, supra* n. 38, para. 35.

[45] In this regard, see the cases of *National Union of Belgian Police v. Belgium*, No. 4464/70, ECHR (1975) Series A, No. 19; *Schmidt and Dahlström v. Sweden*, No. 5589/72, ECHR (1976) Series A, No. 21; *Swedish Engine Drivers' Union v. Sweden*, No. 5614/72, ECHR (1976) Series A, No. 20 and *Young, James and Webster v. United Kingdom, supra* n. 37.

[46] No. 30668/96, ECHR judgment of 2 July 2002.

[47] Para. 48 of the judgment. It should be noted that here the Court followed the analysis developed by Judges Martens and Matcher in their dissenting opinion in the *Gustafsson* case (*supra* n. 35), itself based upon the Social Charter. They argued that an 'indissoluble link . . . , in the context of industrial relations, exists between trade-union freedom (as a special form of positive freedom of association), the right to bargain collectively and the right to take collective action in order to protect occupational interests. As is illustrated inter alia by the twin Articles 5 and 6 of the European Social Charter (and the pertinent conclusions concerning these provisions of the Committee of Independent Experts), under international labour law the right to bargain collectively is, if not an objective of, then at any rate a corollary of both the positive freedom of association of trade unions and its necessary derivative, the freedom of the unions to protect their occupational interests by collective action.' (Dissenting opinion, para. 6.)

has inscribed this freedom within a new problematic, making it possible to move beyond certain limits imposed by a number of documents, such as the ECHR and the ICCPR, amongst others.

The traditional jurisprudence of the Committee on this issue is in itself remarkable. In effect, the Committee has managed to read into the provisions of Article 1(2), which sets out the commitment of the parties 'to protect effectively the right of the worker to earn his living in an occupation freely entered upon', a right to non-discrimination in employment-related matters as well as the prohibition on forced labour,[48] the latter also being proscribed by Article 4 of the ECHR and Article 8 of the ICCPR.[49] It is important to note, however, that even if the right not to be forced into an employment not to one's liking is protected in these two latter documents, it is also in these contexts subject to numerous exceptions that explain, in part at least, the rarity of claims based upon a violation of this right, as well as the fact that those that have been brought have been largely unsuccessful. Amongst these exceptions there is one that, in the course of the last decade, has proved particularly problematic, given the nascent tendency to oblige the army to take steps to protect fundamental rights:[50] that concerning military service, or civil service carried out in its place. These problems were primarily linked to conscientious objection to military service, and to the consequences of this—disciplinary measures, the imposition of a longer period of civil service, etc. The logical consequence of this exception was that the persons concerned could not be protected under Article 4 of the ECHR or Article 8 of the ICCPR. Lawyers for the claimants were thus required to use their imagination in order to find other foundations to support their arguments. Before the ECtHR, they resorted mainly to the freedom of thought, conscience, and religion (Article 9). Before the UN Human Rights Committe (HRC), they appealed above all to the principle of non-discrimination (Article 26 of the ICCPR). In terms of the ECHR, all of these cases concluded with a finding of non-violation. The findings of the HRC were more mixed: it held that there had been a violation of the Covenant in two cases

---

[48] *Conclusions I*, at 15.

[49] See also the ILO Convention Concerning Forced Labour (1930) No. 29 and that Concerning the Abolition of Forced Labour (1957) No. 105.

[50] Remarkable examples of this can be found in the jurisprudence of the ECtHR (the application of guarantees of a fair trial to military disciplinary or penal proceedings; for the most important case, see *Engel v. The Netherlands*, ECHR (1976) Series A, No. 22; for a case involving France, see *Serves v. France*, No. 20225/92, ECHR (1997) VI, but also in that of the European Court of Justice (the application of the principle of equality of treatment between men and women): see Case C-273/97, *A.M. Sirdar v. The Army Board and Secretary of State for Defence* [1999] ECR I-7403; Case C-285/98, *T. Kreil v. Bundesrepublik Deutschland* [2000]ECR I-69, in the conclusions handed down by the ILO (strict interpretation of the derogation clause relative to the armed forces contained in Convention No. 87): in particular, the Committee on Freedom of Association, case No. 1279, *Union of Workers in the Manufacturing Establishments of the Armed Forces v. Portugal*, Vol. LXVIII, 1985, Series B, No. 1, Report of the Committee of Freedom of Association, paras. 119–40; case No. 1664, *Ecuadorian Confederation of Free Trade Unions v. Ecuador*, Vol. LXXVI, 1993, Series B, No. 1, Report of the Committee of Freedom of Association, paras. 279–90) and even in the Human Rights Committee of the United Nations (see *infra* n. 51).

in which the excessive length of civil service relative to military service had been contested;[51] but it rejected other arguments, notably where the applicant claimed to be the victim of discrimination in relation to civilian workers.[52] The extreme prudence, discomfort even, shown by the enforcement organs in these cases is manifestly not due only to the fact that the documents in question do not explicitly protect conscientious objection, but also, and perhaps above all, to the fact that the organization of civil service as a result of conscientious objection is excluded from the scope of the prohibition of forced labour.

Hence the significance of the decision of the European Committee of Social Rights of 25 April 2002, in claim No. 8/2000, *Quaker Council for European Affairs v. Greece*, in which it held an excessively long period of civil service (up to thirty-nine months, when military service lasted between three and twenty-one months) to be a violation of Article 1(2) of the Charter. This decision is above all interesting because it limited the force of the exception present in the other instruments; or, more accurately, it moved beyond it. In considering that civil service as a substitute for military service could constitute a restriction on the right to earn a living in an occupation freely entered upon, the Committee removed its status as an exception and made it the object of supervision; a supervision that, although minimal, is effective. Also interesting about this decision is that it enriched the problematic of forced labour. The basic idea that led to the finding against Greece in this case is that, above a certain threshold, an obligation to perform a service such as civil service can constitute an obstacle to the exercise of the right to earn a living in an occupation freely entered upon. Is this an obstacle that constrains one not to work, which would transform it into a new, negative form of 'forced labour'? The Committee denies this, but it may well be suspected that this is purely out of respect for the ECHR, which had been cited in the case. It is submitted that, objectively, the notion of 'forced labour' now covers three hypotheses: first is the classic situation in which an individual is obliged to perform a certain labour against his will; secondly, and equally classically, where the individual is obliged against his will to continue in work that he had voluntarily accepted at the outset; and thirdly, the new category, is when he is restricted by external forces from entering into the employment market. In this there are undoubtedly new prospects for the protection of individuals.

B. The Attraction of Civil Rights as Extensions of Social Rights

If there is one aspect that can give full sense to the affirmation that the Charter is the 'counterpart' of the ECHR, it is the case law of the supervisory organs set up

---

[51] Human Rights Committee, 69th Session, 10–28 July 2000: *Maille v. France* (Communication No. 689/1996, doc. CCPR/C/69/D/689/1996); *Vernier and Nicolas v. France* (Communication Nos. 690/1996 and 691/1996, doc. CCPR/C/69/D/691/1996).

[52] See in particular Human Rights Committee, 37th Session, 23 November 1989, *H.A.E. de J. v. The Netherlands*, Communication No. 297/88, doc. CCPR/C/37/D/297/1988.

by these instruments. Through the bridges that these organs build between the documents, through the development of a global problematic associating civil and political rights on the one hand and social rights on the other, they are effectively contributing to the reversal of what the Secretary General of the Council of Europe referred to as 'the invisibility of the indivisibility' of human rights. The work of the ECtHR is already understood in this manner; it could have been more ambitious still, allowing itself to protect, on the basis of the Convention, most of the rights guaranteed by the Social Charter.[53] It is less often, however, that we understand the efforts of the Committee as working in the opposite direction: that it has come round to protecting certain rights protected by the Convention through an extension of social rights.

The basis for the Committee's approach, as it has stated on a number of different occasions, is a global conception of human rights founded upon the requirements of human dignity. Thus, for example, in interpreting Article 13 of the Charter, which lays down the right to social and medical assistance, the Committee has emphasized since the first supervision cycle that 'the compilers of the Charter were anxious that necessitous persons should not be prevented from exercising their civil and political rights in full or from taking up certain kinds of employment and office. Persons receiving assistance were not to be regarded as second-class citizens, merely because they were unable to support themselves.'[54] In the same way, in the context of Article 15 (the right of physically or mentally disabled persons to vocational training and to professional and social reintegration), it declared that:

The very essence of the Social Charter is to guarantee and respect the dignity of all human beings, irrespective of their physical or mental condition. The idea of human rights implies that the dignity of all individuals must be recognised and respected. In this respect the pro- tection of disabled persons in the field of vocational training and employment is a good example of the vital link between the safeguard of social rights and the guarantee of human dignity.[55]

Or again, to give one last example, when specifying the scope of Article 17 (the right of mothers and children to economic and social protection), the Committee emphasized the impossibility of 'separat[ing] the social and economic protection of mothers and children from the legal provisions governing their situation'. In its view 'objectives of social policy in their regard could not be achieved without taking account of the rights granted to the persons protected and of the duties of those called on to ensure this protection'.[56]

Among the rights brought within the scope of the Social Charter in this manner, the right not to be subject to cruel or degrading treatment (Article 3

---

[53] See in this context the very interesting article by F. Sudre, 'Exercice de jurisprudence-fiction: la protection des droits sociaux par la Cour européenne des droits de l'homme', in Grewe and Benoît-Rohmer, *supra* n. 23, at 145f.   [54] *Conclusions I*, at 64.
[55] *Conclusions XIV-2*, at 63.   [56] *Conclusions IV*, at 103.

ECHR) and the right to respect for private and family life (Article 8 ECHR) appear to be the most significant.

The necessity of respecting the first of these was principally affirmed by the ECSR in the context of the application of the provisions of Article 17, designed to protect children.[57] The principle behind this protection was set down during the 15th supervision cycle in the following terms:

The Committee attaches high importance to the protection of children against all forms of maltreatment or abuse, physical or mental. In accordance with the ECtHR, it emphasizes the fact that children are particularly vulnerable and considers that one of the main objectives of article 17 is to ensure appropriate protection for children in this area... For these reasons, the Committee considers that article 17 requires a legal prohibition on all forms of violence against children, whether in school or in other institutions, in the home or elsewhere. Moreover, it considers that all forms of degrading punishment or treatment inflicted on children must be prohibited by law and that this prohibition must be matched by adequate civil or criminal sanctions.[58]

This interpretation of the principle has not gone unnoticed, as it may appear, in some respects, to be more demanding than that of the ECtHR. The proof of this is that there are currently five complaints pending before the ECSR, all alleging the violation of the Charter on the grounds that the states in question have not effectively prohibited either the corporal punishment of children, or any other form of degrading punishment or treatment of children, and that they have not established any adequate civil or criminal sanctions.[59]

The necessity of protecting the right to private life runs through much of the case law of the ECSR. For example, in the context of Article 13 (the right to social and medical assistance), the Committee, noting that the law in one state attempted to avoid abuse of the system by allowing social security agencies increased control over the files of welfare applicants, and even to participate in file sharing, was concerned as to whether adequate measures had been taken to safeguard the privacy of the individuals concerned.[60] In the same manner, in considering the obligation on states to ensure the social and economic welfare of mothers and children, the Committee noted that they also had a duty to supervise the conditions under which children are taken into care[61] in order to guarantee that their rights to privacy, in terms of their correspondence and telephone

---

[57] This article provides that, in order to ensure the effective exercise of the right of mothers and children to social and economic protection, the Contracting Parties will take all necessary measures to achieve this goal, including the creation and maintenance of appropriate institutions and services.

[58] *Conclusions XV-2*, at 30 (non-official translation).

[59] These complaints were introduced by the World Organization Against Torture. They were brought against Greece (Complaint No. 17/2003), Ireland (Complaint No. 18/2003), Italy (Complaint No. 19/2003), Portugal (Complaint No. 20/2003), and Belgium (Complaint No. 21/2003).

[60] *Conclusions XV-1*, at 342.

[61] This position draws notably on the case law of the ECtHR. See in particular *Olsson v. Sweden*, ECHR (1988) Series A, No. 130.

conversations, to the protection of property and to maintain contact with relations are respected. Interference in this context will only be tolerated on the grounds of the safety, physical and mental health or development of the child, or for the protection of others.[62] It has also extended its supervisory role to include the nature of sentences handed down to delinquents, as well as to the conditions of their detention.[63] Considerations relevant to the protection of normal family life can be found in the jurisprudence relating to Articles 16 (the right of the family to social, legal, and economic protection) and 19 (the right of migrant workers and their families to protection and assistance), particularly in terms of family reunification and deportation. This jurisprudence tends not only to support the family as the 'fundamental unit' of society, but also a certain conception of the family based on the notion of equality between spouses. These examples, moreover, are by no means exhaustive of the trend.

In conclusion, it is important to note that we must be wary of reaching conclusions based on what has been said above regarding the superiority of rights belonging to one category or those belonging to the other. The most important and interesting points are to be found elsewhere; in the dynamic intersection between the bodies charged with the protection of human rights, particularly in Europe, that hold that social rights, on the one hand, and civil and political rights on the other are interdependent, and working towards the same goal: the protection of each human being. These dynamics exist. The task now is to shed light on them.

[62] *Conclusions XV-2*, at 28–30.   [63] Ibid.

PART III

THE EUROPEAN UNION

7

Anchoring the European Union to the European Social Charter: The Case for Accession

OLIVIER DE SCHUTTER*

I. INTRODUCTION

When, in 1956, the ILO Group of Experts presided over by B. Ohlin studied the potential impact on the protection of social rights and social protection of the creation of a European organization aiming at economic integration, the overall conclusion was highly optimistic.[1] There was no need in principle to provide for a harmonized level of protection of social rights in the future European Economic Community, the experts wrote, because: 'International competition in a common market would not prevent particular countries from raising workers' living standards and there is no sound reason to think that freer international markets would hamper in any way the further improvement of workers' living standards, as productivity rises, through higher wages or improved social benefits and working conditions.'[2] The report of the experts on 'Social Aspects of European Economic Co-operation', the important influence of which on the final shaping of the Treaty of Rome is too well known to be recounted here,[3] therefore found that there was no need for a 'European regional arrangement for closer economic co-operation' (the European Economic Community) to be given the power to legislate in the

---

* Co-ordinator of the EU Network of Independent Experts on Fundamental Rights. This chapter is written in a personal capacity.
  [1] International Labour Office, *Social Aspects of European Economic Co-operation. Report by a Group of Experts*, Studies and Reports, New Series, No. 46 (1956) (hereinafter: 'Ohlin Report').
  [2] Ibid., at 115.
  [3] On the influence the Ohlin Report exercised on the Treaty of Rome, see especially C. Barnard, 'The Economic Objectives of Article 119', in T. Hervey and D. O'Keeffe (eds), *Sex Equality Law in the European Union* (1996); P. Davies, 'The Emergence of European Labour Law', in W. McCarthy (ed.), *Legal Intervention in Industrial Relations: Gains and Losses* (1993), at 313–59; S. Deakin, 'Labour Law as Market Regulation: the Economic Foundations of European Social Policy', in P. Davies, A. Lyon-Caen, S. Sciarra, and S. Simitis (eds), *European Community Labour Law: Principles and Perspectives* (1996), at 62–93; J. Kenner, *EU Employment Law: From Rome to Amsterdam and Beyond* (2003), at 2–6.

social field. According to the authors, differences in productivity between workers in different countries should by necessity translate into differences in remuneration and other advantages, such differences being unavoidable, and indeed desirable, in a context in which the liberalization of international trade ought to promote allocative efficiency.

There were two exceptions to this view, however. One was equality of remuneration between men and women, as the experts noted that, in industries where a large proportion of female labour was employed, differences between the Member States might lead to distortions of competition. The other exception concerned weekly working hours and paid holidays because, the report said, 'it may be that in a particular country working hours are very much longer in one industry than in others—for example because workers are very weakly organized in that industry. As a result the industry in question may have significant advantage compared with competitors in other industries where working hours are at the level that is customary in the country concerned.'[4] Did this necessarily require harmonization of those guarantees within the structure of the European organization for economic cooperation which was, the following year, to become the European Economic Community? The Ohlin group considered that an alternative would be to ensure that all six Member States of the new organization were parties to the same international instruments for the protection of social rights. With respect to the principle of equal pay for equal work, the Report refers to Article 2 of the draft European Social Charter (ESC) drawn up by the Council of Europe in 1955.[5] As regards working time, the experts suggested that 'consideration might be given to the possibility of general acceptance by European countries of such standards as are laid down in the ILO Hours of Work (Industry) Convention, 1919, in certain other ILO Conventions relating to hours of work, or perhaps in a new instrument or instruments which might be established through the machinery of the ILO with a view especially to application in Europe'.[6]

We now know how right Maurice Byé was when, in his dissenting opinion appended to the Ohlin Report, he criticized the perhaps too idealistic views of his colleagues on the virtues of the mobility of the factors of production—including workers—and on the common market's capacity to ensure, as if by a miracle, the gradual improvement of social and working conditions. Indeed, although the Ohlin Report had a lasting influence on the balance between social rights and economic freedoms in the economic Constitution of the Community, the establishment of the internal market has progressively led to the development of a

---

[4] Ohlin Report, *supra* n. 1, at 34–35.

[5] Ibid., at 63. This provision was to become Art. 4 of the European Social Charter as opened for signature and ratification in Turin on 18 October 1961, which provides for 'the right of men and women workers to equal pay for work of equal value'.

[6] Ohlin Report, *supra* n. 1, at 72. Reference could have been made in this respect as well to the draft European Social Charter (ESC) of the Council of Europe (see Arts. 2(1) and 4(2) of the 1961 ESC (providing for reasonable daily and weekly working hours and the right of workers to an increased rate of pay for overtime work)).

social dimension of the European Community, especially after the adoption of the Single European Act of 1986 which sought to create the internal market 31 December 1992. The *acquis* of the Community in the social field has, ever since, been very significant, albeit lacking coherence and systematicity. While much progress has been made, one dimension however has been omitted, although it was present in the Ohlin Report: the international dimension. The EU Member States have widely diverging approaches to internationally protected social rights in general, and to the ESC in particular. Only ten Member States have ratified the Revised European Social Charter of 3 May 1996 ((Rev)ESC),[7] which came into force on 1 July 1999 and takes matters further than not only the list of nineteen rights contained in the ESC of 1961, but also the four additional rights contained in the Additional Protocol of 5 May 1988.[8] In both the 1961 Charter and the 1996 Revised Charter, the commitments of the Member States are variable, because the States may choose, within certain limits, whether or not to accept as binding the substantive provisions contained in those instruments.[9] The resulting asymmetry between the Member States has not been compensated for by the development of social rights at the European level. Although there have been remarkable achievements in European social legislation, particularly in the fields of equal treatment between women and men[10] and protection from discrimination on a number of grounds,[11] but also in the adoption of measures for the approximation of the national laws of the Member States which have as their objective the establishment and functioning of the internal market,[12] most of the guarantees of the ESC may only be implemented within the Union by the adoption of directives which may impose only minimum requirements on the Member States,[13] which

---

[7] CETS No. 163.

[8] The EU Member States who are parties to the (Rev)ESC are Belgium (since 1 May 2004), Cyprus and Estonia (1 November 2000), Finland (1 August 2002), France (1 July 1999), Ireland (1 January 2001), Italy (1 September 1999), Portugal (1 July 2002), and Slovenia and Sweden (1 July 1999).   [9] See Art. 20(1) ESC and Art. A(1) (Rev)ESC.

[10] Art. 141 EC.   [11] Art. 13 EC.

[12] Art. 95 EC. See, e.g., on the choice of Art. 95 EC as the legal basis for the adoption of Directive 2001/37/EC of the European Parliament and of the Council of 5 June 2001 on the approximation of the laws, regulations and administrative provisions of the Member States concerning the manufacture, presentation and sale of tobacco products (OJ 2001 L194/26), the judgment of the Court of 10 December 2002 in Case C-491/01, *The Queen v. Secretary of State for Health, ex parte British American Tobacco (Investments) Ltd and Imperial Tobacco Ltd* [2002] ECR I-11453. The Court confirms that, 'provided that the conditions for recourse to Article 95 EC as a legal basis are fulfilled, the Community legislature cannot be prevented from relying on that legal basis on the ground that public health protection is a decisive factor in the choices to be made' (para. 62). Thus, Art. 95 EC may serve as a legal basis for the enactment of measures implementing the requirements of Art. 11 (Rev)ESC, which concerns the right to protection of health.

[13] See Art. 137(2)(b) EC (stating that the Council may adopt, in the fields of improvement in particular of the working environment to protect workers' health and safety, working conditions, social security, and social protection of workers, protection of workers where their employment contracts have been terminated, the information and consultation of workers, representation and collective defence of the interests of workers and employers, conditions of employment for third-country nationals legally residing in Community territory, the integration of persons excluded from the

implies that they are a product of negotiation often settling on the lowest common denominator. And the open method of coordination of social policies[14] only results in weak incentives on the Member States to protect social rights beyond the minimum levels of protection prescribed under European legislation or at the levels at which the other Member States offer such protection.

This chapter argues for the accession of the Union to the (Rev)ESC. It will focus on the legal questions which this proposal raises. The political argument in favour of the Union acceding to the (Rev)ESC may be easily summarized. Despite the reference which Article 136 EC makes to the 1961 Charter,[15] neither in the social field to which that reference applies, nor in the other fields in which the Union may legislate in order to implement the guarantees of the ESC,[16] is the Union bound to respect the minimal levels of protection of social and economic rights including, but not limited to, the fundamental social rights of workers, which the Charter defines for the Member States. And because the undertakings of the Member States under the ESC system are variable in scope, there is a risk that those States which are least committed to complying with the full range of guarantees set out under the ESC will receive a premium for such an uncooperative attitude. Because of the level of their international undertakings, only they, for instance, will be able to rely on exceptions carved into certain directives imposing minimum requirements, or to implement those directives without offering a higher level of protection than is strictly necessary under those directives to the individuals under their jurisdiction. Only if the Union is bound to comply with the minimum standards defined by the (Rev)ESC when it adopts legislation in the fields covered by the Charter will the Member States not be incentivized to undercut the

labour market, and equality between men and women with regard to labour market opportunities and treatment at work, by means of directives, 'minimum requirements for gradual implementation, having regard to the conditions and technical rules obtaining in each of the Member States').

[14] See Art. 137(2)(a) EC (stating that the Council 'may adopt measures designed to encourage cooperation between Member States through initiatives aimed at improving knowledge, developing exchanges of information and best practices, promoting innovative approaches and evaluating experiences, excluding any harmonisation of the laws and regulations of the Member States', not only in the fields listed in the previous note, but also for protection from social exclusion and modernization of social protection).

[15] According to Art. 136 EC, '[t]he Community and the Member States, having in mind fundamental social rights such as those set out in the European Social Charter signed at Turin on 18 October 1961 and in the 1989 Community Charter of the Fundamental Social Rights of Workers, shall have as their objectives the promotion of employment, improved living and working conditions, so as to make possible their harmonisation while the improvement is being maintained, proper social protection, dialogue between management and labour, the development of human resources with a view to lasting high employment and the combating of exclusion'.

[16] Certain examples are given below: see, p. 141f. Other examples abound. Art. 31 EU, e.g., may be used as a legal basis for defining certain crimes at the level of the Union, which may protect important interests protected under the ESC. See, e.g., Council Framework Decision 2004/68/JHA of 22 December 2003 on combating the sexual exploitation of children and child pornography (OJ 2004 L13/44), which may be seen as an important contribution to the implementation of Art. 7(10) ESC or the (Rev) ESC in the Union.

other States in the inter-jurisdictional regulatory competition, and will they be encouraged, instead, to raise standards under their own jurisdiction.

For instance, Article 2(1) of the ESC, which the (Rev)ESC has not amended, obliges the Contracting Parties 'to provide for reasonable daily and weekly working hours, the working week to be progressively reduced to the extent that the increase of productivity and other relevant factors permit'. Five Member States have not acceded to this provision of the Charter.[17] It would be unacceptable, however, if, in the implementation of the Working Time Directive,[18] these Member States were to benefit from this situation by not implementing the Directive at the same level as the other Member States. Indeed, as recalled by Advocate General Tizzano in the *BECTU* case, 'the objective of ensuring a comparable minimal level of protection as between the various Member States . . . meets the requirement, dictated by the need to prevent distortion of competition, of avoiding any type of social dumping, that is to say, in the last analysis, ensuring that the economy of one Member State cannot derive any advantage from adopting legislation which provides less protection than that of the other Member States'.[19] However, the directives adopted under Article 137 EC may still not comply with the minimal levels set by Article 2(1) and (3) of the ESC, thus making it possible for the Member States whose range of commitments under the Charter is less extensive to benefit from that position.[20]

The remainder of this chapter will seek to answer the most important questions raised by the proposal for the accession of the Union to the ESC. Section II recalls the historical background. It shows that, far from being a novel idea, the accession of the Union to the ESC was seriously considered both in 1989 and in 1994–1996, and was then dismissed for reasons which either have not been made public or remain unconvincing. Section III turns to the current context, and seeks to identify the main arguments which may, today, justify reconsideration of the proposal, at a time when the Union has demonstrated its commitment to fundamental rights by adopting a Charter of Fundamental Rights and is about to accede to the other main human rights instrument of the Council of Europe, the European

---

[17] These States are Austria, Denmark, Latvia, and the UK (among the States Parties to the ESC), and Sweden (which is party to the (Rev)ESC).

[18] Directive 2003/88/EC of the European Parliament and Council of 4 November 2003 concerning certain aspects of the organization of working time, OJ 2003 L299/9. This directive codifies the changes made to Council Directive 93/104/EC of 23 November 1993, concerning certain aspects of the organization of working time (OJ 1993 L307/18). Directive 93/104/EC has been amended by Directive 2000/34/EC of the European Parliament and of the Council (OJ 2000 L195/41).

[19] Opinion of Tizzano AG of 8 February 2001 in Case C-173/99, *BECTU* [2001] ECR I-4881, at para. 45.

[20] Indeed, neither in the proposal presented by the European Commission in September 2004 for a revision of Directive 2003/88/EC, nor in the extended impact analysis which accompanies the proposal, was the ESC even mentioned. See Proposal of the Commission for a Directive of the European Parliament and of the Council amending Directive 2003/88/EC concerning certain aspects of the organization of working time, COM(2004)607 final of 22 September 2004; and the extended impact assessment of the proposal, SEC(2004)1154 of the same date.

Convention on Human Rights. Section IV examines whether the Union has the power to accede to the ESC in the absence of a clear provision authorizing such accession, either in the current Treaties or in the Treaty establishing a Constitution for Europe. Section V comments briefly on the scope of Union law, and seeks to explain why, although it may influence the exercise by the Union of its powers to impose the rights contained in the (Rev)ESC, the accession of the Union to that instrument should not lead to the transfer to the Union of new powers, nor to giving it new tasks. Finally, Section VI of this chapter seeks to identify the impact which accession could have on the status of the (Rev)ESC in the legal order of the Union. Although the (Rev)ESC should not in principle be recognized as having direct effect in the legal order of the Union—and, thus, will normally not be invoked by individual litigants before the European Court of Justice or the Court of First Instance—we may see it being relied upon before European or national courts in exceptional circumstances.

II. THE BACKGROUND

On 16 April 2003, at the signing by the new Member States of the Accession Treaty to the European Union (EU), the Secretary General of the Council of Europe, Mr Walter Schwimmer, invited the Union to become an associate member of the Council of Europe. On the following 5 May, he expressed the hope that the Union would accede, not only to the European Convention on Human Rights (ECHR), but also to the European Cultural Convention and the ESC.[21] The idea of such membership had also been put forward by the EU network of independent experts on fundamental rights.[22]

The idea of such accession is not new. In 1984, it was foreshadowed by the 'Spinelli' draft of a Treaty on the European Union.[23] In April 1989, at a colloquium on the future of social policies in Europe organized at Utrecht, the proposal was put forward that the institutions of the European Communities should solemnly affirm their commitment to uphold the ESC by adopting a unilateral solemn declaration

---

[21] The decision to include the second instrument mentioned in this list may cause some surprise. It obviously has been influenced by the Declaration on the future role of the Council of Europe in European construction, adopted and signed at the 84th Session of the Committee of Ministers on 5 May 1989, on the 40th anniversary of the organization, which noted that '[t]he European Convention on Human Rights, the European Social Charter, the European Cultural Convention and many other instruments, actions and institutions within the Council of Europe constitute a vital contribution to the process of European construction. We are resolved to preserve these gains as well as to enhance and to develop them further for the benefit of the widest possible Europe' (para. 14). This passage of the Declaration, however, appears under the title 'Priority lines of intergovernmental action', rather than under the title 'Relations with the European Community'.

[22] See the Report on the situation of Fundamental Rights in the Union in 2003, March 2004, p. 19 at www.europa.eu.int/comm/justice_home/cdf/index_en.htm.

[23] See Art. 4(2) of the Draft EU Treaty of 14 February 1984.

to that effect,[24] rather than persist in the drafting of a Community Charter of Fundamental Social Rights of their own, distinct from that of the Council of Europe. In May 1989, a few months before the adoption at the Strasbourg European Council by eleven of the twelve Member States of the European Economic Community (EEC) of the Community Charter of the Fundamental Social Rights of Workers, the Parliamentary Assembly of the Council of Europe called upon the Community institutions to adopt a common declaration, like that adopted on 5 April 1977 by the Assembly, the Council, and the Commission on fundamental rights,[25] 'aiming to establish the ESC as an unquestionable source of fundamental rights and principles in the European Community'.[26] At the same time it invited the Commission of the European Communities to take an active part in the revision process of the ESC. This participation ought, said the Assembly, to contribute to this process in particular 'with respect to representation of the Commission, the European Parliament and the Community legal order in its future reporting and supervision procedures'. Recommendation 1107 (1989), which accompanied this resolution, encouraged the Committee of Ministers of the Council of Europe to view 'the future of the Social Charter of the Council of Europe together with the protection of basic social rights in the context of the Communities' in the light of the current movement towards cooperation between the two organizations.

When it took that position in May 1989, the Parliamentary Assembly of the Council of Europe was acting in a particularly favourable context.[27] In 1986, the Preamble to the Single European Act referred to respect for the 'fundamental rights recognised in the constitutions and laws of the Member States, in the Convention for the Protection of Human Rights and Fundamental Freedoms *and*

---

[24] Although the proposal was inspired by the precedent of the Common Declaration of the (EC) Institutions on Fundamental Rights of 5 April 1977, the draft of such a solemn declaration, like that put forward by Prof. P. Van Dijk in a memorandum annexed (Annex D) to the Council of Europe's Report on the ESC and eventual membership of the EU (*rapporteur* Mr Foschi) (Doc. 6138 of 31 October 1989), contained a final line in which the European Parliament, the Council, and the Commission were to have expressed 'their wish to open a dialogue with the Council of Europe with a view to examining the possibilities and the means for adapting certain substantive and procedural clauses of the European Social Charter . . . as well as the modalities of accession of the European Communities to the Charter'. In that respect, the Declaration which was proposed would have gone further than the example provided by the Common Declaration of 5 April 1977 on fundamental rights.   [25] OJ 1977 C103/1.

[26] Resolution 915 (1989) on the future role of the ESC, adopted on 9 May 1989 on the report prepared within the Social, Health and Family Affairs Committee (Doc. 6031, *rapporteur* Mr Foschi). See also the text approved by the Commission on social matters of the Parliamentary Assembly of the Council of Europe at its meeting in Strasbourg of 25 September 1989, addressed to the President of the Commission of the European Communities, J. Delors (appearing in Annex C of the Council of Europe's Report on the Social Charter and the eventual accession of the European Community (*rapporteur* Mr Foschi), Doc. 6138, 31 October 1989).

[27] In this context see B. Hepple, 'The Implementation of the Community Charter of Fundamental Social Rights', 53 *MLR* (1990) 643; E. Vogel-Polsky and J. Vogel, *L'Europe sociale 1993: illusion, alibi or réalité?* (1991), at 204–18; L. Betten, 'Prospects for a Social Policy of the European Community and its Impact on the Functioning of the European Social Charter', in L. Betten (ed.), *The Future of European Social Policy* (1989), at 101; and Kenner, *supra* n. 3, at 110–15.

the European Social Charter, particularly freedom, equality and social justice'. Since this amounted to an affirmation that fundamental social rights should be respected within the European Economic Community,[28] it might have appeared logical for such affirmation to constitute a first step towards the incorporation of the ESC itself—and not merely of certain of its guarantees—in the Community legal order. In an Opinion of 22 February 1989, the European Economic and Social Committee stated its preference for an improved integration into the Community legal order of the 'basic social guarantees' stipulated by the instruments of the International Labour Organization as well as the ESC, instead of the adoption of a Charter of Fundamental Social Rights specific to the European Community. The Economic and Social Committee considered that the right path for the Community was not to 'devise a new instrument, but to enshrine fundamental social guarantees in the Community legal systems, with its distinctive supranational features'. It noted:

At different international levels, the social partners and governments have managed to agree on the definition of fundamental social rights, whether under the United Nations, the International Labour Organization, the Council of Europe or the OECD. It is all the more urgent that, in the context of a single market, certain social rights be anchored in the Member States so as to constitute a coherent and interdependent set forming part of the common heritage of the Member States. The idea is not to invent rules, but primarily to take account of those already established and accepted on other levels, and, secondly, to define these rights by taking account of the new needs resulting from the setting up of the internal market and facilitating its harmonious functioning.[29]

This route was not followed. On the contrary, the European Commission chose to promote the adoption, in the form of a Solemn Declaration accompanied by an Action Programme, of a 'Community Charter of Fundamental Social Rights'. A first draft of this Charter was published by the Commission at the end of May 1989.[30] Eleven of the twelve States at the Strasbourg European Council finally adopted an amended version of this text, which was now centred on the fundamental social rights of workers more than on those, generally, of the individual—which explains the change of title which resulted.

The decision to ensure the protection of fundamental social rights in the EU, not by the incorporation of the ESC of the Council of Europe, but rather by amendments made to the EC Treaties and secondary Community law, has been

[28] It was at this moment that reinforcement of fundamental social rights was presented as the indispensable counterweight to the establishment by 31 December 1992 of the internal market, the achievement of which was provided for by the Single European Act. See Economic and Social Council, Opinion on the Social Aspects of the Internal Market, 19 November 1987, OJ 1987 C356/8, at 31.

[29] ECOSOC, Opinion on Community fundamental social rights, Doc. ECOSOC 270/89 of 22 February 1989. ECOSOC also suggested 'adopting the necessary procedure so that the content and the extent of these principles and [Community] fundamental rights may be interpreted while respecting the norms already recognised in the instruments of international social law'.

[30] COM(89)248 of 31 May 1989.

confirmed on two significant occasions since the adoption of the Community Charter of Fundamental Social Rights of Workers. When the work undertaken by the Committee for the revision of the ESC resulted in the draft of a revised ESC, the version proposed in October 1994 contained the following provision:[31]

Article L. Accession by the European Community

After its entry into force, the Committee of Ministers of the Council of Europe may invite the European Community to accede to this Charter, by decision taken on the majority required by Article 20(d) of the Council of Europe's Statute, and by a unanimous vote of the representatives of the Contracting States entitled to sit on the Committee. The specific modalities for the accession and the consequences for the functioning of the system of supervision shall be determined by the Committee of Ministers.

This Article was sidelined following the discussion of the text of the new treaty by the Committee of Ministers of the Council of Europe. It would, however, have had the advantage that accession of the European Community—the Union today—could be achieved without a protocol of amendment of the (Rev)ESC, a protocol submitted in principle for ratification by all the States Parties to it.[32] It is true that the requirement of ratification according to their respective constitutional procedures by all the States Parties to the (Rev)ESC may be avoided by recourse to the so-called 'opting out' procedure, according to which a protocol of amendment envisaging the accession of the EU could enter into force at the expiry of a set period beginning on the date of its opening for accession unless one of the contracting parties notified its objection before the expiry of this period—in which event recourse would be had to the usual procedure of signature and ratification by all the States Parties.[33] But, given the substantive importance of a protocol of amendment to the (Rev)ESC permitting the accession of the EU, it is doubtful whether recourse to such procedure would be considered

[31] Charter Rel. (84)23 of 14 October 1994, Art. L contained a second paragraph, not reproduced here, relating to the moment of entry into force of the (Rev)ESC with regard to the European Community in the event of its ratification by it.

[32] See Parliamentary Assembly of the Council of Europe, Report giving an opinion on the draft revised European Social Charter (*rapporteur* Mr Rathbone), Doc. 7243 of 13 February 1995, at point 6.3.3. The procedure to be followed for the amendment of the (Rev)ESC is set out in its Art. J. In this particular case, Art. J(4) would apply: as a protocol on the accession of the EU to the ESC would bear upon the definition of the undertakings of the parties to the Charter and on the mechanisms of control (Parts III and IV), and not merely on the list of objectives (Part I) or the material rights (Part II), the protocol of accession of the EU could come into force only after notification by all the parties to the (Rev)ESC that they had accepted it.

[33] See on this formula R. Brillat, 'Le participation de la Communauté européenne aux conventions du Conseil de l'Europe', XXXVII *AFDI* (1991) 819, especially at 822. Protocols permitting the participation of the EEC in a number of agreements concluded in the framework of the Council of Europe have entered into force by using this technique. Examples are the European Agreement on the Exchange of Therapeutic Substances of Human Origin of 1958 (CETS No. 26, OJ 1987 L37/1), the Agreement on the Temporary Importation, free of duty, of Medical, Surgical and Laboratory Equipment for use on free loan in Hospitals and other Medical Institutions for purposes of Diagnosis or Treatment of 1960 (CETS No. 33, OJ 1986 L131/47), and the European Agreement on the Exchanges of Blood-Grouping Reagents of 1962 (CETS No. 39, OJ 1987 L37/31).

acceptable.[34] Therefore, the rejection by the Committee of Ministers of the Council of Europe of Article L of the draft (Rev)ESC relating to the Accession of the European Community has not merely political significance: such a rejection has also produced precise legal consequences.

In their own way, the discussions which preceded the adoption of the Charter of Fundamental Rights by the institutions of the Union at the Nice Summit of December 2000 also illustrated the tendency to relegate the ESC to the category of instruments destined to remain outside the legal order of the Union itself, while the Union would follow its own path in order to ensure the protection of fundamental social rights in its field of activities. The fate of the ESC stands in striking contrast with that of the European Convention on Human Rights, which has in fact—materially, if not yet institutionally—been incorporated into the legal order of the EU. The contrast between these two Council of Europe instruments cannot be ignored. The (Rev)ESC has inspired the formulation of many provisions of the EU Charter of Fundamental Rights. But the EU Charter has failed to include many of its guarantees, where it has replicated the totality of the rights and freedoms of the ECHR and its additional protocols. Moreover, whereas it was agreed that the provisions of the EU Charter of Fundamental Rights corresponding to provisions of the ECHR should be read in accordance with the interpretation given to these provisions by the European Court of Human Rights,[35] there is no similar article prescribing that the provisions of the EU Charter of Fundamental Rights be read in the light of the development of the jurisprudence of the European Committee of Social Rights.

III. THE CURRENT CONTEXT

The adoption of the Community Charter of Fundamental Social Rights of Workers in 1989 and the revision of the ESC in 1994–1996 were missed opportunities. The time may have come, now, to address the question of the accession of the Union to the (Rev)ESC in new terms. Given the reinforcement of

[34] The analogy is more that of Amendments to the Convention for the protection of individuals with regard to automated processing of personal data (STE No. 108) allowing for the accession of the European Communities, adopted by the Committee of Ministers of the Council of Europe at its 675th meeting on 15 June 1999. All the States Parties have to notify their acceptance of these amendments before they can come into force. Only after their entry into force can the European Communities accede to the Convention.

[35] See Art. 52(3) of the EU Charter of Fundamental Rights, appearing in the provisions relating to the scope of the rights guaranteed in the Charter: 'Insofar as this Charter contains rights which correspond to rights guaranteed by the [European Convention on Human Rights], the meaning and scope of those rights shall be the same as those laid down by the said Convention.' Although its title has been changed (it is now entitled 'Scope and interpretation of rights and principles'), this provision has been left unmodified in the version of the EU Charter which will constitute Part II of the Treaty establishing a Constitution for Europe: see Art. II-112(3).

the ESC following its revitalization since 1989–1990, one of the outcomes of which was the adoption of the (Rev)ESC on 3 May 1996, it is becoming less and less easy to justify maintaining its isolation from the Union's legal order. The ESC defines for the EU Member States obligations within the international legal order that they are no longer permitted to ignore; neither should it be possible for them to ignore those obligations when building the social rights component of the internal market. Recent developments have given renewed urgency to this question. The ESC has been significantly reinforced since the mid-1990s. The risk of conflicts between the ESC and EU law has increased, particularly given the exercise of the competences attributed to the EU in the areas covered by the (Rev)ESC. The inclusion of social rights in the EU Charter of Fundamental Rights attests to a readiness to subject the development of EU law to respect for these rights, which should now also translate in the international sphere. The prospect of the accession of the Union to the European Convention on Human Rights makes the case for accession to the (Rev)ESC even more compelling. These arguments are developed more fully below.

A. The Reinforcement of the ESC

The first reason why building bridges between the Union and the (Rev)ESC now appears more urgent than ever is that the system of the ESC has been significantly reinforced since the early 1990s. The strengthening of the system of the ESC is the result of a process of revitalization which, perhaps ironically in the context of this study, had been provoked initially in particular by the fear that the Social Charter of the Council of Europe would be marginalized, following the adoption in 1989 of a catalogue of fundamental social rights of workers peculiar to the European Community. Indeed, the choice made then by the EC was seen to indicate that it would build another 'Social Europe' alongside the *acquis* achieved within the Council of Europe in the field of social rights, rather than accede to that *acquis* or incorporate it without seeking to adapt it to its own specificities or to the specific role fundamental social rights ought to play in the construction of an internal market.[36] The European Social Charter therefore was to be improved—made more relevant to the needs of the times. The process of revitalization of the Charter led to the completion of the list of rights contained in the 1961 Charter by the 1988 Additional Protocol, and then by the adoption in 1996 of the (Rev)ESC, which will be progressively substituted for the original text as the states proceed towards its ratification. It also led to a better division of tasks between the European Committee of Social Rights (originally the Committee of Independent Experts) and the Governmental Committee: according to the redefinition of their respective roles which was achieved by the adoption of the Turin Protocol of 1991,

---

[36] See Prof. P. Van Dijk's memorandum of May 1989, *supra* n. 24, at point 18f, on the need to create a human rights instrument adapted to European social policy.

the quasi-judicial interpretation of the Charter should be left to the independent experts, whereas the Governmental Committee should seek to draw the conclusions following from the findings of the experts, and may, in doing so, explicitly take political factors into account.[37] Finally, the Additional Protocol to the ESC Providing for a System of Collective Complaints was adopted on 9 November 1995 and entered into force on 1 July 1998.[38] The introduction of this last mechanism further accentuated the quasi-jurisdictional nature of the task of the European Committee of Social Rights. Indeed, the collective complaints mechanism is based on the idea that the social rights of the Charter are justiciable, a development which should create a powerful incentive for the national courts to allow these rights to be invoked before them more frequently, and of course will influence our understanding of the nature of the obligations imposed on the States Parties to the ESC.

Hitherto, this change has not persuaded the European Court of Justice to take the view that, in its task of ensuring the observance of the law in the application of the EC Treaty,[39] it ought also to ensure the protection of the rights contained in the ESC. At the present time, the contrast between civil and political rights, on the one hand, and social rights, on the other, remains striking: if the European Court of Justice does not hesitate to count the former among the general principles of Community law whose respect it ensures—by according a 'special significance' to the ECHR[40]—on the other hand it has never elevated social rights to the same status;[41] and if the ESC of 18 October 1961 has sometimes served as a guide to the interpretation of Community law,[42] it has not been taken into account by the European Court of Justice in the same way as has the ECHR, one Advocate

[37] Protocol amending the ESC, opened for signature at Turin on 21 October 1991 (ECTS No. 142). Although this Protocol has not yet entered in force due to the insufficient number of ratifications by States Parties to the ESC, the modifications to the procedure of examination of the state reports which could be brought about without modification of the original text of the ESC were implemented in the practice of the bodies involved. More importantly, the spirit guiding the Turin Protocol, with a reaffirmation of the independence of the Committee of Independent Experts (now European Committee of Social Rights) and of its monopoly of the interpretation of the requirements of the Charter, has influenced the developments within the Charter since.   [38] ECTS No. 158.

[39] Art. 220 (ex Art. 164) EC.

[40] Joined Cases 46/87 and 227/88, *Hoechst AG v. Commission* [1989] ECR 2859, at para. 13.

[41] It is true that the ECJ has included among the general principles of Community law the right to freedom of association, including the exercise of trade union rights (Case 36/75, *R. Rutili* [1975] ECR 1219, at para. 32), the free exercise of a profession (Case 4/73, *Nold* [1974] ECR 491), or, in various guises, the prohibition of discrimination (see, among many other examples, Case C-13/94, *P v. S and Cornwall County Council* [1996] ECR I-2143). But these rights are at the crossroads of civil and political and social rights, in the classical understandings of those categories. They are seen mostly to impose prohibitions, rather than obligations of performance.

[42] Case 149/77, *Defrenne (No. 3)* [1978] ECR 1365 (the reference to the ESC leads the Court to ground its affirmation according to which 'the elimination of discrimination based on sex is part of the fundamental rights', at para. 28); Case 24/86, *Blaizot* [1988] ECR 379 (before replying in the affirmative to the question whether university courses in veterinary medicine should be considered as part of vocational training in the sense of Art. 128 EEC, the Court notes that 'Article 10 of the European Social Charter, to which most of the Member States are Contracting Parties, treats University education as a type of vocational training', at para. 17).

General having explained that the 'structure' of the ESC was such 'that the rights which it enshrines are more political objectives than constraining rights, and the signatory states were bound to do no more than choose, from among those listed, the rights which they decided to protect'.[43] In the *Bergemann* case, Advocate General Lenz suggested to the Court that, although the ESC itself, in Part III, made it clear that the Charter only bound the States Parties in the international legal order, and therefore did not establish any direct right to the protection of individuals, nevertheless the ratification of the Charter demonstrated the existence of a common political will of these States, and should be seen as recognizing a set of common values potentially relevant to the interpretation of directly applicable law.[44] But the Court did not follow his suggestion. This is not to say that the Community judicature is indifferent to social rights. These rights, however, appear in the case law as objectives which it is legitimate for the EU Member States to wish to pursue, rather than as 'claim rights' which individuals should be recognized as possessing.[45]

B. The Risk of Conflicts between the ESC and Union Law

The refusal of the European Court of Justice hitherto to consider that the ESC should influence the Community judicature in its development of the general principles of law the observance of which it should ensure in applying and interpreting Union law—a refusal which the adoption of the EU Charter of Fundamental Rights and its current incorporation into the European Constitution will only partly compensate for—carries with it the risk of conflicts of interpretation between the European Court of Justice and the European Committee of Social Rights.[46] The European Court of Justice accepts that certain fundamental social rights—in so far as the Member States may seek to protect them at the national level—may constitute overriding requirements relating to the public interest capable of justifying restrictions on the free movement of goods[47] or

---

[43] Opinion of Jacobs AG in Case C-67/96, *Albany International BV* [1999] ECR I-5751.

[44] See Case 236/87, *Bergemann* [1988] ECR 5125, at para. 28 of the Opinion.

[45] For further developments see O. De Schutter, 'La garantie des droits et principes sociaux dans la Charte des droits fondamentaux de l'Union européenne', in J.-Y. Carlier and O. De Schutter (eds), *La Charte des droits fondamentaux de l'Union européenne: Son apport à la protection des droits de l'homme en Europe* (2002), at 117. For a systematic presentation of the status of social rights in the ECJ's case law see K. Lenaerts and P. Foubert, 'Social Rights in the Case-law of the European Court of Justice', in P. Van der Auweraert et al. (eds), *Social, Economic and Cultural Rights: An Appraisal of Current European and International Developments* (2002), at 159.

[46] On the question of relations between the ESC and EU law, see generally F. Vandamme, 'Les droits sociaux fondamentaux en Europe', *JTDE* (1999) 49; J.-F. Akandji-Kombé, 'Charte sociale et droit communautaire', in J.-F. Akandji-Kombé and S. Leclerc (eds), *La Charte sociale européenne* (2001), at 149; and J.-F. Flauss, 'Les interactions normatives entre les instruments de droit européen relatives à la protection des droits sociaux', in J.-F. Flauss (ed.), *Droits sociaux et droit européen: Bilan et perspective de la protection normative* (2002), at 87.

[47] See Case C-120/95, *Decker* [1998] ECR I-1831, at paras. 39 and 40.

on the freedom to provide services,[48] or as justifying restrictions on competition law.[49] However, the ESC is not a necessary source of reference for the identification of these rights. It cannot therefore be ruled out that a Member State will be under an obligation in Community law to renounce the protection of certain fundamental social rights, or, more plausibly, to renounce their protection at a certain level, even where, by ensuring this protection, it would be intending to fulfil its obligations under the ESC. Of course, no such conflict will occur where Union law only imposes minimum requirements on the Member States, as is the case where directives are adopted in the social field on the basis of Article 137 EC, in order to achieve the objectives defined in Article 136 EC by the Member States and the Community, 'having in mind fundamental social rights such as those set out in the European Social Charter signed at Turin on 18 October 1961 and in the 1989 Community Charter of the Fundamental Social Rights of Workers'.[50] However, taking into account, for example, the distrust which the European Committee of Social Rights has expressed about the 'activation' of social benefits— with the possible impact this development entails on the right of the worker to earn his living in an occupation 'freely entered upon'[51]—and the tendency of the Member States of the Union to consider that, in the areas covered by Community directives, these define the level of the minimal requirements they are to comply with—so that the more generous provisions of the ESC could be sidelined[52]—the

---

[48] See Case 279/80, *Criminal Proceedings against A.J. Webb* [1981] ECR 3305; Case C-113/89, *Rush Portuguesa* [1990] ECR I-1417, at para. 17; Case C-272/94, *Guiot* [1996] ECR I-1905, at para. 16; Case C-158/96, *Kohll* [1998] ECR I-1931, at para. 41; Joined Cases C-369/96 and C-376/96, *Arblade* [1999] ECR I-8453, at para. 36; Case C-165/98, *Mazzaleni and ISA* [2001] ECR I-2189, at para. 27; Case C-164/99, *Infringement Proceedings against Portugaia Construções Lda* [2002] ECR I-787, at paras. 20 and 21.

[49] See Case C-67/96, *Albany* [1999] ECR I-5751.

[50] In order to achieve the objectives laid down for the Community social policy by Art. 136 EC (ex Art. 117 EEC), Art. 137 EC, in its current wording, provides that the Council 'may adopt, in [certain fields], by means of directives, minimum requirements for gradual implementation...' (Art. 137(3)(b) EC). Art. 137(4) EC adds—which is redundant where directives imposing only minimum requirements are concerned—that the provisions adopted pursuant to Art. 137 EC 'shall not prevent any Member State from maintaining or introducing more stringent protective measures compatible with this Treaty'. The Treaty of Nice (OJ 2001 C180/1) made important amendments to Art. 137 EC, in particular in order to constitutionalize the open method of coordination. However, the provisions cited here were already in the previous version of Art. 137 EC (see, respectively, Art. 137(2) and (5) EC).

[51] According to the European Committee of Social Rights, the right of the worker to earn his living in an occupation freely entered upon (Art. 1(2) ESC (the text was unchanged in the (Rev)ESC)) could be incompatible with the imposition of sanctions on persons who have refused to take the employment offered to them, unless the employment offered clearly corresponds to their qualifications: see *Conclusions XVI-1* (2002), at 11 (United Kingdom); *Conclusions XVI-1* (2002), at 98 (Belgium).

[52] According to a particularly well-placed author, the European Committee of Social Rights 'has experienced, in certain situations where legislation was submitted to its appreciation, some difficulties in imposing its views in fields where the Community, according to the Committee, has opted for a too minimal level of protection. Where Community directives have covered...a field, the EU Member States consider that this constitutes the minimal level of satisfactory requirements, and these States are reluctant to accept more generous interpretations of the corresponding provisions of the European Social Charter, often more generously worded': Vandamme, *supra* n. 46, at 55.

risk that such a conflict may develop in the future does not seem to be purely theoretical.

A related but distinct argument is based on the risk of an obstacle to the full effectiveness of Union law where situations of conflict would arise between the obligations it imposes on Member States and the obligations of the ESC. Without an alignment between the fundamental social rights recognized in the legal order of the EU and the rights set out in the (Rev)ESC it cannot be ruled out that certain Member States will invoke Article 307 (ex Article 234) EC in order to comply with the obligations imposed on them by the ESC, despite the obstacle this represents for the fulfilment of their obligations in the context of the EU. Article 307 EC aims to facilitate the accession of states to the Union, where pre-existing international obligations would constitute an obstacle to full compliance with their obligations in the legal order of the Union from the moment of accession.[53] To this end, this provision lays down that the rights and obligations which exist, before accession, between one or more Member States of the one part and one or more third states of the other 'are not affected' by Union law. The effects of EU law have to be suspended, even if the source of the incompatibility has not disappeared, in such a way as to allow the Member State to respect the obligations it accepted in the international legal order prior to its accession to the Union.[54] These commitments naturally remain in force in the international legal order: with respect to third states, the accession treaty of a state to the EU constitutes *res inter alios acta*, which may not result in legal consequences opposable to those third states.[55] Uncontroversial under general international public law,[56] the rule has been used, notably, in order to permit the EU Member States to comply with the obligations imposed on them by the ILO Convention (No. 89) of 9 July 1948

---

[53] See Case 812/79, *Attorney General v. Juan C. Burgos* [1980] ECR 2787, at para. 10 (stating that Art. 234 EEC seeks to 'remove any obstacle to the performance of agreements previously concluded with non-member countries which the accession of a Member State to the Community may present').

[54] It may be deduced from the reason for the existence of this rule that it comes into play only when the execution by a Member State of its obligations resulting from an earlier agreement could still be required by third countries who are parties to the agreement: see Case C-124/95, *Centro-Com* [1997] ECR I-81, at paras. 56–57; Joined Cases C-364 and 365/95, *T. Port GmbH & Co* [1998] ECR I-1023, at paras. 60–61.

[55] In issue here is only the international obligation *of the Member State* with regard to one or more third states. It is naturally a different question whether *the Community/Union*, of its own part, ought to succeed to the international obligations of Member States, and to bind itself with regard to third states parties to agreements concluded by such Member States before their accession. The reply is in principle in the negative: as the ECJ explains, although there exists an obligation imposed on the Union institutions by virtue of Art. 307(1) EC, not to impede the performance of the obligations of the Member States arising out of a prior agreements, 'that duty of the Community institutions is directed only to permitting the Member State concerned to perform its obligations under the prior agreement and does not bind the Community as regards the non-Member country in question': Case 812/79, *Burgos, supra* n. 53, at para. 9.

[56] See the reference made by the ECJ to Art. 30(4)(b) of the Vienna Convention on the Law of Treaties of 23 May 1969 in its judgment in Case C-466/98, *EC Commission v. United Kingdom of Great Britain and Northern Ireland* [1997] ECR I-9427, at para. 24.

concerning Nightwork of Women Employed in Industry.[57] As a result of this rule, if an incompatibility were to exist between the obligations of an EU Member State as a Party to the ESC and its obligations as a Member State of the European Union, risking impeding the full effectiveness of Union law, it could be eliminated only at the price of restricting the obligations accepted in the framework of the ESC by that State. Indeed, Article 307 EC provides for such an exception only to the extent that the incompatibility remains strictly temporary. Article 307(2) EC states in this regard that: 'To the extent that such [prior] agreements are not compatible with this Treaty, the Member State or States concerned shall take all appropriate steps to eliminate the incompatibilities established. Member States shall, where necessary, assist each other to this end and shall, where appropriate, adopt a common attitude.' Thus, if an incompatibility subsists, Article 307(2) EC imposes an obligation on the EU Member State to denounce the international agreement it had concluded before the moment of its accession to the Union.[58] It was, moreover, such a solution for which France opted after the European Court of Justice delivered its judgment in the *Stoeckel* case, which concluded that the prohibition of nightwork by women, where nightwork by men is not prohibited, was incompatible with Article 5 of Directive 76/207:[59] on 26 February 1992, France denounced ILO Convention (No. 89) of 9 July 1948 concerning Nightwork of Women Employed in Industry, without waiting for the ECJ to deliver a judgment formally confirming its obligation to do so under Article 307(2) EC.[60]

Article 307 EC will be reinstated, with purely formal amendments, as Article III-435 of the European Constitution. It still remains to be ascertained, however, with respect to which EU Member States this provision might play a role, if situations were to emerge in which the ESC-based obligations of a State acceding to the Union would create an obstacle for the fulfilment of its obligations as a new

---

[57] See Case C-158/91, *Lévy* [1993] ECR I-4287 (the Court admitted that Art. 234 EEC (now Art. 307 EC, after amendment), could be an obstacle to sanctioning the State Party to that convention for not respecting Council Directive 76/207/EEC of 9 February 1976 on the implementation of the principle of equal treatment for men and women as regards access to employment, vocational training and promotion, and working conditions (OJ 1976 L39/40), on the point where an incompatibility existed). See on this point the Opinion of Tesauro AG of 16 January 1997 in Case C-197/96, *EC Commission v. France* [1997] ECR I-1491 at 1491–95.

[58] See Case C-62/98, *Commission v. Portugal* [2000] ECR I-5171, and, in the literature, Manzini, 'The Priority of Pre-existing Treaties of EC Member States within the Framework of International Law', 12 *EJIL* (2001) 781.   [59] Case C-345/89 [1991] ECR I-4047.

[60] France was nevertheless found to have violated Art. 5 of Directive 76/207/EEC by a judgment of 13 March 1997 (Case C-197/96, *Commission v. France* [1997] ECR I-1489). Although France had denounced ILO Convention 89, it had retained in the Labour Code Art. L 213.1 which was at the source of the incompatibility. Although that provision was not applied by the public authorities, which recognized that they were prohibited from relying upon it because of the incompatibility, the Court recalled that 'the incompatibility of national legislation with Community provisions, even provisions which are directly applicable, can be finally remedied only by means of national provisions of a binding nature which have the same legal force as those which must be amended' (point 14). See also, for a finding in similar circumstances of the failure of Italy to comply with Community law, Case C-207/96, *Commission v. Italy* [1997] ECR I-6869.

member of the Union. The European Court of Justice has taken the view that Article 307 EC can be invoked only when an international agreement has been concluded by one or more Member States with one or more third states prior to the accession of that or those Member States to the EU, and that no exception may be made where the incompatibility has its source in a later agreement, concluded after the date of the accession, even where that later agreement replaces a previous agreement while retaining the clause having caused the incompatibility with the obligations imposed by the Union on its Member States.[61] Thus, when a Member State has ratified the (Rev)ESC, which was opened for signature on 3 May 1996, it will no longer be allowed provisionally to invoke Article 307 EC in order to derogate from the obligations imposed on it in the context of the EU by arguing that it was bound by such rule appearing in the ESC, prior to its accession to the European Union:[62] despite the fact that it replaces an earlier treaty, to which its contracting parties remain bound until they ratify the new treaty, the (Rev)ESC is formally a new treaty, which creates new rights and obligations between the contracting parties. As a result, Article 307 EC should be invoked by only two categories of Member States: those who were parties to the 1961 Charter before their entry into the Union, who have not, since they acceded to the Union, become parties to the 1996 (Rev)ESC; and those who joined the Union on 1 May 2004 and were then parties either to the (Rev)ESC or (unless they have since become a party to the (Rev)ESC) to the 1961 Charter. Austria,[63] Denmark,[64] Spain,[65] and the United Kingdom[66] belong to the first category. Cyprus, the Czech Republic, Estonia, Hungary, Latvia, Lithuania, Malta, Poland, Slovakia, and Slovenia belong to the second. But one must draw a still further distinction between the situation of the states bound at the time of their accession to the Union by the 1961 Charter and those bound at the moment of their accession by the Revised Charter of 1996. In the first case, the substitution of the (Rev)ESC for the ESC will have the effect, in future years, of prohibiting reliance on Article 307 EC or its successor vis-à-vis the institutions of the Union: that is the case with

---

[61] See Case C-466/98, *supra* n. 56, at paras. 26–29.

[62] This is, e.g., the situation with Ireland, bound by the ESC of 1961 at the time of its accession to the Communities in 1973, but which has since ratified the (Rev)ESC of 1996. The situation of Sweden is similar: bound by the 1961 ESC before its accession to the EU, it has since substituted its undertakings under the (Rev)ESC for its previous undertakings under the 1961 ESC.

[63] Austria, however, signed the (Rev)ESC on 7 May 1999. When, following its ratification, that treaty comes into force with regard to it, Art. 307 EC will no longer be able to be raised against the institutions of the Union.

[64] Denmark, however, signed the (Rev)ESC on 3 May 1996. When, following its ratification, that treaty comes into force for it, Art. 307 EC will no longer be able to be raised against the institutions of the Union.

[65] Spain, however, signed the (Rev)ESC on 23 October 2000. When, following its ratification, this treaty comes into force for it, Art. 307 EC will no longer be able to be raised against the institutions of the Union.

[66] The UK however signed the (Rev)ESC on 7 November 1997. When, following its ratification, that treaty comes into force for it, Art. 307 EC will no longer be able to be raised against the institutions of the Union.

Austria, the Czech Republic, Denmark, Hungary, Latvia, Malta, Poland, Slovakia, Spain, and the United Kingdom. In the second case, Article 307 EC may be relied upon as long as the incompatibility which had been found to exist has not been eliminated. This is the case with Cyprus, Estonia, Lithuania, and Slovenia.

It may be difficult to identify situations in which the risk of conflict may materialize, thus justifying the use of Article 307 EC (or Article III-435 of the European Constitution). As many provisions of the (Rev)ESC of 1996 have found their inspiration in primary or secondary Community law, such risks should not be overestimated. Moreover, Article 137(2) EC provides that only directives imposing minimum requirements may be adopted in order to fulfil certain of the objectives defined in Article 136 EC, which the Member States have defined 'having in mind fundamental social rights such as those set out in the European Social Charter signed at Turin on 18 October 1961 and in the 1989 Community Charter of the Fundamental Social Rights of Workers'. These are the promotion of employment, improved living and working conditions, proper social protection, dialogue between management and labour, the development of human resources with a view to lasting high employment and the combating of exclusion.[67] This obviously limits the risk of conflicts occurring between the obligations of the EU Member States under Union law and under the ESC as, in implementing such directives, they remain free to afford a higher level of protection to workers.

The risk of conflict, on the other hand, has not been eliminated. The jurisprudence of the European Committee of Social Rights is dynamic: its development may lead to the imposition on the States Parties to the Charter of obligations the scope and extent of which were not necessarily predictable at the outset, arising out of the text itself. And the European Committee of Social Rights has clearly stated that a state party may not use the pretext of obligations imposed on it under EU law in order to restrict the scope of obligations incumbent upon it by virtue of the ESC:

> The Committee attaches the greatest importance to the fact that the contracting parties to the Charter take account of that treaty when they adopt, within the European Union, directives in the fields covered by the Charter. The Committee hopes moreover that the contracting parties, when they are to implement European Union directives into their national law, shall comply with their obligations under the Charter. This arises in particular with regard to directives which have not yet been incorporated into the national law of a certain number of contracting parties.[68]

Finally, in a number of areas covered by the (Rev)ESC—other than those currently enumerated in Article 137(1) EC—the European Community/Union

---

[67] Art. 137 EC has been substantially modified by the Treaty of Nice, as already mentioned. However, the principle that only directives imposing minimum requirements may be adopted has been retained.   [68] *Conclusions XIV-1*, at 27.

has been given competences which permit it not merely to adopt directives or framework laws imposing minimum requirements on Member States, but also to adopt harmonization measures. This is the case in particular with measures taken with a view to setting up the internal market, on the basis of Articles 94 and 95 EC.[69] Where this is the case, if European legislation protects fundamental social rights at a lower level than that prescribed by the ESC—or its revised version—the Member States will no longer be able to comply with obligations imposed upon them by virtue of the ESC without infringing their obligations under EU law.

C. The Impact of the EU Charter of Fundamental Rights on the Status of Social Rights within the Union Legal Order

The adoption of the EU Charter of Fundamental Rights by a solemn declaration of the Council, the European Parliament, and the European Commission at the Nice Summit in December 2000, now followed by the incorporation of the Charter in the body of the Constitution, marks a true improvement in the protection of fundamental social rights in the legal order of the Union. It is true that most of the social rights recognized by the Charter—in particular those found in its Title IV ('Solidarity')—are to be exercised in accordance with Union law and national laws and practices: although their constitutional value is recognized, their precise significance continues to depend on the way in which the Union's constituent power (in other parts of the Constitution) or the legislature has chosen to protect them. Yet the recognition of the fundamental character of such rights transforms their status. One cannot rule out a development according to which a non-retrogression obligation will be imposed, as rights which previously figured only in the secondary law of the Union can be invoked as rights of constitutional status, creating an obstacle to the adoption of Union legislative acts which restrict these guarantees. At a minimum, secondary law which gives effect to social rights recognized in the Charter will be extensively interpreted, in accordance with the object of legislation aimed at the protection of fundamental rights.[70] Thus it is

---

[69] For the example of health protection law (Art. 11 ESC), see p. 137.

[70] See Joined Cases 75 and 117/82, *Razzouk and Beydoun v. EC Commission* [1984] ECR 1509: recognizing that the principle of equality of treatment between the sexes 'forms part of the fundamental rights the observance of which the Court has a duty to ensure', the Court considered that, therefore, 'in relations between the Community institutions, on the one hand, and their employees and the dependants of employees, on the other, the requirements imposed by the principle of equal treatment are in no way limited to those resulting from Article 119 of the EEC Treaty or from the Community directives adopted in this field' (at paras. 16 and 17). The recognition of the principle of equal treatment between women and men, in other terms, means that the understanding of its scope cannot be limited to the implementation of that principle in secondary, or even in primary, Community law. Likewise, in *P v. S and Cornwall County Council, supra* n. 41, the fundamental character of the right not to be discriminated against on the ground of sex led the Court to admit that the scope of Council Directive 76/207/EEC of 9 February 1976 on the implementation of the principle of equal treatment for men and women as regards access to employment, vocational training and promotion, and working conditions (OJ 1976 L39/40) 'cannot be confined simply to discrimination

that, in the context of a case on the interpretation of the 1993 Working Time Directive[71] concerning the right to annual paid holidays—recognized in Article 31(2) of the Charter of Fundamental Rights—Advocate General Tizzano laid the emphasis on the fundamental character of the right concerned, which should influence the interpretation of the Directive. He wrote:

in proceedings concerned with the nature and scope of a fundamental right, the relevant statements of the Charter cannot be ignored; in particular, we cannot ignore its clear purpose of serving, where its provisions so allow, as a substantive point of reference for all those involved—Member States, institutions, natural and legal persons—in the Community context. Accordingly, I consider that the Charter provides us with the most reliable and definitive confirmation of the fact that the right to paid annual leave constitutes a fundamental right.[72]

The improvement of this constitutional protection within the Union by the adoption of a catalogue of fundamental rights including social rights—and the precise consequences which will flow from the inclusion of the Charter in the Treaty establishing a Constitution for Europe for the status of fundamental social rights in the Union—makes the accession of the Union to the ESC more likely. If the Union already ensures protection for social rights, it will be easier for it to accept international obligations imposing the same protection.

D. *The Impact of the Accession of the Union to the ECHR*

Having failed to seize the opportunities created by the inter-governmental conferences of 1996–1997 and 1999–2000 for the revision of the treaties, which led respectively to the treaties of Amsterdam and of Nice,[73] the Heads of State and Government agreed, in adopting the Treaty establishing a Constitution for Europe, to provide a legal basis for the accession of the Union to the ECHR.[74]

---

based on the fact that a person is of one or other sex. In view of its purpose and the nature of the rights which it seeks to safeguard, the scope of the directive is also such as to apply to discrimination arising, as in this case, from the gender reassignment of the person concerned' (at para. 19).

[71] Council Dir. 93/104/EC of 23 November 1993 concerning certain aspects of the organization of working time (the 'Working Time Directive') (OJ 1993 L307/18). One phrase in the directive has been annulled by the ECJ at the request of the UK, which considered that the directive could not be described as founded on Art. 118A EC (now, after amendment, Art. 137 EC). See Case C-84/94, *UK v. Council* [1996] ECR I-5755.

[72] Opinion of 8 February 2001 in Case C-173/99, *BECTU, supra* n. 19, at para. 28.

[73] In the course of the negotiations which resulted in a political agreement at the European Summit of Nice in 2000, the representatives of the Member States failed to agree on a proposal from Finland designed to confer on the European Community the competence to accede to the ECHR. See the document of the Finnish Delegation to the IGC: CONFER 4775/00 of 22 September 2000, 'Competence to accede to the European Convention for the Protection of Human Rights and Fundamental Freedoms'.

[74] This was required by the Opinion delivered by the European Court of Justice on 28 March 1996, concluding that the European Community could not rely on its implicit powers in order to accede to the ECHR, because of what the Court called the 'constitutional significance' of such a change in the regime of protection of human rights in the legal order of the Community. See Opinion

The Constitution provides in Article I-9(2) that '[t]he Union shall accede to the European Convention for the Protection of Human Rights and Fundamental Freedoms. Such accession shall not affect the Union's competences as defined in the Constitution.' The Member States of the Council of Europe have also given a clear political signal in that direction, by the adoption on 13 May 2004 of Protocol No. 14 to the ECHR, which contains a clause authorizing the accession of the Union to the ECHR,[75] the technical modalities of which, in any event, remain to be negotiated and will lead to the preparation of another Protocol amending the ECHR.

This perspective makes it even more urgent to re-examine the question of the accession of the Union to the ESC. The complementarity of these two major instruments of the Council of Europe illustrates the principle of the interdependence and indivisibility of human rights. It would be unfortunate, on a symbolic level, if these two instruments were divorced, and were treated differently by the Union. Indeed, it has been generally recognized that one of the principal merits of the EU Charter of Fundamental Rights was to combine in one single instrument different categories of fundamental rights which, too often, have been treated separately. Accession of the Union to the ECHR without any gesture being made in the direction of the accession of the Union to the (Rev)ESC would risk being interpreted as a new mark of the Union's lack of commitment to social rights. The political risk is real.

IV. THE QUESTION OF THE EXTERNAL POWERS OF THE EU

Both the European Community and the EU are to be considered as having international legal personality.[76] However, in the absence of a general power of the

---

2/94 [1996] ECR I-1759. The Court stated in that Opinion that the Community institutions do not have at their disposal a 'general power to enact rules on human rights or to conclude international conventions in this field', although it did not question that respect for human rights constituted a 'condition of lawfulness of Community acts': see paras. 27 and 34. On this Opinion, see, *inter alia*, De Schutter and Lejeune, 'L'adhésion de la Communauté européenne à la Convention européenne des droits de l'homme. A propos de l'avis 2/94 de la Cour de justice des Communautés européennes' [1996] *Cahiers de droit européen* 555; Gaja, 'Opinion 2/94', 33 CMLRev. (1996) 973.

[75] Protocol 14 to the ECHR, amending the control system of the Convention, Art. 17 (amending the existing Art. 59 ECHR).

[76] The Treaty of Rome attributes such international legal personality to the EC: see Art. 281 EC (ex Art. 210 EC Treaty). With respect to the Union, this personality derives from the competence which it has had since the entry into force of the Treaty of Amsterdam on 1 May 1999, in Art. 24 EU, to conclude international agreements with states or international organizations. Such agreements bind the Union as such, and not merely the Member States acting together in the framework of the EU Treaty; indeed the State which abstains from voting in the Council when the latter concludes an international agreement can make a formal declaration, in which case 'it shall not be obliged to apply the decision, *but shall accept that the decision commits the Union*' (Art. 23(1)(2) EU) (emphasis added). The existence of such competence to conclude international agreements suffices to create the international legal personality. There is no requirement of a formal attribution of such personality, for

Community or the Union in the field of fundamental rights,[77] the limits imposed on the exercise of its international powers are a serious obstacle to its accession to international instruments for the protection of human rights. It is, nevertheless, submitted that, even under the current definition of the external powers of the Union, accession to the (Rev)ESC cannot be ruled out. The process of constitutionalization of the law of the Union calls, in any event, for a renewed reflection on the relationship of the Union with the international law of human rights. It should be emphasized that the explicit attribution to the Union, in the Treaty establishing a Constitution for Europe, of a power to accede to the ECHR—rather than, generally, to international human rights instruments—cannot lead to a reading *a contrario*: the *travaux préparatoires* make it clear that the accession of the Union to other international human rights instruments may not be excluded, under the general principles regulating the exercise of external powers by the Union.[78]

A. The Implied External Powers of the EU

Of course, the external competences of the Union remain regulated, as are its internal competences, by the principle of conferral.[79] However, the competence of the Union to conclude international agreements, like that of the European Community, 'arises not only from an express conferment by the Treaty . . . but may equally flow from other provisions of the Treaty and from measures adopted, within the framework of those provisions, by the Community institutions'.[80] The existence of an implied external competence of the EC today is admitted either where it corresponds to internal competences of the Community (first hypothesis) or where the conclusion by the Community of an international agreement appears necessary to attain, in the course of the operation of the common market, one of the objectives of the Community as defined by the Treaty (second hypothesis).

The first hypothesis corresponds to the idea, expressed in the *ERTA* case of 1971, that 'with regard to the implementation of the provisions of the Treaty the system of internal Community measures may not . . . be separated from that of external relations'.[81] Therefore, 'whenever Community law has created for the institutions of the Community powers within its internal system for the purpose of attaining a specific objective, the Community has the authority to enter into the international commitments necessary for the attainment of that objective even in

---

instance, in the act constituting the international organization: see ICJ, *Opinion relating to Reparation for Injuries Incurred in the Service of the United Nations* [1949] ICJ Rep 174.

[77] See Opinion 2/94, *supra* n. 74, at para. 20.

[78] See in particular the commentary to what was then Art. 7 of the Draft Constitution for Europe as discussed within the European Convention: CONV 724/03, Annex 2, Draft text with commentaries, at 58.   [79] See Art. I-11(1) of the Treaty establishing a Constitution for Europe.

[80] See Case 22/70, *Commission v. Council (European Road Transport Agreement)* [1971] ECR 265, at para. 16.   [81] Ibid., at para. 19.

the absence of an express provision in that connexion'.[82] This is the case either when the internal power 'has already been used in order to adopt measures which fall within the attainment of common policies', or, even in the absence of such internal measures, 'in so far as the participation of the Community in the international agreement is . . . necessary for the objectives of the Community'.[83] Transposed to the question of the accession of the EU to the ESC, this doctrine implies that the existence of an implied external competence may be deduced from the adoption by the European Community of a number of acts which seek to implement the rights figuring in the (Rev)ESC. The views of the European Court of Justice on the subject of the competence of the Community to accede to ILO Convention No. 170 concerning safety in the use of chemicals at work are transposable: in so far as the Community has been given certain powers to adopt measures aiming at the protection of the rights of workers within the Community, the corresponding external powers must also be recognized.[84] Article 136 EC states that the Community and the Member States, 'having in mind fundamental social rights such as those set out in the European Social Charter signed at Turin on 18 October 1961 and in the 1989 Community Charter of the Fundamental Social Rights of Workers, shall have as their objectives the promotion of employment, improved living and working conditions, so as to make possible their harmonisation while the improvement is being maintained, proper social protection, dialogue between management and labour, the development of human resources with a view to lasting high employment and the combating of exclusion'. Article 137(2)(b) EC—which was amended by the Treaty of Nice in order to introduce the open method of coordination in the social field—provides that, in order to fulfil these objectives, directives may be adopted in certain areas, imposing minimum requirements for gradual implementation. A number of the directives adopted on that legal basis in fact implement rights recognized in the (Rev)ESC. These provisions have in substance been retained in the Treaty establishing a Constitution for Europe, respectively at Articles III-209 and III-210(2)(b). This clearly favours transposing the *ERTA* doctrine in the field of fundamental social rights of workers.

The second hypothesis is based on the use of Article 308 EC (ex Article 235 EC Treaty) on the implied powers of the Community, which provides that the Council, acting unanimously, can take the necessary measures '[i]f action by the Community should prove necessary to attain, in the course of the operation of the common market, one of the objectives of the Community, and [the EC Treaty] has not afforded the necessary powers . . .'.[85] Currently, Article 2 EC lists

---

[82] See Opinion 1/76 (Draft Agreement establishing a European laying-up fund for inland waterway vessels) [1977] ECR 741, at para. 3.   [83] Ibid., at para. 4.

[84] See Opinion 2/91 (Convention No. 170 of the International Labour Organization concerning safety in the use of chemicals at work) [1993] ECR I-1061, at paras. 14–17.

[85] On the use of the provision in such context see Opinion 2/92 (Power of the Community or of One of its Institutions to Participate in the Third Revised Decision of the OECD Council on National Treatment) [1995] ECR I-521.

among the objectives of the Community, *inter alia*, 'a high level of employment and of social protection, equality between men and women, . . . the raising of the standard of living and quality of life, and economic and social cohesion and solidarity among Member States', all of which demonstrate clear links to the rights protected under the (Rev)ESC. Under the European Constitution, the use of the flexibility clause[86] in order to adopt measures promoting fundamental rights will be facilitated in so far as 'equality, the rule of law and respect for human rights' are cited among the values of the Union (Article I-2), and the Union has among its objectives as listed in Article I-3 the promotion of those values.[87]

The Constitutional Treaty confirms this reading in Article III-323(1):

The Union may conclude an agreement with one or more third countries or international organisations where the Constitution so provides or *where the conclusion of an agreement is necessary in order to achieve, within the framework of the Union's policies, one of the objectives referred to in the Constitution*, or is provided for in a legally binding Union act or is likely to affect common rules or alter their scope. (Emphasis added.)

The constitutional obstacle which the European Court of Justice identified in its Opinion 2/94 of 28 March 1996 to the use of the implied powers clause in order to achieve the accession of the European Community to the ECHR may not be presumed to apply with equal weight to the envisaged accession to the (Rev)ESC. The 'constitutional significance' of the accession which was then envisaged resulted, in the view of the Court, from the fact that the European Community would be subordinated to a precise institutional system, comprising a Court having the competence to deliver enforceable judgments, and undertakings in the context of a treaty the provisions of which were generally recognized as having direct effect, resulting in their assimilation—without complementary execution measures adopted by the Union legislature—to Community law. Opinion 2/94 of 28 March 1996 rules out the use of Article 235 of the EC Treaty (now Article 308 EC) in order to achieve this accession, in so far as it would entail:

a substantial change of the current regime for the protection of human rights, in that it would comprise the insertion of the Community in a distinct international institutional system as well as the integration of all the provisions of the Convention in the Community legal order. Such a modification of the human rights protection regime in the Community, whose institutional implications would be fundamental for both the Community and its Member States, would be of constitutional significance and would by its nature go beyond the limits of Article 235 [now Article 308 EC]. It could only be achieved by the means of a modification of the Treaty.

---

[86] See Art. I-18 of the Constitution.

[87] Moreover, among the objectives of the Union Art. I-3(3) mentions in particular 'a highly competitive social market economy, aiming at full employment and social progress', and states further that the Union 'shall combat social exclusion and discrimination, and shall promote social justice and protection, equality between women and men, solidarity between generations and protection of the rights of the child'.

Whatever the validity of the argument raised against the use of the flexibility clause in order to realize the accession to the ECHR, it does not seem that accession to the (Rev)ESC by means of that clause would meet the same constitutional objection. The provisions of the (Rev)ESC do not pretend to be directly applicable in the internal legal orders of the contracting parties, and there is nothing to suggest that the Union legal order would be more generous in its recognition of a direct effect to the provisions of the Charter than have been the national legal orders, which are generally hostile to such recognition. The supervisory powers which the European Committee of Social Rights exercises by examining the reports periodically submitted by the States Parties, although they can lead to recommendations by the Committee of Ministers of the Council of Europe, do not have an authority comparable to that of binding judgments. As for the collective complaints mechanism, provided the EU chooses to accept it at the moment of its accession to the (Rev)ESC, it may not change this situation in any fundamental way. The common view still is that expressed in the report submitted to the Foreign Affairs Committee of the French Senate by A. Boyer,[88] according to which 'the introduction of a right of collective complaints affects only the method of prompting supervision without calling into question the conditions under which this supervision shall be exercised. Indeed, the final decision still remains in the hands of a political organ, the Committee of Ministers, called upon to adopt a decision based primarily on considerations of political opportunity. The recommendations adopted will not obviously have any legally binding character. The supervision procedure of the European Social Charter and that of the European Convention on Human Rights therefore have nothing in common.' Although this view is, in fact, hardly tenable, it nevertheless does illustrate the general perception, still dominant at least in the world of politics, that supervisory procedures in the field of internationally protected social and economic rights cannot be truly assimilated to adjudicatory procedures, as these rights are not really rights at all, but rather objectives expressed to be desirable on the international plane. Whether well founded or not, however, this perception, although not a decisive element in its own right, does suggest that the obstacle identified by Opinion 2/94 of the Court with respect to the accession of the European Community to the ECHR may not have the same weight here, because the constitutional implications of accession to the (Rev)ESC may not be compared to those of the accession to the ECHR, even if it is combined with accession to the Collective Complaints Protocol.

More fundamentally, perhaps, it may be worth questioning the adequacy of the classical case law of the European Court of Justice on the extent of the Community's external powers, where the question of accession to an international

---

[88] Report 160 (98–99). This report contributed to what became Act 99–173 of 10 March 1999 authorizing the approval of the Additional Protocol to the ESC providing for a system of collective complaints [1999] *Journal Officiel de la République Française* 3631.

instrument protecting human rights is raised. By acceding to such instruments the States Parties undertake to respect certain minimum standards for the benefit of the people under their jurisdiction, which implies in the first place that they will not adopt any measures which violate these standards. In so far as the undertaking is purely negative (formulated as an obligation to abstain from), it is irrelevant whether or not the parties have the competence to take measures which implement the given standard. It is only where the undertaking is also to adopt certain measures—to fulfil positive obligations (to act)—that the question of competences may play a role. The accession of the Union to international instruments adopted in the field of human rights does not necessarily have to have an impact on the extent of its competences. Quite the contrary; such accession must in principle be considered neutral from the point of view of the division of competences between the Union and the Member States.[89] If necessary, a specific clause could record this neutrality.[90] This, however, results from the very principle of attributed competences, according to which the Union cannot exercise competences which it has not been given by the Member States, even for the sake of better complying with obligations the Union has undertaken on the international plane.

B. *The Absence of an Exclusive External Power of the EU*

Even if it were to be admitted, the existence of a competence of the Union to accede to the (Rev)ESC ought not to be confused with the *exclusive* character of such competence. The progress which the Union has made in social matters naturally does not imply that it should be recognized as having a competence *exclusive* from that of the Member States to accede to an instrument such as the (Rev)ESC. This would only be the case if, by ratifying the (Rev)ESC—or, previously, the ESC—the Member States would be affecting the acts adopted in the framework of the Union under what is now Article 137 EC and what will be Article III-210 of the European Constitution.[91] This is not the case, however. Indeed, there is no conflict between the two groups of rules, which only impose certain minimal

---

[89] *Mutatis mutandis*, Art. 28 of the International Covenant on Economic, Social and Cultural Rights (ICESCR), for instance, adopted by the UN General Assembly on 16 December 1966 (Res. 2200 A (XXI)) states that '[t]he provisions of the present Covenant shall extend to all parts of federal States without any limitations or exceptions'. This provision, however, cannot be construed as having the effect of investing the federative entities within each state with competences which those entities are denied under the constitutional organization of their state.

[90] Such clause could seek inspiration from Art. I-9(2), 2nd sentence, of the Treaty establishing a Constitution for Europe, which says that the accession of the Union to the ECHR 'shall not affect the Union's competences as defined in the Constitution'. It could also be formulated along the lines of Art. 51 of the Charter of Fundamental Rights.

[91] Under this provision, framework laws may be adopted in certain defined fields in order to achieve the objectives identified in Art. III-209 for the Union and the Member States, 'having in mind fundamental social rights such as those set out in the European Social Charter signed at Turin on 18 October 1961 and in the 1989 Community Charter of the Fundamental Social Rights of Workers'.

levels of protection, leaving to the individual states the freedom to take measures raising the level of protection. Article H of the (Rev)ESC (relations between the Charter and domestic law or international agreements)[92] states that the Charter 'shall not prejudice the provisions of domestic law or of any bilateral or multilateral treaties, conventions or agreements . . . under which more favourable treatment would be accorded to the persons protected'. Article III-210 of the European Constitution, like Article 137 EC today, provides for the adoption by the Council of framework laws *imposing only minimum requirements*. On this point again the reasoning of the European Court of Justice in Opinion 2/91, delivered on the subject of the Community's competence to accede to ILO Convention No. 170, is transposable.[93]

We should, however, bear in mind, of course, that the guarantees of the (Rev)ESC transcend the domains listed in Article III-210 of the European Constitution, domains in which the Union may support and complement the action of the Member States, particularly by the adoption of European framework laws imposing minimum requirements. Thus, for instance, Article 11 of the (Rev)ESC guarantees the right to health protection. Regularly reiterating that, under Article 11(1) of the Revised Charter, national health systems must respond appropriately to avoidable health risks (that is risks that can be controlled by human action) and must guarantee the best possible results,[94] the European Committee of Social Rights requests from the States Parties who have accepted this provision, information about the legislative framework concerning nutrition prophylaxis, production, transport, commercialization, and labelling of food products, including those for newborn children, veterinary prophylaxis and infectious diseases of livestock, slaughterhouses, and conservation of meat and fish stocks, or use of phytosanitary products. It inquires, in particular, about measures to counteract the outbreaks of such diseases as New Variant Creutzfeldt–Jakob disease and the emergence of new food products derived from biotechnology.[95] The Committee also requests information about the wording and the size of warning inscriptions on tobacco products.[96] It is clear that the requirements developed in the jurisprudence of the Committee in a field such as public health may, for example, affect the rules adopted within the Union concerning the use of genetically modified micro-organisms,[97] product safety,[98] or the sale of tobacco products,[99] in the form of harmonization measures which go further than the imposition of minimum requirements.

---

[92] Corresponding to Art. 32 ESC.   [93] Opinion 2/91, *supra* n. 84, at para. 18.

[94] *Conclusions 2003-1*, at 146 (France).   [95] *Conclusions 2003-1*, at 285 (Italy).

[96] *Conclusions 2003-1*, at 395 (Romania).

[97] See Directive 2001/18/EC of the European Parliament and of the Council of 12 March 2001 on the deliberate release into the environment of genetically modified organisms and repealing Council Directive 90/220/EEC, OJ 2001 L106/1.

[98] Directive 2001/95/EC of the European Parliament and of the Council of 3 December 2001 on general product safety, OJ 2002 L11/4.

[99] See Directive 2001/37/EC of the European Parliament and of the Council of 5 June 2001 on the approximation of the laws, regulations and administrative provisions of the Member States

The ECJ encountered this difficulty in its Opinion 2/91.[100] Indeed, some of the undertakings imposed by ILO Convention No. 170 were covered by directives adopted by the European Community on the basis of provisions of the Treaty of Rome providing for the possibility of approximating the national legislations with a view to the establishment of the internal market.[101] Moreover these directives—in contrast to social directives based on ex Article 118 of the EC Treaty (now Article 137 EC)—are adopted 'with a view to achieving an ever greater degree of harmonization and designed, on the one hand, to remove barriers to trade resulting from differences in legislation from one Member State to another and, on the other hand, to provide, at the same time, protection for human health and the environment'.[102] The Court deduced from this that: 'In those circumstances, it must be considered that the commitments arising from Part III of Convention No. 170, falling within the area covered by [such] directives . . . , are of such a kind as to affect the Community rules laid down in those directives and that consequently Member States cannot undertake such commitments outside the framework of the Community institutions.'[103] In the operative part of its Opinion, the Court reasoned that 'the conclusion of ILO Convention No 170 is a matter which falls within the joint competence of the Member States and the Community' (at paragraph 39). According to the Court, the cooperation which is required between the Member States and the Community and which is imposed in the context of an agreement or a convention which falls in part under the competence of the Community and in part under that of the Member States extends to 'the implementation of commitments resulting from that Convention' (at paragraph 38).

C. Conclusions

In the current situation, the Union Member States carry out the obligations imposed on them by the ESC or its revised version in the absence of any coordination—in this specific context—between them and the EU. This situation constitutes an anomaly. The accession of the Union to the (Rev)ESC would constitute the most satisfactory answer to this anomaly. Until such accession is envisaged, better coordination between the Member States and the EU seems to be required. This development would merely be a recognition, in the field of external relations, of

concerning the manufacture, presentation and sale of tobacco products (OJ 2001 L194/26) and, on the use of Art. 95 EC as the legal basis chosen for the adoption of this Directive, the judgment of 10 December 2002 in *British American Tobacco, supra* n. 12.

[100]   See *supra* n. 84.

[101]   The applicable provisions were Arts. 100 and 100A of the EC Treaty, now Arts. 94 and 95 EC. Art. III-172 of the European Constitution now provides that 'European laws or framework laws shall establish measures for the approximation of the provisions laid down by law, regulation or administrative action in Member States which have as their object the establishment and functioning of the internal market', under the conditions and according to the procedures it defines.

[102]   Opinion 2/91, *supra* n. 84, at para. 25.   [103]   Ibid., at para. 26.

the expansion in the category of shared competences between the Union and the Member States, which the European Constitution defines as residuary in its delineation of the different categories of competences.[104]

V. THE QUESTION OF THE LIMITED SCOPE OF APPLICATION OF UNION LAW

A second objection which the scenario of accession may raise is that it will result in extending the powers of the EU in the fields covered by the (Rev)ESC, or in a creeping extension of the scope of application of EU law, which the institutions— particularly the European Commission—may be tempted to justify by the need fully to implement the requirements of the revised Charter. This fear, however, is based on a misunderstanding. The accession of the Union to the (Rev)ESC would imply that, in the international legal order, the Union accepts as the aim of its policy in the fields covered by the Charter the attainment of the conditions in which the rights and principles listed in the (Rev)ESC may effectively be realized[105] and that it agrees to comply with a certain number of provisions of that instrument.[106] These undertakings ought not, without infringing the principle of conferral[107] and that of speciality of the Union—which, as an international organization, differentiates itself in this regard from a state[108]—invest the Union with new competences or tasks. Neither should these undertakings result in an extension of the scope of the law of the Union.

However, to the extent that they act within the sphere of application of Union law, the Member States will be under an obligation to respect the rights and principles of the revised Charter that the Union will have agreed to. Inspired by current Article 300(7) EC (ex Article 228(7) of the EC Treaty), Article III-323(2) of the European Constitution provides that '[a]greements concluded by the Union are binding on the institutions of the Union and on its Member States'.[109]

---

[104] See Art. I-14(1) of the European Constitution, according to which '[t]he Union shall share competence with the Member States where the Constitution confers on it a competence which does not relate to the areas referred to in Articles I-13 [exclusive competences of the Union] and I-17 [categories of supporting, coordinating or complementary actions]'. On this link and this development see Dehousse and Maczkovics, 'Les arrêts *open skies* de la Cour de justice: l'abandon de la competence externe implicite de la Communauté?', *JTDE* (2003), at 236.   [105] Part I of the (Rev)ESC.

[106] Appearing among the Arts. forming Part II of the (Rev)ESC.

[107] Art. I-11(2) of the European Constitution states: '[u]nder the principle of conferral, the Union shall act within the limits of the competences conferred upon it by the Member States in the Constitution to attain the objectives set out in the Constitution. Competences not conferred upon the Union in the Constitution remain with the Member States.'

[108] N. Bernard, 'A "New Governance" Approach to Economic, Social and Cultural Rights in the EU', in T. Hervey and J. Kenner (eds), *Economic and Social Rights under the EU Charter of Fundamental Rights* (2003), at 247 and 248.

[109] In the terms of Art. 300(7) EC '[a]greements concluded under the conditions set out in this Article shall be binding on the institutions of the Community and on Member States'. Although

But the undertakings given by the Union in the context of the (Rev)ESC will be obligatory as far as the Member States are concerned *only in the sphere of application of the law of the Union*. A violation by a Member State of any provision of the (Rev)ESC which has been accepted by the Union shall not be considered a violation of the obligations of that state under Union law, unless it is acting under Union law in the adoption of the particular behaviour or act which creates the violation. The situation of the Member States vis-à-vis the (Rev)ESC shall not be affected by the accession of the Union in situations which present no link to Union law. In fact, the question is exactly the same as that raised by the perspective of the accession of the Union to the ECHR: although the EU Member States may have differing undertakings under the ECHR (they have not, for example, all ratified all the additional protocols to the Convention), these undertakings will not be expanded by reason of the accession of the Union, because the states will be bound by the undertakings of the Union only where they act under Union law, *not* in situations which are unconnected to Union law.[110] The Protocol amending the (Rev)ESC in order to authorize the accession of the Union could contain a specific provision on this point, with a view to clarifying any ambiguity that might still remain. Such provision could be based on the model furnished by the 'field of application' provision of the Charter of Fundamental Rights.[111] It would read:

The provisions of the Revised European Social Charter which are accepted by the Union are addressed to the institutions, bodies, offices and agencies of the Union with due regard for the principle of subsidiarity and to the Member States only when they are implementing Union law. They shall therefore respect the rights and observe the principles set out in Part II of the Revised European Social Charter[112] and promote the application thereof in

under Art. 24(5) EU, as amended by the Treaty of Nice, no agreement will be binding on a Member State whose representative in the Council states that it has to comply with the requirements of its own constitutional procedure, the principle according to which the Union's undertaking binds the institutions of the Union and the Member States is equally applicable in this context. Moreover, the principle of loyal cooperation implies that even the states not bound by the agreement should abstain from putting obstacles in the way of the Union conforming to it.

[110] The question is posed in a similar manner to that which was put forward by the UK in 1993–1996, when the question of the accession of the EC to the ECHR was revived under the Belgian presidency of the Union of 1993. The UK did not at the time acknowledge the direct applicability of the ECHR before its national courts, a situation which has since been remedied in part by the adoption of the Human Rights Act 1998. The UK authorities therefore expressed the fear that accession by the Community would have the effect of leading it to impose the recognition of the direct applicability of the ECHR on the national legal order of the UK, in so far as the ECHR, becoming part of EU law, would be recognized as having a status equivalent to that accorded to Community law by virtue of the European Communities Act 1972. In reality, this argument (known as the 'back door argument') misunderstood that the ECHR, obligatory for the Community as for its Member States (Art. 228(7) of the EC Treaty, now Art. 300(7) EC), could be invoked only in the sphere of application of Community law.

[111] Art. 51 of the Charter, Art. II-111 of the European Constitution.

[112] It should be noted that the (Rev)ESC refers to the rights and principles it contains, using terminology similar in that respect to that of the EU Charter of Fundamental Rights itself.

accordance with their respective powers and respecting the limits of the powers of the Union as conferred on it in the European Constitution.

The accession of the Union to this Charter does not extend the field of application of Union law beyond the powers of the Union or establish any new power or task for the Union, or modify powers and tasks defined in the European Constitution.

An important proviso must be made, however. Even if such a clause is inserted into the Protocol providing for the accession of the Union to the (Rev)ESC, this does not imply that such accession will not have an impact on the way the Union exercises the powers attributed to it by the Member States, and which it may use in order to implement the Charter. It is one thing to say that accession will not confer new powers upon the Union, or impose new tasks on it; it is quite another to say that it will have no influence on the exercise by the Union of the powers it has been given—and there may well be such an influence. Indeed, the examples given in the introduction to this chapter are based on the premise that, where certain powers have been conferred upon the Union which it may exercise in order to contribute to the protection of the rights in the (Rev)ESC, the Union may be under an obligation, in well-defined circumstances, to exercise those powers for that purpose. After the Union has acceded to the Charter, it will, of course, be under an obligation to respect the rights the latter contains. However, those rights should also be protected and promoted, in so far as the institutions of the Union remain, by ensuring that they are effectively guaranteed, within the limits of the powers which have been attributed to those institutions.[113]

This admittedly is an audacious proposition, the risks of which cannot be underestimated. For instance, on the basis of Article 13 EC, the Council has adopted Directives 2000/43/EC[114] and 2000/78/EC,[115] which prohibit direct and indirect discrimination based on age, religion, or belief, and age, disability, and sexual orientation in the fields of employment and occupation and prohibit discrimination an grounds of race or ethnic origin even beyond these fields. These are remarkable instruments, arguably among the most important pieces of secondary legislation adopted at Union level in order to implement fundamental rights. In certain respects, however, they remain under the protection from discrimination imposed under the ESC. Although Article 1(2) of the Charter explicitly refers only to an obligation to 'protect effectively the right of the

---

[113] This deliberately paraphrases the wording of the same question by Working Group II, 'Incorporation of the Charter/accession to the ECHR', in the European Convention. See the Final Report of Working Group II, WG II 16, CONV 354/02, 22 October 2002, at 13, on the consequences which could result from the accession of the Union to the ECHR: ' "positive" obligations of the Union to take action to comply with the ECHR would arise only to the extent to which competences of the Union permitting such action exist under the Treaty'.

[114] Directive of 29 June 2000 implementing the principle of equal treatment between persons irrespective of racial or ethnic origin, OJ 2000 L180/22.

[115] Directive of 27 November 2000 establishing a general framework for equal treatment in employment and occupation, OJ 2000 L303/16.

worker to earn his living in an occupation freely entered upon', the European Committee of Social Rights has interpreted this provision as imposing on the states which have accepted it an obligation to protect all beneficiaries[116] from discrimination in employment either on all grounds or, at least, on the grounds of political opinion, religion, race, language, sex, age, and health.[117] The Committee mentions a number of measures which should be encouraged because, in its own words, they 'promote the full effectiveness of the efforts to combat discrimination according to Article 1 § 2 of the Revised Charter'. Thus, the states bound by this provision should in that respect recognize 'the right of trade unions to take action in cases of discrimination in employment, including on behalf of individuals'. They should allow for 'the possibility of collective action by groups with an interest in obtaining a ruling that the prohibition of discrimination has been violated'.[118] They should also set up a specialized body to 'promote, independently, equal treatment, especially by providing discrimination victims with the support they need to take proceedings'.[119] Moreover, in the view of the Committee, legal measures may not be enough: concrete measures should, moreover, be taken in order to encourage full equal treatment in employment.[120] All these requirements transcend those set as minimum requirements by the Equal Treatment Directives.

We may note also, for instance, that Council Directive 2000/78/EC prohibits discrimination on grounds of disability in employment and an occupation. But under the (Rev)ESC more is required. When the revised Charter was adopted, Article 15 was amended in order to reinforce the right to independence, social

---

[116] See the Appendix to the Social Charter, 'Scope of the Social Charter in terms of persons protected'. Foreigners are included under the substantive provisions of the Charter 'only insofar as they are nationals of other Contracting Parties lawfully resident or working regularly within the territory of the Contracting Party concerned'.

[117] In recent Conclusions relating to Italy, the European Committee of Social Rights examined the provisions which protect workers from discrimination in employment in the Italian legal system. Finding that neither Art. 3 of the Constitution nor Art. 15 of Act No. 300/1970 (the Workers' Statute)—which prohibits any agreement or act discriminating against a worker because of his or her political opinions, religion, race, language or sex—offer protection against discrimination based on age or health, the ECSR concluded that this omission should be remedied under para. 2 of Art. 1 of the Charter (*Conclusions 2002* (Italy), at 75). In its Conclusions relating to Romania on the same provision of the Charter and during the same cycle of supervision, the ECSR noted expressly that health-based discrimination was prohibited in the Romanian legal system, despite not being explicitly mentioned in the applicable regulations (*Conclusions 2002* (Romania), at 117–21).

[118] See *Conclusions 2002* (Italy), at 75.   [119] *Conclusions 2002* (Slovenia), at 174–76.

[120] In its first conclusions on Italy, the Committee of Independent Experts noted 'regretfully' that it has been 'unable to find in the first report of the Italian Government sufficient particulars on the admission of women to certain posts, notably in the civil service; it considered that the rights guaranteed by the Charter, especially in the matter of non-discrimination against women, required not only that the State remove all legal obstacles to admission to certain types of employment, but also that positive, practical steps be taken to create a situation which really ensured complete equality of treatment in this respect': *Conclusions I* (released on 1 January 1970), at 15–16. See also the Conclusions adopted during that same supervision cycle on the UK: *Conclusions I*, at 16.

integration, and participation in the life of the community of persons with disabilities, and to move beyond an approach centred (in the 1961 version of that provision) on rehabilitation and social resettlement. Article 15(3) of the (Rev)ESC, which concerns the integration and participation of persons with disabilities in the life of the community, has been read by the European Committee of Social Rights as requiring the adoption of positive measures to achieve integration in housing, transport, telecommunications, and cultural and leisure facilities. As Article 15(3) of the (Rev)ESC refers to participation in normal life of persons with disabilities, the European Committee of Social Rights also requires that 'persons with disabilities and their representative organizations should be consulted in the design, and ongoing review of such positive action measures and that an appropriate forum should exist to enable this to happen'.[121] Moreover, Article 15(3) of the (Rev)ESC 'requires the existence of anti-discrimination (or similar) legislation covering both the public and the private sphere in the fields such as housing, transport, telecommunications, cultural and leisure activities, as well as effective remedies for those who have been unlawfully treated'.[122] Would it not be desirable for the Union, when it legislates in order to guarantee equal treatment to persons with disabilities, to take those requirements into account, in order to ensure that all the Member States—not all of whom are bound by Article 15 of the (Rev)ESC—comply with those standards? Once the Union has acceded to the (Rev)ESC, will it not be obligatory for the Union to do so?

The question whether positive obligations will be imposed on the basis of the (Rev)ESC after the accession of the Union may be a contentious one, although this would simply result from the assimilation of the ESC to the ECHR, with respect to the consequences flowing from the accession of the Union to these instruments. If the principle is agreed that positive obligations may be derived from the Charter, the question becomes that of the conditions under which such obligations may be imposed. If the Union and the Member States share competences in certain areas, in which circumstances should the Union act, in order to achieve the objective of implementing the (Rev)ESC? The principles of subsidiarity and proportionality will have to govern the allocation of tasks between the Member States and the Union. A decisive question for the future—which accession of the Union to the ECHR will oblige us to address in any event—is how these principles, relatively easy to apply where the objective is to establish an internal market in which fundamental freedoms of movement are guaranteed and in which competition is not distorted, are to be transposed to a situation in which the objective is that of the effective protection and promotion of fundamental rights.

---

[121] *Conclusions 2003-1*, at 168 (France—Art. 15(3)); *Conclusions 2003-1*, at 507 (Slovenia—Art. 15(3)).
[122] *Conclusions 2003-1*, at 170 (France—Art. 15(3)); *Conclusions 2003-1*, at 298 (Italy—Art. 15(3)); *Conclusions 2003-2*, at 508 (Slovenia—Art. 15(3)); *Conclusions 2003-2*, at 614 (Sweden—Art. 15(3)).

VI. THE IMPACT OF THE ACCESSION OF THE EU TO THE REVISED ESC

A. *The Principle: The Absence of Direct Effect*

According to the case law of the European Court of Justice, the provisions of international agreements concluded by the Union and the acts adopted by the organs set up under such agreements 'from the time of their entry into force form an integral part of the Community legal order'.[123] The result is that the legislation of the Union, like the national laws of the Member States, must take into account the provisions of such agreements, the European Court of Justice having the jurisdiction to ensure that they are respected.[124] The manner in which the national legal order of each Member State defines its relationships with public international law is in this respect immaterial: uniform application of the agreement throughout the Union rules out the ability of each Member State to view the effects of an international agreement in terms of its own national law. The Court of Justice indicated in the *Kupferberg* judgment of 26 October 1982 that this was the result of the Community nature of the provisions contained in an international agreement concluded by the Community, which, from the time of its entry into force, becomes part of Community law. The uniform application throughout the Community of the provisions of such an international agreement prevents their effects from being made to vary according to whether their application is a matter, in practice, for the Community institutions or for the Member States, and, in the latter case, according to the attitude of each state to the effects accorded to international agreements.[125]

In order for an international agreement concluded by the Union to produce direct effects, however—giving litigants subjective rights which they can invoke before their national authorities or before a Community Court—'the spirit, the economy and the terms' of the agreement must be examined.[126] In the case relating to the common organization of the market in bananas and its compatibility with the General Agreement on Tariffs and Trade (GATT), the Court thus concluded that this Agreement was characterized by 'the great flexibility of its provisions, in particular those conferring the possibility of derogation, the measures to be taken when confronted with exceptional difficulties and the settlement of conflicts between the contracting parties',[127] and that, therefore, the GATT could

---

[123] Opinion 1/91 (Draft agreement between the Community, on the one hand, and the countries of the European Free Trade Association, on the other, relating to the creation of the European Economic Area) [1991] ECR I-6079, at para. 37.

[124] On this point see in particular Lenaerts and De Smijter, 'Some Reflections on the Status of International Agreements in the Community Legal Order', in G. C. Rodriguez Iglesias et al., *Mélanges en hommage à Fernand Schockweiler* (1999), at 347.

[125] Case 104/81, *Kupferberg* [1982] ECR 3641, at para. 14.

[126] See Case C-280/93, *Germany v. Council* [1994] ECR I-3641, at para. 14.

[127] Ibid., at para. 106.

neither be invoked by an individual within the Community in order to challenge the lawfulness of a Community act, nor be relied upon by the Court in order to assess the lawfulness of a regulation in an action brought by a Member State for the annulment of a Community act. This same conclusion would probably be reached with regard to the (Rev)ESC. Article I of the Charter, which concerns the 'implementation of the undertakings given', clearly indicates that complementary measures of execution, by legislation, by the conclusion of collective agreements, or by 'other appropriate means', are required before the provisions of the Charter can be invoked before national courts. The Charter does not, moreover, impose on the parties a requirement that they guarantee an effective remedy to individuals protected who allege that the rights given to them in the Charter have been violated.[128] According to the Appendix to the Charter, which forms an integral part of it,[129] 'it is understood that the Charter contains *legal obligations of an international character*, the application of which is submitted solely to the supervision provided for in Part IV thereof [which refers in turn to the supervisory mechanism of the European Social Charter, as well as to the Additional Protocol to the European Social Charter providing for a system of collective complaints]'. In principle, as intended by its authors, the provisions of the Charter are not aimed at giving individuals subjective rights which can be given effect to before national authorities, and in particular before the national courts. From this point of view, 'the spirit, the economy and the terms' of the (Rev)ESC are comparable to those of the GATT, and the same legal consequences should in principle be attached to them.

The Court of Justice attaches particular weight to any indications in the text itself of an international agreement the Union's accession to which is envisaged. The Court in fact holds generally that, in order to determine the effects which the Community legal order may recognize the provisions of an agreement concluded by the Community with a third State as having, the intention of the authors of the treaty should play a decisive role, 'in conformity with the principles of public international law':

Community institutions which have power to negotiate and conclude an agreement with a non-member country are free to agree with that country what effect the provisions of the agreement are to have in the internal legal order of the Contracting Parties. Only if that question has not been settled by the agreement does it fall for decision by the Courts having jurisdiction in the matter, and in particular by the Court of Justice within the framework of its juridiction under the Treaty, in the same manner as any question of interpretation relating to the application of the agreement in the Community.[130]

---

[128] Equally significant is the fact that the exhaustion of remedies available within the national legal order of the States Parties is not a condition of admissibility of the collective complaints lodged under the Additional Protocol to the ESC providing for a system of collective complaints.

[129] See Art. N of the (Rev)ESC (emphasis added).

[130] See Case 104/81, *Kupferberg, supra* n. 126, at point 17.

Therefore, the accession of the Union to the (Rev)ESC will not in general imply that individuals will be able to rely on the Charter in order, in particular, to seek the annulment of certain acts adopted by the Union which might be seen as violating the Charter. In three specific situations, however, they will be able to invoke the Charter. First, where the European Committee of Social Rights has identified certain situations of non-conformity with the requirements of the Charter, these findings may be relied upon directly. Secondly, the provisions of the Charter may be invoked against acts adopted by the Union when they seek to implement the obligations of the Union. Thirdly, where an act of the Union would refer explicitly to the European Social Charter, this reference may justify invoking that instrument in the context of an action for the annulment of that act, or in the context of an appreciation of its validity. The following paragraphs briefly explain each of these situations, in which the presumption that the (Rev)ESC is not recognized as having direct effect in the legal order of the Union, may be overcome.

B. *The Impact of the Findings of the European Committee of Social Rights*

In order to clarify the conditions under which, after it has been acceded to by the Union, individuals will be able to invoke the (Rev)ESC before the European Court of Justice, we should first consider the supervision mechanisms laid down by the ESC, to which Article C of the (Rev)ESC refers in its turn. This supervision is based on the appreciation by a committee of independent experts—the European Committee of Social Rights—of situations which are referred to it either by the Contracting Parties to the Charter, in the reports which the parties submit on a biennial basis in accordance with Articles 20 and 21 of the ESC, or by the authors of collective complaints under the Additional Protocol of 1995. The Governmental Committee reports to the Committee of Ministers of the Council of Europe on the basis of the conclusions reached by the European Committee of Social Rights upon its examination of the states' reports, which are 'positive' or 'negative' according to whether the situation described does or does not appear to conform to undertakings made by the party concerned. The Committee of Ministers, relying on the report made to it by the Governmental Committee, can address individual recommendations to the state whose laws or practices have been considered by the European Committee of Social Rights to be in violation of its obligations under the Charter. When dealing with a collective complaint, the European Committee of Social Rights may adopt a decision finding that a State Party has failed to comply with its obligations. It reports to the Committee of Ministers of the Council of Europe. Again, that body addresses an individual recommendation to the state found to be in violation.

At paragraph 39 of Opinion 1/91 (the 'First EEA Opinion'),[131] the European Court of Justice remarked that where an international agreement provides for its

---

[131] See *supra* n. 123.

own system of courts with jurisdiction to settle disputes between the Contracting Parties to the agreement, and, as a result, to interpret its provisions, the decisions of that court will be binding on the Community institutions, including the Court of Justice, which will also be bound by those decisions when it is called upon to rule on the interpretation of the international agreement, in so far as that agreement is an integral part of the Community legal order. The lesson from this Opinion is that where, by the conclusion of an international agreement comprising a mechanism for the judicial settlement of disputes, the Union has agreed to submit to the authority of this mechanism, the European Court of Justice—as part of its task to ensure that the law is respected in the legal order of the Union—is bound by the findings of the courts created by that agreement. The question whether 'the economy, the terms, and the spirit' of the international agreement justify recognizing its direct effect then becomes secondary to the obligation on the Union institutions, including the Court, to conform to the decisions delivered by the judicial system set up by the international agreement in issue. It is thus necessary to pose the question whether this reasoning can be transposed, *mutatis mutandis*, into the context of the (Rev)ESC, or whether the supervision procedures set up within the latter do not have a sufficiently 'judicial' character for the disputes which arise out of it to be considered obligatory for the European Court of Justice.

The recent case law of the Court demonstrates a clear tendency to enlarge the scope of situations in which it may examine the compatibility of legislative acts adopted by the Union or the Community where the Union or the Community is bound by an international agreement which sets up a judicial supervisory mechanism. In the two judgments of 30 September 2003 in the *Biret* cases,[132] although the Court refused to consider that a decision of the WTO Dispute Settlement Body could compensate in that instance for the lack of direct effect of the WTO rules as described above, it was clearly critical of the reasoning of the Court of First Instance, according to which there was an 'inescapable and direct link between the decision and the plea alleging infringement of the SPS Agreement [on the Application of Sanitary and Phytosanitary Measures]' and which considered therefore that the decision of the Dispute Settlement Body 'can only be taken into consideration if the Court had found that Agreement to have direct effect in the context of a plea alleging the invalidity of the directives in question [imposing on the Member States to prohibit the importation into the Community of beef and veal from farm animals to which certain substances with hormonal action had been administered]'.[133]

According to the European Court of Justice, a decision by an international court, binding upon the Union, may oblige the institutions of the Union, including

---

[132] Case C-93/02 P, *Biret International SA v. Council* [2003] ECR I-10497 (full Court), at paras. 55–59, and Case C-94/02 P, *Biret & Co v. Council* [2003] ECR I-10565 (full Court), at paras. 58–62.
[133] Case T-174/00, *Biret International SA v. Council* [2002] ECR II-17, at para. 67, and Case T-210/00, *Biret & Co v. Council* [2002] ECR II-47, at para. 77.

the Court of Justice, to apply it and, if necessary, to overcome their doubts about the direct applicability of the instrument which that court has authoritatively interpreted. It appears to be difficult to rely on the conclusions adopted by the European Committee of Social Rights on the basis of biennial reports submitted by States Parties in order to apply this doctrine.[134] However, this doctrine may play a role where the European Committee of Social Rights would arrive at a finding of non-conformity with the requirements of the Charter in the context of a decision adopted on the basis of a collective complaint filed against the Union, provided, of course, that, upon acceding to the ESC, the Union would also agree to being subjected to that particular control mechanism. Such a finding might encourage the Court of Justice to overcome its doubts about the direct applicability of the Charter: it might be seen to compensate, by its specificity, for the lack of precision of the Charter provisions being invoked against the Union.

The European Court of Justice's attitude to such a situation may not be easy to second-guess. After it has considered a collective complaint, the European Committee of Social Rights makes its 'legal assessment of the complaint'. It draws up a report containing this assessment, which is sent to the Committee of Ministers of the Council of Europe. The Committee of Ministers adopts a resolution on the basis of that report, and it 'must adopt a recommendation addressed to the state concerned' if the conclusions of the European Committee of Social Rights are negative. The Explanatory Report to the Additional Protocol on Collective Complaints makes it clear that the Committee of Ministers 'cannot reverse the legal assessment made by the Committee of Independent Experts [now named the European Committee on Social Rights]. However, its decision (resolution or recommendation) may be based on social and economic policy considerations.'[135] The intervention of the Committee of Ministers deprives the mechanism in part of the quasi-judicial character it would have if the European Committee of Social Rights were able to adopt a final decision on its own. Moreover, Article 12 of the Additional Protocol reaffirms, in order to 'avoid any ambiguity',[136] the principle according to which—also in the context of the collective complaints system—the Charter contains only legal undertakings of an 'international' character, that is to say, not imposing on the parties the requirement to recognize its direct invocability before their own authorities. This seems to constitute an obstacle to the recognition of the enforceable character of the findings of the European Committee of Social Rights as contained in the reports it submits to the Committee of Ministers, and likewise to that of the resolution or recommendations adopted by the Committee of Ministers.

---

[134] These conclusions, however, may encourage the ECJ to recognize the direct effect of the (Rev)ESC in a more indirect way, in so far as such conclusions clarify the requirements of the Charter and therefore, by adding to their specificity, may progressively make them more precise, and therefore directly applicable.

[135] Explanatory Report to the Additional Protocol to the European Social Charter providing for a system of collective complaints, at para. 46.   [136] Ibid., at para. 54.

We may therefore be sceptical of the possibility that the reasoning adopted by the European Court of Justice in Opinion 1/91—reasoning according to which the decisions of an international court created by an agreement to which the Union is a party can bind the Court of Justice and thus compensate for the absence of direct effect in its provisions—could apply in the context of the ESC. This scepticism is further reinforced by the fact that the Court of Justice appears to want to subordinate the recognition of the 'judicial' character of the instance concerned, left authoritatively to interpret the instrument to which the Union is a party, to conditions which the European Committee on Social Rights seems not to comply with. Not so very long ago, the European Court of Justice for instance denied the Human Rights Committee set up in the context of the International Covenant on Civil and Political Rights the character of a 'judicial instance', in order to draw from that conclusion certain consequences concerning the authority of its interpretation of the Covenant.[137] And we have already noted the sceptical attitude adopted by Advocate General Jacobs in the *Albany International* case towards the ESC, the binding character of which he would have been prepared even to deny.[138]

C. The Adoption of Acts of the Union Implementing the ESC

Secondly, a specific situation will arise when the European legislature adopts measures expressly intended to ensure that the undertakings assumed by the Union in the context of the ESC are given effect to. In such a case, it will be justified to examine the compatibility of these measures with those undertakings. Indeed, the Court confirmed in the *Nakajima All Precision Co Ltd* judgment of 7 May 1991 that, when an act of secondary law has been adopted in order to implement a particular obligation assumed by the Community in the international legal order, it must comply with those international obligations.[139] This exception to the conditions normally imposed to the recognition of the direct applicability of international obligations binding upon the Union corresponds to the specific hypothesis in which the European legislature adopts a measure in order to comply

---

[137] See Case C-249/96, *Grant v. South West Trains* [1998] ECR I-621.

[138] See *supra* n. 43.

[139] Case C-69/89 [1991] ECR I-2069, at para. 31. See also Case *Kupferberg, supra* n. 126, at para. 11; Case 266/81, *SIOT* [1983] ECR 731, at para. 28; Case C-149/96, *Portugal v. Council* [1999] ECR I-8395, at para. 29. In the context of the undertakings of the European Community in the framework of the WTO for instance, the Court of First Instance confirms that 'it is only where the Community intended to implement a particular obligation assumed in the context of the WTO, or where the Community measure refers expressly to the precise provisions of the WTO agreements, that it is for the Community judicature to review the legality of the Community measure in question in the light of the WTO rules': Case T-174/00, *Biret International, supra* n. 134, at para. 63. The criticisms addressed by the ECJ to the reasoning of this judgment—in the decision it adopted in the *cassation* proceedings which the judgment led to—do not bear upon the quoted passage, but rather on the consequences attached to the presence of a decision adopted by the WTO Dispute Settlement Body.

with its international undertakings, and thus may be said to have itself agreed to establish the link between the adoption of that measure and those international obligations. It could hardly be justified to extend the scope of this exception to all those cases in which the Union legislature—within the limits of its attributed competences—has adopted certain measures in order to achieve an objective of the Union which also corresponds to an obligation contained in the Revised Charter. However, where the European legislature acts explicitly in order to carry out the obligations imposed on it in the international legal order by the Revised Charter, the European Court of Justice will be able to verify whether the act adopted indeed fulfils the requirements of the Charter.

D. *The Reference by the Union Legislature to the Revised ESC*

A third situation in which the invocability of the ESC could be asserted results from the *Fediol* case, which gave rise to a judgment of the European Court of Justice of 22 June 1989.[140] In the context of an action to annul a decision adopted by the Commission which the applicant alleged to be illegal under GATT, the invocability of that Agreement was in issue, the Court having on several prior occasions found that its provisions did not have direct effect.[141] The EEC Oil Industry Federation (Fediol) challenged the rejection of the complaint it had filed against certain competitors, stating that the Commission ought to have considered that the commercial practices of these competitors were contrary to the GATT rules. At paragraph 19 of its judgment, the Court notes that the absence of direct effect of these rules, implying that they 'were not capable of conferring on citizens of the Community rights which they can invoke before the courts', does not imply that 'citizens may not, in proceedings before the Court, rely on the provisions of GATT in order to obtain a ruling on whether conduct criticized in a complaint lodged under Article 3 of Regulation No 2641/84 constitutes an illicit commercial practice within the meaning of that regulation'. Indeed, according to Article 2(1) of Regulation 2641/84,[142] 'illicit commercial practices' means 'any international trade practices attributable to third countries *which are incompatible with international law* or with the generally accepted rules'. The Court could therefore conclude that the GATT provisions invoked by Fediol 'form part of the rules of international law to which Article 2(1) of [the Regulation] refers', which justifies reliance upon them by the applicant in its action for annulment of the decision of the Commission.

In *Fediol*, the invocability of the GATT rules was admitted only by reason of the reference made to these rules by the Community legislature: where it is adopted in the precise context of a regulation making such a reference, the

---

[140] Case 70/87, *Fediol v. Commission* [1989] ECR 1781.
[141] See Joined Cases 21–24/72, *International Fruit Company* [1972] ECR 1219; Case 9/73, *Schlueter* [1973] ECR 1135; Case 266/81, *SIOT, supra* n. 140; Cases 267–269/81, *SPI and SAMI* [1983] ECR 801.   [142] OJ 1984 L252/1 (emphasis added).

decision of the Commission depends for its legality on compliance with the GATT provisions.[143] It is nevertheless remarkable that the absence of direct effect of such rules, which the ECJ habitually deduces from its spirit, its economy, and its terms—'the General Agreement', said the Court in the formula which has already been quoted, is characterized by 'the great flexibility of its provisions, in particular those conferring the possibility of derogation, the measures to be taken when confronted with exceptional difficulties and the settlement of conflicts between the contracting parties'—does not create an obstacle to the Court applying the terms of the Agreement when it finds itself invited to do so by the Community legislature. Its view that the provisions of the GATT have no direct effect, says the Court, does not prevent it 'from interpreting and applying the rules of GATT with reference to a given case, in order to establish whether certain specific commercial practices should be considered incompatible with those rules. The GATT provisions have an independent meaning which, for the purposes of their application in specific cases, is to be determined by way of interpretation'.[144]

The *renvoi* effected by the Community legislature, however, is the decisive element. A general reference to the ESC as the source of inspiration, as in Article 136 EC (ex Article 117 EC Treaty) or in Article III-209 of the Treaty establishing a Constitution for Europe, is not enough. Similarly, despite the fact that many provisions of the EU Charter of Fundamental Rights are based on provisions of the ESC or the (Rev)ESC,[145] this cannot be seen to imply that any violation of the (Rev)ESC by an act of the institutions of the Union or of the Member States acting within the sphere of application of Union law should be considered a violation of the EU Charter of Fundamental Rights, even if, following the accession of the Union to the (Rev)ESC, this instrument is obligatory for the Union in the international legal order. After such accession, Union law, including the Charter of Fundamental Rights, will have to be interpreted in the light of the Revised

---

[143] The Court reasons that 'since Regulation No 2641/84 entitles the economic agents concerned to rely on the GATT provisions in the complaint which they lodge with the Commission in order to establish the illicit nature of the commercial practices which they consider to have harmed them, those same economic agents are entitled to request the Court to exercise its powers of review over the legality of the Commission's decision applying those provisions' (at para. 22).

[144] Case 70/87, *Fediol v. Commission* [1989] ECR 1781, at para. 20.

[145] The formulations chosen in the Explanations adopted by the Presidium of the Convention having elaborated the Charter of Fundamental Rights, and later updated by the Presidium of the Convention having drafted the Constitutional Treaty (see Doc. CONF 828/03, and Declaration (No. 12) concerning the explanations relating to the Charter of Fundamental Rights, appended to the Treaty establishing a Constitution for Europe, OJ 2004 C310/1), vary. Article 15(3) of the Charter of Fundamental Rights (according to which nationals of third countries who are authorized to work in the territories of the Member States are entitled to working conditions equivalent to those of citizens of the Union) 'is based on' Art. 19(4) ESC; Art. 23(1) of the Charter of Fundamental Rights ('Equality between women and men must be ensured in all areas, including employment, work and pay') 'draws on' Art. 20 of the (Rev)ESC, just as Art. 25 (rights of the elderly) 'draws on' Art. 23 of the (Rev)ESC; Art. 27 of the Charter of Fundamental Rights (which guarantees the right of workers to information and consultation within the undertaking) is said simply to 'appear in' the (Rev)ESC, at Art. 21.

Charter, as is usual with the international undertakings of the Union.[146] However, the reference to the (Rev)ESC as a source of inspiration does not constitute a true reference back to this instrument, in the same way as compatibility with the requirements of the Charter of Fundamental Rights would be subordinated to compatibility with the requirements of the (Rev)ESC.

E. Conclusions

In sum, for all its symbolic value, the accession of the Union to the (Rev)ESC would not have such far-reaching consequences as some may fear, even if, as would be desirable, such accession were accompanied by the ratification of the Additional Protocol to the ESC providing for a system of collective complaints. By acceding to the (Rev)ESC, the Union would be undertaking, in the international legal order, to promote the objectives of the Charter and to respect the provisions of Part II of the Charter which it would have accepted. This will entail Union law having to be interpreted, in so far as possible, in accordance with this undertaking.[147] But the specificities of the Revised Charter, like the attitude the European Court of Justice has had in the past with regard to this instrument, lead one to suppose that the Charter will not be considered directly applicable in the legal order of the Union. The Charter will be invocable before the European Court of Justice only where, in specific circumstances, the Union legislature has adopted an act by means of which it sought to implement a precise obligation imposed on the Union by the Charter, or where the Union legislator has explicitly referred to the Charter in order to make the validity of a regulatory or an executive act depend on its compatibility with the Charter. As for the Member States, they will, of course, be bound by the international obligations of the Union. However, the obligation imposed on the Member States loyally to cooperate with the institutions of the Union, in particular in order to facilitate compliance by the Union with its international obligations, does not extend to areas in which no powers have been conferred upon the Union, nor even to areas where the Union shares with the Member States a power to act but has not exercised its power. The obligation of the Member States to cooperate with the Union in the fulfilment of its international obligations does not extend beyond the situations in which they are acting in the field of application of Union law. Therefore, the fear which is sometimes expressed, that the accession of the Union to the (Rev)ESC might result in modifying the status accorded to that instrument in the domestic legal orders of the Member States, is misplaced.

---

[146] To the extent that the provisions of the Charter of Fundamental Rights of the EU are explicitly inspired by certain provisions of the (Rev)ESC, they must be interpreted in its light: see Case T-395/94, *Atlantic Container Lines AB and others v. European Community* [2002] ECR II-885, at para. 147.

[147] See, on this point, Case C-341/95, *Gianni Bettati* [1998] ECR I-4355; Case C-61/94, *EC Commission v. Germany* [1996] ECR I-3989.

8

The Trajectory of Fundamental Social Rights in the European Union

BRUNO DE WITTE

I. INTRODUCTION

This chapter will elaborate a simple argument about the appearance and evolving role of fundamental social rights in the European Union legal order. That simple argument is that, despite some indications to the contrary, fundamental social rights have had a very distinct trajectory in EU law, and still today have a position and role in EU law which is rather different from those of other fundamental rights.[1]

The view proposed here, that the trajectory of social rights in the EU legal order is distinct, seems to be contradicted by two important facts: (a) that the European Court of Justice (ECJ) when developing its case law on the protection of fundamental rights as general principles of EC law drew no principled distinction between social rights and other fundamental rights; and (b) that the EU Charter of Rights of 2000 includes social rights alongside other rights, and that it even transcends the traditional dichotomy between two main categories of rights by grouping all rights in a single document which is subdivided in a set of unprecedented categories: Dignity, Freedoms, Equality, Solidarity, Citizens' Rights, Justice. These two legal facts may give the impression that the trajectory of fundamental social rights is very much part of the overall trajectory of fundamental rights in EU law, and the reader could, accordingly, be referred to general accounts of fundamental rights protection in the EU. However, I will argue that this first impression is deceptive and that, in reality, there is a separate story to be told about the recognition of social rights and the role they play in the European Union legal order. Whereas rhetorical support is given to the idea of the indivisibility of rights, the legal regime of social rights remains quite distinctive. The fact that social rights are treated *differently* does not mean that they play a *less prominent* role than civil and political rights. In some ways, as will be argued at the end of this chapter,

---

[1] For the purpose of this chapter, I define fundamental social rights as the rights contained in the European Social Charter, in its various versions.

their significance for the future development of the EU legal order may be more fundamental.[2]

II. THE DISTINCTIVENESS OF SOCIAL RIGHTS IN THE FUNDAMENTAL RIGHTS CASE LAW OF THE ECJ

The European Community is still not a party (and neither is the EU) to any of the important international social rights instruments: the European Social Charter, the UN Covenant of Economic, Social and Cultural Rights, and the main conventions of the ILO. In this respect, the EU finds itself in a very different position from that of its Member States. To the extent that the Member States have transferred powers to the EU in fields covered by these international instruments, they can no longer fully ensure compliance with their international obligations, and there arises a potential gap in the protection of social rights. The same is true for the social rights protection offered by the constitutions of many Member States: to the extent that relevant policy competences are transferred to the EU level, those constitutional provisions lose their legal grip as standards for the guidance and control of state action. This phenomenon is well known and is not essentially different for social rights, as compared to civil rights.

The 'gap' is filled—this, too, is well known—by the fact that the EU institutions are bound to respect fundamental rights *as a matter of EU law itself.* This basic constitutional rule derives from two different sources of primary EU law: a written source in Article 6(2) EU Treaty, and a parallel but much older unwritten source in the case law of the ECJ about the general principles of Community law.

There can be hardly any doubt that social rights are included among the (unwritten) fundamental rights recognized by the ECJ as part of the general principles of Community law. The Court has agreed to include international social rights treaties among the 'sources of inspiration' from which it derives its general principles of EC law; however, practical applications have been very rare indeed, as can be seen from the fact that the one judgment traditionally cited in clear support of this view was delivered twenty-five years ago.[3] General principles of EC law bind not only the EU institutions but also the Member States when

---

[2] For another examination of the evolution of EU fundamental rights from the perspective of their (in)divisibility, see J. Kenner, 'Economic and Social Rights in the EU Legal Order: The Mirage of Indivisibility', in T. Hervey and J. Kenner (eds), *Economic and Social Rights under the EU Charter of Fundamental Rights* (2003), at 1.

[3] Case 149/77, *Defrenne v. Sabena* [1978] ECR I-365. See the detailed assessment of the Court's case law in J.-F. Akandji-Kombé, 'Charte sociale et droit communautaire', in J.-F. Akandji-Kombé and S. Leclerc (eds), *La Charte sociale européenne* (2001), at 149, 153–56; and, earlier, in E. Szyszczak, 'Social Rights as General Principles of Community Law', in N. A. Neuwahl and A. Rosas (eds), *The European Union and Human Rights* (1995), at 211.

acting 'within the scope' of EC law, a notion which is notoriously controversial.[4] But again, there are no judgments yet in which the ECJ or the Court of First Instance has found a Member State to have acted in breach of an unwritten social right. The problem is that social rights usually require positive state action, and the rather rudimentary human rights doctrine of the ECJ so far does not include a 'positive obligations' dimension. This absence has been noted above all by German authors, since it contrasts with the sophisticated and multi-layered fundamental rights doctrine of the German Constitutional Court, in which the derivation of positive state duties from fundamental rights is quite common.[5] If it adopted this approach, the ECJ would have to find that, by *omitting* to adopt certain measures, a Member State had violated an unwritten EC social right. The ECJ, in fact, followed this line of reasoning in a different context, namely that of the protection of the common market freedoms. In a case brought by the Commission against France (known as the *Spanish strawberries* case), it held that France had acted in breach of the free movement of goods by failing to protect the orderly import and sale of Spanish strawberries against violent action by French agricultural organizations.[6] A similar approach could have been adopted in cases involving the protection of fundamental social rights, but the occasion has not so far arisen.

Similarly, the Court has never so far referred to the constitutional traditions common to the Member States as an indirect source of unwritten social rights in the EU legal order (whereas it did refer to them when 'discovering' other fundamental rights). One might even wonder whether social rights are part of this common constitutional tradition, in view of the fact that some Member States do not give them any constitutional recognition, and other States formulate constitutional objectives in the field of employment and welfare but avoid using the language of rights.[7] To the extent that a particular right is sufficiently broadly recognized in national constitutional law as to be part of the 'common constitutional traditions', the further question arises whether there is sufficient common ground in its meaning and interpretation as to make it operational as a general principle of Community law. Yet, all these questions have so far remained theoretical.

The foregoing leads to the inescapable conclusion that the ECJ has played a negligible role, thus far, with respect to the discovery and interpretation of unwritten social rights. This conclusion may seem to be at odds with the opinion of authors who have argued that the ECJ has 'played a socially activist role' throughout the past decades.[8] However, those authors in fact refer to the role played by the ECJ in

---

[4] See P. Craig and G. de Búrca, *EU Law: Text, Cases and Materials* (2003), at 337–49; Ranacher, 'Die Bindung der Mitgliedstaaten an die Gemeinschaftsgrundrechte', *Zeitschrift für Öffentliches Recht* (2003) 97.   [5] See, e.g., L. Jaeckel, *Schutzpflichten im Deutschen und Europäischen Recht* (2001).

[6] ECJ Case C-265/95, *Commission v. France* [1997] ECR I-6959; see Muylle, 'Angry Farmers and Passive Policemen: Private Conduct and the Free Movement of Goods', 23 *ELRev.* (1998) 469.

[7] See the chapter by Cécile Fabre in this volume, and J. Iliopoulos-Strangas (ed.), *La protection des droits sociaux fondamentaux dans les Etats membres de l'Union européenne* (2000).

[8] K. Lenaerts and P. Foubert, 'Social Rights in the Case-Law of the European Court of Justice', *LIEI* (2001) 267, at 293.

protecting the social rights of EU citizens through its inventive interpretation of *written* Community law, both primary and secondary. Examples of this are its case law extending the scope of the 'social advantages' to which EU migrants and their families are entitled in their country of residence, and the judgments in which it recognized qualified rights of cross-border access to education and health care.[9] The ECJ has also adopted a broad interpretation of the individual rights contained in EC legislation in the social policy field, most clearly so with the 1976 Equal Treatment Directive. Those are, indeed, important judicial contributions, but they use the language of equality or of social protection rather than the language of fundamental social rights.

III. THE DEVELOPMENT OF SOCIAL RIGHTS BETWEEN TWO CHARTERS (1989 TO 2000)

A plan to fill this gap in the EC legal order by means of an EC Charter of Fundamental Social Rights was unveiled by Jacques Delors at the 1988 Stockholm meeting of the European Trade Unions Confederation. It was eventually adopted at the Strasbourg European Council meeting in 1989, but not in the form of a binding document—and even this soft-law document was unacceptable for one of the Member States, the United Kingdom.[10] The significance of this Charter for the evolution of EU law is disputed. Was this Charter simply a 'bone to be tossed to organized labor, which had been left out in the 1992 program', as Gillingham claims?[11] That interpretation is difficult to reconcile with the positive attitude of the Delors Commission, which included the Charter in its long-term legal and political strategy. The Commission had started preparing a Social Action Programme to 'operationalize' the Workers' Charter even before that Charter was formally adopted, and the Maastricht Treaty's Social Agreement, adopted a few years later, created new legal competences which allowed the eleven signatory states of the Charter to achieve the Commission's legislative programme. In doing so, they were not hindered by a recalcitrant British government, which had accepted, as part of the overall package deal leading to the conclusion of the IGC at the Maastricht summit of December 1991, that the eleven other Member States could legislate 'on their own' in this field.

Whereas the Workers' Charter did not make much of an impact on the case law of the ECJ,[12] it did leave its mark on a number of social policy directives adopted

---

[9] There is a rich literature on the role of the ECJ in formulating such free movement-related social rights. See, e.g., (in addition to the paper by Lenaerts and Foubert cited *supra* in note 8): M. Aziz, *The Impact of European Rights on National Legal Cultures* (2004), at 110ff.; A. P. van der Mei, *Free Movement of Persons within the European Community: Cross-Border Access to Public Benefits* (2003); and (for the access to health care rights) Tamara Hervey's chapter in this volume.

[10] For a comment written shortly after its adoption see B. Bercusson, 'The European Community's Charter of Fundamental Social Rights of Workers', *MLR* (1990) 624.

[11] J. Gillingham, *European Integration, 1950–2003: Superstate or New Market Economy?* (2003), at 263.   [12] It was referred to in Case C-84/94, *UK v. Council* [1996] ECR I-5755.

in the 1990s, and was often mentioned in their preambles. This has led many commentators to take the view that the 1989 Charter, despite its very soft legal status, was a true springboard for innovative EU social policy. It is difficult, however, to evaluate the true dimension of the policy-making impetus emanating from the Workers' Charter. Would some of the post-1989 EC directives not have been enacted in its absence? Would their content have been different if it had not been for the Charter? The answer to these questions may seem of purely historical importance now, but the situation of the early 1990s is strangely reminiscent of the current situation, after the adoption of the EU Charter of Fundamental Rights in 2000. Then, as now, there was a set of (social) rights that led a twilight legal existence, but nonetheless served as a source of inspiration for the enactment of social policy measures by the EU institutions.

Whatever their concrete impact, those fundamental social rights that were included in the 1989 Charter[13] have had a different legal life from that of other (civil and political) fundamental rights. The latter were more prominently present in the case law of the ECJ (although not that much either[14]), and in the main played a gap-filling role, that is they served to protect citizens against possible encroachments on their rights by the EC institutions in the absence of a written catalogue. The rights formulated in the 1989 Charter, on the contrary, were an embryonic written catalogue that figured less prominently (or rather, not at all) in the case law of the Court.

In the mid-1990s, a vivid discussion developed on whether one should take a step further than the Charter of 1989 and include a set of fundamental social rights (whether those of the Charter or others) in the EC Treaty. This discussion, involving mainly academics, trade unions, and NGOs, took place in the margins of the inter-governmental conference of 1996–1997 that was called to revise the Maastricht Treaty. The political outcome of this debate was disappointing for its promoters, in the sense that the Amsterdam Treaty, which was adopted at the end of that IGC, failed to include a comprehensive list of social rights in primary Community law. Still, the Amsterdam Treaty was said to have marked a 'modest leftward turn'[15] compared to the preceding Treaty texts, due probably to the recent accession of Finland, Sweden, and Austria and to the change of government in the UK just before the Amsterdam summit. The new Treaty text indeed extended the EU's capacity for social regulation of the market, but this change was not accompanied by a major

---

[13] Note that the EC Charter of 1989 was narrowly defined as containing only rights of 'workers' (contrary to the Commission's original view that their personal scope should be formulated more broadly) and therefore did not cover all the ground that is covered by the European Social Charter.

[14] See B. de Witte, 'The Past and Future Role of the European Court of Justice in the Protection of Human Rights', in P. Alston, with M. Bustelo and J. Heenan (eds), *The EU and Human Rights* (1999), at 859, where it was argued that, until the end of the 1990s at least, the fundamental rights case law of the ECJ had formal constitutional importance but little practical relevance.

[15] Pollack, 'A Blairite Treaty: Neo-Liberalism and Regulated Capitalism in the Treaty of Amsterdam', in K. Neunreither and A. Wiener (eds), *European Integration after Amsterdam: Institutional Dynamics and Prospects for Democracy* (2000) 266, at 288.

new role for fundamental social rights, save for the important breakthrough represented by the new non-discrimination provision in the EC Treaty.[16]

Article 6(2) EU Treaty, as amended in Amsterdam, refers to the ECHR as a source of the fundamental rights to be respected by the Union and to be enforced by the ECJ to the extent of its jurisdiction. The European Social Charter is not mentioned in the same breath. In fact, the European Social Charter was demoted, in the course of the IGC, from the draft text of Article 6 to the (non-binding) Preamble to the Amsterdam Treaty. In that Preamble, the Member States confirm their 'attachment to fundamental rights as defined in the European Social Charter . . . and in the 1989 Community Charter of the Fundamental Social Rights of Workers'. Both these legal documents are also mentioned in the body of the EC Treaty—not in a prominent position comparable to that of Article 6 EU, but in the small 'niche'[17] of the social policy chapter. Indeed, Article 136 EC, after its amendment in Amsterdam, states that the 'Community and the Member States' shall pursue the social policy objectives listed in that Article, 'having in mind fundamental social rights such as those set out in the European Social Charter signed at Turin on 18 October 1961 and in the Community Charter of the Fundamental Social Rights of Workers'. One of the questions raised by this enigmatic phrase is what 'having in mind' means. These words clearly imply that the fundamental social rights contained in those instruments are not directly enforceable as a matter of EU law. However, would they, for instance, entitle the ECJ to strike down EC social legislation that obviously ran counter to the rights guaranteed by the ESC and the Community Charter, since it could then be argued that the EU legislator had failed to keep those rights 'in mind'? This does not seem likely.

On the whole, therefore, one can agree with Emmanuelle Bribosia and Anne Weyembergh, who write that the Treaty of Amsterdam failed to recognize the indivisibility of fundamental rights and instead relegated social rights to the back seat.[18] This meagre result of the Treaty reform contrasted with the claims by trade union organizations and other NGOs in the period preceding the adoption of the Amsterdam Treaty, namely that there was a particular justification for including a set of fundamental social rights (rather than civil or political rights) in the Treaty. This view had been echoed in, and fuelled by, documents by academics setting out various concrete proposals for the inclusion of fundamental social rights in the

---

[16] On which, see Mark Bell's chapter in this volume.

[17] The term is borrowed from S. Sciarra, 'From Strasbourg to Amsterdam: Prospects for the Convergence of European Social Rights Policy', in Alston, Bustelo and Heenan (eds), *The EU and Human Rights, supra* n. 14, 473, at 496.

[18] E. Bribosia and A. Weyembergh, 'La consolidation de l'Etat de droit européen', in M. Telò and P. Magnette (eds), *De Maastricht à Amsterdam: L'Europe et son nouveau traité* (1998) 69, at 83: 'A Amsterdam, on a renoncé à consacrer l'indivisibilité des droits civils et politiques et des droits économiques et sociaux. Si l'on s'est soucié d'améliorer la protection juridictionnelle des droits fondamentaux tels qu'issus de la Convention européenne des droits de l'homme, on s'est contenté d'une vague référence aux droits économiques et sociaux et aux instruments qui en assurent la protection.'

Treaties.[19] Their efforts were to no avail in 1996–1997. And yet, only three years later, social rights were officially and comprehensively codified at the EU level, albeit in the context of a general codification of fundamental rights.

IV. THE EU CHARTER OF RIGHTS: INDIVISIBILITY—BUT NOT TOO MUCH

The new Charter of Rights was not meant to modify any of the existing elements of EU fundamental rights law, but only, at least in the view of the Cologne European Council which launched the process of its elaboration, to make the existing law more visible for citizens. Eventually, the Convention which drafted the Charter did not scrupulously respect the limits of this mandate, and acted innovatively by rephrasing existing rights, by selecting certain rights and forgetting others (for example, some of the rights contained in the European Social Charter),[20] and by adding some new ones. One of the major characteristics of this document is that it transcends the dichotomy between social and economic rights on the one hand, and civil and political rights on the other. This feature has been noted by all commentators and praised by most of them. It represents the endorsement of two core ideas that have slowly matured over the years in national constitutional law and in international human rights law, namely: (a) the idea that all rights require some measure of positive action on the part of the state, so that it is no longer correct to make a sharp distinction between rights implying a negative duty of abstention and rights implying a positive duty to act; and (b) the idea that rights that are not self-executing (to use the international law term) or are not 'subjective rights' (to use a term familiar to continental constitutional lawyers) can nevertheless have important legal and political effects.[21]

The decision of the European Council in Cologne in June 1999 had specified that 'account should furthermore be taken of economic and social rights as contained in the European Social Charter and the Community Charter of the Fundamental Social Rights of Workers, insofar as they do not merely establish objectives for action by the Union'. The distinction, alluded to by the European Council, between two types of social rights (those that merely contain objectives

---

[19] B. Bercusson, S. Deakin, P. Koistinen, et al., *A Manifesto for Social Europe* (1996); R. Blanpain, B. Hepple, S. Sciarra, and M. Weiss, *Fundamental Social Rights: Proposals for the European Union* (1996); L. Betten and D. MacDevitt (eds), *The Protection of Fundamental Social Rights in the European Union* (1996). For a concise view of this brief span of social rights activism see S. Sciarra, *supra* n. 17, at 488–93.

[20] See O. De Schutter, 'La garantie des droits et principes sociaux dans la Charte des droits fondamentaux de l'Union européenne', in J.-Y. Carlier and O. De Schutter (eds), *La Charte des droits fondamentaux de l'Union européenne* (2002) 117, at 144–46.

[21] For a commentary focusing on this feature of the Charter from a constitutional law perspective see M.-C. Ponthoreau, 'Le principe de l'indivisibilité des droits: L'apport de la Charte des droits fondamentaux de l'Union européenne à la théorie générale des droits fondamentaux', *Revue française de droit administratif* (2003) 928, particularly at 931.

for action and those that are legally more incisive) was not closely followed by the Charter Convention, which decided to include a number of 'rights' that were formulated as very general policy objectives.[22] The Convention got away with this broad brush approach because it was understood that the Charter would not become legally binding, or at least not immediately. Still, the diaphanous distinction between 'rights' and 'principles', drawn in Article 51(1) of the Charter,[23] was considered by the British government representative to have been 'a key factor in the Herzog Convention reaching agreement on the Charter, particularly in relation to the inclusion of social and economic rights'.[24]

The 'justiciability issue' returned with a vengeance during the recent Convention on the Future of the Union, when some delegates (particularly the UK government representative) made it clear that their agreement to incorporate the Charter in the EU Constitution, and thus make it legally binding, would be conditional on emphasizing more clearly the distinction between 'rights' and 'principles'. This was accepted by Working Group II of the Convention,[25] and it eventually led to the addition of a fifth paragraph to Article II-112 of the European Constitution, which limits the justiciability of provisions containing principles: they shall be 'judicially cognizable' only in the interpretation of implementing measures taken by the EU institutions or by the Member States, and in rulings on their legality.

The distinction which, in the view of the Cologne European Council in 1999, should have been the basis for inclusion in the Charter or not has thus become an internal fault line within the text of the Charter as incorporated in the Constitution for Europe. It is by no means clear how this fault line will operate in practice. Indeed, the Charter does not label its provisions as being either rights or principles (or, rather, the use of those labels to denote single norms in the Charter is quite inconsistent with the nature of the overall distinction drawn in Article II-112). The rights/principles distinction is therefore bound to become a major source of confusion and controversy.[26] This very regrettable lack of precision contrasts with some national constitutions (such as those of Ireland and Spain) which

---

[22] E.g., Art. 38: 'Union policies shall ensure a high level of consumer protection'.

[23] Now Art. II-111 of the Treaty establishing a Constitution for Europe.

[24] Goldsmith, 'The Charter of Rights—A Brake Not an Accelerator', *EHRLR* (2004) 473, at 476.

[25] Brian Bercusson, in his chapter in this volume, calls this 'Working Group II's attack on social rights' and comments that, in doing so, it 'attempts to reverse what was a central compromise in the earlier Convention which drafted the Charter: that social and economic rights should not be separated from traditional "rights" by characterizing them as "principles" which are not justiciable positive rights'.

[26] Both the distinction itself and the lack of clarity in the way it was made have been criticized by many authors, among whom are: G. de Búrca, 'Fundamental Rights and Citizenship', in B. de Witte (ed.), *Ten Reflections on the Constitutional Treaty for Europe* (2003) 11, at 22–25; P. Alston, 'The Contribution of the EU's Fundamental Rights Agency to the Realization of Economic and Social Rights', in P. Alston and O. De Schutter (eds), *Monitoring Fundamental Rights in the EU: The Contribution of the Fundamental Rights Agency* (2005) 159, at 169ff.; S. Prechal, 'Rights v Principles, or How to Remove Fundamental Rights from the Jurisdiction of the Courts', in *The European Union: An Ongoing Process of Integration: Liber Amicorum Alfred E. Kellermann* (2004), at 177; D. Ashiagbor, 'Economic and Social Rights in the European Charter of Fundamental Rights', *EHRLR* (2004) 62, at 71; O. De Schutter, 'Les droits fondamentaux dans le projet européen: Des limites à l'action des

similarly exclude judicial review of some fundamental social rights provisions,[27] but at least clearly indicate which specific provisions are excluded. The drafters' lack of rigour is an invitation to interpretative cacophony, which was already inaugurated by the French *Conseil Constitutionnel* in its decision reviewing the constitutional compatibility of the European Constitution. When referring to the distinction in Article II-112(5) between rights and principles, it affirmed without any qualification and without any further argument that the right to work and the entitlement to social security benefits and social assistance are examples of principles rather than rights.[28]

When trying to apply the dichotomy to the fundamental social rights, it would certainly be too simple to consider that entire chapters of the Charter (say, the chapter on 'solidarity') contain only marginally justiciable principles rather than fully justiciable rights. It is necessary, rather, to proceed on a case-by-case basis, and good arguments can be made for ranging most of the Charter's fundamental social rights in the 'rights' category rather than the 'principles' category. Still, the fact remains that the formulation of Article II-112(5) calls into question, in a very direct way, the promise of indivisibility held by the original text of the Charter.

V. THE IMPACT OF THE EU CHARTER OF RIGHTS: A NEW PLATFORM FOR FUNDAMENTAL SOCIAL RIGHTS PROTECTION?

It is now widely accepted that the legal status of the Charter is not an all-or-nothing issue, and that this formally non-binding document may display, and has already displayed, a variety of 'soft' legal effects. It was pointed out by several authors and, most emphatically, by the European Commission that the Charter can effectively display the same legal effects as a binding instrument because its contents can easily be absorbed into the existing category of general principles of Community law which are, undoubtedly, legally binding and enforceable by the ECJ. The Charter was thus capable of becoming a source of inspiration for the Court in discovering and applying these general principles, alongside the ECHR and national constitutional traditions. The Commission went so far as to say that the 'Charter will offer a clear guide for the interpretation of fundamental rights by the Court of Justice which in the current situation has to use disparate, sometimes uncertain, sources of inspiration'.[29] Several Advocates-General of the ECJ have, in their Opinions

---

institutions à une politique des droits fondamentaux', in O. De Schutter and P. Nihoul (eds), *Une Constitution pour l'Europe: Réflexions sur les transformations du droit de l'Union européenne* (2004) 81, at 110–14.

[27] See C. Fabre's chapter in this volume.

[28] *Conseil Constitutionnel*, Decision No. 2004–505 DC of 19 November 2004, *Traité établissant une Constitution pour l'Europe*, at para. 15.

[29] Commission Communication of 11 October 2000, COM(2000)644, at 5.

given since 2001, supported this view. The ECJ itself has failed so far to refer to the Charter, in order not to interfere with the delicate political debate on the future legal status of the Charter, which was only very recently concluded by the Charter's incorporation as Part II of the European Constitution signed in October 2004.

However, one should not remain fixated on the use or non-use of the Charter by the judicial institutions at the European or national level. More important, certainly for most of the social rights contained in the Charter, is another avenue for giving effect to the Charter, namely through the application of the Charter by the institutions that have authored it: the Council, the Commission, and the European Parliament.[30] The Commission, in particular, has taken active steps to allow such application. By an internal decision of 13 March 2001, it decided that it would systematically examine the compatibility with the Charter of all its proposals and decisions to which the Charter could apply.[31] Since then, there have been many pieces of EC legislation, or proposed EC legislation, the preambles to which include references to the (social) rights of the EU Charter. Obviously, it is not enough for the Commission and the other EU institutions to make ritual reference to the Charter in their legislative and non-legislative instruments. It is more important to know whether this Charter check makes a difference to the actual content of Commission proposals or of European Parliament and Council acts. Only if that proves to be the case will it be possible to say that the Charter, even now when its definitive legal status still depends on the entry into force of the Constitution, makes a contribution to the effective guarantee of fundamental rights in Europe.

It may well turn out that the principal merit of the Charter is not to codify and tighten the limits imposed on the action of the EU institutions, so as to prevent them from encroaching on the sphere of liberty that should be left to citizens. This 'negative' function of fundamental rights protection is currently performed by the ECJ through its case law; existing deficiencies in judicial protection (such as the limited access for individuals to the European Courts and the lack of review of EU action under the second and third pillars) are not remedied by the Charter and only partially addressed in the European Constitution. The role of the Charter, and particularly its social rights provisions, may be more promising in two other respects: that of *limiting the deregulatory impact* of EU law on national labour and welfare policies,[32] and that of formulating *duties to act* for the EU institutions.

---

[30] See further on this point G. de Búrca and Aschenbrenner, 'European Constitutionalism and the Charter', in S. Peers and A. Ward (eds), *The European Union Charter of Fundamental Rights* (2004) 3, at 14–17.

[31] A first application of this policy was made on the same day, 13 March 2001. The Commission's proposal for a Council Directive concerning the status of third-country nationals who are long-term residents contained the following Recital No. 4: '[t]his Directive respects the fundamental rights and observes the principles recognised in particular by the Charter of Fundamental Rights of the European Union' (OJ 2001 C240E/79).

[32] This is what Marie-Ange Moreau calls, in her chapter in this volume, the *barrier effect* (in the original French version of her paper: *l'effet rempart*) of fundamental social rights. For a detailed elaboration of this (possible) function of the Charter see O. De Schutter, *supra* n. 20, at 129ff., and S. Giubboni, *Diritti sociali e mercato* (2003), at 230ff.

As regards the creation of duties to act, one must take into account Article 51 of the Charter (now Article II-111 of the Constitution), which provides that the Charter does not establish any new power or task for the Community or the Union.[33] The intention of the drafters of the Charter was clearly to avoid the mere enumeration of a fundamental right creating a competence for the European institutions to act for the protection of that right. The scope of the rights follows existing EU competences rather than the other way round. However, even though this intention is clear, the actual wording of the clause is misleading by its use of the word 'tasks'. While it makes legal sense to affirm that the Charter does not extend the *powers* of the EU, if one takes 'powers' as meaning 'legal competences', it does not make sense to state that the Charter will not extend the *tasks* of the EU. Indeed, the very purpose of adopting a Charter of Rights was to make it a task for the European institutions to apply the Charter rights in their various activities. By adopting the Charter in their solemn proclamation made in Nice, the three institutions (Commission, Council, and European Parliament) have clearly undertaken the new task of respecting and promoting the rights contained in the Charter. So, whereas Article 51(2) can meaningfully be interpreted as a barrier to the extension of EU *competences* by the indirect means of promoting a Charter right, it cannot mean that the *policies* of the Community and Union remain unaffected by the Charter. That would make a charade of the Charter.

In fact, the first paragraph of the same Article 51 of the Charter imposes an obligation on the Member States and the EU to 'promote the application' of the rights contained within it.[34] Many Charter rights (particularly in the Solidarity and Equality chapters) require positive action for 'the progressive achievement of their full realization' (to use the words of the UN Social Covenant), so that the right becomes meaningful only when seen in conjunction with the measures taken for its effective enjoyment. In other words, the primary law of the Charter is intimately connected with the secondary law consisting of the measures taken for its implementation.

It seems that, for most of the social rights included in the Charter, the EU *does* have competence, whether broad or narrow, to take positive steps to promote their application.[35] The competence of the EU is sometimes quite straightforward, when the wording of the right corresponds to the definition of a sector-specific

---

[33] This 'horizontal clause' has frequently been examined by legal authors; see, among others, P. Eeckhout, 'The EU Charter of Fundamental Rights and the Federal Question', 39 *CMLRev.* (2002) 945, at 979ff.; S. Barriga, *Die Entstehung der Charta der Grundrechte der Europäischen Union* (2002), at ch. 2.

[34] A clause, such as this one, that explicitly calls upon the political institutions to act for the promotion of fundamental rights is innovative, when compared to most national constitutions (see M. Cartabia, 'Articolo 51', in R. Bifulco, M. Cartabia, and A. Celotto, *L'Europa dei diritti. Commento alla Carta dei diritti fondamentali dell'Unione Europea* (2001) 344, at 350).

[35] One should note, however, that the EU is not allowed to regulate, by means of binding norms, the right of association and the right to strike (Art. 137(5) EC Treaty). This competence exclusion is confirmed for the future in Art. III-210(6) of the European Constitution.

EU competence, as is the case for education, health, and the various social policy competences listed in Article 137 EC Treaty. Indeed, there is sometimes an element of circularity in the Charter because some of its social rights have been formulated, by the Charter Convention in 2000, to reflect the core content of *existing* EC directives. The traces of this 'upgrading' of secondary Community law can be seen in the explanatory memorandum to the Charter. Articles 27, 30, and 33 of the Charter are good examples of this approach. In such cases, the basic legislative programme for giving effect to the right is already in place. The effect of the Charter (as incorporated in the Constitution) is to entrench norms of secondary law by including them as norms of primary constitutional law in the EU. One could argue, following UN human rights practice,[36] that the social rights impose a duty of non-retrogression, so that existing legislation may not be modified in a sense that makes it less protective of the social right.

In addition to these cases of clear correspondence between a Charter right and an EU competence, fundamental social rights may also play a 'transversal' role in other competence domains that are less directly linked to a particular social right. This can occur with the Community's internal market competences, which are precisely defined not in sector-specific but in functional terms. The aim to facilitate the free movement of persons, services, or goods justifies the adoption of EC legislation harmonizing national laws and practices in a given domain. This EC legislation typically pursues a twofold aim: that of improving the operation of the internal market, and that of protecting at the European level a public interest which the Member States (or at least some of them) were pursuing in their own divergent ways prior to harmonization. That public interest may, occasionally, be the guarantee of a fundamental social right. A good example of this is the Directive on the protection of posted workers of 1996.[37] The enactment of this Directive was a politically and legally controversial use of internal market competences to favour social policy ends. The Directive was based on Article 57(2) EC Treaty (since renumbered as Article 47(2)), which is the Treaty basis for legislation to facilitate the free movement of services. In fact, this Directive applies to all services crossing intra-Community borders when they involve the sending of personnel abroad by the service provider (the so-called 'posting' of workers). Social policy concerns became dominant during its elaboration:[38] its main policy aim

---

[36] Committee on Economic, Social and Cultural Rights, General Comment No. 3, 1990, para. 9 (reprinted in H. J. Steiner and P. Alston, *International Human Rights in Context* (2000) at 266).

[37] Directive 96/71 of 16 December 1996, OJ 1997 L18/1. The directive is mentioned as an example of EC fundamental rights legislation by De Schutter, *supra* n. 26, at 87.

[38] The original Commission proposal dates from 1991, and the Council adopted it only in 1996. In the interim, a number of host countries had adopted legislation unilaterally imposing some of their domestic labour legislation on posted workers, thus putting added pressure on the other states to agree to the enactment of a directive that would reflect these social policy concerns. See the account by W. Eichhorst, *European Social Policy between National and Supranational Regulation: Posted Workers in the Framework of Liberalised Services Provision*, Max-Planck-Institut für Gesellschaftsforschung, Discussion Paper 98/6 (1998), at 20–26.

became to prevent the undermining of the core labour law rules of the host states by making posted workers subject to those labour laws. From the point of view of the firms providing cross-border services, the Directive forces them to comply with two different sets of labour law (that of their country of establishment and that of the country to which they post workers), which is why some critics have argued that this Directive did not, in fact, *facilitate* the free movement of services (as its legal basis requires), but hindered it. However, from the point of view of the workers (mainly those employed by competing local firms, but also the posted workers themselves), the Directive may be seen as a contribution to the protection of their fundamental social rights.[39]

Another, not too dissimilar, example is provided by European legislation protecting the equal exercise of social rights by foreign residents. As far as *EU citizens* are concerned, their claim to equal protection in the enjoyment of fundamental social rights has long been part of secondary EC law, and is also fully covered by Article 12 EC Treaty. As far as *third-country nationals* are concerned, the legislative developments are more recent and more tentative. The Preamble to the Directive of 2003 on the status of third-country nationals who are long-term residents[40] refers to the Charter of Rights, and its Article 12 guarantees equal treatment for long-term resident foreigners in, among other things, 'education and vocational training, including study grants', and 'social protection, including social security and health care', which are social rights recognized by the Charter. In this manner, the EU's competence (granted by Article 63(4) EC Treaty) to define the legal status of third-country nationals in their country of residence was interpreted by the EU institutions as calling for the adoption of measures to promote the exercise of Charter rights by third-country nationals.[41]

What happens in these cases is the legislative *mainstreaming* of social rights, in particular of their non-discrimination element. This duty to mainstream exists across all EU policies and applies to all fundamental rights contained in the Charter. This duty will become greater if and when the Charter acquires binding constitutional law status on the entry into force of the Constitution of the EU. This Constitution furthermore contains a new, more specific, mainstreaming clause stating that, in defining and implementing all its policies, 'the Union shall take into account requirements linked to the promotion of a high level of employment, the guarantee of adequate social protection, the fight against social exclusion, and a high level of education,

[39] For discussion of the various policy concerns underlying the Directive see P. Davies, 'Posted Workers: Single Market or Protection of National Labour Law Systems?', 34 *CMLRev.* (1997) 571.

[40] Council Directive 2003/109 of 25 November 2003 concerning the status of third-country nationals who are long-term residents, OJ 2004 L16/44.

[41] Compare this with Council Regulation 859/2003 of 14 May 2003, by which the social security exportability scheme that existed for the benefit of migrant EU nationals (the famous Regulation 1408/71) was extended to third-country nationals migrating between two EU countries (OJ 2003 L124/1). The Preamble to this Regulation refers to the right to social security and social assistance contained in the Charter of Fundamental Rights, but without stating in so many words that the adoption of the Regulation was mandated by the Charter text.

training and protection of human health'.[42] This selection of 'mainstreamable' policy objectives overlaps in part with the fundamental social rights of the Charter.

Thus, the question is not so much whether the EC and EU may gain *extra* legislative powers under the Charter for the promotion of human rights (they do not), but whether the *existing* legislative and other powers of the EU will be reoriented and infused with a range of different values and policy considerations after the enactment of the Charter. Among the non-legislative activities that could be displayed by the EU institutions, one may mention: the use of social rights as an instrument of both negative and positive conditionality in the EU's external relations, the full incorporation of social rights among the monitoring functions (however one would describe those) of a future Fundamental Rights Agency,[43] and the use of social rights as substantive indicators within the context of the open method of coordination (OMC) as used in social and educational policy.[44] It has even been suggested recently that, beyond the incorporation of human rights concerns in existing OMC processes, one could also set up a separate open method of coordination wholly devoted to the progressive realization of the Charter rights.[45] Obviously, social rights would lend themselves particularly well to such an approach.

However, one should not nurture too much optimism The practice of the EU institutions, so far, is rather disappointing. It is true that, as was mentioned above, the Charter has been cited in the preambles to some EU instruments since 2001. But evidence of a true change in policy formulation or implementation is rare, and varies from one right to the other, and from one EU policy area to the next. Take the right to *education*, which is one of the social rights of the Charter as these are defined for the purposes of this chapter.[46] The formulation of that right in Article 14 of the Charter (now Article II-74 of the EU Constitution) is not particularly strong,[47] but that does not explain its complete lack of impact on the EU's education policy since 2001. The EU has developed an educational policy for many years now, and is currently revising the aims and instruments of that policy so as to make it an active part of the 'Lisbon process'.[48] However, the benchmarks and indicators that the EU institutions and Member States are identifying in the

[42] Art. III-117. This Art. is preceded by a 'gender equality' mainstreaming clause (Art. III-116) and followed by a 'combating discrimination' mainstreaming clause (Art. III-118).

[43] Alston, *supra* n. 26.

[44] See the chapters by Silvana Sciarra and Stijn Smismans in this volume.

[45] This idea is developed by Smismans in this volume. Other supporters of this idea include: G. de Búrca, 'The Constitutional Challenge of New Governance in the European Union', 28 *ELRev* (2003) 814, at 834; N. Bernard, 'A New Governance Approach to Economic, Social and Cultural Rights in the EU', in Hervey and Kenner, *supra* n. 2, 247, at 267; O. De Schutter, 'The Implementation of Fundamental Rights through the Open Method of Coordination', in O. De Schutter and S. Deakin (eds), *Social Rights and Market Forces: Is the Open Coordination of Employment and Social Policies the Future of Social Europe?* (2005).

[46] That is, the rights contained in one of the versions of the European Social Charter.

[47] See the critical comments by C. Wallace and J. Shaw, 'Education, Multiculturalism and the Charter of Fundamental Rights of the European Union', in Hervey and Kenner (eds), *supra* n. 2, 223, at 235ff.

[48] See, generally, J. Lonbay, 'Reflections on Education and Culture in EC Law', in R. Craufurd Smith (ed.), *Culture and European Union Law* (2004), at 243.

course of that process do not in any way reflect the fact that education is also a fundamental right recognized in the EU Charter,[49] nor is the Charter mentioned in the rare binding legal acts adopted in this field.[50] This is, therefore, an area in which the Charter has not even started to make a rhetorical impact on EU policy, let alone shape the actual content of the policy.[51]

In *social policy*, where EU competences are more clearly affirmed than in education policy, fundamental rights are somewhat more visible. In the Social Policy Agenda presented by the Commission in June 2000 (that is, even before the final adoption of the EU Charter), 'reinforcing fundamental rights and combating discrimination' was selected as one of the main objectives.[52] However, the manner in which this Agenda has since been developed shows a clear concern for the combating of discrimination (which is by far the most active area of EU human rights policy today), but complete neglect for the other fundamental social rights that are relevant to this policy area.[53] The Charter has clearly not yet become an inspirational force for the EU's social policy.

Will this change once the European Constitution enters into force and the Charter of Fundamental Rights acquires full binding force? For social rights even more than for other types of rights, this change of legal status will not entail any direct consequences for the effective enjoyment of fundamental social rights. However, the entry into force of the Constitution will be meaningful. Apart from the effect of this constitutionalization of rights on general polity-building,[54] the Constitution will act as a *platform*[55] for the development of EU policies. Political and civil society actors arguing for more effective protection of particular Charter rights will be able to stand on this constitutional platform to make their voices better heard.

VI. CONCLUSION

In a social policy resolution adopted in 1994, the EU Council of Ministers stated that 'the national identity of the Member States is particularly defined by their

---

[49] See, for instance, the latest document in this field: COM(2003)685 of 11 November 2003, *Education and Training 2010*.

[50] One such binding act adopted after the enactment of the Charter, but which does not refer to it and does not use fundamental rights language, is the 'Europass' decision (Decision 2241/2004 of 15 December 2004 on a single Community framework for the transparency of qualifications and competences, OJ 2004 L390/6).

[51] Contrast this with G. Gori, *Towards an EU Right to Education* (2001), who argues that the fundamental right to education should be a guiding principle of EU law and policy.

[52] COM(2000)379 of 28 June 2000, *Social Policy Agenda*.

[53] See, e.g., EC Commission, *Scoreboard on implementing the Social Policy Agenda*, COM(2004)137 of 1 March 2004, and the Commission's *Communication on the Social Agenda*, COM(2005)33 of 9 February 2005.

[54] See the reflections on this theme by M. Poiares Maduro, 'The Double Constitutional Life of the Charter of Fundamental Rights of the European Union', in Hervey and Kenner (eds), *supra* n. 2, at 269.

[55] I borrow this image from Tamara Hervey's chapter in this volume.

individual paths to solidarity within society and social balance'.[56] This recognition of the primary role of the Member States is probably still valid today, since there have not been major shifts of social policy competences to the EU (nor does the draft Constitution contemplate any such shifts). However, the EU Charter of Rights has contributed to making solidarity (one of the chapter headings of the Charter) a common European value, so that the 'paths' leading to the effective attainment of that value have also, arguably, become less nationally specific and more common to the whole EU. It can certainly no longer be argued that the value of solidarity is any less commonly European than that of freedom or equality. To this extent, indivisibility is now strongly entrenched in EU constitutional law. At a more practical level, the role of fundamental social rights continues to be distinct from that of other fundamental rights. On the one hand, their capacity for judicial enforcement is questioned in the final clauses of the Charter. On the other hand, though, they are at the forefront of the new agenda of human rights protection in the EU, which is less focused on the role of courts and negative protection, and more on constructing a positive human rights policy by and for the EU institutions.[57]

[56] Preamble to the Council Resolution of 6 December 1994 on certain aspects of a European social policy: a contribution to economic and social convergence in the Union, OJ 1994 C368/6.

[57] Such an agenda was formulated a few years ago by Alston and Weiler, 'An Ever Closer Union in Need of a Human Rights Policy: The European Union and Human Rights', in Alston, Bustelo and Heenan (eds), *The EU and Human Rights, supra* n. 14, 3, and developed further by other authors, including in particular: G. de Búrca, 'Convergence and Divergence in European Public Law: The Case of Human Rights' in P. Beaumont, C. Lyons, and N. Walker (eds), *Convergence and Divergence in European Public Law* (2002), at 131; and De Schutter, *supra* n. 26.

9

Social and Labour Rights under the EU Constitution

BRIAN BERCUSSON

I. INTRODUCTION

The focus of attention to social and labour rights in the European Constitution[1] has been on the Charter of Fundamental Rights of the European Union (EU). But it should be noted that the theme of 'Social and Labour Rights in the European Constitution' does not *only* refer to '*fundamental* social and labour rights'. Again, there are many 'social and labour rights in EU *law*', apart from the EU Charter. The *constitutional* context gives specific meaning to questions of social and labour rights in EU law in general, and fundamental social and labour rights in particular.[2]

This volume brings together discourses on social and labour rights in the European Social Charter (ESC) and the law of the EU. The substantive rights involved are often parallel, if not overlapping in content. This is evident, for example, in the reference to the ESC in Article 136 of the EC Treaty and the Preamble to the Treaty on European Union (TEU), and now in the Preamble to Part II and in Article III-209 of the Constitutional Treaty. Specifically, there are references to the ESC in the '*explanations*' attached by the Praesidium of the Convention which drafted the EU Charter to various Articles providing social and labour rights, and, according to the revised Preamble to the EU Charter in Part II of the Constitutional Treaty, '[i]n this context the Charter will be

[1] Draft Treaty establishing a Constitution for Europe, CONV 850/03, 18 July 2003. See now the Treaty establishing a Constitution for Europe adopted by the Member States in the Intergovernmental Conference meeting in Brussels 17–18 June 2004, OJ 2004 C310/1. References to the Treaty hereafter will be to the text in the Official Journal. References to the EU Charter of Fundamental Rights will be to the Charter of Fundamental Rights of the European Union, proclaimed in Nice on 7 December 2000, and adopted by the Commission, the Council and the Member States, OJ 2000 C364/01.

[2] In this chapter the emphasis is on rights in the European Constitution in the sphere of employment and industrial relations. Much attention has been paid to the substantive content of labour rights in this sphere. B. Bercusson (ed.), *European Labour Law and the EU Charter of Fundamental Rights* (2002).

interpreted by the courts of the Union and the Member States with due regard to the explanations [. . .]'.

A major difference between the social and labour rights in the ESC and those in the law of the EU, one which was a prominent theme of the EUI conference at Florence of 18–19 June 2004, is their mechanisms of implementation and enforcement. The central question addressed in this chapter is whether and, if so, how the mechanisms of implementation and enforcement of social and labour rights in the EU are to be reconfigured in light of the European Constitution.

Much of the discussion over implementation and enforcement of social and labour rights in the European Constitution has focused on their justiciability, and, in particular, the role of the European courts, mainly the European Court of Justice (ECJ). This is hardly surprising, since the legal effect of the social and labour rights in the Charter was the subject of some of the sharpest disputes in the Convention which drafted the EU Charter, and these disputes continued when the legal effect of the EU Charter was considered in the Convention on the Future of Europe. Those disputes focused on the specific issue of the *justiciability* of the fundamental social and labour rights in the EU Charter. However, other legal effects for social and labour rights are also canvassed (see Section II. below).

As previously emphasized, (i) not all social and labour rights are fundamental; (ii) not all social and labour rights are in the EU Charter; and (iii) social and labour rights, whether or not fundamental and whether or not in the EU Charter, may be affected by the emergence of a European Constitution. The issue of justiciability of social and labour rights, while important, is only one aspect of the broader issue of implementation and enforcement of social and labour rights. Other mechanisms, including the open method of coordination and the European social dialogue, are emerging in the new constitutional context of the EU (see Section III. below).

II. THE LEGAL EFFECTS OF THE EU CHARTER AND JUSTICIABILITY OF SOCIAL AND LABOUR RIGHTS

A. *The Convention drafting the EU Charter*

The EU Charter emerged in a specific legal context which highlighted sharp divisions of opinion regarding the legal status of the EU Charter and its political and legal consequences. One specific concern was whether social and economic rights, as contrasted with civil and political rights, should be included, and, if so, should be justiciable, or considered 'only' programmatic rights.

One division in the Convention drafting the EU Charter was between those who favoured including social and economic rights and those who wished to exclude them altogether. The latter considered that such rights were not part of the existing *acquis communautaire*, or fell outside the competences of the EU.

Their objective was to ensure that the EU Charter should not in any way become an instrument for the future expansion of EU competences in the social sphere.

Those who wished to include social and economic rights were further divided among those who separated some rights as 'subjective' or 'justiciable' (for example, protection of children and adolescents, dignity at work, protection against dismissal, vocational training, maternity protection, and parental leave) from other rights which were 'programmatic' (for example, health protection, social protection, elderly persons, disabled persons, migrant workers, housing). The strategy would be for such programmatic rights to be placed in a separate chapter and introduced by a clause declaring that the EU recognized as a political objective to create proper conditions for the implementation of that category of rights. Some social rights would be incorporated into the first section of the Charter, alongside justiciable civil and political rights. But there would be a separate, more extensive list of social rights which are not guaranteed by the EU itself (though they may be by some Member States).

Another tactic in this debate was the argument for inclusion of a 'horizontal' clause in the EU Charter which would make it clear that no extension of EU competences was to be allowed through the Charter's provisions. This could be made either generally applicable to the whole of the Charter, or specifically aimed at the clauses on social and economic rights.

The European Council of Nice faced a choice. On the one hand, to reject the Charter would be regarded as a setback for 'Social Europe', confirmation of the primacy of the EU's economic profile in general and of deregulated markets in particular. It would send a negative message about social rights to candidate states in the context of enlargement. On the other hand, some Member States were unequivocal in their refusal to accept a legally binding Charter including social and economic rights, let alone incorporating it into the Treaty.

The outcome gave something to each side. On the one hand, the Charter breaks new ground by including in a single list of fundamental rights not only traditional civil and political rights, but also a long list of social and economic rights. On the other hand, although the EU Charter was approved by the European Council, it was limited to a political declaration. It was not given a formal legal status. The final decision as to its legal status was eventually referred to the Convention on the Future of Europe.

B. *The Convention on the Future of Europe*

The working methods of the Convention on the Future of Europe included the establishment of Working Group II on the EU Charter of Fundamental Rights. The Final Report of Working Group II[3] was presented to the Plenary of the

---

[3] CONV 354/02, 22 October 2002.

Convention on 29 October 2002. It recommended that the EU Charter be integrated into the Treaty. The Convention accepted this recommendation and has incorporated the whole of the EU Charter as Part II of the proposed Constitutional Treaty. The proposal in the Final Report of Working Group II that the EU Charter be integrated into the Constitutional Treaty of the European Union was endorsed in the Draft of Articles 1 to 16 of the Constitutional Treaty produced by the Convention's Praesidium on 6 February 2003.[4]

However, a footnote added: 'The full text of the Charter, *with all the drafting adjustments given in Working Group II's final report* (CONV 354/02) will be set out either in a second part of the Constitution or in a Protocol annexed thereto, as the Convention decides.'[5] The 'adjustments' to the EU Charter proposed by Working Group II on the Charter were described as follows in its Final Report:[6]

It is important to note that these adjustments proposed by the Group do not reflect modifications of substance. On the contrary, they would serve to confirm, and render absolutely clear and legally watertight, certain key elements of the overall consensus on the Charter on which the previous Convention had already agreed . . . all drafting adjustments proposed herein fully respect the basic premise of the Group's work, i.e. to leave intact the substance agreed by consensus within the previous Convention . . .

On the contrary, I suggest that the proposed 'adjustments' may be characterized as an attack on social and labour rights in particular. Further, despite its statement to the contrary, Working Group II reopened questions resolved by the earlier Convention, relying in one case on 'understandings' reported by a few members of that Convention who happened to be in this Working Group, or the 'important guidance provided by the "Praesidium's Explanations"',[7] though the Praesidium itself explicitly denied that it represented the Convention's authority and the Working Group conceded 'they have no legal value'.[8] The Working Group had no authority to reopen these questions, let alone propose 'adjustments' which change the consensus reached in the earlier Convention.[9]

---

[4] CONV 528/03, 6 February 2003.

[5] Emphasis added. This endorsement was reinforced by the Final Report of Working Group XI on Social Europe. However, the Praesidium produced its draft of Articles 1–16 on 6 February 2003, the same day that the Final Report of Working Group XI was presented by its Chair to the Plenary of the Convention. The Praesidium's draft texts were introduced by acknowledging that they 'reflect the reports of the Working Groups on Legal Personality, the Charter, Economic Governance, Complementary Competencies, the Principle of Subsidiarity and External Action, as well as the guidelines that emerged on the basis of their recommendations during the plenary debate'. Manifestly, the draft failed to take account either of the Final Report of Working Group XI, or of any debate on the Report in the Plenary. This failure compounded the Praesidium's inability to recognize the importance of Social Europe by failing to establish a Working Group early in its proceedings.

[6] Section A.II.1.   [7] Section A.II.6.   [8] Section A.III.3.

[9] Professor Gráinne de Búrca has written one of the '*Ten Reflections on the Constitutional Treaty for Europe*' prepared by the European University Institute, a contribution submitted to the Convention by Giuliano Amato (CONV 703/03, 28 April 2003). Professor de Búrca analyses Working Group II's proposed 'adjustments' and recommends that, with one minor exception, they should be rejected. Amato says he does 'not endorse every single word of this study'.

C. *Working Group II's Attack on Social and Labour Rights*

This attack is expressed in an 'adjustment' in the form of an additional paragraph added to Article 52 (Article 52(5)):[10]

The provisions of this Charter which contain principles may be implemented by legislative and executive acts taken by the institutions and bodies of the Union, and by acts of Member States when they are implementing Union law, in the exercise of their respective powers. They shall be judicially cognisable only in the interpretation of such acts and in the ruling on their legality.

This provision aims to prevent 'principles' being interpreted in future as containing elements of positive rights for individuals. This proposal was vainly resisted by members of Working Group II, who complained that it resurrected the distinction between rights and principles which had been rejected by the drafting Convention.[11] It attempts to reverse what was a central compromise in the earlier Convention which drafted the Charter: that social and economic rights should not be separated from traditional 'rights' by characterizing them as 'principles' which are not justiciable positive rights. That Convention decided that all rights should have the same status.[12] This was a compromise in exchange for the Convention's not seeking to assert that the Charter should have legal constitutional status. That final legal status would be determined by the Member States, but the Convention which drafted the Charter rejected the view, advocated by a number of its members, that there should be differences in the legal status of different parts of the Charter.

The language of the Charter uses the word 'rights'. By asserting that 'principles' are different, the Working Group aimed to open the door to transforming some 'rights' into mere 'principles'. The Working Group conceded that it was aiming at social rights when it stated:[13] 'This is consistent both with case law of the Court of Justice and with the approach of the Member States' constitutional systems to "principles" *particularly in the field of social law*' (emphasis added).

However, it is submitted that the 'adjustment' may not have the effect claimed for it. First, challenges to Union acts and those of the Member States as contravening the EU Charter may be referred to the European courts, which may then take judicial cognizance of the Charter's provisions in ruling on the legality of those

---

[10] Now Article II-112(5) of the Treaty establishing a Constitution for Europe.

[11] In criticizing the Working Group's amendments during the Convention Plenary's debate on the Final Report of Working Group II, Olivier Duhamel, a Member of the Convention from the European Parliament, stated they were 'unnecessary and retrograde' and singled out the alleged distinction between 'rights and principles', as did Anne Van Lancker, who specifically identified the distinction between rights and principles as attempting to limit the Charter. The French Government representative, Pierre Moscovici, warned that the distinction between rights and principles could limit the interpretation of those principles.

[12] As affirmed in a dissent in the Working Group by Mme. Elena Paciotti, a Member of the Convention from the European Parliament.   [13] Section A.II.6, at 8.

acts, with consequential effects on the legal rights of individuals. Secondly, the reference to 'principles' in Article 52(5) may not apply to many of the provisions in Chapter IV ('Solidarity') of the Charter, as Articles 27–38[14] are formulated mostly as rights, not principles.

D. *Legal Effects of the EU Charter Incorporated into the Constitutional Treaty*

As part of a Constitutional Treaty, the legal effects of the EU Charter could be significant. Two only will be examined here: direct effect and 'indirect' effect (consistent interpretation).

1. Direct Effect   As with equal pay for men and women (Article 141 EC), the Court could attribute binding direct effect to provisions of the Charter which were considered sufficiently clear, precise, and unconditional. This effect would apply both vertically (against Member States and their 'emanations'), and horizontally (against private persons or bodies). Examples from the Charter might include:

- Article 8(2):[15] 'Everyone has the right of access to data which has been collected concerning him or her, and the right to have it rectified.'
- Article 30:[16] 'Every worker has the right to protection against unjustified dismissal, in accordance with Community law and national laws and practices.'
- Article 29(2):[17] 'Every worker has the right to limitation of maximum working hours, to daily and weekly rest periods and to an annual period of paid leave.'

Provisions of the Charter which are not considered to satisfy the conditions for direct effect may nonetheless be invoked to challenge EU laws, including Commission proposals for legislation, or Member State laws which are said to violate the fundamental rights guaranteed. Such challenges could be mounted in national courts and referred to the European courts under Article 234 EC. Examples might include:

- national legislation transposing the Parental Leave Directive[18] which included derogations denying rights guaranteed by Article 33[19] of the EU Charter: 'the right . . . to parental leave following the birth or adoption of a

---

[14] Now Articles II-87-98 of the Treaty establishing a Constitution for Europe.
[15] Now Article II-68(2) of the Treaty establishing a Constitution for Europe.
[16] Now Article II-90 of the Treaty establishing a Constitution for Europe.
[17] Now Article II-89(2) of the Treaty establishing a Constitution for Europe.
[18] Council Directive 96/34 on the Framework Agreement on parental leave concluded by UNICE, CEEP and the ETUC, OJ 1996 L145/4.
[19] Now Article II-93 of the Treaty establishing a Constitution for Europe.

child'; an example would have been the exclusion of parents with children under five years of age at the date of transposition;

- EU competition law invoked to challenge collective agreements protected by Article 28[20] of the Charter: 'the right to negotiate and conclude collective agreements'.[21]

An illustration of the Charter's potential impact is a case brought by a British trade union (BECTU) challenging the UK Government's implementation of the Working Time Directive.[22] The UK legislation made entitlement to paid annual leave subject to a qualification period of thirteen weeks' employment. There is no such qualification in the Directive. BECTU complained because many of the union's members on short-term contracts were being deprived of their right to paid annual leave under EC law by the UK legislation.

On 8 February 2001 Advocate General Tizzano delivered his advisory Opinion upholding BECTU's complaint. The Advocate General looked at the right to paid annual leave 'in the wider context of fundamental social rights' (paragraph 22). A worker's right to a period of paid annual leave is to be given the same fundamental status as other human rights and guaranteed absolute protection. He points out (paragraph 26) that:

Even more significant, it seems to me, is the fact that that right is now solemnly upheld in the Charter of Fundamental Rights of the European Union, published on 7 December 2000 by the European Parliament, the Council and the Commission after approval by the Heads of State and Government of the Member States.

He freely admits that 'formally, [the EU Charter] is not in itself binding' (paragraph 27). However, he states unequivocally:

I think therefore that, in proceedings concerned with the nature and scope of a fundamental right, the relevant statements of the Charter cannot be ignored; in particular, we cannot ignore its clear purpose of serving, where its provisions so allow, as a substantive point of reference for all those involved—Member States, institutions, natural and legal persons—in the Community context. Accordingly, I consider that the Charter provides us with the most reliable and definitive confirmation of the fact that the right to paid annual leave constitutes a fundamental right. (paragraph 28)

This is the worst nightmare of those who fought against the inclusion of fundamental social and labour rights in the EU Charter. These rights are 'a substantive point of reference', and not only for the Community institutions, but also for Member States (for example, as in *BECTU*, where a Member State is responsible

---

[20] Now Article II-68 of the Treaty establishing a Constitution for Europe.
[21] Case C-67/96 with Joined Cases C-115/97, C-116/97, and C-117/97, *Albany International BV v. Stichting Bedrijfspensioenfonds Textielindustrie* [1999] ECR I-5751.
[22] Case C-173/99, *R. v. Secretary of State for Trade and Industry, ex parte Broadcasting, Entertainment, Cinematographic and Theatre Union (BECTU)* [2001] ECR I-4811.

for transposing an EC directive including the fundamental social right to paid annual leave), and even for private persons, human and corporate.

2. Indirect Effect   The doctrine of 'indirect effect' established by the European Court of Justice with respect to directives requires national courts to interpret national laws consistently with EC law. It would apply with even greater force to the rights guaranteed in the EU Charter incorporated into the Constitutional Treaty.

Recent developments in the doctrine illustrate its potential.[23] The *Pfeiffer* case concerns the German legislation (Arbeitszeitgesetz) implementing the Working Time Directive 93/104/EC.[24] Article 3 of the Arbeitszeitgesetz specifies a working day of eight hours which may be prolonged to ten hours provided the average of eight hours daily work is maintained. Article 7.1.1 allows for derogation from Article 3 by a collective agreement prolonging daily hours of work beyond ten hours. A collective agreement with the German Red Cross provided for such a prolongation so as to allow a working week exceeding forty-eight hours (Article 14.2 of the agreement). The questions referred to the ECJ under Article 234 EC included whether Article 6 of Directive 93/104 had direct effect so as to allow an individual to complain to a national court where the Member State has not correctly implemented the Directive.

The Opinion of Advocate-General M. D. Ruiz-Jarabo Colomer of 6 May 2003 concludes that Article 6.2 of the Directive was sufficiently clear, precise, and unconditional to have direct effect. However, the Advocate-General acknowledges that the ECJ has refused to allow an individual to rely on the direct effect of directives to make claims in national courts against other private individuals. Directives do not have so-called 'horizontal' direct effect (paragraphs 56–57).

The Advocate-General then refers to the ECJ's doctrine of 'indirect' effect of directives, which requires a national court to interpret national law consistently with the objectives of the directive (paragraph 58). The Advocate-General argues that it follows that Article 6.2 of Directive 93/104 overrides Article 7.1.1 of the Arbeitszeitgesetz which allows a collective agreement to prolong the working day beyond ten hours, and Article 14 of the collective agreement must be interpreted so that the workers concerned are not required to work more than forty-eight hours on average (paragraph 59).

---

[23] Advocate-General M. D. Ruiz-Jarabo Colomer in joined Cases C-397/01 to C-403/01, *Bernhard Pfeiffer et al. v. Deutsches Rotes Kreuz Kreisverband Waldshut eV*, 6 May 2003. Second Opinion of 27 April 2004. Decision of the ECJ, 5 October 2004 (not yet reported).

[24] Council Directive 93/104 concerning certain aspects of the organization of working time, OJ 1993, L307/18, as amended by Directive 2000/34, OJ 2000 L195/41. Consolidated in Directive 2003/88 concerning certain aspects of the organization of working time, OJ 2003 L299/9.

The new elements in the Advocate-General's reasoning appear to be:

1. provisions of Directives having direct effect must be taken into account by national courts, but *not only* when they are invoked in claims against Member States ('vertical' direct effect);

2. there is no 'horizontal' direct effect of directives, but the direct effect of Directives means that *not only legislation,*[25] but *also other legal measures* (including *private law measures* such as collective agreements) based on a national law which contravenes directly effective provisions of a Directive must be interpreted consistently with the Directive;

3. in contrast with the ECJ's view that national courts are *not* obliged to disapply national *legislation* where it is impossible to interpret it consistently with EC law,[26] the Advocate-General's view is that national courts *are* obliged to interpret *other legal measures* (here, collective agreements) consistently with the Directive, where these other legal measures are based on national law which is inconsistent with directly effective provisions of a Directive.

This appears to be a new *Pfeiffer* doctrine of 'private indirect effect'. National courts are obliged to interpret private law measures consistently with directly effective provisions of a Directive, where these private law measures are based on national law which is inconsistent with the directly effective provisions of a Directive.

This latter doctrine does not equate to horizontal direct effect. The effect of the directive is achieved through *interpretation* of the (intermediary) private law measure, which itself relies on the national legislation. The link between the directive and national legislation remains the central element, but it is achieved through indirect effect of the directive on the private law measure.

This doctrine has significant implications for social rights in labour law. Contracts of employment are the most important private law measures in labour law. The *Pfeiffer* doctrine seems to state that contracts of employment, based on national law, must be interpreted consistently with the directly effective provisions of directives.

The Advocate-General presented his Opinion on 6 May 2003. In an unusual move, the Court issued an Order on 13 January 2004 reopening the procedure, transferring the case from the sixth Chamber to the Court, and ordering an oral hearing for arguments on 9 March 2004.

The ECJ's Order of 13 January 2004 provides some indications of why this unusual procedural step was taken. In particular, paragraph 9 emphasizes the purpose of Directive 93/104: to protect workers as the weaker party to the employment contract, and adds that effective protection (*effet utile*) must be

---

[25] Case 14/83, *Von Colson and Kamann v. Land Nordrhein-Westfalen* [1984] ECR 1891.
[26] Case C-106/89, *Marleasing SA v. La Comercial Internacionale de Alimentacion SA* [1990] ECR I-4135.

assured by both EU and national courts. In paragraph 10, the ECJ emphasizes that the complaints based on Directive 93/104 are concerned with limiting daily working hours, not monetary compensation, making it difficult to launch a claim against the Member State for the harm caused by the violation of EC law.[27]

These factors indicate doctrinal concerns quite different from those of the Advocate-General. The ECJ's order highlights issues only of direct effect of directives (paragraphs 6–8). There is no reference to doctrinal questions concerned with indirect effect of directives. However, the implications of direct effect are placed in a general context of disputes between private parties (paragraphs 6–7), and specifically, in the employment context where one party, the worker, is in a weaker position (paragraph 9).[28] In this context of directly effective provisions of a Directive as regards a weaker private party, the ECJ focuses on the contrast between the remedy sought for the Member State's failure to implement the Directive (limitation of working hours) and the remedy available under EC law (compensation: *Francovich*) (paragraph 10).

For the ECJ, the direct effect of the directive on national legislation continues to be essential. However, the collective agreement disappears from view, and the doctrine of indirect effect is not invoked. Instead, rather than resorting to the doctrine of indirect effect to resolve the problem, the ECJ looks to the alternative doctrinal source/inspiration of the *Francovich* case.

The ECJ's order states:[29]

. . . the point at issue is whether, *having regard to the particular circumstances of these cases*, it is for the Court to define the consequences which national courts should apply when, in a dispute between private individuals, a provision of domestic law, adopted to transpose the rules laid down in a directive, is deemed incompatible with a provision of the latter in order for that provision to fulfil the requirements of producing direct effect.

The reference to '*the particular circumstances of these cases*' could refer to a number of factors, with important implications for the enforcement of social rights. The protection offered by the directive is to the *weaker party* to the employment contract. Should 'horizontal direct effect' apply where directly effective provisions of directives aim to protect the weaker party in the employment context? This would be a doctrine of '*effet utile*' specific to EC labour law. Directives affording protection to workers can be invoked before national courts to override contracts of

---

[27] Cases C-6/90 and C-9/90, *Francovich and Bonfaci v. Italy*, [1991] ECR I-5357.

[28] '*Ensuite, la directive 93/104 vise à protéger spécifiquement les travailleurs en tant qu'ils sont la partie faible au contrat de travail, protection dont l'effet utile doit être assuré par les juridictions tant communautaires que nationales.*'

[29] Para. 3. My translation (emphasis added) from the French: '. . . *à se prononcer sur le point de savoir si, au regard de circonstances particulières telles que celles des affaires au principal, il y a lieu pour la Cour de préciser les conséquences que doivent tirer les juridictions nationales lorsque, dans le cadre d'un litige entre particuliers, une disposition du droit interne, adoptée aux fins de le point de savoir si, au regard de circonstances particulières transposer les règles édictées par une directive, s'avère incompatible avec une disposition de cette dernière pour autant que cette disposition remplit les conditions pour produire un effet direct*'.

employment which are inconsistent with directives. They are an exception to the general rule precluding horizontal direct effect.

The lack of an *effective remedy* is of special concern in the case of violation of EC labour law directives. *Francovich* only allows financial compensation against the state. *Factortame*[30] allowed for other (interim) remedies.[31] Another remedy would be to require national law to allow directly effective provisions of directives to override inconsistent contracts of employment.[32]

The Grand Chamber (eleven judges) of the European Court of Justice handed down its decision in *Pfeiffer* on 5 October 2004. The Court reached the same conclusion as the Advocate-General, and appears to support the reasoning in the Advocate-General's Opinion. Like the Advocate-General, the Court concludes that Article 6(2) of the Working Time Directive satisfies the criteria for direct effect (paragraph 104).

Referring to *Von Colson and Kamann* and Article 10 EC, the Court added (paragraph 115) (emphasis added):

Although the principle that national law must be interpreted in conformity with Community law concerns chiefly domestic provisions enacted in order to implement the directive in question, it does not entail an interpretation merely of those provisions but requires the national court to consider *national law as a whole* in order to assess to what extent it may be applied so as not to produce a result contrary to that sought by the directive . . .

And crucially (paragraph 116) (emphasis added):

In that context, if the application of *interpretative methods recognised by national law* enables, in certain circumstances, a provision of domestic law to be construed in such a way as to avoid conflict with another rule of domestic law or the scope of that provision to be restricted to that end by applying it only in so far as it is compatible with the rule concerned, the national court is *bound* to use those methods in order to achieve the result sought by the directive.

The 'interpretative methods recognised by national law' must be applied equally to safeguard EC law. For example, if a rule of national law would prohibit contracts of

---

[30] Case C-213/89, *R. v. Secretary of State for Transport, ex parte Factortame Ltd and Others* [1990] ECR I-2433.

[31] See below, Section III.B.1., on the specific need for interim remedies in labour disputes, particularly those involving dismissals, where reinstatement or re-engagement in employment, not compensation is the desired remedy.

[32] There is a final '*particular circumstance*' to this case: the presence of the *collective agreement*. It would be dangerous if the ECJ's conclusions were somehow confined to the case where national provisions allowed for derogations by collective agreement. This could take the form of requiring national courts to interpret *only* collective agreements (somehow analogous to legislation) consistently with directives. Even worse, following the *Francovich* line of reasoning, the ECJ might allow claims for compensation against the authors of collective agreements (as with the Member State, the author of the legislation) which violate directly effective rights in a directive. Similarly, the violation by the EU or a Member State of a fundamental right guaranteed by the Charter in the Treaty would very likely constitute a breach of EU law giving rise to liability under the *Francovich* principle.

employment derogating from legislative minimum standards, that interpretative method must accord the same status to EC law, to prohibit contracts of employment derogating from EC legislation (paragraphs 118–119) (emphasis added):

In this instance, the principle of interpretation in conformity with Community law requires the referring court to do *whatever lies within its jurisdiction*, having regard to the *whole body of rules of national law*, to ensure that Directive 93/104 is fully effective, in order to prevent the maximum weekly working time laid down in Article 6(2) of the directive from being exceeded . . .

Accordingly, it must be concluded that, when hearing a case between individuals, a national court is required, when applying the provisions of domestic law adopted for the purpose of transposing obligations laid down by a directive, to consider the *whole body of rules of national law* and to interpret them, *so far as possible*, in the light of the wording and purpose of the directive in order to achieve an outcome consistent with the objective pursued by the directive . . . the national court must thus do whatever lies within its jurisdiction to ensure that the maximum period of weekly working time, which is set at 48 hours by Article 6(2) of Directive 93/104, is not exceeded.

It may be that there is a subtle difference between the *doctrine* enunciated in the Court's judgment and the Opinion of the Advocate-General. *Both* are clear that national legislation, specifically that implementing a directive, must be interpreted consistently with the directive, 'so far as possible'. The Advocate-General may be read as importing an *EC rule of interpretation* requiring that courts interpret other (private law) measures consistently with a directive, without qualification. The Court appears to say that EC law requires courts only to use interpretative methods *recognized by national law*.

The protection of labour rights has particular salience, as the Court noted in its Order in the *Pfeiffer* case of 13 January 2004, with regard to weaker parties and effective remedies. If not through justiciability, other doctrinal solutions are available so that the social and labour rights in the EU Charter offer a prospect of using EU law to achieve the social objectives of the Constitutional Treaty.

III. JUSTICIABILITY IN THE BROADER CONTEXT OF MECHANISMS OF IMPLEMENTATION AND ENFORCEMENT OF SOCIAL AND LABOUR RIGHTS

The controversy over the justiciability of social and labour rights in the European Constitution has overshadowed the existence of other mechanisms of enforcement. This is highlighted in the case of social rights in the sphere of employment and industrial relations, where recent developments in implementation and enforcement are reflected in provisions of the Constitutional Treaty. These developments may have importance also for the implementation and enforcement of social rights in other spheres.

Justiciability and the role of the courts in the implementation and enforcement of social rights should be analysed in the general context of *other mechanisms of implementation, application and enforcement* of social rights, in this case, the rights of workers and their organizations in the European Union. To do otherwise would be to isolate the ECJ in the 'formal' EU Constitution from the context of enforcement of rights under the 'real' Constitution operating in practice in the field of EU labour law.

Further, to understand the role of social and labour rights in the European Constitution, it is necessary to appreciate the role of the national context of social and labour rights in the Member States, not least as regards implementation and enforcement of social and labour rights.

A. *Mechanisms of Enforcement in National Law*

One account of the application of labour law in national jurisdictions identified three principal mechanisms: through the administration, through the courts and through the social partners (administrative, judicial and industrial relations mechanisms of enforcement).[33] There are differences in the effectiveness and in the importance attached to each of these mechanisms of enforcement among the labour law systems of the Member States. Various mechanisms interact and overlap in different ways within each national jurisdiction.

Within each Member State, an equilibrium among the different mechanisms has been established. This is not to say that all such national equilibria are functionally equivalent. That in some Member States the administrative, judicial or industrial relations mechanism is predominant does not imply that the overall equilibrium in each Member State assures equally effective enforcement. Specifically, the presence or absence of strong mechanisms of judicial enforcement is not determining.

Although there is controversy about the particular efficacy of one or other mechanism in a specific national context, one axiom of labour law should be remembered. The effectiveness of labour law rules is in inverse proportion to the distance between those who make the rules and those who are subjected to them: the greater the distance, the less their effectiveness; the less the distance, the greater their effectiveness.

The presumption is that rules originating from social partners engaged in collective bargaining, being closest to those subject to these rules, achieve a higher level of effectiveness. Conversely, those emerging from legislative or administrative processes, distant from employers and workers, will have relatively less efficacy. Whatever the national equilibrium among the various mechanisms of

---

[33] A. Supiot, 'L'Application du droit du travail en Europe', *Travail et Emploi* (1991), no. 47. A similar framework has been applied to enforcement of EU labour law: 'Enforcement of European Labour Law' in B. Bercusson, *European Labour Law* (1996), Part III, Chs 7–11.

enforcement, the argument is that those systems in which the social partners are more prominent in rule making will be those in which the effectiveness of enforcement is greater.

B. *Effective Enforcement in EU Law*

In EU law, the principle of effective enforcement (*effet utile*) has been the driving force of doctrinal developments ever since the path-breaking decision in *Van Gend en Loos*,[34] in which the European Court of Justice pointed out the need for decentralized enforcement of EC Treaty obligations through national courts by individuals, alongside the established mechanism of administrative enforcement by the European Commission through complaints to the ECJ. Since then, numerous doctrinal developments, indeed revolutions, such as the extension of direct effect to directives, indirect effect (consistent interpretation), state liability, and so on have continued to reinforce the importance of effectiveness.

The role of the European Court of Justice in the enforcement of the social rights of labour under the Constitutional Treaty will be used to illustrate the effectiveness of different mechanisms, both at EU and Member State levels. Two issues will be explored which bear on general questions of the enforcement of social and labour rights in the European Constitution.

First, the increasing prominence of EU labour law in national systems[35] raises complex issues of the *interaction* of *national* enforcement mechanisms and enforcement of *EU* labour laws in the EU Member States. The Constitutional Treaty makes specific provision for this interaction, not least as regards enforcement through an EU judicial structure and the role of the ECJ in this structure (see Subsection 1 below).

Secondly, the *evolution* of EU social and labour policy means the boundaries between different sources and methods of enforcement of EU labour law are becoming increasingly fluid. Again, this evolution, which potentially provides lessons for the implementation and enforcement of social rights in general, is reflected in provisions of the Constitutional Treaty on the open method of coordination and the European social dialogue (see Subsection 2 below).

1. Interaction of National and EU Enforcement Mechanisms   Effective enforcement of EU social and labour rights depends on different Member State rules and practices. Broadly speaking, EU law determines substantive rules, but domestic law determines remedies and procedures.

---

[34] Case 26/62, *NV Algemene Transporten Expeditie Onderneming van Gend en Loos v. Nederlandse Administratie der Belastingen* [1963] ECR 1.

[35] For example, one UK source estimates that 40% of UK employment law derives from EU requirements (Better Regulation Taskforce, Employment Regulation: Striking a Balance (2002), cited in C. Kilpatrick, 'Has New Labour Reconfigured Employment Legislation?', 32 *ILJ* (2003) 135, at 141).

This means there is an important distinction between the full *effectiveness* of rights deriving from EU law, dependent on national remedies and procedure, and the *formal* remedies and procedures, provided by EU law for breaches of EU law.

The case law of the ECJ addresses the issue of enforcement of EU social rights of workers and their organizations by elucidating three principles: equivalence, effectiveness, and proportionality.[36] These principles can be applied to cover not only judicial, but also administrative and industrial relations processes. For example, the incorporation of social rights into collective agreements implies the commitment of the negotiating parties to enforcement, and may both promote compliance and lessen the need for administrative or judicial enforcement. The obvious fact, sometimes overlooked by lawyers, is that when a worker or a workers' representative is confronted with an employer's violation of his or her rights, the first step is not to go to court but to seek to resolve the conflict through discussion. Judicial processes are thus preceded by negotiations engaged in the similar exercise of assessing facts and interpreting rules, including formal legal rules. Collective bargaining, including information and consultation, is an integral process of enforcement of rules in disputes. This also applies to EU social and labour rights, and in particular where they are embodied in an EU social dialogue agreement.

In considering the role of courts, including the ECJ, under the Constitutional Treaty, therefore, the rules on industrial relations processes may be of equal significance to the requirements regarding access to a court and *locus standi* in order to enforce EU social and labour rights. Examples are the *locus standi* of workers' representatives in litigation before national courts or the ECJ. The use of collective actors in judicial enforcement procedures of EU labour law is underdeveloped compared with its relatively widespread use in the Member States. However, recent EU initiatives attribute *locus standi* to interest groups, as in Article 9(2) of the Framework Employment Equality Directive[37] and Article 6(3) in the amended Equal Treatment Directive.[38]

Similarly, administrative processes of enforcement were often established because workers were unable in practice to enforce their rights through judicial processes. Yet EU law has failed to develop specific instruments of administrative enforcement, though effective enforcement may require some administrative intervention to reinforce individual or collective action before courts or through industrial relations processes. The interrelation of

---

[36] Barry Fitzpatrick provides a closely argued analysis of the ebb and flow of the ECJ's doctrine on effective judicial protection based on principles of equivalence, effectiveness and proportionality. See his contribution in J. Malmberg (ed.), *Effective Enforcement of EC Labour Law* (2003), at 43–58. The following Section draws on my Foreword to that book.

[37] Council Directive 2000/78 establishing a general framework for equal treatment in employment and occupation OJ 2000 L303/16.

[38] Council Directive 76/207 on the implementation of the principle of equal treatment for men and women as regards access to employment, vocational training and promotion, and working conditions, OJ 1976 L39/40, as revised by Council Directive 2002/73, OJ 2002 L269/15.

administrative, industrial relations and judicial processes is manifest in many areas of labour law.[39]

An example of exceptional practical significance in enforcement of EU labour rights is the issue of interim decision-making powers. The Swedish Co-Determination Act of 1976 reflects this experience. Labour disputes may be resolved by court proceedings, but these normally take considerable time. The question is which interpretation of the employee's rights or obligations is to prevail while awaiting the court's decision. In the Swedish terminology this is the issue of which party has the 'priority of interpretation'. Other related questions include which of the parties has the burden of bringing the dispute to court to enforce his or her interpretation, and, subsequently, in what circumstances the court may make an interim decision. For example, 'the rules on priority of interpretation and burden of litigation differ largely depending on whom the enforcing party is . . . an administrative authority . . . the workers' representatives . . . or individual employees . . . there are examples where the workers' representatives are given a priority of interpretation, with the rules in the Swedish Co-Determination Act as the most striking example'.[40]

Different processes of enforcement of labour rights through administrative, industrial relations, and judicial mechanisms may have different impacts at individual and collective levels, and can be mutually beneficial. For example, it may be that collective methods of enforcement of labour law are stronger and individual enforcement mechanisms relatively weaker at Member State level, but the reverse is true at EU level. If so, this may offer a positive prospect of the European Court of Justice reinforcing the micro level of national judicial procedures. Decisions of the ECJ have had an impact on national enforcement of social rights through judicial processes.[41]

---

[39] Sylvaine Laulom demonstrates that the nature of administrative intervention is dependent on the area concerned, looking at the three areas of working time, equal treatment at work, and restructuring of the enterprise: 'The administrative processes and the industrial relations processes or judicial processes are strongly interrelated in all the three fields of labour law under study and in all the Member States investigated. But these interrelations are slightly different in the three areas. The task of administrative authorities in the field of working time has a traditional foundation due to the established link between working time and health and safety. Nevertheless, the rising importance of collective bargaining in the regulation of working time can imply some modifications to the functions of administrative bodies . . . [C]oncerning equality, the Member States, where a labour inspectorate has specialized powers, have provided for independent authorities to ensure observance of equality principles. This shows the need for some form of control auxiliary to the collective and judicial enforcement of equality rights.' In Malmberg (ed.), *supra* n. 36 at 109–35.

[40] See Malmberg in Malmberg (ed.), *supra* n. 36, at 159–90.

[41] An example is provided by three time-related questions: (i) how much time is allowed to claim a right before a court?; (ii) when does time begin to run?; and (iii) what are the possible retroactive effects of a claim? A close analysis of the ECJ's case law reveals that '. . . in some cases national time limits to challenge before a court the validity of a dismissal have somehow been "communitarised" by national judges. In Germany and the Netherlands, for example, the *Bundesarbeitsgericht* and the *Hoge Raad* have been ready to extend the time limits laid down in ordinary dismissal cases, when the contested dismissal is allegedly grounded on a transfer of undertaking, contrary to what Community law prescribes.' Antonio Lo Faro characterizes this as a sort of ' "procedural added value" which can sometimes be found when a Community right is claimed before a national court'. Indeed, 'In a burst of Europeanism probably unparalleled in any other Member State, the German legislation excludes whatsoever limitations on the retroactivity of claims brought for the application of Community legislation on equal treatment.' See A. Lo Faro, in Malmberg (ed.), *supra* n. 36, at 190–214.

Conversely, national industrial relations systems could contribute to supporting effective enforcement of EC labour rights at the collective level.[42] The objective is mutual reinforcement of EU and national systems of labour law.

The specific role of the EU institutions, and, in particular, the ECJ is highlighted by the incorporation into the EU Constitution of the EU Charter of Fundamental Rights, including many labour rights and principles. Jonas Malmberg points out that it 'might it be argued that the more fundamental the Community right which is infringed, the more intrusive should be the remedial structure'. He contrasts 'ordinary' labour rights, with 'fundamental social rights': equality, health and safety, and even information and consultation of workers, and asks 'Should it be a factor in Community law enforcement that the level of scrutiny of national remedies, and wider judicial process, should be stricter where fundamental social rights are at issue?'[43] Questions of the enforcement in general, and not only justiciability, of rights and principles will become a focus of attention. Alternatives to judicial processes of effective enforcement of the social and labour rights in the EU Charter may become a central element in this debate.

2. Evolution of EU Labour Policy and its Implications for the Enforcement of Social and Labour Rights   Throughout its history of almost half a century, the European Community has experienced a variety of legal strategies for the formulation and implementation of labour law and social policy. The past decade has witnessed dramatic changes in the EU's methods of labour regulation.

The traditional approach of *judicial enforcement* of labour standards laid down in EU legislation (directives) is constantly under the pressure of new doctrinal developments.[44]

In addition, there has emerged a new *industrial relations* mechanism, the process of social dialogue and European framework agreements between the social partners (Maastricht Treaty, now Articles 138–39 of the EC Treaty).

There is also a new *administrative* mechanism, the 'open method of coordination' (OMC), applied to the European Employment Strategy (EES) (Treaty of Amsterdam, now Articles 125–30 of the EC Treaty).

---

[42] Research at the Swedish National Institute for Working Life aims to contribute to addressing the latter issue by examining the role of European social dialogue agreements in EC labour law. K. Ahlberg et al., *Fixed-Term Work in the EU: A European Agreement Against Discrimination and Abuse* (1999).

[43] This argument is particularly timely in the aftermath of the struggle over the issue of sanctions in Council Directive 2002/14 establishing a framework for informing and consulting employees in the European Community, OJ 2002 L80/29. The incorporation in the final directive of the traditional formula regarding judicial sanctions was a retreat from the Commission's approach in its initial draft proposal seeking more targeted remedies for specific and serious breaches. However, as Article 27 of the EU Charter makes workers' right to information and consultation a fundamental right, the question of what sanctions are required for its effective enforcement, as integrated in Article II-87 of the EU Constitution, may now perhaps be revived. For a detailed account, see B. Bercusson, 'The European Social Model Comes to Britain', 31 *ILJ* (2002) 209.

[44] The *Pfeiffer* litigation, described above, being one illustration.

These new developments have produced new approaches to application and enforcement of labour rights. The context of these changes is the so-called 'Lisbon Strategy', but the Treaty of Nice provided the legal framework for the changes signalled by the Lisbon Strategy, which took shape in the Commission's Social Policy Agenda 2000–2004.

(a) The Context: The Lisbon Strategy

The Lisbon European Council of 23–24 March 2000 articulated a new strategic goal for the EU: 'to become the most competitive and dynamic knowledge-based economy in the world capable of sustainable economic growth with more and better jobs and greater social cohesion'.[45] As well as a new strategic goal, the Lisbon Council highlighted the 'open method of coordination' as a principal process through which this goal was to be achieved.

In its Social Policy Agenda 2000–2004, the Commission confirmed the Lisbon Strategy.[46] Reflecting the approach favoured by the Lisbon Council, the Commission stated (at page 7): 'This new Social Policy Agenda does *not seek to harmonise social policies*. It seeks to work towards common European objectives and increase *co-ordination of social policies* in the context of the internal market and the single currency.'

(b) The Treaty of Nice: From Judicial Enforcement to Administrative Process

The approach emphasizing *coordination* is reflected in the changes to the Social Chapter of the EC Treaty adopted by the Treaty of Nice in December 2000. Article 137(2) EC was amended by the Treaty of Nice in two apparently minor ways.

First, it *added* to Article 137(2)'s provision encouraging cooperation between Member States the phrase '*excluding any harmonisation of the laws and regulations of the Member States*'.

Secondly, this phrase *replaced* the former Article 137(2)'s provision limiting cooperation measures solely '*in order to combat social exclusion*'. Instead, the reference to 'the combating of social exclusion' is inserted into the Treaty of Nice's new Article 137(1)(j) EC.

The replacement in Article 137(2) of the phrase 'in order to combat social exclusion' by the insertion of the new phrase 'excluding any harmonisation of the laws and regulations of the Member States' has two very significant implications. The first is that *coordination/cooperation* is an approach which may henceforth be applied to *all* the social policy areas listed in the revised Article 137(1) EC (not only 'in order to combat social exclusion'). Secondly, in social policy generally, as in the case of employment policy (Article 129 EC), the process of cooperation/coordination *excludes* 'any harmonisation of the laws and regulations of the Member States'.

---

45 Lisbon Presidency Conclusions, para. 5.   46 COM(2000)379 final, section 1.2, at 5.

These amendments to Article 137 EC by the Treaty of Nice mark the new departure in EU social policy signalled by the Lisbon Strategy. EU social policy is *not* primarily to be implemented through the adoption by means of *directives of minimum requirements* (Article 137(2)(b) EC, formerly 137(2)) in the fields listed in Article 137(1)(a–i).

Rather, in all these fields there is the *alternative* of measures designed to encourage *cooperation* between Member States in all social policy fields (Article 137(2)(a)), no longer restricted to combating social exclusion (ex Article 137(2) EC), and explicitly '*excluding* any harmonisation of the laws and regulations of the Member States'.

(c) The Social Policy Agenda 2000–2004: Legislation, Social Dialogue, and Administrative Processes

The European Council at Nice in December 2000, in adopting the Commission's Social Policy Agenda 2000–2004 of 28 June 2000, declared that in its implementation 'all existing Community instruments bar none must be used; the open method of co-ordination, legislation, the social dialogue, the Structural Funds, the support programmes, the integrated policy approach, analysis and research'.[47] The Commission's Social Policy Agenda 2000–2004 also stated that: 'To achieve these priorities, an adequate combination of all existing means will be required' (page 14). Although a *variety* of means were listed, the *scope* of application allocated to each was significant.

The *first* was 'The open method of co-ordination, inspired by the Luxembourg Employment Process and developed by the Lisbon and Feira Councils'. There was *no limit* specified to the scope of matters suitable for the application of this method.

The *third* was stated as follows: 'The Social Dialogue as the most effective way of modernising contractual relations, adapting work organisation and developing adequate balance between flexibility and security'. The role of social dialogue is strictly *limited* to work relationships within the enterprise.

In contrast, the *second* means listed was: 'Legislation: Standards should be developed or adapted, *where appropriate*, to ensure the respect of *fundamental social rights* and to respond to *new challenges*. Such standards can also result from agreements between the social partners at European level'. The scope of legislation required to achieve the European social model is here *limited* to fundamental social rights and new challenges. There is scope for judicial enforcement primarily where the EU adopts legislative measures.

The Commission's Social Policy Agenda was adopted on 28 June 2000. Although adopted some months before the EU Charter of Fundamental Rights was proclaimed in December 2000, it was by then clear that the EU Charter would include fundamental social rights. In the event, the EU Charter contains a

---

[47] Nice European Council, 7–9 December 2000, Annex 1, para. 28.

number of rights in the fields of individual employment and collective industrial relations. One anticipated outcome of the EU Charter, as in the case of its predecessor, the Community Charter of the Fundamental Social Rights of Workers of 1989, is the preparation of a Social Action Programme including legislative standards 'to ensure the respect of fundamental social rights'.

Although there is as yet no sign of such a legislative programme, the adoption of the Constitutional Treaty, incorporating the EU Charter, may provide the necessary stimulus. The scope for engagement by the courts in the enforcement of EU labour law depends on whether such a legislative programme emerges.

On the other hand, the clearly unlimited scope of the open method of coordination as an instrument for achieving the Lisbon Strategy is in clear contrast with the relatively restricted scope of legislation and social dialogue. The emphasis is on the open method of coordination as the instrument for achieving the Lisbon Strategy. The Lisbon Strategy, and the Social Policy Agenda 2000–2004, may succeed or fail depending on the efficacy of its chosen instrument.[48]

(d) The Open Method of Coordination and Social Dialogue: A Decentralized Reporting and Monitoring Procedure (compare the ESC)

In its Communication of 26 June 2002 on the role of social dialogue in European labour law, entitled 'The European social dialogue, a force for innovation and change',[49] the Commission noted, under the heading 'Improving monitoring and implementation', that:

The European social partners have adopted joint opinions, statements and declarations on numerous occasions. More than 230 such joint sectoral texts have been issued and some 40 cross-industry texts . . . However, in most cases, these texts did not include any provision for implementation and monitoring: they were responses to short-term concerns. They are not well known and their dissemination at national level has been limited. Their effectiveness can thus be called into question.

On the question of the perceived lack of effectiveness, the Commission noted that:[50]

Special consideration must be given to the question of how to implement the texts adopted by the European social partners. The recommendations of the High-Level Group on Industrial Relations and Change see the use of machinery based on the open method of coordination as an extremely promising way forward.

The social partners could apply some of their agreements (where not regulatory) by establishing goals or guidelines at European level, through regular national implementation reports and regular, systematic assessment of progress achieved.

---

[48] See 'EU in Danger of Missing Key Employment Targets', *European Industrial Relations Review* (2004), No. 363, at 37–40.   [49] COM(2002)341 final.

[50] Ibid., Section 2.4.1, at 18.

To that end, the Commission recommended:

The social partners are requested to:

- adapt the open method of coordination to their relations in all appropriate areas;
- prepare monitoring reports on implementation in the Member States of these frameworks for action;
- introduce peer review machinery appropriate to the social dialogue.

The significance of this recommendation is highlighted by the Work Programme of the European Social Partners 2003–2005. For example, of the twelve items in the Social Partners' Work Programme under the Employment Heading, only three refer to 'agreements', while nine appear to be eligible for the Commission's recommendation on application of the open method of coordination.[51]

Given the nature of the Social Partners' Work Programme, therefore, the Commission questions the effectiveness in implementation and monitoring of texts other than agreements. Its solution is, first, to clearly identify those areas where 'regulatory agreements' are the chosen instrument. Secondly, where other instruments are proposed (frameworks of actions, declarations, orientations, joint opinions) the OMC method may be adapted as appropriate; in particular, 'monitoring reports on implementation' and 'peer review machinery appropriate to the social dialogue'.

It remains to be seen whether the OMC, hitherto criticized as to its effectiveness when implemented by Member States' administrations in the field of employment policy, is appropriate for the Work Programme of the Social Partners on Employment. If joint opinions and other non-regulatory instruments continue to be ineffective, their failure may imply other, more rigorous steps towards effectiveness, including regulatory agreements and/or legislation.

On the other hand, this evolution of policy and instruments in the employment field has implications for social rights in general. Implementation of a particular European social policy objective (the European Employment Strategy) proceeds through a mechanism originally developed to coordinate national administrations (the OMC). When European policy objectives embrace more general issues of labour standards and employment protection, they engage other EU mechanisms, in this case, the European social dialogue. One scenario: guidelines could emerge from an EU-level social dialogue between EU social partners with mandates from affiliated social partners drawing on experience of national employment pacts, or following on from proposals by the Commission. Affiliated social partners at Member State level could produce National Action Plans to implement the Guidelines embodied in EU framework agreements. The Commission and Council could review and report on implementation and

---

[51] The three appear only in proposals for a 'seminar in view to negotiate a voluntary agreement' on stress at work (2003) and a 'seminar to explore possibility of negotiating a voluntary agreement' on harassment (2004–2005). An additional item refers to the framework agreement on telework signed on 16 July 2002.

supplement this with recommendations in the form of EU legislative proposals where implementation was inadequate.[52]

The question is whether other, wider social policy objectives can similarly engage with the mechanisms developed in the employment field (OMC) and the sphere of labour standards/industrial relations (social dialogue). Perhaps by adding their specific contributions by way of enforcement mechanisms (expert bodies, special access to judicial processes, tailored administrative procedures), they too can provide solutions to the problems of implementation and enforcement of social rights.

The next Subsection highlights one fundamental challenge confronting the protagonists in such mechanisms: their legitimacy. This is a problem particularly for those arms of civil society most frequently engaged in the struggle for social rights. The question of legitimacy is not a new one in the field of labour rights as regards the principal protagonists: trade unions. Interestingly, the new EU Constitution has produced a perhaps unintended development, with important consequences for the legitimacy of the social dialogue as a mechanism for implementing labour standards.

C. *The Unintended Consequence of Constitutional Change: Social Dialogue Agreements as Non-legislative Measures*

1. *The Institutional Position of the Social Partners and Social Dialogue*
The Draft Treaty Establishing a Constitution for Europe was presented by the Convention on the Future of Europe on 18 July 2003.[53] Adopted at the Intergovernmental Conference on 17–18 June 2004, the Constitutional Treaty breaks new ground by acknowledging the social partners among the institutional elements of the EU in Title VI of Part I: 'The Democratic Life of the Union'.

Article I-48: The social partners and autonomous social dialogue

The European Union recognises and promotes the role of the social partners at its level, taking into account the diversity of national systems. It shall facilitate dialogue between the social partners, respecting their autonomy.

The Tripartite Social Summit for Growth and Employment shall contribute to social dialogue.[54]

---

[52] B. Bercusson, 'Institutional Reform and Social and Labour Policy', in U. Mückenberger (ed.), *Manifesto Social Europe* (2001), at 101–28. See also B. Bercusson, 'The Role of the EU Charter of Fundamental Rights in Building a System of Industrial Relations at EU Level', 9 *Transfer: European Review of Labour and Research* (2003), No. 2, at 209–28.

[53] Draft Treaty establishing a Constitution for Europe, CONV 850/03, 18 July 2003.

[54] At the IGC meeting in Brussels on 17–18 June 2004, the final sentence was added at the end of what was Article I-47: 'The Tripartite Social Summit for Growth and Employment shall contribute to social dialogue.' See Provisional consolidated version of the draft Treaty establishing a Constitution for Europe, CIG 86/04, 25 June 2004. This Article has subsequently been renumbered Article I-48; see Treaty establishing a Constitution for Europe, CIG 87/04, 6 August 2004. In what follows I have adopted the numbering and wording of the Constitutional Treaty as it appears in the Official Journal, OJ 2004 C310/1.

2. The Legal Status of Social Dialogue Agreements   The Constitutional Treaty, in Title III: Internal policies and action, Chapter III: Policies in other areas, Section 2—Social Policy, Articles III-209–219 mostly replicates the 'Social Provisions' of the EC Treaty (Articles 136–145), as amended by the Treaty of Nice.

However, one significant alteration illustrates the, perhaps, unintended consequences of constitutional change by characterizing social dialogue agreements as non-legislative measures.

Article III-212 replaces Article 139 EC. In Article III-212(2), instead of Article 139(2)'s reference to a Council 'decision' implementing the social partners' agreement, it is to be implemented 'by European regulations or decisions adopted by the Council':

> Agreements concluded at Union level shall be implemented either in accordance with the procedures and practices specific to management and labour and the Member States or, in matters covered by Article III-210, at the joint request of the signatory parties, by European regulations or decisions adopted by the Council on a proposal from the Commission. The European Parliament shall be informed.

At first glance, this seems dramatically to change the legal nature of implementing measures. The earlier debate over what was meant by 'decision' in Article 139(2) EC was not resolved, but in practice led to '*directives*'.[55] Under the Constitutional Treaty, 'directives' become 'European framework laws'. In the future, it is European regulations or decisions, *not* 'European framework laws', which will implement the social partners' agreements.

It might seem that the wording 'European regulations or decisions' simply replicates the present position of implementation by a 'decision', with the added option of a 'European regulation'. But this is not the case. Both 'European regulation' and 'European decision' are given specific meanings in Article I-33.

However, it does not appear that any change is intended. The legal nature of European regulations and European decisions is defined in Article I-33. Though they are deemed to be 'non-legislative acts', their legal effects are described in terms *identical* to those of the 'legislative acts' (European laws and European framework laws).[56]

It seems the difference between legislative and non-legislative acts is *not* in terms of legal effects, but in terms of the *procedure* of enactment. Article I-34: European laws and European framework laws follow from a Commission proposal and engage the European Parliament and the Council. Article

---

[55] B. Bercusson, *European Labour Law* (1996), at 548–50.

[56] A *European regulation* may have the legal effect: either of a *European law*: 'binding in its entirety and directly applicable in all Member States'; or of a *European framework law*: 'binding, as to the result to be achieved, upon each Member State to which it is addressed, but shall leave to the national authorities the choice of form and methods'. A *European decision* seems to have the legal effect of a *European law*: 'binding in its entirety'.

I-35: European regulations and European decisions engage the Council and the Commission, but not the European Parliament.

If so, the implementation of EU social dialogue agreements through European regulations and European decisions should not change the current procedure under Article 139 EC (new Article III-212). The procedure does not engage the European Parliament.

In sum: the legal effects of European regulations and decisions implementing future agreements should be the same as the directives which implemented past framework agreements.[57] However, the new provision has resulted in two changes which highlight issues in the implementation and enforcement of social rights.

(a) Implementation of Social Rights through Collective Bargaining Mechanisms

Article III-212(2) provides that framework agreements are to be implemented through the new legal measures of European regulations or decisions, and not European framework laws. The change from 'directives' (which become European framework laws) to European regulations and decisions threatened to break a crucial link with Article III-210(4), which replaces Article 137(3) EC.

Article 137(3) EC provides that implementation of directives (to become European framework laws) can be achieved through agreements between management and labour.[58] In a series of decisions, the European Court made clear that agreements between management and labour implementing directives must have the same legal effects as the directive.[59] This is now stated in the second paragraph of Article 137(3). However, the Draft Treaty proposed by the Convention on the Future of Europe on 18 July 2003 included the following provision (Article III-104(4), paragraph 2 of the Draft Constitution):

In that case, [the Member State] shall ensure that, no later than the date on which a *European framework law* must be transposed, management and labour have introduced the necessary measures by agreement, the Member State concerned being required to take any necessary measures enabling it at any time to be in a position to guarantee the results imposed by that framework law.

Article III-104(4) provided that agreements between management and labour are a means for implementing European framework laws, *but not European regulations or decisions*. The result of the change in Article III-106(2) was that the previous link between Article III-104(4) (ex Article 137(3) EC) and Article III-106(2) of the Draft Treaty (ex Article 139(2) EC) was broken.

---

[57] For example, the effects of the current framework agreements/directives (e.g. on parental leave, part-time and fixed-term work) should not be different from future framework agreements which take the form of European regulations or European decisions.

[58] The first paragraph of Article 137(3) EC reads: 'A Member State may entrust management and labour, at their joint request, with the implementation of directives adopted pursuant to paragraph 2.'

[59] B. Bercusson, *European Labour Law* (1996), at 121–26.

This is an important change which was not intended. It blocks the implementation of EU level framework agreements through agreements between management and labour within Member States. In terms of social rights contained in social dialogue agreements, it is vital that national systems of collective bargaining and agreements take the responsibility for their implementation and enforcement. Preventing articulation between EU level agreements and collective agreements implementing these EU level agreements within the Member State strikes at the heart of an EU system of industrial relations.

Fortunately, following representations, the necessary amendments to Article III-104(4) were made allowing Member States to entrust the social partners with the implementation also of regulations and decisions made under Article III-106(2).[60]

(b) Judicial Review of Social Rights Embodied in EU Social Dialogue Agreements

Under the EC Treaty, *equivalence* of legal effects was presumed to exist between the two methods prescribed by Article 139(2): implementing framework agreements through:

(i) 'the procedures and practices specific to management and labour and the Member States', or

(ii) by a 'decision adopted by the Council'.

In practice, framework agreements were implemented through Council decisions in the form of *directives*. These are now characterized as legislative measures: 'European framework laws'.

As noted above, this previous equivalence between the legal effects of directives and EU-level framework agreements is challenged by the new provision in Article III-212(2) of the Draft Constitution. This excludes European framework laws (formerly directives) as the means for implementing EU-level framework agreements. Instead, only European regulations or decisions become the means of implementing EU-level framework agreements.

The result is that the equivalent legal status of European framework laws (legislative acts) and EU-level framework agreements (non-legislative acts: regulations or decisions)—despite their linkage in the amended Article III-210(4)—has been lost.

---

[60] Article III-104(4), now Article III-210(4) of the Constitutional Treaty, reads: 'A Member State may entrust management and labour, at their joint request, with the implementation of European framework laws adopted pursuant to paragraphs 2 and 3 or, where appropriate, with the implementation of European regulations or decisions adopted in accordance with Article III-212. In this case, it shall ensure that, no later than the date on which a European framework law must be transposed, or a European regulation or decision implemented, management and labour have introduced the necessary measures by agreement, the Member State concerned being required to take any necessary measure enabling it at any time to be in a position to guarantee the results imposed by that framework law, regulation or decision.'

Again, this may have unforeseen and unintended consequences. The problem may be illustrated by examining the social rights embodied in the Parental Leave Directive, the first product of the EU social dialogue.[61] In litigation before the European Court of First Instance (CFI) the criterion of 'sufficient collective representativity' was put forward to identify the social partners referred to in Articles 138–139 EC as entitled to engage in the European social dialogue and produce legitimate EU social dialogue agreements.

UEAPME, an organization representing artisans and small and medium enterprises, challenged the legality of the Parental Leave Directive.[62] To do so under Article 230 EC, UEAPME had to show, *inter alia*, direct and individual concern. The CFI held that it could do so if it could show that, UEAPME having been excluded from the negotiations, the agreement had not been negotiated by representative social partners. This view was premised on the equation drawn between the legislative processes involving the social partners reaching agreements transformed into directives, and the legislative process for adopting directives which engage the European Parliament. The CFI said:

. . . the principle of democracy on which the Union is founded requires—in the absence of the participation of the European Parliament in the legislative process—that the participation of the people be otherwise assured, in this instance through the parties representative of management and labour who concluded the agreement which is endowed by the Council acting on a qualified majority, on a proposal from the Commission, with a legislative foundation at Community level. In order to make sure that that requirement is complied with, the Commission and the Council are under a duty to verify that the signatories to the agreement are truly representative (paragraph 89).

For an agreement to be democratically legitimate, the CFI stipulates at paragraph 90 that it must be ascertained: 'whether, having regard to the content of the agreement in question, the signatories, taken together, are sufficiently representative'. The CFI insisted that the representativeness of the parties is to be measured 'in relation to the content of the agreement' (paragraph 90), or 'with respect to the substantive scope of the framework agreement' (paragraph 91). It looked, for example, at who exactly were the workers covered by the agreement (paragraph 94). The implication for the social partners is that agreements may be democratically legitimate when signed by organizations which are only representative as regards the narrow scope of the agreement concerned. This offers the social partners an opportunity, in that agreements negotiated at EU level need not be all-encompassing. On the other hand, it presents them with a challenge in that, taken individually, organizations signing these agreements may be far from representative in general.

---

[61] Council Directive 96/34 on the Framework Agreement on parental leave concluded by UNICE, CEEP and the ETUC, OJ 1996 L145/4.

[62] Case T-135/96, *Union Européenne de l'Artisanat et des Petites et Moyennes Entreprises (UEAPME) v. Council of the European Union* [1998] ECR II-2335.

The Constitutional Treaty's rejection of equivalence between legislative measures and non-legislative measures, the latter including social dialogue agreements embodied in regulations or decisions adopted without the participation of Parliament,[63] undermines the rationale of the decision in *UEAPME*. If the measures concerned are not legislative acts engaging Parliament, the requirement of democratic legitimacy in the form of criteria of representativeness is not applicable. It will be that much more difficult to establish *locus standi* for the purposes of judicial review of social dialogue agreements.[64]

Further, as the CFI in *UEAPME* also insisted that the Commission undertake such review prior to forwarding any agreement, and the Council likewise before making any decision conferring legal status on such an agreement, these institutions would also appear to be precluded from assessing the representativeness of the social partners as a precondition of approval of their agreements—in that sense reflecting the injunction in Article I-48 of the Constitutional Treaty as regards the social partners: 'respecting their autonomy'.

The new constitutional context, therefore, has important consequences for judicial or other review of social dialogue agreements containing social rights.

IV. CONCLUSION

The history of EC law is that of the emergence of a new legal order. This new legal order developed new concepts of implementation and enforcement of EC law. When directives stipulated policy results, but left to Member States the choice of form and method (Article 249 EC), the European Court of Justice developed doctrines testing the adequacy of Member State implementation.

This chapter has examined two developments in the emerging European constitutional order which may hold out promise for the implementation and enforcement of social and labour rights: the role of the EU Charter of Fundamental Rights, and other mechanisms modelled on developments in the field of labour policy.

A. *The EU Charter*

Implementation of the EU Charter aims to build a bridge between *programmatic* (social and economic rights) and *justiciable* (civil and political) rights. The challenge is to *establish* clearly *justiciable rights*, and, further, to *develop*

---

[63] Though, note, the Constitution has added a final additional sentence to Article III-212(2): 'The European Parliament shall be informed.' Cf. the presumably unintended irony evinced in the final sentence of the second paragraph of Article III-213: 'The European Parliament shall be kept *fully* informed.'

[64] It is not clear whether they qualify as a 'regulatory act' under Article III-365(4), the replacement for Article 230 EC.

implementation of *programmatic* social and economic rights: such as health and education, etc.

The tasks of an implementation strategy are threefold. First, with respect to *justiciable* rights, to develop effective implementation, looking to effective sanctions, preventing regressions, removing qualifications, thresholds, exclusions, modifications. Secondly, *moving more social and economic rights towards justiciability*, formulating them as positive and enforceable rights; including effective sanctions. Thirdly, with respect to *programmatic* rights, implementation through effective monitoring of government policy and actions, with possible judicial review of consistency and powers of nullification.

It is important that the EU Constitution acquires the character of a *dynamic* instrument, that Member States have to actively accommodate any new social and labour rights: a form of dynamic subsidiarity.[65] There are lessons to be learned from other international experiences in implementing fundamental social and labour rights, including the procedures of the ILO's Freedom of Association Committee, and the supervision and the collective complaints procedure of the European Social Charter.

B. Other Mechanisms

Developments in EU employment and labour policy have revealed new mechanisms for the implementation and enforcement of rights in that sphere. For the purposes of social and labour rights in general, three issues may be identified for further exploration.

First, the focus of EU social dialogue agreements between the European social partners is on the social rights of workers. However, trade unions and employers have an interest in expanding the scope of their agreements to include wider rights. Trade unions in particular are concerned to expand their constituency to reflect the changing nature of the workforce and, indeed, the future interests of their present constituency (for example, pensions and the elderly). Indeed, the first agreements reached reflected these wider social concerns: Parental Leave, Part-time Work and Fixed-Time Work.[66] The expansion of the scope of social dialogue agreements as the vehicle for the implementation and enforcement of social rights may prove promising.[67]

---

[65] B. Bercusson et al., 'Subsidiarity and Solidarity', in B. Bercusson et al., *A Manifesto for Social Europe* (1996) at 63–74. See also, Bercusson et al., 'A Manifesto for Social Europe', 3 *ELJ* (1997) 189.

[66] Council Directive 96/34 on the Framework Agreement on parental leave concluded by UNICE, CEEP and the ETUC, OJ 1996 L145/4. Council Directive 97/81 concerning the Framework Agreement on part-time work concluded by UNICE, CEEP and the ETUC, OJ 1998 L14/9. Council Directive 1999/70 concerning the framework agreement on fixed-term work concluded by ETUC, UNICE and CEEP, OJ 1999 L175/43.

[67] See B. Bercusson, 'Collective Bargaining and Equal Opportunities Agreements' and B. Bercusson and A. Weiler, 'Analysis of Equal Opportunities Agreements', in European Foundation for the Improvement of Living and Working Conditions, *Equal Opportunities and Collective Bargaining in the European Union: Innovative Agreements: An Analysis* (1999) 1–27 and 29–173.

Secondly, the example set by the social partners raises the question of whether there are equivalent organizations in the field of other social and labour rights which could achieve similar effects in the form of measures, such as agreements, which could achieve similar effects? Civil society does not lack for such organizations.

Thirdly, however, there is the issue of legitimacy. How representative need/must be the organizations purporting to engage in the field of social and labour rights? As illustrated in the case of social dialogue agreements, the parliamentary road to legitimacy is not always appropriate. The concept of representativeness is open to different interpretations, with subtle variations dependent on context, not least the varying context of specific social and labour rights.

In sum, other methods of monitoring social and labour rights are on the EU agenda; specifically, a role for the social partners in monitoring EU Charter rights at the appropriate levels, including the monitoring of Member States' action in the social and employment policy field through the 'open method of coordination'. A new chapter is the opening in the legal enforcement of social and labour rights, both at transnational and national levels.

10

Fundamental Labour Rights
after the Lisbon Agenda

SILVANA SCIARRA

I. INTRODUCTION: WITHIN AND WITHOUT THE OPEN METHOD OF COORDINATION: HOW TO ESTABLISH A LANGUAGE OF RIGHTS IN LABOUR LAW REFORMS

This chapter is focused principally on current developments in European social and employment policies. The intention is to consider the original character of EU legal approaches in these fields and to investigate whether, using the notion of fundamental labour rights, there can be a beneficial expansion of this notion by means of a broader circulation of international sources. 'Circulation' is a notion grounded on the necessary interrelation—and in some cases the interdependence—of sources generated within different legal systems. A 'pluralistic' point of view, not new in Western European legal traditions, reappears in current legal discourse. The main objective of this chapter is to capture developments occurring within national and supranational legal orders, and to interpret their possible outcomes in terms of new entitlements both for individuals and for groups.

The hypothesis on which this chapter is based is that the evolution of labour law at national level has been influenced by EU law, while maintaining its own dominant characteristics. This observation suggests that national diversities enrich the multicultural and multilevel legal environment in which law-making takes place. In the first phase of the so-called Lisbon strategy, national legislatures have been extremely active in furthering labour law reforms. Legislation adopted over the years has intervened significantly in the regulation of individual contracts of employment and, more broadly, has had an impact on the reform of national labour markets.[1] If one bears in mind the original four pillars of the European employment strategy (EES),[2] one soon realizes that there has been a convergence

---

[1] Reforms have been adopted, for example, in Spain, Italy, Denmark, Germany, Poland. Information available at www.eiro.eurofound.eu.int.

[2] Employability, entrepreneurship, adaptability, equal opportunities.

of national legislatures towards similar areas of intervention. A related argument is that national legislatures had a rather predictable canvas on which lines could be drawn and colours could be mixed.[3] Even areas of labour law, such as working time, which was regulated by secondary legislation prior to the Lisbon strategy,[4] have become part of a complex multilevel process of policy-making, whereby the protection of the right to health and safety at the place of work has been confronted by overall objectives such as the 'modernization' of national legal systems and of the European social model.[5] It can also be argued that a common concern, shared by all Member States, to decrease unemployment and increase employment would have brought them towards similar solutions in their national interpretations of the choices to be made and of the priorities to be set.

However, the fact that, from Lisbon onwards, following the Luxembourg process, there was a European strategy and that this was pursued actively and with renewed energy by both the Commission and the Council changed the nature of national responses and framed them within a scheme which slowly acquired its own legal relevance. This point needs to be stressed in response to commentators trying to portray a negative image of soft law techniques. Such portrayals draw a very blurred picture of the duties and obligations of the actors involved in the Open Method of Coordination (OMC). In particular they point to the lack of sanctions against the failure to respond or the incomplete response of national governments. The notion of 'moral' sanction, familiar in international law when the dispute concerns variable interpretations of legal standards and different ways of enforcing them, does not seem strong enough. Neither does it appear convincing to the detractors of the OMC to take into account the delicate equilibrium on which national governments have to base their choices, bringing together constraints imposed by budgetary laws and the growing social expectations of citizens. Such a theoretical dispute on the role of soft law hides, in some cases, a deeper—and perhaps unconscious—fear that Europe is at the origin of all evils and disruptions in national labour law. Rather than falling into the banal category of euro-scepticism, this point of view paradoxically may express the aspirations of those who want more from Europe, and in a more tangible form. It is to such questions that labour law reforms have to refer, within or without the OMC.

I shall argue in favour of maintaining and strengthening the soft law regime in which the EES first flourished. I shall also submit that in such an open process labour law should rediscover a 'language of rights'. In this framework of analysis a

---

[3] For example, reforms in Spain and Poland, available at: www.eiro.eurofound.eu.int. See also the General Report based on national country studies in 15 Member States: S. Sciarra, *The Evolution of Labour Law (1992–2003) General Report* (2004) at http://europa.eu.int/comm/employment_social/labour_law/docs/generalreport_en.pdf.

[4] Council Directive 93/104 EC concerning certain aspects of the organization of working time, OJ 1993 L307/18.

[5] A national case study is presented by C. Barnard, 'The EU Agenda for Regulating Labour Markets: Lessons from the UK in the Field of Working Time', in G. Bermann and K. Pistor (eds), *Law and Governance in an Enlarged Union* (2004) 177.

comparison with sources external to the EU, such as the European Social Charter (ESC), becomes a way of expanding the understanding of an evolving notion of labour rights. The language of rights, therefore, is not self-referential nor limited to the European legal system. Labour standards have been influenced by legal discourses taking place in a broader international context. Similarly, the original discourse evolving within the boundaries of EU law has been listened to and absorbed by other international sources. An historical analysis of European social law and of its evolution confirms the feasibility of such a scheme and of the broader international sources to which reference must continue to be made. The suggestion is to frame Lisbon and the current post-Lisbon review in a line of continuity with previous steps in the consolidation of a European model of multilevel policy-making. This trend should find an interface in the most recent attempts to develop multilevel Constitution-making, and to do so by incorporating sources external to the EU, such as the ECHR.

In a number of European legal systems, in parallel with the vivacious discussion taking place at a supranational level on ways to bind the EU to the observance of international standards on fundamental rights, the ECHR has been viewed by individual Member States as a reliable source to acquire and include in domestic legal systems. This is the case with the Human Rights Act of 1998, which entered into force in the UK in 2000, and which aims at giving further effect to rights already enjoyed under the Convention. Denmark incorporated the ECHR into national law in 1997 and Finland did the same in 1990. In 1995 Finland also promoted a constitutional reform which led to the inclusion in the Constitution of a new chapter on fundamental rights, followed by a review in 2000. Sweden incorporated the ECHR into its national law by means of an Act of Parliament in 1994. Notwithstanding the fact that such a source is not constitutional, courts may not apply legislation which conflicts with the ECHR, since national legislation must comply with its principles.[6] It is neither repetitious nor irrelevant to note that national legal systems were not equally motivated to pay attention to the ESC. Even though the reason may be found in the rich heritage of national constitutional traditions in the field of social rights, the discrepancy between these two Council of Europe sources continues to be striking.

II. RIGHTS AND POLICIES

The interesting—and probably not accidental—combination of rights and policies in the most recent evolution of labour law at the European level is something to be considered before entering into a more detailed analysis of the

---

[6] More detailed information on such developments in these Nordic countries can be found in N. Bruun and J. Malmberg, *The Evolution of Labour Law in Denmark, Finland and Sweden 1992–2003*, http://europa.eu.int/comm/employment_social/labour_law/docs/ell_da_fi_sv.pdf.

OMC. Two framework Directives—the Fixed-term Work and the Part-time Work Directives[7]—refer in their preambles to clause 7 of the Community Charter of the Fundamental Social Rights of Workers, providing for an improvement in working conditions by way of an 'approximation of these conditions while the improvement is being maintained'. They also refer to the Essen European Council, where the notion of employment policies linked to a more flexible organization of work was first conceived. The Fixed-term Work Directive also takes into account the 1999 Council Resolution on Employment Guidelines, inviting the social partners to negotiate 'flexible working arrangements' with particular emphasis on the balance between flexibility and security. This is to say that both Directives, even before the official birth of the OMC at Lisbon, have been framed within employment policies, while reproducing the classical formula, compatible with the completion of the internal market, according to which approximation of legal standards is parallel to improvement.

Both Directives are built around the principle of non-discrimination 'to improve the quality' of work. The Part-time Work Directive at Article 5 specifies that, in order to remove discrimination against part-timers and to facilitate recourse to such contracts of employment, Member States shall 'identify and review obstacles' impeding the expansion of part-time work and try to eliminate them. The Fixed-term Work Directive at Article 5 has a slightly different approach and aims to introduce objective limits in the recourse to such contracts, so as to justify the renewal or the maximum number of renewals of successive contracts.

These measures are different, and so is the nature of the legal command addressed to Member States. Whereas the expression adopted in the Part-time Work Directive is such as to rely on national choices in a soft law mood, the Fixed-term Work Directive indicates clear legal requirements which have to be taken into consideration by national legislatures in transposing the Directive into domestic law.

It is important to underline that in both approaches, while pursuing the expansion of flexible contracts of employment, the quality of such contracts must be maintained and improved. If we correctly interpret the language of employment policies, we can translate into clear legal obligations the vague exhortation addressed to Member States to create 'better jobs' and—one could add in the official language of EU law—jobs governed by 'improved' and 'approximated' standards, so as to enhance the efficient functioning of an integrated market. What is new, in comparison with the 'old' Article 117, now Article 136 TEC? Starting from this wide platform of social policies, partially strengthened, after Amsterdam, by the reference to the 1961 European Social Charter (ESC), harmonization emerged as the most efficient technique. The historical importance of legislation in social policies must be the object of some reconsideration in the

---

[7] Council Directive 1999/70/EC of 28 June 1999 concerning the Framework Agreement on Fixed-term Work concluded by ETUC, UNICE and CEEP, OJ 1999 L175/43; Council Directive 97/81/EC of 15 December 1997 concerning the Framework Agreement on Part-time Work concluded by UNICE, CEEP and the ETUC, OJ 1998 L14/9.

current debate. Negative integration, the most unsettling and unwanted outcome of a closer Union, is not the result of obscure plans put in motion by European institutions, nor the result of an aggressive policy put forward by the ECJ. It is a dangerous symptom of a lack of social cohesion and of uncontrolled competition among social systems, owing to the absence of a minimum platform of rights.[8]

One could argue that significant achievements were reached when harmonization was the leading regulatory technique. The consolidation of the *acquis* in social policies—that on which we base and expand the interpretation of fundamental social rights—was brought about by the so-called 'structural' directives of the 1970s, by the extraordinary evolution of directives on equal treatment, and, later on, by directives on health and safety. Significant examples of secondary legislation expanding beyond social policies—such as the European Works Council Directive and the Posted Workers Directive—are now, not by chance, the object of interesting review by the Commission.[9] Criticism addressed by scholars—including the present writer[10]—against the 'minimalism' of that legislation now meet a worrying silence on the part of both the legislature and the social partners at the European level.[11]

These critical observations about the present, in the light of a reconsideration of the historical premises of social policies, lead us towards one specific point of the analysis to be developed. The OMC was born as an alternative to harmonization. Article 137(2) TEC, as amended at Nice, explicitly keeps harmonization out of the Council's options when dealing with social inclusion and modernization of social protection systems. When harmonization is kept out of the picture, soft law forces interpreters to become familiar with notions such as exchange of information on best practices and mutual learning. Even such language—nebulous and atechnical as it is in the eyes of black-letter lawyers—represents a step forward, when compared with expressions previously adopted in the TEC, such as 'encouragement' and 'promotion'.[12]

The real novelty in the most current debate on rights and policies must be found in a rising awareness of how to avoid the soft law regime in which policies on employment and on social inclusion are flourishing and affecting the structure of rights on which those policies were built and from which they historically

---

[8] M. Poiares Maduro, 'Europe's Social Self: "The Sickness unto Death" ', in J. Shaw (ed.), *Social Law and Policy in an Evolving European Union* (2000) 329.

[9] See: http://europa.eu.int/comm/employment_social/news/2004/apr/ewc_en.html.

[10] S. Sciarra, 'Social Values and the Multiple Sources of European Social Law', 1 *ELJ* (1995) 60.

[11] For example, the Proposal for a Directive on temporary workers encountered significant difficulties which led to the submission of an amended proposal for a directive. Compare the original document, COM(2002)149 of 20 March 2002, with the amended proposal for a Directive of the European Parliament and the Council on Working Conditions for Temporary Workers, COM(2002)701 final of 28 November 2002.

[12] 'The Community and the Member States, having in mind fundamental social rights such as those set out in the European Social Charter signed at Turin on 18 October 1961 and in the 1989 Community Charter of the Fundamental Social Rights of Workers, shall have as their objectives the promotion of employment, improved living and working conditions, so as to make possible their harmonisation while the improvement is being maintained . . .', Article 136 TEC.

originate. Even this novelty is not an historical accident. The strict correlation between rights and policies has been sought and pursued by those who believed in reforming the Treaties, and in doing so by expanding both the 'objectives' of the EU and the reference to external international sources.[13]

We should inquire into why interpreters are alarmed—now more than in the past—by a possible interruption of this slow, and yet significant, interchange between rights and policies. The 'shift' from social policy to employment policy,[14] which took place in a more visible fashion after the launch of the OMC, can, in fact, be perceived as a threatening sign or, even worse, as an obscure and malicious plan of institutional actors. I shall attempt to answer this inquiry by looking at some specific examples arising out of the transposition of the two previously mentioned Directives. I shall then analyse how the lack of traditional sanctions in the OMC soft law regime has been counterbalanced by monitoring mechanisms and how this can be beneficial for the strengthening of fundamental social rights.

III. EMPLOYMENT POLICIES AND THE 'NON-REGRESSION CLAUSE' IN THE DIRECTIVES ON FIXED-TERM WORK AND PART-TIME WORK

These two Directives have been chosen as examples, in order to verify the feasibility of a combination of rights and policies. The result is unique: hard law forces Member States to comply, but soft law implications are such—particularly in the Part-time Work Directive—as to leave legislatures ample room for manoeuvre.

The right not to be discriminated against may be linked to specific compliance mechanisms; obligations generated by soft policies may deviate from legal principles showing a dominant need to comply with non-legal targets, such as an increased flexibility in employment contracts. The scenario is such as to create a trade-off between levels of protection and promotion of employment. Let us look at some specific cases, bearing in mind that in most European countries legislation adopted in both fields provoked adaptations of previous legislation. In civil law countries this also meant amending clauses and regulations in civil or labour codes.

The excessive increase of fixed-term contracts in Spain,[15] saluted as one relevant feature of the new dynamic labour market enhanced by the Conservative Government's reforms, had to be counterbalanced by disincentives to enter into

---

[13] See B. de Witte's chapter in this volume and de Witte, 'The Past and Future Role of the European Court of Justice in the Protection of Human Rights', in P. Alston, with M. Bustelo and J. Heenan (eds), *The EU and Human Rights* (1999) at 859–98.

[14] D. Ashiagbor, 'EMU and the Shift in the European Labour Law Agenda: From "Social Policy" to "Employment Policy" ', 7 *ELJ* (2001) 311; S. Regent, 'The Open Method of Coordination: A New Supranational Form of Governance?', 9 *ELJ* (2003) 190.

[15] Nearly a third of Spanish employees are on temporary contracts, http://www.eiro.eurofound. eu.int/2004/09/feature/es0409104f.html. See the comments by F. Valdés Dal-Ré, 'Recenti riforme del diritto del lavoro in Spagna', *Giornale di diritto del lavoro e di relazioni industriali* (2005).

such contracts. Collective agreements were chosen as the right sources in which to specify the objective reasons for employing such contracts. In Portugal, too, in the new 2003 Labour Code, the attitude is not in favour of fixed-term contracts.[16] In Italy, on the contrary, in the transposition of the Directive—one of the first manifestations of the centre-right administration in the labour law field—the recourse to such contracts has been widened, so as to raise the suspicion that the way in which 'technical, productive organisational and substitutive reasons' has been interpreted may far transcend the purpose of the Directive.[17] In this last example the most debatable innovation consisted in abandoning the previous legal technique—implying a legal definition of cases in which fixed-term contracts were allowed—in favour of a wide formula leaving ample space on this issue to the parties to individual contracts of employment. One of the limits set by the Directive at clause 3 of the annexed framework agreement—namely, the existence of 'objective conditions' for entering the fixed-term contract—is therefore left to the individual parties entering into a contract of employment. This is a reference to a critical interpretation of the non-regression clause, in which comparisons among standards of protection are left to the courts. The non-binding nature of the European Council's guidelines on employment policies within the equally non-binding EES can, however, imply that courts frame their interpretation of legislation within this context. While letting hard law prevail over soft law, they may introduce a value judgement on the balance between flexibility and security. In Germany, in an attempt to favour workers over the age of fifty-two at risk of losing their jobs, no objective reasons are required for entering fixed-term contracts. The 2003 reform introducing this amendment could be challenged on the ground of age discrimination.[18] This is yet another reference to the potential tensions arising from labour market reforms, all having to do with varying—at times conflicting—interpretations of individual fundamental rights. In the United Kingdom the apparent compliance with the Directive in indicating a maximum number of years when stipulating subsequent contracts may be overcome by Article 8(5) of the Regulation, allowing the removal of this limit in collective or workforce agreements.[19] A lot would need to be said in this regard on the scope of such agreements and on how legislation connected to employment policies forces a hierarchy among legal and voluntary sources, allowing the latter ample room for manoeuvre, even when their effect is to lower legal standards.

---

[16] On new developments in the Portuguese Labour Code see: http://www.eiro.eurofound.eu.int/ 2003/05/inbrief/pt0305101n.html. Additionally, on the basis of order No. 255/2002 of 12 March 2002 there are financial incentives for employers who convert a fixed-term contract, on expiry, into an open-ended contract. See: http://www.eiro.eurofound.eu.int/2002/05/feature/pt0205102f.html.

[17] Decree 368 of 6 September 2001, transposing European Directive 99/70 and comments in S. Sciarra, *The Evolution of Labour Law (1992–2003) Report on Italy*, at http://europa.eu.int/ comm/employment_social/labour_law/docs/ell_italy.pdf.

[18] P. Skidmore, 'The European Employment Strategy and Labour Law: A German Case-study', 29 *ELRev.* (2004) 52.

[19] C. Kilpatrick, 'Has New Labour Reconfigured Employment Legislation?', 32 *ILJ* (2003) 135.

Such complex interpretations of national legislatures' choices, involving multiple sources and multiple levels of enforceability, are framed within evolving patterns of employment guidelines and of subsequent responses in national policies. The 2004 Employment Guidelines, more focused on 'effective implementation of reforms through governance', recommend in some cases (France is one example) the facilitation of the transition from fixed-term to open-ended contracts.[20] Once more, the political willingness of all actors involved in the process strikes a balance in favour of a successful Open Method, based on totally unpredictable variables.

Other examples can be selected, when looking at the transposition of the Part-time Work Directive. The range of solutions adopted is wide. We move from the Dutch approach—we all recall the emphasis placed on the 'miracle' which occurred in that country in the 1990s[21]—where the intent is to favour voluntary part-time employment, to the Italian recent reform, which moves in a completely opposite direction. In 2003 the Italian legislature, amending legislation previously enacted for the transposition of the Directive, introduced very flexible clauses—described as 'elastic clauses'—whereby individual workers, even in the absence of collective agreements, may give their consent to the employer's request. Overtime, too, can be agreed upon at an individual level. The Italian example shows very clearly that the interpretation of Article 5 of the Directive, namely the removal by the state of obstacles impeding the expansion of part-time work, can raise serious doubts about the lower standards guaranteed to individual workers. The notion of what should be described as compliance on the part of Member States, when soft law policies are intertwined with the enforcement of fundamental rights, needs to be investigated further.

A very controversial provision, present in both Directives under discussion, is the so-called non-regression clause, according to which implementation of the Directives 'should not constitute valid ground for reducing the general level of protection afforded to workers'. This clause may give rise to opposing views. It may appear that EU law interferes with the choices of national legislatures, setting a platform of rights which is not to be lowered. This would not, however, represent an impediment to national parliaments in legislating. They should remain sovereign and free to intervene, even amending previous legislation in accordance with their own standards of what a 'valid ground' is.

The fundamental right not to be discriminated against, the inspiring principle in both Directives, finds itself at the crossroads of opposing policies. It is not as easy as it may appear to argue that measures attempting to treat part-time and fixed-term workers in a disparate way, lowering pre-existing individual and collective guarantees, should be considered illegal. The notion of lower standards itself is at stake, when it falls between other measures adopted by national legislatures to remove obstacles to the introduction of more flexible working conditions.

---

[20] Proposal for 2004 Employment Guidelines, COM(2004)239 final, of 7 April 2004, at 16.
[21] J. Visser and A. Hemerijck, *A Dutch Miracle: Job Growth, Welfare Reform and Corporatism in the Netherlands* (1997).

It remains to be seen how national courts will be able to refer cases to the ECJ, specifying how non-compliance of national law with EU law occurs by reason of the violation of a fundamental right. The principle of equal treatment among comparable workers, a powerful binding principle for national judges, must therefore include the evaluation of the objective criteria according to which fixed-term workers entered into their contracts. Similarly, the violation of the fundamental right not to be discriminated against may be grounded in national legislation lacking measures 'to prevent abuse' in the excessive use of successive fixed-term contracts, as is stated in clause 1 of the framework agreement.

It can be argued that, for those who are entitled to the fundamental right in question, the organizational rules observed at the place of work represent the precondition for access to the right itself. Managerial discretion—as in the case of non-objective reasons leading to fixed-term contracts—should be held to be contrary to the principle of equal treatment. It is hard—but not impossible—to maintain that such an interpretation of a fundamental right could even open the way to a preliminary ruling procedure. As for part-time work, the non-regression clause is followed by a caveat indicating that Member States and social partners, 'in the light of changing circumstances', should not see their 'right' to adopt different provisions circumscribed. This truism, which confirms Member States' sovereign legislative powers, finds a limit in the principle of non-discrimination between comparable full-time workers. If nothing else, this confirms the role of fundamental rights not only as a binding guideline for national legislatures, but also as a limit to all deregulatory policies which may imperil the full enforceability of the principle itself. The difficult comparison among legal standards and the equally difficult evaluation of what less favourable treatment may be must be left to national judges, steeped as they are in the historical and interpretative context of the overall system of individual and collective guarantees in each legal system.

A first conclusion to be drawn after looking at these selected examples is that atechnical notions such as flexibility or modernization, widely adopted in the language and in the practice of European soft law, do not provide a serious guide for the interpreter, whereas fundamental rights and principles do. At the present stage of European integration through law, a virtuous combination of soft policies and hard law implementation mechanisms seems a valuable solution. It may lead us towards a fundamental rights strategy, capable of feeding and strengthening the employment strategy.

IV. MONITORING AND SANCTIONING IN THE EUROPEAN EMPLOYMENT STRATEGY

In the absence of traditional sanctions to be imposed on Member States involved in the European Employment Strategy, there was a need to attract them into an open coordination scheme, thus urging them towards the achievement of common targets. The peer review mechanism, an important requirement within the process of cooperation among Member States enhanced by the EC, cannot be described as a traditional sanction. In the evaluation of National Action Plans (NAPs) the Council wields its institutional powers in its capacity as 'soft regulator'. The lack of specific indicators in employment policies—unlike those applied to social inclusion policies within the OMC[22] proved that the analysis of legislation in the process of being enacted or simply announced by national governments as part of their political agendas, had to be based on changing parameters. Similarly, the impetus that the Council wanted to give to change existing laws was not inspired by strictly legal criteria and has been abandoned. Since 'open' meant that the method had to respect states' prerogatives and competence, the coordination could be no more than a mere indication of possible common directions to follow, and not of how to follow them. Consequently, unlike in the coordination of macro-economic policies, no real warnings or sanctions could be issued against Member States. The request put forward at the Nice Council was to arrange a mid-term review of the Luxembourg process, which began at Lisbon, and to investigate even further into the actual impact of the OMC on national performances. The Nice Social Agenda[23] pursued 'quality in work' as an important objective, and so did the Employment Committee, working on quality indicators.[24]

All this activism inside European institutions and other relevant bodies prepared the ground for a series of country studies. They disclosed, in some cases, that interesting changes were taking place inside national administrations in order to comply with the OMC.[25] Member States took seriously their duty to comply with soft policies, at least in building up their own internal infrastructures and in promoting adaptations of domestic deliberative procedures. In this exercise one can find traces of significant self-criticism by the Commission, which has developed in several Communications into possible ways to improve the means and—mostly importantly—to reach the objective of a 'high level of employment'.[26] A practice of monitoring, applied to employment policies, is yet another way of governing complex processes of change by learning and by adapting to such complexity. The Commission does not make light of the difficulties of guaranteeing a transition between different forms of work, nor can it deny that the two worlds of

[22] Social Protection Committee, *Report on Indicators in the Field of Poverty and Social Exclusion*, October 2001, available at: http://europa.eu.int/comm/employment_social/soc-prot/soc-incl/indicator_en.htm. Comments in M. Ferrera, M. Matsaganis, and S. Sacchi, 'Open Coordination against Poverty: The New EU "Social Inclusion Process" ', 12 *Journal of European Social Policy* (2002) 227.

[23] Presidency Conclusions, Nice European Council Meeting 7, 8, and 9 December 2000, Annex I, European Social Agenda, para. 26.

[24] Report by the Employment Committee, Indicators of Quality in Work, 23 November 2001.

[25] Impact evaluation of the European Employment Strategy, http://europa.eu.int/comm/employment_social/employment_strategy/impact_en.htm.

[26] Communication from the Commission, *Strengthening the Implementation of the European Employment Strategy*, COM(2004)239 final, 7 April 2004.

standard and non-standard contracts may end up mirroring two separate labour markets.[27]

Labour law remains central to all adjustment and change, and so does anti-discrimination law. However, through the analysis of soft law documents produced in the realm of the OMC, labour lawyers perceive a distinct shift in the adoption of regulatory techniques. Rather than pursuing outcomes—as in directives—the aim is to promote 'processes and methods'.[28] This change of perspective is not without worries, even when it is contextualized and made functional to specific—possibly temporary—needs of the supranational legal order and to its reorganization of political priorities. To quote another example, a close examination of the employment strategy related to EU anti-racism policy and to the implementation of the Race Directive gives rise to criticism, in as much as it shows that there are points of divergence, despite the apparently common objective of combating discrimination by way of including the excluded in the labour market.[29]

I want to describe as 'co-ordinated reformism' the combination of soft promotion of national responses and hard implementation of fundamental rights. In this interchange of regulations, external and objective expertise is required in order to strengthen a criticism which cannot otherwise be translated into sanctions.[30] A recent product of this course of action is the report produced by the Employment Taskforce chaired by Wim Kok.[31] The already mentioned 2004 Employment Guidelines were inspired by this report and referred to it when revitalizing the European strategy and calling on Member States to make a renewed common effort. This is a confirmation of the fact that the OMC uses monitoring in place of sanctioning. Within the employment strategy the adjective 'open' seems to dominate the noun 'method' and consequently transforms the final outcome into a looser coordination. The acknowledgement of diversities—among national legal systems as well as among regulatory techniques inside each national system—may seem to contradict the obligation to coordinate. Such an obligation, referred to by both the Commission and the Council, appears now—almost paradoxically—to be expanded and in a sense complicated by the appearance of the OMC in other fields, in particular in the coordination of social

---

[27] Communication from the Commission, *The Future of the European Employment Strategy. A Strategy for Full Employment and Better Jobs for All*, COM(2003)6 final, 14 January 2003, at 14.

[28] D. Ashiagbor, 'The European Employment Strategy and the Regulation of Part-time Work', in S. Sciarra, P. Davies, and M. Freedland (eds), *Employment Policies and the Regulation of Part-time Work in the European Union* (2004) 37. See also Regent, *supra* n. 14.

[29] M. Bell, 'Combating Racial Discrimination through the European Employment Strategy', 6 *Cambridge Yearbook of European Legal Studies* (2004) 55.

[30] I have analysed the role of expertise in the elaboration of social inclusion policies and found that it has a significant impact on setting the agenda of the Commission. See S. Sciarra, 'The "Making" of EU Labour Law and the "Future" of Labour Lawyers', in C. Barnard, S. Deakin, and G. Morris (eds), *The Future of Labour Law: Liber Amicorum Sir Bob Hepple QC* (2004) 201.

[31] European Commission, *Jobs, Jobs, Jobs, Report of the Employment Taskforce chaired by W. Kok*, November 2003, at http://europa.eu.int/comm/employment_social/employment_strategy/pdf/etf_en.pdf.

inclusion policies. The links between the latter and employment policies make them complementary to each other in several cases.

In this unsettled scenario the 'constitutionalization' of the OMC in Part I of the Treaty establishing a Constitution[32] may make it a victim of its own success. The OMC will be symbolically visible as a constitutional provision, and yet remain a method, as such unenforceable and non-binding. Its acquired relevance in the Treaty will, perhaps, impose on EU institutions—the Commission and the Council, but not the ECJ—the obligation to search for more precise and normative monitoring mechanisms. It is therefore of some importance to suggest that this innovation in Part I should be closely linked with the new opening Articles in Part III. Bringing about mainstreaming as an alternative technique to traditional sanctions, the opening Articles of Part III may indicate a new path to national courts. The 'aim' to eliminate inequalities and to promote equality between women and men, as in Article III-116, is common to all activities referred to in Part III. Mainstreaming also applies to employment, social protection, and social inclusion policies, as well as to education, training, and the protection of health (Article III-117). A broad anti-discrimination clause is provided in Article III-118, while the three following Articles deal with environmental and consumer protection and with animal welfare. The inclusion of mainstreaming Articles in the Treaty, like the constitutionalization of the OMC, appears to be a confirmation of existing practices. The EU Race Directive[33] and the related anti-racism policy are linked and connected with other measures and actions by reason of a mainstreaming principle.[34] Gender mainstreaming has also been adopted in European social policies.[35]

If we connect the OMC with a close observation of mechanisms of integration through hard law, we can see new perspectives ahead, despite the apparent institutional weakness of social and employment policies. Enforcement could become a widespread technique and the object of monitoring through independent bodies. It is for this reason that another process, parallel to that described so far, becomes relevant for the present analysis.

V. . . . AND IN THE ENFORCEMENT OF SOCIAL RIGHTS

The Charter of Fundamental Rights approved at Nice opened a wide-ranging and unprecedented discussion among lawyers and created a beneficial interchange

---

[32] Treaty Establishing a Constitution for Europe, OJ 2004 C310/1, Article I-15.

[33] Council Directive 2000/43/EC of 29 June 2000 Implementing the Principle of Equal Treatment between Persons Irrespective of Racial or Ethnic Origin, OJ 2000 L180/22.

[34] Bell, *supra* n. 29. See also J. Shaw, *Mainstreaming Equality in European Union Law and Policymaking* (2004), in particular at 22ff.

[35] U. Mückenberger, 'Gender Mainstreaming', in U. Mückenberger, *Manifesto Social Europe* (2001) 269. See also M. Bell, 'Equality and the European Union Constitution', *ILJ* (2004), at 252, indicating that: 'Aside from anti-discrimination legislation, the mainstreaming concept is a parallel attempt to secure equality through means other than litigation.'

among different disciplinary approaches. Social rights included in the Charter are another sign of a slow and yet continuous progression, allowing social and employment policies to emerge and gain autonomy from other policies. We need to investigate how monitoring the enforcement of social rights and sanctioning Member States when they do not respect them can contribute to strengthening soft law regimes under the OMC.

A group of independent experts, chaired by Olivier De Schutter, is currently experimenting with a widespread monitoring of fundamental rights in EU Member States.[36] Both the methodological and the theoretical implications of this sophisticated exercise are very relevant in the field of social and labour law, particularly when it comes to establishing criteria of comparability among labour standards in the enforcement of employment policies. While adopting fundamental rights as parameters in the implementation of the OMC, the independent experts are looking for ways of strengthening the weak basis of soft law machinery. 'Guiding policies in a more systematic manner in such a way that they are drawn up to take into account the objective of implementing fundamental rights'[37] is what the experts aim at. In the future this whole process could beneficially be monitored by an independent agency.[38] This rich collection of data could bring about a circular, self-reproducing, perfect harmony between rights and policies.

The point to be emphasized is that 'mutual evaluation' and 'collective learning' should be based on objective criteria and on comparable standards of implementation. This would subtract evaluation—so far the only available sanction—from the climate of political negotiation which seems to characterize the OMC. One cannot ignore that soft law procedures in the coordination of employment policies are thought of as functional to the Council's broad economic guidelines, thus permitting mutual learning among national governments in a limited and restricted area whose borders are defined by EU macro-economic priorities. The

[36] EU Network of Independent Experts in Fundamental Rights (CFR-CDF) *Report on the Situation of Fundamental Rights in the European Union and its Member States in 2002* (2003) at http://europa.eu.int/comm/justice_home/fsj/rights/network/rapport_2002_en.pdf and EU Network of Independent Experts in Fundamental Rights (CFR-CDF) *Report on the Situation of Fundamental Rights in the European Union in 2003* (January 2004), at http://www.fd.uc.pt/hrc/network/report_2003.pdf.

[37] Section 5 in the Introduction to the *Report for 2002*, *supra* n. 36, at 25.

[38] See now the Communication from the Commission, The Fundamental Rights Agency. Public Consultation Document, COM(2004)693 final, 25 October 2004. See also the recent proposal put forward by President Barroso for 'locking in' a culture of fundamental rights in EU legislation. The idea is to screen systematically all Commission legislative proposals for compatibility with the Charter of Fundamental Rights and favour 'impact assessment' of the impact of legislation on individual rights. See European Commission Press Release, Brussels 27 April 2005 at www.europa.eu.int/rapid/pressReleaseAction.do. Compare also the critical analysis of A. Andronico and A. Lo Faro, 'Defining Problems: Open Method of Coordination, Fundamental Rights and Governance', in O. De Schutter and S. Deakin, *Social Rights and Market Forces: Is the Open Coordination of Employment and Social Policies the Future of Social Europe?* (2005). Their auspices are that fundamental rights be expanded as procedural rights within OMC, rather than leaving to such a 'method' the function to protect them.

initial assumption is that the OMC—as previously stated—is a regulatory technique alternative to harmonization. This does not imply that the market has already reached an ultimate level of integration. It can be argued, in fact, that a final and conclusive period of market integration is almost incompatible with the unique nature of the EU, characterized by the fact that integration at all levels is a permanently open process. Positive integration appears to be the only elective way of avoiding distortions of competition in a changing legal environment, when fundamental rights are at stake.

I suggest that the OMC, by insinuating flexible measures into the regulation of employment contracts, may create a potentially less stable environment for the guarantee of fundamental rights. I therefore submit that the OMC should be driven by policies which gradually implement a minimum level of rights, in order to establish minimum guarantees for individuals. Fundamental rights of the last generation, such as the right to training, follow individuals throughout their working lives and have become increasingly relevant in allowing transition from one occupation to another. They should, therefore, be constructed and implemented as rights detached from employment contracts and attached to working and career paths of a flexible nature. The right to the protection of personal data—to take another relevant example—can be enforced differently in different phases of the working life and should follow the individual, rather than the contract of employment. The right to the reconciliation of family and working life can also have a different impact in different cycles of the individual's professional development and become an essential link to the fulfilment of other fundamental human rights. Even the right of access to employment services should be thought of as a fundamental right responding to the different needs of individuals in different phases of their working lives.

Within the framework of the OMC we can re-think a traditional distinction between fundamental freedoms and fundamental rights of a procedural nature, the latter being dependent for their full enforcement on the state's active intervention. Drawing on this distinction it is possible to see how fundamental freedoms—positive and negative freedoms of association—rather than being constructed, as happens under most European national constitutions, as preconditions for the exercise of other rights, are in reality inaccessible to marginal workers and to the socially excluded. In the new, vast universe of precarious and flexible workers an historical paradox can be presented as a theoretical framework in which to develop a practice of fundamental rights. Procedural rights, such as the right to training, the right to reconciliation of work and family life, and the right of access to employment services, may gradually become instrumental to the progressive emancipation of precarious and economically dependent workers. When such fundamental rights are fully granted by active state intervention, even access to fundamental freedoms may become enforceable in practice. What we are witnessing at the moment in most countries is the inability of traditional social partners to represent in traditional ways the most marginal and precarious groups within the labour force and the newly emerged economic actors, such as employment and temporary work agencies.

VI. CONCLUDING REMARKS: THE RELEVANCE OF THE EUROPEAN SOCIAL CHARTER

One of the most positive remarks made by commentators on the Nice Charter has to do with the fact that all fundamental rights are assembled in a single document, thus overcoming the segregation of social rights in a different source document, as in the Council of Europe's European Social Charter. The latter has, however, been an interesting point of comparison and inspiration, both for the monitoring exercised by independent experts and for the Collective Complaints Protocol, which was added in 1995 and entered into force in 1998.[39] The original system of monitoring and sanctioning enforced under the ESC has always been praised by European labour lawyers, including among them leading figures who served on the Committee as independent experts.[40] In the academic discussion preceding the 1996 IGC, an independent evaluation of the enforcement of social rights—as opposed to rights justiciable in courts—was advocated by a group of labour lawyers.[41] That reference was intended to pave the way for innovative solutions within the European debate on fundamental rights, with an emphasis on so-called collective social rights, some of which were—and still are—explicitly left out of EU competence.[42] That debate also yielded arguments in favour of a clearer visibility of the ESC among the external sources referred to in European Treaties. The latter suggestion was partially followed up in subsequent reforms of the Treaties and even in the drafting of the Constitution,[43] but the impact of this source remains inadequate.

The current discussion, in view of the ratification of the Treaty establishing a Constitution, seems to go into different directions, when accession to the ECHR—not to the ESC—is envisaged. Social rights are still at the crossroads of differing interpretations, especially because of the unclear distinction between

---

[39] Additional Protocol to the European Social Charter Providing for a System of Collective Complaints, ETS No. 158.

[40] O. Kahn-Freund, 'The European Social Charter', in F. G. Jacobs (ed.), *European Law and the Individual* (1976) 10ff.

[41] R. Blanpain, B. Hepple, S. Sciarra, and M.Weiss, *Fundamental Social Rights: Proposals for the European Union* (1996).

[42] The right to organize and the right to strike and lock out are excluded from EU competence (Art. 137(5) TEC). Criticism of the notion of 'collective' social rights is voiced by T. Novitz, 'Are Social Rights Necessarily Collective Rights?—A Critical Analysis of the Collective Complaints Protocol to the European Social Charter', *EHRLR* (2002) 50.

[43] References are in S. Sciarra, 'La constitutionnalisation de l'Europe sociale, entre droits sociaux fondamentaux et soft law', in O. De Schutter and P. Nihoul (eds), *Une constitution pour l'Europe. Réflexions sur les transformations du droit de l'Union européenne* (2004).

principles and rights inserted into the final clauses of the Charter, now inserted in Part II of the Constitution. Meanwhile, several links can be established in EU law between social rights and employment policies. A number of possible future expansive interpretations are possible to imagine. Article 125 TEC describes the employment strategy, specifying that it is 'particularly for promoting a skilled, trained and adaptable workforce'. Legal measures adopted to enhance flexibility, thus improving employment figures, should not lead to degrading working conditions or to diminished guarantees. One could argue that the fundamental right to dignity, much emphasized in the structure of the Nice Charter, is infringed when no fair balance can be established between management prerogatives and workers' compliance with them. Jobs 'on call' or extreme forms of part-time work may be taken as examples. In such employment contracts there is often disproportionate discretion left to the employer, both in the working time arrangements and more generally in establishing working conditions. In all such cases there may be an instrumental reference to the supremacy of EU law and EU targets. Choices of national legislatures that do not respect fundamental social rights may not be justified as a necessary compliance with the Council's guidelines issued under the OMC.

Furthermore, recourse to descriptive and non-legal terms such as 'modernization' does not justify the adoption of legal measures which infringe fundamental rights. Specific social indicators must correspond to such broad definitions of political programmes, so that the evaluation of national responses to the OMC remains based in a well-grounded measurement of social change. The issue of comparability must, once more, be recalled as a necessary starting point in all attempts to learn from one another. It can be argued that monitoring and reporting, especially when such actions are carried out by truly independent bodies, can be a way to alert national actors—be they individuals or groups—to pursue litigation before national courts. These are cases in which fundamental social rights can be interpreted by national courts as minimum levels of guarantees not to be waived or reduced. Fundamental social rights can also be sources of inspiration for national legislatures, even though no duty to legislate can be envisaged. In fields in which secondary law is already enforceable, further improvements of existing standards could become a strategy for mutual learning. A good example is the reconciliation of family and working life, a field in which numerous links with employment policies can be discerned.

Circulation of international standards, an idea proposed in the opening of this chapter, is one way to enhance further developments in the language of rights. However, one cannot deny that the collective complaints procedure, the most challenging novelty in the apparatus of ESC sanctions, in the field of labour rights, has not yet fulfilled its full potential, due also to a lack of activity on the part of the European social partners.[44] The list of organizations listed in Article 1 of the Additional Protocol may also need re-thinking, if one had to take into

---

[44] See the contributions by J.-F. Akandji-Kombé, R. Brillat and O. De Schutter in this volume.

account groups of non-standard workers and other categories of economically dependent workers, or other groups at risk of being discriminated against on all grounds provided for by EU law. I have tried to indicate how raising awareness of the respect for fundamental social rights may also result in interventions of national courts, by way of preliminary ruling procedures.

Moreover, the originality of regulatory techniques in the EU, as indicated in the description of the OMC and its current enforcement, requires that unique forms of monitoring be put in place. Recourse to independent expertise should not be left in the discretion of governments alone. Independence should result from a combination of well-established expertise in the field and distance from governments and the social partners. In the EU tradition independent agencies have the role of making specialized contributions in specific fields, relieving European institutions of the urgent need to sanction or to evaluate Member States' performances. The proposal to establish a Fundamental Rights Agency follows in this direction. In expanding the remit for the creation of a Centre on racism and xenophobia, it is suggested that the Agency be organized on thematic lines. This trend could be confirmed by the announced creation of a European Gender Institute.[45] It is also worth noting that one of the main tasks of the Agency should be the 'collection and analysis of objective, reliable and comparable data at European level'.[46]

One of the points that has been strongly advocated in this chapter is the objectivity of data on which all evaluations and possible complaints should be based. There may be a need to bring the culture of fundamental labour rights more closely to the attention of institutions active in pursuing further protection of human rights. A separation among areas of fundamental rights and the means of enforcing them may seem counter-intuitive if we look at their universality, which is aimed at in the Charter of Fundamental Rights and in the yet-to-be-ratified Constitution. However, international sources proceed in the direction of specifying areas and means of protection, sometimes exposing new spheres of human rights to the challenges of international law.[47] It may be worth exploring the specificity of social rights at the present stage of evolution in national and supranational law, and to do so while leaving behind the inferiority complex that, over the years, has characterized such a large area of scholarship and policy-making. To avoid the separation of labour rights, we must learn to treat them as citizens' rights.

---

[45] COM(2004)693 final, *supra* n. 38, at 4 and 5. See also the conclusions of the European Council of Brussels (17–18 June 2004) for the creation of a European institute specializing in equality between men and women, para. 45.

[46] COM(2004)693 final, *supra* n. 38, at 8.

[47] An example, relevant to the present discussion, is the Council of Europe's Convention for the Protection of Individuals with regard to Automatic Processing of Personal Data, ETS No. 108.

11

How to Be Fundamental with Soft Procedures? The Open Method of Coordination and Fundamental Social Rights

STIJN SMISMANS*

I. INTRODUCTION

Soft law is certainly not a new invention in European policy-making. Yet, the use of non-binding instruments to provide policy guidance in European governance has increased particularly over the last decade. A central role in this evolution is played by the Open Method of Coordination (OMC), a cyclical benchmarking procedure coordinating national policies by providing guidance and assessment at the European level. OMC procedures have been introduced for such different areas as macro-economic policy, employment policy, social inclusion and enterprise policy, and the Lisbon Summit of the European Council in 2000 placed the OMCs within a broader strategy aiming at providing a framework for competitiveness and social cohesion. These coordination procedures of national policies are called 'open' both because of their assumed openness to the participation of stakeholders, and because of their openness in terms of objectives and instruments, which can more easily be adjusted to changing needs than traditional regulatory policy based on legislative standards.

Yet, while the participatory nature of the OMC is contested,[1] also its openness in terms of capability to adjust to changing needs has raised criticism. In contrast to common legislative standards, the flexible benchmarks set by the OMC could

---

* A previous version of this chapter appeared as the URGE Working Paper No. 2/2005 of the Research Unit on European Governance of the Collegio Carlo Alberto Foundation of Moncalieri, Turin (website: www.urge.it).

[1] K. Jacobsson and A. Vifell, 'Integration by Deliberation? Dynamics of Soft Regulation in the Case of EU Employment Policy', Paper presented at the ECPR Conference, 26–28 September 2002, Bordeaux; M. Barbier, C. De la Porte, and P. Pochet, 'European Briefing. Digest', 12 *Journal of European Social Policy* (2002), at 242; S. Smismans, 'EU Employment Policy: Decentralisation or Centralisation through the Open Method of Coordination?', in R. Toniatti, F. Palermo, and M. Dani (eds), *An Ever More Complex Union: The Regional Variable as Missing Link in the EU Constitution* (2004) (also at http://www.iue.it/PUB/law04–1.pdf); T. Nanz and C. De la Porte,

arguably lead to regulatory competition resulting in a race to the bottom in terms of social standards. However, given the lack of legislative competence and/or political will, the adoption of social standards through European regulation is not a realistic alternative, and might not—given the diversity of welfare systems—even be desirable. Therefore, recourse to fundamental social rights may appear as an attractive solution, in the sense that in the absence of social legislation at European level, fundamental social rights may appear as a hard standard which OMC processes would have to respect, thereby avoiding deregulatory tendencies.

However, the relation between the 'soft' OMC procedure and the (assumed) 'hard' fundamental social rights may be more complex than appears at first sight. To assess this relationship, the second section of this chapter will briefly clarify the nature of both the OMC and fundamental social rights. It recalls that on the one hand, the OMC—while being a soft law procedure—may have 'hard effects', and that, on the other hand, fundamental social rights are less 'hard' than their fundamental nature may lead us to expect. The relation between OMC and fundamental social rights is thus not an automatic one in which the soft OMC procedure would be backed by the hard guarantees of fundamental social rights.

There is, though, a common ground where the OMC and fundamental social rights may meet. The third section of this chapter will analyse this meeting place, using the example of the European Employment Strategy (EES). The role of fundamental social rights in terms of justiciable rights *ex post* is likely to remain very limited in the context of the OMC on employment, but fundamental rights may play a programmatic role *ex ante* in the EES. In addition, the technique of the OMC could be used in developing a real European fundamental rights policy.

However, I will argue in the last section of this chapter that in order for this fundamental rights policy to be effective, it should be based on a participatory process and be linked with other OMC procedures.

II. THE HARD EFFECTS OF SOFT LAW AND THE SOFTNESS OF FUNDAMENTAL SOCIAL RIGHTS

A. *The Hard Effects of the OMC*

It may be useful to recall here the basic features of the OMC. According to the Conclusions of the Lisbon Summit, the OMC is characterized by the following elements: the fixing of European guidelines; the establishment of quantitative and qualitative indicators and benchmarks; the translation of these guidelines in national and regional policies; and a periodic monitoring, evaluation, and peer review.[2]

'OMC—An Important Tool to Improve Transparency and Democratic Participation? The Case of Pension Reform from the Perspective of Deliberative Democracy', 11 *JEPP* (2004) 267.

[2] European Council Presidency Conclusions, 23/24 March 2000.

Yet, there are important differences among the various OMC procedures. The periodicity of guidelines differs, as well as the specificity of the quantitative and qualitative targets. Some OMC procedures are described or referred to in the Treaty, whereas others have been established without any Treaty reference. Moreover, while none of the OMC procedures can lead to binding European norms, the potential 'threat of sanction' differs, with some OMC procedures having, for instance, the option to adopt specific recommendations, putting Member States under pressure to follow the guidelines.[3]

This chapter focuses on the OMC in the field of employment, which has served largely as a reference point for the development of this method in other sectors. Enshrined in the EC Treaty, the OMC in employment constitutes the backbone of the European Employment Strategy.[4] It is a cyclical process structured around the yearly issuing of European Employment Guidelines, prepared by the Commission and adopted by the Council, after consultation of the European Parliament, the Economic and Social Committee, the Committee of the Regions and the Employment Committee. The Member States 'shall take into account' these guidelines in the development and implementation of their national employment policies. Each Member State is to make an annual report (the National Action Plan (NAP)) on 'the principal measures to implement its employment policy in the light of the guidelines for employment', outlining how it plans to respond to the guidelines and what progress has been made. The NAPs are sent to the Commission and the Council which prepare on this basis a joint report to the Spring European Council. On the basis of this analysis, and at the initiative of the Commission, new guidelines will be drafted[5] and the Council may make (non-binding) recommendations to Member States concerning their employment policies.[6]

The effects of this soft coordination mechanism remain difficult to ascertain. The difficult empirical assessment has just begun[7] and the Commission's evaluation

---

[3] For an overview, see S. Borrás and K. Jacobsson, 'The Open Method of Co-ordination and New Governance Patterns in the EU', 11 *JEPP* (2004), at 185–208.

[4] For an overview of the literature, see C. De la Porte and P. Pochet, 'The European Employment Strategy: Existing Research and Remaining Questions', 14 *Journal of European Social Policy* (2004), at 71–79.

[5] Since 2003 the implementation of the guidelines has been prioritized rather than spending resources on the drafting of new ones. The OMC in employment is still based on an annual cycle, but the guidelines will be revised profoundly only every three years. In 2004, for instance, the Council simply confirmed the 2003 guidelines, while issuing general and individual recommendations.

[6] For a more detailed description of the procedure and relation with other OMC procedures, see S. Smismans, 'Reflexive Law in Support of Directly Deliberative Polyarchy: Reflexive-Deliberative Polyarchy as a Normative Frame for the OMC', in O. De Schutter and S. Deakin (eds), *Social Rights and Market Forces: Is the Open Coordination of Employment and Social Policies the Future of Social Europe?* (2005).

[7] See, for instance, K. Jacobsson and H. Schmid, 'Real Integration or Just Formal Adaptation?—On the Implementation of the National Action Plans for Employment', in C. De la Porte and P. Pochet (eds), *Building Social Europe through the Open Method of Co-ordination* (2002), at 60–95.

of five years of OMC-employment[8] certainly does not present an uncontested success story. However, while the precise impact of the 'soft' OMC procedure remains unclear, the first years of experience show at least its important potential in the diffusion of a cognitive framework defining in which terms and with which priorities debates on certain policies, such as employment, should take place in the Member States.[9] This framework defines the conceptual borders beyond which any alternative becomes increasingly more difficult to defend and even to imagine.[10] Analysing the EES, Jacobsson reminds us of Gramsci arguing that 'the most effective form of political control is to make one's conception of the world hegemonic, to set the political agenda in such a way that ideology becomes conceived of as natural or normal.'[11] Thus, while not binding and not immediately discernible as having direct effects, soft procedures such as the OMC may have a very important impact in the longer run. Armstrong, for instance, argues that the policy space which Member States occupy in the field of social inclusion, coordinated within an OMC, is more institutionally shaped by other OMC processes and the values they incorporate than by the direct pressures of directly effective EU economic law.[12]

Moreover, the impact of the introduction of the OMC should not only be measured by the way it influences national policies. The OMC in employment, for instance, has strongly reconceptualized the role of EC labour law. The 'expanding nature' of the EES on the European social dimension[13] has been described as a shift from social policy to employment policy.[14] EC labour law is increasingly thought of as a tool for European employment policy, and one can see 'a re-orientation from an approach to labour market regulation which had as its core a strong concept of employment protection and high labour standards, to an approach which prioritises employment creation, and minimises the role of social policy, since social policy is seen as potentially increasing the regulatory

---

[8] Taking stock of five years of the European Employment Strategy, COM(2002)416 final, 17 July 2002.

[9] E. Szyszczak, 'The Evolving European Employment Strategy', in J. Shaw (ed.), *Social Law and Policy in an Evolving European Union* (2000), at 211; Léonard, 'Industrial Relations and the Regulation of Employment in Europe', 7 *European Journal of Industrial Relations* (2001), at 34; P. Syrpis, *Legitimising European Governance: Taking Subsidiarity Seriously within the Open Method of Coordination*, EUI Working Paper Law, 02/10 (2002), at 40; K. Jacobsson, 'Soft Regulation and the Subtle Transformation of States: The Case of EU Employment Policy', 14 *JEPP* (2004), at 361.

[10] Barbier applies to the EES the concept of 'référentiel' borrowed from Jobert and Muller. See Barbier, 'Une "Europe sociale" normative et procédurale: le cas de la stratégie coordonnée pour l'emploi', *Sociétés contemporaines* (2002) and B. Jobert and P. Muller, *L'Etat en action, politiques publiques et corporatismes* (1987).   [11] Jacobsson, *supra* n. 9, at 366.

[12] K. Armstrong, 'Tackling Social Exclusion through OMC: Reshaping the Boundaries of EU Governance' in T. Börzel and R. Cichowski (eds), *The State of the Union: Law, Politics and Society* (2003), vol. 6, at 180.

[13] N. Bruun, 'The European Employment Strategy and the "Acquis Communitaire" of Labour Law', 17 *IJCLLIR* (2001), at 309.

[14] D. Ashiagbor, 'EMU and the Shift in the European Labour Law Agenda: From "Social Policy" to "Employment Policy"', 7 *ELJ* (2001), at 311.

burden'.[15] This has been particularly clear for what has long been the core of European social intervention, namely occupational health and safety policy (OH&S). Under pressure of the priority given to employment, OH&S policy has in the 1990s been deprived of many of the resources it could build on, and its strongly regulatory approach has to a great extent been replaced by a soft persuasive policy whose effectiveness can be questioned.[16]

Finally, the impact of the OMC on the European social dimension can only be understood by taking into account how the different OMC procedures relate to one another. As shown by the example of social inclusion given by Armstrong, referred to above, the OMC in this field is strongly constrained by the framework set by the OMC on employment, which in its turn is shaped by the cognitive framework of the Broad Economic Policy Guidelines (BEPG). It has been argued that the OMC, as a strategy for reincarnation of the European welfare state, is subservient to the ideologies, path-dependencies and structures of Economic and Monetary Union, as institutionalized in the BEPGs.[17] The Lisbon process, centred around a discourse of economic growth and competitiveness rather than around social citizenship, and the encouragement of coordination of social and economic policies has resulted not so much in economic policy being sensitive to social concerns, but to a colonization of the welfare state by the economic policy-making process.[18]

Therefore, seen from the perspective of the protection of social rights, the OMC may, at the same time, be too soft and too hard. Too soft because, while not being able to set binding social standards at European level, nor does it guarantee that it would lead to the protection of social rights at national level given its language of quantitative objectives[19] and the predominance of the economic framework.

Too hard, because despite its non-binding nature, it may impose a cognitive framework, outside of which it may prove increasingly difficult to take policy initiatives. This cognitive framework is likely to shape 'the European social

[15] Ibid., at 311.

[16] For more detail, see S. Smismans, *Law, Legitimacy and European Governance, Functional Participation in Social Regulation* (2004), Ch. 2. In addition to the priority given to employment, the bad implementation record of the occupational health and safety (OH&S) regulatory framework has been another reason for the shift to 'persuasive policy-making'. Yet, bad implementation does not explain the low policy priority given to OH&S.

[17] D. Chalmers and M. Lodge, *The Open Method of Coordination and the European Welfare State*, Discussion Paper ESRC, Centre for Analysis of Risk and Regulation (June 2003), at 2.

[18] Ibid., at 10. This economic bias obviously relates to the deep structure of the EC's economic constitution; G. de Búrca, 'The Constitutional Challenge of New Governance in the European Union', 28 *ELRev.* (2003), at 820.

[19] S. Ball, 'The European Employment Strategy: The Will but Not the Way?', 30 *ILJ* (2001), at 353. On the role of Eurostatistics in the EES, see Jacobsson, *supra* n. 9, at 361–63. Given the importance of statistical indicators in the EES, Antoine Lyon-Caen and Joëlle Affichard argue that in order for the OMC to be 'open', reflexivity should extend to the presentation and use of the indicators, opening-up statistical expertise to constructive criticism, in particular from other fields of expertise. See A. Lyon-Caen and J. Affichard, 'From Legal Norms to Statistical Norms: Employment Policies Put to the Test of Coordination', in De Schutter and Deakin (eds), *supra* n. 6.

dimension' both in influencing national policies and conceptualizing the nature of European intervention.

One should thus be cautious about presenting the OMC by definition as 'a step forward' for Europe's social dimension. The introduction of the OMC has often been presented in this way since it allows the EU to intervene in social policy issues for which it had previously no competence. However, European engagement of this kind does not necessarily guarantee a high or higher protection of social standards. This does not imply that the operation of the OMC will necessarily be to the detriment of social standards, nor does it argue that the EU Member States would be better off without any coordination. Yet, one should acknowledge that it is in the nature of the OMC as an 'open' process which can go in different directions, that it does not offer any guarantee for the protection of social rights. Therefore, and given that the adoption of a strong regulatory social framework at EU level may be neither feasible nor desirable, it would be entirely justified to ask whether fundamental social rights can offer such a guarantee within the context of the coordination of national policies. Yet, this attractive line of reasoning may soon meet with disappointment when confronted with the soft nature of fundamental social rights.

B. *The Softness of Fundamental Social Rights*

Whereas the 'soft OMC' may have hard effects, fundamental social rights may be softer than the term 'fundamental rights' seems to suggest. While human rights may be 'fundamental', they are not necessarily 'hard' in terms of their justiciability or the existence of sanctions for their breach. The discourse of fundamental human rights has been strongly framed by international law and the international documents codifying these rights. It is influenced by the 'softness' of these international instruments which are characterized by weak sanction mechanisms and broadly defined principles. In particular, fundamental social rights—together with economic and cultural rights—are often said to be 'soft' in that they are not readily justiciable and may even be merely manifestations of a political or social programme, in contrast to civil and political rights which can be invoked in court against State action which fails to respect them. This difference is often justified by the fact that the latter are more easy to ensure since they are largely 'negative rights', that is they offer protection against state action, whereas the former are generally 'positive rights' that require positive action from the state and therefore strongly depend on the available socio-economic resources of a country, which implies limits to the possibility of claiming relief. Increasingly, however, it is argued that the opposition between 'negative' civil and political rights on the one hand, and 'positive' social rights on the other, is artificial since the former may also entail positive duties on the state, whereas the latter may also imply an obligation for the state not to intervene.[20]

---

[20] E.g. T. Jasudowicz, 'The Legal Character of Social Rights from the Perspective of International Law as a Whole', in K. Drzewicki, C. Krause, and A. Rosas (eds), *Social Rights as Human Rights*.

Yet, while arguments to place social rights on the same ground as other fundamental rights are increasingly to be found, international documents most often still deal with them separately and provide for different enforcement mechanisms.

Within the context of the EU, the difficult trajectory of social rights seeking to find their place in a process that has been primarily concerned with the building of a common market should also be recalled. Although social considerations have been taken into account in the interpretation and design of internal market rules, these have mainly been conceptualized as derogations from (economic) rights, and were thus to be interpreted narrowly according to the case law of the Court.[21] 'EU social rights are not conceived as rights corresponding to social entitlements that EU citizens can claim with regard to the European polity. They are conceived, instead, either as an instrument of undistorted competition or as a guarantee that such competition will not affect the level of social protection afforded by the Member States.'[22]

In the fundamental rights regime of the EU, social rights have occupied a secondary position, contrary to the values of economic freedom that are promoted by market integration.[23] Although the Court has recognized fundamental social rights as part of the general principles of Community law, they have rarely found their way into the case law, and there is no case in which the Court has required the Member States or the EU to take 'positive action' in order to respect an (unwritten) fundamental social right.[24]

The adoption of the Charter of Fundamental Rights of the European Union (EUCFR) in 2000, now agreed to be included in the Constitutional Treaty, opened the way to a strengthened position for fundamental social rights. Not only does it provide a written catalogue of fundamental rights with binding and 'constitutional' value—if the Constitutional Treaty is ratified—but it also appears, at first sight, to place social rights at the same level as economic, civil, and political rights by merging them into a single text without a clear distinction. However, as has already been extensively debated in the literature,[25] the potential impact of the Charter is strongly shaded by its 'horizontal clauses' aiming at protecting the

---

A European Challenge (1994), at 23; V.-P. Viljanen, 'Abstention or Involvement? The Nature of State Obligations under Different Categories of Rights', in ibid., at 43. Cécile Fabre, while recognizing the difference between negative and positive rights, argues that the distinction is irrelevant to arguments for or against constitutional social rights. See C. Fabre, *Social Rights Under the Constitution* (2000), at 65.

[21] N. Bernard, 'A "New Governance" Approach to Economic, Social and Cultural Rights in the EU', in T. Hervey and J. Kenner (eds), *Economic and Social Rights under the EU Charter of Fundamental Rights—A Legal Perspective* (2003), at 253.

[22] M. Poiares Maduro, 'The Double Constitutional Life of the Charter of Fundamental Rights of the European Union', in Hervey and Kenner (eds), *supra*, n. 21, at 285.

[23] Ibid., at 284.   [24] See B. de Witte's chapter in this volume.

[25] See, for instance, T. Hervey and J. Kenner (eds), *Economic and Social Rights under the EU Charter of Fundamental Rights: A Legal Perspective* (2003), *supra* n. 21; and G. de Búrca, 'Beyond the Charter: How Enlargement Has Enlarged the Human Rights Policy of the EU', in De Schutter and Deakin (eds), *supra* n. 6.

sovereignty of the Member States. The negotiation on the introduction of the Charter into the Constitutional Treaty further stressed these limits, in particular by introducing a distinction between rights and principles.[26] The latter are 'judicially cognisable only in the interpretation of' legislative and executive acts implementing them. Although the Charter does not indicate which provisions are rights and which principles, (most of) the social provisions are likely to be considered principles rather than rights, given their vague formulation and the legacy of the past.

III. WHERE OMC AND FUNDAMENTAL SOCIAL RIGHTS MAY MEET

A. *The European Employment Strategy and Fundamental Social Rights*

Theoretically one can broadly distinguish between two ways in which fundamental social rights can relate to the EES. On the one hand, they can provide a standard to be respected by the EES, and which is *ex post* justiciable. On the other hand, they can have a programmatic *ex ante* function in guiding European employment policy.

1. *Fundamental Social Rights as an* Ex Post *Justiciable Standard*

(a) Guidelines and Fundamental Social Rights

The EES has been built on several so-called pillars, among which are the importance of 'entrepreneurship' and the encouragement of 'adaptability'.[27] The entrepreneurship pillar combines a 'classical' industrial relations policy based on the idea that entrepreneurial activity will create employment in terms of dependent work, with a more innovative idea of an employment policy that would encourage the autonomy and initiative of individuals, and would thus identify in independent work and entrepreneurship a valid alternative to dependent work.[28] While the first dimension does not necessarily include employment protection in terms of qualitative standards and rights, the second increases further the risk of a non-protected workforce since independent workers have traditionally lacked many of the protective measures from which dependent workers could profit. Encouraging entrepreneurship as a core dimension of employment policy might increase the use and abuse of the status of 'independent worker' for functions which would otherwise be ensured by 'dependent contracts'. Could fundamental social rights provide a justiciable basis for sanctioning such an abuse?

---

[26] See B. Bercusson's chapter in this volume.

[27] Until 2002, the EES was explicitly built on four 'pillars', namely employability, entrepreneurship, adaptability, and equal opportunities. While this four pillar structure formally disappeared in the 2003 guidelines, these ideas remained central features of the EES.

[28] M. Dani, *Lo sviluppo dell' imprenditorialità nello spazio constitutionale europeo: le politiche pubbliche tra sostegno ed emancipazione* (2005) at 3.

The notion of 'adaptability' in the EES apparently aims at modernizing work organization in order to increase employment, while reconciling more flexibility with security and high occupational status. While adaptability may offer the benefit of reconciling work with family life, the framework of competitiveness and employment provided by the EES may also lead to the kind of flexibilization that puts at risk social rights. The serial use of short time contracts, for instance, frequently leads to workers not being able to take an annual period of (paid) leave. This contrasts with the fundamental social right to an annual period of paid leave, as recognized in Article 31(2) of the EUCFR. Could this provision be relied upon to contest the (assumed) effects of the EES?

The scope for justiciability of fundamental rights in the context of the EES appears strongly limited. This limitation results from the 'soft character' of both the OMC and of fundamental social rights.

The OMC, as a soft procedure of coordination of national policies, does not lead to the adoption of European legislation, but only provides guidance and assessment. Are these guidelines justiciable? Could one directly challenge the guidelines for failing to respect fundamental rights? The action for annulment under Article 230 EC explicitly excludes recommendations and opinions as acts that could be reviewed. The case law confirms that only binding measures come within the scope of the action for annulment,[29] which seems to preclude any possibility of bringing aspects of the soft OMC procedure before the Court of Justice on this basis. Moreover, contesting via the preliminary ruling procedure (Article 234 EC) the validity of EES guidelines or recommendations for not respecting fundamental social rights appears equally unlikely. As Bernard rightly argues, although the Court has referred to the difference of wording between Articles 230 and 234 to establish its jurisdiction in the context of the preliminary ruling procedure to *interpret* non-binding acts adopted by the institutions, it would be difficult to understand why the *validity* of a category of act would be open to challenge under Article 234 EC but not under Article 230 EC.[30]

While it appears impossible to contest directly the validity of soft measures as guidelines and recommendations for violation of fundamental social rights, it should be acknowledged that the OMC is not entirely detached from hard law. There are two ways in which OMC procedures can relate to hard law. First, the guidance provided by OMC procedures is intended to be translated into national policies, which may include the adoption of national legislation. While being a soft procedure, the OMC will thus at a certain stage (also) result in hard law. Secondly, while the OMC procedure as such does not lead to European legislation, the cognitive framework provided by OMC procedures may, nevertheless, influence European regulation in those areas where the EU does have legislative

---

[29] Bernard, in Hervey and Kenner (eds), *supra* n. 21, at 256.   [30] Ibid., at 257.

competence. It is in this double interaction between OMC and hard law that one may imagine fundamental social rights entering judicial procedures. Yet, even in this case, account should be taken of the limits imposed by the 'soft' nature of fundamental social rights.

(b) National Legislation Implementing OMC Guidelines

Can fundamental social rights provide a threshold for national legislation which is framed in the context of an OMC? Could a judicial challenge be mounted to national legislation implementing an OMC guideline, on the ground of infringement of fundamental social rights? It should be recalled that in relation to the action of the Member States, the EUCFR only applies 'when they are implementing Union law' (Article 51(1) EUCFR). Does national legislation adopted within the framework provided by an OMC fall under this definition?

The concept of 'Union law' need not be reduced to European legislation, European binding acts of a general nature, but it should be seen also as including European binding acts of an individual nature, and also non-binding acts. Union law can be defined as the broad category of all European acts and their interpretation over which the Court of Justice has jurisdiction. The ECJ has clearly confirmed that the preliminary ruling procedure of Article 234 EC confers on the Court jurisdiction to rule on the 'validity and interpretation of *all acts* of the institutions of the Community without exception'.[31] In the case at hand, the Court confirmed its jurisdiction to interpret via a preliminary ruling a recommendation, despite its non-binding character. The ECJ further specified that 'the national courts are bound to take recommendations into consideration in order to decide disputes submitted to them, in particular where they cast light on *the interpretation of national measures adopted in order to implement them* or where they are designed to supplement binding Community provisions'.[32]

The 'implementation of Union law' is thus not limited to binding European acts, but can also refer to the implementation of non-binding European acts. The adoption of a national measure to implement a recommendation issued in the context of an OMC procedure would thus fall under the definition 'implementation of Union law'. Some authors, however, have argued that this would be more difficult to sustain in relation to the broader policy guidelines that are issued within OMC procedures.[33] This reasoning is defensible in so far as it might be difficult to identify whether a national measure constitutes the implementation of such a broadly defined guideline. However, one could argue that where NAPs explicitly identify national legislation as the implementing measure of European policy guidelines, they provide us with a clear indication that we are dealing here with the 'implementation of Union law'.

---

[31] Case C-322/88, *Salvatore Grimaldi v. Fonds des maladies professionnelles* [1989] ECR I-4419, indent 8 (emphasis added). [32] Ibid., at 4421, indent 18 (emphasis added).
[33] Bernard *supra* n. 29, at 258.

However, even if it is accepted that national legislation implementing an OMC guideline/recommendation can be defined as 'implementation of Union law', and therefore that the EUCFR applies, it is still necessary to take into account the limits imposed by the Charter's distinction between rights and provisions.

The possibility to use a fundamental social right as a justiciable provision to challenge national legislation based on the EES seems extremely limited given that the Court will most likely remain very reluctant to recognize the social provisions of the Charter in terms of subjective rights providing direct entitlements. There might be some very rare exceptions to this: it would be very strange, for instance, for Article 23 EUCFR on sex equality not to be justiciable, given that this principle has always been a justiciable and directly effective right in Community law. Thus, for instance, if a national law intended to implement the EES guideline to encourage lifelong learning excluded women from such programmes, this law could be challenged with reference to the fundamental social right recognized in the Charter. Yet, beyond sex equality—for which the Treaty already provided a solid basis to challenge national legislation—it remains to be seen whether the Court will recognize other social provisions of the Charter as justiciable rights. The Court is even reluctant to recognize fundamental social rights in the interpretation of European legislation (see below). The situation in which the legality of a national law implementing the EES could directly be challenged on the basis of an 'unwritten' fundamental social right and independently of any European regulatory framework[34] seems extremely unlikely.

Therefore, the role of fundamental social rights in relation to national legislation implementing the EES may be less in the provision of a justiciable basis to challenge such legislation, but rather in the support for such national legislation where it contributes to the realization of social rights—in potential conflict with economic freedoms. As argued above, the EES is built on a permanent tension between ensuring competitiveness and social cohesion. Adaptability, for instance, need not lead to the downgrading of social standards by introducing flexible contracts. Adaptability can also lead to the creation of new social rights aiming at reconciling work with family life. National legislation implementing OMC guidelines in this sense may find support in this interpretation by reference to the fundamental social rights of the Charter.

Moreover if such national legislation derogates at the same time from EU law, such as the free movement rules, it should be possible to use the fundamental social rights of the Charter in defence of such national derogations. The Court has already allowed fundamental rights to be invoked where Member States derogate from EU law,[35] and it would therefore be logical to accept such reasoning where similar derogations take place in the context of an OMC, given that in that case

---

[34] For the possibilities when European regulation does exist, see below.
[35] Case 5/88, *Wachauf* [1989] ECR 2609 and Case C-260/89, *Elliniki Radiophonia Tileorassi AE v. Domitiki Etairia Pliroforissis and Sotiris Kouvelas* [1991] ECR I-2925.

the Member States are 'implementing Union law' and should thus not only 'respect the rights' and 'observe the principles' of the Charter, but should also 'promote the application thereof' (Article 51 EUCFR).

Fundamental social rights can thus be used in the interpretation of national legislation implementing the EES, both to support the social rights dimension *within* the EES in contrast to the economic and competitiveness dimension of the strategy, and *outside* the EES to support derogations from the economic constitution of the EU.[36]

(c) European Legislation Related to the Cognitive Framework of the OMC

In addition to the relation between the OMC and national legislation framed in that context, the OMC in question may also be related to legislation adopted at the European level. It is clear that the OMC has generally been developed for certain policy areas in which the EU has no legislative competence, and in some cases precisely because the transfer of such competence to the European level has been considered undesirable. However, this does not imply that the OMC takes place in a vacuum, entirely separated from regulatory initiatives for issues on which the EU does have competence to adopt hard law. In fact, while aiming at coordinating national policies, the OMC might also influence the cognitive framework within which European legislation is adopted. This is, for instance, the case with the EES. As argued above, EU labour law has increasingly been influenced by the broad cognitive framework for employment provided by the OMC.

While the EES encourages 'adaptability', including flexible solutions in regulating working time, Directive 2003/88/EC, replacing Directive 93/104/EC, lays down minimal requirements for the protection of health and safety of workers in organizing working time. Although defining 'minimal requirements', this regulation is characterized by strong flexibility allowing for a large number of derogations. While adaptability in working time may be won at the benefit of reconciling work with family life, the framework of competitiveness and employment provided by the EES may also lead to a further interpretation of the Working Time Directive in the direction of flexibilization according to sectors and local needs and at the cost of social rights.[37] Therefore, the recognition of the fundamental right

---

[36] If one accepts that national legislation in the context of an OMC is 'implementing Union law', this use of fundamental social rights would respect the requirements of Article 52(5) EUCFR regarding 'principles': 'The provisions of this Charter which contain principles *may be implemented* by legislative and executive acts taken by Institutions and bodies of the Union, and *by acts of Member States when they are implementing Union law*, in the exercise of their respective powers. They shall be judicially cognisable only in the interpretation of such acts and in the ruling on their legality' (emphasis added).

[37] Analysing the implementation of the Working Time Directive in the UK, C. Barnard, S. Deakin and R. Hobbs argue that 'the Directive is at risk of degenerating into a weak and partial mechanism for the realization of social rights'; Barnard, Deakin and Hobbs, 'Reflexive Law, Corporate Social Responsibility and the Evolution of Labour Standards: The Case of Working Time', in De Schutter and Deakin (eds), *supra* n. 6.

of every worker to a limitation of maximum working hours, to daily and weekly rest periods and to an annual period of paid leave, as provided in Article 31(2) EUCFR, may serve as a counterbalance in the judicial interpretation of the Directive and of the EES.

Two remarks should be made here. First, even in the interpretation of European legislation, the Court has been reluctant to recognize fundamental social rights. In *BECTU*,[38] for instance, the Court agreed that the United Kingdom did not respect the provisions on annual leave provided by the Working Time Directive, but it shied away from the language of fundamental rights, preferring instead to characterize the right to paid annual leave as 'a particularly important principle of Community law', albeit one 'from which there can be no derogations'.[39] The EUCFR, the possible inclusion of which in the Constitutional Treaty was being debated at that time,[40] had not been referred to by the Court, which only mentioned the Community Social Charter which was cited in the Working Time Directive's preamble.

Secondly, although fundamental social rights might be invoked in this way, and they could *de facto* constitute a threshold against a race-to-the-bottom effect of the EES on European legislation, in terms of judicial proceedings the issue will most likely be argued in terms of the relationship between the Directive in question and fundamental rights, without any reference to the OMC.

However, the EES and European social regulation are not necessarily moving in the same direction. For instance, analysing policy towards older workers, Paul Skidmore[41] has revealed the tension between the EES and European social policy based on the EU's legislative competences. Encouraging measures to tackle the unemployment of younger and older workers, the EES may lead to national labour law provisions favouring particular age groups in the workforce, which may result in a contrast with the Framework Directive 2000/78/EC[42] on equal treatment in employment and occupation. The Framework Directive, adopted on the basis of the anti-discrimination clause of Article 13 EC, prohibits age discrimination, but also states that 'differences of treatment on grounds of age shall not constitute discrimination, if, within the context of national law they are objectively and reasonably justified by a legitimate aim, including legitimate employment policy, labour market and vocational training objectives, and if the means of achieving that aim are appropriate and necessary' (Article 6(1)). Courts may thus be faced with the task of deciding whether a national measure adopted in the context of the EES does constitute 'legitimate employment policy' and where this is the case whether the measure is then proportionate. In general the

---

[38] Case C-173/99, *R v. Secretary of Trade for Industry, ex parte BECTU* [2001] ECR I-4881.
[39] Compare with Case C-133/00, *Bowden and others v. Tuffnells Parcels Express Ltd* [2001] ECR I-7031; see J. Hunt, 'Fair and Just Working Conditions', in Hervey and Kenner (eds), *supra* n. 21, at 60–63. [40] This may also explain the Court's reluctance to intervene in the political debate.
[41] P. Skidmore, 'The European Employment Strategy and Labour Law: A German Case-Study', 29 *ELRev.* (2004), at 52–73. [42] OJ 2000 L303/16.

ECJ's case law on discrimination has demonstrated the Court's strict adherence to a principle of formal equality with only narrow derogations.[43] This is likely to be followed also in relation to age discrimination, even if 'justified' by the employment policy of the EES. Can fundamental social rights play a role in deciding on this tension between EES and European social regulation? In the case at hand, the old worker 'privileged' by national measures would most likely have little to win from a reference to fundamental rights. Whereas Article 21 EUCFR clearly prohibits discrimination on grounds of age, the Charter does not provide clear entitlements to which one could refer in order to justify such privileged treatment. In particular, the Charter does not include the right to work.[44]

The potential tension between Directives based on the anti-discrimination clause of Article 13 EC and the OMC is also noted in the field of social inclusion. According to Kenneth Armstrong, OMC and anti-discrimination Directives may be complementary policy instruments to combat social exclusion, but they create, nevertheless, 'a tension between a conception of social inclusion premised on pathways out of exclusion and policy diversity between states on the one hand, and an ideal of civil and political inclusion premised on equality guarantees and uniform EU entitlements'.[45] If this tension were to enter the sphere of judicial scrutiny, the use of fundamental rights would favour the second pathway since they identify general entitlements. Yet, in the absence of strong uniform EU social entitlements, in terms of legislation or fundamental rights as defined in the EUCFR, reference to fundamental rights would mostly end up in ensuring formal equality, which may precisely put at risk national social entitlements taking into account 'difference'.

To summarize, the possibility of reference to fundamental social rights in a judicial context in order to limit, interpret, or steer the effects of an OMC is not entirely to be ruled out. However, as a justiciable threshold against a potential race-to-the-bottom effect of the OMC, fundamental social rights may not offer very much. Guidelines and Recommendations as such cannot be directly challenged. It is also very unlikely that a national law implementing the EES could be challenged by reference to a fundamental social right as enshrined in the EUCFR. Instead, fundamental social rights might enter into the judicial debate in relation to the *interpretation* of national or European legislation influenced by the EES. Thus it could strengthen a social rights interpretation of national law implementing the EES—rather than a race-to-the-bottom interpretation of the Strategy—and strengthen the position of such national legislation against the EU's economic constitutional framework. It could equally strengthen the social rights interpretation of European legislation in the context of the cognitive framework provided by the EES, or help to address the tension between the former and the latter.

---

[43] Ibid., at 60.

[44] A remarkable absence in the EUCFR, in contrast for instance to the European Social Charter. See D. Ashiagbor's chapter in this volume.   [45] Armstrong *supra* n. 12, at 177.

It is undoubtedly the case that a judicial interpretation of the EES in terms of respecting and even promoting social rights will have more chance the more the EES takes up *ex ante* the language of social rights in terms of its policy objectives.

2. Fundamental Social Rights as Ex Ante *Inspiration of the EES* While fundamental social rights demonstrate serious limits in terms of justiciability, in particular if they are expected to provide a threshold against a race to the bottom interpretation of the OMC, they may play an important role *ex ante* in defining the policy objectives of the EES. The *ex ante* role of fundamental social rights as a normative discourse that can guide policy has been illustrated by the way in which the 1989 Community Charter of the Fundamental Social Rights of Workers inspired European social policy, and in particular the adoption of Directives.[46]

However, fundamental social rights need not necessarily serve as a basis for a legislative policy agenda at the European level, they can also serve as normative objectives and as an inspiration for the programmatic steering of national policies through the OMC. Fundamental social rights are realized through the development of social policies, which remain largely in the hands of the Member States. However, OMC procedures, such as those in the field of employment, social inclusion, and pensions, aim to set the cognitive framework for these policies. If this cognitive framework is defined in terms of economic and statistical targets without the language of fundamental rights this may undermine at national level the direct link between fundamental social rights and the policy instruments needed to realize them. It is therefore desirable that these OMCs take up the language of fundamental social rights.

Would this, however, conflict with the emphasis of the EUCFR on the importance of respect for the division of powers between the EU and its Member States in order to protect their national sovereignty? By adopting the language of fundamental social rights in the OMC, the EU would not exercise any additional competence. It would fit precisely with the idea that fundamental social rights do not necessarily require the creation of common legislative standards at the European level, but can be realized even while taking into account national diversity. EU Institutions and Member States would simply 'respect the [Charter's] rights, observe the principles and promote the application thereof in accordance with their respective powers . . .' (Article 51(1)). *Vice versa*, if OMC procedures at the EES do not take up the language of fundamental rights they are likely to fall short of the requirement to respect and promote the application of the Charter's rights and principles given their power to influence the cognitive framework for policy instruments which help to realize such rights.

---

[46] B. Wendon, 'The Commission as image-venue entrepreneur in EU social policy', 5 *JEPP* (1998), at 344. Since 2001 a comparable evolution can be noticed in relation to the EUCFR, see B. de Witte's chapter in this volume.

In order to integrate the language of fundamental social rights into the EES it would be advisable to include in the Employment Title of the EC Treaty a reference to fundamental social rights and the EUCFR as explicit principles and objectives of this policy. Whereas in relation to social policy the Social Chapter of the EC Treaty requires the Community and the Member States to 'have in mind fundamental social rights such as those set out in the European Social Charter (ESC) and in the 1989 Community Charter of the Fundamental Rights of Workers', such requirement is lacking in relation to employment policy.[47]

However, the main challenge is to integrate the language of fundamental social rights into the content of the EES, via the guidelines and recommendations. Some of the benchmarks set in the EES could be framed with reference to the realization of specific fundamental social rights. Such language strengthens the cognitive framework in which national policies and legislation could then take rights seriously. Moreover, it would broaden the space to provide an *ex post* 'social rights interpretation' of the OMC by the judiciary, as indicated above.

B. The OMC at the Service of a Fundamental Rights Policy

Using the example of the EES, I have argued that fundamental social rights may function both as an *ex post* (interpretative rather than entitling) justiciable threshold and an *ex ante* programmatic inspiration for the OMC. Several authors have identified an additional relation between fundamental social rights and the OMC, namely that the OMC could be used as a technique to give concrete contextual substance to these abstract rights.[48]

This fits with the programmatic use of fundamental social rights as a source of inspiration for policy-making, but strengthens this use in a double way. First, the introduction of an OMC specifically on fundamental rights, for instance via an annual cycle of national reports to be assessed at the European level, would contribute to defining and interpreting fundamental rights in concrete contexts and on the basis of concrete experiences, in relation to Europe's economic constitution, and would allow for the exchange of best practices. Secondly, such a cyclical assessment combined with the possibility of addressing recommendations to particular states would create political peer pressure for changes in policy. This double advantage is illustrated by the experience of the review procedure of the European Social Charter of the Council of Europe which may be of inspiration here.[49]

---

[47] The Constitutional Treaty does not introduce such a reference for employment. It is also worth noting that the reference to fundamental social rights in relation to social policy remained unchanged, i.e. mentioning the ESC and the 1989 Community Charter, without introducing an extra reference to Part II (EUCFR) of the Constitutional Treaty.

[48] de Búrca, *supra* n. 18, at 28; de Búrca, in De Schutter and Deakin (eds), *supra* n. 25; Bernard, in Hervey and Kenner (eds), *supra* n. 21, at 247; Armstrong, in Börzel and Cichowski (eds), *supra* n. 12, at 180; O. De Schutter, 'The Implementation of Fundamental Rights through the Open Method of Coordination', in De Schutter and Deakin (eds), *supra* n. 6.

[49] See B. Casey, 'The European Social Charter and Revised European Social Charter', in C. Costello (ed.), *Fundamental Social Rights: Current European Legal Protection and the Challenge*

Governments are required to provide reports on their implementation of the Charter, which are then assessed by the European Committee of Social Rights, composed of independent experts. This Committee determines for each provision whether or not the national situation is consistent with the Charter. This review process requires the experts to interpret the Charter and it has contributed significantly in providing doctrinal substance to what are often very generally framed provisions.[50] The European Committee of Social Rights subsequently addresses a report to the Governmental Committee that prepares the decisions of the Committee of Ministers. The latter adopts a resolution for the supervision cycle as a whole and can adopt recommendations addressed at individual countries.

Such a political reporting mechanism on fundamental rights also has advantages over *ex post* judicial sanctioning mechanisms. An OMC can provide both *ex post* assessment and *ex ante* guidance for a real fundamental rights policy. Neither does it depend on the initiative of an individual complainant. Moreover, those most in need of fundamental social rights protection often lack the knowledge and resources to go to court. Finally, although it appears difficult to maintain a rigid distinction between political and civil rights on the one hand, and economic and social rights on the other, one cannot ignore the fact that the recognition of a fundamental social right very often implies a difficult assessment of costs and available resources. A participatory political procedure may often be a better forum than judicial proceedings to make such an assessment.[51]

IV. THE LANGUAGE OF RIGHTS: A MINORITY LANGUAGE? THE NEED FOR PARTICIPATORY PROCEDURES

As noted by Olivier De Schutter, the current political setting is a favourable one for thinking about a fundamental rights policy in the EU in which an OMC may find a place.[52] Not only has the EUCFR and its inclusion in the Constitutional Treaty placed fundamental rights at the centre of the European constitutional debate, but the European Council in Brussels in December 2003 also decided to convert the European Monitoring Centre on Racism and Xenophobia into a Fundamental Rights Agency. The Monitoring Centre, which has as its main task the collection of data, would extend its remit to the field of fundamental rights.

---

of the EU Charter on Fundamental Rights (2000), at 55–74; and see R. Brillat's chapter in this volume.

[50] See R. Brillat and J.-F. Akandji-Kombé in this volume.

[51] R. Wieruszeski, 'Some Comments Concerning the Concept of Economic and Social Rights', in Drzewcki, Krause, and Rosas (eds), *supra* n. 20, at 69; M. Craven, 'A View from Elsewhere: Social Rights, International Covenant and the EU Charter of Fundamental Rights', in Costello (ed.), *supra* n. 49, at 86; Bernard, in Hervey and Kenner (eds), *supra* n. 21, at 266.

[52] De Schutter, in De Schutter and Deakin (eds), *supra* n. 48.

The Commission established a consultation process late in 2004 to prepare a proposal in this direction.[53] Even while awaiting further institutional initiatives for what might become an EU fundamental rights policy, several lessons can be drawn from existing institutions.

It has been argued for instance that existing European information agencies are too detached from policy-making, and that they fail to trigger policy initiatives or to influence the implementation of policy. The 2002 assessment made of the Monitoring Centre, for instance, was very critical and suggested, among other things, that the Centre should strengthen its links with the Member States.[54] Comparable comments have been made regarding the European Agency for Safety and Health Protection at Work.[55]

If hopes are built primarily on an agency which gathers information, fundamental rights may remain a minority language that has no real influence on policies. The same risk is present in the functioning of the Network of Independent Experts set up in 2002 by the European Commission at the recommendation of the European Parliament.[56] The Network, composed of one expert per Member State, provides an annual report, addressed to the Commission, assessing the application of the EUCFR, and may be called to deliver an opinion on specific questions raised by the Commission. Yet, while providing valuable reports it risks remaining an exercise confined to a small group of experts without actually triggering any political consequences.

It has been argued that the novelty of the OMC resides precisely in the fact that, compared to previous forms of soft law, data collection and reporting mechanisms in the EU, it provides for a 'high level political participation' through the Council and the European Council, in contrast to monitoring procedures which are typically managed at the administrative level.[57] The OMC thus has greater potential to generate political engagement than other forms of soft law and monitoring.

However, creating an OMC process on fundamental rights provides no guarantee that fundamental rights protection will be a strong feature of European policy-making. Two potential weaknesses of the OMC which emerge from the experience with existing OMC procedures should be considered.

First, despite 'high level' political involvement through the Council and European Council, the practice of OMC procedures has often been described as technocratic, centred around a limited group of representatives from national administrations, and—despite rhetorical promises—weak in including stakeholders

---

[53] Communication from the Commission, The Fundamental Rights Agency. Public consultation document. COM (2004)693 final, 25 October 2004.

[54] Commission européenne, Evaluation de l'Observatoire européen des phénomènes racistes et xénophobes, May 2002, at: http://europa.eu.int/comm/employment_social/fundamental_rights/pdf/origin/eumc_eval2002_fr.pdf.   [55] Smismans, *supra* n. 16, at 294.

[56] See http://europa.eu.int/comm/justice_home/cfr_cdf/index_en.htm.

[57] Borrás and Jacobsson, *supra* n. 3, at 189.

or ensuring bottom-up involvement.[58] While this puts into doubt the democratic quality of the OMC, the lack of involvement may equally impede its effectiveness by not reaching those who implement policies in practice. In the field of fundamental rights, the importance of involving civil society actors in a reporting system such as the OMC is illustrated by the experience of the European Social Charter. Until 1998, civil society actors were only involved in the annual review procedure through the participation of representatives of the European social partners' organizations as observers in the meetings of the Governmental Committee. Although Article 27 ESC provided the Governmental Committee with the opportunity also to consult other civil society organizations, this has never been done in practice.[59] As argued by the former head of the ESC Section at the Council of Europe, the limited role assigned to employers' and workers' organizations in the old ESC system and the total exclusion of the NGOs had reduced their interest in the Charter and was, therefore, one of the main effectiveness problems of the ESC, given their important influence on national policies in this area.[60]

Secondly, the experience with existing OMCs has raised awareness of the need to 'streamline' or coordinate the various coordination methods. Initially, OMC procedures—despite often dealing with interrelated policy issues—proceeded with their own policy cycles, involving different actors, and ignoring what happened in the parallel procedures. Yet, the OMC has more recently demonstrated the potential for 'reflexivity', by taking into account what is happening beyond that particular coordination mechanism.[61]

More than for any other policy sector, an OMC on fundamental rights should avoid enclosing itself within its own cyclical process. Fundamental rights should inspire all policy areas. Put differently, the language of rights should not confine itself to a ghetto with only fundamental rights experts being involved in an OMC on fundamental rights, but instead should be able to influence other OMCs. The prospect of having an OMC dealing with fundamental rights on the one hand, and an OMC dealing with employment on the other, each functioning entirely independently, should be avoided. Instead, the language of fundamental rights, although developed and fine-tuned within an OMC dealing specifically with fundamental rights, should then be able to influence the EES and to provide a counterbalance to the competitiveness discourse in this Strategy.

Thus, an OMC on fundamental rights could have an advantage over an information-based agency in that it could create a degree of high-level political involvement. But the language of fundamental rights should reach outside and beyond the OMC on that topic. In that sense, particular attention should be given

---

[58] See *supra* n. 1.

[59] M. Fuchs, 'The European Social Charter: Its Role in Present-Day Europe and Its Reform', in Drzewcki, Krause, and Rosas (eds), *supra*, n. 20, at 158.　　　　[60] Ibid., at 159.

[61] See Smismans, in De Schutter and Deakin (eds), *supra* n. 6.

to creating elements of reflexivity and interaction with other OMC procedures, for instance by streamlining their policy cycles, and by creating the widest possible participatory structures able to propagate the language of fundamental rights beyond a closed circle of experts.

The advantage of having an OMC does not imply that an information agency would not also have a role to play. One should rather look at how these policy instruments might be combined in order to compensate for one another's weaknesses.[62] Profiting from the reform of the Monitoring Centre on Racism, the future institutional setting for a European fundamental rights policy could be structured around the following three features.

First, the Fundamental Rights Agency would focus on the collection of data *and* providing an analysis of this data, which would be collected through a network involving national administrations, experts, and civil society actors. In order to avoid information collection being merely a compilation of dispersed and non-comparable data (a criticism made both of the Monitoring Centre and the Bilbao Agency on occupational health and safety), it should also have a research function and should develop the capacity to analyse critically the received data. The competence to engage in research has, for instance, been a strong reason for satisfaction with the Dublin Foundation for Living and Working Conditions, in contrast to the criticism of the Bilbao Agency which lacks such a competence.[63] The Network of Independent Experts could play a central role in providing the capacity for critical analysis, for instance, by linking into the Agency structure as a scientific committee.[64]

This data collection would lead to annual reports on the state of fundamental rights in each Member State, and to reports on specific topics. National administrations currently play a role in information gathering, but they should not be monopoly players, since they are both party and judge in the implementation of fundamental rights. Experience with agencies, such as the Bilbao Agency, has shown the risk that a monopolizing position of national administrations in the agency's network may negatively influence the quality of the information provided.[65] On the other hand, the experience of the European Committee of Social Rights in the context of the ESC, has shown the strong added value of reporting and of an assessment involving experts. Using the Fundamental Rights Agency for national reporting, with its resources in terms of having a fixed secretariat, and building on expertise—provided by the Network of Independent

---

[62] I have argued in a comparable way in favour of an OMC in the field of occupational health and safety in combination with the role of the Bilbao Agency dealing with this field, in order to overcome the shortcomings of the latter. See Smismans, *supra* n. 16, at 302–04.   [63] Ibid., at 301.

[64] The assessment of the Monitoring Centre also called for a scientific committee, in order to leave the Management Board more space to deal with the real management issues. See Commission européenne, Evaluation de l'Observatoire européen des phénomènes racistes et xénophobes, May 2002, at: http://europa.eu.int/comm/employment_social/fundamental_rights/pdf/origin/eumc_eval2002_fr.pdf.   [65] Smismans, *supra* n. 16, at 295–96.

Experts—and civil society involvement could offer an advantage over an OMC in which national administrations would be the central players.

Secondly, while using the Agency for national reporting, these reports should nevertheless be integrated in a cyclical OMC procedure creating a degree of political engagement; that is, national reports should be taken up by the Commission, in order to propose assessments and recommendations to the Council and European Council, to be streamlined with other OMC procedures. Again the ESC experience could be interesting here. One of the main reasons for the reforms of the 1990s has been the tension between the expert analysis of the European Committee of Social Rights (then Committee of Independent Experts) and the political assessment by the Governmental Committee, a tension which was resolved in favour of the expert judgement of the European Committee.[66]

Thirdly, civil society actors should be involved in the reporting system. This should be done, above all, by involving them in the agency network in gathering information. However, their position could also be enhanced by introducing a collective complaints procedure such as has been done in the ESC (and which entered into force in 1998).[67] Such a collective complaints procedure could compensate for the significant shortcomings in the justiciability of fundamental rights, in particular social rights, not least in the context of OMC procedures.

V. CONCLUSION

The OMC can be seen both as a potential asset or as a threat for social standards. In the absence of (the political will to adopt) binding social norms at the European level, the OMC could steer national (social) policies in the same direction and, therefore, could reduce the risk of a race-to-the-bottom effect due to regulatory competition. Yet, if dominated by Europe's economic constitutional framework, statistical and quantitative benchmarks, the OMC might also undermine the social-rights-oriented cognitive framework of national social policies.

Fundamental social rights could then appear as a threshold below which the OMC should not go. Yet, in terms of justiciability, fundamental social rights seem to offer little in relation to the OMC. One cannot directly challenge the validity of OMC guidelines or recommendations, and it is equally very unlikely that one could challenge a national law implementing an OMC guideline by reference only to fundamental social rights, independently of any European regulatory framework. Instead, fundamental social rights may help in the interpretation of national law implementing an OMC in relation to the EU's constitutional and regulatory framework, as well as in interpreting the latter where related to the cognitive framework provided by an OMC.

---

[66] See also R. Brillat's chapter in this volume.
[67] Casey, in Costello (ed.), *supra* n. 49, at 68–75.

However, the most important use of fundamental social rights in relation to the OMC is likely to be in their programmatic nature, in giving definition to the direction and objectives of OMC procedures. Such a programmatic use would be strengthened by using the OMC as a technique for reporting on and guiding a fundamental rights policy in itself.[68] However, particular attention should be given to ensuring that such a fundamental rights OMC would be able to spread the language and orientation of fundamental social rights into other OMCs. The current proposal to transform the European Monitoring Centre on Racism and Xenophobia into a Fundamental Rights Agency provides a good occasion to think about the best institutional setting to realize this aim, which should be done by creating an appropriate balance between expert assessment, civil society involvement, and political engagement.

[68] The creation of an OMC fundamental rights in the EU may seem to duplicate already existing reporting mechanisms such as that of the ESC. Yet, its added value lies particularly in the fact that the EU is more politically salient, and that it would create better opportunities to link with EU policies, including OMCs. See also de Búrca, in De Schutter and Deakin (eds), *supra* n. 25.

PART IV

ESC JURISPRUDENCE AND THE EU *ACQUIS*: THE COMMON CORE AND THE ADDED VALUE

12

The Right to Work

DIAMOND ASHIAGBOR

I. INTRODUCTION

What meaning can be attached to the idea of a 'right to work' in the European context? Although prominently placed in the European Social Charter, the Community Charter of the Fundamental Social Rights of Workers and the EU Charter of Fundamental Rights, the right to work nevertheless remains a socio-economic right which most starkly begs the question of how such rights can be realized in practice, and against whom: on which institutions could a corresponding duty be imposed—the state, employers, or trade unions?

The 'right to work' is a right fraught with definitional problems. Within the 1961 European Social Charter, and unchanged in the Revised European Social Charter of 1996, the emphasis is very much on the obligation of states to attain the goal of full employment, with the right to work seen primarily as necessitating state action in respect of employment and labour market policy, placement services, and training, and only secondarily as requiring protection of workers' rights within employment. In contrast, the language of the Community Social Charter and the EU Charter of Fundamental Rights reveals a conception of the right to work principally in terms of freedom to choose an occupation and the (economic) freedom of movement of workers within the territory of the EU. Can these two perspectives on the right to work be reconciled? What of alternative perspectives, which conceive of the right to work as a right enforceable against trade unions, or in relation to the actions of employers—in terms of protection from discrimination in engagement and guarantee of what might be called job security?

This chapter will explore the significance of the 'right to work' within the European Social Charter and EU law, in particular interrogating the interaction between the two systems, and the extent to which they succeed in fully explicating this right and providing mechanisms for its realization. Of importance to this task are conceptualizations of the right to work which, whilst not explicitly referenced in either the European Social Charter or the EU Charters, are nevertheless implicit in the rights discourse within these two systems. In addition to the notion of the right to work as a means of leveraging the unemployed or underemployed onto the labour market, this chapter will also consider discourses around the right to work which view this right as a means of realizing social citizenship.

II. THE RIGHT TO WORK: ECONOMIC FREEDOM OR STATE OBLIGATION?

The European Social Charter reads as follows:

Article 1—The right to work

With a view to ensuring the effective exercise of the right to work, the [Contracting] Parties undertake:

1 to accept as one of their primary aims and responsibilities the achievement and maintenance of as high and stable a level of employment as possible, with a view to the attainment of full employment;
2 to protect effectively the right of the worker to earn his living in an occupation freely entered upon;
3 to establish or maintain free employment services for all workers;
4 to provide or promote appropriate vocational guidance, training and rehabilitation.[1]

Within the European Social Charter, therefore, the primary locus of the right to work is in the struggle for full employment. Neither the EU Charter nor the Community Charter of 1989 speak directly to the goal of full employment, but instead both EU Charters locate the core of the right to work in the freedom to earn a living in a freely chosen occupation. An equivalent provision to Article 1(2) of the European Social Charter is contained in Article 15 of the EU Charter of Fundamental Rights, paragraph 1 of which proclaims that '[e]veryone has the right to engage in work and to pursue a freely chosen or accepted occupation'. From the outset, however, one is confronted with tensions between the two systems of rights. The fact that the right to work contained in Article 15 applies to 'everyone' is significant, since other rights inextricably linked to the right to work do not have such broad coverage. In the absence of a clear statement as to the active scope of application of the EU Charter (that is who should be protected), the beneficiaries of each right vary from article to article. Within Article 15 itself for example, a clear distinction is made between the right to engage in work and to pursue a freely chosen occupation (open to all) and the right to seek employment, to work, to exercise the right of establishment and to provide services in any Member State, which is open only to 'citizens' of the EU in keeping with the EC Treaty—such free movement rights are not extended to nationals of third countries.

---

[1] European Social Charter 1961; word in square brackets refers to text deleted from the original European Social Charter of 1961 by the Revised European Social Charter of 1996.

So, although the EU Charter self-consciously draws inspiration and legitimacy from other international statements of rights, referring in its preamble to the Social Charters adopted by the Community (in 1989) and by the Council of Europe (in 1961), nevertheless the fact that the EU Charter must operate within the constraints of EU competence serves to limit a complete identification between the EU Charter and the ESC: in the EU context, as distinct from the world of the Council of Europe, beneficiaries of rights to be enjoyed in conjunction with the right to work are sometimes 'workers', sometimes economically active citizens of EU Member States seeking to exercise rights for free movement granted by the EC Treaty, and sometimes all those legally resident within the Union.[2]

That said, to underline the close interaction between the European Social Charter and the EU Charter, Article 15 is described by the Text of the explanations relating to the complete text of the Charter as 'draw[ing] upon' Article 1(2) of the European Social Charter.[3] Although this explanatory document issued by the Praesidium which oversaw the drafting of the Charter has limited legal value[4] and is simply intended to clarify the provisions of the Charter, it nevertheless plays an important part in the attempt to ground the EU Charter in pre-existing rights, and to gain legitimacy by association with the long-established Council of Europe system.

How successful is this attempt to locate the right proclaimed in the EU Charter in the European Social Charter? The primary orientation of the right to work in the EU Charter and the Community Charter of 1989 is very much toward the freedom of a natural or legal person to be economically active across the territory of the EU. This much is apparent in the case law of the European Court of Justice referred to in the Explanatory Document: the jurisprudence adduced as evidence of the Union's longstanding respect for the right to work indeed reveals a concern to protect the fundamental right to pursue one's business activity, a concern initially prompted by the desire to ensure the Community institutions respected the rights already enshrined in Member States' constitutions.[5]

Article 15(2) of the EU Charter—which reiterates the three freedoms guaranteed by Articles 39, 43, and 49 of the EC Treaty—further underlines how the EU's

[2] The different categories of beneficiaries of rights under the EU Charter continues to be relevant if one conceptualizes the right to work as encompassing a right to receive minimum subsistence since, here too, the EU Charter restricts rights to those 'residing and moving legally within the European Union': see below.

[3] *Text of the explanations relating to the complete text of the Charter* (hereinafter 'Explanatory Document'), CHARTE 4473/00, 11 October 2000.

[4] Article II–112 (7) of the Constitution, which was one of the last amendments made to the constitutional text before it was signed, reads: 'The explanations drawn up as a way of providing guidance in the interpretation of the Charter of Fundamental Rights shall be given due regard by the courts of the union and of the Member States.'

[5] For example, Case 4/73 *Nold* [1974] ECR 491, paras. 12 to 14; See also Case 44/79 *Hauer* [1979] ECR 3727, and Case 234/85 *Keller* [1986] ECR 2897.

perspective on the right to work is preoccupied with rights necessary for the functioning of integrated markets, and in particular the free flow of the factors of production essential for a common or internal market.

Having characterized the EU's representation of the right to work as being concerned with freedom to undertake economic activity, in contrast to the ESC's characterization of the right as a duty on states to promote employment, it would be inaccurate to imply that EU discourse knows nothing of full employment. Rather, it is more appropriate to say that full employment permeates EU discourse at the level of policy-making, not via the language of rights. The difference between the EU discourse and that contained in the ESC is that discussions on full employment are not conceptualized as concerning individual (or even collective) rights, but rather as a matter of economic, employment, and social policy, in particular, within the context of the European Employment Strategy and the Lisbon Strategy.

III. THE RIGHT TO WORK AS AGAINST THE STATE

A. *Full Employment and the European Social Charter*

The right to work is one of the central rights protected by the European Social Charter and, as the European Committee of Social Rights pointed out during its first supervision cycle, it is 'of fundamental importance within the context of the Charter, for the effective exercise of several essential rights is inconceivable unless the right to work is guaranteed first'.[6] The right to work is deemed essential for the realization of a number of other rights contained in the European Social Charter, such as the rights to just conditions of work (Article 2), to safe and healthy working conditions (Article 3), to fair remuneration (Article 4), to organize and bargain collectively (Articles 5 and 6). Despite the centrality of the right to work, it has always been clear that it falls far short of requiring states to guarantee a job for everyone who wants one.[7] Instead, the European Committee of Social Rights has consistently interpreted the obligation on states to maintain 'as high and stable a level of employment as possible' and to strive for 'full employment' as requiring the Contracting Parties to adopt a 'coherent economic policy' with this aim in mind, with the emphasis on means rather than results. In other words, states are obliged to adopt policies moving in the general direction of full employment (and to specify as much, so that the European Committee of Social Rights can assess progress made) rather than to demonstrate actual improvement in employment rates; indeed an increase in

---

[6] Council of Europe, European Committee of Social Rights, *Conclusions I* (first supervision cycle, 1969–70), at 13.

[7] Council of Europe, *European Social Charter: A Short Guide* (2000), at 119.

unemployment during a particular cycle does not automatically result in a conclusion that a state is in non-compliance.[8]

What do the European Social Charter, and the European Committee of Social Rights, therefore mean by 'full employment'? Some indication is given in the first supervision cycle, in which the European Committee of Social Rights stated that 'if a state at any time abandoned the objective of full employment in favour of an economic system providing for *a permanent pool of unemployed*, it would be infringing the Social Charter'.[9] Historically, the concept of full employment has been used to mean 'having always more vacant jobs than unemployed men',[10] that is, seeing employment at a living wage as a basic human right. But another approach, dominant amongst economists, views full employment as the minimum unemployment rate which puts no upward pressure on inflation—the 'natural rate of unemployment' or 'non-accelerating inflation rate of unemployment' (NAIRU).[11] In other words, an economy with full employment is an economy where employment is as high as it can be, without labour shortages that lead to rising wages and hence prices. But it is clear that the level of unemployment under this version of full employment could be very different from the level at which everyone who wants a job has got one.[12] It is submitted that a better way to define full employment—a definition compatible with the overarching framework of the 'right' to work—is nearer to the Beveridgean perspective. Ultimately, though, any definition of full employment has also to include notions of what constitutes an acceptable 'job';[13] however, on this point the European Committee of Social Rights is silent, save for the implication elsewhere in the European Social Charter, that rights amount to minimum labour standards.

Nevertheless, it is arguable that the obligation to achieve full employment in the European Social Charter, as interpreted by the European Committee of Social Rights, is a weak one which does little to give meaning to the nebulous 'right' to work. This was further exacerbated by the decision on the part of the European Committee of Social Rights during the eighth supervision cycle not to adopt conclusions on states' compliance with the full employment goal, instead merely to 'review' policies pursued and measures taken to achieve this objective.[14] Rather, the strategy adopted

---

[8] This interpretation was repeated throughout the conclusions in the first 7 supervision cycles; see in particular, Council of Europe, European Committee of Social Rights, *Conclusions III*, at 3, where the ECSR stated that 'a large increase in the rate of unemployment would not prevent the Committee from concluding that the Charter was being satisfied, so long as a substantial effort is made to improve the labour market situation'.

[9] Council of Europe, *supra* n. 6, at 14 (emphasis added).

[10] W. Beveridge, *Full Employment in a Free Society* (1944), at 18; See also A. Britton, 'Full Employment in the Industrialized Countries', 136 *International Labour Review* (1997) 293.

[11] See H. Lachs Ginsburg et al., 'Editorial Introduction: The Challenge of Full Employment in the Global Economy', 18 *Economic and Industrial Democracy* (1997) 5, at 7–8.

[12] E. Crooks, 'How Full is Full Employment?' BBC News Online, Business, Monday 27 September 1999, 20:15 GMT, http://news.bbc.co.uk/1/hi/business/the_economy/459370.stm.

[13] See E. Lee, 'Is Full Employment Still Desirable and Feasible?', 18 *Economic and Industrial Democracy* (1997) 35, at 47.

[14] L. Samuel, *Fundamental Social Rights: Case Law of the European Social Charter* (2002) 2nd edn., at 16.

by the European Committee of Social Rights has been to monitor states' progress ever more closely, a strategy with strong resonances to that adopted by the EU.

Essentially, what Article 1(1) of the European Social Charter requires is a shift in policy on the part of Contracting Parties, not through the imposition of a detailed policy agenda on states, but through the evaluation and monitoring of national policies for convergence towards the agreed goal. To this end, the European Committee of Social Rights obliges states to report back on strategies to combat long-term unemployment, the gender employment gap, and regional and sectoral disparities.[15]

Such indirect efforts to influence policy by setting the parameters within which an issue is to be conceptualized exhibits close similarity with the methodology of the EU's Employment Strategy, which adopts a soft law approach to governance of Member States' employment policies, by means of annual guidelines.[16]

B. *What does the EU's Understanding of 'Full Employment' Add to the Right to Work?*

The goal of full employment has been high on the EU policy agenda since the Lisbon European Council in 2000, but the discourses employed within the European Employment Strategy rarely speak of fundamental or human rights. Launched in 1997 following the inclusion of a new Title on Employment in the EC Treaty, the European Employment Strategy was given new impetus at Lisbon, where EU Member States set themselves the goal of full employment based on developing the 'knowledge economy' and modernizing welfare states. Again, there is no clear definition of full employment, but an indication of the meaning is given in the targets set for Member States: that they raise their overall employment rates to as close as possible to 70 per cent by 2010, and the female employment rate to more than 60 per cent.[17]

However, as with the goal of full employment in the European Social Charter, it is far from clear how this goal could be translated into a legal duty in the EU context. At best, key parts of the European Employment Strategy, such as the pursuit of 'employability' lack a 'precise legal standing'.[18] At worst, the full employment discourse could be seen as downgrading other components of the right to work, such as rights within employment.

From the earliest days of the European Employment Strategy, the emphasis was on facilitating mutual learning by Member States so they could share knowledge

---

[15] See Council of Europe, European Committee of Social Rights, *Conclusions XIV–1*.

[16] See D. Ashiagbor, 'Soft Harmonization: The "Open Method of Coordination" in the European Employment Strategy' (2004) 10:2 *EPL* 305–32.

[17] Presidency Conclusions, Lisbon European Council, 23 and 24 March 2000, Bull. EU 3/2000, 7, at para. 30.

[18] S. Sciarra, 'The Employment Title in the Amsterdam Treaty: A Multi-Language Legal Discourse', in D. O'Keefe and P. Twomey (eds), *Legal Issues of the Amsterdam Treaty* (1999) 157, at 165.

of best practices to improve their records on employment. The shape of the Employment Title changed in the course of the negotiations during the Intergovernmental Conference leading to the Treaty revision: from a common to a coordinated policy; away from harmonization, toward coordination of national policies. Consequently, tools for comparison of national practices—such as targets, indicators, statistics—become central. That this form of governance (by means of benchmarking, guidelines and indicators) has its own complexities has become apparent both within the EU Employment Strategy and, to a lesser extent, within the European Social Charter.

In the 1998 supervision cycle (XIV-1) the European Committee of Social Rights concluded that assessing states' compliance with Article 1(1) was impossible on the basis of bare unemployment indicators alone; account must also be taken of additional factors, such as trends in the nature of employment, the design of national labour market policies and the budgetary commitment to these policies. The European Committee of Social Rights accordingly asked all Contracting Parties to supply information in the subsequent reports on a fuller range of unemployment, employment, and labour market policy indicators.[19] The development of a new indicator-based method of assessment of the national situation enabled the Committee to begin to adopt conclusions on Article 1(1) once again. Such developments mirror the shift which has taken place within the EU Employment Strategy, where employment indicators have grown in number, type, and complexity from the relatively straightforward first generation of indicators in 1997,[20] in part to reflect post-Lisbon priorities such as quality in work and the promotion of employment as a means to combat social exclusion. The mutual influence between the two systems is further exemplified by the 2002 supervision cycle (XVI-1), in which the European Committee of Social Rights examined twenty-four national reports, using indicators such as the overall activity rate, the unemployment rate among high risk groups and inputs into active labour market policies. Notably, data for each country was also compared with the EU average, contributing to the conclusion that only fourteen states were found to be in conformity with the European Social Charter, with a decision in seven of the others deferred for lack of sufficient information.

C. Can 'Full Employment' Really Fulfil the Promise of the 'Right' to Work?

The EU's Lisbon agenda is careful to qualify the drive for job creation ('more jobs') with a commitment to 'better jobs' through increased quality of new and

---

[19] See Council of Europe, *supra* n. 15, at 33–34.
[20] The original eight indicators related simply to *employment* and *unemployment*, covering: the employment rate, employment growth, employment of those aged 55–64, the employment gender gap; for *unemployment*: the unemployment rate, long-term unemployment, youth unemployment and the unemployment gender gap: see Commission of the European Communities, *Commission Draft for the Joint Employment Report 1997* (1997), at Annex 1.

existing jobs. Nevertheless, it remains to be seen whether the 'disincentive' discourse not far from the surface of debates around employment and economic policy in the EU—that extensive work protection and social benefits are a disincentive to take up work and therefore an obstacle to more jobs[21]—will result in a 'right' to work denuded of substance, amounting to little more than a compulsory work ethic or obligation to accept work. It is in this respect that one needs to revisit the earlier assumption that other rights in the ESC (to just conditions of work, to fair remuneration, and so on) are dependent on the right to work: in fact it would be more accurate to say that these rights are interdependent, since the objective of full employment will serve to undermine the right to work if it is not accompanied by a commitment to the creation of high quality jobs. Moreover, whilst the obligation on states to achieve and maintain 'as high and stable a level of employment as possible' is interpreted by the European Committee of Social Rights to emphasize means adopted by the States, rather than results achieved, nevertheless a wide range of state policies are permitted, provided a state adheres to a 'coherent economic policy'. The Committee has declared the retention of a permanent pool of unemployed to infringe the Social Charter,[22] which has led some commentators to propose that state policy which pursues a neoliberal agenda emphasizing low inflation and is careless as to the decline of manufacturing industry (a policy of the sort pursued by the Thatcher Governments of the 1980s) should also have been declared incompatible with the European Social Charter.[23]

As Bo Stråth points out, one of the reasons the political commitment to (the post-war version of) full employment was abandoned was that it was tied to the existence of labour markets contained within national boundaries, to a belief in Keynesian macro-economics, and to conventions of social responsibility—in particular, that the state would underwrite job security or provide income security— which have been fragmenting.[24] Undoubtedly, the Conservative Governments of the 1980s and 1990s could not be described as aspiring to the post-war ideal of full employment; and neither is the New Labour Government in the UK. However, one way of viewing the position adopted by the European Committee of Social Rights is that social solidarity, possibly with the state acting as employer of last resort, is not necessary for compliance with the European Social Charter. What one might label a diluted form of full employment is also central to the EU's Lisbon agenda: in the EU context, labour market deregulation goes hand-in-hand with a commitment to full employment—indeed the economic orthodoxy is that active labour market policies to help people take up employment, tax-benefit

[21] Council Recommendation of 19 June 2000 on the broad guidelines of the economic policies of the Member States and the Community, OJ 2000 L210/1, at para. 2.1.

[22] Council of Europe, *supra* n. 6, at 14.

[23] See in particular, K. Ewing, 'Social Rights and Human Rights: Britain and the Social Charter— The Conservative Legacy', 2 *EHRLR* (2000) 91.

[24] B. Stråth, 'After Full Employment and the Breakdown of Conventions of Social Responsibility', in B. Stråth (ed.), *After Full Employment: European Discourses on Work and Flexibility* (2001), at 14–15.

reforms to 'make work pay', greater wage dispersal, and more flexible labour markets will lead to higher employment.

D. The Right to Work and Social Citizenship in the EU

If we view this more modest, modern version of full employment as essentially a weak form of the right to work, what would a strong form look like? One possibility is a vision of the right to work which incorporates a sense of social solidarity and social citizenship, perhaps extending to income transfers or minimum income.[25] As will be seen from the above analysis of the EU's Lisbon agenda, the supply-side orientation of EU employment policy leaves little room for a perspective on the right to work which would require a return to the state underwriting income or job security.

Whilst the EU Charter does contain rights or entitlements to social security and social assistance, these are heavily circumscribed.[26] Article 34(1) only goes so far as to say the Union 'recognises and respects' the entitlement (as opposed to 'right') to benefits in cases such as maternity, illness, industrial accidents, old age, and loss of employment; further, such entitlements are subject to 'the rules laid down by Community law and national laws and practices'. As the Explanatory Document confirms, the principle in Article 34(1) is based on three sources: Articles 137 and 140 of the EC Treaty, Article 12 of the European Social Charter, and point 10 of the Community Charter on the rights of workers. Both Articles 137 and 140 EC make it clear that social security is primarily a matter for Member States. In contrast to Article 34(1), Article 34(3) of the EU Charter asserts a right to social and housing assistance, so as to ensure a decent existence for all those who lack sufficient resources, suggesting an enforceable norm. However, this is again subject to 'national laws and practices', such that the Community should refrain from adopting legislation on the basis of this Article, in light of the limited competence of the Community in the field of social assistance and the need to respect national differences. Taken together, the rights contained in the Solidarity chapter of the EU Charter fail to live up to the potential of the Charter's innovative treatment of economic and social rights; grouping such rights under the heading of 'solidarity' has proved insufficient to assist the development of 'social citizenship', so as to benefit not only those EU citizens who fall outside of the category of the economically active 'market citizen' envisaged by the fundamental freedoms of the EC Treaty, but also legally resident third-country nationals.

---

[25] But note, there are a number of tensions between the idea of a right to work/right to economic and social participation on the one hand, and a 'basic income' on the other: see J. A. Noguera and D. Raventós, 'Basic Income, Social Polarization and the Right to Work', paper presented at the 9th International Congress of the Basic Income European Network, Geneva, 12–14 September 2002.

[26] The following draws on D. Ashiagbor, 'Economic and Social Rights in the European Charter of Fundamental Rights', 1 *EHRLR* (2004) 62.

Further, this circumscribed sense of social solidarity has to be seen against a backdrop of a shift within EU policy discourse to what might be called a 'Third Way' approach to welfare provision,[27] signalling a move from state provision of income guarantees and the protection of labour market 'insiders'. The most recent economic policy guidelines for the EU urged Member States to address incentive effects, duration, eligibility, and enforcement of benefit schemes to make them more employment-friendly.[28] This would seem to require Member States which have not already done so to reduce replacement rates, impose job search and other requirements on the unemployed, and reduce the length of time for which benefits are available. For example, in earlier country-specific economic policy guidelines, France was urged to pay 'particular attention' to income guarantee schemes; as for the Netherlands, its reforms should focus on the 'relatively lax eligibility rules', and Sweden is congratulated for its tightened eligibility criteria for unemployment insurance (in terms of occupational and geographical mobility).[29]

The supply-side leanings of the European Employment Strategy, containing echoes of a 'workfare' approach to labour market regulation—namely the suggestion that receipt of benefits is made conditional on participation in active labour market policies—throw out interesting challenges to the view adopted by the European Committee of Social Rights that the right to earn one's living in an occupation freely entered upon encompasses the loss of unemployment benefits for refusal to take up employment (see below).

Such tendencies are also a far cry from a broader conception of the right to work of the sort suggested in the Supiot Report's assertion of 'proactive security' for individuals in the labour market.[30] This report, commissioned by the European Commission, analysed recent changes to the labour market in terms of a disintegration of the Fordist model of employment in four areas: a breakdown in the continuity of employment status throughout an entire lifetime; the disintegration of occupation (or job content); the disintegration in the standardized types of employment status; and the disintegration in the nature and identity of the employer.[31] Rather radically, the report then proposed a redesigned notion of security, to accommodate these changes whilst providing a certain level of

---

[27] Streeck labels this 'supply-side egalitarianism' in the sense that 'Social cohesion is sought, not through equal outcomes, but through equal opportunity; and traditional concepts of solidarity are infused with a bourgeois spirit of efficiency and self-sufficiency, emphasizing individual effort and collective investment in competitiveness at least as much as social entitlements to minimal levels of reward or consumption': W. Streeck, 'Competitive Solidarity: Rethinking the "European Social Model" ', MPIfG (Max Planck Institute for the Study of Societies) Working Paper 99/8 (1999).

[28] Council Recommendation of 25 June 2003 on the Broad Guidelines of the Economic Policies of the Member States and the Community for the period 2003–2005, OJ 2003 L195/1.

[29] Council Recommendation of 15 June 2001 on the Broad Guidelines of the Economic Policies of the Member States and the Community, OJ 2001 L179/1.

[30] A. Supiot et al., *Beyond Employment: Changes in Work and the Future of Labour Law in Europe* (2001). This book originally appeared as *Transformation of Labour and the Future of Labour Law in Europe*, Final Report of the Expert Group established by the European Commission (1998), V/98/776.   [31] Ibid., at 220–21.

protection for workers. In brief, that employment status should be redefined to guarantee the continuity of a career rather than the stability of specific conditions; that employment status should no longer be determined on the basis of the restrictive criterion of 'employment', but on the broader notion of 'work';[32] and that this broadened employment status go hand-in-hand with various types of what are termed 'social drawing rights'.[33] Social drawing rights essentially enable citizens to retain a right to income and other advantages when engaged in socially recognized non-market activities.[34]

The invitation in the Supiot Report to law- and policy-makers to think 'beyond employment' casts new light on what one might mean by rights of access to and participation in the labour market contained in the concept of the 'right to work'. This perspective, reintroducing an element of financial and social solidarity, requires the right to work to be 'anchored in a qualified public commitment to help provide the opportunities to earn a living wage for citizens who need and demand it'.[35]

IV. FREELY UNDERTAKEN WORK AND PROHIBITION AGAINST FORCED LABOUR

The right to freely undertake work in Article 1(2) of the European Social Charter is a broad-ranging right, applying across the spectrum of employment to include self-employment, domestic employment, employment in small firms,[36] part-time employment,[37] and within both public and private sectors.[38]

This right is echoed not only in Article 15 of the EU Charter, on freedom to choose an occupation and right to engage in work, but also in Article 5 of the EU Charter, which prohibits slavery and forced labour, and Article 16 on freedom to conduct a business. The freedom to choose an occupation and the (economic) freedom of movement of workers within the EU is the aspect of the right to work most explicitly recognized in the EU Charter. As discussed above, Article 15 of the EU Charter views the freedom to engage in economic activity as the prime component of a right to work. To this is added a further right, available to EU citizens,

---

[32] For an analysis of the differing conceptions of 'work', 'labour' and 'travail', see B. Stråth 'The Concept of Work in the Construction of Community', in B. Stråth (ed.), *After Full Employment* (2000).

[33] Supiot et al., *supra* n. 30, at 56 and 222.

[34] See D. Marsden and H. Stephenson (eds), *Labour Law and Social Insurance in the New Economy: A Debate on the Supiot Report* (2001).

[35] A. Hemerijck, *Prospects for Inclusive Social Citizenship in an Age of Structural Inactivity*, MPIfG (Max Planck Institute for the Study of Societies) Working Paper, 99/1 (1999).

[36] See D. Harris and J. Darcy, *The European Social Charter* (2001), at 53.

[37] Council of Europe, European Committee of Social Rights, *Conclusions XIII–1*, at 50.

[38] Council of Europe, European Committee of Social Rights, *Conclusions XIII–5*, at 254.

to engage in such activity across a Union without internal borders—reiterating the fundamental freedoms contained in Articles 39, 43, and 49 of the EC Treaty.

A. *Prohibition of Discrimination in Employment*

Although the original European Social Charter of 1961 contained a reference, in its Preamble, to the enjoyment of social rights without discrimination on grounds such as sex, it contained no express, detailed, prohibition of gender (or any other type of) discrimination in employment.[39] Due in part to this lacuna, the right to earn one's living in a freely chosen occupation was used by the European Committee of Social Rights as the main vehicle through which it was able to scrutinize and evaluate states' measures to combat sex discrimination in employment—by considering discrimination in respect of access to employment. During the second supervision cycle, the European Committee of Social Rights adopted the interpretation that Article 1(2) related mainly to the elimination of discrimination in employment, as well as to prohibition on forced labour.

The European Committee of Social Rights therefore concentrated on the achievement of legal and *de facto* equality between men and women with regards to access to employment, as part of its review of the right to work. According to the Committee's jurisprudence, the Contracting Parties are obliged to adopt general legislation prohibiting, at the very least, discrimination on the grounds of sex. The legal prohibition on discrimination was to be backed by further safeguards such that, for example, clauses in collective agreements and contracts of employment which violated the principle of equality must be annulled, victimization by means of dismissal for requesting equal treatment should be prohibited, and anyone dismissed for such a reason should be reinstated. With regard to other grounds of discrimination, the Committee also paid special attention to denials of the right to work on the basis of political opinion (in particular in the context of the duty to loyalty required of civil servants), to trade union membership or activity, and to discrimination against Muslim workers and Roma people. In view of the complexity of concepts of equality and discrimination, it will be immediately apparent that the 'right to work' is an inadequate lens through which to view gender equality, least of all to tackle sex discrimination.[40]

Following the inclusion, in the Revised European Social Charter of both a horizontal commitment to non-discrimination and specific provisions,[41] the European Committee of Social Rights modified its approach, taking into account the

---

[39] The Preamble provides that 'the enjoyment of social rights should be secured without discrimination on grounds of race, colour, sex, religion, political opinion, national extraction or social origin'.

[40] For a fuller critique of concepts of equality and discrimination in EU law and within the ESC, see M. Bell's chapter in this volume.

[41] According to Article E of Part V of the Revised European Social Charter, '[t]he enjoyment of the rights set forth in this Charter shall be secured without discrimination on any ground such as race, colour, sex, language, religion, political or other opinion, national extraction or social origin, health, association with a national minority, birth or other status'; see M. Bell in this volume.

new Article 20 of the Revised Charter (conferring the right to equal opportunities and equal treatment in employment). The Committee decided that for States which had ratified both Article 1(2) and Article 20 it would no longer deal with discrimination based on sex under Article 1(2) but, more logically, under Article 20 of the Revised European Social Charter.

B. Forced and Compulsory Labour

The second aspect of the right to earn one's living in an occupation freely entered upon is the prohibition of forced or compulsory labour. According to the Committee's interpretation, the coercion of any worker to carry out work against his or her will, and without freely expressed consent, is contrary to the Charter. The same applies to the coercion of any worker to carry out work he or she had previously agreed to do, but subsequently no longer wants to carry out. A major preoccupation of the Committee in respect of forced labour has, accordingly, been with the employment of merchant seamen: here, the Committee adopted numerous conclusions on non-compliance where merchant seamen were subject to criminal sanctions for breaches of professional discipline or other contractual obligations, even where such breaches did not endanger either the safety of the ship or the life and health of people on board (for example, by going on strike or leaving the workplace).[42]

When adopting its first conclusions under the Revised European Social Charter in 2002, the Committee decided to develop its case law in relation to the right to earn one's living in an occupation freely entered upon by widening the situations deemed to be forced or coerced labour to include the length of civilian national service, the loss of unemployment benefits for refusal to take up employment, and the consequences of part-time work.[43]

What does this mean for those active labour market policies within the European Employment Strategy which could be equated to a form of workfare? In order to 'make work pay' and encourage the search for jobs, Member States are urged to review aspects of tax and benefit systems such as the conditionality of benefits, eligibility, duration, the replacement rate, the availability of in-work benefits, the use of tax credits, administrative systems, and management rigour.[44] It is instructive to

[42] For example, Council of Europe, European Committee of Social Rights, *Conclusions III* (1973), at 228.

[43] See: Council of Europe, European Committee of Social Rights, *Conclusions 2004*, at 11–12. 'Following negotiations started in 1997 with the trade unions, the Government has made proposals to amend Section 59 of the Merchant Shipping Act 1995—which authorises criminal penalties against striking sailors—so that this would only apply to strike action which could result in serious damage, including loss of vessels, or serious injury, including death, to persons. The report states that negotiations are continuing with the trade unions and that the amendments have not yet been laid before Parliament. Since the legal situation has not yet changed, the Committee considers it not to be in conformity with Article 1§2 of the Charter': Council of Europe, European Committee of Social Rights, *Conclusions XVI–1* (2000) vol. 2, at 679–80.

[44] Presidency Conclusions, Barcelona European Council, 15 and 16 March 2002, Bull. EU 3/2002, 1–56, at para. 32.

consider the example of the UK, one of the EU Member States which has gone furthest down the route of benefits conditionality. The Jobseeker's Allowance, which was introduced nationally in 1996 as part of a radical restructuring of the benefits regime, applies to 76 per cent of unemployed people; it is the basic form of unemployment benefit and is grounded in conditionality—participation in active labour market measures is a condition for receiving this benefit. The 'New Deal', which came into operation from 1998, is the core of the 'welfare to work' part of the UK's employment strategy, and operates within the framework of compulsion established by the Jobseeker's Allowance.[45] The New Deal in fact consists of eight programmes designed to provide intensive support to the unemployed, especially the young and long-term unemployed, lone parents, people with disabilities, those lacking basic literacy and numeracy skills, and ex-offenders.[46] All but two of these programmes are voluntary. The New Deal for Young People, in particular, offers four options: a subsidized job for six months; work in the voluntary sector; work on the Environment Task Force; or full-time education or training for up to twelve months for those who need it. Those who refuse any of these four options will lose benefits, leading to the statement that 'there is no fifth option' for young people.[47]

As discussed above, this work-orientated benefits system adopted within the UK is being matched by EU-level recommendations to other Member States, offering great potential for tensions between the EU and the ESC system. However, this potential for conflict between the two systems has been defused to an extent; having introduced a new subheading in 2002 under which to evaluate states' compliance with rights not to be coerced into employment ('Other aspects of the right to earn one's living in an occupation freely entered upon: Acceptance of a job offer or of a training offer as a condition for maintaining unemployment benefits') in recent conclusions on benefits conditionality, the Committee has tended to adopt the position that where workers may (a) refuse unsuitable offers without withdrawal of their unemployment benefits and (b) where workers have a right of administrative or judicial appeal to an appropriate body following suspension of benefit, then this situation is in conformity with the Charter.[48]

---

[45] J. Peck and N. Theodore, 'Beyond "Employability" ', 24 *Cambridge Journal of Economics* (2000) 729–49, at 735.

[46] *United Kingdom: Employment Action Plan 1999*, at 4–5.

[47] As stated by Andrew Smith MP, the Employment Minister: 'New Figures Reveal That New Deal is Tough on Shirkers', New Deal Press Notices, No. 513/98, 4 November 1998; see also House of Commons, Select Committee on Education and Employment, Fifth Report, *New Deal: An Evaluation*, HC 58, 20 March 2001, at para. 7.

[48] For example: in Greece, in the event of unjustified refusal of suitable employment, a worker forfeits entitlement to unemployment benefits. The same applies where a worker does not participate in necessary training and information activities. However, this measure is not applied where the job in question is unsuited to the worker's age, physical aptitude, qualifications and experience, or where the remuneration offered is not reasonable. Similarly, in Portugal, workers who refuse work without justification lose entitlement to unemployment benefits. However this does not apply when the job in question is incompatible with the worker's age, physical suitability, qualifications and experience. Neither the Greek nor Portuguese situations were held to breach Art. 1(2) of the ESC: Council of Europe, European Committee of Social Rights, *Conclusions XVII-1* (Greece and Portugal).

V. FREE EMPLOYMENT SERVICES AND VOCATIONAL GUIDANCE AND TRAINING

The third and fourth components of the right to work contained in the European Social Charter—the obligation on states to establish free employment services and to provide or promote appropriate vocational guidance, training, and rehabilitation—both find strong echoes in the EU system. The EU Charter provides that 'everyone' has the right of access to a free placement service (Article 29), as well as the right of access to vocational and continuing training (Article 14). Again, both sets of rights in the EU Charter are described as 'based on' or 'drawing upon' the European Social Charter.[49]

A. Free Employment Services

With regard to the right to free employment services, in the first cycle of supervision the European Committee of Social Rights interpreted this provision as placing an obligation on each Contracting Party not only to create or maintain such services throughout its national territory but also to ensure that they were properly operated and, where necessary, supervised in collaboration with both sides of industry.[50] The Committee pointed out in the fourth supervision cycle that both employees and employers have the right to enjoy the free use of employment services—so as to prevent employers passing any placement costs onto workers.[51]

In relation to countries in which private placement agencies operate, the Committee expressed its view that private fee-charging services were not prohibited so long as free placement services were available in all sectors of the economy as well.[52] This perspective, with its presumption that fee-charging or private employment services are to be viewed with suspicion as far as the right to work is concerned, illustrates an interesting tension between, on the one hand, the values of market integration and competition policy within the EU, and on the other, the principle of 'solidarity' informing both the ESC and much of the EU Charter.

In the *Job Centre* case,[53] the European Court of Justice held that the Italian state's monopoly over job placement services was contrary to the principles of free competition, and therefore illegitimate. The judgment came at a time when the job placement system was being reformed in Italy, and is therefore likely to have accelerated the move towards the greater liberalization of labour market mediation in the country.[54] In the view of the ECJ, job placement, like all economic

---

[49] Explanatory Document, *supra* n. 3.

[50] Council of Europe, *supra* n. 6, at 16. On tripartite cooperation on employment services see *Conclusions XV–1*, at 40–41.

[51] See Samuel, *supra* n. 14 at 31.

[52] Council of Europe, European Committee of Social Rights, *Conclusions XII–1*, at 62.

[53] Case C-55/96 *Job Centre* [1997] ECR I–7119.

[54] See S. Sciarra, '*Job Centre*: An Illustrative Example of Strategic Litigation', in S. Sciarra (ed.), *Labour Law in the Courts: National Judges and the European Court of Justice* (2001).

activities, is subject to European Community competition law. In particular, public placement offices were held subject to the prohibition contained in Article 82 of the EC Treaty (abuse of dominant position in the market),[55] and a Member State which prohibits private employment services ('any activity as an intermediary between supply and demand on the employment market') is also in breach of the Treaty. This was particularly so in Italy where public job placement offices were unable to offer an adequate service in the field of intermediation between labour supply and demand. Thus the state's monopoly penalized the users of the service.

The potential has always existed for a very serious clash between EU competition law (or the law of the single market) and the regulatory objectives of individual Member States, particularly where Member States wish to preserve areas such as social policy from the logic of market integration in order to recognize other values, such as social cohesion or solidarity. The only surprise is that it was relatively late in the day, in cases such as *Job Centre* and *Albany*[56] that the issue came before the European Court of Justice. But now that the EU institutions are seized of the matter, the question of how any tension between the values of the market and human rights, especially socio-economic rights, will be resolved may be conceptualized as follows: it is not the case that the logic of the internal market will always trump 'solidarity' or other social values, but rather that the EU, and the ECJ, will require any trade-off between the competing values to be decided within the parameters set by internal market law. Increasingly, state activities will be 'caught' by internal market law, which will then apply its own logic to determine if alternative values are to be permitted to justify exceptions to free trade.

B. *Vocational Guidance and Training*

By Article 1(4) of the ESC the Contracting Parties undertake 'to provide or promote vocational guidance, training and rehabilitation'. The provision contains obligations that are elaborated in more detail in Article 9 (the right to vocational guidance), Article 10 (the right to vocational training), and Article 15 (the right to rehabilitation). For that reason the Committee decided during the first supervision cycle that Contracting Parties which have ratified these three articles, are not required to include in their biennial reports particulars concerning the application of Article 1(4), leaving the assessment on Article 1(4) to the supervision cycles on non-hard-core provisions of the European Social Charter.[57]

In the twelfth supervision cycle the European Committee of Social Rights adopted the following position: since the purpose of Article 1 was to ensure the

---

[55] Art. 82 EC: 'Any abuse by one or more undertakings of a dominant position within the common market or in a substantial part of it shall be prohibited as incompatible with the common market in so far as it may affect trade between Member States.'

[56] Case C-67/96, *Albany International BV* v. *Stichting Bedrijfspensioenfonds Textielindustrie* [1999] ECR I-5751.   [57] Council of Europe, *supra* n. 6, at 16.

effective exercise of the right to work, in order to satisfy the requirements of Article 1(4) a state must not only have institutions providing vocational guidance, training, and rehabilitation, but must also ensure access to these institutions for all those interested, including foreigners, nationals of the Contracting Parties to the Charter, and people with disabilities.[58]

The right to vocational and continuing training in the EU Charter is subsumed within the wider right to education, but it is important to distinguish the two. As with free placement services, a right so strongly articulated in both the EU Charter and the European Social Charter has the potential to fall foul of EU internal market law. Measures taken by an EU Member State under one set of EU obligations (for example, the duty within the European Employment Strategy to promote the development of human resources and implement an active labour market policy) run the risk of falling foul of another EU obligation (in particular, Article 87 EC on state aids) if financial support, incentive measures, or subsidies are seen to favour certain undertakings. The European Commission has accordingly issued a number of clarifications: that a training aid measure intended to reduce the costs which certain firms would normally have to bear, in their own interest, to improve their employees' skills, confers on them an advantage over their competitors and is likely to distort competition, in breach of Article 87.[59]

A broader difficulty, however, with the obligation on states to provide or promote training is the extent to which it can realistically be relied upon by workers. By emphasizing the fact that workers should improve their skills, education, and training so as to be mobile and adaptable, the concept of 'employability' within EU employment policy appears to downplay the responsibilities of employers to provide secure employment.[60] Such individual responsibility for training and labour market mobility could hardly be said to amount to a 'right' to vocational training.

VI. THE RIGHT TO WORK AS AGAINST THE EMPLOYER OR TRADE UNION

Since both the European Social Charter and the EU Charter are directed to states,[61] the right to work is silent as to the role of employers or trade unions,

---

[58] Council of Europe, *supra* n. 52, at 67 and *Conclusions XII–2*, at 57.

[59] Communication from the Commission, Framework on Training Aid, OJ 1998 C343/7, at para. 7. For an analysis of the interaction between competition law and national employment measures, see S. Ball, 'The European Employment Strategy: The Will but not the Way?' 30 (2001) *ILJ* 353, at 363–66.

[60] S. Deakin and H. Reed, 'The Contested Meaning of Labour Market Flexibility: Economic Theory and the Discourse of European Integration', in J. Shaw (ed.), *Social Law and Policy in an Evolving European Union* (2000), at 95.

[61] More accurately, Art. 51(1) of the EU Charter makes it clear that its provisions are addressed to 'the institutions and bodies of the Union . . . and to the Member States only when they are implementing Union law'.

beyond the implicit duty on states to ensure they do not permit the right to work, however understood, to be restricted by private action. For the right to work to be meaningful as against employers, it would most likely necessitate rights not to be arbitrarily refused employment, rights to be given work, and rights not to be dismissed unfairly[62]—begging the question whether conceptualizing these employment rights as subsets of the right to work aids their realization. The first and third rights are dealt with elsewhere in the (Revised) European Social Charter: Article E of Part V on non-discrimination; Article 20 on sex discrimination in employment; and Article 24 on the right to protection in cases of termination of employment.

To some, the right to work is synonymous with unfettered freedom of contract, namely freedom from the sort of state interference which empowers trade unions to regulate terms and conditions of employment jointly with employers. In the US, the 'right to work' is a term of art in the industrial relations field, referring to the principle behind state legislation designed to outlaw various union-security measures, particularly the 'closed shop' under which workers are required to join a union within a specified time after beginning employment. For such legislation to be characterized as enforcing the 'right to work' is somewhat misleading, since such laws do not guarantee employment, but rather affect the balance of power between management and labour, weakening the bargaining power of unions, and potentially reducing workers' job security.[63]

In Europe, both the European Social Charter and the EU Charter take a different view on the balance to be struck between freedom of association and the individual's right to work. According to the Appendices to the 1961 Charter and to the Revised European Social Charter, Article 1(2) shall not be interpreted as prohibiting or authorizing any union security clause or practice. Commenting on the litigation under the European Convention on Human Rights concerning the closed shop in the then British Rail, Bob Hepple pointed to the artificiality of opposing an individual 'right to work' against the traditional methods of protecting jobs through union strength.[64]

VII. CONCLUSION

A common criticism levelled at social and economic rights is that they do not deserve the label of 'rights', since their justiciability is questionable as they require

---

[62] See B. Hepple, 'A Right to Work?', 10 *ILJ* (1981) 65.

[63] There are at least three national organizations in the US which campaign vociferously for the 'right to work', defining this as the 'right of every free American to work for a living without being compelled to belong to a union': see the National Institute for Labor Relations Research, http://www.nilrr.org/; see also the National Right to Work Legal Defense Foundation, which defines itself as a 'non-profit organization providing free legal aid nationwide to thousands of employees whose human and civil rights have been violated by compulsory unionism abuses': http://www.nrtw.org/; and the National Right to Work Committee: http://www.nrtwc.org/.

[64] Hepple, *supra* n. 62, at 81.

positive state action, typically in the form of expenditure. Both the European Social Charter and the EU Charter make important contributions to challenging this characterization of social and economic rights, with the EU Charter in particular holding out the promise of an end to the traditional hierarchy between civil and political rights on the one hand, and socio-economic rights on the other, through its innovative use of 'chapters' and the unconventional distribution of social rights throughout the Charter.

With regard to the right to work, however, we are confronted with a set of obligations which can be difficult to individualize and which, more clearly than other socio-economic rights, can rightly be classified as programmatic, in particular, concerned with social and economic policy. Even if we are in accord with Jon Elster's argument that there is some value in talking of a 'right' to work, in order to do justice to the ideal of self-realization through work,[65] nevertheless, the above survey of the right within the European Social Charter and the EU Charter suggests an absence of a coherent, cohesive core to the idea of a right to work.

---

[65] J. Elster, 'Is There (or Should There Be) a Right to Work?', in A. Guttman (ed.), *Democracy and the Welfare State* (1988).

13

Walking in the Same Direction? The Contribution of the European Social Charter and the European Union to Combating Discrimination

MARK BELL*

I. INTRODUCTION

Combating discrimination is a relatively deep-rooted element of European Union law. The right to equal pay for women and men was one of the most visible elements of European social policy contained in the 1957 EEC Treaty and this was later complemented by legislation on equal treatment for women and men in the fields of employment and social security.[1] This prominent location has been reaffirmed in recent years. Three core Directives have been adopted that prohibit discrimination throughout the employment relationship: the Racial Equality Directive;[2] the Framework Employment Directive;[3] and the Revised Equal Treatment Directive.[4]

Alongside the evolving contribution of the European Union, the role of the Council of Europe in combating discrimination has gradually expanded. Most attention has focused on Article 14 of the European Convention on Human Rights.[5] Recent debate has centred on the prospects for strengthening the

---

* This chapter was completed during a Jean Monnet Fellowship at the Robert Schuman Centre for Advanced Studies, European University, Florence.

[1] See further, E. Ellis, *EC Sex Equality Law* (1998).

[2] Council Directive 2000/43 implementing the principle of equal treatment between persons irrespective of racial or ethnic origin, OJ 2000 L180/22. This Directive also covers a range of areas outside employment, including goods and services, education, and health care.

[3] Council Directive 2000/78 establishing a general framework for equal treatment in employment and occupation, OJ 2000 L303/16. This forbids discrimination on the grounds of religion or belief, disability, age, and sexual orientation.

[4] Council Directive 2002/73 amending Directive 76/207 on the implementation of the principle of equal treatment for men and women as regards access to employment, vocational training and promotion, and working conditions, OJ 2002 L269/15.

[5] See further, Gerards, 'The application of Article 14 ECHR by the European Court of Human Rights', in J. Niessen and I. Chopin (eds), *The Development of Legal Instruments to Combat Racism in a Diverse Europe* (2004).

Convention through Protocol 12, which aims to provide a broader and more autonomous right to non-discrimination.[6] In contrast, the 1961 European Social Charter has been described as leading a 'twilight existence' for most of its history.[7] Nonetheless, a variety of reforms in the 1990s resulted in a general 'revitalisation' of the Charter.[8] On the one hand, the basic provisions of the Charter were overhauled and updated through the 1996 Revised European Social Charter.[9] This contains a horizontal commitment to non-discrimination throughout the scope of the Charter,[10] as well as several substantive provisions closely related to issues of equality and discrimination.[11] Alongside this enhancement in the content of the Charter, the process for monitoring the implementation of its provisions was refreshed. A Protocol agreed in 1991 sought to improve the periodic reporting and review mechanism.[12] The most innovative change, however, was the introduction of a Collective Complaints Protocol,[13] which permits complaints of breaches of the Charter to be brought by certain Social Partners or NGOs. Around one-third of the complaints lodged so far have concerned issues of equality and discrimination.[14] The parallel development of EU law and the European Social Charter has resulted in an expanding area of overlap in their activities. Clearly, this presents possibilities for synergy, together with risks of regulatory competition or even conflicts in standards. This chapter compares three principal themes in the discrimination law of the Union and that flowing from the Charter. First, the concepts of equality and discrimination underpinning the law are interrogated. This is followed by an analysis of the scope of the law, in particular, how the law responds to diversity and different forms of discrimination. The final section focuses on the approach to implementation and enforcement of anti-discrimination law.

II. CONCEPTS OF EQUALITY AND DISCRIMINATION

A. *The General Principle of Equality and Non-discrimination*

The general principle of equality and non-discrimination can be found within both EU law and the European Social Charter. The Court of Justice has consistently

---

[6] See further, J. Schokkenbroek, 'A New European Standard Against Discrimination: Negotiating Protocol No. 12 to the European Convention on Human Rights', in J. Niessen and I. Chopin (eds), *The Development of Legal Instruments to Combat Racism in a Diverse Europe* (2004).

[7] D. Harris and J. Darcy, *The European Social Charter* (2001), at 12.   [8] Ibid.

[9] European Social Charter (Revised), CETS No. 163.   [10] Article E.

[11] For example, Articles 20, 26, and 27.

[12] Protocol amending the European Social Charter, CETS No. 142. Although not yet ratified, most of its amendments are already applied in practice: Harris and Darcy, *supra* n. 7, at 15.

[13] Additional Protocol to the European Social Charter Providing for a System of Collective Complaints, CETS No. 158.

[14] By 28 June 2004, 27 complaints had been lodged and 10 of these raised issues relating to discrimination. See further: http://www.coe.int/T/E/Human%5FRights/Esc/5%5FCollective%5F complaints.

recognized this as one of the (unwritten) general principles governing EU law. For example, in *Ruckdeschel*, it referred to 'the general principle of equality which is one of the fundamental principles of Community law. This principle requires that similar situations shall not be treated differently unless differentiation is objectively justified.'[15]

A similar approach can be found in the law relating to the European Social Charter. Article 1(2) of both the 1961 Charter and the 1996 Revised Charter requires signatories 'to protect effectively the right of the worker to earn his living in an occupation freely entered upon'. In the 1961 Charter, this was interpreted in the light of a statement in the preamble that 'social rights should be secured without discrimination on grounds of race, colour, sex, religion, political opinion, national extraction or social origin'. As discrimination would restrict the free choice of occupation for workers, states were under a duty to prohibit discrimination.[16] In the 1996 Revised Charter, Article E provides a firmer foundation: 'the enjoyment of the rights set forth in this Charter shall be secured without discrimination on any ground such as race, colour, sex, language, religion, political or other opinion, health, association with a national minority, birth or other status'. Moreover, Part V of the 1996 Revised Charter clarifies that 'a differential treatment based on an objective and reasonable justification shall not be deemed discriminatory'.

The general nature of this concept of equality leads McCrudden to describe it as 'equality as mere rationality'.[17] Any unjustified distinction can be brought within the scope of the principle. For example, *Ruckdeschel* concerned a production refund that was provided to manufacturers who turned maize into starch, but not for those who turned maize into Quellmehl. In *Syndicat national des professions du tourisme v. France*,[18] the European Committee of Social Rights held that Article 1(2) of the Revised Charter was breached by discrimination between different categories of tour guides.[19] The breadth and flexibility of this principle reveals a symmetrical approach to equality. The focus is on providing the same treatment, once it can be established that the persons are in a comparable situation. There are, however, a number of weaknesses in this approach.

First, there is no apparent recognition of patterns of discrimination and disadvantage. The symmetrical vision fails to accord priority to tackling disadvantage and the entrenched inequality experienced by specific groups.[20] Yet, this context is crucial to understanding if formal equal treatment will result in full equality in practice. For example, a requirement to work overtime at short notice may apply

---

[15] Cases 117/76 and 16/77, [1977] ECR 1753, Rec. 7 of judgment.

[16] L. Samuel, *Fundamental Social Rights—Case Law of the European Social Charter* (2002), at 25.

[17] C. McCrudden, 'Theorizing European Equality Law', in C. Costello and E. Barry (eds), *Equality in Diversity—The New Equality Directives* (2003), at 19.

[18] Complaint No. 6/1999, 10 October 2000.

[19] For example, only certain categories of tour guides were permitted access to sites such as Versailles.

[20] O. Arnardóttir, *Equality and Non-Discrimination under the European Convention on Human Rights* (2003), at 23.

equally to all workers, however, this will be more difficult for workers with family responsibilities. This has the effect of placing women at a disadvantage as they remain disproportionately responsible for childcare and the care of other family members.

The application of a formal equal treatment rule is also restricted by the need to locate another person with different characteristics in a comparable situation. This requirement proves difficult to meet in practice because labour markets are often segregated by characteristics such as sex, race, and nationality. The European Committee of Social Rights has highlighted this difficulty in relation to enforcing equal pay for women. In contrast to the approach of the Court of Justice,[21] the Committee has endorsed the need for women working in segregated areas of the labour market to be able to make an objective job evaluation by comparison with workers of other employers.[22]

B. *Indirect Discrimination*

Both EU law and the Charter have moved beyond the general principle of equality and an approach based exclusively on formal equal treatment. This is frequently depicted as a shift in favour of a substantive concept of equality.[23] As a first step, there has been recognition in both legal orders of indirect discrimination, in other words, situations where the application of an apparently neutral rule or practice places a particular group of persons at a particular disadvantage.

EU legislation on sex equality did not originally specify whether the principle of equal treatment extended to situations of indirect discrimination. Nonetheless, the Court of Justice gradually developed a concept of indirect discrimination. This case law stemmed from litigation concerning the less favourable treatment of part-time workers, who remain disproportionately women.[24] Ultimately, a statutory definition of indirect discrimination was introduced through Directive 97/80.[25] This focused on situations where 'an apparently neutral provision, criterion or practice disadvantages a substantially higher proportion of members of one sex'. The reference to a 'substantially higher proportion' clearly pointed to the relevance of statistical analysis in establishing the (indirect) discriminatory effect of employment practices. Whilst determining the appropriate pools of comparison has proven to be a complex task within sex equality litigation,[26] it was evident that statistical evidence would frequently be unavailable in other types of discrimination litigation, especially on the grounds of religion and sexual orientation. Therefore,

---

[21] Case C-256/01, *Allonby v. Accrington & Rossendale College* [2004] 1 CMLR 35, Rec. 50 of judgment.

[22] Council of Europe, *Equality Between Women and Men in the European Social Charter* (2000), para. 67.

[23] D. Schiek, 'A New Framework on Equal Treatment of Persons in EC Law?', 8 *ELJ* (2002) 290.

[24] E.g. Case 170/84, *Bilka-Kaufhaus GmbH v. Weber Von Hartz* [1986] ECR 1607.

[25] Council Directive 97/80, OJ 1998 L14/6, Art. 2(2).

[26] Case C-167/97, *R v. Secretary of State, ex parte Seymour-Smith and Perez* [1999] ECR I-623.

the 2000 anti-discrimination Directives adopted a broader standard based on demonstrating that a practice would place persons of particular race, religion, age, disability, or sexual orientation at 'a particular disadvantage'.[27] Interestingly, the 2002 Revised Equal Treatment Directive amends the definition of indirect sex discrimination to conform to the approach taken in the 2000 Directives.[28]

The concept of indirect discrimination has also evolved within the framework of the Charter. On the one hand, the interpretations of Article 1(2) of the Charter do not appear to have clarified whether the principle of non-discrimination includes indirect discrimination.[29] On the other, indirect discrimination has been recognized by the European Committee of Social Rights in the context of other Charter provisions. Article 19 includes rights to equal treatment for migrant workers. In its analysis of this provision, the Committee has referred to 'de facto' inequality arising from the application of neutral rules, such as residence requirements, which place migrant workers at a disadvantage in practice.[30] More recently, the European Committee of Social Rights clarified in *Autism-Europe v. France* that Article E of the Revised Charter 'not only prohibits direct discrimination but also all forms of indirect discrimination'.[31]

Although indirect discrimination is increasingly recognized within the Charter, it remains hazy and lacks the specific definition found within the EU legislation. Crucially, the Directives have separated direct discrimination from indirect discrimination with the consequence that the former can normally only be justified by reference to a specific legislative exception. In contrast, all forms of discrimination remain open to justification in the broad formula found within the Charter. This echoes the approach taken in the case law of the Court of Human Rights under Article 14 of the Convention.[32]

C. Positive Action

A substantive concept of equality recognizes that the effects of persistent inequality across different areas of life (such as housing, education, health care) may make it difficult for certain groups to compete on an equal basis in the labour market. The deeply entrenched disadvantage faced by many Roma communities in Europe is a clear example where equal treatment is unlikely to result in equality in practice.[33] Employers may be able to provide objective justification for imposing qualification requirements when advertising job vacancies, yet, the systematic disadvantage of Roma communities within educational systems in some states render such

---

[27] Art. 2(2)(b), Directive 2000/43; Art. 2(2)(b), Directive 2000/78.
[28] Art. 2(2), Directive 2002/73.
[29] Samuel, *supra* n. 16, at 25–31; Harris and Darcy, *supra* n. 7, at 47–53.
[30] P. Boucaud, *Migrant Workers and Their Families* (1996), at 39–40.
[31] *Autism-Europe v. France*, Complaint No. 13/2002, 4 November 2003, para. 52.
[32] See further, Gerards, *supra* n. 5.
[33] B. Hepple, 'Race and Law in Fortress Europe', 67 *MLR* (2004) 1, at 8.

requirements exclusionary in practice.[34] In order to break the cycle of disadvantage, positive actions may be adopted in order to secure greater equality of opportunity. Where the goal is to achieve a fair representation of different groups within the labour market, this may ultimately lead in the direction of more interventionist measures, such as preferential treatment or quotas, with a view to securing equal results.

The European Union has cautiously endorsed a limited role for positive action, whilst rejecting measures that aim at equal results. The three core Directives on discrimination in the labour market all permit Member States to allow positive action.[35] In the case of gender equality, this is reinforced by Article 141(4) EC, which authorizes positive action 'with a view to ensuring full equality in practice'. Nevertheless, the EU legislation does not impose any obligation on the Member States to initiate positive action or even to permit the voluntary adoption of positive action by employers. The tentative nature of these interventions is confirmed in the Revised Equal Treatment Directive. Member States are obliged to 'encourage' employers to take action to prevent discrimination[36] and to 'encourage' employers to provide information on equality within the business, which 'may include statistics on proportions of men and women at different levels of the organisation'.[37] Alongside the weak duty to facilitate positive action, the Court of Justice has placed firm limits on the extent of such measures. In a series of cases, the Court has clarified that measures conferring absolute and unconditional preferential treatment for women at the point of employment selection constitute unlawful discrimination.[38]

The most express recognition of the role for positive action in the Charter was introduced by Article 1 of the 1988 Additional Protocol, which deals with equal opportunities and equal treatment for women and men. This provision was subsequently incorporated into the 1996 Revised Charter and Part II of the Appendix to the Revised Charter clarifies that the prohibition on sex discrimination 'shall not prevent the adoption of specific measures aimed at removing de facto inequalities'. In contrast to EU law, the case law of the Charter has not yet fleshed out the limits to positive action.[39]

Whilst the contours of positive action under the Charter remain rather vague, the European Committee of Social Rights has occasionally emphasized the positive duty on Member States to take actions beyond the introduction of anti-discrimination legislation. With regard to Article 19 and migrant workers, the Committee stated: 'the Contracting Parties should not limit the fulfilment of their

---

[34] Para. 36, ECRI, 'Second Report on Hungary', CRI (2000) 5.

[35] Art. 5, Directive 2000/43; Art. 7, Directive 2000/78; Art. 2(8), Directive 2002/73.

[36] Art. 2(5), Directive 2002/73.   [37] Art. 8b(4), Directive 2002/73.

[38] See further, Tobler, 'Positive Action under the Revised Second Equal Treatment Directive', in Association française des femmes juristes and European Women Lawyers Association (eds), *L'egalité entre les femmes et hommes et la vie professionnelle—le point sur les développements actuels en Europe* (2003).   [39] Council of Europe, *supra* n. 22, para. 62.

obligations under this article to ensuring non-discrimination between their own nationals and foreigners but should pursue a positive and continuous course of action'.[40] Similarly, the Committee has interpreted the various provisions relating to gender equality as requiring states to have 'active policies' for the implementation of equality.[41] This emphasis on positive duties compares favourably with EU anti-discrimination legislation, which has primarily focused on the provision of avenues for individual enforcement of equal treatment rights, rather than imposing proactive obligations on states.

D. Overview

In considering the concepts of equality and non-discrimination deployed by the Union and through the European Social Charter, a common starting point can be identified. This is premised on the Aristotelian notion that equality means 'treating equals equally and unequals unequally'.[42] Both systems have recognized over time that identical treatment will not be sufficient to achieve full equality in practice. A gradual shift can be traced and there is a trajectory in favour of a more substantive concept of equality. The nature of EU legislation has demanded greater precision in the definition of discrimination. Moreover, individual litigation has forced the Court of Justice to spell out the limits to positive action. In contrast, the periodic monitoring of national practice by the European Committee of Social Rights has allowed its praxis to evolve incrementally, whilst retaining a broad discretion for national authorities.

III. DIVERSITY AND DISCRIMINATION

One of the most evident trends in anti-discrimination law has been the gradual expansion in the list of prohibited grounds of discrimination. This is evident in national legal reforms, but also in law from the European Union and the Council of Europe. Whilst the extension in the scope of anti-discrimination law is often welcomed as a sign of progress, it poses new challenges and dilemmas. On the one hand, certain aspects of anti-discrimination law are of equal relevance, irrespective of the ground of discrimination. For example, the need to protect individuals against victimization subsequent to making a complaint of discrimination seems just as relevant to cases of sex discrimination as to cases of religious discrimination. On the other, there are specificities relating to each of the grounds. For example, issues of race discrimination are frequently bound up with matters of immigration, citizenship, and nationality. In order to respond effectively to diversity, law may

---

[40] *Conclusions I*, at 81, cited in Boucaud, *supra* n. 30, para. 66.
[41] Council of Europe, *supra* n. 22, para. 45.
[42] *Autism-Europe v. France*, Complaint No. 13/2002, 4 November 2003, para. 52.

need to distinguish between the grounds of discrimination and to adopt different strategies. Yet, there is a risk that this results in an unequal level of protection, often referred to as a hierarchy of equality.

A. *Identifying Suspect Grounds of Discrimination*

The previous section indicated that a general principle of equality was present in both EU law and under the Charter. The very generality of this principle obviates the need for an exhaustive list of protected grounds. Nonetheless, a substantive concept of equality seeks to move beyond bare neutrality and a completely symmetrical approach to equal treatment. Consequently, it becomes valuable to identify certain groups systematically vulnerable to discrimination.

EU law has elaborated a pluralistic response to the question of diversity. Beyond the general principle of equality, Article 21 of the (non-binding) Charter of Fundamental Rights incorporates a lengthy list of prohibited grounds of discrimination, which is also non-exhaustive.[43] This applies throughout the scope of EU law, but it does not generate autonomous rights to non-discrimination. In other words, even if the Charter was legally binding, it would not provide a free-standing right to equal treatment irrespective of 'genetic features'. It would simply demand that there is no discrimination on this ground throughout EU law. Whilst this is more explicit than the general principle of equality, the underlying concept is comparable.

In addition to the long list in Article 21, the EU Charter of Fundamental Rights contains a series of clauses on cultural, religious, and linguistic diversity; gender equality; the rights of children; older people and people with disabilities.[44] Without analysing the precise content of each article, the selection of groups provides an indication to the legislator that these are particularly suspect grounds of discrimination and areas where positive interventions may be required. Indeed, this is also foreseen in the Union's legislative competences for combating discrimination. Unlike the long list of grounds found in Article 21 of the EU Charter, further legislation generating autonomous rights to non-discrimination is only anticipated in respect of nationality,[45] sex,[46] racial or ethnic origin, religion or belief, age, disability, and sexual orientation.[47] The implication is that these are grounds where discrimination is so pervasive that the general right to equality will not be sufficient; instead, legislation installing protection against discrimination will be demanded. In adopting this legislation, the Union has chosen to draw further distinctions between the discrimination grounds. Whilst protection against racial discrimination extends beyond the workplace to include other areas,

---

[43] Art. 21(1) states: 'Any discrimination based on any ground such as sex, race, colour, ethnic or social origin, genetic features, language, religion or belief, political or any other opinion, membership of a national minority, property, birth, disability, age or sexual orientation shall be prohibited.'
[44] Arts 22–26.   [45] Art. 12 TEC.   [46] Art. 13 TEC and Art. 141 TEC.
[47] Art. 13 TEC.

such as the provision of goods and services or education, discrimination on the grounds of religion or belief, age, disability, and sexual orientation is only forbidden in the fields of employment and vocational training. The differences in the material scope and substantive content of the core anti-discrimination Directives do not always follow a clear rationale, leading to a debate surrounding the existence of an 'equality hierarchy' within the legislation.[48]

The Preamble to the 1961 European Social Charter included reference to an exhaustive list of prohibited grounds of discrimination: 'race, colour, sex, religion, political opinion, national extraction or social origin'. Whilst the Charter also contained provisions relating to children and disabled persons,[49] these were not framed in terms of equal treatment, rather they were premised upon protection and social assistance. The 1996 Revised Social Charter represents a decisive shift in approach. Article E provides a longer and non-exhaustive list of grounds in respect of which there should be no discrimination in the enjoyment of the rights provided by the Charter. In *Autism-Europe v. France*,[50] the European Committee of Social Rights held that disability, although not mentioned explicitly in Article E, was covered by the open-ended reference to non-discrimination on any 'other status'.

The Revised Charter also contains several free-standing rights to non-discrimination. There is a specific provision on gender equality in employment and training,[51] as well as the right to equal opportunity for workers with family responsibilities.[52] Existing provisions from the 1961 Charter on equal treatment for migrant workers and equal pay for men and women are retained.[53] It should also be noted that Article 5 on the right to organize has been consistently interpreted as prohibiting discrimination based on trade union activity or membership.[54] Nonetheless, there is a significant difference here with the EU legal framework. A free-standing right to non-discrimination in employment on grounds of race, religion, age, or sexual orientation remains implicit, even in the Revised Charter.

B. Equal Protection and Recognizing Diversity

Both legal frameworks have combined general guarantees of non-discrimination with specific responses to different forms of discrimination. In this area, there are several points of convergence, yet also some striking differences.

1. Gender Equality Clear parallels can be identified in relation to gender equality. The 1961 Social Charter was at its most concrete with respect to 'the

[48] M. Bell and L. Waddington, 'Reflecting on Inequalities in European Equality Law', 28 *ELRev.* (2003) 349.   [49] Arts. 7 and 15 respectively.
[50] *Autism-Europe v. France*, Complaint No. 13/2002, 4 November 2003, para. 51.
[51] Art. 20.   [52] Art. 27.   [53] Arts. 19(4) and 4(3) respectively.
[54] Harris and Darcy, *supra* n. 7, at 50.

right of men and women workers to equal pay for work of equal value'.[55] The 1988 Additional Protocol complemented this with a free-standing right to equal opportunity and equal treatment in employment and training. Finally, the 1996 Revised Charter took a number of further steps. First, it requires action to protect workers from sexual harassment under the aegis of 'the right to dignity at work'.[56] Furthermore, there is recognition of the connection between gender equality and the reconciliation of work and family responsibilities. In relation to pregnancy and maternity, the Revised Charter simultaneously enhances the rights of women in comparison with the 1961 Charter, whilst dismantling some of its more paternalistic elements. Therefore, the right to paid maternity leave is moderately extended (from twelve to fourteen weeks) and the prohibition on women performing 'dangerous, unhealthy or arduous' work is curtailed to those who are pregnant, have recently given birth, or are 'nursing their infants'.[57]

This trajectory is comparable to the evolution of EU gender equality law. It too commenced with a focus on equal pay for women and men, later supplemented by legislation on equal treatment in employment and training. Moreover, the 2002 Revised Equal Treatment Directive addresses both harassment (as a violation of dignity) and the rights of women in respect of pregnancy and maternity. These overlaps are not unconnected coincidences. On the contrary, the influence of EU legislation on the Social Charter norms is manifest. For example, the 1988 Additional Protocol identifies three exceptions to the principle of equal treatment irrespective of sex. These concern pregnancy and maternity; positive action; and where sex is a genuine occupational requirement.[58] This reflects the model earlier adopted in the 1976 Equal Treatment Directive.[59]

2. Migrant Workers   Alongside equal pay for women and men, the other express equality provision in the 1961 Charter was Article 19 on migrant workers and their families. Paragraph 4 obliges states to: 'secure for such workers lawfully within their territories . . . treatment not less favourable than that of their own nationals in respect of the following matters: (a) remuneration and other employment and working conditions; (b) membership of trade unions and enjoyment of the benefits of collective bargaining; (c) accommodation'.

The European Committee on Social Rights has emphasized that the different circumstances of migrant workers implies that formal equal treatment in law may not be sufficient: 'equality in law does not always and necessarily ensure equality in practice. Hence, additional action becomes necessary owing to the different

---

[55] Art. 4(3).   [56] Art. 26.   [57] Art. 8 in both the 1961 and 1996 Charters.

[58] Art. 1(2)–(4).

[59] Art. 2(2)–(4), Council Directive 76/207 on the implementation of the principle of equal treatment for men and women as regards access to employment, vocational training and promotion, and working conditions, OJ 1976 L39/41.

situation of migrant workers as compared to nationals.'[60] The crucial constraint that greatly weakens the potential contribution of Article 19 is the personal scope of the Charter. Both the 1961 and 1996 Charters are limited to the nationals of the Contracting States, therefore, third-country nationals are not included.[61]

The principle of non-discrimination on the ground of nationality is firmly entrenched in the EU legal order. In respect of migrant workers, Article 39(2) EC prohibited discrimination in employment. This was supplemented with Regulation 1612/68, which further guaranteed equal treatment in relation to any 'social and tax advantages'.[62] Initially, these rights were subject to the same personal scope restrictions as found in the European Social Charter; namely, they were primarily attached to migrant workers, rather than all migrants, and they were limited to nationals of the EU Member States. The insertion of a chapter on Union citizenship in the EC Treaty[63] paved the way for the Court of Justice to reconstruct the right to non-discrimination as an aspect of citizenship and to decouple this from the exercise of economic activity.[64] Extending non-discrimination rights to third-country nationals has proven more complex, but concrete steps have now been taken. The Long Term Residents Directive provides that third-country nationals with more than five years of legal residence in a Member State will be entitled to equal treatment with EU nationals in a variety of areas, including employment, education, social protection, and goods and services.[65] Admittedly, these rights to equal treatment are subject to significant exceptions. For instance, Member States may retain pre-existing rules restricting certain types of employment to EU nationals.[66] Equal treatment in social protection may be limited to 'core benefits'.[67] Even though the Long Term Residents Directive is only a recent step forward and hedged with qualifications, it signals a clear distinction between the equality rights provided by EU law and those provided by the European Social Charter.

3. Racial Discrimination   Perhaps the most obvious divergence that has opened up between Union law and the European Social Charter is in respect of racial discrimination. Although race is included as a prohibited ground of discrimination in both the preamble to the 1961 Charter and Article E in the Revised Charter, there are no free-standing rights to equal treatment irrespective of race. Matters of race discrimination have been principally considered by the European Committee of Social Rights under two different headings. First, Article 1(2) has been interpreted as guaranteeing a general right to non-discrimination in employment. In its review of

---

[60] *Conclusions V*, at 123, cited in Boucaud, *supra* n. 30, para. 94.
[61] Appendix to 1961 and 1996 Charters, para. 1.   [62] Art. 7(2), OJ Spec Ed. II (1968) 475.
[63] By the 1993 Treaty on European Union.
[64] For example, Case C-85/96, *Sala* [1998] ECR I-2691; Case C-184/99, *Grzelczyk* [2001] ECR I-6193.
[65] Art. 11, Council Directive 2003/109 of 25 November 2003 concerning the status of third country nationals who are long-term residents, OJ 2004 L16/44. There are certain exceptions to the personal scope of the Directive, for example, students or asylum-seekers do not acquire rights.
[66] Art. 11(3)(a), Directive 2003/109.   [67] Art. 11(4), Directive 2003/109.

individual state practice under Article 1(2) the Committee has criticized, for example, restrictions in the British Race Relations Act 1976 on compensation for unintentional indirect discrimination.[68] Nevertheless, Harris and Darcy note that race discrimination 'has not been as systematically examined by the Committee as discrimination on grounds of sex'.[69]

There is also evidence that race discrimination has been considered in the context of Article 19 on migrant workers.[70] In a recent report on Greece, the Committee made express reference to measures being adopted in order to implement the Racial Equality Directive in its analysis of the situation of migrant workers.[71] The connection made with the Directive illustrates the potential for synergy between the two legal frameworks. It seems evident that race discrimination has been hitherto rather marginal in the Social Charter. In contrast, the European Union has constructed a significant legal framework on this type of discrimination. The Racial Equality Directive covers a broad material scope and contains several positive obligations for state action, most notably a duty to establish a body for the promotion of equal treatment.[72] In the same way that EU gender equality law appears to have influenced the development of norms and standards under the Social Charter, the Racial Equality Directive may assist in raising the profile of racial discrimination.

C. Overview

The origins of both legal frameworks focused on discrimination on grounds of sex and against migrant workers. In recent years, a broader understanding of the prohibited grounds of discrimination has emerged, most strongly in EU law. The expansion in the range of grounds has been combined with recognition of diversity. Most notably, the legal framework on gender equality is more elaborate within the Social Charter than that pertaining to other grounds. This is particularly attuned to issues of pregnancy, maternity, and family responsibilities. In contrast, EU law has also developed specific legislation on racial discrimination, alongside some initial steps on the rights of third-country nationals. In this respect, a visible gap has emerged between the strength of EU equality legislation and that found in the Social Charter.

IV. PUTTING THE LAW INTO PRACTICE

In considering the implementation of European equality law, a distinction can be drawn between mechanisms for enforcement within national legal systems and

---

[68] European Committee of Social Rights, *Conclusions XVII-1*, Vol. 1 (2004), at 308.

[69] Harris and Darcy, *supra* n. 7, at 52.

[70] For example, see comments on Belgium: Committee of Independent Experts, *Conclusions XIV-1*, Vol. 1 (1998), at 138.   [71] European Committee of Social Rights, *supra* n. 68, at 87.

[72] Art. 13, Directive 2000/43.

mechanisms to compel states to respect their European legal commitments. In the context of EU law, the distinction between the two levels is clearly blurred by the possibility for individual litigants to enforce EU equality law within domestic legal proceedings, even against private parties (the principle of direct effect). Nonetheless, this distinction is a helpful means of clarifying the different dimensions to the topic of enforcement. Three strands to enforcement mechanisms can be identified within both legal frameworks: individual enforcement, collective enforcement, and monitoring of state practice.

A. Individual Enforcement

EU equality legislation has shifted considerably over time, with a gradual reduction in the discretion accorded to Member States as regards procedures and sanctions for enforcing equality legislation within domestic legal systems. The 1976 Equal Treatment Directive simply required states to establish a 'judicial process' for individual complaints.[73] Subsequent decisions of the Court of Justice expanded on this general obligation, in particular by concentrating on the effectiveness of remedies.[74] The perceived gaps in the original Equal Treatment Directive visibly influenced recent EU equality legislation. Each of the three core anti-discrimination Directives contains specific requirements designed to assist individual enforcement of the legislation. Notably, the burden of proof shifts from the complainant to the respondent where the complainant establishes 'facts from which it may be presumed that there has been direct or indirect discrimination'.[75] Measures must also be introduced to protect individuals from any victimization in response to proceedings to enforce equality legislation.[76]

The European Social Charter lacks any express provision relating to national procedures for enforcement of its rights or the effectiveness of remedies. In this respect, it is weaker than the Convention on Human Rights, where Article 13 guarantees the right to 'an effective remedy'. Nonetheless, the European Committee of Social Rights has adopted a purposive interpretation of the Charter. States will not be in compliance merely by enacting formal rules; on the contrary, there must be 'effective practical application of normative provisions'.[77] In the context of equality rights, over time the Committee has identified a range of measures that states should enact in order to comply fully with the Charter. These tend to coincide with directions in EU equality legislation; for example, the Committee has emphasized the need for protection against victimization and

---

[73] Art. 6.

[74] S. Parmar, 'The European Court of Justice and Anti-Discrimination Law: Some Reflections on the Experience of Gender Equality Jurisprudence for the Future Interpretation of the Racial Equality Directive', in J. Niessen and I. Chopin (eds), *The Development of Legal Instruments to Combat Racism in a Diverse Europe* (2004), at 152–53.

[75] Art. 8(1), Directive 2000/43; Art. 10(1), Directive 2000/78; Art. 4(1), Council Directive 97/80 on the burden of proof in cases of discrimination based on sex, OJ 1998 L14/6.

[76] Art. 9, Directive 2000/43; Art. 11, Directive 2000/78; Art. 7, Directive 2002/73.

[77] Committee of Independent Experts, *supra* n. 70, at 36.

procedures permitting a shift in the burden of proof.[78] The Committee has also been willing to make specific assessments of the quality of national remedies. For example, it determined that maximum compensation of thirty-nine weeks of salary for sex discrimination in Danish law was 'not sufficient to deter the employer'.[79]

The key distinction between Union law and the Charter in the area of individual remedies concerns the possibility for individuals to enforce European equality rights in the absence of national implementation. The principle of direct effect, elaborated in response to equal pay litigation,[80] provides individuals with the option of directly invoking EU equality legislation within domestic proceedings. In contrast, the enforceability of the European Social Charter within domestic legal proceedings will depend entirely on the national legal system and how it incorporates international treaties.[81] Crucially, there is no procedure that permits individual disputes to be brought before the European Committee of Social Rights, a sharp contrast to the option of individual complaint under the Convention on Human Rights.

B. *Collective Enforcement*

Whilst EU law places a premium on individual enforcement, it remains relatively weak in respect of collective enforcement. There is no obligation on states to extend autonomous legal standing for organizations to bring complaints of discrimination. Instead, organizations only have a role to assist individual complainants.[82] Similarly, the Racial Equality and Revised Equal Treatment Directives oblige national equal treatment bodies to provide 'independent assistance to victims of discrimination in pursuing their complaints',[83] but there is no duty on the state to afford independent legal standing to these bodies. The European Committee of Social Rights has recommended that states go further. In the context of enforcing equal pay, it has advised states to extend legal standing to trade unions and to consider allowing class actions by affected individuals.[84] More recently, the Committee has also requested information from states on the legal standing afforded to NGOs to bring complaints of discrimination.[85]

The concrete difference between Union law and the Social Charter concerns the option for collective enforcement at the European level. In relation to EU law, the capacity of organizations to challenge Member State non-compliance will

---

[78] Samuel, *supra* n. 16, at 91–92.

[79] Committee of Independent Experts, *Conclusions XV-1*, Vol. 1 (2000), at 173.

[80] Case 43/75, *Defrenne v. SABENA* [1976] ECR 455.

[81] See further the chapter by Gisella Gori in this volume.

[82] Organizations are entitled to intervene in support or on behalf of complainants with their consent: Art. 7(2), Directive 2000/43; Art. 9(2), Directive 2000/78; Art. 6(3), Directive 2002/73.

[83] Art. 13(2), Directive 2000/43; Art. 8a(2)(a), Directive 2002/73.

[84] Samuel, *supra* n. 16, at 90.

[85] European Committee of Social Rights, *supra* n. 68, at 21 (Denmark), at 307 (UK).

depend on national procedural requirements. If national law provides a procedure through which organizations can initiate in the domestic courts a complaint regarding failure to implement EU equality legislation, then this may be subsequently referred to the Court of Justice. For example, in *MRAX v. Belgium*,[86] an anti-racism organization successfully challenged certain Belgian immigration rules as incompatible with EU free movement legislation. Yet, their ability to commence judicial review proceedings at the national level depended on Belgian civil procedure. There is no option for an organization to lodge directly a complaint at the Court of Justice concerning non-compliance by a Member State. This prerogative is reserved to the Commission and the Member States.[87]

The European Social Charter is highly innovative in providing a specific route for collective complaints concerning national breaches of the Charter. Three types of organization have the right to lodge complaints: international organizations of employers and trade unions;[88] international NGOs with consultative status at the Council of Europe; and 'representative national organisations of employers and trade unions within the jurisdiction of the Contracting Party against which they have lodged a complaint'.[89] In addition, states may choose to accept the right of national NGOs to lodge complaints against them.[90] Eleven states have ratified the Collective Complaints Procedure, although only one (Finland) has chosen to permit complaints from national NGOs.[91] The Governmental Committee of the European Social Charter maintains a list of international NGOs with the right to lodge complaints. This list currently covers fifty-eight organizations, many with an obvious interest in issues of discrimination (for example, European Disability Forum, European Roma Rights Centre).[92] From the perspective of tackling discrimination, the collective complaints procedure has considerable virtue. Individual litigation depends heavily on the willingness of individuals to bear the financial and emotional costs that are often inherent in pursuing a complaint. Disputes framed around individuals are also less apposite when confronting systematic patterns of inequality. Where certain social groups are subject to disadvantage and exclusion across different aspects of life, individual complaints are unlikely to capture the web of mechanisms through which inequality is perpetuated. In contrast, the possibility for collective complaints allows a focus on the cumulative situation. This is certainly evident from some of the complaints already lodged. In *Autism-Europe v. France*,[93] the complainant successfully demonstrated that across a

---

[86] Case C-459/99, [2002] ECR I-6591.   [87] Arts 226 and 227 TEC.
[88] Currently, European Trade Union Confederation, the Union of Industrial and Employers' Confederations of Europe and the International Organisation of Employers.
[89] Art. 1, Additional Protocol to the European Social Charter providing for a system of collective complaints, CETS No. 158.   [90] Ibid., Art. 2.
[91] Based on the situation on 14 May 2004. Available at: http://conventions.coe.int/Treaty/Commun/QueVoulezVous.asp?NT=158&CM=8&DF=14/05/04&CL=ENG.
[92] Full list available from: http://www.coe.int/T/E/Human%5FRights/Esc/5%5FCollective%5F complaints/Organisations%5Fentitled/List_of_NGOs.asp#TopOfPage.
[93] Complaint No. 13/2002, 4 November 2003.

range of indicators France was failing to provide sufficient educational resources for people with autism. In *Quaker Council for European Affairs v. Greece*,[94] the complainant demonstrated a number of mechanisms through which Greece in practice deterred conscientious objectors from accessing the civilian alternative to military service.

The weakness of the collective complaint system lies in the subsequent enforcement of decisions finding a violation. There is no procedure for the award of compensation or mandatory positive actions on the part of the state respondent.[95] At best, the Committee of Ministers can adopt a recommendation addressed to the state in question, which is then obliged to report on its actions to give effect to the recommendation in its next periodic report.[96] In this sense, Cullen describes it as 'a system designed to discover failures of implementation rather than to remedy violations of rights'.[97] Indeed, there is a genuine risk that states use the 'soft' reporting obligation as a means to obfuscate the need to comply with the Committee's decision. For example, in 2004 the Committee noted various subsequent reforms to the organization of military service in Greece, but nonetheless alternative civilian service remained more than double the length of military service and the earlier decision had not been respected.[98]

C. Monitoring of State Practice

Both legal frameworks contain external mechanisms at the European level to control whether equality rights are correctly implemented by national authorities. Within the EU, the Commission has a mandate to supervise the enforcement of Union legislation, with the option of bringing infringement proceedings to the Court of Justice to challenge non-compliance. The Racial Equality and Framework Directives include a specific obligation on Member States to communicate information to the Commission on the application of the Directives at five year intervals, commencing in 2005.[99] In contrast, the Revised Equal Treatment Directive contains a more limited obligation on Member States to communicate information once every four years on any measures of positive action that they have adopted.[100] The European Union Monitoring Centre on Racism and Xenophobia (EUMC) also keeps under review national law and policy on racial discrimination. Moreover, the Commission's periodic reports on the application

---

[94] Complaint No. 8/2000, 25 April 2001.

[95] T. Novitz, 'Are Social Rights Necessarily Collective Rights? A Critical Analysis of the Collective Complaints Protocol to the European Social Charter', *EHRLR* (2002) 50, at 54.

[96] Arts 9 and 10, Collective Complaints Protocol.

[97] H. Cullen, 'The Collective Complaints Mechanism of the European Social Charter', 25 *ELRev.* (Human Rights Supplement) (2000) 18, at 27.

[98] European Committee of Social Rights, *supra* n. 68, at 70.

[99] Art. 17, Directive 2000/43; Art. 19, Directive 2000/78.

[100] Art. 2(3), Directive 2002/73.

of the Directive must take into account the views of the EUMC.[101] In December 2003, the European Council decided in principle to convert the EUMC into a Human Rights Observatory.[102]

Periodic monitoring of state practice through a national reporting system is the primary method through which enforcement of the European Social Charter is verified. National reports on implementation of the Charter are first considered by an independent expert committee, the European Committee of Social Rights. This reaches 'Conclusions' on whether or not national law and practice are in conformity with the Charter. These Conclusions are then considered by the Governmental Committee, which consists of one representative of each Contracting State. The Governmental Committee identifies those issues where it would be appropriate to make a recommendation addressed to an individual state and makes a proposal to this end for a decision from the Committee of Ministers.[103]

Although this is a more systematic process of monitoring than that applicable under Union law, it contains a number of weaknesses. First, states may be able to defer potential criticism through the submission of insufficient or ambiguous information. The European Committee of Social Rights is frequently forced to postpone reaching a firm conclusion on the compatibility of state practice and to request further information in future national reports.[104] Even where sufficient information exists to conclude that national law or practice is in breach of the Charter, the final decision on whether to make a recommendation rests with a political body, rather than an independent adjudicator. Moreover, recommendations are not legally binding.[105] In essence, the periodic reporting system is largely dependent on political persuasion and cajoling in order to promote voluntary compliance.

With regard to combating discrimination, the work of the European Commission against Racism and Intolerance (ECRI) should also be taken into account. ECRI is an expert advisory committee established in 1994 to strengthen the work of the Council of Europe on combating racism. Amongst its activities, it has developed a 'country-by-country' periodic review of national law and practice on racism. This has generated a series of detailed reports that provide an independent assessment and critique of the national situation.[106] At the end of each report, there is an opportunity for government comments, which often aim to respond to the criticisms made. Although there is no subsequent formal procedure, such as that applicable under the European Social Charter, the work of ECRI provides an additional, and more focused, mechanism through which national practice can be subjected to independent and external critical analysis.

---

[101] Art. 17, Directive 2000/43.

[102] See further, European Parliament, 'Working Document on the Proposal for a Council Regulation on the European Monitoring Centre on Racism and Xenophobia' (Rapporteur: Sweibel), PE 339.635, 25 March 2004.   [103] See further, Harris and Darcy, *supra* n. 7, Ch. 3.

[104] Ibid., at 311.   [105] Ibid., at 400.

[106] The reports are available from: http://www.coe.int/T/E/human_rights/Ecri/1-ECRI/ 2-Country-by-country_approach/default.asp#TopOfPage.

V. CONCLUSION

In any comparison of Union law and the European Social Charter, it is quite evident that the former enjoys stronger mechanisms to compel national authorities to fulfil their legal commitments. This is especially true from the perspective of an individual victim of discrimination. The potential for individuals to rely on the doctrine of 'direct effect' has played a crucial role in the elaboration of EU norms on gender equality. Despite the limitations regarding the enforcement of the European Social Charter, it contains a number of valuable innovations, from which the Union could learn. The Collective Complaints Protocol is a novel mechanism that provides a useful counterbalance to the heavy emphasis on individual litigation found within EU law. In the field of discrimination and inequality, developing a collective perspective on enforcement appears essential given the obstacles to individual complaints. Whilst the recent Directives attempt to alleviate some of the main deterrents to successful individual litigation, they fail to confront the need for parallel mechanisms of collective enforcement.

The rapid expansion in the scope of EU anti-discrimination law, together with the greater focus on discrimination issues found within the Revised European Social Charter reveal a gradual convergence in the scope of both legal frameworks. Clearly, certain differences remain. EU law has developed targeted protection against racial discrimination through the Racial Equality Directive. In the framework of the Council of Europe, issues of racism are more commonly addressed in the activities of ECRI than through the European Social Charter. Alternatively, the Charter covers discrimination based on trade union membership or activity, a topic that has been largely overlooked in EU anti-discrimination law. Notwithstanding such divergences, in the sphere of employment discrimination there is an obvious overlap in both frameworks. The challenge for the Union and the Council of Europe is to promote greater cooperation and coordination with a view to ensuring that each provides added value, rather than mere duplication. Considering the work of the European Committee of Social Rights, it seems evident that their review of national practice will often coincide with an analysis of national implementation of EU anti-discrimination legislation. From the perspective of the Union, this promises a constructive and independent source of information. In return, the importance attached to the Charter reporting system could be elevated if it was clear that the Conclusions of the Committee would have an impact within the EU legal framework. Therefore, potential exists for fruitful cooperation that could ultimately benefit the effective implementation of anti-discrimination law within both legal frameworks.

14

The European Social Charter and EU Anti-discrimination Law in the Field of Disability: Two Gravitational Fields with One Common Purpose

GERARD QUINN*

I. INTRODUCTION

This chapter explores the synergy that currently exists and can be further developed between the Council of Europe and the European Union in order to secure the full and equal enjoyment of all human rights for persons with disabilities. More specifically, it explores the complementarity between the existing case law of the European Social Charter and the future potential of the Framework Employment Directive on the ground of disability.

Historically, the Council of Europe has had very extensive involvement in the disability debate and from an early date.[1] However, and broadly speaking, much of its involvement had been animated by social policy and the provision of social support. While this focus was beneficial in itself, it did tend to reinforce (howsoever unwittingly) an attitude that too readily accepted the absence of persons with disabilities from the mainstream of life. That is to say, it accepted their absence as 'normal'. And this was despite the fact that the Council of Europe was—and still is—Europe's premier regional human rights organization. That is changing—especially since the early 1990s and nowhere more so than in the thinking and evolving non-discrimination case law of the European Committee of Social Rights.

---

* This chapter is dedicated to the memory of Stephen Livingstone.
[1] For a representative sample of Council of Europe publications in the field see, Council of Europe, *Rehabilitation and Integration of People with Disabilities* (2003), *Assessing Disability in Europe—Similarities and Differences* (2002), *Access to Social Rights for People with Disabilities in Europe* (2003), *Legislation to Counter Discrimination against Persons with Disabilities* (2003), *Discrimination against Women with Disabilities* (2003), *Safeguarding Adults and Children with Disabilities against Abuse* (2003).

More recently, the European Union (EU) has become heavily engaged in the disability rights debate from the perspective of non-discrimination law and policy. The increasing engagement of the EU on the subject reflects the more general turn of the EU towards human rights especially throughout the 1990s. Disability was an early beneficiary of the drive to create a 'People's Europe'.[2] The advent of Article 13 in the Treaty of Amsterdam was a pivotal moment. For the first time ever, disability was specifically mentioned in the treaties establishing and animating the Union. This carried huge symbolic importance. More concretely, it led to the Framework Employment Directive combating discrimination, *inter alia*, on the ground of disability in the employment context.[3]

It is true that the EU tends to have mixed motives in advancing the equality and non-discrimination agenda. On the one hand, it tends to view equality as a productive factor in any rational market-driven economy—as something that makes for more rational market behaviour and which therefore helps to underpin and not undermine the wealth creating capacity of the European common market space. While one may decry a purely economic rationale to equality it does have its uses. And it happens to be particularly powerful in the disability context since most market decisions by employers in the past have been driven less by a rational appraisal of the true merits of individuals and more by prejudice against disability. On the other hand, the EU also sees the equality/non-discrimination agenda as a civilizing factor that helps to elevate the quality of democratic life more generally and is therefore worth pursuing for itself.[4] At times it is difficult to identify which of these two rationales—advancing economic rationality or securing human rights— has the upper hand in EU policy. While they can sometimes conflict they have indisputably propelled the EU to the vanguard of the disability debate in Europe.

This chapter starts with a deceptively simple question: what does the non-discrimination ideal as exemplified in EU law (which has its true provenance in civil rights) have to offer a social rights perspective on disability and, conversely, what does a social rights perspective on disability as exemplified in the European Social Charter have to offer the civil rights approach? An exploration of this question goes to the limits of the non-discrimination ideal unless it can attach itself to—and help to animate—the material basis for human freedom. And indeed, such an exploration serves to underscore the reality that social programmes alone will not do unless tied to an agenda that moves beyond maintaining people and towards positioning them to enter and remain in society.

One conceptually important and hitherto unexplored bridge between civil rights generally and EU anti-discrimination law in particular with social rights (and specifically the European Social Charter) resides in the concept of equality.

---

[2] For the historical background to the EU's involvement on the disability issue see G. Quinn, 'The Human Rights of People with Disabilities under EU Law', in P. Alston et al. (eds), *The EU and Human Rights* (1999) 281.   [3] Council Directive 2000/78, OJ 2000 L306/16.

[4] See generally M. Bell, *Anti-Discrimination Law and the European Union* (2002).

At a deep level the European Convention on Human Rights (ECHR) is not merely about the intrinsic worth of each human being and their dignity; it is also about their equal inherent self-worth. Obviously, Article 14 of the ECHR plays a pivotal role in keeping space open for vulnerable groups by regulating and limiting the kinds of choices Governments make. This concern to regulate and limit Governmental choice is tied to a deeper and broader European vision of democratic society. The drafters of the ECHR were very much alive to the reality that the slide toward totalitarianism usually begins with discrimination against unpopular groups or causes.[5] If left unchecked such an impulse toward exclusion and discrimination leads to a closure of political and civil space and ultimately to the implosion of the political order.

Important though it is, the ECHR does not exhaust the Council of Europe's weaponry against the impulse toward exclusion and discrimination. A consistent commitment to human autonomy and freedom requires some degree of social solidarity in order to make the allure of freedom real for those who require assistance. Any political order that is blind to material need is blind to the political economy of freedom itself. This is the key to the much vaunted—but little understood—thesis of the interdependence and indivisibility of both sets of rights. This brand of equality—or egalitarianism—leads to the identification of several human needs and categorizes them as human rights. So, some notion of equality is deeply embedded in all socio-economic rights.

While the equality ideal is obviously emblazoned on civil and political rights it is less visibly so in the socio-economic rights sphere. One recurring problem in the socio-economic rights sphere, however, is that once the right in question is identified and its ingredients delineated (for example, right to housing) one is apt to leave to one side its wellspring in equality. Thus, the right in question tends to become fossilized and detached from its underlying or animating principles. Parenthetically, this is why it is so important for treaty monitoring bodies in the socio-economic rights field periodically to refer the various substantive rights back to notions of dignity and equality. Otherwise the rights tend to become ends in themselves rather than the means to the higher end of human freedom and choice. In other words, the socio-economic rights could end up placing individuals in a cage rather than on a pedestal. This is not merely an academic point. It would appear especially true in the context of disability where social programmes have sometimes seemed as much designed to purchase or 'compensate' for the absence of the 'other' rather than to respect difference and create space for difference in the mainstream.

There is another reason why treaty monitoring bodies in the socio-economic rights field should be conscious of the equality ideal. Most governments have a vast web of redistributive social programmes in place covering a wide range of

---

[5] See, for example, the contribution of Mr Ungoed-Thomas in the debates leading up to the adoption of the ECHR: 'Have these freedoms, give effect to these freedoms and you will ensure that each state remains democratic', Vol. II, *travaux preparatoires*.

contingencies and most groups. However, and international legal norms notwithstanding, most of these programmes respond to politics and not to law (whether domestic or international). Such democratic responsiveness is, on balance, a good thing. Rights, ideally, should inform the democratic process and not supplant it. However, a corrective is sometimes needed since 'normal' politics can predictably fail to deliver for certain groups who lack political clout or impact (so-called 'discrete and insular minorities')—or worse still, they may be deliberately targeted or ignored. Invoking the substantive rights on their own may not be enough to reach issues of equity between groups—some notion of equality is also needed. This appears to hold especially true in the context of disability where there has never been a close relationship between the numbers affected (estimated at 10 per cent of any given population) and their access to power.

Indeed, treaty monitoring bodies in the socio-economic rights sphere should also be aware that governments may be tempted to sideline certain disfavoured or unpopular groups by setting their level of social entitlements (or the conditions of eligibility) in such a way as to effectively exclude or segregate them. The pernicious doctrine of 'separate but equal' has long been rejected in the civil and political rights sphere. Yet treaty monitoring bodies have to be aware that governments may try to achieve indirectly through social policy what they are explicitly forbidden to achieve directly.[6] This is an added reason why the equality/non-discrimination ideal is so important in the socio-economic rights sphere. While there is no doubt that the weight of social support for persons with disabilities in the past served a useful and indispensable function there is equally little doubt that much of it came at the cost of compounding their isolation and reducing their range of choice. The legacy of segregation still exists in the disability context across Europe. It will take some time to dissipate and the equality/non-discrimination norms would appear to be one of the strongest weapons available to combat it.

How then stands the equality/non-discrimination ideal across the normative architecture of Europe? At the moment the Framework Employment Directive is of limited use in the disability context since its material scope is confined to employment. More accurately put, its undoubted positive symbolic and practical value in the employment context will be hugely accentuated once a series of flanking measures are adopted in fields such as education, which will ensure that persons with disabilities have the marketable skills necessary to make themselves attractive to prospective employers. Anti-discrimination law generally applies a rust solvent to doors that have remained shut for too long. Such legislation does not, in itself, enable people to pass through those doors. Unfortunately, we may have to wait for some years before additional measures are adopted, if only to give time to test the efficacy of the Framework Employment Directive in the courts.

---

[6] This is known as the doctrine of unconstitutional conditions under US Constitutional law: see Sullivan, 'Unconstitutional Conditions', 102 *Harvard Law Review* (1989) 1415 ('[this doctrine] reflects the triumph of the view that government may not do indirectly what it may not do directly over the view that the greater power to deny a benefit includes the lesser power to impose a condition on its receipt').

Likewise, Article 14 of the ECHR is of limited use since it only attaches to the material scope of the various rights protected under the Convention itself.[7] Protocol 12 to the European Convention on Human Rights—which will significantly expand the material scope of the relevant non-discrimination provision—is not yet in force. And nobody knows how the European Court of Human Rights will deal with it once it is in force. It is probably fair to say they may well adopt a cautious approach at least for the first few years of its life.

However, the non-discrimination norm in the European Social Charter (both in the 1961 Charter and more particularly in the 1996 Revised version) already applies across a very broad range of fields of relevance to the lives of persons with disabilities such as education, housing, mobility, social security, employment, etc. So there already exists a non-discrimination norm at European level with a broad scope of material application. It is remarkable how infrequently it is referred to. Perhaps it reflects the relative invisibility of the European Social Charter. Hopefully the veil of invisibility that has so indecently concealed the positive thrust of the Charter (especially in recent years) is now being removed. Perhaps it reflects an implicit judgment about the relative weight of the Social Charter and its case law before the European Court of Justice. That too should change since instruments like the Framework Employment Directive allow for an opportunity of a deliberative dialogue between bodies concerned with cognate issues. Or perhaps it follows on from the relatively 'weak' enforcement machinery of the Charter relying as it does on a Governmental Committee and the Committee of Ministers at the political level. Yet it would be a mistake to telescope the value of the Charter into an analysis of the outcomes it could legally drive. The primary value of the Charter, I suggest, does not reside in the 'enforceability' or otherwise of its Conclusions with respect to State Reports or on its Decisions on Collective Complaints. Rather its value resides in how effectively it can become an expositor of social values—values that supposedly lie at the heart of social Europe.

An examination of the case law of the European Committee of Social Rights could therefore prove helpful in understanding the role of the equality norm in the socio-economic sphere with respect to disability and may be influential in helping to frame how the relevant issues will arise for consideration before the European Court of Justice.

Ultimately this chapter goes to the synergy that ought to evolve between the EU and the Council of Europe—bodies that I previously described as 'twins separated at birth'.[8] Disability is a good test of the current and future fit between these two different organizations and the values they espouse.

---

[7] These limitations to Article 14 are familiar and may be exaggerated. See e.g. R. Wintemute, 'Within the Ambit: How Big is the Gap in Article 14 European Convention on Human Rights?', *EHRLR* (2004) 366.

[8] G. Quinn, 'The European Union and the Council of Europe on the Issue of Human Rights: Twins Separated at Birth?', 46 *McGill Law Journal* (2001) 845.

II. THE EUROPEAN SOCIAL CHARTER—REFRESHING SOCIAL RIGHTS THROUGH EQUALITY

The Council of Europe has been involved in the disability field almost since its inception. This should be no surprise given the sheer numbers of war wounded at the close of hostilities in 1945. Nor should it be any surprise that the focus of the Council's early activities was on rehabilitation.

The baseline document setting out the Council of Europe's policy in the disability field is Recommendation R (92) of 1992: 6 *A Coherent Policy for the Rehabilitation of People with Disabilities*, which was adopted following a first Ministerial Conference on disability in Paris in 1991. Despite its title, much of this recommendation focuses on the equalization of opportunities for persons with disabilities. It predated and complements an analogous United Nations General Assembly Resolution by one year: the *United Nations Standard Rules of the Equalisation of Opportunities for Persons with Disabilities* (1993).[9] A second Council of Europe Ministerial Conference on disability was held in Malaga in 2003 and produced the Malaga Political Declaration[10] which declares in part that: 'Our main aim in the next decade is to improve the quality of life of people with disabilities and their families, putting the emphasis on their integration and full participation in society, since a participative and accessible society is of benefit to the whole population'.[11] Significantly, the Declaration went on to provide a (political) 'undertaking' on the part of the Ministers gathered to: 'work within anti-discriminatory and human rights frameworks towards mainstreaming equality of opportunity for people with disabilities throughout all policy areas'.[12] This political steer is important since it shows how much European thinking in disability has changed away from welfare and towards equal effective human rights. It also shows the emphasis placed on non-discrimination as a key tool in advancing the human rights agenda.

A Ten Year Action Plan is currently being drawn up in the Council of Europe on the basis of the Malaga Political Declaration. Among other things, it should lead to an updated version of Recommendation R (92) 6.

Curiously, although there was—and still is—a wealth of intergovernmental activities on disability, there was very little of significance taking place within the Council's human rights machinery.[13] Only recently has the European Court of

---

[9] GA Res. 48/96, 20 December 1993. See generally T. Degener and Y. Koster-Dreese, *Human Rights and Disabled Persons: Essays and Relevant Human Rights Instruments* (1995).

[10] Political Declaration of the Second Ministerial Conference of Ministers Responsible for Integration Policies for People with Disabilities, 7–8 May 2004, Malaga, Spain: available at http://www.coe.int/T/E/Social_Cohesion/soc-sp/Integration/03_Ministerial_Conferences/ 2nd_Conference_Malaga_2003/TopOfPage.   [11] Ibid., at para. 17.

[12] Ibid., at para. 30.

[13] Much of these activities take place within a Partial Agreement Structure: website available at http://www.coe.int/T/E/Social_Cohesion/soc-sp/Integration.

Human Rights become involved—with mixed results and still much untapped potential.[14] A variety of human rights instruments appear to have been somewhat underused in the disability context although there are recent signs that the Convention for the Prevention of Torture is being used much more systematically, for example, to target abuses within mental institutions.[15]

My focus, however, is the case law of the European Committee of Social Rights. All substantive articles of the Revised Charter (social security, education, etc.) have some application to persons with disabilities. Yet the Revised Charter has also carried forward from its 1961 predecessor with a revised and expanded Article 15 that looks more particularly to the rights of persons with disabilities without prejudice to the application of the rest of the instrument.

A. Article 15 of the European Social Charter of 1961—Rehabilitation with a Nod Towards Equality

The original European Social Charter of 1961 lacked an explicit prohibition against discrimination.[16] However, the Preamble contained a reference to the non-discrimination principle which has been used by the European Committee of Social Rights from time to time to inform its analysis.[17]

With respect to disability the 1961 Charter was a creature of its times and reflected the then prevalent rehabilitation philosophy. Article 15 of the 1961 Charter reads:

Article 15—The right of physically or mentally disabled persons to vocational training, rehabilitation and social resettlement.

With a view to ensuring the effective exercise of the right of the physical or mentally disabled to vocational training, rehabilitation and resettlement, the Contracting Parties undertake:

1. to take adequate measures for the provision of training facilities, including, where necessary, specialised institutions, public or private;

2. to take adequate measures for the placing of disabled persons in employment, such as specialised placing services, facilities for sheltered employment and measures to encourage employers to admit disabled persons to employment.

---

[14] For a good overview of the Court's case law see generally, L. Clements and J. Read, *Disabled People and Human Rights: A Review of the 1998 Human Rights Act for Children and Adults with Disabilities in the UK* (2003).

[15] For a review of these instruments see G. Quinn, and T. Degener, 'Survey of International, Comparative and Regional Disability Law Reform', in M. L. Breslin and S. Yee (eds), *Disability Rights Law and Policy: International and National Perspectives* (2002) 3, at 57–91.

[16] See generally, D. Harris and J. Darcy, *The European Social Charter* (2001) and L. Samuel, *Fundamental Social Rights: Case Law of the European Social Charter* (2002).

[17] The relevant part of the Preamble reads: 'Considering that the enjoyment of social rights should be secured without discrimination on grounds of race, colour, sex, religion, political opinion, national extraction or social origin'.

Notice that the very title of the Article uses the phrase 'disabled person'. Although certainly open to debate, that term is used infrequently nowadays in order to emphasize that a person's individuality and humanity comes before their disability. That is, the modern view is that the physical or mental impairment only becomes a disability because society fails to respect the difference posed by the impairment. The question of the definition of disability is one that the Committee has raised on many occasions (see below). Its main concern is to ensure that the definition used does not stigmatize the person and places a consistent focus where it should be—on how the person is treated by third parties.

In terms of its material scope, Article 15(1) focuses mainly on vocational training and rehabilitation. It is fairly clear that its primary beneficiaries were originally envisaged as the war wounded or victims of industrial accidents. Article 15(2) seems to assume the normalcy of separate facilities instead of placing them clearly on the defensive. Extrapolating further, its underlying ethic was perhaps more one of 'fixing the person' rather than social integration. To a certain extent it might be said that it accepted the philosophy of 'separate but equal' for persons with disabilities.

To be fair, however, the European Committee of Social Rights had always adopted a much broader vision of Article 15 of the 1961 Charter and even went so far as to conclude negatively in the past against Ireland and Norway for insufficient results under Article 15(1)[18] The Committee also concluded negatively in the past against the United Kingdom on the basis of different treatment towards non-nationals with disabilities.[19] It also concluded negatively against Italy on the basis of the large number of persons with disabilities seeking employment.[20]

More recently, the European Committee of Social Rights has begun to reinvigorate Article 15 of the 1961 Charter with the newer rights-based approach to disability. In the process, it has reawakened the link between the non-discrimination ideal and the substantive rights of the Charter. In doing so it is only catching up with the rest of the Council of Europe machinery and especially with the trans-European values expressed in Recommendation R (92) 6.

Normally (but not invariably) when its case law (or interpretive approach) changes the Committee does not immediately conclude negatively against a Contracting Party where its laws or practices are deemed to fall short of the required benchmarks. Instead, it sets out its new normative understandings of the relevant provisions and then poses a number of pointed questions to the Contracting Parties. The responses to those questions then place the Committee in a better position to evaluate conformity with the new benchmarks announced in successive cycles of supervision.

The questions put under Article 15 of the 1961 Charter from 2003 onwards reveal a decisive change of direction. Take the Committee's *Conclusions XVI–2* for 2003

---

18 *Conclusions I*, at 208 (Ireland) and at 73 (Norway).
19 *Conclusions VII*, at 84 (United Kingdom).   20 *Conclusions XIII–2*, at 222 (Italy).

and Denmark, for example. In those Conclusions the Committee asked: 'what steps, if any, have been made or are planned to move away from a medical definition of disability toward a more social definition such as that endorsed by the WHO in its International Classification of Functioning (ICF: 2001)'.[21] This is important since the Committee is letting it be known that it favours a definition that places an emphasis on how people are treated rather than on their medical condition as such. This 'de-medicalisation' of the definition of disability is widely seen as a bridge to a human rights understanding of disability.

The Committee then stressed that Article 15(1) favours integration into ordinary (that is, mainstreamed) training arrangements and asked Denmark for relevant information on vocational training. It stated: 'The Committee wishes to receive updated information on the measures in place to encourage the integration of adults with disabilities into mainstream training'.[22] With respect to Austria in the same set of Conclusions the Committee interpreted 'vocational training' to sweep in the general system of education on a theory that it is impossible to hermetically seal vocational training from the general education system since there are many points of intersection between the two. It then specifically asked Austria: 'How many students with disabilities are attending mainstream secondary and vocational schools and how many still attend separate special schools?' It further asked . . . 'whether resources follow the child and whether parents are informed of this when deciding whether to opt for special or integrated education'.[23] On the question of the application of equality or non-discrimination rules in an educational context the Committee stated that it wished to receive from Austria: 'Information on how equal access and equal treatment is guaranteed in education and vocational training '. . . and whether the relevant Constitutional provision may be litigated by individuals'.[24] In the 2003 set of Conclusions the Committee did not go so far as to require non-discrimination legislation in the education field since 'education' as such is not explicitly mentioned in Article 15 of the 1961 Charter. However, it does require such legislation under Article 15 of the Revised Charter, the text of which does explicitly cover education (see below).

With respect to Article 15(2) (employment) of the 1961 Charter the Committee concluded negatively against Denmark in 2003 on the basis that it did not yet have in place legislation combating discrimination on the ground of disability in the employment sphere.[25] In other words, the Committee views non-discrimination legislation as essential to comply with Article 15(2) of the 1961 Charter. While it did not take the opportunity to elaborate on the minimum content of such legislation, it is very clear that it had in mind the obligation of 'reasonable accommodation' which is a hallmark of comparative disability discrimination legislation throughout the world and which is also one of the key features of the Framework Employment Directive.

---

[21] *Conclusions XVI–2*, Vol. 1 (2003), at 224.   [22] Ibid., at 245.   [23] Ibid., at 52.
[24] Ibid.   [25] Ibid., at 229.

The Committee also concluded negatively against Denmark in 2003 with respect to Article 15(2) of the 1961 Charter because the working terms and conditions of those employed in sheltered workshops were quite different to those of persons working in the open labour market. There the Committee: '. . . notes that the right to fair remuneration and just conditions of employment apply to all workers including workers with disabilities whether they are employed in sheltered facilities or in the open labour market'.[26] This is important since civil society as well as states tend to accept too readily the principle of 'separate but equal' when it comes to sheltered employment. Furthermore, the Committee asked Denmark to inform it of the extent to which trade unions are active in sheltered employment and what percentage of the workforce in such enterprises belong to unions. The Contracting Parties cannot, as such, be held responsible if trade unions decline to operate in the sheltered employment context. Yet their presence in the field is a good barometer of the extent to which such employment is generally treated as part of the general scheme of employment.

Essentially, from the 2003 Conclusions onwards, the Committee is setting its face firmly against the notion of 'separate but equal' under Article 15 of the 1961 Charter. In other words, the Committee has begun to interpret Article 15 of the 1961 Charter in a manner consistent with the principles of equality and non-discrimination so as to ensure that the substantive rights in question create genuine opportunities in the mainstream of life. This process of revitalization was only likely to continue and intensify under Article 15 of the Revised Charter. And it has.

B. *Article 15 in the Revised European Social Charter of 1996—Equality with a Nod to Rehabilitation*

It will be recalled that the Revised Charter—unlike the 1961 Charter—now contains an explicit provision prohibiting discrimination: Article E. It reads: 'The enjoyment of the rights set forth in this Charter shall be secured without discrimination on any ground such as race, colour, sex, language, religion political or other opinion, national extraction or social origin, health, association with a national minority, birth or other status.'

The Appendix of the Revised Charter (which is stated to form an 'integral part' of the text) further provides that 'a differential treatment based on an objective and reasonable justification shall not be deemed to be discriminatory'. To date, this portion of the Appendix has not received much scrutiny by the Committee.

One threshold issue was whether, or how, Article E would interact with the various substantive rights. That Article E had a role to play in the interpretation of the substantive rights was definitively answered in the affirmative in the Committee's Decision in Collective Complaint 13 (see below). That it should

---

[26] Ibid., at 229.

have been doubted was more curious. Paradoxically, it did not help that the prohibition was placed in a non-numbered paragraph. Presumably the intention was to underscore its transversal character. Yet its very physical separateness from the body of the text could easily have been used as an argument to marginalize it. One benefit of having it placed in the body of the text would have been that states would have to report on their overall non-discrimination legislation as it touched on social rights.

With respect to the substantive rights themselves, the process of revitalizing the Charter had pronounced and positive effects in the context of Article 15. The purpose of the various amendments and additions was stated by the relevant drafting committee to be for the purpose of the: '. . . extension of the scope of the rights in the Charter in order to cover as much as possible in the measures proposed in [Recommendation R (92) 6]'.[27] This is important for it clearly links the amended and expanded Article 15 of the Revised Charter in the minds of the framers with the overall orientation and philosophy of Recommendation R (92) 6. It is therefore clear that Recommendation R (92) 6 constitutes a valuable reference tool for the interpretation of Article 15.

Article 15 in the Revised Charter now reads:

Article 15—the right of persons with disabilities to independence, social integration and participation in the life of the community.

With a view to ensuring to persons with disabilities, irrespective of age and the nature and origin of their disabilities, the effective exercise of the right to independence, social integration and participation in the life of the community, the Parties undertake, in particular:

1. to take the necessary measures to provide persons with disabilities with guidance, education and vocational training in the framework of general schemes wherever possible or, where this is not possible, through specialised bodies, public or private;

2. to promote their access to employment through all measures tending to encourage employers to hire and keep in employment person with disabilities in the ordinary working environment and to adjust the working conditions to the needs of the disabled or, where this is not possible by reason of the disability, by arranging for or creating sheltered employment according to the level of disability. In certain cases, such measures may require recourse to specialised placement and support services;

3. to promote their full social integration and participation in the life of the community in particular through measures, including technical aids, aiming to overcome barriers to communication and mobility and enabling access to transport, housing, cultural activities and leisure.

The contrast between the bald text of the new Article 15 with its 1961 predecessor is sharp. It can be seen even in the title of the new Article which refers to 'independence, social integration and participation in the life of the community'. So from

[27] Committee on the European Social Charter (Charte-Rel), Final activity report, CHARTE/REL (94), 19 October 1994, at 43.

the very beginning the ethos of the new Article 15 is startlingly different and much more consonant with Recommendation R (92) 6.

Paragraph 1 to Article 15 now explicitly refers to 'education' and would appear to place separate or segregated facilities much more clearly on the defensive. This is not to say that such facilities may not be required. But it is to say that there is heavy onus on the Contracting Parties to prove their necessity. Paragraph 2 seems more directed toward employment in the open labour market and similarly seems to place separate facilities on the defensive. Paragraph 3 is wholly new and deals with the web of programmatic or positive action measures needed to break down barriers and make participation in the mainstream more possible. It resonates to a very high degree with Recommendation R (92) 6.

The new Article 15 has already been extensively interpreted by the Committee. In its General Introduction to the 2003 Conclusions under the Revised Charter the Committee stated that it: '. . . considers that this provision reflects and advances the change in disability policy that has occurred over the last decade or more away from welfare and segregation and towards inclusion and choice. In light of this the Committee emphasises the importance of the non-discrimination norm in the disability context and finds that this forms an integral part of Article 15 of the Revised Charter. It is fortified in its views on Article 15 with reference to Article E on non-discrimination'.[28] In a way the Committee genuflected before the intentions of the framers and began to view the new Article 15 in a much broader light. And, significantly, it tied its understanding of the requirements of Article 15 to Article E on non-discrimination.

Take the Committee's Conclusions with respect to France in 2003 under the Revised Charter as an illustrative example. With respect to Article 15(1) the Committee stated that the explicit reference to 'education' 'brings important aspects of the right to education for children with disabilities within the remit of that sub-paragraph'.[29] It went on to say:

Already under Article 15.1 of the 1961 Charter, the Committee had assessed general education schemes to test them for their level of inclusiveness and had held that States were required to make tangible progress towards the development of inclusive educational systems.

In so far as Article 15.1 of the Revised Charter explicitly mentions 'education' the Committee considers necessary the existence of non-discrimination legislation as an important tool for the advancement of the inclusion of children with disabilities into general or mainstream educational systems and confer an effective remedy on those who are found to have been unlawfully excluded or segregated or otherwise denied an effective right to education.[30]

It will be remembered that the Committee stopped short of requiring such legislation under Article 15 in the 1961 Charter but now felt no compunction, since the word

---

[28] European Social Charter (Revised), Conclusions 2003, Vol. 1, at 10.
[29] Ibid., France, at 158.   [30] Ibid., France, at 158.

'education' is explicitly mentioned under Article 15(1) of the Revised Charter. More particular questions were then posed to France (and to other Contracting Parties) along the following lines:

With respect to the modalities of the right to an equal effective education in the mainstream the Committee wishes to receive information on the following issues:

(1) whether and how the normal curriculum is adjusted to take account of disability, (2) whether and how individualised educational plans are crafted for students with disabilities, (3) whether and how resources follow the child (including support staff and other technical assistance) to enable such plans to be implemented, (4) whether and how testing or examining modalities are adjusted to take account of disability and whether the fact that examinations are taken under non-standard conditions is revealed to third parties who, the Committee feels, have no right to such information, (5) whether the qualifications that eventuate are the same for all children or whether different qualifications ensue. If so, are these qualifications officially recognised or validated and do they have the same functional value to the individual as the mainstream qualification? In order to evaluate this the Committee is interested to learn what the relative progression rates are for such children into employment or further education.

This line of questioning effectively and succinctly expresses the equality agenda in the disability context. It is clear therefore that some notion of equality and non-discrimination animates the Committee's thinking with respect to the revised Article 15.

The Committee went on to pose particular questions in the context of special education in order to elicit information regarding progression rates onto mainstream employment or further education or vocational training. Note here the emphasis placed on the dialectic between mainstream and separate provision with a default setting that favours mainstreaming. The Committee asked whether general teacher training incorporates special needs education as an integral component. This is quite important. If teacher training programmes merely bolt extra modules on special needs education some years after primary training, then the subliminal message sent to novices is not to expect difference in the classroom and, if it occurs, to view it (and the children) as a problem. However, if they are required to take such special needs training as an integral part of their basic training from the outset, then they should be better placed to accept the presence of disabled children as 'normal' and better equipped to adjust their teaching practices.

Furthermore, and pointedly, the Committee stated its view that anti-discrimination legislation was required under Article 15(1). It stated: 'The Committee recalls that the legal situation of persons with disabilities calls for comprehensive anti-discrimination legislation, in particular in the field of education and training, providing for effective remedies'.[31] It went on to seek more information from France about its relevant legislation. In the future, one can expect the Committee

---

[31] Ibid., France, at 163.

to develop a coherent theory as to what such legislation ideally ought to contain. But it is fair to assume from the content of the above list of questions to France that the Committee would look for provisions in the legislation that would enable a Contracting Party reasonably to accommodate or adjust their systems in order to respect the difference of disability.

With respect to Article 15(2) of the Revised Charter (employment), and with respect to its 2003 Conclusions on France, the Committee recalled that non-discrimination legislation had previously been called for under Article 15(2) of the 1961 Charter and '*a fortiori*, this reasoning also applies to Article 15(2) of the Revised Social Charter'.[32] It then posed a number of detailed questions to France about its relevant anti-discrimination legislation. Importantly, it asked France to provide further information on how the 'concept of reasonable accommodation is incorporated in the legislation'.[33] To put the matter another way, it sees the obligation as a key requirement in any such anti-discrimination legislation. More broadly, the Committee posed a detailed set of questions designed essentially to elicit information about the degree to which French employment practices are orientated toward the mainstream or the open labour market.

With respect to Article 15(3)—which is wholly new to the Revised Charter— the Committee set out its understanding of its basic requirements in its 2003 Conclusions. Again with respect to France (as well as other Contracting Parties) the Committee stated:

Article 15.3. describes the positive action to be implemented in order to achieve the goals of social integration and participation of disabled persons. It focuses on the positive action measures needed to achieve these goals in fields such as housing, transport, telecommunications, cultural and leisure facilities. Such measures must not be pursued in isolation and should be programmed to complement each other, on a clear legislative basis.[34]

So the mere existence of such measures is not enough. They must be programmed to be complementary and they must possess a clear legislative base. Often such measures are in conflict with one another which can place individuals in very difficult positions. For example, to gain disability benefit many claimants will have to show 'inability to work'. And yet the obligation of 'reasonable accommodation' under anti-discrimination legislation may be the difference to enabling them to work. Eligibility for the former should not be allowed to determine automatically the applicability of the latter. And often such measures lack a clear legislative base, which makes it much more difficult for individuals to know their rights, to predict official behaviour, and to challenge particular actions.

The Committee went on to state that Article 15(3) requires that: 'persons with disabilities and their representative organisations should be consulted in the design and ongoing review of such positive action measures and that an appropriate forum should exist to enable this to happen'.[35] This is critically important

---

[32] Ibid., France, at 163.   [33] Ibid., France, at 164.
[34] Ibid., France, at 168.   [35] Ibid., France, at 168.

since many such measures are sometimes taken in 'the best interests' of persons with disabilities and yet in complete ignorance of their expressed wishes.

Significantly, and with respect to the non-discrimination principle, the Committee went on to state: 'Article 15.3. requires the existence of non-discrimination (or similar) legislation covering both the public and the private sphere in . . . fields such as housing, transport, telecommunications, cultural and leisure activities as well as effective remedies for those who have been unlawfully treated'.[36] This is an interesting innovation. In a sense, the Committee is looking for ways to subjectivize some of the entitlements provided by way of traditional positive action measures. Generally such measures are crafted in general terms with proxies for individual need in mind. If fossilized through time (which is a natural tendency in any programme delivery system) they may become very detached from what individuals actually need. As a corrective or reality-check to this natural tendency the Committee is interested to explore ways of enabling individuals to challenge how such measures are designed and delivered. Non-discrimination legislation may be one way of doing it. But space is left open by the Committee for 'similar legislation' having the equivalent effect. There is clear resonance between this insistence of the Committee on complementarity, clarity, and legality with respect to service provision and the Malaga Political Declaration, which states that the Ministers undertake (politically): 'To promote the provision of quality services, responding to the needs of individuals with disabilities which are accessed via published eligibility criteria, based on thorough and equitable assessment, shaped by the disabled person's own choices, autonomy, welfare and representation, with proper safeguards, regulation and access to independent adjudication of complaints . . .'.[37] It will be recalled in this regard that General Comment 9 adopted by the UN Committee on Economic, Social and Cultural Rights on 'the domestic application of the covenant' in 1998 emphasized that where administrative remedies are used they must be 'accessible, affordable, timely and effective'.[38]

C. *Collective Complaint 13*—Autisme-Europe v. France *(1994)*

Although not widely known, there are at least eight European-level disability NGOs listed as entitled to bring Collective Complaints before the Committee. They include major players such as the European Disability Forum, the European Blind Union, Disabled Persons International, and Mental Health Europe.[39]

Only one Collective Complaint has been brought by disability groups so far, which was decided by the Committee in 2003: *Autisme-Europe v. France*. The

---

[36] Ibid., France, at 170.   [37] Malaga Political Declaration, at para. 34.
[38] E/C.12/1998/24, CESCR, 3 December 1998, at para. 9.
[39] The full list of NGOs entitled to maintain such Complaints is set out in the website of the Social Charter: http://www.coe.int/T/E/Human_Rights/Esc.

Complaint was declared admissible by the Committee on 12 December 2002 and the Committee's Decision on the Merits was reached in November 2003.[40] A public hearing on the Complaint took place in September 2003 in Strasbourg.

The essence of the allegations of the complaint was, as set out in the Committee's Decision on Admissibility, that France had not satisfactorily implemented Articles 15 and 17 of Part II and Article E of Part V of the Revised Charter due to the low rates of integration or targeted provision for the educational rights of children and adults with autism. Article 17, in the relevant part, reads:

17. The Rights of children and young persons to social, legal and economic protection

With a view to ensuring the effective exercise of the right of children and young persons to grow up in an environment which encourages the full development of their personality and their physical and mental capacities, the parties undertake, either directly or in co-operation with public and private organisations, to take all appropriate and necessary measures designed:

1.a. to ensure that children and young persons, taking account of the rights and duties of their parents, have the care, the assistance, the education and the training they need, in particular by providing for the *establishment or maintenance of institutions and services sufficient and adequate for this purpose.*[41]

In its Decision on Admissibility the Committee summed up the Complaint as follows:

With regard to Article 15 and 17, whether taken together or in conjunction with Article E, Autisme-Europe alleges that, although France has enacted positive law that seems, *de jure*, to accord fully with the requirements of the Charter, it has nevertheless failed to secure the effective, *de facto*, and non-discriminatory enjoyment of the rights in question, due, primarily, to inadequate and separate budgetary provisions.

With regard to Article E (Part V), Autisme-Europe alleges that France is infringing the principle of non-discrimination laid down in Article E in that autistic people are not enjoying the right to education recognised in Article 17 of Part II. This follows from the fact that autistic people do not benefit from educational institutions or services, in the ordinary system or under special supervision, of an adequate standard and in sufficient number.[42]

Under French law, children with disabilities can be mainstreamed into ordinary classrooms (so-called 'individual mainstreaming') with the financial support of the general education budget (which is a privileged budget within the French system). Or they may be mainstreamed into ordinary classes with the support of extra auxiliary staff or as part of a group (so-called 'collective mainstreaming'). Financial assistance for this latter form of integration comes from the sickness insurance fund and, in the case of autism, through special appropriations

---

40 Both Decisions are available on the Social Charter website.   41 Emphasis added.
42 Complaint No. 13/2002, Decision on the Merits, December 2002, paras. 3–4.

within the fund targeting their needs (even though they may not be sick as such). If mainstreaming is not possible, then a series of specialized institutions are provided for and the salaries of teaching staff in these institutions are paid through the general education budget.

At the September 2003 hearing Autisme-Europe did not pursue the argument that French law as such violated the Revised Charter. It argued instead that the implementation of the law or the *de facto* situation violated the Revised Charter: 'More specifically, the complainant . . . argued that, in practice, insufficient provision is made for the education of children and adults with autism due to identifiable shortfalls—both quantitative and qualitative—in the provision of both mainstream education as well as in the so-called special education sector'.[43] Much of the argument of Autisme-Europe revolved around statistics which were debated vigorously by both sides. Five interrelated sets of arguments were pursued: (1) that special education institutions and services were not available in the numbers required; (2) that the separate budgetary arrangements for such education rendered it nearly impossible to make adequate provision; (3) that early intervention measures were inadequate; (4) that insufficient progress had been made in the direction of mainstreaming; and (5) that administrative unwieldiness and lack of appropriate teacher training inhibited the achievement of the legislative goals.

As to the allegation that there simply were not enough supported places in specially tailored institutions, the complainant argued that only a minority of children or adults with autism had adequate educational provision and that various catch-up plans were unlikely to reach the majority of such persons for the foreseeable future. The Committee summed up the argument as follows: 'According to the complainant, on average 300 places have been created annually since 1995, which represents an annual increasing rate of 0.7% in comparison with the official needs. At this pace, it will take one hundred years to absorb the deficit of places and this without taking account of the natural increase of the autistic population, which, on the basis of the official figures, it estimates will grow by 160 persons per year'.[44] In reply the Government acknowledged that the catch-up plan of 1995–2000 had fallen short of real needs but nevertheless insisted that their current efforts were adequate to comply with the requirements of the Charter.

As to the argument concerning the impact of separate budgetary provision, the complainant argued: '. . . because of the budget mechanism chosen, persons with disabilities do not in practice (despite the legislation) benefit from the right to education because they cannot do so for as long as the funding of special education placements remains outside the national education system and is treated as "social assistance" or "care" to which health or social-action expenditure limits apply'.[45] As far as persons with autism are concerned, the complainant specifically argued that, unless France alters its budgetary and financial policy, the shortfall on

---

[43] Ibid., at para. 16.   [44] Ibid., at para. 22.   [45] Ibid., at para. 28.

educational provision for autistic persons will never be made up and the qualitative needs will never be met. The Government contested the inferences drawn by the complainant as to the impact of financing mainstreaming and special education through the sickness insurance fund.

As to the alleged inadequacy of early intervention—which is particularly important in the case of autistic children—the complainant argued that such provision is virtually non-existent and that the figures provided by the Government were not sufficiently disaggregated between early intervention offered to all disabled children and early intervention offered to autistic children.

As to the allegation concerning mainstreaming, the complaint argued that the process had been too slow. The Committee stated:

According to [a report of the French Senate] ... only 7% of children with disabilities ... are integrated into ordinary schools. According to the Ministry of Education, mainstreamed disabled children and young people amount to 1.3% of the total school population in each department, while the Court of Auditors rates their integration to less than 1%. At the hearing, the complainant asserted that out of 6,000 children with autism who could be mainstreamed only 250 are individually integrated, that is about 5%. Another 400 are collectively integrated [special classes in mainstream schools], making a total of 650 on a total school population of 15 million children, teenagers and students.[46]

The Government contested the various statistical arguments and affirmed that mainstreaming is a legislative priority in France. The complainant also argued: 'That there are no binding rules requiring the teaching staff of specialised educational facilities to be specifically trained to cater for autistic persons and that the training of staff is in fact non-existent. This appears to be confirmed by official sources'.[47] The Government responded by pointing to a series of initiatives that are and can be expected to adequately provide for special training needs.

The Decision of the Committee on the merits is interesting at two levels. At one level it provides an adequate basis for its decision in the instant case as one might expect. At another more transcendent level it gives a clear indication of the animating values that the Committee see at the heart of the Charter and that should animate its interpretation into the future. And this is where the value of the Decision—indeed the Charter—lies.

First of all the Committee decided that the issues arising within and between Articles 15, 17, and E were so intertwined as to be considered together.[48] It next reflected on the nature of the expanded Article 15 of the Revised Charter. It reiterated the sentiments it previously expressed in the General Introduction to the Conclusions on the Revised Charter of 2003 (see above) and added that: 'The underlying vision of Article 15 is one of equal citizenship for persons with disabilities and, fittingly, the primary rights are those of "independence, social integration and participation in the life of the community"'.[49] The addition of

---

46 Ibid., at para. 34.   47 Ibid., at para. 40.   48 Ibid., at para. 47.
49 Ibid., at para. 48.

'education' into the new expanded Article 15(1) was specifically commented on by the Committee. It stated: 'Securing a right to education for children and others with disabilities plays an obviously important role in advancing these citizenship rights. This explains why education is now specifically mentioned in the revised Article 15 and why such an emphasis is placed on achieving that education "in the framework of general schemes wherever possible"'.[50] So the Committee linked education to the broader agenda of securing independence and participation. Importantly, it also emphasized the default setting of the revised Article 15 towards 'mainstreaming'.

With respect to Article 17 the Committee noted that the right to education contained therein is predicated on the need to ensure that children and young persons grow up in an environment that encourages the 'full development of their personality and of their physical and mental capacities'. It went on to say: 'This approach is just as important for children with disabilities as it is for others and arguably more so in circumstances where the effects of ineffective or untimely intervention are ever likely to be undone'.[51] The Committee also explicitly viewed Article 17 as embodying the modern approach of mainstreaming and that it, in particular 'requires the establishment and maintenance of sufficient and adequate institutions and services for the purpose of education'.[52] Article 17 was then combined with Article 15 in the sense that the latter covers both children and adults whereas the former only covers children and young persons. Indeed, there was a natural link between Articles 15 and 17 in this case since Article 17 was very explicit on the institutions and services required whereas Article 15 was more explicit on the philosophy that should inform these institutions.

The view of the Committee on Article E is worth quoting in full. The Committee stated that it considers that:

[T]he insertion of Article E into a separate Article in the Revised Charter indicates the heightened importance the drafters paid to the principle of non-discrimination with respect to the achievement of the various substantive rights contained therein. It further considers that [the function of Article E] . . . is to help secure the equal effective enjoyment of all the rights concerned regardless of difference. Therefore, it does not constitute an autonomous right which could in itself provide independent grounds for a complaint. It follows that the Committee understands the arguments of the complainant as implying that the situation as alleged violates Articles 15.1 and 17.1 when read in combination with Article E of the Revised Charter.[53]

So the overarching role of Article E is to ensure the 'equal effective enjoyment' of the substantive rights covered by the Revised Charter. The Committee went on to explain why it considered disability to be covered by the reference to 'other status' within Article E. This was necessary since Article E does not explicitly include disability as one of the prohibited grounds of discrimination (unlike—and embarrassingly unlike—Article 13 of the Treaty of Amsterdam). Interestingly, the

---

[50] Ibid.   [51] Ibid., at para. 49.   [52] Ibid., at para. 49.   [53] Ibid., at para. 51.

Committee fortified this reasoning by referring to the (political) 'undertaking' in the Malaga Political Declaration reaffirming the non-discrimination approach to disability at a European Ministerial level.

Saying that the non-discrimination framework of reference applies is one thing: working out its implications in this context is quite another task. In this regard the Committee referred explicitly to the case law of the European Court of Human Rights to the effect that the non-discrimination ideal is also violated by failing to take positive steps to take due account of differences where they occur.[54] The Committee stated: 'Human difference in a democratic society should not only be viewed positively but should be responded to with discernment in order to ensure real and effective equality'.[55] To a certain extent this shows sensitivity to the advances made in equality thinking by the European Court of Human Rights. This does not necessarily mean that it is pegged to the case law of the Court. One inhibiting factor in the development of the 'positive rights' philosophy of the Court is the reality that the civil and political rights of the ECHR were not primarily designed to serve positive ends, at least in the sense meant by Isaiah Berlin and others. Such positive obligations emerge in the afterglow of essentially negative rights. The situation under the Charter is quite different. Unlike the ECHR, it is specifically designed to provide for positive rights. So the equality/non-discrimination ideal takes on a different function. It need not be used to generate positive rights—they are already posited under the instrument. Rather, it calls for sensitivity in the delivery of those rights toward difference.

In this vein the Committee went on to develop its theory of discrimination to embrace indirect discrimination as well as direct discrimination. It stated that such indirect discrimination: '. . . may arise by failing to take due and positive account of all relevant differences or by failing to take adequate steps to ensure that the rights and coactive advantages that are open to all are genuinely accessible by and to all'.[56] In Complaint No 1 (1998) the Committee had already emphasized that the implementation 'of the Charter requires the States Parties to take not merely legal action but also practical action to give full effect to the rights recognised in the Charter'.[57] It took the opportunity to reiterate this point and added: 'When the achievement of one of the rights in question is exceptionally complex and particularly expensive to resolve, a State Party must take measures that allows it to achieve the objectives of the Charter within a reasonable time, with measurable progress, and to an extent consistent with the maximum use of available resources'.[58] In other words, if the relevant obligations were primarily

---

[54] Ibid., at para. 52. The Committee cited the Decision of the Court in *Thlimmenos v. Greece* [2000] ECHR 161 (6 April 2000).   [55] Ibid., at para. 52.

[56] Ibid.

[57] *International Commission of Jurists v. Portugal*, Complaint No. 1 (1998), Decision on the merits, at para. 32.   [58] Decision on the merits of Collective Complaint No. 13, at para. 53.

obligations of conduct, then what was required were tangible steps in the direction of achieving results. In setting the pace and in determining how such steps should be taken the Committee emphasized that: 'States Parties must be particularly mindful of the impact their choices will have for groups with heightened vulnerabilities as well as for other persons affected including, especially, their families on whom falls the heaviest burden in the event of institutional shortcomings'.[59] This was relevant in the instant complaint since the majority of autistic children who could not be placed in school were left with their families to cope with. The Committee then concluded:

In the light of the afore-mentioned [considerations] . . . the Committee notes that in the case of autistic children and adults . . . France has failed to achieve sufficient progress in advancing the provision of education for persons with autism . . . [The Committee] . . . considers that, as the authorities themselves acknowledge, and whether a broad or narrow definition of autism is adopted, that the proportion of children with autism being educated in either general or specialist schools is much lower than in the case of children, whether or not disabled. It is also established that there is a chronic shortage of care and support facilities for autistic adults.[60]

The Committee of Ministers adopted a Resolution on 10 March 2004 on the Complaint.[61] After recounting the essence of the Decision of the European Committee of Social Rights the Committee of Ministers took note: 'Of the statement made by the respondent Government indicating that the French Government undertakes to bring the situation into conformity with the Revised Charter and that measures are being taken in this respect (see Appendix to this Resolution)'.[62] The Committee of Ministers also anticipated that France would indicate in its next periodic report covering the relevant provisions of the Revised Charter the improvements made to bring the situation into conformity. The Appendix to the Resolution set out some of the steps already being taken by France in the field of autism.

III. THE EUROPEAN UNION—ACHIEVING SOCIAL ENDS THROUGH CIVIL RIGHTS LAW[63]

The purpose of this section is to explore the question whether the above case law under the Social Charter serves a useful purpose in the context of EU anti-discrimination law.

---

[59] Ibid., at para. 54.   [60] Ibid.

[61] Resolution ResChS (2004), *Autisme-Europe v. France*, Collective Complaint No. 13/2002, (875th meeting of the Minister's Deputies).   [62] Ibid., at para. 1.

[63] See generally, L. Waddington, *Disability Employment and the European Community* (1995). See also W. Van Oorshot and B. Hvinden (eds), *Disability Policy in European Countries* (2001) and S. M. Machado and R. De Lorenzo (eds), *European Disability Law* (1997).

A. Background to the Framework Employment Directive in the Disability Context

The European Union was founded pragmatically to leverage political unity through economic integration. Although the initial and ultimate goal was inescapably political, the means initially chosen were purely economic. This familiar theme impacts on how the disability issue has been framed during successive periods within the Institutions of the Union.

The sad reality was that the disability issue was not a priority within the Community. From an economic perspective it should have been, since labour market irrationality based on prejudice towards the abilities and talents of persons with disabilities signals a market failure that should be redressed to everyone's material advantage—including that of the taxpayer. The view taken for a long time was that the exclusion of persons with disabilities from the labour market was 'natural' and not driven by implicit social choices. In any event, it may have made little difference to expose employers to the need to make more rational assessments of the marketable skills of persons with disabilities since they had, by definition, few such skills due to their exclusion or segregation in the sphere of education.

Interestingly, things began to change slowly in the 1980s due to outside factors. The relative success of Section 504 of the US Rehabilitation Act (an anti-discrimination measure) helped to fuel the rise of civil society in the United States.[64] In the language of political sociology, 'interest aggregation' in the shape of new and potent NGOs was beginning to lead to 'interest articulation' in the shape of coherent policy demands that legislators could understand. It was only a matter of time before this new consciousness was reflected on a world stage.

The inauguration of the United Nations World Decade in Favour of Persons with Disabilities in the early 1980s was the spur that led to the creation of a Disability Unit within the old DG V of the European Commission (now DG Employment and Social Affairs). Throughout the 1980s and much of the 1990s it spent much of its energy managing a European Action Programme in favour of people with disabilities (Helios I & II). One of its effects—whether intended or not—was to create an 'epistemic community' of disability activists and NGOs. Slowly but surely their inarticulate sense of grievance and hurt was translated into the language of rights—a language that could be understood by power and especially by the European Commission as it sought ways to connect with the peoples of Europe in order to rejuvenate the European project.

Predictably enough, nothing much came of the UN World Decade at a global level. If it was a failure, it was a highly useful failure. Demands were made in the late 1980s for the drafting of a full thematic human rights treaty on the rights of persons with disabilities. This was killed off by offering instead a new super Resolution of the

---

[64] See generally, P. Blanck, E. Hill, C. D. Seigal, and M. Waterstone (eds), *Disability Civil Rights Law and Policy* (2004).

UN General Assembly entitled the Standard Rules for the Equalisation of Opportunities for Persons with Disabilities (1993). Fortuitously, at around the same time the European Commission was reflecting aloud about the future of EU Social Policy. Its Green Paper of 1993 contained a gem. It stated: 'Social segregation, even with adequate income maintenance and special provision, is contrary to human dignity and corrosive of social solidarity and community morale'.[65] This signalled a real turning point. The subsequent White Paper committed the Commission to find a way to express the UN Standard Rules in EU policy. The auguries were good. Ministers of Education acting in Council had already signalled a willingness to move away from segregation in education.[66] A landmark Communication was issued by the Commission in 1996 entitled 'Equality Opportunities towards Persons with Disabilities—toward a New EU Strategy'.[67] What was striking was not the text itself—but the values that so clearly animated it. Indeed, in a sister Resolution, the Council endorsed these values.[68] The strategy has recently been renewed.[69]

The EU—unlike the Council of Europe—has always been relatively open toward the participation of civil society. This openness proved crucial in the mid-to-late 1990s on the disability issue. In a series of important publications the European disability NGOs provided clear analyses of the need for enhanced competencies at Union level to combat discrimination directed against persons with disabilities. In this they echoed a deafening chorus emanating from many different issue-specific groups. Cumulatively the arguments were unanswerable.

B. *The Framework Employment Directive and Disability*

The application of the Framework Employment Directive on the ground of disability will be the subject of a very extensive study soon to be produced by the European Commission's Network of Independent Legal Experts on Disability. The focus of this Section is not so much on how that Directive is currently being implemented—nor indeed on its general provisions which apply as much on the disability ground as on other grounds—but on the question whether the thrust of the case law of the Social Charter could serve any useful purpose to courts and ultimately the European Court of Justice with respect to its interpretation. That, in turn, depends on what the key interpretive issues are likely to be when unpacking the Directive from a disability perspective.

---

[65] Green Paper: European Social Policy—Options for the Union, COM(93)555, at 48.

[66] Resolution of the Council and the Ministers for Education meeting within the Council of 31 May 1990 concerning integration of children and young people with disabilities into ordinary systems of education, OJ 1966 C162/2.

[67] COM(96)406, Equality for Opportunity for People with Disabilities—A New Community Disability Strategy.

[68] Resolution of the Council and of representatives of the Governments of the Member States meeting within the Council of 20 December 1996 on equality of opportunity for people with disabilities, OJ 1997 C12/1.

[69] COM(2003)650, Equal Opportunities for People with Disabilities—A European Action Plan.

It will be recalled that the purpose of the Directive is to 'lay down a general framework for combating discrimination' on various grounds including disability in the employment context 'with a view to putting into effect in the Member States the principle of equal treatment' (Article 1). The concept of discrimination is defined under Article 2 as follows:

1. For the purposes of this Directive, the 'principle of equal treatment' shall mean that there shall be no direct or indirect discrimination whatsoever on any of the grounds referred to in Article 1.

2. For the purposes of paragraph 1:

   (a) direct discrimination shall be taken to occur whether one person is treated less favourably than another is, has been, or would be treated in a comparable situation, on any of the grounds referred to in Article 1;

   (b) indirect discrimination shall be taken to occur where an apparently neutral provision, criterion or practice would put persons having a particular . . . disability . . . at a particular disadvantage compared with other persons unless:

      (i) that provision, criterion or practice is objectively justified by a legitimate aim and the means of achieving that aim are appropriate and necessary; or

      (ii) as regards persons with a particular disability, the employer or any person or organisation to whom this Directive applies, is obliged, under national legislation to take appropriate measures in line with the principles contained in Article 5 in order to eliminate disadvantages entailed by such provision, criteria or practice.

One issue that may well arise is whether persons with disabilities are in fact 'in a comparable situation' vis-à-vis others.

As originally proposed by the Commission the obligation of reasonable accommodation would have been contained in Article 2 and failure to discharge it would be deemed a form of discrimination. It was apparently moved during negotiations in Council to a new Article 5 not because no link could be posited between non-discrimination and the obligation itself, but more because such detail was felt out of place in a headline article dealing with discrimination. The reference to 'reasonable obligation' under the heading of 'indirect discrimination' was intended to cover British sensibilities, since their legislation at the time (Disability Discrimination Act 1995) did not cover 'indirect discrimination' and they sought a reassurance that the notion of 'reasonable accommodation' (which was covered by their law) would be sufficient to discharge their obligations with regard to 'indirect discrimination'.

Article 5 then goes on to expound on the obligation of 'reasonable accommodation'. It reads:

In order to guarantee compliance with the principle of equal treatment in relation to persons with disabilities, reasonable accommodation shall be provided. This means that employers shall take appropriate measures, where needed in a particular case, to enable a person with a disability to have access to, participate in, or advance in employment, or to undergo training, unless such measures would impose a disproportionate burden on the employer. This burden shall not be disproportionate when it is sufficiently remedied by measures existing within the framework of the disability policy of the Member State concerned.

This provision matches closely similar provisions under US as well as much comparative discrimination law.

An interesting—and somewhat unexpected—twist was added to Article 7 dealing with positive action on the disability ground. Article 7(2) reads: 'With regard to disabled persons, the principle of equal treatment shall be without prejudice to the right of Member States to maintain or adopt provisions on the protection of health and safety at work or measures aimed at creating or maintaining provisions or facilities for safeguarding or promoting their integration into the working environment'. There is a danger that if read restrictively this provision could well rationalize a common practice reported from many Member States whereby health and safety law is used (abused) to exclude or otherwise segregate disabled workers.

IV. CONCLUSIONS—THE GRAVITATIONAL FORCE OF THE CASE LAW OF THE EUROPEAN SOCIAL CHARTER ON THE INTERPRETATION OF EU ANTI-DISCRIMINATION LAW

What, then, is the added value of the case law of the Social Charter in looking at similar issues that arise under the Framework Employment Directive?

The most important contribution occurs at the level of ideas and values. Using the non-discrimination ideal the Committee has effectively rejected any notion of 'separate but equal' in the disability context. It sees the non-discrimination ideal as a carrier of a vision of an inclusive society. Likewise, the European Court of Justice should be encouraged to view the Framework Employment Directive as a tool—an incredibly powerful tool—to insert greater rationality into the decision-making process of employers, to create openings for the undoubted human talent that lies behind disability to flourish, and to create a diverse life world of benefit to all. The Committee endorses the view that rights—including social rights—do not exist merely for their own sake. They help create the conditions for an active life. In other words, one of the most important dimensions to freedom is the right to belong.

Another useful insight from the case law of the Charter is its insistence that the legal definition of disability should not be an occasion to dwell on the medical peculiarities of the person. If allowed to focus on the medical impairment, then the legal definition might have the unintended effect of shifting the blame for exclusion onto their medical condition and reinforce the perception that the resulting exclusion is somehow 'natural'. In holding to this view the Committee is conscious of the reality that people do not exclude themselves: social arrangements exclude people. The Committee has achieved this result in the field of social rights. At least as much should be expected in the field of civil rights and under the Framework Employment Directive. It bears emphasizing that the Framework Employment Directive does not itself define disability. In keeping with the spirit of the case law of the European Social Charter which is directly influenced by the human rights approach to disability, the European Court of Justice should take care to ensure that the definitions adopted by Member States should not get in the way of tackling discriminatory behaviour and the resulting social exclusion.

Yet another valuable contribution from the Committee has been its insistence on (1) the existence of non-discrimination law and (2) that such law should respond appropriately to the human difference of disability by providing for the obligation of 'reasonable accommodation'. The obligation of 'reasonable accommodation' in such legislation which the Committee now insists on simply amounts to an adjustment of the non-discrimination norm to meet the circumstances of persons with disabilities. It is sensitivity to differences that places persons with disabilities in a 'comparable situation' as required by Article 1 of the Framework Employment Directive. In this regard the European Committee of Social Rights built upon the understanding of equality put forward by the European Court of Human Rights. Conceptually, the concept of 'reasonable accommodation' is no different to maternity leave which responds appropriately to gender difference. Indeed, maternity leave could itself be seen as a form of 'reasonable accommodation' on the gender ground.

In sum, the European Committee of Social Rights has shown through its relevant case law that it is possible to refresh social rights using the non-discrimination ideal—an ideal which is more commonly accentuated in the civil rights field. And that is highly relevant to how the European Court of Justice should go about the essential task of framing the relevant issues from within the lenses of non-discrimination law. If the Council of Europe and the European Union are indeed twins separated at birth, then they might move a little closer if the non-discrimination ideal becomes a bridge between social and civil rights, which can only benefit the vibrancy of the European social model.

15

We Don't See a Connection: The 'Right to Health' in the EU Charter and European Social Charter

TAMARA K. HERVEY*

I. INTRODUCTION

This chapter considers the expressions of the internationally recognized 'right to health' in the EU's *acquis* and the 'jurisprudence' and 'soft law' of the European Social Charter (ESC). Expressions of the 'right to health' are found in Article 35 of the European Union's Charter of Fundamental Rights and Freedoms (EUCFR) (titled, 'The right to health care'), and in Article 11 of the (Revised) European Social Charter ((Rev)ESC)[1] (titled, 'The right to protection of health'). While the European Committee of Social Rights (ECSR) has made tentative beginnings in developing a body of 'jurisprudence' elaborating the content of Article 11 (Rev)ESC, and the Committee of Ministers has issued non-normative indicative guidance ('soft law') relevant to the provision, such elaboration of the formal expression of the 'right to health' in EU law remains severely limited. Further, the EU institutions appear unaware of the relevance or potential application of the 'right to health' in various particular contexts. The relevant legal documentation does not make any express links to Article 11 (Rev)ESC, even where policy measures cover fields of activity that fall within the 'right to health', at least as conceptualized in the ESC context. The chapter explores two possible reasons for this failure to make a connection. The first is that it expresses a statement to the effect that the 'right to health' is already effectively guaranteed within the Member

* This chapter draws on T. K. Hervey, 'The Right to Health in EU Law', in T. K. Hervey and J. Kenner (eds), *Economic and Social Rights under the EU Charter of Fundamental Rights* (2003), 193, and on T. K. Hervey and J. M. McHale, *Health Law and the European Union* (2004), Chs 4, 9 and 10. I am grateful to the participants in the conference, *Economic and Social Rights*, 18–19 June 2004, EUI, Florence, especially to Gisella Gori, Gráinne de Búrca and Bruno de Witte; and to my colleagues in the Human Rights Law Centre, University of Nottingham, for their constructive comments. The usual disclaimer applies.   [1] 1961 and 1996.

States of the EU. The second is that the lack of connection is explicable by reference to the debate on the division of competence between the EU and its Member States.

The structure of the chapter is as follows. A brief introduction to the 'right to health' in international and national constitutional law (see Section II) provides some legal context. This is followed by an introductory analysis of the right to health under the (Rev)ESC (Section III) and the EUCFR, now found in the Constitutional Treaty (CT) (see Section IV).[2] The main body of the chapter (Section V) contains an exploration of the construction of a 'right to health' in the *Conclusions* of the ECSR,[3] and equivalent laws and policies in the context of the EU. This focuses on a number of elements of the ECSR's 'jurisprudence', representing examples of some of the key strands of national law and policy regarded as mandated by Article 11 (Rev)ESC. This analysis reveals that, while the EU is active in many of the policy areas that 'fit' within Article 11 (Rev)ESC, the EU does not draw an explicit link with the 'right to health' in those contexts. A concluding section of the chapter (Section VI) draws out two possible reasons for that lack of connection.

II. THE 'RIGHT TO HEALTH' IN INTERNATIONAL AND NATIONAL CONSTITUTIONAL LAW

Arguments over the nature, content, form and structure of social rights, such as the right to health, may make their inclusion in charters of fundamental rights controversial.[4] As is the case with other rights, the phrase 'right to health' is shorthand, encapsulating entitlements with respect to health care and health protection.[5] Just as the 'right to life' does not mean the 'right to eternal life', so the right to health does not mean a right to be healthy, or a claim to maintain or attain perfect health.[6] Further, it is often argued that social rights, such as the right to health, do not merit the term 'rights', being merely a luxury affordable only by developed states.[7] Indeed the cost of health care is also a problem for wealthy

---

[2] Solemnly proclaimed at Nice in December 2000; OJ 2000 C364/1.

[3] Here, I am following the views of several contributors to this collection (R. Brillat, J.-F. Akandji-Kombé) to the effect that the work of the ECSR is (quasi) jurisprudential or judicial, and the approach of my co-panellists at the conference, P. Koncar and M. Bell.

[4] M. Craven, 'A View from Elsewhere: Social Rights, International Covenant and the EU Charter of Fundamental Rights', in C. Costello (ed.), *Fundamental Social Rights: Current European Legal Protection and the Challenge of the EU Charter on Fundamental Rights* (2001) 77.

[5] V. A. Leary, 'The Right to Health in International Human Rights Law', 1 *Health and Human Rights* (1994) 3; B. Toebes, *The Right to Health as a Human Right in International Law* (1999), at 16–18 and 24.

[6] B. Toebes, 'The Right to Health', in A. Eide, C. Krause, and A. Rosas (eds), *Economic, Cultural and Social Rights* (2001) 170.

[7] H. Steiner and P. Alston, *International Human Rights in Context: Law, Politics, Morals* (2000), at 300–05.

states.[8] The main emphasis of such social rights consists in a *claim on* the public authorities for protection and assistance, rather than the *freedom from* state interference that is said to characterize civil and political rights.[9] It is argued that treating such matters as 'rights' devalues the currency of (civil and political) rights, and justifies inappropriate state intervention in the functioning of free market economies.[10] Worse, a strong claim of right may serve as proxy for appropriate political debate leading to the proper allocation of socio-economic resources, and may in fact bring about a substantively unjust result in terms of their allocation.[11] Alternatively, in spite of the official position that human rights are indivisible and interrelated,[12] social rights are often seen as 'second class' rights,[13] aspirational only and programmatic in nature. As they constitute a 'positive' claim on the state, rather than a 'negative' freedom from state interference, such rights are not seen as enforceable by individuals before judicial bodies. However, as will be seen, the right to health encapsulates a cluster of rights, not all of which fall within the category of 'positive rights', and even if they do, may have value in terms other than individual judicial enforcement.[14]

While I agree that we should reject the rhetoric of 'rights' if it is inappropriate in terms of the aims to be achieved by espousing and promoting such rights,[15] I tend towards the view that, as others have argued, if the value of civil and political rights is appreciated, it is certainly worth exploring what may be gained by

---

[8] Leary, *supra* n. 5, at 13. Recent reforms of national health care systems have been, at least in part, driven by a desire to contain spiralling costs, see, e.g., R. B. Saltman, J. Figueras, and C. Sakellarides (eds), *Critical Challenges for Health Care Reform in Europe* (1998); R. B. Saltman, 'A Conceptual Overview of Recent Health Care Reforms', 4 *European Journal of Public Health* (1994) 287; Dunning Report, *Choices in Health Care: A Report by the Government Committee on Choices in Health Care, the Netherlands* (1992); C. Barker, *The Health Care Policy Process* (1992), at 151–57; R. Freeman, *The Politics of Health in Europe* (2000), at 66–85.

[9] See further A. Rosas and A. Eide, 'Economic, Social and Cultural Rights: A Universal Challenge' and A. Eide, 'Economic, Social and Cultural Rights as Human Rights', in Eide, Krause and Rosas, *supra* n. 6.   [10] See Steiner and Alston, *supra* n. 7, at 237.

[11] See contributions of Minow, Anderson and Mandler, Human Rights Program, Harvard Law School and François-Xavier Bagnoud, Center for Health and Human Rights Workshop, *Economic and Social Rights and the Right to Health*, September 1993, www.law.harvard.edu/programs/HRP/Publications/economic1.html, at 4.

[12] See Universal Declaration of Human Rights, Vienna World Conference on Human Rights Declaration, para. 5.

[13] Vienna World Conference 1993, UN Committee on Economic, Social and Cultural Rights UN Doc. E/1993/22, Annex III, paras. 5 and 7, cited Steiner and Alston, *supra* n. 7, at 238, 'The reality is that violations of civil and political rights continue to be treated as though far more serious and more patently intolerable, than massive and direct denials of economic, social and cultural rights.'

[14] Cf. A. Von Bogdandy, 'The European Union as a Human Rights Organization? Human Rights and the Core of the European Union', 37 *CMLRev.* (2000) 1307, at 1316 'the very essence of a right is that it is accorded immediate protection by the courts'.

[15] 'If our commitment to rights arises out of our humane concerns about the object of those rights—such as good health or health care—then we should feel free to eschew rights rhetoric for other serviceable forms of argument: theories of political community, of distributive fairness and social justice, or of maximising utility' (Steiner, Harvard Law School Workshop, *supra* n. 11, at 2).

applying the notion of rights to social entitlements such as the 'right to health'.[16] Further, the realization that, in practice, civil and political rights may be rendered meaningless without the means to enjoy them has led some to argue that social rights are *higher* in value than civil and political rights.[17] Civil and political rights also have economic costs and impose economic burdens; this has not been an insurmountable impediment to their utility and widespread support. Civil and political rights may also be (or have been) under-determined in terms of substantive content. It follows that, like civil and political rights, social rights may become more determined through the historical contexts provided in human rights practice. If human rights most urgently need defending where they are most denied, a rights agenda is by definition aspirational; but this does not necessarily reduce it to mere rhetoric.[18] The various roles of soft law and the existence of alternative enforcement mechanisms extend the value of rights beyond their formal judicial enforceability. Not least, in human rights practice and NGO work, the rhetoric of rights buys time and attention from those in power: 'Rights talk buys ten minutes of their attention. I use it like a magic wand.'[19]

It has been observed that 'health and human rights are complementary approaches to the central problem of defining and advancing human well-being'.[20] Indeed, current public health practice, in particular in HIV/AIDS, is drawing clear links between health and human rights protection. The vulnerability of certain individuals or groups to disease, disability, and premature death may be clearly linked to the extent to which the human rights and dignity of those individuals are protected.[21] This realization may be linked to the notion of the interdependence and indivisibility of human rights—the right to health cannot be effectively protected without respect for other recognized rights and *vice versa*. Rights discourse as applied to health may therefore be useful or appropriate for this reason.[22] Further, rights discourse may help to emphasize the importance of health status in terms of the survival and quality of life of individuals, expressing the fundamental values of a socio-political order. A notion of a 'right' to health moves away from the conceptualization of health as simply a medical, technical problem, by emphasizing health as a social good.[23] Moreover, using the

---

[16] Gostin, Harvard Law School Workshop, *supra* n. 11, at 7.

[17] 'What permanent achievement is there in saving people from torture, only to find that they are killed by . . . disease that could have been prevented?', Eide and Rosas, in Eide, Rosas and Krause, *supra* n. 9, at 7; 'Of what use is the right to free speech to those who are starving and illiterate?', Steiner and Alston, *supra* n. 7, at 237.

[18] D. Beetham, 'What Future for Economic and Social Rights', 43 *Political Studies* (1995) 41, cited in Steiner and Alston, *supra* n. 7, at 255.

[19] Osborn, Harvard Law School Workshop, *supra* n. 11, at 7.

[20] Mann, Gostin et al., 'Health and Human Rights', 1 *Health and Human Rights* (1994) 7.

[21] Mann, Gostin et al., *supra* n. 20, cite the example of women in East Africa who are vulnerable to HIV infection: 'women's vulnerability to HIV is now recognized to be integrally connected with discrimination and unequal rights, involving property, marriage, divorce and inheritance'.

[22] Leary, *supra* n. 5.   [23] Ibid., at 8.

terminology of the right to health emphasizes the notion of individualization of health as a social right.[24] In addition, the 'visibility' of rights, applied in the context of health, may help to raise the profile of health entitlements, not necessarily through justiciability, but rather the normative cachet of rights.[25] Finally, although international human rights law primarily addresses the individual as the holder of human rights, the full enjoyment of individual human rights may, in some circumstances, require the protection of *groups* of persons. This perspective has prompted the notion of a 'third generation' of human rights, as a response to the phenomenon of global interdependence.[26] The right to health is not generally regarded as such a 'third generation' human right in itself, but may be closely related to the rights to peace, to a protected environment, and to development. If the benefits of a rights discourse as applied to collectively held rights[27] are accepted, a collective notion of a right to health may be useful in this respect.

The Preamble to the Constitution of the World Health Organization, 1946, was the first international instrument to explicitly formulate a 'right to health'.[28] The right to health is now found in several international human rights conventions,[29] including Article 11 of the (Rev)ESC, and also in Article 35 EUCFR. The right to health is also found in a number of national constitutions.[30]

---

[24] This is illustrated, for instance, by the practice of the UN Committee on Economic, Social and Cultural Rights in its role as supervisory organ of the ICESCR. The Committee has developed an understanding of social rights as not simply generalized policy goals, but also, in some circumstances, as individual entitlements, through either the freedom-related dimension of rights (in the context of health, a freedom from state intervention in health), or through the combination of social rights with other 'foundational' rights, in particular rights to dignity, due process and non-discrimination; see Craven, *supra* n. 4, at 82–86.

[25] 'A rights approach offers a normative vocabulary that facilitates both the framing of claims and the identification of the right holder. This means that the addressee of the rights or duty bearers … have the duty to provide the entitlement, not to society in general, but to each member. This standing has very important implications for efforts to seek redress in cases where the entitlement is not provided or the right violated.' A. Chapman, *Exploring a Human Rights Approach to Health Care Reform* (1993).

[26] See K. Vasak, 'A Thirty Year Struggle', *UNESCO Courier* (November 1977) 29, cited Rich, 'Right to Development: A Right of Peoples', in J. Crawford (ed.), *The Rights of Peoples* (1988).

[27] For discussion and elaboration, see Rich, *supra* n. 26, at 53–54.

[28] Toebes, *supra* n. 5, at 15; Toebes, in Eide, Krause and Rosas, *supra* n. 6, at 171.

[29] See Universal Declaration of Human Rights, 1948, Art. 25; International Covenant on Economic Social and Cultural Rights, 1966, Art. 12; Convention on the Elimination of All Forms of Discrimination Against Women, 1979, Art. 12; Convention on the Rights of the Child, 1989, Art. 24; European Social Charter, 1961, Arts 11 and 13; Revised European Social Charter, 1996, Arts 11 and 13; Convention on Human Rights and Biomedicine, 1996, Art. 3; Protocol of San Salvador, 1988, Art. 10. See Toebes, in Eide, Krause and Rosas, *supra* n. 6, at 173.

[30] See, for instance, Art. 23 of the Belgian Constitution; Ch 2, s 19(3) of the Finnish Constitution; Art. 70 D of the Hungarian Constitution; Arts 39(e) and (f), 46 and 47 of the Indian Constitution; Art. 32 of the Italian Constitution; Art. 11(5) of the Luxembourg Constitution; Art. 22(1) of the Netherlands Constitution; s 15 of Art. 2 of the Philippines Constitution; Art. 64(1) of the Portuguese Constitution; Art. 27 of the South African Constitution; and Art. 43 of the Spanish Constitution. See Toebes, in Eide, Krause and Rosas, *supra* n. 6, at 174.

The right to health, as found in international and national law, has multiple and contested meanings,[31] with respect both to the types of obligations it imposes and the substantive content of those obligations. The notion of a 'right to health' tells us little unless we know what kinds of duties states and other holders of public power such as the EU have to enable people to realize it.[32] Human rights are said to impose three types of obligations on the holders of public power: obligations to respect, to protect, and to fulfil.[33] Thus the right to health may be used to mean a negative obligation to *respect* people's health, to restrain the holders of public power from infringing the health of individuals. For instance, it may provide a curb on state acts which encroach upon people's health, such as environmental pollution. It may require states not to impede individuals or groups of people from access to available health services.[34] Or the right to health may involve a positive obligation on the part of the state or other polity, to *protect* health. This would require taking legislative action, for instance to ensure (equal) access to health services if they are provided by third parties, or to provide health care to the impoverished; or to protect people from health infringements by third parties.[35] Or the right to health may involve more extensive action on the part of the state or other polity, to *fulfil* the right to health, by facilitating its enjoyment or by providing the means for so doing. In the context of obligations imposed on states, this may require states to adopt a national health policy, and moreover, to devote a sufficient proportion of national revenues to health. It may require states to create the conditions where all people within the state have access to health services, and to the necessary preconditions for good health, such as clean water and adequate sanitation.[36]

The specific meaning of rights becomes clear through their application in international and national judicial and quasi-judicial fora.[37] As the focus of this chapter is on the ESC and the EU, an introduction to the scope of the 'right to health' in each of those two contexts is now set out, before turning to a detailed analysis of selected examples from the 'jurisprudence' and 'soft law' of the ESC on the 'right to health', and equivalent provisions of EU law.

---

[31] See Minow, Harvard Law School Workshop, *supra* n. 11, at 4.

[32] See Steiner and Alston, *supra* n. 7, at 267; Nussbaum, Harvard Law School Workshop, *supra* n. 11, at 7.

[33] See H. Shue, 'The Interdependence of Duties', in P. Alston and K. Tomasevski, *The Right to Food* (1984); see also e.g. Committee on Economic Social and Cultural Rights, General Document No. 12, (1999) UN Doc. E/C.12/1999/5, cited in Steiner and Alston, *supra* n. 7, at 267; A. Eide, 'Economic, Social and Cultural Rights as Human Rights', in Eide, Krause and Rosas, *supra* n. 6, at 23.

[34] Toebes, in Eide, Krause and Rosas, *supra* n. 6, at 179–80.

[35] Toebes, in Eide, Krause and Rosas, *supra* n. 6, at 180.

[36] Toebes, in Eide, Krause and Rosas, *supra* n. 6, at 180.

[37] As Leary, *supra* n. 5, points out, 'it is not unusual for the full implications of a right enshrined in a bill of rights or a human rights treaty to be perceived only gradually: rights proclaimed in national constitutions and in international legal instruments are expressed in succinct language whose meaning is rarely self-evident'. For further elaboration of the international 'right to health', and a call for the human rights system to engage further with the 'right to health', see P. Hunt, *Reclaiming Social Rights* (1996), Ch 3.

III. THE 'RIGHT TO HEALTH' UNDER THE ESC

Article 11 (Rev)ESC[38] reads as follows:

The right to protection of health

With a view to ensuring the effective exercise of the right to protection of health, the Contracting Parties undertake, either directly or in co-operation with public or private organisations, to take appropriate measures designed *inter alia*:

1. to remove as far as possible the causes of ill-health;
2. to provide advisory and educational facilities for the promotion of health and the encouragement of individual responsibility in matters of health;
3. to prevent as far as possible epidemic, endemic and other diseases, as well as accidents.

Article 11 (Rev)ESC covers the 'protection of health'. This is a wider notion than treatment for those who are suffering from ill-health (health care), as it also covers the broader determinants of good health (health protection, establishing the preconditions for good health). The actual text of the provision makes no explicit reference to a national health care system. However, the *Conclusions* of the ECSR confirm that Article 11 ESC obliges states to have in place such a health care system. States comply with the provision if they provide evidence of six enumerated elements of the 'right to health'.[39] First, there must be a health care system which includes 'public health arrangements making generally available medical and para-medical practitioners and adequate equipment consistent with meeting its main health problems ensuring a proper medical care for the whole population'.[40] Secondly, special measures are required to protect the health of members of various 'vulnerable' groups, and ensure their access to the health care system. Thirdly, general public health protection measures 'aimed at preventing air and water pollution, protection from radio-active substances, noise abatement, food control, [and] environmental hygiene' are required. Health protection and the promotion of good health is also to be achieved through the control of alcoholism, tobacco, and drugs. Fourthly, in order to fulfil the obligation to 'provide advisory and educational facilities for the promotion of health and the encouragement of individual responsibility in matters of health', states must provide a system of health education. Fifthly, the obligation in subparagraph 3 is fulfilled by providing 'measures such as vaccination, disinfection and the control of epidemics, providing the means of combating epidemic and endemic diseases'. Also, states are required to follow a policy of accident prevention.[41] Sixthly, and

[38] Only a minor amendment to the original ESC, the addition of the phrase 'as well as accidents', has been made.

[39] *Case Law on the European Social Charter*, Strasbourg 1982, at 104; *Conclusions I*, at 59, Committee of Independent Experts, First Conclusions; and see Toebes, *supra* n. 5, at 155–59.

[40] *Case Law on the European Social Charter, Conclusions I, supra* n. 39.

[41] Revised European Social Charter, Explanatory Report, Art. 56.

finally, although again the text is not explicit on the matter, Article 11 (Rev)ESC requires 'the bearing by collective bodies of all, or at least a part, of the cost of health services'.[42]

Where a 'positive' obligation, entailing public expenditure, such as that in Article 11 (Rev)ESC is at issue, states may not generally claim lack of resources as justification for failing to meet the obligation.[43] However, the obligations on states under Article 11 (Rev)ESC are 'of a very general kind'.[44] To a large extent, each state has a wide discretion to decide on its own measures to achieve the aims of Article 11. The ECSR observed that Article 11 covers a large field, and consequently it is difficult to conclude that states have failed to fulfil their obligations in respect of that provision.[45]

A. Related Provisions in the (Rev)ESC

In addition to Article 11, the (Rev)ESC includes a number of other provisions closely related to the 'right to health'. Article 3 (Rev)ESC on the right to safe and healthy working conditions concerns the achievement of healthy working environments, and thus directly engages the health of workers. Article 7 (Rev)ESC, on the right of children and young persons to protection, provides that persons under fifteen years of age are not to be employed, except in 'light work without harm to their health, morals or education', and also an exclusion of persons under eighteen years of age from employment in 'dangerous or unhealthy' occupations. The right of employed women to the protection of maternity, found in Article 8 (Rev)ESC, protects the health of both the mother and the newborn infant. Article 13 (Rev)ESC provides:

The right to social and medical assistance

With a view to ensuring the effective exercise of the right to social and medical assistance, the Parties undertake:

1. to ensure that any person who is without adequate resources and who is unable to secure such resources either by his own efforts or from other sources, in particular by benefits under a social security scheme, be granted adequate assistance, and, in case of sickness, the care necessitated by his condition;

. . .

4. to apply the provisions referred to in paragraphs 1, 2 and 3 of this article on an equal footing with their nationals to nationals of other Parties lawfully within their

---

[42] *Case Law on the European Social Charter, Conclusions I, supra* n. 39.

[43] See D. J. Harris and J. Darcy, *The European Social Charter* (2001), citing the example of the reunification of Germany, where the Committee expected the standards of the ESC to be met in the whole of Germany straightaway; see *Conclusions XII-2*, at 74 (Germany). Harris and Darcy contrast the situation under the International Covenant on Economic, Social and Cultural Rights, 993 UNTS 3, in this respect, see ICESCR, Art. 2(1).

[44] *Case Law on the European Social Charter, Conclusions I, supra* n. 39.

[45] Ibid.; see Toebes, *supra* n. 5, at 156–57.

territories, in accordance with their obligations under the European Convention on Social and Medical Assistance, signed at Paris on 11 December 1953.

In this context, 'medical assistance' means the provision of free health care or of the financial assistance necessary to meet the costs of necessary medical treatment to those in need.[46] However, the details of where or how the care is given are left to the discretion of the states.[47] Article 15 on the rights of persons with disabilities may resonate with a right to health, in cases where the disability arises from ill health. Article 23 on the rights of elderly persons explicitly includes a reference to 'health care and services necessitated by their state'. Given the known links between health, housing, poverty, and social exclusion, Articles 30 and 31 (Rev)ESC may also be relevant. Finally, the horizontal non-discrimination clause in Article E (Rev)ESC may be extremely important in terms of implementation of the rights contained in the (Rev)ESC, as a connection with non-discrimination may often 'firm up' a 'positive' right, such as the right to health, and assist in its enforceability.[48]

B. *Legal and Practical Effects of Article 11 (Rev)ESC*

Other contributions to this book have elaborated the legal and practical effects of the provisions of the (Rev)ESC.[49] The ESC binds states in international law to comply with the obligations to which they agree therein. Although not all states that are parties to the (Rev)ESC have signed Article 11 (Rev)ESC, all the Member States of the EU have done so. Unlike under the Council of Europe's ECHR, or in the context of the EU's *acquis communautaire*, there is no procedure that allows *individuals* to bring claims before the ECSR that their rights under the (Rev)ESC have been breached. Enforceability of the (Rev)ESC by individuals thus depends on national law with respect to the incorporation of international treaties.[50] National courts are under an obligation to interpret relevant provisions of national law to be consistent with the obligations under the (Rev)ESC. In some

---

[46] Although the wording of Art. 13(1) does not necessarily establish an individually enforceable right (see M. Scheinin, 'Economic and Social Rights as Legal Rights', in Eide, Krause and Rosas, *supra* n. 6), the Committee takes the view that it does. For instance, in the case of the UK, the obligations under Article 13(1) mean 'that social assistance ... must be guaranteed to those in need "as of right" and not depend solely on a decision at the administration's discretion', see *Case Law on the European Social Charter*, 1993, *Supplement No 3*, 121 (UK), cited by Hunt, *supra* n. 37, at 115. More recently, the ECSR has sought further information as to whether social assistance is granted 'as of right' with respect to Hungary and the Slovak Republic (*Conclusions XVI-2*, at 434 and 787) Bulgaria and Romania (*Conclusions*, March 2004, at 67 and 325) and has concluded that France is not in conformity with Art. 13 (Rev) ESC, as social assistance is not available to persons under age 25 as of right (*Conclusions*, March 2004, at 203–04).

[47] ECSR, General Introduction, *Conclusions XIII-4*, at 57. For further discussion of Article 13 (Rev)ESC, and its relations with EU law, see J. Tooze, 'Social Security and Social Assistance', in Hervey and Kenner (eds), *supra* n. **; see also Harris and Darcy, *supra* n. 43, at 165–76.

[48] Ibid.

[49] See the contributions of R. Brillat, J.-F. Akandji-Kombé, G. Gori, and P. Alston in this volume. See also, in general, Harris and Darcy, *supra* n. 43, especially Ch 3.

[50] See G. Gori's chapter in this volume for an overview.

circumstances, national law may be judicially reviewable for lack of compliance with the (Rev)ESC, although this is dependent upon the precise arrangements for such judicial review proceedings within each state.

Under the monitoring procedure, states that have agreed to Article 11 (Rev)ESC must make periodic reports to the ECSR on their national implementing measures. The ECSR considers both the formal legal position with respect to compliance, and also the practical position,[51] reaching a binding decision, which cannot be overturned by any other institution involved in the monitoring procedure. Although from 2001 the ECSR has considered Article 11(Rev)ESC in some greater depth, overall, however, Article 11 (Rev)ESC has been relatively underdeveloped, compared, for instance, to the provisions on 'economic' rights relating to the employment relationship.[52] The wide area of discretion given to states in implementing Article 11 means that states are relatively rarely found to be non-compliant[53] with its provisions in the ECSR *Conclusions*, which form the keystone of the monitoring procedure.[54] Enforcement of the (Rev)ESC is now also possible through a collective complaints procedure, where states have agreed to its application.[55] Article 11 (Rev)ESC has yet to be the basis of a finding of non-compliance under the collective complaints mechanism. Given the possibilities for developing a collective notion of the 'right to health', in particular the health protection elements thereof,[56] this is probably also indicative of a relatively underdeveloped provision of the (Rev)ESC.

IV. THE 'RIGHT TO HEALTH' IN EU LAW

We now turn to the 'right to health' in the EU Charter of Fundamental Rights and Freedoms 2000 (EUCFR), now found in Part II of the Constitutional Treaty

[51] See *ICJ v. Portugal (Merits)* 7 IHRR 525, at 530, 'the aim and purpose of the Charter, being a human rights protection instrument, is to protect rights not merely theoretically, but also in fact', cited in Harris and Darcy, *supra* n. 43, at 25.

[52] Professor David Harris, former member of the Committee of Independent Experts (now ECSR), during the conference which preceded the publication of this book, described the approach of the Committee to Article 11 ESC as 'reactive, rather than proactive', noting that suggestions to collaborate with WHO (Europe) in developing Art. 11 ESC were rejected while he was a member of the Committee.

[53] As opposed to deferral of *Conclusions*, due to lack of adequate information, which is more frequent under Art. 11 (Rev)ESC.

[54] For further details on the monitoring and reporting procedure, see Harris and Darcy, *supra* n. 43, Ch 3.

[55] See H. Cullen, 'The Collective Complaints Mechanism of the ESC', 25 (Supp HR) *ELRev.* (2000) 18; T. Novitz, 'Are Social Rights Necessarily Collective Rights?', 2002 *EHRLR* 50, R. Brillat, 'A New Protocol to the European Social Charter Providing for Collective Complaints' 1996 *EHRLR* 52.

[56] See *supra*, p. 309. Since this chapter was completed, the ECSR has received two collective complaints involving Art. 11 (Rev)ESC, No. 22/2003 and No. 30/2005. Both are in the context of health and safety at work, although No. 30/2005 also concerns protection of the health of the population in general.

(CT) agreed on 18 June 2004.[57] The first thing to note is that the Charter does not include a 'right to health' as such. Article 35 EUCFR concerns the 'right to health *care*', and provides that, 'Everyone has the right of access to preventive health care and the right to benefit from medical treatment under the conditions established by national laws and practices. A high level of human health protection shall be ensured in the definition and implementation of all Union policies and activities'. This provision has two elements: an expression of individual entitlement and a mainstreaming obligation. The individual entitlements ('everyone has the right . . .') are both to medical treatment in the case of ill-health, and to preventive health care. This latter could potentially encompass the notion of the preconditions for good health, as elaborated in the international and national practice on the (collective) right to health. The fact that the title of this provision is the 'right to health *care*' may therefore be of less relevance than it appears. The second sentence repeats the 'mainstreaming' provision in Article 152(1) EC,[58] and extends the obligation placed on the EU institutions in the context of *Community* policies and activities to *Union* policies and activities. This element of the Charter may be seen as a kind of 'super-mainstreaming'[59] expression of the values that underpin EU law and policy.

A. *Related Provisions in the EUCFR*

The EU Charter contains a number of other provisions relevant for the right to health. Article 1 on human dignity may be said to be the basis of all elements of the right to health. Its close relative is Article 3 on the integrity of the person, which draws from and is stated to be consistent with[60] the European Convention on Human Rights and Biomedicine. Article 8 EUCFR[61] on the protection of personal data may be relevant in the context of patients' records and medical research data. Article 13 EUCFR on the freedom of the arts and sciences may be relevant to medical research. The EUCFR includes general provisions on the rights of the elderly (Article 25 EUCFR) and persons with disabilities (Article 26 EUCFR), which may relate to the right to health. In the work context, Article 31 EUCFR entitles workers to 'working conditions which respect [their] health, safety and dignity',[62] and Article 32 EUCFR protects young people at work.

---

[57] As the Constitutional Treaty has yet to be ratified by the 25 Member States of the EU, and may indeed never be ratified, discussion here will refer to the EU Charter of Fundamental Rights, 'solemnly proclaimed' in 2000, which is currently a measure of EU 'soft law'. However, the effects of the Charter as part of a Constitutional Treaty will be considered below.

[58] See CHARTE 4473/00 CONV. 49, 10 November 2000.

[59] J. Kenner, *EU Employment Law: From Rome to Amsterdam and Beyond* (2002), at 544.

[60] See *supra* n. 58.

[61] Based on Art. 286 EC, Directive 95/46 (OJ 1995 L281/31) and also Art. 8 ECHR and the Council of Europe Convention of 28 January 1981 for the Protection of Individuals with regard to Automatic Processing of Personal Data, which has been ratified by all Member States.

[62] In Case C-84/94, *UK v. Council (Working Time)* [1996] ECR I-5755, para. 15, the ECJ adopted a broad notion of the concept of 'health and safety at work', drawing explicitly on the World

Finally, Article 21 EUCFR on the non-discrimination principle is important: 'Any discrimination based on any ground such as sex, race, colour, ethnic or social origin, genetic features, language, religion or belief, political or other opinion, membership of a national minority, property, birth, disability, age or sexual orientation shall be prohibited.' The phrase 'any ground such as' is crucial here, as it implies that other suspect grounds, for instance citizenship or nationality,[63] might also found a complaint of discrimination. The provision draws on Article 13 EC, Article 14 ECHR, and Article 11 of the Convention on Human Rights and Biomedicine, with respect to genetic heritage. 'Insofar as this provision corresponds to Article 14 of the ECHR, it applies in compliance with it.'[64]

B. *Legal and Practical Effects of Article 35 EUCFR*

At the time of its promulgation, the legal status of the Charter was left to be determined at a later date.[65] The Constitutional Treaty incorporates the Charter wholesale as Part II of the Treaty.[66] The legal significance of such an incorporation is that the provisions of the EUCFR will no longer be 'soft law' (persuasive, a reference point for interpretation of hard law), but will, if the Constitutional Treaty enters into force, become 'hard' or binding primary EU law, placing enforceable obligations on the institutions and Member States of the EU.[67] The practical significance of such an incorporation is more difficult to predict, and there are differences of opinion among legal commentators in this respect.[68] Article I-9 CT

Health Organization's definition of health as a 'state of complete physical, mental and social well-being that does not consist only in the absence of illness or infirmity'.

[63] But see Art. 21(2) EUCFR.   [64] See *supra* n. 58.

[65] See Cologne European Council Conclusions, June 1999. Apparently at least 6 Member States are, or at least were, against the Charter being incorporated into the Treaties, see L. Betten, 'The EU Charter on Fundamental Rights: A Trojan Horse or a Mouse?', 17 *IJCLLIR* (2001) 151, at 152, citing *The Times* and the *Guardian*, 20 June 2000; see also B. de Witte, 'The Legal Status of the Charter: Vital Question or Non-Issue?', 8 *MJ* (2001) 81, at 82.

[66] See Doc. CIG 50/03, as amended by CIG 81/04 and CIG 85/04 of 18 June 2004.

[67] The enforcement provisions of EU law include Art. 226 EC, under which the European Commission brings a defaulting Member State before the ECJ; and the doctrine of 'direct effect', according to which certain provisions of the EC Treaty (those that meet preconditions of justiciability, that is, are clear, precise, and unconditional) are enforceable at the suit of individuals before national courts. This sets EU law apart from (most) other species of international law. Treaty provisions have also been found to be directly effective as between individuals. See Case 26/62, *Van Gend en Loos* [1963] ECR 1; Case 43/75, *Defrenne v. SABENA (No. 2)* [1976] ECR 455; Case 39/72, *Commission v. Italy* [1973] ECR 101; Case 9/70, *Grad v. Finanzamt Traunstein* [1970] ECR 825; Case 104/81, *Kupferberg* [1982] ECR 3641; Case 41/74, *Van Duyn v. Home Office* [1974] ECR 1337; Case 148/78, *Ratti* [1979] ECR 1629; Case 152/84, *Marshall v. Southampton and South-West Hampshire Area Health Authority* [1986] ECR 723. For discussion, see, e.g., P. Pescatore, 'The Doctrine of Direct Effect: An Infant Disease of Community Law', 8 *ELRev.* (1983) 155; P. Craig, 'Once Upon a Time in the West: Direct Effect and the Federalization of EEC Law' 12 *OJLS* (1992) 453; S. Prechal, 'Does Direct Effect Still Matter?', 37 *CMLRev.* (2000) 1047.

[68] See for instance M. Dougan, 'The Convention's Draft Constitutional Treaty: A "Tidying-Up Exercise", that Needs Some Tidying-Up of Its Own', Federal Trust Papers, http://www.fedtrust.co.uk/

provides that 'the Union shall recognise' the 'rights, freedoms and principles' of the EUCFR,[69] and that fundamental rights, found in the ECHR and the common constitutional traditions of the Member States are 'general principles' of EU law.[70] This provision appears to suggest that the incorporation of the EUCFR merely codifies the existing position, as developed by the European Court of Justice. In fact, by its reference only to the Union, and not to the Member States, Article I-9 CT apparently does not go as far as the existing jurisprudence, which places an obligation on Member States to respect fundamental rights as 'general principles' of EU law when they are implementing EU law,[71] or when they are derogating from their Treaty obligations.[72] The former of these two obligations is explicitly reflected in Article II-111(1) CT.[73] In any case, the point here is that the EUCFR appears to be aimed principally at the 'institutions, bodies, offices and agencies' of the EU,[74] rather than at those of its Member States.

Whatever one's take on this matter, it may be that the *social* rights in the EUCFR will lack the quality of individual justiciability, even if the EUCFR is 'hardened up' as a legal instrument.[75] The Cologne Conclusions state that: 'in drawing up such a Charter account should furthermore be taken of economic and social rights as contained in the European Social Charter and in the Community Charter of Fundamental Social Rights for Workers *insofar as they do not merely establish objectives for action by the Union*' (emphasis added). The original Charter does not, however, elaborate on the distinction implicit here between 'economic and social rights' and mere 'objectives for action'.[76] Drawing on the wording of the Charter, Hepple suggests that the provisions on economic and social rights

---

uploads/constitution/27_03.pdf (2003); P. Craig, 'What Constitution Does Europe Need? The House that Giscard Built: Constitutional Rooms with a View', Federal Trust Papers, http://www.fedtrust.co.uk/uploads/constitution/26_03.pdf (2003); P. Eeckhout, 'The EU Charter of Fundamental Rights and the Federal Question', 39 *CMLRev.* (2002) 945; Schwarze, 'Constitutional Perspectives of the European Union with Regard to the Next Intergovernmental Conference', 8 *EPL* (2002) 241; de Witte, *supra* n. 65; J. Wouters, 'Editorial', 8 *MJ* (2001) 3 and the other contributions to this special issue of the journal, Vol. 8 (1); Betten, *supra* n. 65; B. Hepple 'The EU Charter of Fundamental Rights', 30 *ILJ* (2001) 225; K. Lenaerts and P. Foubert, 'Social Rights in the Case-Law of the European Court of Justice: The Impact of the Charter of Fundamental Rights of the European Union on Standing Case-Law', 28 *LIEI* (2001) 267; Lord Goldsmith, 'A Charter of Rights, Freedoms and Principles', 38 *CMLRev.* (2001) 1201.

[69] Art. I-9(1) CT.
[70] Art. I-9(2) CT provides that the EU shall seek accession to the ECHR; this proposal need not concern us here.   [71] Case 5/88, *Wachauf* [1989] ECR 2609.
[72] Case C-260/98, *ERT* [1991] ECR I-2925.
[73] It is not clear whether the omission of the latter was deliberate or not, see further Eeckhout, *supra* n. 68, at 977–79, and, more generally, G. de Búrca, 'The Drafting of the European Union Charter of Fundamental Rights', 26 *ELRev.* (2001) 126.
[74] Art. II-111(1) CT. The words 'offices and agencies' have been added from the original EUCFR text, reflecting the proliferation of such bodies within the EU.
[75] See Goldsmith's argument in terms of 'principles' as opposed to 'rights and freedoms', in Lord Goldsmith, *supra* n. 68. Cf. M. Gijzen, 'The Charter: A Milestone for Social Protection in Europe?', (2001) 8 *MJ* 33, at 42, 'the Charter has the potential to become the first legally binding document which guarantees both fundamental socio-economic rights and which provides, at the same time, for a system of individual petition'.   [76] Hepple, *supra* n. 68, at 228.

within it fall into three categories: clear individual rights; rights that 'the Union recognizes and respects'; and pure objectives. Article 35 EUCFR falls into the third category. This is also reflected in the constitutional traditions of some Member States, which draw a distinction between justiciable rights and 'directive principles of social policy'.[77] This might pose obstacles to the development of the right to health care in the EUCFR as an individually justiciable right,[78] even if the Charter becomes binding EU law.[79]

It seems that an attempt to constitutionalize this position was made in the final text of the CT. Article II-112 CT contains a new paragraph (5), not in the original EUCFR, which states that: 'The provisions of this Charter which contain principles may be implemented by legislation and executive acts taken by institutions and bodies of the Union, and acts of the institutions when they are implementing Union law, in the exercise of their respective powers. They shall be judicially cognisable only in the interpretation of such acts and in the ruling on their legality.' This suggests that 'principles' (as opposed to 'rights') can never be directly effective in EU law. While it is not entirely clear which provisions of the EUCFR contain such 'principles', it seems unlikely that the mere phrase 'everyone has a right' will be sufficient to determine a provision as containing a 'right'.[80] It seems that the new provision refers to the chapter on 'Solidarity', of which Article 35 EUCFR is a part, and its inclusion was necessary to secure UK and Irish agreement on the Constitutional Treaty.[81]

However, even if some provisions remain non-justiciable at the suit of individuals, the provisions in Part II of the CT may be relevant for a number of reasons. For instance, Part II of the CT clearly imposes obligations on the institutions of the EU. Article II-111(1) CT, understood in the context of Article I-2 CT on the EU's values and Article I-9 on fundamental rights, suggests a positive obligation on the institutions to take full account of the EUCFR when performing their legislative tasks.[82] To the extent that the provisions of the EUCFR are construed by the European Court of Justice or the Court of First Instance as expressing previously existing 'general principles of EU law',[83] those provisions may in effect become the basis for judicial review[84] of action of the EU institutions, both administrative and legislative. Review of acts of the Member States *implementing* EU law,[85] or

---

[77] Ibid. See, for instance, the Spanish Constitution and the Irish Constitution, Art. 45.

[78] Lenaerts and Foubert, *supra* n. 68, at 271, 'It seems, however, obvious, that the social rights contained in the Charter cannot as such serve as a basis for claims by EU citizens against the Community or a Member State. They should rather be seen as a "touchstone" against which Community and Member State action can be tested.'

[79] See S. Douglas-Scott, 'The Charter of Fundamental Rights as a Constitutional Document', 2004 *EHRLR* 37.   [80] See A. McColgan, 'Editorial', 2004 *EHRLR* 2.

[81] See *Financial Times*, 17 June 2004. And see B. Bercusson's chapter in this volume where he makes the case that this is an attack on social rights, pp. 172–74.

[82] Kenner, *supra* n. 59, at 531.

[83] Or, as the British delegation on the EUCFR insisted, 'a showcase of existing rights'.

[84] Under Arts 230 TEC and 234 TEC; also potentially under Art. 68 TEC.

[85] Case 5/88, *Wachauf v. Germany* [1989] ECR 2609. On the intricacies of what constitutes 'implementing' in this context, see Douglas-Scott, *supra* n. 79.

derogating from EU law when exercising one of the 'four freedoms',[86] may also be possible on this basis. The EU Commission has powers to ensure that Member States comply with obligations in EU law under the procedure in Article 226 EC, which involves judicial proceedings before the ECJ, with the ultimate sanction of a penalty payment.

Further, the inclusion of social rights in the EUCFR and now the CT, the explicit references to the ESC and (Rev)ESC in the Preamble, and the notion of 'indivisibility' of rights in the EUCFR, may encourage courts applying EU law to draw on the ESC and (Rev)ESC. The EUCFR and CT bring the jurisprudence of the European Court of Human Rights even more firmly within EU law.[87] Although there is no express mention of the ECSR, some have argued that the European Court of Justice is now required, in cases concerning the interpretation of provisions derived from the ESC (which of course includes Article 35 EUCFR) to consider the *Conclusions* of the ECSR.[88] Moreover, the right to health, taken in addition to other general principles of EU law, either expressed in the EUCFR or not, may form a basis for the development of individually enforceable rights to health. For instance, the right to health could conceivably be combined with the right to dignity in Article 1 EUCFR, the right to non-discrimination in Article 21 EUCFR, or the right to good administration in Article 41 EUCFR.[89] Alternatively, even if the provision on the right to health care is simply an expression of an objective, merely setting tasks to be translated into enforceable rights by secondary EU or (largely) national law, the status of these secondary provisions may be affected by their relationship with a fundamental right set out in the Charter. Such provisions may take on a 'constitutionalized' status, as has been the case, for instance with the European Court of Justice's development of the secondary legislation on sex equality.[90]

Further, Part II of the CT will be used to interpret existing EU law,[91] and the EUCFR has already been so used, at least by some Advocates-General before the ECJ.[92] It may also play a role as a platform for the development of new measures of EU law.[93] Although Article II-111(2) CT explicitly states that the Charter does not give any new powers or tasks to the EU institutions, it may provide a source of

---

[86] Case 260/89, *ERT v. DEP & Sotirios* [1991] ECR I-2925.

[87] Art. 52(3) EUCFR; Art. II-112(3) CT; see also Art. I-9(2) CT, which provides that the EU shall seek accession to the ECHR.

[88] Kenner, *supra* n. 59, at 537; B. Casey, 'The European Social Charter and Revised European Social Charter'; and B. Fitzpatrick, 'European Union Law and the Council of Europe Conventions', in Costello (ed), *supra* n. 4.

[89] For discussion of this right, see Case T-54/99, *Max.mobil* [2002] ECR II-313.

[90] Directive 76/207, OJ 1976 L39/40 as encapsulating a fundamental right, see Cases 75 and 117/82, *Razzouk and Beydoun* [1984] ECR 1509, para. 16; see von Bogdandy, *supra* n. 14.

[91] This is implicit in Art. II-112(7) CT, which provides that the explanatory guidance on the EUCFR, drawn up by the Praesidium of the Charter Convention, 'shall be given due regard by the courts of the Union and of the Member States'.

[92] See, for instance, Advocate-General Tizzano in Case C-173/99, *R v. Secretary of State for Trade and Industry, ex parte BECTU* [2001] ECR I-4881, para. 28.

[93] Non-binding legal provisions (or soft law) have played this role in the EU in the past. On the roles of soft law, see, e.g., L. Cram, *Policy-making in the EU: Conceptual Lenses and the Integration*

inspiration for the EU legislature, may constrain or direct the substantive contents or focus of EU law and policy (through the 'super-mainstreaming' element of some of its provisions) and may consequently give added support to certain actors in the legislative process.[94] In terms of social rights, the Charter may increase the influence of the (Rev)ESC in the EU's legal order, or those of its Member States.[95] Less tangibly still, the Charter may be seen as an important expression of the *values* underpinning the EU as a polity,[96] and thus may influence legislative, administrative, and judicial activity in perhaps more subtle ways.

V. THE 'RIGHT TO HEALTH' IN THE ESC AND THE EUCFR

This brief overview of the provisions on the (Rev)ESC and the EUCFR on the 'right to health' has revealed a number of similarities, and also a number of key differences between the approaches to the 'right to health' in each legal context. The *legal effects* of the two provisions differ, although to some extent the formal differences between obligations in EU law in general and those in international law are less stark in this context, as the EUCFR is not (yet) a part of 'hard' EU law, and even if it becomes so, there remains a question mark over the legal effects of the 'social rights' provisions of Part II of the CT, in particular their justiciability at the suit of individuals. Legally speaking, both provisions are a reference point in the interpretation of other provisions of law (in the EU context, mainly secondary EU legislation; in the (Rev)ESC context, national laws which are assumed to intend to comply with international obligations of the states that are parties to the (Rev)ESC). Differences in *practical effect* are not possible to elaborate with any great certainty at this stage, as the practical effects of the provisions of the EUCFR are as yet largely untested.[97] It is possible that, as elaborated above, the two bodies of law may contribute alike to construction of provisions of secondary EU law or national law, and that this process may lead to a common understanding of the

---

Process (1997), at 107–11; K. C. Wellens and G. M. Borchardt, 'Soft Law in European Community Law', 14 *ELRev.* (1989) 267; J. Kenner, 'The EU Employment Title and the "Third Way": Making Soft Law Work?', 15 *IJCLLIR* (1999) 33; see also specifically in the context of social policy, Betten, *supra* n. 65, at 152. For examples in the areas of sex equality and racism/xenophobia see, respectively, C. Hoskyns, *Integrating Gender* (1996); R. Geyer, *Exploring European Social Policy* (2000), at 164–71.

[94] For example, Waddington has shown how the disability lobby exerted its influence on the EU policy-making process, moving from a 'charity-based' to a 'dignity-based' provision; see L. Waddington, *Disability, Employment and the European Community* (1995).

[95] Gijzen, *supra* n. 75, at 47; see also J. Kenner, 'Economic and Social Rights in the EU Legal Order—The Mirage of Indivisibility', in Hervey and Kenner, *supra* n.**.

[96] B. Hepple, 'Social Values in European Law', (1995) *CLP* 39. A. Lyon-Caen, 'Fundamental Social Rights as Benchmarks in the Construction of the EU', in L. Betten and D. McDevitt (eds), *The Protection of Fundamental Social Rights in the European Union* (1996), at 45; Kenner, in Hervey and Kenner, *supra* n. 95; Douglas-Scott, *supra* n. 79.

[97] Commentators differ in their interpretations of this matter; see *supra* n. 68.

effects of 'social rights', such as a 'right to health', in which (Rev)ESC and EUCFR become involved in a process of mutual cross-fertilization. However, it is likely to be too soon to find significant evidence of this as yet.

The main focus of this chapter is on the *content* of the right to health under the (Rev)ESC and the EUCFR, and the question of the extent to which the EU institutions have referred to or been inspired by the (older) provision in the (Rev)ESC on the 'right to health'. As noted above, the content of social (human) rights provisions (as with all human rights provisions) becomes revealed through the practice of their application. In the context of the right to health under the (Rev)ESC, in practice this means their application through the reporting procedure, and its principal outcome, the regular *Conclusions* of the ECSR.[98] The sections of these *Conclusions* on Article 11 (Rev)ESC form the organizing structure of this part of the chapter. In addition, the 'soft law' Recommendations of the Committee of Ministers, although non-normative, play a role in elaborating guidance on the proper interpretation of the (Rev)ESC. A number of these Recommendations are relevant to Article 11,[99] and are also considered below.

The more recent *Conclusions* of the ECSR structure the sections on Article 11 (Rev)ESC under several headings, referable to the subparagraphs of Article 11 itself. These are as follows:

Removal of the causes of ill-health
    State of health of the population—General indicators
    Health care system
Advisory and educational facilities
    Developing a sense of individual responsibility
    Counselling and screening
Prevention of diseases
    Policies on the prevention of avoidable risks
    Prophylactic measures

Each of these is in turn divided into several elements. The conclusion to be drawn from this is, presumably, that these elements, in the view of the ECSR, constitute the content of the 'right to health' under Article 11 (Rev)ESC.

---

[98] There has, as yet, been no successful complaint on the basis of Art. 11 (Rev)ESC, under the complaints mechanism; but see *supra* n. 56.
[99] Examples include Recommendation No. (1999) 21 of the Committee of Ministers of the Council of Europe on criteria for the management of waiting lists and waiting times in health care (30 September 1999) (discussed below); Recommendation No. (2001) 12 of the Committee of Ministers of the Council of Europe on the adaptation of health care services to the demand for health care and health care services of people in marginal situations (10 October 2001); Recommendation No. (2000) 3 of the Committee of Ministers of the Council of Europe on the right to the satisfaction of basic material needs of persons in situations of extreme hardship (19 January 2000); Recommendation No. (1998) 11 of the Committee of Ministers of the Council of Europe on the organisation of health care services for the chronically ill (18 September 1998).

For the purposes of this chapter, there is space to consider only two selected elements in any depth. In particular, the general health indicators, regarded as important under Article 11(1) (Rev)ESC[100] are not elaborated, for reasons of space, and because there is no obvious point of contact with the EU's *acquis*. The elements chosen for analysis here are those with respect to hospital waiting lists and waiting times, and those concerning smoking. These represent one example of the 'health care' branch of the right to health, and one example of the 'health protection' branch. Brief coverage of other elements puts these into context, and also adds further to the overall conclusions. For each element, the *Conclusions* of the ECSR are elaborated and any relevant references to the Recommendations of the Council of Europe's Committee of Ministers are made. A comparison is then drawn with the activities of the institutions of the European Union, in particular the ECJ, and, drawing from these, the approach of the EU's *acquis communautaire* to the 'right to health' in the EU context.

A. *Health Care: Timely Access to (Hospital) Treatment*

Under Article 11(1) (Rev)ESC, states are required to 'take appropriate measures . . . to remove as far as possible the causes of ill-health'. The ECSR considers that this requires States Parties to have in place a health care system, which guarantees access to health care.[101] The ECSR is interested in the financial arrangements of such health care systems, although this is not an explicit heading for discussion of the 'right to health' in the ECSR *Conclusions*. Collective bodies must bear 'all, or at least a substantial part, of the cost of the health services'.[102] Both 'social insurance' and 'national health systems' are recognized as valid mechanisms for fulfilling the obligations under the (Rev)ESC.[103] In particular, the ECSR is interested in coverage under the system, both in terms of whether any individuals are left with inadequate access to health care, and in terms of which types of health care services are covered (for example, are dental services covered?). So, for instance, the ECSR deferred its conclusions on Cyprus in 2001, noting that in the vast majority of States Parties to the ESC, 98–100 per cent of the population is covered by the health care system, whereas in Cyprus, 13 per cent of the population is not covered at all, and a further 20 per cent entitled only to reduced-cost

---

[100] Mortality rates for the 'vulnerable groups' of infants and mothers are considered to be a key indicator as to whether a health system as a whole is functioning well or not. A particularly high infant or maternal mortality rate raises a problem of conformity with Art. 11(1) (Rev)ESC; see *Conclusions XIII-3*, Turkey, at 357–58.   [101] *Conclusions I*, at 59.

[102] *Conclusions I*, at 59.

[103] For discussion of the differences between these two main types of national health system found within the EU and Council of Europe states, see Hervey and McHale, Ch 4, *supra* n. **; A. P. Van der Mei, *Free Movement of Persons within the European Community: Cross-Border Access to Public Benefits* (2003); E. Mossialos and M. McKee, *EU Law and the Social Character of Health Care* (2002); E. Mossialos et al. (eds), *Funding Health Care: Options for Europe* (2002).

health care.[104] The ECSR also asks what measures are taken to prevent health care costs from being an excessive burden on people with low incomes.[105] Ratios of health care professionals (including specialists) to populations are considered. The ECSR is also interested in the cost of pharmaceuticals, reimbursement rules, and cost-sharing schemes. This is directly relevant to the question of preventing health care costs from being excessively burdensome on people with low incomes.[106] So, for instance, in the case of Belgium, the ECSR found in 2001 that, although patients' levels of contribution to expenses had increased steadily since 1980 (a 'steady worsening' of the situation), this was offset by national measures that reduced the impact of cost-sharing on disadvantaged groups, and thus access to health care in Belgium is in compliance with Article 11(1) (Rev)ESC.[107]

The ECSR has established that its *Conclusions* consider not only the formal legal position, but also the practical implications of the national regulations in force with respect to particular protected rights.[108] In the context of Article 11 (Rev)ESC, the ECSR has found that access to health care must be provided 'without undue delay'.[109] In order to assess conformity of national situations, the ECSR pays attention to the average waiting time for admission to hospital under states' health care systems, and the way in which waiting lists are managed.[110] The content of the 'right to health' has been further elaborated in this context by Recommendation No. (99) 21 of the Committee of Ministers of the Council of Europe on *Criteria for the Management of Waiting Lists and Waiting Times in Health Care*.[111] This states that 'the final objective of a health care system should be to eliminate both undue delays in access to health care and undue waiting lists altogether'. The Recommendation notes that a system of waiting times or waiting lists 'usually translates society's wish to ensure a fundamental principle: that access to health care should be available to all according to their needs, and regardless of their ability to pay'. The Recommendation describes 'access to care irrespective of the client's ability to pay' as a 'central principle'.

In both the Committee of Ministers' Recommendation and the 'jurisprudence' of the ECSR, the language used in this context ('final objective', 'fundamental principle', 'central principle') resonates with the discussion above with respect to some social rights under the EUCFR, including Article 35 EUCFR, being categorized as mere 'principles' or 'pure objectives', rather than clear individual rights.[112] It also resonates with the distinction, present in the constitutional

---

[104] *Conclusions XV* (2001), Vol. 2 (Cyprus). The ECSR noted that in order to be in conformity with Article 11(1) ESC, 'the health care system must offer care accessible to the largest number, which presupposes sufficiently broad coverage of the population, and at best universal coverage'.

[105] *Conclusions XVI-2* (2003), at 427, 644; *Conclusions XV* (2002), Vol. 1, (Austria).

[106] Ibid.   [107] *Conclusions XV* (2001), Vol. 1 (Belgium).   [108] Ibid.

[109] This requirement refers mainly to the situation in several states whose health services are essentially provided on a universal basis, where waiting lists apply for health care and treatment.

[110] *Conclusions XV-2*, at 128, 269, 491, 557, 598–99; *Conclusions XVI-2* (2003), at 161, 427, 644–45, 775.

[111] Adopted 30 September 1999, at the 681st Meeting of the Ministers' Deputies.

[112] See Hepple, *supra* n. 68.

traditions of some Member States, between justiciable rights and 'directive principles of social policy'. The implication here is that the right to health under the (Rev)ESC, or at least that element of it relevant to the universal and timely access to health care, regardless of financial means, does not represent a 'hard' or individually enforceable right, but rather a softer legal obligation.

The ECSR has found manifest lack of conformity with Article 11(1) (Rev)ESC in the situation where poor organization of primary health care 'has led to queues and long waiting times', waiting times for some specialized services were three years, and the hospitals concerned did not create waiting lists according to the patients' state of health.[113] The ECSR observed that the organizational problems in the relevant primary health care system lead to low moral among health care staff, and that the long waiting lists encourage 'under the table payments'. This is clearly not consistent with the principles of equitable and transparent access to health care, set out in the Recommendation, which, as a measure of 'soft law', provides guidance on the interpretation of Article 11 (Rev)ESC. The ECSR deferred its conclusion on compliance with Article 11(1) in the case of a situation where duration of waiting lists was long in absolute terms, the situation was not improving (here the average waiting time for admission to hospital increased from thirty-five to forty-five days within five years, the number of persons waiting more than twenty-six weeks for primary care doubled in two years, and the total numbers of patients on waiting lists also increased), and simultaneously the number of hospital beds continued to decrease. Further information was sought on the way in which waiting lists were managed.[114] The WHO has set an objective of three hospital beds per 1000 inhabitants for developing countries, and the ECSR takes the view that figures lower than this are not compliant with Article 11(1) (Rev)ESC.[115] That said, a mere decrease in the total number of hospital beds does not in itself imply lack of compliance with Article 11(1) (Rev)ESC.[116] Nor does a mere increase in the number of patients on waiting lists.[117] Nor, once a waiting list system is established, does the mere breach of its guidelines in itself constitute a failure to comply with Article 11(1) (Rev)ESC. Norway set a maximum six month waiting time for patients who do not need emergency treatment, but who require treatment to avoid serious complications. During the reference period, the number of cases where this maximum wait was not respected actually increased. However, taking into account other information, in particular the patient's right to choose a hospital, the ECSR resolved to wait until the next report before passing judgement.

[113] *Conclusions XVI-2* (2003), at 644–45 (Poland).
[114] *Conclusions XV-2* (2001), Vol. 2, at 596–600 (UK); see also *Conclusions XV* (2001), Vol. 1 (Denmark).
[115] *Conclusions XV-2* (2001), Vol. 2, at 257–60 (Turkey); see also *Conclusions XV* (2001), Vol. 1 (Spain), in which the ECSR found that a density of hospital beds of 3.9 per 1000 inhabitants constituted a 'weak point' in the situation with respect to Art. 11(1), but deferred its conclusions under the next examination of Art. 11.
[116] *Conclusions XV-2* (2001), Vol. 2, at 47–50 (Germany).
[117] *Conclusions XV* (2001), Vol. 1 (Norway).

The European Court of Justice and other institutions of the EU have also engaged with the question of hospital waiting lists, and patients' rights in this context. However, this engagement has been indirect, rather than through the direct application of Article 35 EUCFR.[118] The question of hospital waiting lists has arisen in the context of jurisprudence on the freedom to provide and receive services across borders in the EU, a matter covered by the (directly effective) Article 49 EC, which provides that 'restrictions' on the freedom to provide services within the EU 'shall be prohibited'. Controversially, the ECJ has found that, in some circumstances, health care reimbursed under a national social security scheme may fall within Article 49 EC.[119] The ECJ has found that a system requiring prior authorization where treatment is sought from a health care provider with whom the insurance fund has not entered into an agreement (which would in practice include health care providers in other states) constitutes *prima facie* a 'restriction' in the sense of Article 49 EC.[120] However, restrictions on the freedom to provide and receive services may be justified in various circumstances. In this context, relevant objective public interest justifications include the social protection provided by,[121] and financial viability of,[122] national social security systems, and consumer protection.[123]

One of the main situations[124] in which patients may seek health care services in a state different from their own is that where the waiting times in the home state are such that patients face a significant delay before receiving treatment. In the

---

[118] It was noted *supra* that Art. 35 EUCFR is, in any case, not directly effective at present, and is unlikely to be so even if the EUCFR is incorporated into the Treaty, which will take place if the CT is ratified.

[119] The essential characteristic of remuneration is that it constitutes consideration for the service in question; Case 263/85, *Belgian State v. Humbel* [1988] ECR 5365, para. 17. Remuneration need not come directly from the recipient of the services; Case 352/85, *Bond van Adverteerders* [1988] ECR 2124. In certain circumstances, medical treatment or health care reimbursed under a national social security scheme may fall within Article 49 EC; Case C-158/96, *Kohll v. Union des Caisses de Maladie* [1998] ECR I-1931, para. 29; it is also the case where *intramural* treatment (within a hospital) is reimbursed by a national sickness insurance fund, even where such reimbursement is on the basis of regulated pre-set scales of fees; Case C-157/99, *Geraets-Smits and Peerbooms* [2001] ECR I-5473 paras. 55–58; Case C-368/86, *Vanbraekel* [2001] ECR I-5363, para. 42; Case C-385/99, *Müller-Fauré and Van Riet (Van Riet)* [2003] ECR I-4509. The Court has not yet ruled on the application of the Treaty to the provision of health care services under a national health system financed largely by public taxation. The English High Court has ruled that the principles developed by the Court in *Geraets-Smits* and *Müller-Fauré* do apply in the context of the UK NHS, funded largely through public taxation; see *R (on the application of Yvonne Watts) v. Bedford Primary Care Trust and Secretary of State for Health* [2003] EWHC 2228 (Admin), 1 October 2003. This case has now been referred to the ECJ. [120] Case C-385/99, *Van Riet*, *supra* n. 119, paras. 37–45, para. 103.

[121] Case C-272/94, *Guiot and Climatec* [1996] ECR I-1905.

[122] Case C-120/95, *Decker* [1998] ECR I-1831; Case C-158/96, *Kohll* [1998] ECR I-1931; Case C-157/99, *Geraets-Smits and Peerbooms* [2001] ECR I-5473; Case C-368/86, *Vanbraekel* [2001] ECR I-5363; Case C-8/02, *Leichtle*, judgment of 18 March 2004, (not yet reported).

[123] Case 205/84, *Commission v. Germany* [1986] ECR 3755, para. 30; Case C-288/89, *Gouda* [1991] ECR I-4007, para. 27; Case C-76/90, *Säger* [1991] ECR I-4221, para. 15; Case C-275/92, *Schindler* [1994] ECR I-1039, para. 58.

[124] Others include where a particular health care service is not available in their home state, or where various elements of quality of care suggest a better service in another state, including value for money, or higher health care professional standards.

Van Riet case,[125] the patient sought authorization from her Dutch sickness insurance fund to be treated in a Belgian hospital, because the treatment could be carried out much sooner in Belgium. This was refused, but in the meantime, the treatment was carried out in Belgium and reimbursement was sought. The Dutch national court referred to the European Court of Justice on the question whether the Dutch system, which provided that, where treatment is sought from a health care provider with whom the insurance fund has not entered into an agreement, prior authorization[126] is required, was compatible with EU law. The Court relied on previous rulings to confirm the application of Article 49 EC in such circumstances. Where the Court went further than in earlier jurisprudence, however, was with respect to what is a legitimate ground on which prior authorization could be refused under the Dutch system. The Court considered the criterion of 'without undue delay', holding that such an assessment must be based on an assessment of the individual patient's medical condition. Further, a refusal to grant prior authorization based not on fear of wastage resulting from hospital overcapacity, but solely on the ground that there are waiting lists within that Member State for the hospital treatment concerned cannot amount to a proper justification.[127] This is because arguments to the effect that such waiting lists are necessary, at least as argued before the Court in this case, amounted in the view of the Court to no more than a consideration of a 'purely economic nature',[128] which can never justify a restriction on a fundamental freedom in EU law.[129]

Particularly where there are long waiting times for hospital treatment, in spite of some clarification in *Van Riet*, there is scope for disagreement over what constitutes 'undue delay'. In *Watts*,[130] before the English High Court, Munby J considered a claim by a patient, who, facing a delay in receiving a hip replacement operation, first sought permission to receive the treatment abroad and have it paid for by the national health authority (Bedford Primary Care Trust), and on refusal, subsequently travelled to France for the operation, and claimed reimbursement from the Trust or the Secretary of State for Health. Watts failed at first instance on the facts, as she was unable to show that she faced an 'undue delay', as, at the time she had the operation abroad, she was facing a delay of only 3–4 months.[131] However, the case has been appealed, and subsequently referred to the European Court of Justice.

The *Van Riet* and *Watts* cases illustrate the potential use of EU law by litigants seeking to avoid waiting times for health care services under their national health (insurance) systems. States use hospital waiting lists in effect as a tool to constrain spending. Waiting lists also arise as a logical consequence of policy decisions about

---

125 Case C-385/99, *Van Riet, supra* n. 119.
126 Such authorization is granted only where it is a medical necessity.
127 Case C-385/99, *Van Riet, supra* n. 119, para. 92.   128 Ibid.
129 Ibid., para. 72, citing Case C-398/95, *SETTG* [1997] ECR I-3091 and Case C-158/96, *Kohll, supra* n. 119.   130 See *supra* n. 119.
131 The UK High Court did find that a delay of one year, for such an operation, where the patient suffered considerable pain and mobility difficulties, would be 'undue'; *Watts, supra* n. 119, para. 158.

resource allocation. The ruling in *Van Riet*, that a refusal to authorize hospital treatment in another Member State *solely* on the grounds that there are waiting lists for the treatment concerned in the home Member State does not constitute a justification for a restriction on the freedom to provide services, implies a loss of control at national level over the use of hospital waiting lists. The ability of certain (litigious) patients to utilize EU law in circumstances such as those arising in *Van Riet* may be regarded as an inappropriate judicial interference with political processes. In general, then, these kinds of pressures may jeopardize the overall structure of national health (insurance) systems, and their financial and administrative arrangements. Overall, however, the ability of states to justify their arrangements on the basis that they are necessary for the financial viability of their health care systems reduces significantly the potentially disruptive impact of EU internal market law in this context.[132]

I have previously considered what, if any, difference the application of a notion of a 'right to health' might make in this context.[133] What is important for the analysis in this chapter is simply the following. Nowhere in the jurisprudence on freedom to receive cross-border health care services has there been reference to Article 35 EUCFR, Article 11 (Rev)ESC, or a 'right to health'. Neither the ECJ nor its Advocates-General (nor indeed those representing the litigants before it) have taken the view that the question of timely access to health care is an element of the 'right to health'. No reference or linkage is made to the relevant jurisprudence of the ESC.

This finding is largely confirmed by reference to actions of EU institutions other than the European Court of Justice. There is (as yet?) no relevant legislation on the question of cross-border health care, but there has been a recent move towards considering health care and long term care using the 'open method of coordination'.[134] This has reached the stage of a Commission Communication on 'Modernising social protection for the development of high-quality, accessible and sustainable health care and long term care: support for the national strategies using the "open method of coordination" '.[135] This document reveals no explicit

---

[132] See further Hervey and McHale, *supra* n. **, Ch 4.

[133] See Hervey, in Hervey and Kenner, *supra* n. **. The conclusion is that a difference in discourse might be found, but differences in substantive outcome are highly unlikely.

[134] The OMC process, originally established in the context of coordination of 'broad economic policy guidelines' and a 'European employment strategy', uses soft law mechanisms of guidelines (agreed by the Member States), exchange of best practice, benchmarking of national standards against those of the best performing Member States, and national action plans according to which Member States' national policies are to converge on these guidelines. The OMC process was subsequently applied to social inclusion, pensions, and a similar process exists in the environmental sphere. For a selection of literature on the OMC, see Kenner, *supra* n. 93; C. De La Porte, 'Is the Open Method of Coordination Appropriate for Organising Activities at European Level in Sensitive Policy Areas?', 8 *ELJ* (2002) 38; K. A. Armstrong, 'Tackling Social Exclusion through OMC: Reshaping the Boundaries of EU Governance?', in T. Börzel and R. Cichowski (eds), *State of the Union: Law, Politics and Society* (Vol. 6) (2003) 170; S. Regent, 'The Open Method of Coordination: A New Supranational Form of Governance?', 9 *ELJ* (2003) 190; F. W. Scharpf, 'The European Social Model: Coping with the Challenges of Diversity', 40 *JCMS* (2002) 645.   [135] See, in particular, COM(2004)304 final.

references to Article 35 EUCFR, or to Article 11 (Rev)ESC, or indeed the use of rights discourse with respect to a 'right to health' in this context.[136]

The exception is in one (but only one) of five themes of the report of the High Level Process of Reflection on patient mobility and healthcare.[137] This Process was set up by the Council, in part in response to the litigation on the free movement of patients.[138] The Process has no formal status in the EU's legislature, but will be indirectly influential on both the Council, whom it advises, and the Commission. In the report, issued in December 2003, an express reference is made to Article 35 EUCFR, in the context of patients' rights, under the theme of 'European cooperation to enable better use of resources'. The report calls for 'greater clarity at European level' on the 'rights, entitlements and expectations' of patients. However, the detail here appears to refer to protection of personal data, informed consent, and obligations of professionals with respect to patients. These are matters that are covered by other provisions of the EUCFR,[139] and indeed potentially the ECHR, but do not fall within the scope of the (Rev)ESC. There is no reference to Article 11 (Rev)ESC in this document. Neither is there any reference to the 'right to health' under any of the other themes, which included 'access and quality'. Rather, matters concerning the personal and material coverage of national health systems, timely treatment, price, and cost-sharing, all matters considered relevant to Article 11 (Rev)ESC by the ECSR, again do not appear to be conceptualized in terms of rights.

B. Health Protection: Anti-smoking Regulation

The *Conclusions* of the ECSR reveal a significant concentration on the 'health protection' elements of a right to health, especially environmental health. Under Article 11(3), states are required 'to prevent as far as possible epidemic, endemic and other diseases . . .'. Several elements of the right to health may be elaborated from the ECSR *Conclusions*. First, the ECSR is interested in national measures to reduce environmental risks, in particular to combat air pollution, water pollution, risks from asbestos, ionizing radiation, and protection against noise.[140] In the case of the Member States of the EU, many of these national provisions may be responding to measures of EU environmental law, and indeed on occasions the ECSR reports refer explicitly to provisions of EU law.[141] As far as I am aware,

---

[136] This echoes the findings in B. de Witte's chapter in this volume, with respect to education, pp. 166–67.

[137] Commission, Outcome of the High Level Process of Reflection on Patient Mobility and Healthcare Developments in the EU, 9 December 2003, HLPR/2003/16. The findings are echoed in the Commission's Follow-Up Communication COM(2004)301 final.

[138] The Council's High Level Group on Patient Mobility and Healthcare, see europa.eu.int/comm/dgs/health_consumer/library/press/press270_en.pdf and http://europa.eu.int/comm/dgs/health_consumer/library/press/press301_en.pdf.   [139] See *supra* pp. 315–16.

[140] *Conclusions XVI-2* (2003), at 163–65; *Conclusions XV* (2001), Vol. 1 (Austria).

[141] See, e.g., *Conclusions XVI-2* (2003), at 430.

there is little or no explicit reference to social (human) rights in the development, implementation, or interpretation of EU environmental law.[142]

Secondly, the ECSR is also interested in food safety.[143] This is a response to particular recent threats or potential threats to health posed by the production of food in the European context, in particular, BSE/nvCJD and genetically modified foodstuffs. Both of these matters are also the subject of significant regulatory activity in the EU institutions. Recently, the regulation of food in the EU has come under scrutiny, and has undergone a period of reform.[144] The reform process culminated in a number of measures, central to which is Regulation 178/2002/EC.[145] However, again, the language of rights is absent from these measures, and the 'right to health' does not appear to underpin their conceptualization in the EU context.

Thirdly, the ECSR considers measures taken by states to combat smoking.[146] This is justified by the Committee's observations that smoking is a major cause of avoidable death in developed countries and is associated with a wide range of diseases (cardiac, circulatory, pulmonary diseases, and cancers). Cancer remains one of the biggest causes of death in the Council of Europe states. The link between tobacco consumption and health problems, in particular between smoking and lung cancer, is well established. The World Health Organization confirms that tobacco is the single greatest cause of preventable disease and death.[147] In the EU, 83 per cent of lung cancers in men are caused by smoking tobacco. Lung cancer is by far the most common fatal cancer in the EU, with an estimated annual death rate per 1,000 in the EU of 447.9.[148] The ECSR examines

[142] A CELEX search of EU legal documentation (preparatory legislative documents, legislation, case law of the ECJ) revealed no references to Art. 35 EUCFR or Art. 11 (Rev)ESC in the context of EU environmental law.   [143] *Conclusions XVI-2* (2003), at 165.

[144] This is for a number of interrelated reasons, chief amongst which is the fallout from the BSE/nvCJD crisis. See, in general, M. Westlake, '"Mad Cows and Englishmen": The Institutional Consequences of the BSE Crisis', in N. Nugent (ed.), *European Union 1996: The Annual Review*, at 11; E. Vos, 'EU Food Safety Regulation in the aftermath of the BSE Crisis', 23 *Journal of Consumer Policy* (2000) 227.

[145] OJ 2002 L31/1. For the proposal see COM(2000)716. There is a separate and detailed EU regulatory scheme for genetically modified foods, see in particular Regulation 258/97, the 'Novel Foods Regulation', OJ 1997 L258/1. This regime is the subject of intense debate in the context of the WTO. See, for instance, J. Scott and E. Vos, 'The Juridification of Uncertainty: Observations on the Ambivalence of the Precautionary Principle within the EU and the WTO', in C. Joerges and R. Dehousse, *Good Governance in Europe's Integrated Market* (2002); J. Scott, 'The Precautionary Principle Before the European Courts', in R. Macrory (ed.), *Environmental Principles in the EU and the Member States* (2004).

[146] *Conclusions XVI-2* (2003), at 165; *Conclusions XV* (2001), Vol. 1 (Austria).

[147] The WHO has been considering smoking and its effects on health since at least the 1970s, see WHO Expert Committee Report, *Smoking and its effects on health* (1975). Successive World Health Assemblies have adopted resolutions aimed at combating smoking, see S. Fluss, 'The Development of National Health Legislation in Europe: The Contribution of International Organizations', 2 *European Journal of Health Law* (1995) 193–237.

[148] See Commission Press Release MEMO/01/190 *Cancer and Cancer Research in the European Union*, 22 May 2001; see also P. Watson, 'Europe Agrees Complete Ban on Tobacco Advertising by 2006', 315 *British Medical Journal* (1997) 1559, citing research suggesting over 500,000 deaths per annum in the EU are tobacco related.

national legislation aimed at preventive measures, such as restrictions on tobacco advertising and education campaigns. Again, explicit reference is occasionally made to EU law measures.[149]

In its 2001 *Conclusions* with respect to Austria, the ECSR notes with approval the 'strengthening' of the new national legislative framework for combating smoking, which entered into force in 1995. A similar example is the 2001 *Conclusions* on Denmark, in which the ECSR requests that the next report 'provide information on the measures taken to tighten the ban on [tobacco] advertising'. As Danish law already prohibits TV and radio advertising of any tobacco product, and requires information on the dangers of smoking to appear on packaging, the implication is that the ECSR regards even greater restrictions as at least desirable in achieving the 'right to health'. Likewise, the ECSR sought further information from Iceland, where the level of tobacco consumption is the second highest in the EU and EEA, and urged Iceland to strengthen its tobacco supply control policy and possibly its legislative framework.[150] The ECSR suggested that a ban on young people smoking and on the sale of tobacco products to young persons was a key element of an achievable anti-smoking policy in its 2001 *Conclusions* with respect to Portugal. The ECSR found Greece to be not in conformity with Article 11(3) ESC, on the basis that Greece has by far the highest level of annual per capita cigarette consumption in the EU and EEA, and the figure continues to rise steadily. The ECSR found that the Greek policy of regulating tobacco sales was 'clearly inadequate', and asked what measures were intended to tackle the situation, suggesting toughening existing legislation, for instance by prohibiting the sale of tobacco to young people, banning smoking in public places, and banning billboard advertising and advertising in the printed media.

In the EU context, the anti-smoking elements of policy development have taken place within the broader construct of the EU's internal market law, which has a strong emphasis on the free movement of goods and services (which include in this context tobacco products themselves and, crucially, tobacco advertising). These measures can be constructed as having a deregulatory effect on national measures aimed at the protection of the right to health through restricting sale and advertisement of tobacco products.[151] The EU institutions have taken various types of action towards combating cancer. In the health promotion context, these have focused on the promotion of lifestyles that do not increase the risk of cancer, especially lung cancer. The EU has financed anti-cancer programmes since the 1980s, and has also sought to regulate the composition, presentation, and sale of tobacco products and the advertising of tobacco products within the EU. Previous 'Europe against Cancer' programmes, funded by the EU, have now been subsumed within the new public health framework,[152] which runs from 1 January

---

[149] See, e.g., *Conclusions XVI-2* (2003), at 431   [150] *Conclusions XV* (2001), Vol. 1 (Iceland).
[151] See, for instance, T. K. Hervey, 'Up in Smoke: Community (anti) tobacco law and policy', 26 *ELRev.* (2001) 101; Hervey and McHale, *supra* n. **, Ch 9.
[152] Decision 1786/2002 adopting the new public health framework, OJ 2002 L271/1.

2003 to 31 December 2008.[153] Again, the legislative instruments establishing these programmes make no reference to Article 35 EUCFR or to Article 11 (Rev)ESC.

The regulation of tobacco products has taken place at EU level since the late 1980s, in the context of internal market legislation. Article 95 EC (formerly Article 100a EC) gives the EU competence to adopt measures which have as their object the establishment and functioning of the internal market. In putting forward proposals for such measures, the Commission must take as a base a high level of protection in matters such as health and consumer protection.[154] Thus, EU-level measures harmonizing the marketing and production of tobacco products have a strong health promotion element. Such legislation concerns three broad areas: consumer protection in the form of health information (and essentially warnings) on tobacco products, especially cigarettes; consumer protection in terms of the lawful composition of tobacco products;[155] and measures concerning the advertising of tobacco products.[156]

The orientation of these measures, and the discourse surrounding their adoption and interpretation, has been profoundly affected by the judicial review of the original Tobacco Advertising Directive 98/43/EC,[157] which, although purporting to be an internal market measure, imposed a wide-ranging prohibition on advertising of tobacco products in the EU. As the Directive was based on the internal market provisions of Article 57(2) (now 47(2)), 66 (now 55) and 100a (now 95) EC, in order to be lawfully adopted, the Directive must have had an internal market rationale. Perhaps with a view to showing that this was so, Article 1 of the Directive provided that its objective was 'to approximate the law, regulations and administrative provisions of the Member States relating to advertising and the sponsorship of tobacco products'. The *content* of the Directive, however, could be construed as suggesting otherwise, and it was this issue that was at the heart of the legal challenges to the validity of the Directive in *Tobacco Advertising* and *Imperial Tobacco*.[158] The Court concluded that the Directive was not properly enacted on the basis of Articles 100a, 57(2), and 66 EC. For our purposes, what is interesting is the extent to which elements of the EU's regulatory activity that might be read as implicitly supporting a 'right to health', in particular the health protection and promotion elements of these regulatory measures, have subsequently been significantly downplayed.

---

[153] Decision 1786/2002, Art. 1(2).   [154] Art. 100a(3) TEC, now Art. 95(3) TEC.

[155] Now see Tobacco Products Consolidation Directive 2001/37, OJ 2001 L194/26. The Directive brings together the pre-existing provisions on manufacture, presentation, and sale of tobacco products in the EU. It reduces the maximum permitted tar level of cigarettes from 12mg to 10mg per cigarette, and introduces ceilings of 1mg nicotine and 10mg carbon monoxide per cigarette, from 1 January 2004. Rules on labelling, in particular with respect to mandatory health warnings, make up most of the remainder of the Directive.

[156] See Directive 2003/33, OJ 2003 L152/16.   [157] Directive 98/43, OJ 1998 L213/9.

[158] Case C-376/98, *Germany v. European Parliament and Council* [2000] ECR I-8419; Case C-74/99, *R v. Secretary of State for Health and others, ex parte Imperial Tobacco* [2000] ECR I-8599.

The main provision now covering the manufacture, presentation, and sale of tobacco products is the Tobacco Products Consolidation Directive 2001/37/EC.[159] The aim of this Directive is to eliminate differences in national regulations concerning manufacture, presentation, and sale of tobacco products.[160] Such differences constitute a hindrance to trade, and thus impede the establishment and functioning of the internal market. Unlike earlier directives,[161] Directive 2001/37/EC downplays health promotion; for instance, no explicit reference is made in its preamble to the 'Europe against Cancer' programmes. However, the public health elements of the Tobacco Products Consolidation Directive have been emphasized in other contexts, for instance, in a joint statement issued by David Byrne (Commissioner for Consumer and Health Protection) and Dr Gro Harlem Brundtland, Director General of the WHO, during Dr Brundtland's visit to the Commission in September 2000.[162]

The main provision of EU law regulating tobacco advertising is now Directive 2003/33/EC.[163] The Directive prohibits tobacco advertising in the press and printed media, and on the internet or by email, save those publications intended exclusively for the tobacco trade.[164] All radio advertising of tobacco products is prohibited, and radio programmes may not be sponsored by tobacco companies.[165] Events taking place in several Member States, or otherwise having cross-border effects, may likewise not be sponsored by tobacco companies.[166] The new Directive explicitly provides that Member States may not prohibit the free movement of products or services complying with the Directive.[167] Unsurprisingly, and in line with the provisions discussed above, the Directive makes no explicit reference to the 'right to health'.

Again, therefore, the overall conclusion, at least with respect to the element of a 'right to health' concerning anti-tobacco policies, is that the EU institutions appear to ignore the linkage between relevant policy measures and a 'right to

---

[159] OJ 2003 L152/16.   [160] Directive 2001/37, Preamble, Recitals 2 and 3.

[161] See e.g. Directive 89/633, Preamble, Recitals 4 and 5.

[162] The visit was for discussion of the negotiations for the WHO's Framework Convention on Tobacco Control (FCTC): see http://europa.eu.int/comm/dgs/health_consumer/library/press/press75_en.html. Agreed by the WHO's member states on 17 March 2003, the FCTC is the latest WHO anti-tobacco initiative. The Commission regards the Consolidation Directive as 'complementary' to the FCTC, but it seems likely that the Directive formed part of the basis for the Commission's negotiating position. See, Information Meeting on the negotiations on the Framework Convention on Tobacco Control, held by the Commission, 13 November 2000: http://europa.eu.int/comm//health/ph/programmes/tobacco/who_minutes_en.htm. For instance, the FCTC echoes the Directive in that it prohibits terms such as 'light', 'mild', or 'low tar', that could lead people to think that one particular tobacco product is less harmful than others. See WHO Press Release *Agreement on Global Tobacco Control*, 17 March 2003.

[163] OJ 2003 L152/16. See also the 'Television without Frontiers' Directive 89/552, OJ 1989 L298/23, Art. 13. The preamble to the Directive gives no explicit justification for this measure, merely notes that 'it is necessary to prohibit all television advertising promoting cigarettes' Directive 89/552, Preamble, Recital 17.   [164] Directive 2003/33, Art. 3.

[165] Directive 2003/33, Art. 4.   [166] Directive 2003/33, Art. 5.

[167] Directive 2003/33, Art. 8.

health' as part of the (Rev)ESC and indeed the EUCFR. Even if the EU institutions originally recognized the question of anti-tobacco policy as an element of the 'right to health', implicit in the construction of such policies as centrally concerned with protection of health and the promotion of the conditions of good health, both explicitly recognized by the ECSR, such discourse has been significantly downplayed of late. It is probably no coincidence that this change of direction coincides with the ruling of the ECJ in *Tobacco Advertising*.

VI. CONCLUSION

What are we to make of these findings? Article 35 EUCFR, on the 'right to health', is part of EU law; indeed, it is part of the EU's Constitutional Treaty. On its face at least, this provision echoes Article 11 (Rev)ESC, to which all Member States of the EU are parties. The EU and the Member States share responsibility for several policy areas which clearly connect to the 'right to health'. These include environmental policy, food regulation, tobacco regulation, and access to timely provision of health care services, at least in a cross-border context. And yet, the institutions of the EU appear, in virtually all cases, to have studiously ignored the connection between the 'right to health' as developed by the 'jurisprudence' under the (Rev)ESC, and various relevant EU policies. Here, this chapter's findings on the *internal* application of the 'right to health' in EU law and policy echo those of Alexandra Gatto's chapter with respect to its *external* application.[168]

Although this chapter has considered only a few areas of EU law and policy, exploration of further areas is unlikely to alter the overall findings. Article 35 EUCFR has not been mentioned by any ruling of the ECJ, CFI, or Opinion of its Advocates-General.[169] Article 35 EUCFR features in the Preambles of only two EU legislative provisions: Regulations 1567 and 1568/2003/EC on development aid.[170] Even where the EU's *acquis* grants rights to health care that are not based on the entitlements of citizenship, as in the context of Directive 2003/9/EC on minimum standards for reception of asylum seekers,[171] this is by reference to the

---

[168] See A. Gatto's contribution to this volume, at p. 361.

[169] Searches of CELEX on the terms 'Charter of Fundamental Rights' and, within findings, 'Article 35' revealed only the Regulations on development aid discussed below. A CELEX search on the term 'European Social Charter' revealed only 92 documents, none of which mentions Article 11 (Rev)ESC.

[170] Regulation 1567/2003 on aid for policies and actions on reproductive and sexual health and rights in developing countries, OJ 2003 L224/1; Regulation 1568/2003 on aid to fight poverty diseases (HIV/AIDS, tuberculosis, and malaria) in developing countries, OJ 2003 L224/7. For further discussion of economic and social rights in the EU's development policy, see A. Gatto's chapter in this volume.

[171] OJ 2003 L31/18, Art. 15, which provides that 'Member States shall ensure that applicants receive the necessary health care which shall include, at least, emergency care and essential treatment of illness'.

provisions of Articles 1 EUCFR on human dignity, not by reference to a 'right to health'.[172]

One possible explanation for the lack of reference to Article 11 (Rev)ESC in the *acquis communautaire* is that it expresses a strong message from the EU institutions that, while a 'right to health' may not be guaranteed in some third countries, (hence the references in the development aid Regulations), a 'right to health' is not a problem *within* the Member States of the EU. The implication is that, to the extent to which Article 35 EUCFR places obligations on the Member States, or the institutions of the EU,[173] these are being met. If this is the explanation, it contradicts the, as yet limited, but nevertheless existent, *Conclusions* of the ECSR on Article 11 on the right to health protection, which find that in some cases, some EU Member States are deficient in their guarantee of the rights under Article 11, or at least supply insufficient information to assess conformity.

Alternatively, a more compelling explanation may be that the discourse of the 'right to health', in conceptualizing internal health care and health protection matters, is problematic in the EU context for another reason. Both in the cross-border services example elaborated above, and more strongly in the tobacco regulation example, the question of division of competence between EU and national institutions appears to form an undercurrent to the regulatory and jurisprudential activity of the EU institutions. If matters such as cross-border provision of health care and regulation of tobacco are conceptualized as concerning the 'right to health', this suggests that the EU institutions are competent to regulate such a right, and may even be responsible for its achievement. Such a conclusion is highly contentious, for a number of reasons. The implication that the Member States have ceded (some) competence in the area of securing a 'right to health' might mean that matters relating to national welfare provision (here, health care services) are no longer a matter for national determination. To the extent that EU competence means harmonization,[174] the implication is that this means a move towards a standardized 'EU' provision, for instance, in health protection, with a loss of local control, and responsiveness to local conditions. There may also be an implication that governments of Member States can no longer be held responsible for some elements of the 'right to health' under Article 11 (Rev)ESC.

The problems associated with EU competence for the 'right to health' have been recognized in the context of the EU's developing constitutional law and practice. For instance, the ECJ's conclusions in the 'constitutional' ruling on *Tobacco Advertising*, may imply that the 'right to health' is not a component of competence under Article 95 EC. Article 95 EC is constructed as a restricted legal

---

[172] See Preamble, Recital 5. Reference is also made to Art. 18 EUCFR on the right to asylum.

[173] See discussion *supra* pp. 317–18.

[174] As Barnard points out, there has been a 'seismic shift' away from the basic philosophy of 'if it moves (or even if it doesn't), harmonize it'; C. Barnard, *The Substantive Law of the EU: The Four Freedoms* (2004), at 535.

basis, concerned with creating and maintaining the internal market, explicitly not as a *general* legal basis provision granting the EU legislature power to regulate the internal market.[175]

The contentious position of social rights, such as the 'right to health', within the EU's legal order, has also been recognized in the Treaty, through the process of Treaty reform. Originally, there was no legal basis for 'health' in the EC Treaty at all. When Article 129 EC was introduced into the Treaty at Maastricht, it explicitly excluded any harmonization of national laws designed to protect and improve public health. This was carried over to the renumbered Article 152 EC, and will be taken forward into the CT, if ratified, in Article III-278.[176] The governments of the Member States appear to be concerned to limit the 'spill over' effects of EU law, particularly internal market law, into areas of national welfare provision, such as those concerning the health care elements of a 'right to health'.

Moreover, as we saw above, the status of social rights in general, including the 'right to health' within the EU's legal order has been seen as problematic in the context of the negotiations of the EUCFR and the Constitutional Treaty. It appears that significant efforts have been taken to avoid the direct application, and in particular the enforceability, of provisions such as Article 35 EUCFR in the legal orders of the Member States. This may be because of nervousness about the effect of the full force of EU law, as developed by the ECJ, being applied to social rights, which have traditionally been implemented through mechanisms other than their individual justiciability, at least in the European context. Overall, then, we might expect the EU's *acquis* to continue to ignore any connections with Article 11 (Rev)ESC, on the 'right to health'.

[175] See para. 83.

[176] Art. I-12(6) CT expressly provides that EU competence is to be determined by specific provisions in Part II CT. Art. III-14(2)(k) CT, in accordance with Art. I-12(5) CT, gives EU competence to 'support, coordinate or supplement' the actions of Member States in the field of public health. Certain exceptional 'common safety concerns in public health matters' are matters of shared competence', by reference to Art. I-14(2)(k) CT.

PART V

BEYOND EUROPE'S BORDERS

16

The Integration of Social Rights Concerns in the External Relations of the European Union

ALEXANDRA GATTO*

I. INTRODUCTION

In the field of external relations, the European Union (EU) first outlined its policy on development, democracy, and human rights in 1991[1] and has had a human rights policy since that date. Despite the recognition of the indivisible character of civil and political and economic, social, and cultural rights,[2] however, greater emphasis has been placed on the promotion of civil and political rights. In spelling out the priorities for the EU's human rights policy Cassese and other authors have emphasized the need for greater attention to be paid to social rights, in both internal and external policy.[3] Such concern is echoed by Alston and Weiler,[4] who have drawn attention to the scant attention paid to social rights in policy statements on human rights; the low priority accorded to funding social development; and the distinction between social sector funding and support for economic, social, and cultural rights.

Although since 1995 the EU has introduced a human rights clause into all its economic and external agreements, the relevance accorded to social rights in external relations is still undefined. Only recently has the EU tried to explain the

* I would like to thank Professor Gráinne de Búrca and Professor Bruno de Witte for all their guidance during the writing of this chapter as well as all those who commented on a draft version at the conference 'Social Rights in Europe/Droits Sociaux en Europe', held at the EUI on 18–19 June 2004.

[1] Commission Communication of 25 March 1991 on Human Rights Democracy and Development Co-operation, SEC(91)61 final.

[2] EP Resolution of 25 March 1991 on Human Rights Throughout the World 1995–1996 and the Union's Human Rights Policy, OJ 1997 C20/99, at para. 6.

[3] A. Cassese et al., *Leading by Example: A Human Rights Agenda for the European Union for the Year 2000* (1998), at 5–6.

[4] P. Alston and J. H. H. Weiler, '*An Ever Closer Union' in Need of a Human Rights Policy: The European Union and Human Rights*, Harvard Jean Monnet Working Paper 1/99 (1999).

specific relevance of social rights in its relations with third countries. However, the definition of the scope of social rights that the EU seeks to promote is flawed by the discrepancy between declaration of intent and practice.

Against this background, this chapter seeks to offer an overview of the instruments used by the European Union in its external relations to promote respect for human rights and, in particular, for economic, social, and cultural rights. This chapter is divided into four parts. First, it outlines the legal and policy background against which the issue of the integration of social rights in the external relations of the European Union will be tackled and traces the introduction of human rights concerns into EU external relations, with particular regard to the introduction of human rights clauses in European Community (EC) external agreements and the alternative tools available for the promotion of social rights (see Section II below). Secondly, it looks at the references to social rights in the main development assistance programmes between the European Union and Mediterranean, Asian and Latin American (ALA), Eastern European,[5] and African Caribbean and Pacific (ACP) countries. The analysis also includes the European Initiative for Democracy and Human Rights (EIDHR) and Regulations 975 and 976/1999 (hereinafter the 'Human Rights Regulations')[6] which are horizontal, not country-specific instruments (Section III). Section IV examines the common commercial policy of the EC. Finally, some concluding remarks are made upon the basis of the above analysis. These are related to some of the critical issues at stake in the integration of social rights in the external relations of the European Union.

II. THE LEGAL AND POLICY BACKGROUND OF SOCIAL RIGHTS IN EU EXTERNAL RELATIONS

A. *The Human Rights Clause and Social Rights*

The inclusion of a clause calling for respect for human rights in external agreements as well as in EC unilateral instruments is one of the EC's most widely used tools for the promotion of human rights in third countries.

An explicit reference to human rights was included for the first time in the Preamble to the Third Lomé Convention (1984). However, only in the Fourth Lomé Convention (1989) was a human rights clause included in the text of the Agreement. In its first formulation the clause was merely exhortatory, since its breach did not constitute grounds for the suspension of the agreement.

---

[5] The PHARE programme, originally aimed at providing technical assistance to Hungary and Poland, and subsequently extended to countries eligible for accession to the EU, is not analysed in the context of this chapter, given the specific pre-accession focus of the assistance.

[6] Council Regulations 975 and 976/1999, OJ 1999 L120/1 and L120/00.

Two years later, in the Luxembourg European Council's Declaration on Human Rights, it was proposed to include human rights clauses in agreements with third countries as an element of an active human rights policy. The Declaration was followed up by the 1991 Resolution on human rights, democracy, and development which sets out the basic tenets of EC human rights and development policy. Given the expansion of the EC's treaty relations and the increasing references to human rights in its agreements, the Commission issued a communication which purported to include social clauses in all economic and cooperation agreements with third countries, and this was then approved by the Council in 1995. As a result, the human rights clause was introduced as an essential element of the agreement. According to the wording of this standard clause, '[r]espect for the democratic principles and human rights . . . underpin[s] the internal and external policies of the Parties and constitute[s] an essential element of partnership and of this Agreement'.[7] This clause is usually supplemented by a non-execution clause, which applies in the event of failure by one of the contracting parties to fulfil an obligation under the agreement.[8]

As well as in external agreements, human rights clauses have also been introduced into unilateral EC measures. These unilateral instruments cannot create rights for or obligations on third parties. Consequently, the EC cannot invoke the human rights clauses in these instruments to justify the adoption of sanctions as a response to human rights violations.

Usually the positive and negative dimensions of the human rights clauses are distinguished. On the one hand they express the common interest of contracting parties in human rights. Human rights constitute a relevant issue during consultations, and positive measures can be taken to improve the human rights situation of a country. On the other hand, the relations between the parties are conditional upon respect for human rights and can be severed in the event of a human rights violation (sanction-based approach).

As stated above, the wording of human rights clauses usually makes a generic reference to respect for human rights. Some of the clauses also refer to the Universal Declaration of Human Rights (UDHR). This raises the problem of the identification of the human rights contained in such clauses. In particular, the question arises of what room is left for social rights in the context of the human rights clauses.

Even though a clear-cut answer is not available, the repeated calls for respect for the principles of indivisibility and interdependence of all human rights point in the direction of the inclusion of economic and cultural rights on the same footing as civil and political rights. This hypothesis is confirmed by the fact that, referring to the human rights clause, the Commission said that it also encompasses core

---

[7] Art. 2 of the Partnership Agreement between the EC and its Member States, and Ukraine, OJ 1998 L49/3.

[8] Other types of human rights clauses are also present in agreements concluded before 1995. For an extensive analysis see M. Bulterman, *Human Rights in the Treaty Relations of the European Community: Real Virtues or Virtual Reality?* (2001), at 156 and E. Fierro, *The EU's Approach to Human Rights Conditionality in Practice* (2003).

labour standards as set out in the eight core ILO Conventions.[9] The same was said on the occasion of the communication from the Commission to the Council on the trading system and internationally recognized labour standards,[10] the opinion of the Committee on Foreign Affairs, Security, and Defence Policy,[11] and in the report on the proposal for a Council Decision concerning the conclusion of the Framework Agreement for trade with Korea.[12]

It is not entirely clear whether human rights clauses effectively contribute to the guarantee of human rights. The efficiency of human rights clauses in fostering human rights is not entirely convincing. The first reason behind the limited success of the human rights clauses is the technical specifications that in practice constrain the use of conditionality. The effectiveness of conditionality depends on the feasibility of the objectives, the proportionality of the envisaged measures, and the existence of credible indicators and supervisory mechanisms. In addition, political considerations can justify occasional or recurrent decisions to refrain from using sanctions as a response to the violation of a human rights clause. The second restriction on the use of conditionality is the very identification of human rights.

The effectiveness of conditionality becomes even more problematic where social rights are concerned. First, the use of a separate social clause, as opposed to a general human rights clause, could lead to the misleading interpretation that social rights do not fall within the category of human rights. This objection can be countered by the consideration that when social rights are explicitly and concretely identified they can more easily be implemented. On the other hand, in the case of human rights broadly defined one may risk applying a minimum standard and overlooking many human rights violations.[13]

Secondly, the respect for more socially oriented conditionality is less immediately acceptable in recipient countries, because it may have unforeseen political effects.[14]

---

[9] Cf. Commission Communication of 18 July 2001 'Promoting Core Labour Standards and Improving Social Governance in the Context of Globalisation', COM(2001)416 final, and Commission Communication of 18 September 2002 on 'Trade and Development—Assisting Developing Countries to Benefit from Trade', COM(2002)0513 final.

[10] Commission Communication of 21 July 1996 'The Trading System and Internationally Recognized Labour Standards', COM(1996)402 final.

[11] Legislative resolution embodying the Parliament's opinion on the proposal for a Council Decision of 28 June 1996 concerning the conclusion of the Framework Agreement for Trade and Co-operation between the European Community and its Member States, of the one part, and the Republic of Korea, of the other part, COM(1996)141-C4-0073/97- 96/0098(CNS), OJ 1999 C104/59.

[12] Proposal for a Council Decision concerning the conclusion of the Framework Agreement for Trade and Co-operation between the European Community and its Member States, of the one part, and the Republic of Korea, of the other part, *supra* n. 11.   [13] Cf. Fierro, *supra* n. 8, at 365.

[14] D. Schmid, 'The Use of Conditionality in Support of Political Economic and Social Rights: Unveiling the Euro-Mediterranean Partnership's True Hierarchy of Objectives?', paper presented at the Fifth Mediterranean Social and Political Research Meeting of the Mediterranean Programme of the Robert Schuman Centre for Advanced Studies at the European University Institute, Florence and Montecatini Terme, 24–28 March 2004—Workshop No. 14 'Economic and Social Rights in the Euro-Mediterranean Area and the Impact of the Euro-Mediterranean Free Trade Areas', jointly organized with the Euro-Mediterranean Human Rights Network (EMHRN), at 29.

Developing countries tend to view social clauses with suspicion, as they can be used for protectionist purposes. Even worse, the application of sanctions can have a detrimental effect on the populations of third countries whose governments do not comply with social and human rights standards.

We may conclude that the integration of social rights in the external relations of the European Union is currently hampered by the shortcomings inherent in conditionality. On the one hand, the implementation of human rights clauses— which include both civil and political rights and economic, social, and cultural rights—generally emphasizes civil and political rights. On the other hand, social rights are not adequately taken into account by the social clause (such as that in the Regulation applying a scheme of generalized tariff preferences (hereinafter 'the GSP Regulation')), as it focuses exclusively on a limited number of labour rights.

A possible way forward is to transcend the social clause debate and to find and explore new approaches, while improving the existing human rights clauses in EU agreements with a view to pursuing a more systematic approach to economic, social, and cultural rights.[15]

B. *Alternative Tools for the Integration of Social Rights: The Involvement of the Private Sector in Development and Corporate Social Responsibility*

The EU has recently taken up the suggestion of enhancing traditional instruments for the promotion of social rights through measures such as linking compliance with labour rights and human rights to trade access and development aid. At the same time, the EU has developed new approaches, such as the involvement of private and local actors in promoting respect for social rights. A similar trend exists in other recent initiatives such as the UN Global Compact and the UN Norms for Transnational Corporations; the revision of the Organization for Economic Co-operation and Development (OECD) Guidelines; and the ILO Tripartite Declaration of Principles concerning multinational enterprises and social policy.

The positive interrelation between development and the promotion of human rights in third countries in the context of EU trade and development cooperation policies[16] was recognized for the first time in the Communication on the promotion of human rights and democratization. This document contains an express reference to the role of companies, since European multinationals were called upon to use their influence in any developing country 'to support rather than undermine that country's own effort to achieve sustainable development'.[17] This

---

[15] Cassese et al., *supra* n. 3, at 60.

[16] Cf. O. De Schutter, 'The Accountability of Multinationals for Human Rights in European Law', in E. Brems and P. Vanden Heede (eds), *Bedrijven en Mensenrechten* (2003), at 48.

[17] See Commission Communication of 8 May 2001, 'The European Union's Role in Promoting Human Rights and Democratisation in Third Countries', COM(2001)252 final.

approach was further specified in the Communication 'Promoting Core Labour Standards and Improving Social Governance in the Context of Globalisation'.[18] The use of bilateral dialogue with developing countries, of development assistance to build capacity, and of additional trade incentives under the GSP Regulation where countries comply with minimum social standards was envisaged.[19]

In the Communication on Corporate Social Responsibility, emphasis was placed on voluntary and non-binding mechanisms of implementation, such as social labels and codes of conduct. States beneficiaries of EU preferences and development are to ensure that corporate responsibility schemes are objective, transparent, and non-discriminatory. Coherence among different codes and reference to ILO standards are recommended. Nevertheless, these codes 'are to be regarded as complementary to government action'.[20] In other words, the risk is that such schemes will be ineffective and that, ultimately, domestic sanctions are needed.

It is suggested that Corporate Social Responsibility can provide an important step forward, in that responsibility for the attainment of better labour and environmental standards is placed directly on companies rather than states. It follows, therefore, that Corporate Social Responsibility initiatives can contribute to the reduction of the negative impact of foreign investment on the local community, environment, and respect for social rights by defining the standards of behaviour of companies.

More recently, it has been recognized that the private sector can play a key role in the reduction of poverty, which currently constitutes the central aim of EU development policy, fully in line with the UN Millennium Declaration. In September 2002 the Commission issued a Communication on trade and development,[21] which defines the importance of the relationship between trade, development, and the integration of developing countries in the world economy. The communication conceives of several measures aimed at improving the delivery of trade-related assistance in key areas and at enhancing coordination and coherence within the EU and with international organizations. The overall objective is to help developing countries to acquire the expertise necessary to deal with the challenges of global trade and, by the same token, to improve their institutional regulatory capacity. In this context, the importance for developing countries of improving the investment climate for the business sector has been emphasized. Training programmes for negotiators and administrators establish, and technical assistance for sustainability impact assessments review existing coordination mechanisms of Member States, and sharing of *best practices* is seen as a key tool for achieving the objective set out in the communication.[22]

---

[18] *Promoting Core Labour Standards, supra* n. 9. In particular, the basic tenets of the EU's approach are set out in para. 3 and further action at the European Union and international level at para. 5.

[19] De Schutter, *supra* n. 16, at 62.   [20] *Promoting Core Labour Standards, supra* n. 9, at 20.

[21] Cf. *Trade and Development, supra* n. 9.

[22] Roundtable European Multi-stakeholder Forum on Corporate Social Responsibility of 7 April 2003, 'Roundtable on the Development Aspects of Corporate Social Responsibility'.

The importance of working together with the private sector has been stressed in the context of two recent communications on health[23] and education.[24] In both cases, the accent was placed on the need for new incentives for multinationals and other private companies in the development of the public good and on the enhancement of cooperation with private investors to improve their responsibility for health in developing countries. Also set out was an overall framework for the promotion of stakeholder dialogue through the establishment of discussion. The present Communication on health reiterates the European Union's approach set out in the Commission Communication Promoting Core Labour Standards and Improving Social Governance in the Context of Globalization.[25] This envisages the use of bilateral dialogue with developing countries; development assistance to build capacity; and additional trade incentives under the GSP where countries comply with minimum social standards.

Considerable emphasis was placed on dialogue with developing countries' civil societies and building capacity in order to promote convergence. It is recognized that civil societies, NGOs, and trade unions can play a role in raising awareness of respect for fundamental rights and promoting compliance with the Corporate Social Responsibility principle by monitoring corporate practice on the ground.

Finally, the Communication on Participation of non-state actors in EC Development Policy[26] reiterates[27] the relevance of all the components of civil society in contributing to developments, and it sets out the basic components of its involvement in practice.

III. THE INTEGRATION OF SOCIAL RIGHTS IN DEVELOPMENT AND COOPERATION POLICIES OF THE EUROPEAN UNION

A. *The EC Development Assistance Programmes*

1. The MEDA Programme The MEDA programme is the principal financial instrument of the European Union for the implementation of the Euro-Mediterranean Partnership. The programme offers technical and financial support measures to accompany the reform of economic and social structures in the Mediterranean countries.[28] The legal basis of the MEDA programme is Council

---

[23] Commission Communication of 23 March 2002 on 'Health and Poverty Reduction in Developing Countries', COM(2002)0129 final, at 10.

[24] Commission Communication of 6 March 2002 on 'Education and Training in the Context of the Fight against Poverty in Developing Countries', COM(2002)116 final.

[25] *Promoting Core Labour Standards, supra* n. 9, at para. 5.

[26] Commission Communication on 'Participation of Non-State Actors in EC Development Policy', COM(2002)598 final.

[27] Commission Communication, 'Towards a Global Partnership for Sustainable Development', COM(2002)82 final.

[28] Algeria, Egypt, Israel, Jordan, Lebanon, Morocco, Palestinian Authorities, Syria, Tunisia, and Turkey.

Regulation 1488/96 (hereinafter 'the MEDA Regulation')[29] which was amended in November 2000.[30]

The relevance of the economic and social dimension is repeatedly stressed throughout the Regulation. As noted by Schmid,[31] between MEDA I and MEDA II attention to social issues was increased.[32] Article 1, as amended in 2000, reads as follows:

1. The Community shall implement measures in the framework of the principles and priorities of the Euro-Mediterranean partnership to support the efforts that Mediterranean non-member countries and territories listed in Annex I (hereinafter referred to as 'Mediterranean partners') will undertake to reform their economic and social structures, improve conditions for the underprivileged and mitigate any social or environmental consequences which may result from economic development.

The development of economic and social cooperation, taking due account of the human and cultural dimension and of achieving 'long-term stability and prosperity, in particular in the fields of economic transition, sustainable economic and social development and regional and cross-border cooperation',[33] is listed among the objectives of the Regulation. Practical measures for the enhancement of social conditions, such as the improvement of social services, especially in the areas of health, the fight against poverty, the strengthening of democracy, and respect for human rights, are described in detail in Annex II to the MEDA Regulation. These interventions take the form of an adjustment mechanism covering various sectors such as health insurance and education. Aid is also targeted at the most vulnerable social groups through specific action to encourage social and economic stability and cohesion.

Respect for human rights and fundamental freedoms constitutes an essential element of the Regulation, the violation of which will justify the adoption of appropriate measures. As noted,[34] this human rights clause contains a general reference to human rights as such, but it is not reinforced by an express reference to specific human rights instruments such as the ICESCR.

Thus, in contrast to other programmes, MEDA accords the utmost relevance to human rights. Social rights concerns, in particular, are allayed by means of interventions in all fields of the social sector. However, it has been pointed out[35]

---

[29] Council Regulation 1488/96, OJ 1996 L189/1, modified by Council Regulation 2698/2000, OJ 2000 L311/1 (hereinafter 'MEDA Regulation').

[30] The main areas and objectives of the programme are directly derived from those of the 1995 Barcelona Declaration in which the parties recognized 'the importance of social development' which, in their view, must go hand in hand with any economic development. They attach particular importance to respect for fundamental social rights, including the right to development. Commission Européenne 1995. Info-note n. 52/95. Conference euro-mediterraneenne de Barcelone. Declaration Final.

[31] Cf. Schmid, *supra* n. 14.   [32] Ibid., at 25.

[33] Art. 2 of the MEDA Regulation, *supra* n. 29.   [34] Cf. Fierro, *supra* n. 8, at 357.

[35] I. Byrne, 'Placing Economic Social and Cultural Rights at the Heart of the Euro Mediterranean Partnership', paper presented at the Fifth Mediterranean Social and Political Research Meeting of the Mediterranean Programme of the Robert Schuman Centre, *supra* n. 14, at 15.

that the social dimension plays an ancillary role vis-à-vis political and economic stability, rather that operating on its own merits. Although support for social and economic equilibrium in the Mediterranean countries is included among the main areas of intervention of the MEDA programme under bilateral cooperation,[36] these interventions are indeed aimed at reducing the adverse effect of economic transition and strengthening political stability.

Development projects which support the rights to education, health, the environment, and rural development are currently financed by 41 per cent of the total budget of MEDA.[37] Support for economic transition and the development of the private sector accounts for 30 per cent.[38] Even if it is premature to assess the impact of many of the current projects, some general conclusions can be drawn from previous evaluations of EU development aid in the Mediterranean region. According to an evaluation carried out by the Commission in 1998 which covered the first three years of the MEDA programme, a distinct lack of human rights focus was observed. Moreover, further coordination between poverty, gender, environment, and trade and structural adjustment policies should be achieved.

2. The TACIS Programme The TACIS programme, which was created in 1991, is the European Community's main instrument for cooperation with the countries of Eastern Europe, the Caucasus, and Central Asia.[39] The programme, consisting mainly of technical assistance, is currently based on Council Regulation 99/2000,[40] which replaced the 1996 Regulation.[41] It has the objectives of promoting transition to a market economy and reinforcing democracy and the rule of law in partner states. Covering the 2000–2006 period, it is based on the principles and objectives set out in the partnership and cooperation agreements and in the trade and economic cooperation agreements concluded between the Union and these countries.

The 1996 TACIS Regulation contained a clause providing for suspension for human rights violations.[42] Thus, when an essential element for the continuation

---

[36] European Commission, Report from the Commission to the Council and the European Parliament, Parliament Annual Report of the MEDA programme 2000, available at http://www.europa.eu.int/comm/europeaid/reports/meda_2000_en.pdf.

[37] For 2000–2006, the MEDA programme has been given €5,350 million out of the Community budget accompanied by substantial loans from the European Investment Bank, which amounted to €6,400 million for the 2002–2007 period.

[38] Sources available at http://europa.eu.int/comm/.

[39] E.g., Armenia, Azerbaijan, Belarus, Georgia, Kazakhstan, Kyrgyz Republic, Moldova, Russian Federation, Tajikistan, Turkmenistan, Ukraine, and Uzbekistan.

[40] Council Regulation 99/2000, OJ 2000 L12/1. As the present TACIS Regulation is due to expire at the end of 2006, the Commission is currently in the process of devising a new TACIS Regulation.   [41] Council Regulation 1279/1996, OJ 1996 L165/1.

[42] Art. 3(11) stated: '[w]hen an essential element for the continuation of co-operation though assistance is missing, in particular in cases of violation of democratic principles and human rights, the Council may on a proposal from the Commission, acting by qualified majority, decide upon appropriate measures concerning assistance to a partner state'.

of cooperation is missing, the Council may, on a proposal from the Commission and acting by qualified majority, decide upon appropriate measures.[43]

The current Regulation also introduces positive measures in support of human rights and democracy.[44] References to social rights concerns can be found both in the Preamble and in the body of the Regulation. In addition to a general reference to respect for human rights, minority rights, and the rights of indigenous peoples,[45] the Preamble also explicitly refers to social rights concerns by stating that '[t]he long-term sustainability of reform will require due emphasis on the social aspects of reform and the development of the civil society'. Article 2(6) recognizes that the programme should be implemented through '[m]easures which take into account the following criteria: the need for sustainable economic development, the social impact of reform measures, the promotion of equal opportunities for women, the sustainable use of natural resources and respect for the environment'. These measures are spelled out in Annex II as support for the reform of the health, pension, social protection, and insurance system; and assistance to alleviate the social impact of industrial restructuring by the development of employment services and retraining. Other measures relate to the reform of the institutional legal and administrative systems. They include, *inter alia*, support for the implementation of international commitments and the strengthening of civil society, education, and training.[46]

Similarly to the MEDA programme, assistance with the effort of moving from centrally planned to market economies is understood as a reinforcing factor for democracy. However, Article 3(3) acknowledges that special attention should be paid to the social aspects of transition.

3. The ALA Programme   Council Regulation 443/92[47] (hereinafter 'the ALA Regulation') provides the legal basis for financial and technical assistance to ALA countries The ALA Regulation emphasizes human rights by including a political commitment to their protection, a human rights clause comprising both positive and negative measures, and the possibility of granting funds for the promotion of human rights and democratic principles. Article 1 of this Regulation states that 'the Community shall attach the utmost importance to the promotion of human rights, support for the process of democratization, good governance, environmental protection, trade liberalization and strengthening the cultural dimension, by means of an increasing dialogue on political, economic and social issues conducted in the mutual interest'.

---

[43] The clause was implemented in the case of Belarus. Cf. Fierro, *supra* n. 8, at 369.

[44] Cf. Arts. 1 and 2 of Regulation 99/2000, *supra* n. 40.   [45] Ibid., Preamble, at Recital 5.

[46] The financial reference amount for these 6 years is €3,138 billion. Each year the budgetary authority decides on the annual appropriations within the limits of the Union's financial perspective. EU assistance is generally provided in the form of grants.

[47] Council Regulation 443/92, OJ 1992 L52/01.

Social rights are not given autonomous recognition. However, the Regulation emphasizes the important role that positive initiatives in relation to human rights and fundamental freedoms can play as preconditions for real and lasting economic and social development.[48] The priorities of financial and technical assistance listed in Article 5 include food, security, and the environment. It is also stated that all cooperation projects should take into account the human and cultural dimensions of development. The protection of special groups, such as women, children, and ethnic minorities, in contrast, is recognized autonomously.

B. The Cotonou Agreement

The Cotonou Agreement[49] introduced significant changes as a response to the disappointing outcome of the Lomé Conventions,[50,51] and to the incorporation into the EC Treaty of a new set of Articles on development.[52]

A human rights clause was introduced for the first time in the body of the text of the Fourth Lomé Convention[53] of 1989. This provision was replaced by an essential element clause as a result of the 'mid term review'[54] of the Fourth Lomé Convention. In both the Fourth and the reviewed Conventions social rights were placed on the same footing as civil and political rights[55] and both Preambles referred to the ICESCR as one of the main instruments of international human rights law.[56] The Convention went on to list a variety of social rights in areas such as environmental protection, rural promotion,[57] cultural development,[58] education and training,[59] the advancement of women,[60] and access to health care.[61]

The recognition of social rights is enhanced a little in the Cotonou Agreement. As in the Fourth Lomé Convention, respect for human rights, democratic principles, and the rule of law is an essential element of the partnership.[62] Article 96 allows for

---

[48] Cf. ibid., Art. 2.

[49] Partnership Agreement between the members of the African, Caribbean and Pacific Group of States (ACP) of the one part, and the European Community and its Member States, of the other part, signed in Cotonou on 23 June 2000, 2000/483/EC, OJ 2000 L317/3.

[50] C. Cosgrove, 'Has the Lomé Convention Failed ACP Trade?', 48 *JIA* (1994) 223.

[51] Co-operation with the ACP countries started in 1957 with the signing of the Treaty of Rome, which made provision for the association of the OCTs (Overseas Countries and Territories) with the EC, as it was then. In 1963, the first co-operation agreement was signed at Yaoundé, and this was renewed in 1969. Following the accession of the UK in 1973, a new agreement, the Lomé Convention (which included certain Commonwealth countries), was signed in 1975. It was renewed in 1979, 1984, and 1990.   [52] Title XX on development, and in particular Art. 177 EC Treaty.

[53] Art. 5 of the ACP-EEC Convention, OJ 1991 L229/1.

[54] The mid-term review, provided for by Art. 336 of the Lomé Convention, was concluded in Mauritius on 4 November 1995.   [55] Art. 5(2) of the IV Lomé Convention.

[56] Singularly reference is made also to regional human rights instruments such as the European Convention on Human Rights, the African Charter on Human and People's Rights, and the American Convention on Human Rights.   [57] Art. 49 of the IV Lomé Convention.

[58] Ibid., Arts 139–40.   [59] Ibid., Art. 151.   [60] Ibid., Art. 153.

[61] Ibid., Art. 154.   [62] Art. 9 of the Cotonou Agreement.

the suspension of cooperation in the event of serious violations by the States Parties of the essential elements. Article 9(1) further states that respect for fundamental social rights, democracy based on the rule of law, and transparent and accountable governance is an integral part of sustainable development. The indivisibility of all human rights, encompassing civil and political and economic, social, and cultural rights, as enshrined in international instruments, is recognized in Article 9(2).

In Cotonou, priority was placed on the reduction of poverty.[63] Gender, environment, institutional development, and capacity building were introduced as thematic and cross-cutting issues in line with the other cooperation programmes examined above. These themes are intended to be taken into account in all areas and at all levels and phases of EC-ACP development cooperation as a whole, as laid down by the Council Regulation of 1995 on the integration of equality between men and women. The mainstreaming of gender equality is also an integral part of the 2001–2006 action plan in the field of development cooperation.[64]

Measures for the promotion of health, education, and food are enshrined in Article 25 of the Cotonou Agreement, which deals with general and sectoral policies of EC-ACP cooperation. The aim of cooperation is to improve access to basic infrastructures and services and, in particular, to reduce the inequality of access to these resources. Article 25(1) states that:

... co-operation shall aim at: improving education and training, and building technical capacity and skills, improving health systems and nutrition, ensuring adequate food supply and security; integrating population issues into development strategies in order to improve reproductive health care, primary health care, family planning and prevention of female mutilation, promoting the fight against HIV and AIDS, increasing the security of the household water and improving access to safe and adequate sanitation; improving the availability of affordable and adequate shelter; and encouraging the promotion of participatory methods of social dialogue as well as aspects for basic social rights.[65]

Even if reference is made to respect for basic social rights, the terminology of rights is rather vague in this Article and reference is not made to the ICESCR as referred to in the Preamble to the Cotonou Agreement.

On the other hand, recognition of the relevance of labour rights is clear and accompanied by the reference to respect for ILO Conventions relating to specific labour rights. According to Article 50(1), the Parties reaffirm their commitment to internationally recognized labour standards, in line with the ILO's 1998 'Declaration on Fundamental Principles and Rights at Work' and, in particular, freedom of association and the right to collective bargaining, the abolition of forced labour, the elimination of the worst forms of child labour, and non-discrimination in employment. Moreover, echoing the World Trade Organization's (WTO) ministerial declaration of 1998, at Article 50(3) the Parties reaffirm that

---

[63] Ibid., Art. 1.

[64] Cf. EU Guidelines on Human Rights Dialogues, Annex 15 to Council of the European Union, *EU Annual Report on Human Rights 2002* (2002) (hereinafter 'The Annual Report'), at 259.

[65] Art. 25(1)(a)–(g) of the Cotonou Agreement.

labour standards should not be used for protectionist purposes, and they agree to cooperate to promote core labour standards, *inter alia*, by exchange of information, education, and raising awareness.

Such express reference to labour rights, as opposed to the general wording used in relation to other social concerns, suggests that labour rights represent one of the few areas in which respect for universal standards of basic economic, social, and cultural rights is accepted by the European Union. Furthermore, the fact that the consideration of labour rights comes into Chapter V of the Cotonou Agreement, on trade-related areas, also provides a more coherent framework for the EU's link between trade and social rights. Article 50 of the Cotonou Agreement in fact refers to the same set of labour rights enshrined in the GSP Regulation. However, two differences can be discerned.

First, the Cotonou Agreement, in contrast to the GSP Regulation, lacks a reference to specific ILO Conventions relating to the protection of core labour rights. Far from being a mere difference in wording, it seems to indicate that in the Cotonou Agreement the 1998 ILO Declaration itself is used as the relevant source of international law for the protection of labour rights, instead of the individual ILO Conventions. To take this argument a step further, while the inclusion of the protection of labour rights has been extended for the first time to EC-ACP cooperation, this protection relies on an even weaker instrument of international law. The 1998 ILO Declaration, is, in fact, not accompanied by the supervisory mechanisms which are required for the ILO Conventions.[66]

Secondly, while in the GSP Regulation non-compliance with labour rights may constitute a basis for negative measures—withdrawal of special incentives— labour rights in Cotonou involve only positive measures, such as cooperation, awareness raising, and capacity building, and cannot constitute a basis for unilateral sanctions. Labour rights as enshrined in Article 50, in fact, are not mentioned in Article 96, which envisages the suspension of cooperation in the event of failure to fulfil an obligation stemming from respect for human rights, democratic principles, and the rule of law referred to in Article 9(2).

Another feature of Cotonou which is of particular relevance for the purpose of this chapter is the inclusion of non-state actors in the ACP-EU Partnership. According to the broad definition adopted in the Agreement,[67] non-state actors include the private sector, economic and social partners, trade union organizations, and civil society in all its forms according to national characteristics. According to Article 2, while central government remains the main partner in cooperation, other actors, including the private sector, should participate. Moreover non-state actors shall, where appropriate:

... be informed and involved in consultation on cooperation policies and strategies, on priorities for cooperation especially in areas that concern or directly affect them, and on the

---

[66] For criticism of the reference to the 1998 ILO Declaration in bilateral and regional free trade agreements see P. Alston, 'Core Labour Standards and the Transformation of the International Labour Rights Regime', 15 *EJIL* (2004) 3, at 457.   [67] Art. 6 of the Cotonou Agreement.

political dialogue; be provided with financial resources, under the conditions laid down in this Agreement in order to support local development processes; be involved in the implementation of cooperation projects and programmes in areas that concern them or where these actors have a comparative advantage; be provided with capacity-building support in critical areas in order to reinforce the capabilities of these actors, particularly as regards organisation and representation, and the establishment of consultation mechanisms including channels of communication and dialogue, and to promote strategic alliances.[68]

Despite the declared objective of involving non-state-actors, in both the definition and implementation of strategies and priorities that were previously under the exclusive jurisdiction of governments, the lack of provision for funding non-state actors and the lack of clarity about procedures may render their participation difficult in practice.[69]

Most of the funding for development of and cooperation with the ACP states is provided by the European Development Fund (EDF). The main purpose of the EDF is financially to assist the development of ACP countries, on the basis of long-term concerted programmes, particularly on rural development, industrialization, and economic infrastructure.[70] The EDF provides funding for any projects or programmes which contribute to the economic, social, or cultural development of countries. However, human rights funding is not automatically included in the indicative programmes of the ACP country support strategies, but instead depends on the availability of resources. Furthermore, the omission of a rights element from social sector expenditure in areas such as health and education implies that economic, social, and cultural rights are of lesser importance in development policy.[71]

It could be argued that the use of human rights language would not make any difference to projects undertaken in the field of health or education. However, adopting human rights language and a human rights approach would strengthen development projects from different points of view.[72] First, a human rights approach would entail the participation of all citizens in the planning and implementation of development programmes. Secondly, the principle of non-discrimination would be emphasized in planning and implementing development

---

[68] Ibid., Art. 4.

[69] K. Arts, 'ACP-EU Relations in a New Era: The Cotonou Agreement', 40 *CMLRev.* (2003) 95, at 101.

[70] It must also be added that an EU Water Fund was established, with a budget of €1 billion, to help give people in the ACP countries signatory to the Cotonou Agreement access to drinking water and adequate sanitation. Cf. Commission Communication, 'Establishment of an EU Water Fund', COM(2003)211 final, not published in the OJ.

[71] See O. Sheehy, 'The Positive Application of Human Rights within EU-ACP Development Co-operation', in Conference Proceedings, 'The Relationship between Africa and the European Union', organized by ECSA of South Africa, University of the Western Cape, 22–23 January 2004, available at http://www.uwc.ac.za/ECSA-SA/conf2004_prog.htm.

[72] P. Alston, 'What's in a Name: Does It Really Matter if Development Policies Refer to Goals, Ideals or Human Rights?' in H. Helmich (ed.), *Human Rights in Development Cooperation* (1998), at 22, SIM Special No., at 101.

programmes.[73] For instance, while the promotion of access to health would be achieved by any infrastructure or any intervention which provided better sanitation, recognizing a right to health would also entail the provision of equal access to people living in rural and in urban areas, to men and women, and the entitlement of particularly weak groups such as the elderly or children to preferential treatment. Another consequence of a human rights-based approach is that it emphasizes the accountability of the state to its citizens, while also prohibiting trade-offs[74] and preventing states from reneging on rights that have been previously obtained.

C. The European Initiative for Democracy and Human Rights

An analysis of the integration of social rights in development cooperation programmes cannot ignore the European Initiative for Democracy and Human Rights (EIDHR). This funding programme, created in 1994 at the initiative of the European Parliament,[75] rationalizes the different human rights budgets by grouping together the budget headings of the European Commission for the promotion of human rights, democratization, and conflict prevention policies. The EIDHR supplies complementary funding to the EU's programmes carried out with third countries' governments such as the TACIS, ALA, MEDA, and PHARE. On the contrary, projects funded by the EIDHR can be implemented with the assistance of non-governmental partners, particularly NGOs and international organizations, and the funding can be used without the host governments' consent or when other EU programmes have been suspended in the country concerned.

Council Regulations 975 and 976/1999[76] set out the legal basis for EIDHR activities. The legal basis of the first Regulation is in the development cooperation chapter of the Treaty that specifically refers to human rights. Since there was no express legal basis in the Treaty for the funding of human rights projects in non-developing countries, Article 308 had to be used, and a separate Regulation was needed. However, in the future the two Regulations could be merged, since Article 181(a) of the EC Treaty (added by the Treaty of Nice) now also expressly allows for human rights activities in non-developing countries.

At first sight, the texts of the two Regulations accord the same relevance to economic, social, and cultural rights and to civil and political ones. The Preambles to both Regulations acknowledge the principles of indivisibility and of the interdependence of all human rights. The mutually supportive relationship between economic and social development and the achievement of civil and political rights

---

[73] K. Tomaševski, *Development Aid and Human Rights Revisited* (1993), at 153.

[74] The question arose in particular in the cases of conflict between resettlement projects and the rights of indigenous populations. Cf. Van Boven, 'The Right to Development and Human Rights', 28 *Int'l Com J Review* (1982) 55; M. Jerv, 'Social Consequences of Development in a Human Rights Perspective' (1998) *Human Rights and Development Yearbook* 43.

[75] EP Opinion of the Committee on Foreign Affairs, Human Rights, Common Security and Defence Policy of 25 April 2001 on Human Rights in the world in 2000 and the EU Human Rights Policy, AD/438117EN.doc, at 4.   [76] Council Regulations 975 and 976/1999, *supra* n. 6.

is emphasized.[77] In the Regulations, the ICESCR—together with the UDHR and the International Covenant on Civil and Political Rights (ICCPR)—is defined as one of the main catalysts for the European Community's action to promote human rights and democratic principles. Moreover, the promotion and protection of both civil and political rights and economic, social, and cultural rights[78] is regarded as one of the objectives of the EC's technical and financial assistance. However, the fact that civil and political rights are mentioned twice in Article 2 of Regulation 975/99 points to a prevailing perception of human rights as civil and political rights. More significantly, Regulation 975/99 lists a wide range of activities that may be carried out to promote civil and political rights without providing a similar elaboration of economic, social, and cultural rights.[79]

The different attention afforded to economic, social, and cultural rights in the context of the EIDHR is not limited to these normative deficiencies, but is also reinforced by the thematic priorities identified by the Commission.[80] Indeed, the Commission retains the power to define the priorities, as well as planning and administering the operations undertaken. Democratic control is limited to the Commission's obligation to report annually to the Parliament on the EIDHR's activities.

From the outset, the principal aims of the EIDHR have included the strengthening of democratization, good governance, and the rule of law; electoral activities; the strengthening of the legal system and the institutions; conflict prevention and resolution; support of civil society; initiatives for the abolition of the death penalty; support for measures to combat xenophobia, racism, and discrimination against indigenous people; human rights education and the raising of awareness in civil society; and freedom of expression and independence of the media. More recently, priorities have expanded to include activities for the protection of children, the fight against torture, and the death penalty, and in support of the setting up of international tribunals and international criminal courts. Only in 2000 were economic, social, and cultural rights mentioned as a separate priority, while they usually go under the general heading of support for human rights. However, this sporadic textual recognition has not upset the overall balance, which remains in favour of support for civil and political rights, as evidenced by the array of activities linked to the observation and monitoring of elections.

The emphasis placed on civil and political rights is partly counterbalanced by the inclusion of cross-cutting issues such as gender equality, women's rights, and the fight against poverty. Even if these themes are not listed as one of the priority areas set by the Commission, they are considered as overarching objectives of the EU's development policy, which need to be taken into account in the implementation of the budget.

---

[77] See ibid., Preambles, at Recitals 5, 6, and 7.
[78] Art. 2 of Regulation 975/1999 and Art. 3 of Regulation 976/1999, *supra* n. 6.
[79] Sheehy, *supra* n. 71, at 14.
[80] Commission staff working document, European Initiative for Democracy and Human Rights Programming Document 2002–2004, Brussels, 20 December 2002, 1REV 1, Final, 6–11.

The distribution of funding mirrors the priority themes laid down by the Commission on an annual basis. The EIDHR channels funding via three types of projects: those identified by calls for proposals; targeted projects which are financed in cooperation with other actors, such as national governments and international organizations;[81] and micro-projects administered by Commission delegations in third countries and aimed at promoting small-scale projects in collaboration with local civil society. The EIDHR's budget increased from €200,000 in 1997 to €102 million in 2001.[82] In 2005–2006 it is programmed to reach €207 million.[83]

According to the Commission, an analysis of the projects funded reveals that those aimed directly at the promotion of social rights, such as a project for the strengthening of the trade union movement in Tunisia,[84] are sporadic.

Among social rights, education and health enjoy preferential treatment and are more often present in projects. Examples of these priority areas include significant funding for centres for the rehabilitation of torture victims in almost all regions[85] and support for more targeted projects, such as the campaign to eradicate female genital mutilation in Africa. Relevant funding was also provided for the creation of Master's degrees in several locations with a view to improving consciousness of and education on human rights law and the promotion of campaigns favouring access to education.[86]

A great number of projects also aim at or include the promotion and protection of targeted groups, such as women,[87] children, and ethnic minorities. It can be argued that these projects indirectly favour the enjoyment of social rights by vulnerable groups by providing access to services or by reducing disparities in the enjoyment of social rights by these groups.

It should also be taken into account that a number of projects set multifaceted objectives. For instance, the promotion of education is often paired with raising awareness on civil and political rights, or the rehabilitation of torture victims is

---

[81] This can take place only if a particular organization has a *de facto* and *de jure* monopoly on the ground.   [82] European Parliament, *supra* n. 75, at 4.

[83] Commission Staff Working Document, European Initiative for Democracy and Human Rights Programming for 2005–2006 available at http://europa.eu.int/comm/europeaid/projects/eidhr/pdf/eidhr-programming-2005-2006_en.pdf.

[84] Friedrich Ebert-Stiftung—Tunisian Office, *Strengthening Trade Union Movement in Tunisia*, *EU Annual Report on Human Rights 2002* (2002).

[85] See, e.g., the project of the International Rehabilitation Council for Torture Victims (IRCT) on the Implementation of the Istanbul Protocol; the projects of the Behandlungszentrum für Folteropfer Ulm for the Rehabilitation of torture victims which provides medical, therapeutic, and psycho-social support and integration work; the Redress Trust project on Improving Torture Survivors' Access to Justice and Reparation Worldwide; The Swedish Red Cross, *The Swedish Red Cross Centres for Victims of Torture*, *EU Annual Report on Human Rights* (2001) and (2002).

[86] Cf. the project in collaboration with UNICEF for capacity building for monitoring and implementation of Children's Rights in Bosnia-Herzegovina, *EU Annual Report on Human Rights* (2002).

[87] Cf. Heinrich Böll Foundation, 'The Promotion of Women's Rights Through Empowerment, Awareness and Legal and Political Reform, Regional / Mediterranean: Egypt, Jordan, Lebanon, West Bank & Gaza' in *EU Annual Report on Human Rights* (2002).

accompanied by the empowerment of women.[88] Others generically refer to the promotion of human rights. As a result, it is difficult to be certain what the impact of these projects would be on the enjoyment of social rights as such.

IV. THE INTEGRATION OF SOCIAL RIGHTS IN THE COMMON COMMERCIAL POLICY OF THE EUROPEAN UNION

A. *Labour Rights in the EU's Generalized System of Preferences*

The Generalized System of Preferences (GSP) scheme is one of the best examples of the introduction of social rights concerns into the external relations of the EU. However, the social rights promoted in this context are limited to labour rights.

The special incentive arrangements for the protection of labour rights, available on request to countries implementing some labour standards, provide for additional reductions of up to half of the already reduced GSP tariff rate.[89] The range of labour rights included as a condition for the concession of special arrangements and as a cause of temporary withdrawal from these arrangements resulted in progressive expansion through this revision process.[90]

When the labour rights incentive was introduced, the countries concerned had to demonstrate that they had adopted and implemented in their national legislation the ILO Conventions on the freedom of association (Convention 87), on the rights to organize and to bargain collectively (Convention 98), and on the minimum age for admission to employment (Convention 138).[91] On the other hand,

---

[88] Cf. a project for the rehabilitation of victims of torture and inhuman treatment, e.g. a psychotherapeutic centre for women and children in Tuzla, Bosnia-Hercegovina, managed by the association Vive Zene, *EU Annual Report on Human Rights 2003* (2003).

[89] For details see *User's Guide to the European Union's Scheme of Generalized Tariff Preferences P5* (2003), available at http://europa.eu.int/comm/trade/gsp/gspguide.htm.

[90] The regime had already been set out in Regulations 3281/94, OJ 1994 L348/1 and Regulation 1256/96, OJ 1996 L169/1, which contained the previous GSP Regulation. However, the provisions relating to the incentive arrangement needed a complementary Regulation to enable them to be put into practice. This was not approved until 1998 by Regulation 1154/98, OJ 1998 L109/1. For a commentary on the Community GSP, see B. Atkinson, 'Trade Policy and Preferences', in C. Cosgrove-Sacks (ed.), *The European Union and Developing Countries* (1999), at 305.

[91] Art. 11 of Council Regulation 2820/98, OJ 1998 L357/1 reads: '1. Without prejudice to the following Articles, the reductions specified in Article 10 shall apply to products originating in the beneficiary countries listed in Annex III on condition that the authorities of those countries have applied to the Commission in writing to take advantage of the special arrangements for their originating products, giving details of:—their domestic legislation incorporating the substance of the standards laid down in ILO Conventions No. 87 and No. 98. Concerning application of the principles of the right to organise and to bargain collectively and Convention No. 138 concerning the minimum age of admission to employment; the full text of such legislation must be attached, together with an official translation into one of the Community languages,—the measures taken to apply and monitor these provisions effectively, any sectoral restrictions on their application, any breaches observed and a breakdown of such breaches by production sector,—a commitment by the government of the country in question to take full responsibility for monitoring application of the special

withdrawal from the GSP benefits was envisaged where any form of forced labour or export of goods made by prison labour was possible.[92]

This regime was criticized because the EU chose a narrow selection of ILO Conventions and labour standards, and it applied a double standard. The range of labour rights to be granted additional tariff incentives differs from those taken into account in the event of the withdrawal of GSP privileges. This system could not only lead to paradoxical situations (for example, a country that has forbidden trade unions and collective bargaining, even if not qualified for additional concessions, could still enjoy the same GSP privileges as one that respects all democratic freedoms) but also has the potential to undermine the universal character of fundamental rights, such as the right to freedom of association.[93]

In line with what was suggested by the Commission in its communication on promoting core labour standards, the EC-GSP Regulation we have reviewed strengthened the social incentive scheme by providing for further improved market access opportunities, by making the scheme more transparent, and by extending the basis to all of the four core labour standards in the 1998 Declaration. The provision for temporary withdrawal has been extended by broadening the basis to severe and systematic violations of any of the core labour standards.

By adding the ILO Conventions on forced labour and on non-discrimination in respect of employment and occupation, the new Regulation 2501/2001[94] brought the special incentive clause into line with the definition of 'core labour' standards adopted by the ILO.[95] Temporary withdrawal is envisaged in the event of serious and systematic violation of the freedom of association, the right to collective bargaining, or the principle of non-discrimination in respect of employment and occupation or the use of child labour, in addition to the above-mentioned use

arrangements and the relevant administrative cooperation procedures. 2. The Commission shall publish a notice in the Official Journal of the European Communities, announcing that such a request has been made by a beneficiary country and stating that any relevant information concerning the request may be sent to the Commission by any interested natural or legal person; it shall specify the period within which interested parties may make known their views'.

[92] Ibid., Art. 22 states: '1. The arrangements provided for by this Regulation may at any time be temporarily withdrawn in whole or in part, in the following circumstances: (a) practice of any form of slavery or forced labour as defined in the Geneva Conventions of 25 September 1926 and 7 September 1956 and International Labour Organization Conventions No. 29 and No. 105; (b) export of goods made by prison labour . . .'.

[93] G. Tsogas, 'Labour Standards in the Generalized System of Preferences of the European Union and the United States', 3 *European Journal of Industrial Relations* (2000) at 369–70.

[94] Art. 14(2) of Council Regulation 2501/2001, OJ 2001 L346/1 states: '. . . The special incentive arrangements for the protection of labour rights may be granted to a country the national legislation of which incorporates the substance of the standards laid down in ILO Conventions No. 29 and No. 105 on forced labour, No. 87 and No. 98 on the freedom of association and the right to collective bargaining, No. 100 and No. 111 on non-discrimination in respect of employment and occupation, and No. 138 and No. 182 on child labour and which effectively applies that legislation.'

[95] See Proposal for a Council Regulation applying a scheme of generalized tariff preferences for the period 1 January 2002 to 31 December 2004, COM(2001)293 final, 12 June 2001, at para. 32 of the Explanatory Memorandum; and the position of the Commission as expressed in *Promoting Core Labour Standards*, *supra* n. 9. Cf. De Schutter, *supra* n. 16, at 60.

of slavery, forced labour, and prison labour.[96] The only difference left between these two provisions relates to the use of prison labour.

The development and definition of core labour standards in the ILO 1998 'Declaration on Fundamental Principles and Rights at Work and its Follow-up' was a factor which contributed to a broader recognition of labour rights in the GSP. Express reference to the Declaration is made in Recital 18 of the Preamble and as evidence of the EU's reliance on the ILO's work the assessments, decisions, and conclusions by the ILO supervisory body should serve as a point of departure for considerations on eligibility for special incentives and for investigations into whether withdrawal from GSP would be justified.

For a country to be granted preferential treatment, it has to present a request to the EU Commission which not only demonstrates that it has incorporated the substance of the relevant ILO Conventions in domestic legislation, but also proves that effective implementing and monitoring mechanisms are in place.

The new GSP Regulation[97] introduced some changes to the review and consultation process[98] which improved, in part, the degree of transparency and participation in the procedure. The examination of a request for a special incentive is advertised by the publication of a notice in the Official Journal of the European Communities, in order to allow all interested parties to submit written observations. The authorities of the applying country are involved throughout the evaluation process, but the Commission reserves the right to ask for inspections to ensure compliance with the standards.[99]

The special incentive arrangements can be withdrawn temporarily if the beneficiary country fails to fulfil its obligations. If information on alleged practices in violation of the above labour rights is received by the Commission or by a Member State the Commission may begin an official investigation.[100] A decision may be reached after internal consultations between the Commission and the GSP Committee. However, interested parties are invited to contact the Commission and to participate in the investigation. The case of Burma remains the only one so far in which the negative aspects of the labour rights clause have

---

[96] Art. 26 Council Regulation 2501/2001, OJ 2001 L346/1 states: '. . . 1. The preferential arrangements provided for in this Regulation may be temporarily withdrawn, in respect of all or of certain products, originating in a beneficiary country, for any of the following reasons: (a) practice of any form of slavery or forced labour as defined in the Geneva Conventions of 25 September 1926 and 7 September 1956 and ILO Conventions No. 29 and No. 105; (b) serious and systematic violation of the freedom of association, the right to collective bargaining or the principle of non-discrimination in respect of employment and occupation, or use of child labour, as defined in the relevant ILO Conventions; (c) export of goods made by prison labour . . .'.

[97] Previously the provisions relating to these incentives appeared under Title II (Arts 8 to 21) of Council Regulation 2820/98, OJ 1998 L 357/1 (last amended by Council Regulation 416/2001, OJ 2001 L60/43); they now appear under Title III (Arts 14 to 20, labour standards, and 21 to 24, environmental standards) of Council Regulation 2501/2001, OJ 2001 L346/1.

[98] De Schutter, *supra* n. 16, at 59.

[99] Art. 16(3) of Regulation 2501/2001, *supra* n. 94 states: '. . . The Commission may carry out assessments in the requesting country. The Commission may be assisted in this task by the Member States . . .'.   [100] Arts 26 to 34 of Regulation 2501/2001, *supra* n. 94.

been applied.[101] Additional preferences were withdrawn in that case by reason of the existence of forced labour in the country.[102]

B. Future Development of the GSP and the WTO India Case

The room left for further development and the enhancement of labour rights special incentives, however, was recently questioned in the case brought before the WTO by India against the EC. India's complaint referred to the legitimacy of EC GSP special incentives, and in particular the special arrangement to combat drug production and trafficking[103] was challenged.[104]

Although this case does not directly deal with labour rights preferences,[105] its outcome is relevant to the overarching question of this chapter in two regards. First, the compatibility of special incentives schemes with WTO law was under discussion. Secondly, the opinion of the WTO Dispute Settlement Body on this issue could provide an indication about a similar case involving labour rights incentives.

In March 2002, India requested consultations with the EC about its GSP scheme.[106] India asserted that the EU's special arrangement relating to drug production and trafficking was not compatible with Article 1 of the GATT and not justified by the 'enabling clause'.[107] Preferences are permitted under the enabling clause only 'in order to increase export earnings, to promote industrialization and to accelerate the rates of economic growth of developing countries'.[108] However, differentiation between developing countries would have constituted discrimination not permitted by the enabling clause.

India's argument was rejected in the Appellate Body's (AB) report published on 7 April 2004, which reversed the conclusions of the WTO panel issued in December 2003.[109] The panel had interpreted the term *non-discriminatory* in the enabling clause[110] to mean that identical tariff preferences under GSP schemes

---

[101] See Fierro, *supra* n. 8, at 371–76 for a detailed account of the Burma case.

[102] Council Regulation 552/97, OJ 1997 L85/8.

[103] Art. 10 of Regulation 2501/2001, *supra* n. 94.   [104] Ibid., Art. 25.

[105] Initially, India challenged the special incentives for the protection of labour rights and the environment and for combating drug production. Subsequently, India decided to limit the complaint to the special incentives against drugs production and trafficking. Cf. European Communities—Conditions for the granting of tariff preferences to developing countries, WT/DS246/AB/R, 7 April 2004, point 4.

[106] For a detailed analysis of the special working group report see S. De La Rosa, 'Observations après le rapport du groupe spécial "Communautés européennes—Conditions d'octroi de préférences tarifaires aux pays en development". Vers une remise en cause du SPG communautaire à la carte?', Revue de l'Association Française pour les Nations Unies—Section Aix-en Provence, Dossier spécial: L'Asie, redécouverte d'un Continent, No. 15 (2003) 2.

[107] Decision on Differential and More Favourable Treatment Reciprocity and Fuller Participation of Developing Countries, GATT document L/4903, 28 November 1979, BISD 26S/203.

[108] Request for Consultations by India, WT/DS246/1, March 2002, at 12.

[109] European Communities—Conditions for the granting of tariff preferences to developing countries, WT/ DS246/R, adopted by the Panel on 28 October 2003, published on 1 December 2003.   [110] Para. 2(a), note 3 of the enabling clause.

should be provided to all developing countries, without differentiation. Yet, two exceptions were considered admissible: differentiation in favour of least-developed countries and in the case of *a priori* import limitations for products originating in particularly competitive developing countries.[111] Consequently, the EC's drugs arrangement was found to be discriminatory because its scheme did not provide identical tariff preferences to all developing countries and it did not fall into one of the above-mentioned exceptions.[112]

Following the EC's appeal in January 2004,[113] the AB[114] overturned the strict interpretation of the term *non-discriminatory* in the enabling clause suggested by the panel. The AB read the enabling clause as authorizing preference-granting countries to respond positively to needs that are not necessarily common or shared by all developing countries. This may entail different treatment among different beneficiary countries.[115] Nonetheless, the criteria according to which differential treatment is provided should be transparent and objective.

According to the AB, the EC's special drugs arrangement, as set out in Regulation 2501/2001, does not provide for mechanisms or objective criteria that would allow other developing countries similarly affected by the drug problem to be included among beneficiary countries. In addition, the Regulation in question does not specify the criteria according to which a country would be removed from the group of beneficiary countries.

The importance of this decision is twofold. On the one hand, some concerns about the WTO compatibility of special arrangements provided by developed countries' GSP schemes have been dispelled.[116] On the other hand, the AB expressly noted that the EC's special incentive arrangements on the protection of labour rights and of the environment, in contrast to the drugs arrangement, included detailed procedures describing the processes and criteria that apply to a request by a country to become a beneficiary.[117] According to this analysis, then, it seems that the labour incentives of the EC-GSP Regulation are not in conflict with the proscriptions of the WTO.

V. CONCLUSION

This chapter has sought to offer an analysis of the degree to which social rights are enshrined in the external relations of the EU and the mechanisms available for their promotion.

---

[111] Panel report, *supra* n. 109, at para. 7.116.   [112] Ibid., at para. 7.177.

[113] Notification of an appeal by the European Communities, WT/DS246/7, 8 January 2004.

[114] European Communities—Conditions for the granting of tariff preferences to developing countries, WT/DS246/AB/R, 7 April 2004.   [115] Ibid., at para. 7/162.

[116] Cf. R. Howse, 'India's WTO Challenge to Drug Enforcement Conditions in the European Community Generalized System of Preferences: A Little Known Case with Major Repercussions for "Political" Conditionality in US Trade Policy', available at http://faculty.law.umich.edu/rhowse/Drafts_and_Publications/Howse3.pdf .   [117] See *supra* n. 97.

The relevance of human rights is recognized to varying degrees in all the above-mentioned EU aid programmes through the inclusion of human rights clauses. The interdependence of human rights and the relationship between the promotion of human rights and development are clearly spelled out in the above-mentioned regulations. The protection of economic, social, and cultural rights is rarely expressly referred to. Social concerns—broadly defined—constitute a key component of technical and financial assistance. In particular, measures aiming at the improvement of education, health, food, security, and the protection of vulnerable groups are expressly envisaged.

However, the overall impression is that, both in legal texts and in the implementation of programmes, there is a reluctance to adopt a social rights language. Even if the EU is clearly engaged in the promotion of social rights through financial and technical assistance, it is not explicit about it. Even if the omission of social rights language does not in itself mean that these programmes will be less beneficial to the enjoyment of social rights, it is symptomatic of a reluctance by the EU to recognize the relevance of social rights in development cooperation.

This attitude is in contrast to the declared link between human rights and development cooperation, as spelt out in the Commission's most recent documents. The call for better integration of core labour standards in, for instance, Community development policy has not yet been integrated into the EU's development assistance programmes.

One exception is assistance to ACP countries. The Cotonou Agreement expressly exhorts parties to respect core labour standards as enshrined in the 1998 ILO Declaration. However, the promotion of core labour standards is not accompanied by sanctions, since failure to fulfil core labour standards does not lead to the suspension of cooperation. Moreover, there is no reference to the relevant ILO Conventions.

It is difficult to carry out an assessment of the impact of assistance programmes on social rights. The analysis is hindered by restricted access to projects. With the exception of MEDA and ACP cooperation, comprehensive and regular evaluations are not available. Moreover, external evaluations are rare.[118] As a result, it is difficult to determine what part of the budgets of these programmes is actually devoted to social rights.

In this context, the EIDHR has contributed to the simplification of the funding of human rights programmes in the external relations of the EU by the progressive streamlining of human rights budgets. Moreover, accountability and transparency are enhanced thanks to regular, comprehensive, and detailed reports.

However, an emphasis on the promotion of civil and political rights can be observed. This is partly due to the above-mentioned normative deficiencies of

---

[118] See, e.g., German Development Institute, *Evaluation on EC Positive Measures in Favour of Human Rights and Democracy (1991–1993)* (1995).

Regulations 975 and 976/1999[119] which make limited reference to social rights. Moreover, the priority areas, as defined by the Commission, have not produced an increasing recognition of social rights. On the contrary, a key role has been given to activities aiming at the promotion of civil and political rights, accompanied by the response to occasional priorities such as the setting up of international tribunals.

As a result, economic, social, and cultural rights are hardly represented in the projects funded by the EIDHR. On the other hand, although projects do not include the promotion of social rights within their objectives, many of them have an indirect beneficial impact on the promotion and enjoyment of social rights. In addition, by involving local NGOs in the management and implementation of the project, the EIDHR also contributes to the strengthening of civil society in the countries in which it operates.

As explained above, EC legislation rarely refers expressly to economic, social, and cultural rights. The basic term of reference for the 'EC human rights clause' in external agreements has for long been the Universal Declaration on Human Rights.[120] Even if the Declaration is not a legally binding instrument, it plays an important role in giving substance to the universal human rights referred to in the EU's human rights clauses and the external agreements[121] and regulations. The Universal Declaration on Human Rights itself refers to a number of rights which belong to the sphere of economic, social, and cultural rights. It includes the right to social security and other economic, social, and cultural rights which are indispensable for the dignity, freedom, and free development of the personality of each human being (Article 22), the right to work, to rest, and leisure (Article 24), the right to an adequate standard of living (Article 25), the right to education (Article 26), and the right to participate in cultural life. More specific reference to social rights is enshrined in the International Covenant on Economic, Social and Cultural Rights (ICESCR), usually referred to in combination with the ICCPR, as the most relevant international human rights instruments.[122] The Cotonou Agreement and the regulation establishing the Generalized System of Preferences refer to a number of ILO Conventions. Recently, a call for respect for the OECD Guidelines for multinational corporations has been introduced in the Joint Declaration annexed to the 2000 EU Association Agreement with Chile. Similar considerations are likely to be introduced in future EU agreements with ACP and Latin American countries.

It follows that in its external relations it seems that the EU prefers to refer to the most universally known and most widely accepted human rights instruments. This

---

[119] See *supra* n. 6.   [120] Cf. Human Rights Regulations, *supra* n. 6 .

[121] Cf. Bulterman, *supra* n. 8, at 174; B. Brandtner and A. Rosas, 'Human Rights and the External Relations of the European Community: An Analysis of Doctrine and Practice', 9 *EJIL* (1998) 468, at 490; and P. Alston et al. (eds), *The EU and Human Rights* (1999), at 707.

[122] Cf. Arts. 2 and 3 of the Human Rights Regulations, *supra* n. 6.

contrasts with the definition of social rights within the Union, which is based on European instruments such as the European Convention for the Protection of Human Rights and Fundamental Freedoms and the European Social Charter.[123] Neither of these two instruments, nor the EC Charter of Fundamental Social Rights is mentioned in the EU's external unilateral (the Human Rights and the GSP Regulations) or bilateral instruments (Cotonou Agreement) examined above.

In contrast, the PHARE programme, originally aimed at providing technical assistance to Hungary and Poland, and later extended to countries eligible for accession to the EU, contained references to the European Social Charter. In the context of Enlargement the Commission has included economic and social rights in its discussion on the fulfilment by the ten candidate countries of the Copenhagen criteria. The Commission's Opinions consider whether or not these countries have adhered to the European Social Charter (other conventions considered include the European Convention on Human Rights, the European Torture Convention, and the main UN instruments). This may be indicative of the fact that adherence to European instruments for the protection of economic, social, and cultural rights is linked to the criteria necessary for EU membership, rather than merely to the development of aid relations.

The preference for internationally agreed standards—as opposed to EC legal instruments—is probably indicative of a concern not to impose European standards at the external level in order to avoid criticism of neo-colonialist or protectionist attitudes towards third countries. These allegations were *in nuce* contained in the recent allegations by India against the EC's GSP system.

As concerns the content of social rights referred to in the aforementioned external relations instruments of the European Union, the reference to social rights is made mainly in general terms. Such rights are mentioned as social rights without further specification. Health, food, and education are often mentioned either as objectives of the EC's development cooperation or as the target of specific projects. However, they are not described as rights. As explained above, far from being a mere linguistic choice, it seems to denote that the EU has not fully endorsed a human rights approach in its development cooperation policy.[124] This contrasts with the efforts made at the international level progressively to integrate human rights into development policies and poverty reduction strategies.[125] This approach has been reaffirmed in draft guidelines on a human rights approach to poverty reduction strategies,[126] recently issued by the Office of the High

---

[123] E. Szyszczak, 'Social Rights as General Principles of Community Law', in A. Neuwahl and A. Rosas (eds), *The European Union and Human Rights* (1995), at 213.

[124] Tomaševski, *supra* n. 73, at 71.

[125] Cf. G. Nankani, J. Page, and L. Judge, 'Human Rights and Poverty Reduction Strategies: Moving Towards Convergence?', in P. Alston and M. Robinson, *Human Rights and Development: Towards Mutual Reinforcement* (2005).

[126] United Nations Office of the High Commissioner for Human Rights, *Draft Guidelines: A Human Rights Approach to Poverty Reduction Strategies*, 10 September 2002.

Commissioner for Human Rights that offer practical advice for the integration of human rights into poverty reduction strategies.

In addition, gender equality,[127] the fight against poverty, and, more recently, access to clean water are regarded as cross-cutting issues, and they constitute over-arching objectives of the EU's development cooperation policy. This explains their close link with and their impact on the enjoyment of social rights.

In this context, labour rights enjoy preferential treatment. Not only are they expressly mentioned in two of the main external relations instruments (the GSP and the Cotonou Agreement) but they are also listed in them and accompanied by a reference to the relevant Conventions of the ILO. Moreover, the recitals to the GSP Regulation state that reference should be made to the comments of the ILO's governing bodies for the interpretation of the labour rights mentioned in the Regulation.

The application of negative measures is usually related to the promotion of civil and political rights.[128] Moreover economic sanctions, such as the withdrawal of aid or the termination of preferential trade arrangements, usually have an undesir-able effect on social and economic rights. A different comment can be made about the so-called horizontal measures, which promote targeted groups such as women, children, and indigenous peoples. Community programmes in this sector are in the main promoted through the EIDHR, and special references to the needs of these groups are contained in some of the development cooperation programmes (for instance, the MEDA programme).

Having outlined in Section I the shortcomings of human rights clauses in the promotion of social rights, it has been suggested that other ways forward need to be explored. In addition to traditional instruments for the promotion of social rights, the EU's development cooperation also emphasizes the role of tech-nical assistance and encourages cooperation and awareness building at local level. This may encourage the major involvement of companies in the promotion of civil and political rights. In the MEDA programme, for instance, the TÜSIAD, the main Turkish business organization, was actively involved in the promotion of civil and political rights in Turkey. On the other hand, the TÜSIAD paid less attention to income redistribution and the provision of social safety nets.[129] In line with the principles underlying EC development policy, the Cotonou Agreement also envisages the participation of non-state actors, including companies, in development programmes.

---

[127] Council Resolution of 20 December 1995 on 'Integrating Gender Issues in Development Co-operation'. This resolution is largely based on the Commission Communication on 'Integrating Gender Issues in Development Co-operation', COM(1995)423 final, 18 September 1995. See also Commission Communication, 'Programme of Action for Mainstreaming Gender Equality in Community Development Co-operation', COM(2001)295 final.

[128] Cf. B. Simma, J. B. Aschenbrenner and C. Schulte, 'Human Rights Considerations in the Development Co-operation Activities of the EC', in Alston et al., *supra* n. 121, at 580.

[129] Schmid, *supra* n. 14, 32.

The above analysis shows that for the EU to promote social rights in its external relations both the normative and operational frameworks have to be improved. In addition, recent initiatives on the involvement of the private sector in development policy and corporate social responsibility can provide a complementary tool for raising awareness and encouraging the involvement of local communities in developing countries which are the beneficiaries of the application of higher social standards.

17

European Fundamental Social Rights in the Context of Economic Globalization

MARIE-ANGE MOREAU

I. INTRODUCTION

The major stages of the construction of social rights in Europe demonstrate an irresistible increase in the strength of fundamental social rights.[1] The super-imposition of different texts, and difficulties in the way their provisions are expressed, have often led to diminished awareness of them. They obey different logics, depending upon the institutions that apply them: the Council of Europe has left its mark on the European Social Charter, whereas the Charter of Fundamental Rights is the product of the evolution of the Union itself through the various Treaties. It is this 'trajectory' of social rights[2] that explains the sophistica-tion and diversity of their legal construction in Europe. From the perspective of citizens, as 'citizen-workers', it is clear that the adoption at Nice of the Charter of Fundamental Rights represents extraordinary progress.[3]

It would be useful, in order to get a precise idea of the place occupied by fundamental social rights in the context of the phenomenon of globalization, to study exactly what each right, recognized equally by the ECHR,[4] the European

---

[1] An earlier study has illustrated, in the context of a comparison with South Africa, the drawbacks for the beneficiaries of this sophistication, namely citizens and workers: Moreau 'L'utilisation des droits sociaux fondamentaux par les travailleurs dans l'Union européenne', in J.-Y. Cherot and T. Van Reenan (eds), *Les droits sociaux à l'âge de la mondialisation* (2005).

[2] This term is used by B. de Witte in this volume. The author of this contribution prefers to use the term 'fundamental social rights' not only precisely to show the difference between civil and political rights versus social rights but also clearly to indicate the specific nature of these rights as fundamental rights. On the difficulty see V. Champeil-Desplats 'Les droits et libertés fondamentaux en France: genèse d'une qualification', in A. Lyon-Caen, and P. Lokiec (eds), *Droits fondamentaux et droit social* (2005) 11–40.

[3] J. Ziller, 'L'Europe sociale dans la Constitution pour l'Europe', *Droit social* (2005) 188–99.

[4] On the weak position of social rights in the ECHR, see J.-Y. Cherot, 'La fonction des normes relatives aux droits fondamentaux dans l'ordre juridique communautaire. La question de l'insertion des droits sociaux fondamentaux dans l'union européenne', in Cherot and Van Reeuan (eds), *supra*

Social Charter[5] and the Charter of Fundamental Rights of the European Union,[6] guarantees. The selection of fundamental social rights protected, the degree of precision with which they are articulated,[7] along with the geographic scope of the protection afforded by each instrument must all be distinguished in terms of their usefulness.[8] However, the detailed analysis carried out in the various chapters of this book—of the general influence of the Charter and its integration into the Constitution, of specific questions such as the right to work (the major absentee from the Charter of the European Union), the complementarity of the provisions giving protection against discrimination, and rights linked to social protection and health[9]—may usefully be complemented by a more 'global' analysis which confronts the trend towards the recognition of social rights in Europe with the phenomenon of economic globalization.

The phenomenon of globalization is sometimes compared to a river, made up of many different streams: it is a current that is sometimes tumultuous, sometimes peaceful, which transforms, changes its course, tears at the banks of the river and destroys them, or, on the contrary, sometimes deposits there a fertile silt; at least, until the next storm. This metaphor illustrates nicely the difficulty of grasping the phenomenon, and the wide diversity of its effects.[10] It is sufficient, in the context of this chapter, to emphasize certain points that allow an account to be provided of the role played by European fundamental social rights in this process.

It seems impossible[11] to limit an analysis of globalization to the increase in international trade. This increase, encouraged and regulated by the rules of the

---

n. 1; Akandji-Kombé, 'Le développement des droits fondamentaux dans les traités', in S. Leclerc, J.-F. Akandji-Kombé and M.-J. Redor (eds), *L'Union européenne et les droits fondamentaux* (1999) 31; L. Dubin, *La protection des normes sociales dans les échanges internationaux* (2003).

[5] See the contributions on the European Social Charter in this volume.

[6] See in particular J.-Y. Carlier and O. De Schutter (eds), *La Charte des droits fondamentaux de l'Union européenne* (2002); O. De Schutter, 'L'affirmation des droits fondamentaux dans la Charte des droits fondamentaux de l'Union européenne', in Lyon-Caen and Lokiec (eds), *supra* n. 2, at 145–83; B. Bercusson, *European Labour Law and the EU Charter of Fundamental Rights* (2003); Benoît-Rohmer, 'La Charte des droits sociaux fondamentaux de l'Union européenne', 12 *RUDH* (2000) 2; G. Braibant, 'La Charte des droits fondamentaux', *Droit social* (2001) 69; Vittorio, 'La Charte des droits fondamentaux de l'Union européenne', *Revue de droit de l'Union européenne* (2001) 27; J. Dutheil de la Rochère, 'La Charte des droits fondamentaux, quelle valeur ajouté? Quel avenir?', 443 *Revue du Marché Commun et de l'Union européennen* (2000) 674; G. de Búrca, 'The Drafting of the European Union Charter of Fundamental Rights', 26 *ELRev.* (2001) 126.

[7] It is important to emphasize the fact that the rights guaranteed by the European Social Charter are in most cases clearly and precisely articulated, which confers on the Charter a normative force that cannot be ignored.

[8] For a very interesting study see M. Bonnechere, 'Droits sociaux fondamentaux: vers un droit commun pour l'Europe', *Semaine sociale Lamy*, no. 1187, 25/10/04, at 5–9 and no. 1188, 02/11/04, at 5–9.

[9] It is very interesting to note that the evolution of some rights, such as those against discrimination, has progressed along similar lines (see M. Bell's contribution to this volume), whereas in terms of the right to health this is not at all the case (see T. Hervey's contribution to this volume).

[10] See the report by the World Commission on the Social Dimension of Globalization, available at www.ilo.org.

[11] Some economists refuse to see beyond the classical 'H.O.S.' analysis, and acknowledge any specificity to the [current] stage of globalization. The argument of this chapter follows instead the

WTO, is accompanied by diversification and specialization in the strategies of multinational firms and by the amount of direct investment, in the context of an unprecedented financialization of markets. It is the *interdependence* of all of these factors that accounts for the new phase of economic globalization that began in the 1990s.[12] As a result, in order to understand the role of social rights in Europe, it is important to emphasize the specific role played by multinational companies: around half of all international trade takes place in intra-firm relations. Multinational companies are therefore the essential actors,[13] who must decide whether or not to establish a presence on the European market.

There is thus clearly a paradox here that needs to be emphasized: the construction of fundamental social rights has been within the vertical and hierarchical normative structure of states, who are guarantors of, and charged with ensuring respect for, these social rights, whereas the 'privileged' actors in the context of economic globalization are transnational companies that operate on the horizontal, economic plane.

It is thus interesting to examine the role played by social rights, as established by the ECHR, the European Social Charter, and the Charter of Fundamental Rights of the European Union, as 'market conditions' that affect the strategic choices of economic actors. They perform, like all regulatory norms, a specific structuring function within the European market. This structuring of the market around social rights, on top of the current guarantees it provides to businesses and workers, is a powerful guarantee of social quality, generating costs linked to these rights; it thus has a number of different aspects and consequences that merit attention. This first observation will be expanded in Section II below.

The most obvious consequence of the interdependence of the factors that condition the strategies of multinational corporations is a generalized 'opening up' of territories to competition, creating in the process not only pressure towards more or less important modes of deregulation ('bottom down'), but also strong fears over the loss of identities. The proclamation and the rise in strength of European social rights has created a double response to the anxiety, more often than not justified, that has arisen over the potentially devastating effects of globalization: the first is a 'barrier' effect and the second a 'dissemination' effect, both of which, for different reasons, contribute to the creation of a new response. This will be examined in Section III below.

---

analysis carried out by C. A. Michalet (see n. 12 below) who illustrates very clearly the ruptures in economic processes between the 'international' configuration, that came to an end in the 1960s, the 'multinational' configuration in the 1970s and the global period since the beginning of the 1990s. It is important to stress that we can trace a connection between these phases and the evolution of legal norms: M. A. Moreau and G. Trudeau, 'Les normes de droit du travail confrontées à l'évolution de l'économie, de nouveaux enjeux pour l'espace régional', 127 *JDI* (2000).

[12] C. A. Michalet, *Qu'est ce que la mondialisation* (2002); C. Pottier, *Les multinationales et la mise en concurrence des salaires* (2003).

[13] Ibid.; W. Andreff, *Les multinationales globales* (1996); J.-L. Mucchielli, *Multinationales et mondialisation* (1998).

Nevertheless, the mechanisms put in place in Europe have not sufficiently tamed the potential for volatility that comes with economic globalization. Multinational corporations operate in the transnational, and often in the 'global' sphere, with the effect that economic strategies pay no heed to national borders. Even if these social rights are enacted at the European and/or Community levels, it is states which remain responsible for ensuring that they are respected, at least in the case of the European Social Charter and the Charter of Fundamental Rights. However, the most active economic actors, multinational companies, remain the objects of state policy only for as long as the European market concerns them. This means that they can easily decide to evade these policies, subject to the imperatives of the market. It is thus important to examine the extent to which the current procedures are insufficient: claims founded upon violations of social rights do not make sufficient use of the strength of the market itself in order to develop respect for social rights, and do not provide sufficient means to the beneficiaries of these rights to respond to the transnational strategies of companies when the rights are violated. This will be examined in Section IV.

II. THE STRUCTURING OF THE EUROPEAN MARKET AROUND SOCIAL RIGHTS

The question of the role of fundamental social rights proclaimed within a certain territory or region has given rise to important debates, since—according to some—the rules of the market in the context of a liberal economy require a search for the highest possible degree of profitability.[14] This search is carried out on a global scale by opening up competition between countries as to which of them offers the most efficient conditions for economic investment. The elements taken into consideration are not only social costs but also all other economic (the market to be conquered, transportation, quality of products, etc.), legal (taxation, company law), cultural and political (stability) factors.[15] They vary according to the strategy adopted by a multinational company seeking to conquer a particular market: a market presence strategy, a minimization of costs strategy, a combination of the two in a 'global' strategy, or an oligopolistic strategy.[16]

It is clear that the European internal market represents an attractive opportunity, even more so since enlargement: each time a multinational company wishes to establish itself on the European market as a strategic market choice, the rules of the Union, thanks to the mechanisms for the support of the economic freedoms,

[14] Michalet, *supra* n. 12, at 95f.

[15] Mucchielli, *supra* n. 13, at 148f. See for example p. 182, on the determining factors of the setting up of Japanese subsidiaries by country and by zone with the following elements: satisfactory infrastructure; size of domestic market; conditions of distribution; production capacity, above all for spare parts; transportation network; ease of hiring English-speaking personnel; existence of Japanese firms on the market; ability to educate children of Japanese personnel; possibility of obtaining segments of the final product.   [16] Michalet, *supra* n. 12, at 117.

allow it a wide choice over the location of the company seat, the management of subsidiaries and branches, the movement of goods, etc. The choice made by the Union to use the force of social rights in order to structure the market is thus essential, as it complements economic comparative advantages with a view to ensure social quality standards.[17]

A few examples here will suffice to illustrate the manner in which the market is structured by fundamental social rights:

- the structuring of the market by the right to organize, the right to collective bargaining, and, since the Charter, the right to strike, allows for professional relations to be conducted on the basis of social dialogue;
- the right to vocational training helps to guarantee the skills of the labour force through the development of professional adaptability;
- the right to just and equitable conditions of work compels respect for the health, security and dignity of workers, and ensures that economic competition is not based upon an absence of legal protection;
- equality between men and women requires that there be no discrimination between male and female sections of the workforce, which ensures competition for employment will not be based upon the automatic disqualification of women;
- the right of access to social security benefits ensures the health of citizens and workers, etc.

These fundamental social rights are an essential part of the 'European social model', which determines the conditions in which companies can set up business on the European market.

The remarkable role played by the jurisprudence of the ECJ in this context must be emphasized.[18] The Court of Justice[19] had to find a means of protecting social rights in the face of economic freedoms and competition law, the pillar of the competitive order.[20] The Court's decision to allow the right to collective bargaining to prevail—without subjecting it to the intricate rules of competition law[21]—in the *Albany* case is noteworthy;[22] as is the decision by the Court to

---

[17] B. Hepple, *Labour Laws and Global Trade* (2005).

[18] It is more important than the jurisprudence of the ECtHR in this regard, in particular regarding the right to organize.

[19] See in particular the very detailed article by O. De Schutter, 'La garantie des droits et principes sociaux dans la Charte des droits fondamentaux de l'Union européenne', in Carlier and De Schutter (eds), *supra n.* 6, at 117.

[20] M. Rainelli, L. Boy and H. Ullrich (eds), *L'ordre concurrentiel: Mélanges en l'honneur d'Antoine Pirovano* (2003).

[21] S. Sciarra, 'Market Freedom and Fundamental Rights', in B. Hepple (ed), *Social and Labour Rights in a Global Context* (2002) 105.

[22] Case C-67/96, *Albany* [1999] ECR I-5751; Joined Cases C-115/97, C-116/97 and C-117/97, *Brentjens* [1999] ECR I-6025; Case C-219/97 *Maatschappij* [1999] ECR I-06121. De Schutter, *L'affirmation, supra* n. 6, at 176–77.

protect the social protection mechanisms based upon solidarity,[23] even where they are likely to confer a dominant position on one actor; and the decision to uphold certain protective measures, such as those concerning working at night, in the face of the requirements of the free movement of goods goes in the same way.[24]

These are all examples of the 'balancing of economic freedoms and social rights', to use Olivier De Schutter's expression, that illustrate that the regional European sphere is structured around social rights, even though the dominant logic is that of a competitive market. As a final example, consider the balancing performed by the Court, in 2003,[25] between the right to demonstrate and freedom of expression, on the one hand, and the free movement of goods on the other. This case illustrates that the ECJ is seeking to carry out this balance between fundamental rights in a fair and proportionate manner.[26] The Court thus tries to find an equilibrium, which provides strong guarantees of stability to companies investing in the European market.[27]

European fundamental social rights thus have, in the context of globalization, the function of structuring the European market in terms of social quality, guaranteed for those companies that establish themselves there. As a result, multinational companies have a choice of localization that allows them to 'play' on variations in national legislation, in particular in fiscal and social matters, without, however, affecting the 'hard core' (*socle*) of social rights.

This *socle*, however, cannot prevent distortions of competition from arising due to the existence of twenty-five different national legislations. Hourly labour costs within the Union varied on a common scale[28] from 6 (Portugal) to 28 (Germany),[29] and now, after enlargement, from 1 to 29, a fact that explains the importance of direct investment in the new Member States. The most obvious movement has occurred in the automobile industry: German companies, for example, have invested massively in the Czech Republic and Slovakia (Volkswagen); however, important investments have also been made in Spain and Portugal (Volkswagen and Renault), and even in France (Toyota).

'Delocalisation' or 'relocalisation' movements in the European Union occur both inside this regional space and at its periphery. At the current moment, for example, an important trend towards the relocation of production or business

---

[23] Joined Cases C-159/91 and C-160/91, *Poucet and Pistre* [1993] ECR I-637. See the analysis by F. Baron, *Marché intérieur et droit social dans l'Union européenne* (1998), at 290f.

[24] As regards the doubts about the ECJ's future choices on the question of solidarity after the adoption of the constitution, see De Schutter, *L'affirmation*, supra n. 6, at 182.

[25] Case C-112/00, *Eugen Schmidberger* [2003] ECR I-5659.

[26] De Schutter, 'L'affirmation', supra n. 6, at 141–182.

[27] In foreign investment strategies, economic and above all political stability remain major factors in any decision. It is clear that the democratic guarantees provided by Europe in the context of the enlargement to twenty-five members are essential. On the role of political stability even in a constructed regional context such as NAFTA, see the example of Mexico. Pottier, *supra* n. 12. In terms of investment choices in Asia, the existence of democracy in India, in the context of its competition with China, will very probably be an important factor in the future.

[28] Based on social indicators made by Eurostat.   [29] Pottier, *supra* n. 12, at 140.

premises away from Ireland can be noted. A number of American companies established in Ireland, because of its skilled labour force, low costs, and above all its fiscal advantages in terms of company tax, are revising their localization policies within the European Union.[30] This trend has been caused by changes in fiscal legislation and the new possibilities offered by Eastern Europe, combined with new international opportunities. Yet, these relocalization trends, with the consequences that they bring in terms of employment—damaging for the country abandoned, beneficial to the new host country—are not often based on the prospect of benefiting from the violation of social rights.[31]

The decision taken in the European Union to structure the market through the affirmation of fundamental social rights also allows for, as its limit and its consequence, the choice of relocation at the periphery of the Union, in particular in the Maghrieb countries.[32] To the extent that peripheral countries have comparative advantages allowing them to compete seriously with the countries of the Union, it is essential that the Union compels them to respect a solid core of social rights. The vague and ineffective guarantees contained in association agreements, specifically with Morocco and Tunisia, do not really address this danger.[33] It is possible at the present time to speak of 'harmful social competition'[34] to describe the non-respect of social rights guaranteed by agreements or treaties concluded with countries on the periphery of the union,[35] due to the specific harm created by unfair competition in the context of globalization.[36] Most important, however, is that this 'harmful social competition' cannot be practised within the Union itself, despite the presence of twenty-five countries with extremely different levels of development.

III. THE RESPONSE OF FUNDAMENTAL SOCIAL RIGHTS TO 'GLOBAL' COMPETITION

The proclamation of fundamental social rights in the Nice Charter, and the interaction between the Charter of 1961 and the ECHR, have led to the creation of a strong movement within the European Union that encourages and supports,

[30] The basic choice is between transferring to the new, incoming countries, or to countries outside the EU (notably in India for technology and call centres). *Le Monde*, 19 February 2004.

[31] Even if we know that the manner in which these rights are guaranteed varies according to each country of the Union.   [32] Pottier, *supra* n. 12, at 142.

[33] Here, in order to emphasize the economic effect of such social clauses, reference to their humanitarian and social importance has been omitted. See A. Gatto's chapter in this volume.

[34] The term 'harmful fiscal competition' was used in the context of European tax harmonization, and in the elaboration of a code of conduct to define all measures that should be banned within the union due to their unfair effects (strict fiscal definition).

[35] See the contribution of A. Gatto in this volume.

[36] With the major difficulties involved in finding arrangements of conditionality capable of avoiding such competition, see the debates surrounding the evolution of the European GSP in L. Dubin, *supra* n. 4 and A. Gatto's contribution to this volume.

in a dynamic fashion, a genuine 'centrality of fundamental social rights'.[37] This centrality can be observed at once in the debates that impact upon national rights, in the trend towards constitutionalization of social rights, and the reinforcement in all countries of internal mechanisms for the enforcement of these rights. It can also be observed at the international level, thanks in particular to the work of the International Labour Office in the context of the application of the Declaration concerning the fundamental rights of workers in 1998. The corresponding development in the European Union is the enactment of the Charter of Rights: if the Constitution for the European Union enters into force, the Charter will be at the heart of the effort to strengthen social rights within the Union.[38]

Even if we leave on the side the importance of this question here, it is possible to note that, at the present time, despite the lack of effective mechanisms of protection of fundamental social rights, this base does allow for the creation of a genuine 'barrier' against the risks of deregulation, and at the same time encourages the trend towards the 'dissemination' of social rights within the framework of 'soft law'.

A. The 'Barrier' Effect

This defensive function is guaranteed by the Charter of Fundamental Rights of the Union and would have been consolidated by the integration of the Charter into the Constitution. The power of neo-liberal thinking within the Union, even if it became less dominant during 2004, still creates a significant risk that the region will favour an economic model of unlimited competition.[39] The most obvious danger comes, without doubt, from the approach adopted within the framework of the European Employment Strategy, which, in several ways, could call into question the principles affirmed in the Charter.[40]

Developments in Britain during the Thatcher era provide a relatively recent example that demonstrates that where there is a political determination to deregulate labour law, there will be no effective limit on the legal plane.[41] This is further attested to by the opposition of the UK to the horizontal application of the Charter or, indeed, to any measure that could be used as a 'Trojan horse' for the creation of new social rights entitlements.

The 'barrier' effect is particularly important in the context of enlargement. A number of social rights guaranteed by the Charter have been the object of

[37] This term was used by the ILO and taken up by Isabelle Daugareilh. I. Daugareilh (ed.), *Mondialisation, travail et droits fondamentaux* (2005).

[38] Ziller, *supra* n. 3.

[39] M. Regini, 'The Dilemmas of Labour Market Regulation', in G. Espin-Andersen and M. Regini (eds), *Why Deregulate Labour Markets?* (2000) Ch 1.

[40] See the contribution of S. Sciarra in this volume.

[41] See for example the examples of deregulation contained in Espin-Andersen and Regini, *supra* n. 39, and in particular the contribution by S. Deakin and H. Reed, 'River Crossing or Cold Bath? Deregulation and Employment in Britain in the 1980s and 1990s', in Espin-Andersen and Regini (eds), *supra* n. 39, at 115.

European Community directives, thus allowing for the concrete and effective application of these rights in the new Member States. The obligation to adopt the *acquis communautaire* illustrates the commitment of the Union to safeguarding important rights such as the right of information and consultation of workers, the right of access to health and social security benefits, the right to equal treatment between men and women, etc. Of course, it will take a certain number of years for these social rights to be applied in reality. To give just one example, the end of the Communist period led, except in Poland, to the artificial creation of a structure of industrial relations (which existed on paper only) based upon the independence of trade unions and employers' associations. It will necessarily take several years before a genuine process of collective bargaining can take root. One of the first challenges of enlargement will be to ensure that the social policy directives are applied in an equivalent way in the new Member States. However, it is important to emphasize that the new Member States will not be allowed to adopt lower levels of protection of EC labour standards in order to increase their comparative advantage and thus enable them to 'catch up'.

Even for those rights that do not fall within the scope of Community competence, such as the right to association or the right to strike (due to the exclusion clause in Article 137 of the EC Treaty), the 'barrier' effect should also operate fully. The fact remains, however, that this 'barrier' effect will be more or less important depending upon the interpretation given by the Court of Justice. In the *BECTU* case,[42] the Advocate-General did not hesitate to make reference to the Charter in order to oppose British legislation that restricted the right to paid holidays; thus demonstrating one possible way of reinforcing the social rights contained in the Charter.[43]

B. The 'Dissemination' Effect

The 'dissemination' effect is evidently more diffuse. It has already been a feature of the jurisprudence of the Court, in the context of the construction of fundamental social rights for European Union citizens. This jurisprudence has the benefit of creating a concept of European citizenship that is autonomous of the various free movement rights. The European citizen can be a genuine beneficiary of social rights.[44]

This effect can be observed both in the context of the actions of social partners and those of civil society actors. It was anticipated in the Social Agenda

---

[42] Case C-173/99, *BECTU* [2001] ECR I-4881, Conclusions of Advocate-General Tizzano.

[43] It is important to recall, however, that a number of rights are subject to national legislation and practices.

[44] See Cases C-85/96, *Martinez Sala* [2001] I-26918, Rec. I.2691; C-413/99 *Baumbast* [2002] ECR I-7091; C-224/98 *D'Hoop* [2002] ECR I-6191; C-184/99 *Grzelczyk* [2001] ECR I-6193. M.-A. Moreau, 'Les droits fondamentaux des travailleurs dans l'union européenne', in Daugareilh (ed), *supra* n. 37.

2004–2005, published by the European Commission, that the social rights of workers would be strengthened through the mechanism of bipartite or tripartite negotiation:[45] whether with regard to the protection of personal data, the fight against stress[46] or harassment, or guidelines for restructuring,[47] each of these subjects is dependent upon social partners' voluntary action to give substance to the rights proclaimed in the Charter.

The agreements signed in the framework of Article 138 EC Treaty, such as the parental leave agreement, fixed-term contract agreement, or part-time agreement are a sign of the strength of the principle of equal treatment within the Union.[48] It is thus possible to maintain that the processes of negotiation at the European level are a means for the elucidation and concretization of social rights.

It is also interesting to note that sectoral social dialogue is used in the Union in order to generate codes of conduct, which may then be applied within companies that are 'global' in scope. The most important negotiations have been successful, one in the leather sector, and one in the sugar sector.[49] As the codes of conduct have been elaborated within the institutional framework of the European Commission, their content has been inspired by European social rights. It is important to stress here that what are presented as 'self-regulation' mechanisms in transnational companies can also possess a degree of Community legitimacy, and their content may respect the social rights of the Community legal order.

These codes, which belong to the category of 'soft law', also assume the status of agreements within the context of sectoral social dialogue. They have thus a 'borrowed' legitimacy and a content that allows for the diffusion of Community fundamental social rights. Such codes of conduct can be applied in all countries in which companies establish themselves, and notably in Asia. They thus enable, in an original fashion, the dissemination of European social rights. It is also interesting to note that the voluntary code of conduct developed in the leather sector has become obligatory in certain Member States: thus, in France, it became the object of an administrative decree.[50]

The same trends are beginning to emerge in the context of negotiations taking place within the framework of European Works Councils charged with elaborating codes of conduct: the model of rights guaranteed in the Charter is a reference model, like the rights contained in the 1998 Declaration of the International

---

[45] Commission Communication, 'Partenariat pour le changement dans une Europe élargie. Renforcer la contribution du dialogue social européen', COM(2004)557 final.

[46] European Agreement on Stress in the Workplace, signed on 11 June 2004, currently going through an approval process by the central bodies: *Liaisons sociales Europe* No. 107, 24.6.2004.

[47] The Agreement which was concluded in June 2003 and fixed only the general outlines for action without creating any binding obligations was rejected by the ETUC in October 2003. This text illustrates the limits of soft law in the context of social dialogue.

[48] COM(2004)557 final, *supra* n. 45.

[49] See the analysis in *Liaisons sociales Europe*, No. 14 at 6, and No. 105 at 3. For other sectors see COM(2004)557 final, *supra* n. 45.

[50] Decree of 10 May 2004, *Journal officiel* 19 May 2004 at 8891; *Liaisons sociales Europe*, No. 105 at 3.

Labour Office. Collective bargaining then plays its role, but it seems that European fundamental social rights do play an indirect role in these new forms of transnational regulation.

Lastly, it may well be that the 'dissemination' effect, whatever impact the Charter itself may have, will influence national judges: in terms of social concerns, we have seen in the past that, despite the fact that the 1989 Charter had no binding force whatsoever, national judges were prepared to use the rights guaranteed therein.[51] The strength of the model, and its foundation upon constitutionally guaranteed rights, means that it will be a source for national judges, even although, according to the Community legal order, it has no horizontal direct effect. We can also note the emergence of a 'horizontal indirect effect' through the extension of the requirements of those social rights guaranteed by the directives to the law of contracts.[52] Social actors, and in particular European trade unions, will also make use of the Charter as a basis for action: before it had even been integrated into the Constitution, it was notable that agreements made reference to fundamental social rights, particularly in the context of agreements signed by the European Works Councils.

The integration of the Charter of Fundamental Rights into the European Union legal system links together the Community legislature and all actors who contribute to the normative construction of the Union: it will be a direct source for all actions brought by institutions, and an indirect source for all other actors in the context of their own normative activity, judicial[53] or contractual.

Therefore, from the strength of the model itself to its influence on contract law, there has been an effective and widespread dissemination of European fundamental social rights.

IV. THE INADEQUACY OF THESE RESPONSES IN TERMS OF VIOLATIONS OF FUNDAMENTAL SOCIAL RIGHTS

If we consider again the specificity of this stage of globalization, marked by the strategies of multinational companies at different levels and the reactions of countries faced with the need to attract direct investment onto their territory, it is readily evident that violations of social rights, either on the territory of the European Union itself or in that of third countries, can be used as a form of comparative advantage.

For example, the fact that the maximum limit on weekly working hours, set at forty-eight hours by the Directive of 23 November 1993, which is systematically

---

[51] In the context of the first judgment handed down in the case of the closure of the Renault factory in Vilvorde. Tribunal de Grande Instance de Nanterre (Référés) 4 April 1997. Comité de Groupe Europeén Renault (C.G.E.) c./Société Renault, *Droit social* 1997, at 504.

[52] See the analysis in this volume by B. Bercusson, following the *Pfeiffer* case in 2003.

[53] It is interesting to note that the President of the ECJ clearly stated, in an interview given to the newspaper *La Tribune*, that the Charter would be a point of reference for the Court. Interview in *Liaisons sociales Europe*, No. 107, 24/06/04.

exceeded in the UK,[54] is effectively a means of allowing British companies to adjust to the demands of competition; controls on health and safety in the enterprise are chronically ineffective in Greece; the difficulties in ensuring respect for the age limits in employing children in the agricultural sector in Southern European countries are well known; and these are just a few examples of social rights that have not merely been proclaimed but have also been the object of binding measures within the Union, and are nonetheless not respected.[55] Despite this, up until now the statistics concerning direct investment in Europe do not indicate that these 'shortcomings' in respect for social rights have been significant. They do not seem to have affected localization policies.

It could, however, be different if such violations of fundamental social rights become the rule in the newly acceding countries. A lack of respect for the *acquis communautaire*, and for the principles proclaimed in the Charter that refer to it, could lead to a noticeable worsening of the conditions of competition in the Union. The most sensitive area will perhaps be that of collective bargaining and the right of association. Violations of fundamental social rights in neighbouring countries linked to the EU by association agreements is an even more sensitive question, as they could effectively promote the delocalization of firms. It is thus extremely damaging that the collective procedure opened up by the instruments that guarantee social rights are only of limited effectiveness, even if the new complaints procedure in place since 1996 within the framework of the European Social Charter is better adapted to the context of globalization. It is regrettable that the institutions have not yet adapted to the global economic context, which requires that collective procedure be reinforced by the pressure made by the market on firms.

A. The Inadequacy of Remedies in Cases of Violations of Fundamental Social Rights

There is no room here to give a detailed analysis of the various possibilities that exist in Europe for complaining against violations of fundamental social rights.[56] Only those characteristics illustrative of their inadequacy in the context of globalization will be emphasized here.

The lack of horizontal applicability of the social rights guaranteed in the Charter has already been noted. If, however, we consider workers, trade unions, and citizens, it is clear that the absence of direct claims significantly limits the impact of the guarantee given by the European Union to civil society. The possibilities for action before national tribunals are, of course, more developed within the context of the ECHR, but the place accorded to social rights therein is very

---

[54] A question highly debated for the revision of this directive on working time in the EU.
[55] Including, since 1996, the use of the collective complaints procedure, see *supra* n. 50.
[56] See various other contributions in this volume.

limited.[57] The rise in claims before national courts that invoke Articles 6, 8, 11, 14, and the First Protocol illustrate, however, the extraordinary desire of citizens to benefit from European fundamental social rights.[58]

To the extent that, in the context of Community law, claims of violation are addressed to the Commission (infringement complaint), citizens are not in control of the process and are dependent, within the framework of the infringement procedure, on the diligence and discretion of the Commission. The EU Charter of Rights does not create additional remedies, so that its enforcement will take place through the traditional channels of Community law.[59] In other situations, the states are the objects of reports dealing with violations of the norms of the ILO or the European Social Charter. The sanctions, which are purely moral or political, are applied to states, and not to economic actors.

Another of the specificities of globalization is that the search for maximum profitability depends in part upon the speed of decision-making processes. It was partly in order to remedy this inefficacy of the reports mechanism that the collective complaints procedure was established in 1996.[60] Even if it constitutes genuine progress in terms of the potential publicization of violations of the rights guaranteed by the Charter, it also leads only to a recommendation addressed to the state. This procedure still lacks visibility and above all requires a higher media profile. Trade unions have not, for strategic reasons,[61] made systematic use of this procedure, even if there has been a constant increase in the number of complaints since 1996. The speed at which states react, assuming that they do react, is slow, and does not correspond at all to the speed at which economic decisions are taken. To demonstrate this, it is sufficient to refer to the complaints that have been dealt with in the renewed context of the Charter of 1961: from the moment a complaint is lodged to its definitive resolution, in the best of cases, one year will pass; sufficient time for a delocalization and two restructurings . . .

Although it undoubtedly provides a new weapon to actors, the legal character of the collective complaints mechanism is limited in that it cannot result in a genuine sanction, or in an injunction to put an end to the violation. Moreover, it is still not well known.[62]

---

[57] Cherot, *supra* n. 4. On the other hand, see Bonnechere for a coherent interpretation between the different sources by the judges, *supra* n. 8.

[58] For a very precise and interesting analysis of the case law see Bonnechere, *supra* n. 8.

[59] This can happen either by way of directives or by collective agreements transformed into directives (Articles 138–39 EC).

[60] S. Grevisse, 'Le renouveau de la Charte sociale européenne', *Droit social* (1990) 884; J.-F. Akandji-Kombé, 'L'application de la Charte sociale européenne: la mise en œuvre de la procédure de réclamation collective', *Droit social* (1997) 888, and 'Actualités de la charte sociale européenne, chronique des décisions', *RTDH* (2003) 113; A. Roux, 'La Charte sociale européenne', in Cherot (ed.), *supra* n. 1. See also the references cited by P. Alston in this volume.

[61] It seems that trade unions do not make use of their position as external actors to bring the Charter mechanism into play because they are seeking the establishment in the European Social Charter of a tripartite system of control along the lines of the model of the ILO.

[62] Roux, *supra* n. 60, at 5.

These procedures, conforming to the classical pyramid structure of legal orders, are not adapted to deal with the transnational dimension of the strategies of multinational companies, and are thus not well suited to the context of economic globalization.

In one respect, however, the collective complaints procedure does represent an important development: the complaint mechanism takes into account that fundamental social rights violations can be detected in a variety of ways and allows not only national and international employers or workers organizations to act as a complainant, but also certain international NGOs and representative national NGOs. This diversification of the actors capable of bringing a claim of violation of fundamental social rights is a significant step forward in the struggle to make these rights effective. To the extent that it opens up these rights to international organizations, trade unions and NGOs, it enables the identification of violations that concern several countries, or even the regional area in its entirety.

The collective complaints procedure thus has great potential for encouraging transnational action, that could be fulfilled if its decisions are given a higher media profile by the Council of Europe.[63] In the context of globalization, the evolution of transnational NGOs and actors, since transnational actors are also capable of violating social rights on the transnational level, is essential. It is therefore extremely important to move away from the idea that violations are always specific to particular nations, and that they can be stopped by the state concerned; even if, at the current time, it seems no violations of the Charter with a specifically transnational dimension have arisen, it is not impossible that they will in the future. Violations in several countries at once are frequent. The fact that the procedure can be initiated on the same question in several countries of the Union simultaneously contributes to a strengthening of protection at the European level.

This transnational character of the procedure can be taken even further: contrary to the complaints procedure established by the North American Agreement on Labor Cooperation (NAALC) joined to NAFTA, the European procedure does not require that at least two organizations from the region act in concert.[64] The European procedure, therefore, unlike the North American one, does not encourage transnational alliances between organizations with the objective of denouncing social rights violations taking place in another country (for example, large American trade unions acting in concert with a small Mexican union in order to denounce a violation of the right to organize in Mexico or the US).[65]

Lastly, there is no individual complaints procedure in place in the context of the European Social Charter equivalent to the San Salvador Additional Protocol to

---

[63] Which would be contrary to the diplomatic logic that dominates within the framework of the Charter.

[64] E. Mazuyer, 'Le traitement juridique des normes du travail dans les intégrations regionales (Communaute Europeene—ALENA)' (EUI PhD thesis, Florence, 2002) and references therein; Dubin, *supra* n. 4, at 272f; Moreau and, Trudeau, *supra* n. 11, at 915.

[65] Mazuyer, *supra* n. 64.

the American Convention on Human Rights of 1998 (not yet in force), which grants a right of individual recourse for the right to organize if the alleged violation can be attributed directly to a State Party. The existence of such a possibility of individual complaint would, however, be consistent with the logic of the attempt, since 1996, to increase the impact of the European Social Charter. Moreover, the Parliamentary Assembly of the Council of Europe clearly pronounced itself in favour of the introduction of such a system in 1999.[66] There is, therefore, unlike the North American context, no collective right of complaint based upon violations of individual rights, a fact that also reduces the possibility of achieving a higher media profile.

B. The Inadequacy of the Transnational Media Profile

It is in terms of this last point that these procedures are insufficient. It is well known that the powerful impact that the North American Parallel Agreement had on the development of social rights was due to the decision to hold public inquiries, with Canadian, American, and Mexican television cameras providing live coverage of the public debates (examination, cross-examination) over violations of the right to organize by Sony, Sprint, McDonalds, etc.

The power of the procedure came, contrary to all expectations,[67] from this media attention that created negative publicity for multinational companies, which are very attached to their image on the market. The public character of the hearings was abolished by President Bush, which led to a drastic reduction in the number of complaints being lodged. A detailed examination of the effects of the social clause procedure[68] in NAFTA illustrates, in a context in which actors can organize their interests or profit from a violation of fundamental rights, the power of the market itself. Companies are only concerned about their position in a given market; it is only through sanctions that flow from that market itself that changes in behaviour can be hoped for.

The new social movements, whether anti-globalization or '*alter-mondialistes*', have learned this lesson well. Their actions display two characteristics: they are transnational, and seek to create negative effects for companies in terms of their markets. Campaigns for the denunciation of violations of social rights, boycott

---

[66] Recommendations in 1978, 1991, and also in 1999. See Roux, *supra* n. 60.

[67] The social clause introduced in NAALC may give rise to hopes that a new mechanism capable of leading, at the end of the procedure, to an economic sanction would have a certain influence over respect for fundamental rights. For reasons linked to the manner in which the established procedure was constructed (organized), this social clause has not had the impact that was expected, even although it was the most widely used complaints mechanism (procedure). On this point see the important literature cited by Mazuyer, *supra* n. 64.

[68] M. A. Moreau and G. Trudeau, 'La clause sociale dans l'accord de libre-échange nord-Américain', *RIDE* (1995) 393; P. Staelens, 'La clause sociale: position des pays en développement et du Mexique dans le cadre de l'Alena', *Bull. de droit comparé de droit du travail et de la sécurité sociale* (1996) 57; Dubin, *supra* n. 4, at 265–82.

demands transmitted to all countries in which the company in question operates, petitions and even virtual demonstrations, etc.: these are the new forms of collective action that have been developed in response to the reality of globalization.[69]

It seems that the sophistication of media techniques and technological transmissions is a force well adapted to the specificity of violations of social rights; it is therefore extremely important that the institutions charged with protecting European fundamental social rights should find new ways of increasing the media profile of violations.

[69] K. A. Elliott and R. B. Freeman, *Can Labor Standards Improve Under Globalisation?* (2003). See in particular 127f on the anti-sweatshop campaigns.

Bibliography

*Larissa Ogertschnig**

TABLE OF CONTENTS

I. GENERAL LITERATURE ON SOCIAL RIGHTS IN EUROPE

Costa J.-P., 'Vers une protection juridictionnelle des droits économiques et sociaux en Europe?', *Les droits de l'homme au seuil du troisième millénaire: Mélange en hommage à Pierre Lambert* (Brussels, Bruylant, 2000).

Costello C. (ed.), *Fundamental Social Rights: Current European Legal Protection & the Challenge of the EU Charter of Fundamental Rights* (Dublin, Irish Centre for European Law, 2001).

* Many thanks to Itziar Gómez for making available a list of Spanish literature for this bibliography.

DRZEWICKI K., KRAUSE C., AND ROSAS A. (eds), *Social Rights as Human Rights: A European Challenge* (Turku/Åbo, Institute for Human Rights, Åbo Akademi University, 1994).

EIDE A., 'Future Protection of Economic and Social Rights in Europe', in A. Bloed, L. Leicht, M. Nowak, A. Rosas (eds), *Monitoring Human Rights in Europe: Comparing International Procedures and Mechanisms* (Dordrecht, Boston, Norwell, MA, Martinus Nijhoff Publishers in co-operation with the International Helsinki Federation for Human Rights, Kluwer Academic Publishers, 1993) 187–219.

——, KRAUSE C., AND ROSAS A. (eds), *Economic, Social, and Cultural Rights: A Textbook* (1st edn., The Hague, Martinus Nijhoff Publishers, Kluwer Law International, 1995)

——, KRAUSE C., AND ROSAS A. (eds), *Economic, Social, and Cultural Rights: A Textbook* (2nd and rev. edn., The Hague, Martinus Nijhoff Publishers, Kluwer Law International, 2001).

FLAUSS J.-F. (ed.), *Droits sociaux et droit européen: bilan et prospective de la protection normative* (Brussels, Bruylant/Nemesis, 2003).

KATROUGALOS G. S., 'The Implementation of Social Rights in Europe', 2 *Columbia Journal of European Law* (1996) 277–316.

MATSCHER F. (ed.), *Die Durchsetzung wirtschaftlicher und sozialer Grundrechte: Eine Rechtsvergleichende Bestandsaufnahme. The Implementation of Economic and Social Rights: National, International, and Comparative Aspects. La mise en œuvre des droits économiques et sociaux: Aspects nationaux, internationaux et droit comparé* (Kehl am Rhein, Engel Verlag, 1991).

VAN DER AUWERAERT P., DE PELSMAEKER T., SARKIN J., AND VAN DE LANOTTE J. (eds), *Social, Economic and Cultural Rights: An Appraisal of Current European and International Developments* (Antwerp, R. Bayliss, 2002).

II. THE EU AND SOCIAL RIGHTS

1. General

ALSTON P., 'The Contribution of the EU's Fundamental Rights Agency to the Realisation of Economic and Socials Rights', in P. Alston, and O. De Schutter (eds), *Monitoring Fundamental Rights in the EU: The Contribution of the Fundamental Rights Agency* (Oxford, Hart Publishing, 2005) 158.

——, with BUSTELO M., AND HEENAN J., *The EU and Human Rights* (Oxford, New York, Oxford University Press, 1999).

BAQUERO CRUZ J., 'La protección de los derechos sociales en la Comunidad Europea tras el Tratado de Amsterdam', 4 *Revista De Derecho Comunitario Europeo* (1998) 639–66.

BERCUSSON B., 'Fundamental Social and Economic Rights in the European Community', in A. Cassese, A. Clapham, and J. Weiler (eds), *Human Rights and the European Community: Methods of Protection* (Baden-Baden, Nomos, 1991) 195–290.

——, DEAKIN S., KOISTINEN P. et al., *A Manifesto for Social Europe* (1st edn., Brussels, European Trade Union Institute, 1996).

——, DEAKIN S., KOISTINEN P. et al., *A Manifesto for Social Europe 2000* (Brussels, European Trade Union Institute, 2000).

BERNARD N., 'A "New Governance" Approach to Economic, Social and Cultural Rights in the EU', in T. Hervey, and J. Kenner (eds), *Economic and Social Rights Under the EU Charter of Fundamental Rights: A Legal Perspective* (Oxford, Portland, OR, Hart Publishing, 2003) 247–68.

BETTEN L., 'The Protection of Fundamental Social Rights in the European Union— Discussion Paper', in L. Betten, and D. MacDevitt (eds), *The Protection of Fundamental Social Rights in the European Union* (The Hague, Kluwer Law International, 1996) 3–30.

——, 'The Amsterdam Treaty: Some General Comments on the New Social Dimension', 13 *IJCLLIR* (1997) 188–92.

——, AND MacDEVITT D. (eds), *The Protection of Fundamental Social Rights in the European Union* (The Hague, Kluwer Law International, 1996).

BLANPAIN R., HEPPLE B., SCIARRA S, AND WEISS M., *Fundamental Social Rights: Proposals for the European Union* (Leuven, Peeters, 1996).

BONNECHÈRE M., 'Quelle garantie des droits sociaux fondamentaux en droit européen?', 10 *Europe* No. 7 (2000) 4–8.

BUNDESMINISTERIUM FÜR ARBEIT UND SOZIALORDNUNG, MAX-PLANCK-INSTITUT FÜR AUSLÄNDISCHES UND INTERNATIONALES SOZIALRECHT, AKADEMIE DER DIÖZESE ROTTENBURG STUTTGART (eds), *Soziale Grundrechte in der Europäischen Union* (Baden-Baden, Nomos, 2001).

BUTT M. E., KÜBERT J., AND SCHULTZ C. A., *Fundamental Social Rights in Europe*, Social Affairs Series, SOCI 104-02/2000 (2000).

CLAUWAERT S., *Fundamental Social Rights in the European Union: Comparative Tables and Documents* (Brussels, European Trade Union Institute, 1998).

CONTIADES X. I., 'Social Rights in the Draft Constitutional Treaty', in I. Pernice, and M. Poiares Maduro (eds), *A Constitution for the European Union: First Comments on the 2003 Draft of the European Convention* (Baden-Baden, Nomos, 2004) 59–73.

DELL'OLIO F., 'Supranational Undertakings and the Determination of Social Rights', 9 *JEPP* (2002) 292–310.

DE WITTE B., 'Economische, sociale en culturele rechten: de rol van de Europese Gemeenschap', in F. Coomans, A. Heringa, and I. Westendorp (eds), *De toenemende betekenis van economische, sociale en culturele mensenrechten* (Leiden NJCM-Boekerij, 1994) 8.

——, 'Protection of Fundamental Social Rights in the European Union: The Choice of the Appropriate Legal Instrument', in L. Betten, and D. MacDevitt (eds), *The Protection of Fundamental Social Rights in the European Union* (The Hague, Kluwer Law International, 1996) 63.

EICHENHOFER E., 'Unionsbürgerschaft—Sozialbürgerschaft?', *Zeitschrift für Ausländisches und Internationals Arbeits- und Sozialrecht* (2003) 404–17.

EUZÉBY A., AND MARQUES R. M., 'Mondialisation de l'économie et concurrence fiscale: des menaces pour le modèle social européen', *Revue du marché commune et de l'Union européenne* (2003) 310–16.

GARCÍA HERRERA A. M., 'Derechos sociales y tratados comunitarios: evolución normativa', in J. Corcuera Atienza (ed.), *La protección de los derechos fundamentels en la Unión Europea* (Madrid, Dykinson, 2002) 309–70.

GIL Y GIL J. L., 'Los derechos sociales en la Carta de los Derechos Fundamentales de la Unión Europea', 8 *Relaciones Laborales: Revista Crítica de Teoría y Prática* (2003) 93–118.

GIUBBONI S., 'I diritti sociali fondamentali nell'ordinamento communitario: Una rilettura alla luce della Carta di Nizza', 8 *Diritto dell'Unione Europea* (2003) 325–56.

——, 'Verso la costituzione europea: la traiettoria dei diritti sociali fondamentali nell'ordinamento comunitario', 4 *Rivista del Diritto della Sicurezza Sociale* (2004) 489–503.

GREWE C., 'Les droits sociaux constitutionnels: propos comparatifs à l'aube de la Charte des droits fondamentaux de l'Union européenne', 12 *Revue universelle des droits de l'homme* (2000) 85–92.

HEPPLE B., 'Social Values and European Law', 48 *CLP* (1995) 39–61.

HEPPLE B., 'Towards a European Social Institution', in C. Engels, and M. Weiss (eds), *Labour Law and Industrial Relations at the Turn of the Century: Liber Amicorum in Honour of Professor Roger Blanpain* (The Hague, Kluwer Law International, 1998) 291–304.

JIMENA QUESADA L. (ed.), *Escritos sobre derecho europeo de los derechos sociales* (Valencia, Tirant lo Blanch, 2004).

JOERGES C., AND RÖDL F., *'Social Market Economy' as Europe's Social Model?*, EUI Working Paper Law, 2004/08 (2004).

KENNER J., 'Economic and Social Rights in the EU Legal Order: The Mirage of Indivisibility', in T. Hervey, and J. Kenner (eds), *Economic and Social Rights Under the EU Charter of Fundamental Rights: A Legal Perspective* (Oxford, Portland, OR, Hart Publishing, 2003) 1–25.

KESSLER F., AND LHERNOULD J.-P. (eds), *Code annoté européen de la protection sociale* (Paris, Groupe Revue Fiduciaire, 2003).

LARSSON A., 'A Comment on the "Manifesto for Social Europe"', 3 *ELJ* (1997) 304–07.

LHERNOULD J.-P., 'Les avantages sociaux en droit communautaire', *Droit social* (1997) 388.

LO FARO A., 'The Social Manifesto: Demystifying the Spectre Haunting Europe', 3 *ELJ* (1997) 300–04.

LUNDBERG E., 'The Protection of Social Rights in the European Community: Recent Developments', in K. Drzewicki, C. Krause, and A. Rosas (eds), *Social Rights as Human Rights: A European Challenge* (Turku/Åbo, Institute for Human Rights, Åbo Akademi University, 1994) 169–99.

MAESTRO BUELGA G., 'Los derechos sociales en la Unión Europea: una perspectiva constitucional', 46 *Revista Vasca De Administración Pública* (1996) 119–42.

———, 'Constitución económica y derechos sociales en la Unión Europea', 7 *Revista De Derecho Comunitario Europeo* (2000) 123–56.

MOREAU M.-A., 'Tendance du droit social communautaire: les droit sociaux en quête de reconnaissance', *Droit social* (1994) 614–17.

———, 'L'utilisation des droits sociaux fondamentaux par les travailleurs dans l'Union européenne', in Cherot J.-Y. (ed.), *Les droits sociaux à l'âge de la mondialisation* (Marseille, Presses Universitaires d'Aix-Marseille, 2005).

NEAL A. C. (ed.), *Fundamental Social Rights at Work in the European Community* (Aldershot, Ashgate Publishing Limited, 1999).

NIELSEN R., AND SZYSZCZAK E., *The Social Dimension of the European Union* (Copenhagen, Copenhagen Business School Press, 1997).

PINELLI C., 'Diritti e politiche sociali nel progetto di trattato costituzionale europeo', 4 *Rivista del Diritto della Sicurezza Sociale* (2004) 477–87.

POIARES MADURO M., 'Striking the Elusive Balance Between Economic Freedom and Social Rights in the EU', in P. Alston, with M. Bustelo, and J. Heenan (eds), *The EU and Human Rights* (Oxford, New York, Oxford University Press, 1999) 449–72.

ROBIN-OLIVIER S., 'La référence aux droits sociaux fondamentaux dans le traité d'Amsterdam', *Droit social* (1999) 609–20.

ROBLEDO C. M., 'La seguridad social y la protección social en el proceso de configuración de la política social comunitaria: de la Carta comunitaria de los derechos sociales fundamentales de los trabajadores y el Protocolo sobre politica social del Tratado de la

Unión Europea, de Maastricht, al Tratado europeo de Amsterdam', 158 *Noticias De La Unión Europea* (1998) 75–82.

Rodière P., *Droit social de l'Union européenne* (2nd edn., Paris, L.G.D.J, 2002).

——, (ed.), *La citoyenneté européenne face au droit social et droit du travail. European Union Citizenship in the Context of Labour and Social Law* (Cologne, Bundesanzeiger, 1997).

Rodríguez-Piñero M., 'De Maastricht a Amsterdam: derechos sociales y empleo', 14 *Relaciones Laborales* (1998) 1–9.

—— and Casas M., 'In Support of a European Social Constitution', in P. Davies, and A. Lyon-Caen (eds), *European Community Labour Law Principles and Perspectives: Liber Amicorum Lord Wedderburn of Charlton* (Oxford, Clarendon Press, 1996).

Rosas A., 'Economic, Social and Cultural Rights: An EU Perspective', in M. Pentikäinen (ed.), *EU-China Dialogue: Perspectives on Human Rights, with Special Reference to Women* (Rovaniemi, Northern Institute for Environmental and Minority Law, 2000) 90–102.

Sajó A., 'Social Rights: A Wide Agenda', 1 *European Constitutional Law Review* (2005) 38–43.

Scharpf F. W., 'The European Social Model', 40 *JCMS* (2002) 645–70.

Schmitter P., and Bauer M., 'A (Modest) Proposal for Expanding Social Citizenship in the European Union', 11 *Journal of European Social Policy* (2001) 55–65.

Schulte B., 'Soziale Rechte im Europäischen Recht: Fragestellungen und Diskussionsansätze', in B. Schulte, and W. Mäder (eds), *Die Regierungskonferenz Maastricht II: Perspektiven für die Sozialgemeinschaft* (Bonn, Dümmler, 1996) 150.

Sciarra S., 'From Strasbourg to Amsterdam: Prospects for the Convergence of European Social Rights Policy', in P. Alston, with M. Bustelo, and J. Heenan (eds), *The EU and Human Rights* (Oxford, New York, Oxford University Press, 1999) 473–501.

——, 'The Employment Title in the Amsterdam Treaty: A Multi-Language Legal Discourse', in D. O'Keeffe, and P. Twomey (eds), *Legal Issues of the Amsterdam Treaty* (Oxford, Hart Publishing, 1999) 157–70.

Szyszczak E., 'Protecting Social Rights in the European Union', in A. Eide, C. Krause, and A. Rosas (eds), *Economic, Social, and Cultural Rights: A Textbook* (2nd and rev. edn., The Hague, Boston, MA, Martinus Nijhoff Publishers, Kluwer Law International, 2001) 493–513.

Teyssie B., and Antonmattei P. H. (eds), *Les normes sociales européennes* (Paris, Editions Panthéon-Assas, L.G.D.J., 2000).

Tomasovsky D., 'Die Sozialen Rechte im Primärrecht der EG', *Die Union* (2001) 21–32.

Vaughan-Whitehead D., *EU Enlargement Versus Social Europe? The Uncertain Future of the European Social Model* (Cheltenham, Northampton, Edward Elgar, 2003).

Waddley M., 'Social Protection in the European Union', in R. Burchill, D. Harris, and A. Owers (eds), *Economic, Social and Cultural Rights: The Implementation in United Kingdom Law* (Nottingham, University of Nottingham Human Rights Law Centre, 1999).

Weiss M., *Fundamental Social Rights for the European Union* (Amsterdam, Hugo Sinzheimer Institute, 1996).

Zacher H. F., 'Wird es einen Europäischen Sozialstaat geben?', 37 *Europarecht* (2002) 147–64.

Ziller J., 'L'Europe sociale dans la Constitution pour l'Europe', *Droit social* (2005) 188–99.

ZORBAS G., 'Certains aspects de la mise en œuvre des droits sociaux et économiques dans la Communauté économique européenne', in F. Matscher (ed), *Die Durchsetzung wirtschaftlicher und sozialer Grundrechte: Eine Rechtsvergleichende Bestandsaufnahme. The Implementation of Economic and Social Rights: National, International, and Comparative Aspects. La mise en œuvre des droits économiques et sociaux: Aspects nationaux, internationaux et droit comparé* (Kehl am Rhein, Engel Verlag, 1991) 141–84.

ZULEEG M., 'Social Rights in the European Community', in B. von Maydell, and A. Nussberger (eds), *Social Protection by Way of International Law: Appraisal, Deficits and Further Development* (Berlin, Duncker & Humboldt, 1996) 59–67.

2. The European Court of Justice and Social Rights

AKANDJI-KOMBÉ J.-F., 'Jurisprudence communautaire récente en matière de droits fondamentaux (1er decembre 1996–30 novembre 1997)', *Cahier de droit européen* (1998) 353–88.

BALL C. A., 'The Making of a Transnational Capitalist Society: The Court of Justice, Social Policy, and Individual Rights under the European Community's Legal Order', 37 *Harvard International Law Journal* (1996) 307–88.

BARBERA M., 'Not the Same? The Judicial Role in the New Community Anti-Discrimination Law Context', 31 *ILJ* (2002) 82–91.

BELL M., 'Shifting Conceptions of Sexual Discrimination at the Court of Justice: From P v. S to Grant v. SWT', 5 *ELJ* (1999) 63–81.

CARACCIOLO DI TORELLA E., AND MASSELOT A., 'Pregnancy, Maternity and the Organization of Family Life: An Attempt to Classify the Case Law of the Court of Justice', 26 *ELRev.* (2001) 239–60.

DAVIES P., 'Market Integration and Social Policy in the Court of Justice', 24 *ILJ* (1995) 49–77.

FENWICK H., AND HERVEY T., 'Sex Equality in the Single Market: New Directions for the European Court of Justice', 32 *CMLRev.* (1995) 443–70.

FLYNN L., 'Equality between Men and Women in the Court of Justice', 18 *Yearbook of European Law* (1998) 259–87.

GIESEN R., 'Posting: Social Protection of Workers vs. Fundamental Freedoms?' 40 *CMLRev.* (2003) 143–58.

JACQUESON C., 'Union Citizenship and the Court of Justice: Something New Under the Sun? Towards Social Citizenship', 27 *ELRev.* (2002) 260–81.

KILPATRICK C., 'Community or Communities of Courts in European Integration? Sex Equality Dialogues between UK Courts and the ECJ', 4 *ELJ* (1998) 121–47.

LENAERTS K., AND FOUBERT P., 'Social Rights in the Case-Law of the European Court of Justice: The Impact of the Charter of Fundamental Rights of the European Union on Standing Case-Law', 28 *LIEI* (2001) 267–96.

——— ———, 'Social Rights in the Case-Law of the European Court of Justice', in P. Van der Auweraert, T. De Pelsmaeker, J. Sarkin, and J. Van de Lanotte (eds), *Social, Economic and Cultural Rights: An Appraisal of Current European and International Developments* (Antwerp, R. Bayliss, 2002) 159.

MOORE M., 'Freedom of Movement and Migrant Workers' Social Security: An Overview of the Case Law of the Court of Justice 1997–2001', 39 *CMLRev.* (2002) 807–39.

O'LEARY S., *Employment Law at the European Court of Justice: Judicial Structures, Policies and Processes* (Oxford, Hart Publishing, 2002).

SIMITIS S., 'Dismantling or Strengthening Labour Law: The Case of the European Court of Justice', 2 *ELJ* (1996) 156–76.

SZYSZCZAK E., 'Social Rights as General Principles of Community Law', in N. A. Neuwahl, and A. Rosas (eds), *The European Union and Human Rights* (The Hague, London, Martinus Nijhoff Publishers, 1995) 207–20.

WATSON P., 'The Role of the European Court of Justice in the Development of Community Labour Law', in K. D. Ewing, C. A. Gearty, and B. A. Hepple, *Human Rights and Labour Law: Essays for Paul O'Higgins* (New York, Mansell Publishing Limited, 1994) 76–105.

3. The EU Charter of Fundamental Rights and Social Rights

ASHIAGBOR D., 'Economic and Social Rights in the European Charter of Fundamental Rights', *EHRLR* (2004) 62–72.

BERCUSSON B. (ed.), *European Labour Law and the EU Charter of Fundamental Rights— Summary Version* (Brussels, European Trade Union Institute, 2002).

——, 'The Role of the EU Charter of Fundamental Rights in Building a System of Industrial Relations at EU Level', 9 *Transfer: European Review of Labour and Research* (2003) 209–28.

BERMEJO G. R., 'Los derechos sociales en la Carta de Derechos Fundamentales de la Unión Europea', in A. A. Herrero de la Fuente (ed.), *La carta de derechos fundamentales de la Unión Europea: una perspectiva pluridisciplinar* (Zamora, Fundación Rei Afonso Henriques de Cooperación Transfronteriza, 2003) 93–112.

BERNSDORFF N., 'Soziale Grundrechte in der Charta der Grundrechte der Europäischen Union—Diskussionsstand und Konzept', *Vierteljahresschrift für Sozialrecht* (2001) 1–34.

BETTEN L., 'The EU Charter on Fundamental Rights: A Trojan Horse or a Mouse?', 17 *IJCLLIR* (2001) 151–64.

CARLIER J.-Y., AND DE SCHUTTER O. (eds), *La Charte des droits fondamentaux de l'Union européenne: son apport à la protection des droits de l'homme en Europe: Hommage à Silvio Marcus Helmons* (Brussels, Bruylant, 2002).

CORRIENTE CÓRDOBA J. A., 'La protección de los derechos económicos, sociales y culturales en la Carta de Derecho Fundamentales de la Unión Europea', 2 *En Anuario De Derecho Europeo* (2002) 117–37.

COSTELLO C., 'Gender Equalities and the Charter of Fundamental Rights of the European Union', in T. Hervey, and J. Kenner (eds), *Economic and Social Rights Under the EU Charter of Fundamental Rights: A Legal Perspective* (Oxford, Portland, OR, Hart Publishing, 2003) 111–38.

—— (ed.), *Fundamental Social Rights: Current European Legal Protection and the Challenge of the EU Charter on Fundamental Rights* (Dublin, Irish Centre for European Law, 2001).

CRAVEN M., 'A View from Elsewhere: Social Rights, International Covenant and the EU Charter of Fundamental Rights', in C. Costello (ed.), *Fundamental Social Rights: Current European Legal Protection and the Challenge of the EU Charter on Fundamental Rights* (Dublin, Irish Centre for European Law, 2001) 77–94.

DE SCHUTTER O., 'La contribution de la Charte des droits fondamentaux de l'Union européenne à la garantie des droits sociaux dans l'ordre juridique communautaire', 12 *Revue universelle des droits de l'homme* (2000) 33–47.

DE SCHUTTER O., 'Donner un avenir à la Charte des droits fondamentaux de l'Union', 6 *Annales d'études européennes de l'université catholique de Louvain* (2002) 75–134.

——, 'La garantie des droits et principes sociaux dans la Charte des droits fondamentaux de l'Union européenne', in J.-Y. Carlier, and O. De Schutter (eds), *La Charte des droits fondamentaux de l'Union européenne: son apport à la protection des droits de l'homme en Europe: Hommage à Silvio Marcus Helmons* (Brussels, Bruylant, 2002) 117–47.

——, 'La garanzia dei diritti e principi sociali nella "Carta dei diritti fondamentali"', in G. Zagrebelsky, S. Della Valle, and J. Luther (eds), *Diritti e costituzione nell'Unione europea* (Rome, GLF editori Laterza, 2003) 192–220.

ENGELS M., 'Soziale Grundrechte in der Europäischen Grundrechtecharta', in T. Frank, A. Jenichen, and N. Rosemann (eds), *Soziale Menschenrechte—Die Vergessenen Rechte* (2001) 77.

GIJZEN M., 'The Charter: A Milestone for Social Protection in Europe?', 8 *MJ* (2001) 33–48.

HEPPLE B., 'The EU Charter of Fundamental Rights', 30 *ILJ* (2001) 225–31.

HERVEY T., AND KENNER J. (eds), *Economic and Social Rights Under the EU Charter of Fundamental Rights: A Legal Perspective* (Oxford, Portland, OR, Hart, 2003).

HILPOLD P., 'Der Schutz Sozialer Grundrechte in der Europäischen Union', 59 *Zeitschrift für Öffentliches Recht* (2004) 351–73.

ILIOPOULOS-STRANGAS J., 'La Charte des droits fondamentaux de l'Union européenne face à la protection constitutionnelle des droits sociaux dans les états membres', in J.-F. Flauss (ed.), *Droits sociaux et droit européen: bilan et prospective de la protection normative* (Brussels, Bruylant/Nemesis, 2003) 11–87.

KOSKINEN P. K., 'Fundamental Social Rights within Limited Social Competences: New Competences for the Community?', in W. Heusel (ed.), *Grundrechtecharta und Verfassungsentwicklung in der EU* (Cologne, Bundesanzeiger, 2002) 83–93.

LÖRCHER K., 'EU-Grundrechtscharta und Soziale Grundrechte', 8 *Europäisches Arbeits- und Sozialrecht* (2000) 105–10.

MEYER J., AND ENGELS M., 'Aufnahme von Sozialen Grundrechten in die Europäische Grundrechtecharta?', *Zeitschrift für Rechtspolitik* (2000) 368–71.

PITSCHAS R., 'Europäische Grundrechte-Charta und Soziale Grundrechte', *Vierteljahresschrift für Sozialrecht* (2000) 207–20.

PONTHOREAU M.-C., 'Le principe de l'indivisibilité des droits. L'apport de la Charte des droits fondamentaux de l'Union européenne à la théorie générale des droits fondamentaux', 19 *Revue française de droit administratif* (2003) 928.

RIEDEL E., 'Solidarität', in J. Meyer (ed.), *Kommentar zur Charta der Grundrechte Europäischen Union* (Baden-Baden, Nomos, 2003) 323–431.

RYAN B., 'The Charter and Collective Labour Law', in T. Hervey, and J. Kenner (eds), *Economic and Social Rights Under the EU Charter of Fundamental Rights: A Legal Perspective* (Oxford, Portland, OR, Hart Publishing, 2003) 67–90.

WEISS M., 'The Politics of the EU Charter of Fundamental Rights', in B. Hepple (ed.), *Social and Labour Rights in a Global Context: International and Comparative Perspectives* (Cambridge, Cambridge University Press, 2002) 73–94.

4. The Community Charter of the Fundamental Social Rights of Workers

ADDISON J. T., AND SIEBERT W. S., 'The Social Charter of the European Community: Evolution and Controversies', 44 *Industrial and Labor Relations Review* (1991) 597–625.

BERCUSSON B., 'The European Community's Charter of Fundamental Social Rights of Workers', 53 *MLR* (1990) 624–42.

BETTEN L., 'Towards a Community Charter of Fundamental Social Rights', 1 *Netherlands Quarterly of Human Rights* (1989) 77–97.

DOWLING D. D. JR., 'From the Social Charter to the Social Action Program 1995–1997: European Union Employment Law Comes Alive', 29 *Cornell International Law Journal* (1996) 43–79.

HEPPLE B., 'The Implementation of the Community Charter of Fundamental Social Rights', 53 *MLR* (1990) 643–54.

SILVIA S. J., 'The Social Charter of the European Community: A Defeat for European Labor', 44 *Industrial and Labor Relations Review* (1991) 626–43.

VOGEL-POLSKI E., 'What Future is there for a Social Europe Following the Strasbourg Summit?', 19 *ILJ* (1990) 65–80.

WATSON P., 'The Community Social Charter', 28 *CMLRev.* (1991) 37–68.

5. The Market, European Monetary Union (EMU), and Social Rights

BARNARD C., AND DEAKIN S., 'Corporate Governance, European Governance and Social Rights', in B. Hepple (ed.), *Social and Labour Rights in a Global Context: International and Comparative Perspectives* (Cambridge, Cambridge University Press, 2002) 122–50.

BROWNE J., DEAKIN S. F., AND WILKINSON F., *Capabilities, Social Rights and European Market Integration*, ESRC Centre for Business Research Working Paper 253, University of Cambridge (2002).

BUZELAY A., 'Libre circulation des travailleurs en Europe et protection sociale', *Revue du marché commun et de l'Union européenne* (2003) 448–53.

DEAKIN S., AND BROWNE J., 'Social Rights and Market Order: Adapting the Capability Approach', in T. Hervey, and J. Kenner (eds), *Economic and Social Rights Under the EU Charter of Fundamental Rights: A Legal Perspective* (Oxford, Portland, OR, Hart Publishing, 2003) 27–43.

EVERSON M., 'The Legacy of the Market Citizen', in J. Shaw, and G. More (eds), *New Legal Dynamics of European Union* (New York, Clarendon Press, 1995) 73–90.

HASSENTEUFEL P., AND HENNION-MOREAU S. (eds), *Concurrence et protection sociale en Europe* (Rennes, Presses Universitaires de Rennes, 2004).

GIUBBONI S., *Diritti sociali e mercato: la dimensione sociale dell'integrazione europea* (Bologna, Il mulino, 2003).

GUILD E., 'How Can Social Protection Survive EMU? A United Kingdom Perspective', 24 *ELRev.* (1999) 22–37.

KENNER J., 'Employment and Macroeconomics in the EC Treaty: A Legal and Political Symbiosis?', 7 *MJ* (2000) 375–97.

POIARES MADURO M., 'Striking the Elusive Balance Between Economic Freedom and Social Rights in the EU', in P. Alston, with M. Bustelo, and J. Heenan (eds), *The EU and Human Rights* (Oxford, New York, Oxford University Press, 1999) 449–72.

SCIARRA S., 'Market Freedom and Fundamental Social Rights', in B. Hepple (ed.), *Social and Labour Rights in a Global Context: International and Comparative Perspectives* (Cambridge, Cambridge University Press, 2002) 95–121.

SYRPIS P., 'Smoke Without Fire: The Social Policy Agenda and the Internal Market', 30 *ILJ* (2001) 271–88.

TEAGUE P., 'Monetary Union and Social Europe', 8 *Journal of European Social Policy* (1998) 117–37.

Tomaševski K., 'From Europe to EUrope to EMUrope: Whither Economic and Social Rights', in F. Coomans, F. Grünfeld, I. Westerndorp, and J. Willems (eds), *Rendering Justice to the Vulnerable: Liber Amicorum in Honour of Theo van Boven* (The Hague, Boston, MA, Kluwer Law International, 2000) 277–88.

Traversa E., 'The Consequences of European Monetary Union on Collective Bargaining and the National Social Security Systems', 16 *IJCLLIR* (2000) 47–54.

6. EU Labour/Social Law

Ashiagbor D., 'EMU and the Shift in the European Labour Law Agenda: From "Social Policy" to "Employment Policy"', 7 *ELJ* (2001) 311–30.

Barbera M., *Dopo Amsterdam: I nuovi confini del diritto sociale comunitario* (Brescia, Promodis Italia, 2000).

Barnard C., 'EC "Social" Policy', in P. Craig, and G. de Búrca (eds), *The Evolution of EU Law* (Oxford, Oxford University Press, 1999) 479–516.

——, *EC Employment Law* (2nd edn., Oxford, New York, Oxford University Press, 2000).

——, 'The Social Partners and the Governance Agenda', 8 *ELJ* (2002) 80–101.

Bercusson B., 'The Implementation of Protocol and Agreement on Social Policy of the Treaty on European Union', 11 *IJCLLIR* (1995) 3–30.

——, *European Labour Law* (London, Charlottesville, Butterworths, 1996).

——, 'Democratic Legitimacy and European Labour Law', 28 *Industrial Law Journal* (1999) 153–70.

——, 'European Labour Law in Context: A Review of the Literature', 5 *ELJ* (1999) 87–102.

Betten L. (ed.), *The Future of European Social Policy* (2nd and rev. edn., Deventer, Boston, Kluwer Law and Taxation Publishers, 1991).

Blanpain R., 'European Social Policies: One Bridge Too Short?' 20 *Comparative Labor Law & Policy Journal* (1999) 497–502.

Brinkman G., 'Lawmaking under the Social Chapter of Maastricht', in P. Craig, and C. Harlow (eds), *Lawmaking in the European Union* (London, Boston, MA, Kluwer Law International, 1998) 239–61.

Cullen H., and Campbell E., 'The Future of Social Policy-Making in the European Union', in P. Craig, and C. Harlow (eds), *Lawmaking in the European Union* (London, Boston, MA, Kluwer Law International, 1998) 262–84.

Davies P. L., Lyon-Caen A., Sciarra S., and Smith S. (eds), *European Community Labour Law: Principles and Perspectives: Liber Amicorum Lord Wedderburn of Charlton* (Oxford, New York, Clarendon Press; Oxford University Press, 1996).

Ebsen I., 'Social Policy in the European Community between Competition, Solidarity and Harmonization: Still on the Way from a Free Trade Area to a Federal System', 2 *Columbia Journal of European Law* (1996) 421–37.

Eichenhofer E., *Sozialrecht der Europäischen Union* (2nd edn., Berlin, E. Schmidt, 2003).

Ewing K. D., Gearty C. A., and Hepple B. (eds), *Human Rights and Labour Law: Essays for Paul O'Higgins* (New York, Mansell, 1994).

Fredman S., 'Social Law in the European Union: The Impact of the Lawmaking Process', in P. Craig, and C. Harlow (eds), *Lawmaking in the European Union* (London, Boston, MA, Kluwer Law International, 1998) 386–411.

Fuchs M., 'Koordinierung oder Harmonisierung des Europäischen Sozialrechts?', *Zeitschrift für Ausländisches und Internationals Arbeits- und Sozialrecht* (2003) 379–90.

——, 'The Bottom Line of European Labour Law (Part I)', 20 *IJCLLIR* (2004), 155–76.

——, 'The Bottom Line of European Labour Law (Part II)', 20 *IJCLLIR* (2004), 423–44.

—— (ed.), *Kommentar zum Europäischen Sozialrecht* (2nd edn., Baden-Baden, Nomos, 2000).

——, AND Marhold F., *Europäisches Arbeitsrecht* (Vienna, Springer, 2001).

Graser A., 'Auf dem Weg zur Sozialunion—Wie "Sozial" ist das Europäische Sozialrecht?', *Zeitschrift für Ausländisches und Internationales Arbeits- und Sozialrecht* (2000) 336–51.

Haunau P., Steinmeyer H.-D., AND Wank R., *Handbuch des Europäischen Sozialrechts* (Munich, C.H. Beck, 2002).

Haverkate G., AND Weiss M. (eds), *Arbeits- und Sozialrecht der EU—Textsammlung* (Baden-Baden, Nomos, 1998).

Hervey T., *European Social Law and Policy* (London, New York, Longman, 1998).

Kaufmann O., 'Das Arbeits- und Sozialrecht als Integrationsmedium: Vergleichende Aspekte', *Zeitschrift für Ausländisches und Internationales Arbeits- und Sozialrecht* (2001) 187–99.

Kenner J., *EU Employment Law: From Rome to Amsterdam and Beyond* (Oxford, Portland, OR, Hart Publishing, 2003).

Krimphove D., *Europäisches Arbeitsrecht* (2nd edn., Munich, C.H. Beck, 2001).

Lorber P., 'Labour Law', in. S. Peers and A. Ward (eds), *The European Union Charter of Fundamental Rights* (Oxford, Portland, OR, Hart Publishing, 2004) 211–30.

Malmberg J., Fitzpatrick B., Gotthardt M., AND Laulom S. et al. (eds), *Effective Enforcement of EC Labour Law* (The Hague, London, Kluwer Law International, 2003).

O'Keeffe D., 'The Uneasy Progress of European Social Policy', 2 *Columbia Journal of European Law* (1996) 241–61.

Ringler J. C. K., *Die Europäische Sozialunion* (Berlin, Duncker & Humblot, 1997).

Samson K., 'Social Policy for a Europe in Transition', in K. Drzewicki, C. Krause, and A. Rosas (eds), *Social Rights as Human Rights: A European Challenge* (Turku/Åbo, Institute for Human Rights, Åbo Akademi University, 1994) 305–14.

Sciarra S., 'Social Values and the Multiple Sources of European Social Law', 1 *ELJ* (1995) 60–83.

——, 'How "Global" is Labour Law? The Perspective of Social Rights in the European Union', in T. Wilthagen (ed.), *Advancing Theory in Labour Law and Industrial Relations in a Global Context* (Amsterdam, North-Holland, 1998).

——, *Labour Law in the Courts: National Judges and the European Court of Justice* (Oxford, Hart Publishing, 2001).

Shaw J., 'Twin-Track Social Europe—The Inside Track', in D. O'Keeffe, and P. M. Twomey, (eds) *Legal Issues of the Maastricht Treaty* (London, New York, Chancery Law Publishing, 1994) 295–312.

——, *Social Law and Policy in an Evolving European Union* (Oxford, Portland, OR, Hart Publishing 2000).

Smismans S., *Law, Legitimacy, and European Governance: Functional Participation in Social Regulation* (Oxford, New York, Oxford University Press, 2004).

Steinmeyer H.-D., 'Der Vertrag von Amsterdam und seine Bedeutung für das Arbeits- und Sozialrecht', *Recht der Arbeit* (2001) 10–22.

SUPIOT A., CASAS M. E., AND DE MUNCK J., et al. (eds), *Beyond Employment: Changes in Work and the Future of Labour Law in Europe* (Oxford, Oxford University Press, 2001).

SZYSZCZAK E., 'Social Policy: A Happy Ending or a Reworking of the Fairy Tale?', in D. O'Keeffe, and P. M. Twomey (eds), *Legal Issues of the Maastricht Treaty* (London, New York, Chancery Law Publishing, 1994) 313–28.

——, *EC Labour Law* (Harlow, Longman, 2000).

TEYSSIÉ B., *Droit européen du travail* (Paris, Litec, 2003).

WEISS M., 'Zur Künftigen Rolle der Europäischen Union im Arbeitsrecht', in P. Hanau, E. Lorenz, and H. C. Matthes (eds), *Festschrift für Günther Wiese zum 70. Geburtstag* (Neuwied, Kriftel, Luchterhand Verlag 1998) 633.

WHITEFORD E., 'Social Policy after Maastricht', 18 *ELR* (1993) 202–22.

7. The European Employment Strategy (EES) and the Open Method of Coordination (OMC)

ADNETT N., 'Modernising the European Social Model: Developing the Guidelines', *JCMS* (2001) 353–64.

ASHIAGBOR D., 'Flexibility and Adaptability in the European Employment Strategy', in H. Collin, P. Davies, and R. Rideout (eds), *Legal Regulation of the Employment Relation* (Deventer, Kluwer, 2000) 373–401.

BALL S., 'The European Employment Strategy: The Will but not the Way?', 30 *ILJ* (2001) 353–74.

BIAGI M., 'The Impact of the European Employment Strategy on the Role of Labour Law and Industrial Relations', 16 *International Journal of Comparative Labour Law and Industrial Relations* (2000) 155–73.

BRUUN N., 'The European Employment Strategy and the "Acquis Communautaire" of Labour Law', 17 *IJCLLIR* (2001) 309–24.

CASEY B., 'The OECD Jobs Strategy and the European Employment Strategy: Two Views of the Labour Market and the Welfare State', 10 *European Journal of Industrial Relations* (2004) 329–52.

DE LA PORTE C., 'Is the Open Method of Co-ordination Appropriate for Organising Activities at European Level in Sensitive Policy Areas?', 1 *ELJ* (2002) 38–58.

——, AND POCHET P., 'The European Employment Strategy: Existing Research and Remaining Questions', 14 *Journal of European Social Policy* (2004) at 71–78.

DE SCHUTTER O., AND DEAKIN S. (eds), *Social Rights and Market Forces: Is the Open Method of Coordination of Employment and Social Policy the Future of Social Europe?* (Brussels, Bruylant, 2005).

GOETSCHY J., 'The European Employment Strategy: Genesis and Development', 5 *European Journal of Industrial Relations* (1999) 117–37.

HOCQUET J.-Y., 'Le comité de la protection sociale (CPS): une instance communautaire pour quoi faire?', *Droit social* (2005) 91–96.

KLOSSE S., 'The European Employment Strategy: Which Way Forward?', 21 *IJCLLIR* (2005) 5–36.

REGENT S., 'The Open Method of Coordination: A New Supranational Form of Governance?', 9 *ELJ* (2003) 190–214.

SCIARRA S., 'Integration Through Coordination: The Employment Title in the Amsterdam Treaty', 6 *Columbia Journal of European Law* (2000) 209–30.

SKIDMORE P., 'The European Employment Strategy and Labour Law: A German Case-Study', 29 *ELRev.* (2004) 52–73.

SZYSZCZAK E., 'The Evolving European Employment Strategy', in J. Shaw (ed.), *Social Law and Policy in an Evolving European Union* (Oxford, Hart Publishing, 2000) 197–220.

WATT A., 'Reform of the European Employment Strategy after Five Years: A Change of Course or Merely of Presentation?', 10 *European Journal of Industrial Relations* (2004) 117–37.

8. EC External Relations, Globalization, and Social Rights

ALSTON P., ' "Core Labour Standards" and the Transformation of the International Labour Rights Regime', 15 *EJIL* (2004) 457–521.

BARNARD C., 'The External Dimension of Community Social Policy: the Ugly Duckling of External Relations', in N. Emiliou, and D. O'Keeffe (eds), *The European Union and World Trade Law* (Chichester, New York, Wiley, 1996) 149–64.

BYRNE I. A., *Placing Economic, Social and Cultural Rights at the Heart of the Euro-Mediterranean Partnership*, Robert Schuman Centre, Mediterranean Programme, Annual Mediterranean Meeting (2004).

CHEROT J.-Y. (ed), *Les droits sociaux à l'âge de la mondialisation* (Marseille, Presses Universitaires d'Aix-Marseille, 2005).

COLE A., 'Labor Standards and the Generalized System of Preferences: The European Labour Incentives', 25 *Michigan Journal of International Law* (2003) 179–207.

CREMONA M., 'The European Union and the External Dimension of Human Rights Policy', in S. Konstadinidis (ed.), *A People's Europe: Tuning a Concept to Content* (Aldershot, Ashgate, 1999) 155–81.

GORI G., 'External Relations in Community Education and Vocational Training Policies', 5 *MJ* (1998) 25–52.

HERKOMMER V., *Die Europäische Sozialklausel: Zollpräferenzen zur Förderung von Kernarbeitsstandards in Entwicklungsländern* (Baden-Baden, Nomos, 2004).

MOREAU M.-A., 'Mondialisation et droit social: quelques observations sur les évolutions juridiques', 16 *RIDE* (2002) 383–403.

NOVITZ T., ' "A Human Face" for the Union or More Cosmetic Surgery? EU Competence in Global Social Governance and Promotion of Core Labour Standards', 9 *MJ* (2002) 231–61.

——, 'The European Union and International Labour Standards: The Dynamics of Dialogue between the EU and the ILO', in P. Alston (ed.), *Labour Rights as Human Rights* (Oxford, Oxford University Press, 2005).

ÖLZ M., 'Die Kernarbeitsnormen der Internationalen Arbeitsorganisation im Licht der Neuen Handelspolitischen "Sozialklausel" der Europäischen Union', *Zeitschrift für Ausländisches und Internationals Arbeits- und Sozialrecht* (2002) 319–59.

RIEDEL E., AND WILL M., 'Human Rights Clauses in External Agreements of the EC', in P. Alston, with M. Bustelo, and J. Heenan (eds), *The EU and Human Rights* (Oxford, New York, Oxford University Press, 1999) 723–54.

ROJO TORRECILLA E., 'Los derechos sociales y laborales ante la globalización económica', in F. Esteve Gracía (ed.) *La Unión Europea y el comercio internacional: límites al libre comercio* (Girona, Universitat di Girona, 2001) 61–80.

ROSAS A., 'Economic, Social and Cultural Rights in the External Relations of the European Union', in A. Eide, C. Krause, and A. Rosas (eds), *Economic, Social, and Cultural Rights: A Textbook* (2nd and rev. edn., The Hague, Boston, MA, Martinus Nijhoff Publishers, Kluwer Law International, 2001) 479–92.

SCHMID D., *The Use of Conditionality in Support of Political, Economic and Social Rights: Unveiling the Euro-Mediterranean Partnership's True Hierarchy of Objectives?*, Robert Schuman Centre, Mediterranean Programme, Annual Mediterranean Meeting (2004).

TSOGAS G., 'Labour Standards in the Generalized System of Preferences of the European Union and the United States', 3 *European Journal of Industrial Relations* (2000) 349–70.

III. THE EUROPEAN SOCIAL CHARTER (ESC)

AKANDJI-KOMBÉ J.-F., 'L'application de la Charte sociale européenne: la mise en œuvre de la procédure de réclamations collectives', *Droit social* (2000) 888–96.

——, 'La procédure de réclamation collective dans la Charte sociale européenne: chronique des décisions du Comité européen des droits sociaux', 12 *Revue trimestrielle des droits de l'homme* (2001) 1035–61.

——, 'Actualité de la Charte sociale européenne: chronique des décisions du Comité européen des droits sociaux sur les réclamations collectives', 14 *Revue trimestrielle des droits de l'homme* (2003) 113–38.

——, 'Actualité de la Charte sociale européenne: chronique des décisions du Comité européen des droit sociaux sur les réclamations collectives (July 2002–September 2003)', 15 *Revue trimestrielle des droits de l'homme* (2004) 225–44.

——, AND LECLERC S., *La Charte sociale européenne* (Brussels, Bruylant, 2001).

ANDREWS J., 'Protocol to the European Social Charter', 13 *ELRev.* (1988) 285–87.

BIERMAN L., AND KEIM G. D., 'On the Economic Realities of the European Social Charter and the Social Dimension of the EC 1992. Comment', 2 *Duke Journal of Comparative and International Law* (1992) 149–62.

BIRK R., 'The Collective Complaint: A New Procedure in the European Social Charter', in C. Engels, and M. Weiss (eds), *Labour Law and Industrial Relations at the Turn of the Century: Liber Amicorum in Honour of Roger Blanpain* (The Hague, Boston, MA, Kluwer Law International, 1998) 261–74.

——, 'Arbeitsrechtliche Neuerungen in der Revidierten Europäischen Sozialcharta von 1996', in G. Köbler, M. Heinze, and W. Hromadka (eds), *Europas Universale Rechtsordnungspolitische Aufgabe im Recht des Dritten Jahrtausends: Festschrift für Alfred Söllner zum 70. Geburtstag* (Munich, Beck, 2000) 137–52.

——, 'Arbeitsrecht und Rechtsvergleichung—Die Kontrolle der Einhaltung der Europäischen Sozialcharta', *Zeitschrift für Vergleichende Rechtswissenschaft* (2001) 48–61.

BRILLAT R., 'A New Protocol to the European Social Charter Providing for Collective Complaints', 1 *EHRLR* (1996) 52–62.

——, 'The European Social Charter', in G. Alfredsson, J. Grimheden, B. G. Ramcharan, and A. De Zayas (eds), *International Human Rights Monitoring Mechanisms: Essays in Honor of Jakob Th. Möller* (The Hague, Boston, Martinus Nijhoff Publishers, 2001) 601–06.

——, 'La Charte sociale européenne', in C. Grewe, and F. Benoît-Rohmer (eds), *Les droits sociaux ou la démolition de quelques poncifs* (2003) 93.

CASEY N., 'The European Social Charter and Revised European Social Charter', in C. Costello (ed.), *Fundamental Social Rights: Current European Legal Protection and the Challenge of the EU Charter on Fundamental Rights* (Dublin, Irish Centre for European Law, 2001) 55–76.

CHURCHILL R., AND KHALIQ U., 'The Collective Complaints System of the European Social Charter: An Effective Mechanism for Ensuring Compliance with Economic and Social Rights?' 15 *EJIL* (2004) 417–56.

COUNCIL OF EUROPE, *The Social Charter of the 21st Century* (Strasbourg, Council of Europe Publishing, 1997).

——, *Social Protection in the European Social Charter* (2nd edn., Strasbourg, Council of Europe Publishing, 2000).

——, *The Protection of Fundamental Social Rights in Europe Through the European Social Charter* (Strasbourg, Council of Europe Publishing, 2001).

——, *Conditions of Employment in the European Social Charter: Study Compiled on the Basis of the Case Law of the European Committee of Social Rights* (2nd edn., Strasbourg, Council of Europe Publishing, 2000).

CULLEN H., 'The Collective Complaints Mechanism of the European Social Charter', 25 *European Law Review—Supplement (Human Rights Survey)* (2000) 18–30.

DALY M., *Access to Social Rights in Europe* (Strasbourg, Council of Europe Publishing, 2002).

DUBOIS-HAMDI C., 'La procédure de réclamations collectives dans le cadre de la Charte sociale européenne (1998–2000): Les premiers enseignements', 33 *Droit en quart monde* (2001) 35–48.

FUCHS K., 'The European Social Charter: Its Role in Present-day Europe and its Reform', in K. Drzewicki, C. Krause, and A. Rosas (eds), *Social Rights as Human Rights: A European Challenge* (Turku/Åbo, Institute for Human Rights, Åbo Akademi University, 1994) 151–67.

GREVISSE S., 'Le renouveau de la Charte sociale européenne', *Droit social* (2000) 884–87.

HARRIS D., 'A Fresh Impetus for the European Social Charter', 41 *International and Comparative Law Quarterly* (1992) 659–76.

——, 'The European Social Charter', in D. Gomien, D. Harris, and L. Zwaak (eds), *Law and Practice of the European Convention on Human Rights and the European Social Charter* (Strasbourg, Council of Europe Publishing, 1996) 377–475.

——, 'The Collective Complaints Procedure', in Council of Europe, *The Social Charter of the 21st Century* (Strasbourg, Council of Europe Publishing, 1997) 100–29.

——, 'The Council of Europe (II): The European Social Charter', in R. Hanski, and M. Suksi (eds), *An Introduction to the International Protection of Human Rights: A Textbook* (2nd and rev. edn., Turku/Åbo Institute for Human Rights, Åbo Akademi University, 1999).

——, 'Lessons from the Reporting System of the European Social Charter', in P. Alston, and J. Crawford (eds), The *Future of UN Human Rights Treaty Monitoring* (Cambridge, Cambridge University Press, 2000).

——, AND DARCY J., *The European Social Charter* (2nd edn., Ardsley, NY, Transnational Publishers, 2001).

HENDRIKS A., 'Revised European Social Charter', 15 *Netherlands Quarterly of Human Rights* (1996) 341–59.

HERINGA A., BOEREFIJN I., AND SCHOKKENBROEK J., 'Towards a New System of Supervision for the European Social Charter', 46 *Review for the Rule of Law* (1991) 42–50.

JAEGER M., 'The Additional Protocol to the European Social Charter Providing for a System of Collective Complaints', 10 *Leiden Journal of International Law* (1997) 69–80.

LECLERC S., 'Les restrictions et limitations à l'application de la Charte sociale', in J.-F. Akandji-Kombé, and S. Leclerc (eds), *La Charte sociale européenne* (Brussels, Bruylant, 2001) 67–91.

LEVY-PUECH D., 'Les engagements souscrits au titre de la Charte sociale par les nouvelles démocraties européennes', in J.-F. Flauss (ed.), *Droits sociaux et droit européen: bilan et prospective de la protection normative* (Brussels, Bruylant/Nemesis, 2003) 143–74.

MIKKOLA M., 'Social Rights as Human Rights in Europe', 2 *European Journal of Social Security* (2000) 259–72.

MOHR M., 'The Turin Protocol of 22 October 1991: A Major Contribution to Revitalizing the European Social Charter', 3 *EJIL* (1992) 362–70.

NOVITZ T., 'Are Social Rights Necessarily Collective Rights? A Critical Analysis of the Collective Complaints Protocol to the European Social Charter', *EHRLR* (2002) 50–66.

ÖHLINGER T., 'Die Europäische Sozialcharta und der Schutz Wirtschaftlicher und Sozialer Rechte durch den Europarat', in M. Nowak (ed.), *Europarat und Menschenrechte* (Vienna, Orac, 1994) 119.

——, 'Standard-Setting Activities by Regional Institutions, Taking the Council of Europe as an Example: The European Social Charter', in B. von Maydell, and A. Nussberger (eds), *Social Protection by Way of International Law: Appraisal, Deficits and Further Development* (Berlin, Duncker & Humblot, 1996) 43–58.

PROUVEZ, N., 'The European Social Charter: An Instrument for the Protection of Human Rights in the 21st Century?', *The Review of the International Commission of Jurists* (1997) 30–44.

SAMUEL L., *Fundamental Social Rights Case-law of the European Social Charter* (2nd edn., Strasbourg, Council of Europe Publishing, 2002).

SUDRE F., 'Le Protocole additionnel à la Charte sociale européenne prévoyant un système de réclamations collectives', 100 *Revue générale de droit international public* (1996) 715–39.

VANDAMME F., 'The Revision of the European Social Charter', 133 *International Labour Review* (1994) 635–56.

——, 'Les droits protégés par la Charte sociale, contenu et portée', in J.-F. Akandji-Kombé and S. Leclerc (eds), *La Charte sociale européenne* (Brussels, Bruylant, 2001) 11–43.

IV. THE EUROPEAN CONVENTION ON HUMAN RIGHTS (ECHR) AND SOCIAL RIGHTS

DAUGAREILH I., 'La Convention européenne de sauvegarde des droits de l'homme et des libertés fondamentales et la protection sociale', 37 *Revue trimestrielle des droits de l'homme* (2001) 123–38.

DE SCHUTTER O., 'The Protection of Social Rights by the European Court of Human Rights', in P. Van der Auweraert, T. De Pelsmaeker, and J. Sarkin, and J. Van De Lanotte (eds), *Social, Economic and Cultural Rights: An Appraisal of Current European and International Developments* (Antwerp, Maklu, 2002) 207–42.

FLINTERMAN C., 'The Protection of Economic, Social and Cultural Rights and the European Convention on Human Rights', in R. Lawson, M. De Blois, and H. G. Schermers (eds), *The Dynamics of the Protection of Human Rights in Europe* (Dordrecht, Boston, Norwell, MA, Martinus Nijhoff Publishers, Kluwer Academic Publishers, 1994) 165–74.

JACOBS F. G., 'The Extension of the European Convention on Human Rights to include Economic, Social and Cultural Rights', 3 *Human Rights Review* (1978) 166–78.

PELLONPÄÄ M., 'Economic, Social and Cultural Rights', in R. St. J. Macdonald, F. Matscher, and H. Petzold (eds), *The European System for the Protection of Human Rights* (Dordrecht, Boston, MA, Martinus Nijhoff Publishers, 1993) 855–74.

PRISO ESSAWE S.-J., 'Les droits sociaux et l'égalité de traitement dans la jurisprudence de la Cour européenne des droits de l'homme. A propos des arrêts *Van Raalte c. les Pays Bas* et *Petrovic c. l'Autriche*', 9 *Revue trimestrielle des droits de l'homme* (1998) 721–36.

SUDRE F., 'La perméabilité de la Convention européenne des droits de l'homme aux droits sociaux', in *Pouvoir Et Liberté—Études Offertes à Jacques Mourgeon* (1998) 467–78.

——, 'Les droits sociaux et la Convention européenne des droits de l'homme', 12 *Revue universelle des droits de l'homme* (2000) 28–32.

——, 'La protection des droits sociaux par la cour européenne des droits de l'homme: "un exercice de 'jurisprudence-fiction' ?" ', 14 *Revue trimestrielle des droits de l'homme* (2003) 755–79.

TULKENS F., 'Les droits sociaux dans la jurisprudence de la nouvelle Cour européenne des droits de l'homme', in C. Grewe and F. Benoît-Rohmer (eds), *Les droits sociaux ou la démolition de quelque poncifs* (Strasbourg, Presses Universitaires de Strasbourg, 2003) 117.

V. THE RELATIONSHIP BETWEEN EU, ESC, AND ECHR AS REGARDS THE PROTECTION OF SOCIAL RIGHTS

AKANDJI-KOMBÉ J.-F., 'Interaction normative entre l'Union européenne et le Conseil de l'Europe en matière de droits sociaux', in C. Schneider (ed.), *L'interaction entre l'Union européenne et le Conseil de l'Europe: Actes de la journée nationale d'études CEDECE de Grenoble, 2–3 déc. 1999* (Strasbourg, Council of Europe, 1999).

——, 'Charte sociale et droit communautaire', in J.-F. Akandji-Kombé, and S. Leclerc (eds), *La Charte sociale européenne* (Brussels, Bruylant, 2001) 149–77.

BETTEN L., 'Prospects for a Social Policy of the European Community and its Impact on the Functioning of the European Social Charter', in L. Betten (ed.), *The Future of European Social Policy* (2nd and rev. edn., Deventer, Boston, MA, Kluwer Law and Taxation Publishers, 1991) 101–41.

DE SCHUTTER O., 'L'interdépendance des droits et l'interaction des systèmes de protection: les scénarios du système européen de protection des droits fondamentaux', 28–29 *Droit en quart monde* (2000) 3–28 .

FITZPATRICK B., 'European Union Law and the Council of Europe Conventions', in C. Costello (ed.), *Fundamental Social Rights: Current European Legal Protection and the Challenge of the EU Charter on Fundamental Rights* (Dublin, Irish Center European Law. 2001) 95–103.

FLAUSS J.-F., 'Les interactions normatives entre les instruments européens relatifs à la protection des droits sociaux', in J.-F. Flauss (ed.), *Droits sociaux et droit européen: bilan et prospective de la protection normative* (Brussels, Bruylant/Nemesis, 2003) 89–112.

FUNK B.-C., 'Die Sozialen Rechte der Grundrechtscharta vor dem Hintergrund des EG-Rechtsbestandes und im Vergleich zur Europäischen Sozialcharta', in A. Duschanek, and S. Griller (eds), *Grundrechte für Europa: Die Europäische Union nach Nizza* (Vienna, New York, Springer, 2002) 39–53.

GOULD M., 'The European Social Charter and Community Law: A Comment', 14 *ELRev.* (1989) 223–26.

HARRIS D., 'The European Social Charter and Social Rights in the European Union', in L. Betten, and D. MacDevitt (eds), *The Protection of Fundamental Social Rights in the European Union* (The Hague, Kluwer Law International, 1996) 107–11.

LARRALDE J.-M., 'Charte sociale et Convention européenne des droits de l'homme', in J.-F. Akandji-Kombé, and S. Leclerc (eds), *La Charte sociale européenne* (Brussels, Bruylant, 2001) 123–47.

RILEY A. J., 'The European Social Charter and Community Law', 14 *ELRev.* (1989) 80–86.

SCHMIDT A., *Europäische Menschenrechtskonvention und Sozialrecht: Die Bedeutung der Straßburger Rechtsprechung für das Europäische und Deutsche Sozialrecht* (Baden-Baden, Nomos, 2003).

STALFORD H., 'Concepts of Family Under EU Law—Lessons from the ECHR', 16 *International Journal of Law, Policy and the Family* (2002) 410–34.

VANDAMME F., 'La justiciabilité des droits sociaux dans la Communauté européenne: comparaison avec la Charte sociale européenne', 20 *Affari Sociali Internazionali* (1992) 101–20.

VI. SOCIAL RIGHTS IN NATIONAL LAW AND NATIONAL IMPLEMENTATION OF ESC, ECHR, AND EU SOCIAL RIGHTS-RELATED LAW

AKANDJI-KOMBÉ J.-F., 'La France devant le Comité européen des droits sociaux', *Droit social* (2001) 977–82.

BERCUSSON B., 'The European Social Model comes to Britain', 31 *ILJ* (2002) 209–44.

——, 'Application du droit national: les interactions entre droits du travail nationaux et communautaires', 100 *Travail et Emploi* (2004) 27–38.

BONNECHÈRE M., 'Charte sociale et droits nationaux', in J.-F. Akandji-Kombé, and S. Leclerc (eds), *La Charte sociale européenne* (Brussels, Bruylant, 2001) 105–21.

BRADLEY A., 'Scope for Review: The Convention Right to Education and the Human Rights Act 1998', 4 *EHRLR* (1999) 395–410.

BREEN C., 'The Right to Education of Persons with Disabilities: Disabled in Interpretation and Application', 21 *Netherlands Quarterly of Human Rights* (2003) 7–37.

BRYDE B.-O., 'Grundrechte der Arbeit und Europa', 56 *Recht der Arbeit—Sonderbeilage Heft 5* (2003) 5–10.

BURCHILL R., HARRIS D., AND OWERS A. (eds), *Economic, Social and Cultural Rights: The Implementation in United Kingdom Law* (Nottingham, University of Nottingham Human Rights Law Centre, 1999).

COUNCIL OF EUROPE, EUROPEAN COMMITTEE OF SOCIAL RIGHTS, *Implementation of the European Social Charter Survey by Country—2002* (Strasbourg, Council of Europe Publishing, 2002).

DARCY J., 'Forced Labour in Greece', 27 *ELRev.* 27 (2002) 218–23.

EWING K., 'Social Rights and Human Rights: Britain and the Social Charter—The Conservative Legacy', *EHRLR* (2000) 91–112.

ILIOPOULOS-STRANGAS J. (ed.), *La protection des droits sociaux fondamentaux dans les états membres de l'Union européenne: Etude de droit comparé* (Athens, Brussels, Baden-Baden, Ant. N. Sakkoulas, Bruylant, Nomos, 2000).

LYON-CAEN A., AND LOKIEC P., *Droits fondamentaux et droit social* (Paris, Dalloz-Sirey, 2004).

NEUBECK X., *Die Europäische Sozialcharta und deren Protokolle: Einfluss und Bedeutung der Sozialrechtlichen Bestimmungen der Europäischen Sozialcharta auf das Deutsche Recht und auf das Recht der Europäischen Union* (Frankfurt/Main, Peter Lang, 2002).

SADURSKI W., *Constitutional Courts in the Process of Articulating Constitutional Rights in the Post-Communist States of Central and Eastern Europe: Part I: Social and Economic Rights*, EUI Working Paper Law, 2002/14 (2002).

SCIOTTI C., 'L'applicabilité de la Charte sociale européenne dans l'ordre juridique des états contractants', in J.-F. Flauss (ed.), *Droits sociaux et droit européen: bilan et prospective de la protection normative* (Brussels, Bruylant/Nemesis, 2003) 175–201.

SUNSTEIN C., 'Against Positive Rights: Why Social and Economic Rights Don't Belong in the New Constitutions of Post-Communist Europe', 2 *East European Constitutional Review* (1993) 35–38.

TOMANDL T. (ed.), *Der Einfluss Europäischen Rechts auf das Sozialrecht* (Vienna, Wilhelm Braumueller, 2000).

ZIFAK S., 'Adjudicating Social Rights: Lessons from the Hungarian Constitutional Experience', 4 *East European Human Rights Review* (1998) 53–96.

VII. THE PROTECTION OF SPECIFIC SOCIAL RIGHTS IN EUROPE (EU, ESC, AND ECHR)

1. Rights of the Disabled

APOSTOLOPOULOU Z., *Equal Treatment of People with Disabilities in the EC: What does 'Equal' mean?*, Jean Monnet Working Paper, No. 9 (2004).

CLEMENTS L. J., AND READ J., *Disabled People and European Human Rights: A Review of the Implications of the 1998 Human Rights Act for Disabled Children and Adults in the UK* (Bristol, Policy Press, 2003).

COUNCIL OF EUROPE—WORKING GROUP ON THE ASSESSMENT OF PERSON-RELATED CRITERIA FOR ALLOWANCES AND PERSONAL ASSISTANCE OF PEOPLE WITH DISABIILTIES, *Assessing Disability in Europe: Similarities and Differences* (Strasbourg, Council of Europe Publishing, 2002).

COUNCIL OF EUROPE—COMMITTEE ON THE REHABILITATION AND INTEGRATION OF PEOPLE WITH DISABILITIES, *Rehabilitation and Integration of People with Disabilities: Policy and Legislation* (7th edn., Strasbourg, Council of Europe Publishing, 2003).

DE SCHUTTER O., AND QUINN G. (eds), *Equality and Disability* (Brussels, Bruylant, 2005).

DEGENER T., AND QUINN G., 'Survey of International, Comparative and Regional Disability Law Reform', in M. L. Breslin, and S. Yee (eds), *Disability Rights Law and Policy: International and National Perspectives* (Ardsley, NY, Transnational Publishers, 2002) 3–129.

Lawson A., and Gooding C. (eds), *Disability Rights in Europe: From Theory to Practice* (Oxford, Portland, OR, Hart Publishing, 2004).

Machado S. M., and De Lorenzo R. (eds), *European Disability Law* (Madrid, Fundacion ONCE, 1997).

Maudinet M., and Council of Europe, Committee on the Rehabilitation and Integration of People with Disabilities, *Access to Social Rights for People with Disabilities in Europe* (Strasbourg, Council of Europe Publishing, 2003).

Quinn G., 'The Human Rights of People with Disabilities under EU Law', in P. Alston, with M. Bustelo, and J. Heenan (eds), *The EU and Human Rights* (Oxford, New York, Oxford University Press, 1999) 281–326.

Steinmeyer, H.-D., and Council of Europe Working Group on Legislation to Counter Discrimination Against Persons with Disabilities, *Legislation to Counter Discrimination against Persons with Disabilities* (Strasbourg, Council of Europe Publishing, 2003).

Tomaševski L., 'The Right to Health for People with Disabilities', in T. Degener, and Y. Koster-Dreese (eds), *Human Rights and Disabled Persons: Essays and Relevant Human Rights Instruments* (Dordrecht, Boston, MA, Martinus Nijhoff Publishers, 1995) 131–46.

Van Oorshot W., and Hvinden B. (eds), *Disability Policies in European Countries* (The Hague, Boston, Kluwer Law International, 2001).

Waddington L., *Disability, Employment, and the European Community* (Antwerp, Maklu, 1995).

——, 'A European Right to Employment for Disabled People?', in T. Degener, and Y. Koster-Dreese (eds), *Human Rights and Disabled Persons: Essays and Relevant Human Rights Instruments* (Dordrecht, Boston, MA, Martinus Nijhoff Publishers, 1995) 106–16.

Whittle R., 'Disability Discrimination and the Amsterdam Treaty', 23 *ELRev.* (1998) 50–58.

——, 'Disability Rights after Amsterdam—The Way Forward', *EHRLR* (2000) 33–48.

——, 'The Framework Directive for Equal Treatment in Employment and Occupation: An Analysis from a Disability Rights Perspective', 27 *ELRev.* (2002) 303–26.

2. Right to Education

Cullen H., 'From Migrants to Citizens? European Community Policy on Intercultural Education', 45 *International and Comparative Law Quarterly* (1996) 109–29.

De Witte B. (ed), *European Community Law of Education* (Baden-Baden, Nomos, 1989).

——, and Post H., 'Educational and Cultural Rights', in A. Cassese, A. Clapham, and J. Weiler (eds), *Human Rights and the European Community: The Substantive Law* (Baden Baden, Nomos, 1991) 123–76.

Freedland M., 'Vocational Training in EC Law and Policy—Education, Employment or Welfare?', 25 *ILJ* (1996) 110–20.

Gori G., 'Union Citizenship and Equal Treatment: A Way of Improving Community Educational Rights?', 21 *Journal of Social Welfare and Family Law* (1999) 405–16.

——, *Towards an EU Right to Education* (The Hague, Boston, MA, Kluwer Law International, 2001).

Lenaerts K., 'Education in European Community Law after Maastricht', 31 *CMLRev.* (1994) 7–41.

McMahon J., *Education and Culture in European Community Law* (London, Athlone Press, 1995).

MENTINK D., AND GOUDAPPEL F., 'The Education Provision in the Charter of Fundamental Rights of the European Union: A Bleak Perspective', 4 *European Journal for Education Law and Policy* (2000) 145–48.

MILNER S., 'Training Policy: Steering between Divergent National Logics', in D. Hine, and H. Kassim (eds), *Beyond the Market: The European Union and National Social Policy* (London, New York, Routledge, 1998).

SHAW J., 'The Nature and Extent of "Educational Rights" under EC Law: A Review', 20 *Journal of Social Welfare and Family Law* (1998) 203–10.

——, 'From the Margins to the Centre: Education and Training Law and Policy', in P. Craig, and G. de Búrca (eds), *The Evolution of EU Law* (Oxford, New York, Oxford University Press, 1999) 555–95.

WALLACE C., AND SHAW J., 'Education, Multiculturalism and the Charter of Fundamental Rights of the European Union', in T. Hervey, and J. Kenner (eds), *Economic and Social Rights Under the EU Charter of Fundamental Rights: A Legal Perspective* (Oxford, Portland, OR, Hart Publishing, 2003) 223–46.

3. Right to Health

DROMMERS J., 'An Introduction to European Union Health Law', 4 *European Journal of Health Law* (1997) 19–41.

HERVEY T., 'Mapping the Contours of European Union Health Law and Policy', 8 *EPL* (2002) 69–105.

——, 'The "Right to Health" in European Union Law', in T. Hervey, and J. Kenner (eds), *Economic and Social Rights Under the EU Charter of Fundamental Rights: A Legal Perspective* (Oxford, Portland, OR, Hart Publishing, 2003) 193–222.

——, AND McHALE J., *Health Law and the European Union* (Cambridge, Cambridge University Press, 2004).

MICHALOWSKI S., 'Health Care Law', in S. Peers, and A. Ward (eds), *The EU Charter and Fundamental Rights* (Oxford, Portland, OR, Hart Publishing, 2004) 287–308.

NEAL A. C., 'Regulating Health and Safety at Work: Developing European Union Policy for the Millennium', 14 *IJCLLIR* (1998) 217–46.

SMISMANS S., 'Towards a New Community Strategy on Health and Safety at Work? Caught in the International Web of Soft Procedures', 19 *IJCLLIR* (2003) 55–83.

THAYER C., 'The European Social Charter and European Health Policies', 6 *Journal international de bioéthique* (1995) 16.

TOEBES B., 'The Right to Health', in A. Eide, C. Krause, and A. Rosas (eds), *Economic, Social, and Cultural Rights: A Textbook* (2nd and rev. edn., The Hague, Martinus Nijhoff Publishers, Kluwer Law International, 2001) 169–90.

VAN DER MEI A. P., AND WADDINGTON L., 'Public Health and the Treaty of Amsterdam', 5 *European Journal of Health Law* (1998) 129–54.

4. Right to Housing

LECKIE S., 'The Right to Housing', in A. Eide, C. Krause, and A. Rosas (eds), *Economic, Social, and Cultural Rights: A Textbook* (The Hague, Martinus Nijhoff Publishers, Kluwer Law International, 1995) 107–23.

ZOON I., 'Denial of Health Care and Lack of Housing for Roma in Romania, Bulgaria and Macedonia', 7 *East European Human Rights Review* (2001) 1–140.

5. Equal Treatment/Non-discrimination

AHTELA K., 'The Revised Provisions on Sex Discrimination in European Law: A Critical Assessment', 11 *ELJ* (2005) 57–78.

BARNARD C., 'Gender Equality in the EU: A Balance Sheet', in P. Alston, with M. Bustelo, and J. Heenan (eds), *The EU and Human Rights* (Oxford, New York, Oxford University Press, 1999) 215–79.

——, 'The Changing Scope of the Fundamental Principle of Equality?', 46 *McGill Law Journal* (2000–2001) 955–77.

BELL M., 'The New Article 13 EC Treaty: A Sound Basis for European Anti-Discrimination Law?', 6 *MJ* (1999) 5–23.

——, *Anti-Discrimination Law and the European Union* (Oxford, New York, Oxford University Press, 2002).

——, 'Beyond European Labour Law? Reflections on the EU Racial Equality Directive', 8 *ELJ* (2002) 384–99.

——, 'The Right to Equality and Non-Discrimination', in T. Hervey, and J. Kenner (eds), *Economic and Social Rights Under the EU Charter of Fundamental Rights: A Legal Perspective* (Oxford, Portland, OR, Hart Publishing, 2003) 91–110.

——, AND WHITTLE R., 'Between Social Policy and Union Citizenship: The Framework Directive on Equal Treatment in Employment', 27 *ELRev.* (2002) 677–91.

BELORGEY J.-M., 'De quelques problemes liés a la prohibition et a l'élimination des discriminations: essai de clarification des concepts et éléments de droit comparé', *Droit social* (2002) 683–89.

COSTELLO C., 'Gender Equalities and the Charter of Fundamental Rights of the European Union', in T. Hervey, and K. Kenner (eds), *Economic and Social Rights Under the EU Charter of Fundamental Rights: A Legal Perspective* (Oxford, Portland, OR, Hart Publishing, 2003) 111–38.

——, AND BARRY E. (eds), *Equality in Diversity—The New Equality Directives* (Dublin, Irish Centre for European Law, 2003).

COUNCIL OF EUROPE, *Equality Between Women and Men in the European Social Charter* (2nd edn., Strasbourg, Council of Europe Publishing, 2000).

DASHWOOD A., AND O'LEARY S. (eds), *The Principle of Equal Treatment in EC Law* (London, Sweet & Maxwell, 1997).

DE BÚRCA G., 'The Role of Equality in European Community Law', in A. Dashwood, and S. O'Leary (eds), *The Principle of Equal Treatment in EC Law* (London, Sweet & Maxwell, 1997) 13–34.

ELLIS E., *EC Sex Equality Law* (2nd edn., Oxford, New York, Clarendon Press, Oxford University Press, 1998).

——, 'Social Advantages: A New Lease of Life?', 40 *CMLRev.* (2003) 639–59.

FOUBERT P., *The Legal Protection of the Pregnant Worker in the European Community: Sex Equality, Thoughts of Social and Economic Policy and Comparative Leaps to the United States of America* (The Hague, Kluwer Law International, 2002).

FREDMAN S., 'Equality: A New Generation?', 30 *ILJ* (2001) 145–68.

——, AND SPENCER S., *Age as an Equality Issue* (Oxford, Portland, OR, Hart Publishing, 2003).

HEPPLE B., 'Race and Law in Fortress Europe', 67 MLR (2004) 1–15.

HERVEY T., 'Sex Equality in Social Protection: New Institutionalist Perspectives on Allocation of Competence', 4 *ELJ* (1998) 169–219.

HERVEY, T., AND O'KEEFFE D. (eds), *Sex Equality Law in the European Union* (Chichester, New York, Wiley, 1996).

LEVY-PUECH D., 'L'égalité entre les femmes et les hommes en matière d'emploi: Charte sociale européenne (révisée) et autres normes du Conseil de l'Europe', in *Le droit social—le droit comparé: Etudes dédiées à la mémoire de Pierre Ortscheidt* (Strasbourg, Presses Universitaires de Strasbourg, 2003) 207–25.

McCRUDDEN C., 'Theorizing European Equality Law', in C. Costello, and E. Barry (eds), *Equality in Diversity—The New Equality Directives* (Dublin, Irish Centre for European Law, 2003).

MALMSTEDT, 'From Employee to EU Citizen—A Development from Equal Treatment as a Means to Equal Treatment as a Goal?', in A. Numhauser-Henning (ed.), *Legal Perspectives on Equal Treatment and Non-Discrimination* (The Hague, Kluwer Law International, 2001) 95–124.

MANCINI G. F., AND O'LEARY S., 'The New Frontiers of Sex Equality Law in the European Union', 24 *ELRev.* (1999) 331–53.

MEENAN H., 'Age Equality after the Employment Directive', 10 *MJ* (2004) 9–38.

MOEBIUS I., AND SZYSZCZAK E., 'Of Raising Pigs and Children', *Yearbook of European Law* (1998) 125–56.

MORE G., 'The Principle of Equal Treatment: From Market Unifier to Fundamental Right?', in P. Craig, and G. de Búrca, *The Evolution of EU Law* (Oxford, Oxford University Press, 1999) 517–54.

PICHAULT C., DE VOS D., HERBERT F., AND JACQMAN J., *Equality in Law between Men and Women in the European Community* (Brussels, Martinus Nijhoff Publishers, 1998).

PRECHAL S., 'Equality of Treatment, Non-Discrimination and Social Policy: Achievements in Three Themes', 41 *CMLRev.* (2004) 533–51.

REES T., *Mainstreaming Equality in the European Union: Education, Training and Labour Market Policies* (London, New York, Routledge 1998).

SCHIEK D., 'A New Framework on Equal Treatment of Persons in EC Law? Directives 2000/43/EC, 2000/78/EC, and 2002/73/EC Changing Directive 76/207/EEC in Context', 8 *ELJ* (2002) 290–314.

SKIDMORE P., 'European Development: EC Framework Directive on Equal Treatment in Employment: Towards a Comprehensive Community Anti-discrimination Policy?', 30 *ILJ* (2001) 126–32.

SZYSZCZAK E., 'Building a European Constitutional Order: Prospects for a Non-Discrimination Standard', in A. Dashwood, and S. O'Leary (eds), *The Principle of Equal Treatment in EC Law* (London, Sweet & Maxwell, 1997) 35–85.

——, 'Remedies in Sex Discrimination Cases', in J. Lonbay, and A. Biondi (eds), *Remedies for Breach of EC Law* (Chichester, New York, Wiley, 1997) 105–115.

WADDINGTON L., 'Testing the Limits of the EC Treaty Article on Non-Discrimination', 28 *ILJ* (1999) 133–51.

——, 'The Development of a New Generation of Sex Equality Directives', 11 *MJ* (2004) 3–11.

——, AND BELL M., 'More Equal than Others: Distinguishing European Union Equality Directives', 38 *CMLRev.* (2001) 587–611.

————, 'Reflecting on Inequalities in European Equality Law', 28 *ELRev.* (2003) 349–69.

WINTEMUTTE R., 'When is Pregnancy Discrimination Indirect Sex Discrimination?', 27 *ILJ* (1998) 23–36.

WOBBE T., 'From Protecting to Promoting: Evolving EU Sex Equality Norms in an Organisational Field', 9 *ELJ* (2003) 88–108.

6. Labour Rights

ADNETT N., AND HARDY S., 'The Parental Leave Directive: Towards a "Family-Friendly" Social Europe?', 8 *European Journal of Industrial Relations* (2002) 157–72.

ALES E., 'L'integrazione europea tra diritti sociali e mercato: il caso degli infortuni sul lavoro', 4 *Rivista del Diritto della Securezza Sociale* (2004) 1–31.

BARBERA M., 'The Unsolved Conflict: Reshaping Family Work and Market Work in the EU Legal Order', in T. Hervey, and J. Kenner (eds), *Economic and Social Rights Under the EU Charter of Fundamental Rights: A Legal Perspective* (Oxford, Portland, OR, Hart Publishing, 2003) 139–60.

BARNARD C., 'Worker's Rights of Participation', in N. A. Neuwahl, and A. Rosas (eds), *The European Union and Human Rights* (The Hague, London, Martinus Nijhoff Publishers, 1995) 185–206.

——, 'Social Dumping and the Race to the Bottom: Some Lessons for the European Union from Delaware', 25 *ELRev.* (2000) 57–78.

BELORGEY, J. M., 'La gestion des conflits du travail en Europe: le choc des cultures', *Droit social* (2002) 1125–30.

BERCUSSON B., 'Collective Bargaining and the Protection of Social Rights in Europe', in K. D. Ewing, C. A. Gearty, and B. Hepple (eds), *Human Rights and Labour Law: Essays for Paul O'Higgins* (New York, Mansell, 1994) 106–126.

BIAGI M. (ed.), *Towards a European Model of Industrial Relations? Building on the First Report of the European Commission* (The Hague, Kluwer Law International, 2001).

BOUCAUD P., *Migrant Workers and Their Families: Protection within the European Social Charter* (Strasbourg, Council of Europe Publishing, 1996).

BRUUN N., *Trade Union and Fundamental Rights in the EU: A Discussion Document on Strategies for the Future* (Stockholm, TCO, 1999).

DEMESY C., 'La liberté syndicale et le droit de négociation collective des militaires', 19 *Revue française de droit administratif* (2003) 546–53.

DRZEWICKI K., 'The Right to Work and Rights in Work', in A. Eide, C. Krause, and A. Rosas (eds), *Economic, Social, and Cultural Rights: A Textbook* (2nd and rev. edn., The Hague, Boston, MA, Martinus Nijhoff Publishers, Kluwer Law International, 2001) 223–43.

GARDE A., 'Partial Harmonisation and European Social Policy: A Case Study on the Acquired Rights Directive', 5 *Cambridge Yearbook of European Legal Studies* (2002) 173–93.

GERMANOTTA P., AND NOVITZ T., 'Globalisation and the Right to Strike: The Case for European-Level Protection of Secondary Action', 18 *IJCLLIR* (2002) 67–82.

GREEN K., 'Labour Standards in the European Union: The Effects on Multinationals', 18 *Houston Journal of International Law* (1996) 497–524.

HEPPLE B. (ed.), *Social and Labour Rights in a Global Context: International and Comparative Perspectives* (Cambridge, Cambridge University Press, 2002).

HUNT J., 'Fair and Just Working Conditions', in T. Hervey, and J. Kenner (eds), *Economic and Social Rights Under the EU Charter of Fundamental Rights: A Legal Perspective* (Oxford, Portland, OR, Hart Publishing, 2003) 45–66.

McGLYNN C., 'A Family Law for the European Union?', in J. Shaw (ed.) *Social Law and Policy in an Evolving European Union* (Oxford, Portland, OR, Hart Publishing, 2000) 223–41.

——, 'Reclaiming a Feminist Vision: The Reconciliation of Paid Work and Family Life in European Union Law and Policy', 7 *Columbia Journal of European Law* (2001) 241–72.

NOVITZ T., *International and European Protection of the Right to Strike: A Comparative Study of Standards set by the International Labour Organization, the Council of Europe and the European Union* (Oxford, New York, Oxford University Press, 2003).

O'HIGGINS P., 'The Interaction of the ILO, the Council of Europe and European Union Labour Standards', in B. Hepple (ed.), *Social and Labour Rights in a Global Context: International and Comparative Perspectives* (Cambridge, Cambridge University Press, 2002) 55–69.

ORLANDINI G., *Sciopero e servizi pubblici essenziali nel processo di integrazione europea: uno studio di diritto comparato e comunitario* (Torino, G. Giappichelli, 2003).

ROJOT J., 'The Right to Bargain Collectively: An International Perspective on its Extent and Relevance', 20 *IJCLLIR* (2004) 513–32.

RYAN B., 'Trade Union Rights and European Community Law', 13 *IJCLLIR* (1997) 305–26.

WHITEFORD E., 'Occupational Pensions and European Law: Clarity at Last?', in T. Hervey, and D. O'Keeffe (eds), *Sex Equality Law in the European Union* (London, Wiley, 1996) 21–34.

7. Social Security Rights

BLANPAIN R. AND COLUCCI M., *European Labour and Social Security Law Glossary* (The Hague, Kluwer Law International, 2002).

BURROWS N., 'Non-discrimination and Social Security in Co-operation Agreements', 22 *ELRev.* (1997) 166–69.

DOUGAN M., AND SPAVENTA E. (eds), *Social Welfare and EU Law* (Oxford, Hart Publishing, 2005).

EICHENHOFER E., 'How to Simplify the Co-ordination of Social Security', 2 *European Journal of Social Security* (2000) 231–40.

EUZÉBY C., 'Repenser la protection social dans l'Union européenne: vers plus de droits fondamentaux universels', 57 *Revue internationale de sécurité sociale* (2004) 10.

HERVEY T., 'Social Security', in T. Hervey (ed.), *European Social Law and Policy* (London, New York, Longman, 1998) 82–109.

MAVRIDIS P., 'La sécurité sociale et les promesses des droits fondamentaux dans l'Union européenne', *Cahiers de droit européen* (2002) 633–77.

PAGANETTO L. (ed.), *Social Protection and the Single European Market: The Evolution of the Social Security Systems and Free Circulation: Problems and Perspectives* (Rome, CEIS Tor Vergata, 1997).

PEERS, S., 'Equality, Free Movement and Social Security', 22 *ELRev.* (1997) 342–51.

PENNINGS F., *Introduction to European Social Security Law* (Antwerp, Oxford, Intersentia, 2003).

PENNINGS F., 'Co-ordination of Social Security on the Basis of the State-of-Employment Principle: Time for an Alternative?', 42 *CMLRev.* (2005) 67–89.

SAKSLIN M., 'Social Security Co-ordination—Adapting to Change', 2 *European Journal of Social Security* (2000) 169–87.

Schrammel W., 'Der Zugang des EU-Rechts zur Sozialen Sicherheit', in T. Tomandl (ed.), *Der Einfluß Europäischen Rechts auf das Sozialrecht* (Vienna, Wilhelm Braumüller, 2000) 1–26.

Steiner J., 'The Principle of Equal Treatment for Men and Women in Social Security', in T. Hervey, and D. O'Keeffe (eds), *Sex Equality Law in the European Union* (London, Wiley, 1996) 111–136.

Tooze J., 'Social Security and Social Assistance', in T. Hervey, and J. Kenner (eds), *Economic and Social Rights Under the EU Charter of Fundamental Rights: A Legal Perspective* (Oxford, Portland, OR, Hart Publishing, 2003) 161–92.

Verschueren H., 'EC Social Security Coordination Excluding Third Country Nationals: Still in Line with Fundamental Rights after the Gaygusuz Judgement?', 34 *CMLRev.* (1997) 991–1017.

White R., *EC Social Security Law* (Harlow, Longman, 1999).

——, 'Social Security', in S. Peers, and A. Ward (eds), *The EU Charter and Fundamental Rights* (Oxford, Portland, OR, Hart Publishing, 2004) 309–21.

Index